CESS RESEARCH STUDIES 2

THE WORKING OF THE ANDHRA PRADESH STATE ROAD TRANSPORT CORPORATION

J. SATYANARAYANA

Foreword by

A.M. KHUSRO

Centre for Economic and Social Studies, Hyderabad
and
CONCEPT PUBLISHING COMPANY, NEW DELHI

First Published 1985

Published by

Naurang Rai
Concept Publishing Company
H-13, Bali Nagar
NEW DELHI-110015 (India)

Printed in India by

Printway India
at Kiran Mudran Kendra, Maya Puri,
NEW DELHI-110064.

FOREWORD

SINCE the commencement of planning in the country, the Public Sector has started assuming increasing importance in the nation's economy. At the state level, the nationalised passenger road transport undertakings occupy an important position, next only to electricity undertakings. The Road Transport Corporation's Act stipulates that a Corporation shall provide "efficient, adequate, economical and properly co-ordinated system of road transport services". It is clear from this provision that the Road Transport Corporations have to provide, on the one hand, efficient services and, on the other, economical services, thereby implying that the economies consequent upon the efficiency shall be passed on to the consumers of the service. However, in practice, most of the road transport undertakings in the country have been incurring losses and building up accumulated losses. The APSRTC is no exception to this. Consequently, there are frequent requests of revision of fares from the State Transport Undertakings to the Government and the resistance of the public to such proposals or revisions of fares. There have also been heated discussions on the floor of the assembly for enquiry into the losses and the working of the APSRTC. There are practically no systematic and detailed investigations into the reasons for the losses of nationalised passenger road transport undertakings in the country to identify the extent to which the inefficiency of the undertakings is responsible for losses and the extent to which external factors are responsible for the same, so that the policy maker and the travelling public know the justification or otherwise of increase in fares. The Government of Andhra Pradesh have, therefore, rightly taken the decision to cause an enquiry to be made into the working of the APSRTC in order to find out the reasons for the losses and to see whether and to what extent these losses can be traced to the very structure of the organisation or the inefficiency of the organisation or whether they can be attributed to external factors. I am happy that this task was entrusted to

Professor J. Satyanarayana, an expert in the area of Transport Economics, who made it a commendable and effective piece of research.

Professor J. Satyanarayana has made a painstaking and incisive analysis of the working of the Corporation and come out with clear findings on the reasons for losses. The report is of relevance and practical use not only to the organisation but also to the policy maker. He has clearly indicated as to how such factors as surplus personnel, governmental policies and attitudes were responsible for losses, in spite of improvement in the operational performance in certain areas.

Another important problem confronting the policy makers in regard to the State Road Transport Undertakings is the issue of a viable/optimal size for nationalised state road transport undertakings and devising a suitable organisational structure for effective and economical functioning of these undertakings. Professor Satyanarayana has made a thorough analysis and evaluation of the existing size and structure of the Corporations and suggested a suitable alternative to the existing set-up. The road transport industry, being a geographically widely dispersed activity and with a need for close contact between the decision maker at the top and the manager of operations at the base, definitely needs the kind of organisation as recommended by Prof. Satyanarayana i.e. small corporations with a two-tier set up.

I am sure that the implementation of the recommendations of Professor Satyanarayana, not only with regard to its working and organisational set up but also in respect of other important areas, such as financial and personnel policies, will go a long way in improving the performance of this important sector of state level public enterprises.

Further, it is to be hoped that this report would be of relevance and value to other state road transport undertakings too in the country.

Chairman A.M. KHUSRO
Centre for Economic and Social Studies
HYDERABAD
April 1985

PREFACE

THE profitability of Andhra Pradesh State Road Transport Corporation has been consistently on the decline since 1973-74 and the organisation started incurring losses since 1977-78. These losses have been consistently on the increase since then, ultimately resulting in a total accumulated loss of Rs. 66.55 crores*, as on March 31, 1982, thus "causing grave concern to the Government". The Government of Andhra Pradesh have, therefore, decided to cause a detailed study of the Corporation to identify the various factors that contributed to heavy losses incurred by the corporation during the recent years and also to study the policies and practices followed by the Corporation in important areas in order to recommend measures for rectifying deficiencies, improving performance and for achieving optimum level of efficiency in its working.

In the light of the above, the Government have entrusted the study to the Centre for Economic and Social Studies, under my supervision, through its G.O.Ms. No. 36 dated 2nd February, 1982. The detailed terms of reference are as follows :

1. Identification of the causes for the losses of the Andhra Pradesh State Road Transport Corporation, since the financial year 1977-78 ;
2. Suitability and adequacy of the corporation's organisational set up ;
3. Cost-fare relationship given optimum utilisation and efficiency ;
4. Recommendations for structural, organisational and financial reforms ;
5. Policy projections.

* The accumulated loss would total up to Rs. 70.36 crores, if the figure of the loss for 1980-81 were to be taken at Rs. 20.72 crores as per "A Performance Profile" prepared by the corporation.

The study is based upon the empirical data, culled out and collected not only from the records of MIS wing of the APSRTC but also from the "Reports on the Performance of Nationalised Road Transport Undertakings" of Central Institute of Road Transport (Training and Research), Pune, the comparable nationalised road transport undertakings, namely, the Gujarat State Road Transport Corporation (GSRTC), the Maharashtra State Road Transport Corporation, apart from some of the State Transport Undertakings of Tamil Nadu. Detailed discussions were held with a number of people at various levels and belonging to various departments, within the organisation and also with the top managements of the undertakings mentioned above. Within the APSRTC, discussions were held with Depot Managers, Divisional Managers, Regional Managers, important functionaries, in some of the departments of Head office, the Vice-Chairman and General Manager, and so on. Further, views were elicited on different aspects, from the Representatives of Officers' Association, Retired Officers' Association, the recognised trade unions, namely, the National Mazdoor Union and the next major Union, the Employees Union.

In the course of the study, the major hurdle has been the availability of data from the APSRTC itself. In spite of willing, helpful and ungrudging co-operation from the Vice-Chairman and General Manager, collection of data has been a serious problem. This is partly because of lack of proper information systems. An instance of the defective information system is the data pertaining to manpower, category-wise and level-wise.

In this context, it is necessary to record one or two discrepancies that have necessarily cropped up in the presentation of data, for the reason that for some purposes latest data could be taken, while for others it could not be done as the latest data do not give details of item-wise costs. These discrepancies arise in the case of operating revenue figures in Tables 1.4 and 1.4 (a), and in the case of financial results of mofussil and city operations as presented in Tables 1.5 and 1.6. In the case of non-operating revenues, the discrepancy in the figures for 1980-81 and 1981-82 arises because of the fact that the data in Table 1.4 are based upon the latest figures, as available from Provisional Annual Accounts, while the details of non-operating revenues in Table

1.4 (a) were obtained from the records of Chief Controller of Stores which may be considered to be more authentic.

As mentioned earlier, the computation of total accumulated losses was based upon the provisional Annual Accounts, whereas the financial results of mofussil and city operations, as presented in Tables 1.5 and 1.6, were collected from the Area MIS office, for the years 1978-79 to 1981-82. Evidently, the reason is that the data for mofussil and city operations which were available did not take into consideration the impact of revised pay scales. To conclude, this discrepancy is because of the limitations of the data available from the corporation.

Broadly the plan of analysis is as follows : At the outset, costs, costs structure, cost-fare relationship and method of cost computation for fare revision are analysed and presented in Chapter 1, even though, in the submission of reports to the Government, this was submitted as the second instalment. In Chapter 2, an evaluation of the existing organisational set up is made and alternative set up was suggested. Finally, capital structure and the Financial Policies and Practices, Personnel Policies and Practices and Management Information Systems are evaluated and recommendations made in respect of them in Chapter 3.

We are thankful to the Government of Andhra Pradesh for entrusting this study to us which enabled us to have an insight into the functioning of the organisation and accorded us an opportunity to serve the cause of public enterprises. I had the opportunity of having detailed discussions on a number of issues with Shri B.N. Jayasimha, Second Secretary to Government, Transport Department, Govt. of Andhra Pradesh. I am thankful to him for his views and for the time given for discussions.

We are deeply indebted to Shri P.S. Rama Mohana Rao, Vice-Chairman and General Manager, APSRTC, who was always willing to meet us and discuss with us at short notice on any issue concerning the study. In fact, he was so voluntary in his help, he invited us to a number of meetings with his Heads and the other Line Managers which gave us an insight into the working of the organisation and the problems that it is confronted with.

I am grateful to Prof. A.M. Khusro, Chairman, Centre for

Economic and Social Studies, and formerly, Member, Planning Commission, for readily agreeing to write a Foreword to the book.

I must acknowledge with thanks the smooth and ready support and help that we have received from the Centre for Economic and Social Studies, and particularly from the then Director, the late Professor Waheeduddin Khan. But for the informality in dealing with a number of issues in the administration of the Project shown by the Director, it would not have been possible to complete the study within the limited time.

I must also thank Professor R. Radhakrishna, Hon. Director, Centre for Economic and Social Studies, for the interest he has evinced in bringing out this publication, at the earliest.

The credit for the successful and timely completion of the study and the preparation of the Report should go to the devoted and unstinting hard work put in by my colleagues in the project, who have, at the cost of their own personal convenience, forgone not only practically every evening but also almost every holiday. Particular mention must be made of Shri M. Shivaji Singh, Divisional Manager, APSRTC whose services have been very kindly spared by the APSRTC to work as a full time Deputy Director in the Project, Dr. V. Viswanadham and Sri P. Subrahmanyam, my colleagues in the Department. I also thank my colleague Dr. P. Jagannadha Rao, who was associated with the study for a major part of the study period.

I should also express my appreciation of the sincere efforts put in by the Research Assistants, Sarvasri K. Gangapa, K. Ravindernath, A. Laxma Reddy, G. Eshwar, K. Prabhakar, Y. Krishna, S.V. Satyanarayana and Miss Hemamalini. Mention must also be made of the voluntary assistance rendered by Dr. C.R. Ananda Rao, my colleague in the Department, Miss G. Lakshmi Kameswari and Miss A. Lalitha.

The burden of typing and stencilling the Report was cheerfully undertaken by Mr. V. Krishnan, Stenographer, Department of Commerce for which I am thankful to him.

Hyderabad, J. SATYANARAYANA
May, 1985.

CONTENTS

ANNEXURES

LIST OF TABLES

LIST OF CHARTS

STATEMENT AND SCHEDULES

1

COSTS, COST-FARE RELATIONSHIPS AND LOSSES

INTRODUCTION

THE main problem that has been confronting the organisation during the recent years is the increasing trend of losses, which has set in is the financial year 1977-78. An attempt is made in this chapter to identify the causes for the losses of Andhra Pradesh State Road Transport Corporation since the year 1977-78.

The profitability of an organisation is a function of both costs and prices, which is equally valid in the case of the passenger road transport industry too. An organisation may incur loss either because the costs go up, the price (the fare in the case of road transport undertaking) remaining the same, or costs remaining the same the price/fare coming down. The second phenomenon of fare coming down does not ordinarily arise in the case of passenger road transport industry for reasons of relative inelasticity of demand for the service, monopoly rights conferred on the services and state regulation of fares. Hence, it follows that the losses in the case of Andhra Pradesh State Road Transport Corporation (APSRTC) must have been because of an increase in costs either in absolute terms, the fare remaining the same, or in relative terms, when cost increase is more than the fare increase, apart from other reasons mentioned in the following paragraphs. In other words, it could be because of cost-fare lag.

The losses arising out of cost-fare lag may be only an apparent reason because cost is a function not only of prices of inputs but also of operational and managerial performance. Hence, a study of losses necessitates not only a study of cost-fare relationship but also the operational and managerial performance.

Besides costs and operational factors, the external factors such as the governmental policies, apart from costs/inflation, which have been referred to above, also influence the profitability of the passenger road transport industry. The Government influences the profitability of an organisation, in the case of the passenger road transport industry, in a number of ways, for example the taxation policy, the social policy thrust on the organisation, the attitude of the regulating agency, of the Government namely the transport authority, and so on.

Broadly the above factors may be analysed in terms of controllable and uncontrollable factors—controllable, within the organisation and uncontrollable by the organisation in view of the external influences. In this context, the controllable items of costs may be identified as the operational aspects of the organisation in terms of such factors/aspects as vehicular utilisation, vehicle utilisation, occupancy ratio, schedule-staff ratio, consumption of stores, inclusive of fuel, tyres and so on. These are strictly within the area of the organisation, capable of being improved by the management by deliberate and systematic efforts. The uncontrollable factors that influence costs are broadly of two categories: (1) inflation, which results in increase in the prices of inputs and (2) Governmental influence, as mentioned earlier.

Apart from the above factors, the organisation may be contributing to its losses because of a number of other reasons which are not strictly operational in their nature. For example, investment of large amount of funds in assets which are not productive and which do not directly contribute to revenues such as construction of bus stations and expenditure on other passenger amenities, maintaining a large fleet of unremunerative and unproductive fleet of staff cars and so on.

It is proposed to discuss the impact of all these factors on the profitability of the organisation and their contribution to losses to the extent they could be identified and quantified.

THE FINANCIAL RESULTS

At the outset, it is proposed to analyse from Table 1.1 the

TABLE 1.1 : **Financial results : 1973-74 to 1981-82**

Year	Total revenue (Rs. in lakhs)	Total expenditure (Rs. in lakhs)	Total margin (Rs. in lakhs)	Effective km. (in lakhs)	Revenue per km. (in paise)	Expenditure per km. (in paise)	Margin per km. (in paise)
1	2	3	4	5	6	7	8
1973-74	4,165.97	3,826.54	339.43	2,611.30	159.54	146.54	13.00
1974-75	5,813.30	5,448.89	364.41	3,090.63	188.09	176.30	11.79
1975-76	7,321.60	7,097.91	223.69	3,695.28	198.13	192.08	6.05
1976-77	8,828.86	8,699.10	129.76	4,277.77	206.39	203.36	3.03
1977-78	10,122.86	10,253.34	(—) 130.48	4,861.87	208.21	210.89	(—) 2.68
1978-79	11,240.25	11,944.85	(—) 704.60	5,106.85	220.10	233.90	(—)13.80
1979-80	13,585.42	14,728.48	(—)1,143.06	5,802.33	234.14	253.84	(—)19.70
1980-81*	16,415.98	18,106.93	(—)1,690.95	6,175.78	265.81	293.19	(—)27.38
1981-82*	19,829.31	22,815.51	(—)2,986.20	6,207.31	319.45	367.56	(—)48.11

Source : 1. For total revenue and expenditure : Annual Accounts Audit Reports, 1973-74 to 1977-78 ; Annual Administration Report, 1978-79 ; Provisional Annual Accounts 1979-80 to 1981-82.

2. For Effective kms. : Annual Administration Reports, 1973-74 to 1978-79 ;] Performance Report, 1979-80 to 1981-82.

*Provisional figures.

financial results of the organization broadly in order to have an idea of the trends in its profitability. For this purpose, the period 1973-74-1981-82 has been chosen, for the reason that the organisation showed a consistently declining trend in its profitability since 1973-74, when it reached the peak of its profitability after losses in the year 1972-73. Earlier to this period the organisation was by and large making profits except for the years 1969-70 and 1972-73, which were exceptional years, when it incurred losses because of two separatist agitations in the State.

In the year 1973-74 the organisation made a profit of Rs. 3.39 crores and, after a gradual decline in its profits up to 1976-77, the Corporation started losing from 1977-78 when it incurred a loss of Rs. 1.30 crores. The losses gradually increased resulting in Rs. 29.86 crores of loss in the year 1981-82. Thus, on the whole, the corporation had accumulated a loss of Rs. 66.55 crores during the short period of five years resulting in capital erosion to the extent of 72.73 per cent, when the capital contributions stood at Rs. 91.50 crores.

A study of the absolute amount of profit/loss, even though gives an idea of the magnitude of profits and losses of an organisation, does not present the profitability of capital employed in the organisation. Hence, a study of its earnings in relation to investment, both in terms of owner's funds and capital invested (long-term funds) is attempted next, from Table 1.2. For the purpose of this study, owner's funds include capital contributions by participating governments and free reserves, and capital invested includes owner's funds and long-term borrowings. In both the cases, the earnings include net profit and interest on capital contributions ; and in the case of the latter aspect of the return on the capital invested, earnings also include interest on long-term borrowings.

An analysis of the Table 1.2 shows that the return on either owners' funds or on capital invested has been consistently on decline resulting in negative return since 1978-79. The return for 1977-78 does not show a negative figure for the reason that when the interest is added back to earnings there was no loss in that Year.

The return on owner's funds/capital invested shows a much higher figure than what is reported by way of return on invest-

TABLE 1.2 : **Return on owner's funds/capital employed**

Year	Earnings Net profit+ interest on capital contribution (Rs. in lakhs)	Investment capital contribution+free reserves (Rs. in lakhs)	Return on Owner's funds (%)	Earnings Net profit+ interest on capital contribution +interest on long term loans (Rs. in lakhs)	Investment Capital contribution+ free reserves+long term loans (Rs. in lakhs)	Return on capital employed (%)	Return on investment as per annual Reports (%)
1	2	3	4	5	6	7	8
1973-74	418.12	1,620.31	25.80	436.10	1,854.35	23.52	13.45
1974-75	453.61	2,601.88	17.43	469.57	2,654.57	17.69	10.67
1975-76	342.46	3,246.74	10.55	397.71	3,290.14	10.15	5.91
1976-77	261.79	4,108.00	6.37	336.16	4,838·95	6.95	2.90
1977-78	31.58	4,551.43	0.69	113.29	5,191.07	2.18	n.a.
1978-79	(—) 493.30	5,815.76	(—) 8.49	(—) 417.70	6,858.22	(—) 6.09	n.a.
1979-80	(—) 842.75	6,694.02	(—)12.59	(—) 690.73	8,532.11	(—) 8.10	n.a.
1980-81	(—)1,318.76	8,078.13	(—)16.33	(—)1,064.02	10,118.06	(—)10.52	n.a.
1981-82	(—)2,533.40	14,344.36	(—)17.66	(—)2,143.51	17,020.24	(—)12.59	n.a.

Source : 1. Annual Administration Reports ;
2. Provisional Accounts.

ment in the Annual Reports of the Corporation. This is because of the fact that the organisation has been treating a sizable portion of the accumulated Depreciation Fund under the heading "Withdrawals from Internal Resources for Capital expenditure", as a part of the investment base for calculating the return on investment. Thus, this method of presentation of return on investment (on Gross Block basis) results in under-statement of return, with implications on the fixation of fares.

The declining profitability during 1974-75 to 1981-82 or the increasing losses since 1977-78 are naturally the result of cleavage between expenditure per km. of vehicles operated and revenue per km. of vehicles operated, the expenditure per km. rising at a faster rate than the revenue per km., the former overtaking the latter since 1977-78. In other words, it means that the margin per km. which was positive in the year 1973-74, gradually declined and became negative since 1977-78, since when the negative margins were on the increase, and touched the highest negative margin of 27.38 paise for every km. of service operated by the organisation. There was a slight decline in this negative margin in the year 1981-82. It would be of interest to see the factors responsible for increase in the expenditure and also the reasons why the expenditure per km. was overshooting the revenue per kilometre. It could be because of a number of factors mentioned earlier, which will be gone into in detail in subsequent analysis of cost structure, cost-fare relationships and operational performance.

But it would be of immediate interest to look into the relationship between the expenditure per passenger km. and the revenue per passenger km. to have an idea of the extent to which the revenue per passenger km. which in a way reflects the fare, covered or not covered the expenditure per passenger km. An idea of this relationship can be had from Table 1.3. It could be seen from the table that the revenue per passenger km. that is the average fare was covering the expenditure per passenger km, that is the average cost of rendering the service, only up to 1976-77 and then onwards it was not covering the expenditure and the deficit had been on the increase since then. This implies that the fares were not covering the costs, since 1977-78, thereby resulting in losses to the organisation. As mentioned earlier, this

TABLE 1.3 : **Revenues, expenditures and margins per passenger kilometre**

Year	Passenger kms. (in lakhs)	Total revenue (Rs. in lakhs)	Revenue per pass km. (in paise)	Total Expenditure (Rs. in lakhs)	Expenditure per pass km. (in paise)	Total Margin (Rs. in lakhs)	Margin per pass km. (in paise)
1973-74	92,652.35	4,165.97	4.50	3,826.54	4.13	339.43	0.37
1974-75	1,01,066.62	5,813.93	5.75	5,448.89	5.39	365.04	0.36
1975-76	1,26,356.69	7,321.60	5.79	7,097.91	5.62	223.69	0.17
1976-77	1,50,303.00	8,828.86	5.87	8,699.10	5.79	129.76	0.08
1977-78	1,77,087.00	10,122.86	5.72	10,253.34	5.79	(—) 130.48	(—)0.07
1978-79	1,97,201.00	11,240.25	5.70	11,944.85	6.06	(—) 704.60	(—)0.36
1979-80	2,24,898.31	13,585.43	6.04	14,728.48	6.55	(—)1,143.06	(—)0.51
1980-81	2,23,625.00	16,415.98	7.34	18,106.93	8.10	(—)1,690.95	(—)0.76
1981-82	2,27,933.00	19,829.31	8.70	22,815.51	10.01	(—)2,986.20	(—)1.31

Source : 1. Annual Administration Reports.
2. Annual Performance Reports.
3. Annual Accounts (Provisional).

relationship between costs and fares will be gone into in a greater detail, at a later stage. But at this stage, suffice it to say that the losses that the organisation has been incurring in the recent years could be attributed to the cost-fare lags to some extent, at least as the losses could not perhaps entirely be attributed to this cost-fare lag alone. It requires a careful and detailed probe to see how far the losses could be attributed to the increase in costs, because of inflation, and how far they are attributable to operational inefficiencies, apart from other reasons.

Operating and non-operating results

Next, it is proposed to analyse the financial results of the organisation, in terms of the operating and non-operating results. In the case of a passenger road transport organisation the operating revenues and expenditures naturally constitute a significant part of the total revenues and expenditures.

Table 1.4 shows that the operating revenues and expenditures constitute a significant part of the total revenues and expenditures, accounting for more than 96 per cent of the total revenues and expenditures. The point of interest is that the percentage of operating revenues and expenditures almost remained the same until 1979-80 and 1978-79 respectively. Obviously, the non-operating revenues and expenditures broadly remained constant in terms of percentage share until 1979-80 and 1978-79 respectively. There was a sudden increase in the percentage share of non-operating expenditure from 1979-80 onwards and a steep decline, in both absolute as well as relative terms, in non-operating revenues during the years 1980-81 and 1981-82. These sudden changes require further probe. Table 1.4 (a) explains the reasons for these sudden changes in the shares of non-operating revenues and expenditures. The non-operating revenues came down considerably, and also its share, in 1980-81, which trend continued in 1981-82 too, essentially because of considerable decline in revenue in sale of scrap (unserviceable) and also to a considerable extent because of a decline in profit on sale of scrapped vehicles. The latter was because of change in the scrapping policy of the organisation in regard to vehicles.

Thus, on the one hand, the non-operating revenues came

TABLE 1.4 : **Operating and non-operating results**

Year	Revenue (Rs. in lakhs)			Expenditure (Rs. in lakhs)			Margin (Rs. in lakhs)		
	Operating	Non-operating	Total	Operating	Non-Operating	Total	Operating	Non-operating	Total
1	2	3	4(2+3)	5	6	7(5+6)	8(2—5)	9(3—6)	10(4—7) or (8+9)
1973-74	4,031.19	134.78	4,165.97	3,723.79	102.75	3,826.54	307.40	32.03	339.43
	(96.76)	(3.24)	(100.00)	(97.31)	(2.69)	(100.00)	(90.56)	(9.44)	(100.00)
1974-75	5,666.79	146.51	5,813.30	5,309.75	139.14	5,448.89	357.04	7.37	364.41
	(97.48)	(2.52)	(100.00)	(97 45)	(2.55)	(100.00)	(97.98)	(2.02)	(100.00)
1975-76	7,127.93	193.67	7,321.60	6,914.49	183.42	7,097.91	213.44	10.25	223.69
	(97,35)	(2.65)	(100.00)	(97.42)	(2.58)	(100.00)	(95.42)	(4.58)	(100.00)
1976-77	8,643.37	185.49	8,828.86	8,467.96	231.14	8,699.10	175.41	(—)45.65	129.76
	(97.90)	(2.10)	(100.00)	(97.34)	(2.66)	(100.00)	(135.18)	(—)(35.18)	(100.00)
1977-78	9,847.93	274.93	10,122.86	9,978.21	275.13	10,253.34	(—)130.28	(—)0.20	(—)130.48
	(97.28)	(2.72)	(100.00)	(97.32)	(2.68)	(100.00)	(99.85)	(0.15)	(100.00)
1978-79	10,980.67	259.53	11,240.25	11,649.96	294.89	11,944.85	(—)669.29	(—)35.31	(—)704.60
	(97.69)	(2.31)	(100.00)	(97.53)	(2.47)	(100.00)	(94.99)	(5.01)	(100.00)
1979-80	13,238.39	347.03	13,585.42	14,243.32	485.16	14,728.48	(—)1,004.93	(—)138.13	(—)1,143,06
	(97.45)	(2.55)	(100.00)	(96.71)	(3.29)	(100.00)	(87.92)	(12.08)	(100.00)
1980-81	16,157.78	258.20	16,415.98	17,476.72	630.21	18,106.93	(—)1,318.94	(—)372.01	(—)1,690.95
	(98.43)	(1.57)	(100.00)	(96 52)	(3.48)	(100.00)	(78.00)	(22.00)	(100.00)
1981-82	19,640.35	188.96	19,829.31	21,970.62	844.89	22,815,51	(—)2,330.27	(—)655.93	(—)2,986.20
	(99.05)	(0.95)	(100.00)	(96.30)	(3.70)	(100.00)	(78.03)	(21.97)	(100.00)

Note : Figures in the brackets are percentages to totals.

Source : 1. 1973-74 to 1977-78—Annual Accounts and Audit Reports;

2. 1978-79—Annual Administration Report ;
3. 1979-80—Provisional Annual Accounts Statement ;
4. 1980-81 and 1981-82 Operating and Non-operating Revenue—Annual Accounts Figures (Provisional).

TABLE 1.4 (a) : **Major items of non-operating revenue and expenditure**

(Rs. in lakhs)

Particulars 1	1973-74 2	1974-75 3	1975-76 4	1976-77 5	1977-78 6	1978-79 7	1979-80 8	1980-81 9	1981-82 10
Non-operating revenue									
(1) Profit on sale of scrapped vehicles	27.29 (20.25)	17.20 (11.74)	49.37 (25.49)	26.59 (14.34)	53.49 (19.46)	58.52 (22.54)	92.00 (26.51)	158.83 (52.18)	178.68 (43.87)
(2) Sale of scrap unserviceable	59.02 (43.79)	44.09 (30.89)	89.97 (46.46)	91.15 (49.14)	87.76 (39.92)	115.31 (44.42)	126.28 (36.39)		
(3) Others	48.47 (35.96)	85.22 (58.17)	54.33 (28.05)	67.75 (36.52)	133.68 (48.62)	85.75 (33.04)	128.75 (37.10)	145.58 (47.82)	228.63 (56.13)
Total non-operating revenue	134.78 (100.00)	146.51 (100.00)	193.67 (100.00)	185.49 (100.00)	274.93 (100.00)	259.58 (100.00)	347.03 (100.00)	304.41 (100.00)	407.31 (100.00)

TABLE 1.4(a) : (*Contd.*)

1	2	3	4	5	6	7	8	9	10
Non-operating expenditure									
(1) Interest on capital	79.37	89.45	118.76	132.03	162.06	211.30	300.31	372.19	453.10
	(76.74)	(64.17)	(64.75)	(57.12)	(58.90)	(71.65)	(61.90)	(59.06)	(53.63)
(2) Interest on loans	17.98	15.96	55.25	74.37	81.71	75.60	152.02	254.74	389.89
	(17.38)	(11.45)	(30.12)	(32.18)	(29.70)	(25.64)	(31.33)	(40.42)	(46.15)
(3) Others	6.08	33.98	9.40	24.74	31.36	7.99	32.83	3.28	1.90
	(5.88)	(24.38)	(5.13)	(10.70)	(11.40)	(2.71)	(6.77)	(0.52)	(0.22)
Total non-operating expenditure	103.43	139.39	183.41	231.14	275.13	294.89	485.16	630.21	884.89
	(100.00)	(100.00)	(100.00)	(100.00)	(100.00)	(100.00)	(100.00)	(100.00)	(100.00)

Note : Figures in the brackets are percentages to the total.

Source : 1. 1973-74 to 1978-79 Annual Administration Reports ;

2. 1979-80 Annual Accounts (Provisional) ;
3. 1980-81 Non-Operating Expenditure is taken from the report "Performance of Nationalised Road Transport Undertakings, 1979-80 and 1980-81" Central Institute of Road Transport, Pune.
4. 1980-81 and 1981-82 Non-operating Revenue Figure P & L A/c. Statement (Provisional) and CCOS Records.

down and on the other the non-operating expenditures had gone up, considerably because of the changing capital structure, resulting in increased long-term borrowings. This, in turn, contributed to increased non-operating expenditure. The interest on long term loans increased by more than 100 per cent between 1978-79 and 1979-80 and by about 66 per cent between 1979-80 and 1980-81, and by more than 50 per cent between 1980-81 and 1981-82. Consequently, the percentage share of interest on loans shot up from about 25 per cent in 1978-79 to a little less than 50 per cent by 1981-82.

Thus, even though the corporation had been incurring non-operating losses since 1976-77, these non-operating losses had been assuming alarming proportions since 1979-80. This state of affairs is essentially because of the fact that the grovernment failed in its responsibility towards a public utility organisation in supplying adequate capital contributions because of which the corporation was forced to resort to high interest bearing loans.

The non-operating losses formed a mere 0.15 per cent in the year 1977-78 but started assuming a major share from 1979-80 onwards and ultimately accounting for 22 per cent of the total losses in the last two years (vide column 9, Table 1.4).

Financial results of mofussil and city operations

A study of the financial results of the corporation in terms of its mofussil and city operations from Table 1.5 shows that the corporation has been incurring losses on mofussil services only since 1978-79, even though it has been incurring losses on the whole since 1977-78. The total accumulated loss amounted to 72.73 per cent of capital contributions as on March 31, 1982, as mentioned earlier. Out of the total accumulated loss of about Rs. 51.55* crores (Rs. 66.55 crores as per revised estimate) since 1977-78 the city services alone accounted for 30.93 per cent during the period, whereas the fleet on the city services (pertaining to twin cities only) constituted about 10 per cent of the total fleet. This share of 30.93 per cent of the total accumulated losses accounted

* These figures are in variance with those in Tables 1.1 and 1.3 because of non-availability of data on the impact of revised pay scales for mofussil and city services for 1981-82.

TABLE 1.5 : **Financial results of mofussil and city operations**

(Rs. in Lakhs)

Year	Mofussil Total revenue	Mofussil Total expenditure	Mofussil Margin	City Total revenue	City Total expenditure	City Margin	Overall Total revenue	Overall Total expenditure	Overall Margin
1973—74	3,680.29	3,182.62	497.67	425.[illegible]2	584.25	(—)159.23	4,105.31	3,766.87	338.44
1974—75	5,259.94	4,699.32	560.62	553.36	749.32	(—)196.46	5,813.30	5,449.14	364.16
1975—76	6,620.99	6,204.39	416.60	700.51	893.51	(—)192.90	7,321.60	7,097.90	223.70
1976—77	8,088.87	7,774.35	314.52	740.[illegible]0	897.04	(—)157.04	8,828.87	8,671.39	157.48
1977—78	9,197.60	9,090.50	107.10	734.35	973.68	(—)239.33	9,931.95	10,064.18	(—) 132.23
1978—79	10,456.84	10,884.90	(—) 428.06	783.41	1,059.95	(—)276.54	11,240.25	11,944.85	(—) 704.60
1979—80	12,704.68	13,545.13	(—) 840.45	380.75	1,183.35	(—)302.61	13,585.42	14,728.48	(—)1,143.06
1980—81	15,194.76	16,516.52	(—)1,321.76	1,221.22	1,590.41	(—)369.19	16,415.98	18,106.93	(—)1,690.95
1981—82	18,053.18	19.131.63	(—)1,078.45	1,497.54	1,905.05	(—)407.41	19,550.82	21,036.68	(—)1,485.86

Sources : 1. 1973-74 to 1977—78 Annual Administration Reports ;
2. 1978-79, The total overall revenue=Operating Revenue+Non-Operating Revenue ; taken from P & L a/c of Annual Admn. Report ;
3. Total overall expenditure 1978-79=Operating expenditure+Non-operating expenditure ; —do—
4. The figures for city from 1978-79 to 1981-82 are collected from M.I.S.

Note : Overall revenue/expenditure=Mofussil revenue/expenditure+City revenue/expenditure.

for by city services takens into consideration the losses incurred by the corporation since 1977-78 only, when the organisation started losing on the whole. In fact, the organisation has been losing on the city services since 1973-74 itself, that is, the period of commencement of the study. In fact city services have been a losing proposition since 1968-69 itself since when separate data are available for city services. The total losses on city services since 1968-69 amount to Rs. 29.50 crores, which would account for 32.24 per cent of the total capital contributions. If we take into consideration the capital contributions in relation to the fleet meantfor city services, and the investment thereon, the organisation had lost more than three times the investment made in the city services, because of its losses on the same. There has been continuous erosion of profits and profitability of the organisation because of city services. To start with, about one-third of the profits on mofussil services were lost on city services in the year 1973-74, which were gradually increasing, resulting in 50 per cent of mofussil profits being set off by the city service losses in 1976-77, and more than twice in the year 1977-78. Thereafter, because of the losses on the mofussil services, and increasing trend of the same, the losses on city services as a percentage were gradually on decline, even though in absolute terms the losses on city services were on the increase. A detailed and separate treatment and analysis of losses on city services and reasons for the same would be analysed in subsequent sections.

Table 1.6 gives an idea of the financial results of mofussil and city operations in terms of paise per kilometre. It could be seen from the table that the overall revenue per km. of operations recorded almost 100 per cent increase during the period 1973-74 to 1981-82, whereas the expenditure per km. increased by 134 per cent resulting in the expenditure per km. surpassing the revenue per kilometre. The phenomenon of the expenditure per km. exceeding the revenue per km. was prevalent since 1977-78. However, the margin per km. in the case of mofussil services was negative only since 1978-79 as was seen in the case of total margin earlier. However, the city services were having negative margins per km. since 1973-74 (the year of commencement of this study) and the negative margin has been on the increase consistently, except for 1975-76 and 1976-77.

In spite of the fact that the city services were losing since the beginning, and the negative margins per km. on the city service were on the increase, there has been improvement in the relative performance of city services vis-a-vis mofussil services, in the sense that the expenditure per km. on mofussil services as a percentage of the expenditure per km. on city services had gone up consistently except for 1976-77 and 1977-78. In other words, the expenditure per km. on city services as a percentage of expenditure per km. on mofussil services declined over the period, implying either a relative improvement in the operational performance of the city services or a relative decline in the operational performance of the mofussil services.

TRENDS IN COST STRUCTURE

From the foregoing analysis we have had an idea of the trend in the profitability and the extent of losses of the corporation since 1973-74. A broad idea of the financial results of mofussil and city operations also has been presented. The losses, as mentioned earlier, could be because of a number of reasons. At the outset, it is proposed to analyse the trends in costs and cost structure so as to have an idea of the extent of increase in costs and the contribution of different items of costs to the increase in total costs. The increase in costs, either in the aggregate or in the case of individual items, could be because of one of the two reasons—(1) inflation and (2) operational inefficiency. After an analysis of the trends in cost and cost structure an attempt would be made to identify the extent of increase in costs in the case of individual items, attributable either to inflation or to inefficiency, to the extent it is possible to isolate, identify and quantify the same.

Table 1.7 gives an idea of the trends in costs and cost structure. During the period 1973-74 to 1981-82, the total cost per km. of operations increased by more than 130 per cent. The highest increase in costs, amongst different individual items, took place in the case of fuel, including lubricants, where the cost per km. increased by more than 220 per cent followed by tyres and tubes with 175.09 per cent increase, interest on capital with 140.13 per cent increase, ignoring the cost of insurance which is a minor item of expenditure. Consequently, the cost per km. of opera-

TABLE 1.6 : **Financial results of**

Year	Effective kms. (in lakhs) District	City	Overall	Mofussil R.P.K. (in paise)	Ex. P.K. (in paise)	Margin per km. (in paise)
(1)	(2)	(3)	(4)	(5)	(6)	(7)
1973-74	2293.89	307.08	2600.97	160.44	138.74	21.70
1974-75	2766.45	324.18	3090.63	190.13	169.87	20.26
1975-76	3335.70	359.58	3695.28	198.49	186.00	12.49
1976-77	3940.04	337.73	4277.77	205.30	197.32	7.98
1977-78	4514.82	347.05	4861.87	203.72	201.35	2.37
1978-79	4758.65	348.20	5106.85	219.74	228.74	(—)9.00
1979-80	5442.05	360.28	5802.33	233.45	248.90	(—)15.45
1980-81	5749.49	425.84	6175.78	264.25	287.25	(—)23.00
1981-82	5761.77	445.54	6207.31	313.33	332.04	(—)18.71

Source : 1. 1973-74 to 1977-78. Annual Administrative Reports ;
2. 1978-79 to 1981-82. MIS and City Division Records.

Note : RPK=Revenue per kilometre.
Ex. P.K.=Expenditure per kilometre.
M.P.K.=Margin per kilometre.

mofussil and city operations (per km.)

City			Overall		
R.P.K. (in paise)	Ex. P.K. (in paise)	M.P.K. (in paise)	R.P.K. (in paise)	Ex. P.K. (in paise)	M.P.K. (in paise)
(8)	(9)	(10)	(11)	(12)	(13)
138.41	190.26	51.85	157.84	144.82	13.02
170.70	231.30	(—)60.60	188.09	176.31	11.78
194.84	248.49	(—)53.65	198.13	192.08	6.05
219.11	265.61	(—)46.50	206.39	202.71	3.68
211.60	280.56	(—)68.96	204.28	207.00	(—)2.72
224.98	304.41	(—)79.43	220.10	233.90	(—)13.80
244.46	328.45	(—)83.99	234.13	253.83	(—)19.70
286.78	373.47	(—)86.69	265.81	293.19	(—)27.38
336.14	427.58	(—)91.44	314.96	338.90	(—)23.94

TABLE 1.7 : **Trends**

Items	1973-74	1974-75	1975-76	1976-77
(1)	(2)	(3)	(4)	(5)
Staff	44.32 (30.24)	43.75 (24.81)	45.16 (23.51)	55.03 (27.06)
Spare parts	13.13 (8.96)	16.50 (9.36)	18.66 (9.72)	18.53 (9.11)
Tyres and tubes	11.28 (7.69)	15.01 (8.51)	20.33 (10.58)	16.78 (8.25)
Fuel including lubricants	24.98 (17.04)	33.37 (18.93)	37.08 (19.31)	37.42 (18.40)
Passenger taxes	—	—	—	—
M.V. Tax and permit fees	24.70 (16.85)	27.79 (15.76)	30.31 (15.78)	31.72 (15.60)
Rent, rates and taxes	0.17 (0.12)	0.28 (0.16)	0.29 (0.15)	0.31 (0.15)
(a) Insurance	0.05 (0.03)	0.79 (0.45)	0.19 (0.10)	0.21 (0.10)
(b) Depreciation	15.30 (10.44)	20.56 (11.66)	20.55 (10.70)	20.66 (10.16)
Total (a+b)	15.35 (10.47)	21.35 (12.11)	20.74 (10.80)	20.87 (10.26)
Interest on capital	3.04 (2.08)	2.89 (1.64)	3.21 (1.67)	3.09 (1.52)
Development rebate reserve	0.03 (0.02)	0.01 (0.01)	—	—
Miscellaneous	9.57 (6.53)	15.36 (8.71)	16.29 (8.48)	19.62 (9.65)
Total	146.56 (100.00)	176.31 (100.00)	192.08 (100.00)	203.36 (100.00)

Source ; 1973-74 to 1978-79 Annual Admn. Reports ; 1979-80 to 1981-82

in cost structure

(paise per km.)

1977-78	1978-79	1979-80	1980-81	1981-82	Percentage increase in costs during the period
(6)	(7)	(8)	(9)	(10)	(11)
61.69 (29.25)	66.64 (28.49)	68.10 (27.00)	82.20 (27.45)	97.31 (28.71)	119.56
16.34 (7.75)	19.14 (8.18)	23.66 (9.38)	28.02 (9.36)	26.79 (7.91)	104.04
17.28 (8.20)	23.22 (9.93)	24.57 (9.74)	24.92 (8.32)	31.03 (9.16)	175.09
37.13 (17.60)	38.99 (16.67)	43.02 (17.06)	63.00 (21.03)	80.77 (23.83)	223.34
—	—	—	—	—	
31.98 (15.16)	35.91 (15.35)	37.92 (15.04)	39.09 (13.05)	40.61 (11.98)	64.42
0.37 (0.18)	0.45 (0.19)	0.47 (0.19)	0.40 (0.13)	0.08 (0.02)	(—)52.94
0.17 (0.08)	0.35 (0.15)	0.53 (0.21)	0.12 (0.04)	0.15 (0.04)	200.00
22.13 (10.49)	24.62 (10.53)	27.09 (10.75)	32.88 (10.98)	32.81 (9.68)	114.44
22.30 (10.57)	24.97 (10.68)	27.63 (10.96)	33.00 (11.02)	32.95 (9.72)	
3.33 (1.58)	4.14 (1.77)	5.14 (2.04)	6.03 (2.01)	7.30 (2.15)	140.13
—	—	—	—	—	
20.47 (9.71)	20.45 (8.74)	21.65 (8.59)	22.84 (7.63)	22.06 (6.52)	130.51
210.89 (100.00)	233.90 (100.00)	252.16 (100.00)	299.50 (100.00)	338.90 (100.00)	131.24

Annual Accounts (Provisional).

tions in the case of some of the items and also their percentage share increased considerably during the period. The cost of fuel including lubricants increased from 24.98 paise in 1973-74 to 80.77 in 1981-82, increasing the share of this item in the cost from 17.04 to 23.83 per cent. Similarly, in the case of tyres and tubes, there was increase in the percentage share of the cost accounted for by this item. In the case of staff, the percentage of cost accounted for by this item declined between 1973-74 and 1981-82, even though, in absolute terms, the increase in staff cost was more than 100 per cent.

Actually the percentage share of this item of cost in 1981-82 was higher than that in any of these years, except in 1973-74 and 1977-78. In the case of depreciation also, the share of this item of cost over the total cost declined during the period even though the cost of depreciation in terms of paise per km. increased by more than 100 per cent. This decline in percentage share is because of the change in the depreciation policy of the organisation in 1975-76 from 4.8 lakh kilometres to 5.5 lakh kilometres. The implication of this is dealt with in greater detail subsequently.

The share of interest on capital out of the total cost increased in recent years because of the change in the capital structure resulting in increased long term external borrowings. This aspect also is discussed in a subsequent section. In the case of other items, there was by and large a decline in the relative share in spite of an increase in absolute terms.

Thus, on the whole, it can be seen that the cost of each item in terms of paise per km. increased by more than 100 per cent except in the case of passenger taxes and rent, rates and taxes. But the percentage share of some of the items of cost such as fuel, tyres and tubes, interest on capital and also staff (if we exclude 1973-74 in the case of this item) increased much more, thereby indicating that the impact of inflation in the case of these items was much more, and/or the efficiency of the organisation in the case of these items declined. A detailed analysis of this follows.

Staff costs

To start with, an analysis of the staff costs and reasons for the increase in the same is attempted, as this item accounts for the maximum share of the total cost—that is, a little less than 30 per cent. The increase in staff cost could be because of excessive staff recruited by the organisation over the years, thereby resulting in decline in its productivity and/or because of increase in the average pay of employees during the period.

The staff position in relation to schedules may be analysed first. Table 1.8 shows clearly that the schedule-staff ratio increased consistently from 1977-78 till 1980-81. The schedule-staff ratio during the period 1977-78—1981-82 was higher when compared with 1968-69 too. During the period 1969-70—1972-73 also, there was an increase in schedule-staff ratio which declined gradually over the next four years. Thus three distinct phases of schedule-staff ratio could be seen : (1) increase during 1968-69—1972-73 ; (2) decline during 1973-74—1976-77; and (3) once again increase during 1977-78—1981-82. Perhaps, the next phase in the cycle has set in the year 1981-82 with a decline in the ratio. A number of reasons could be adduced to these phases : Firstly, the style of leadership of the Chief Executive of the organisation in keeping track of different aspects of the functioning of the organisation and exercising controls ; secondly, the impact of Government policies ; and thirdly the trade union pressures and the incapacity to resist the same on the part of the management.

An idea of the relative growth of staff in different categories of staff also can be had from the table. The table very clearly shows that there was relatively more increase in staff in the categories of (i) drivers and conductors and (ii) others, where the percentage share accounted for by these categories increased from 46.412 to 50.868 and 6.856 to 8.411 respectively, during the fourteen year period. During the period 1977-78—1980-81 too, the percentage share accounted for by these two categories increased. This is of relevance in the context of trend of losses and increasing losses from 1977-78 onwards.

A more precise idea of the categories in which the schedule-staff ratio has increased can be had from Table 1.9 which shows schedule-staff ratio for different categories. A substantial part of the increase in schedule-staff ratio was accounted for by increase in the drivers and conductors per schedule during that period. After an initial increase in the schedule—drivers and conductors

TABLE 1.8 : Staff category-wise

Year	No. of schedules	Officers	Administrative	Traffic	Drivers & conductors	Workshop & maintenance	Others	Total	Staff per schedule
(1)	(2)	(3)	(4)	(5)	(6)	(7)	(8)	(9)	(10)
1968-69	1,926	120 (0.600)	1,265 (6.325)	1,821 (9.106)	9,481 (47.412)	5,939 (29.699)	1,371 (6.856)	19,997 (100)	10.383
1959-70	1,929	121 (0.585)	1,179 (5.706)	1,875 (9.074)	9,992 (48.359)	6,199 (30.001)	1,296 (6.272)	20,662 (100)	10.711
1970-71	2,011	127 (0.570)	1,319 (5.925)	2,249 (10.104)	10,853 (48.759)	6,127 (27.527)	1,583 (7.112)	22,258 (100)	11.068
1971-72	2,106	145 (0.590)	1,596 (6.501)	2,225 (9.063)	11,830 (48.189)	5,948 (24.229)	2,805 (11.426)	24,549 (100)	11.657
1972-73	2,113	158 (0.620)	1,654 (6.492)	2,307 (9.056)	12,275 (48.186)	6,170 (24.220)	2,910 (11.423)	25,474 (100)	12.056
1973-74	2,645	162 (0.559)	1,791 (6.182)	2,687 (9.275)	14,069 (48.565)	6,820 (23.542)	3,440 (11.874)	28,969 (100)	10.952
1974-75	2,905	164 (0.505)	2,156 (6.641)	2,817 (8.677)	16,148 (49.742)	7,733 (23.820)	3,445 (10.612)	32,463 (100)	11.175
1975-76	3,565	223 (0.588)	2,461 (6.499)	3,460 (9.138)	19,655 (51.910)	10,343 (27.316)	1,721 (4.545)	37,863 (100)	10.620
1976-77	4,071	264 (0.612)	2,882 (6.684)	4,688 (10.873)	22,056 (51,156)	11,129 (25.812)	2,096 (4.861)	43,115 (100)	10.591
1977-78	4,498	269 (0.549)	2,899 (5.922)	4,720 (9,642)	24,823 (50.709)	12,877 (26.305)	3,363 (6.870)	48,951 (100)	10.883

1978-79	4,973	324 (0.604)	2,979 (5.555)	5,031 (9.382)	27,258 (50.833)	14,409 (26.871)	3,621 (6.752)	53,622 (100)	10.783
1979-80	5,470	341 (0.566)	3,170 (5.259)	5,649 (9.371)	31,148 (51.670)	15,855 (26.300)	4,120 (6.834)	60,283 (100)	11.021
1980-81	5,784	355 (0.548)	3,931 (6.073)	5,824 (8.997)	33,887 (52.350)	16,197 (25.023)	4,537 (7.009)	64,731 (100)	11.191
1981-82	5,922	356 (0.546)	3,886 (5.956)	6,072 (9.306)	33,188 (50.868)	16.254 (24.913)	5,488 (8.411)	65,244 (100)	11.017

Source : 1968-69 to 1978-79 Annual Administration Reports 1979-80 to 1981-82 MIS Records.
Note : Figures in brackets are percentages to the total staff.

TABLE 1.9 : **Schedule-staff ratio : Category-wise**

Year	Officers	Adminis-trative	Traffic	Drivers & conductors	Workshop & maintenance	Others	Total
(1)	(2)	(3)	(4)	(5)	(6)	(7)	(8)
1968-69	0.062	0.657	0.945	4.923	3.084	0.712	10.383
1969-70	0.063	0.611	0.972	5.180	3.214	0.672	10.712
1970-71	0.063	0.656	1.118	5.397	3.047	0.787	11.068
1971-72	0.069	0.758	1.057	5.617	2.824	1.332	11.657
1972-73	0.075	0.783	1.092	5.809	2.920	1.377	12.056
1973-74	0.061	0.677	1.016	5.319	2.578	1.301	10.952
1974-75	0.056	0.742	0.970	5.559	2.662	1.186	11.175
1975-76	0.063	0.690	0.971	5.513	2.901	0.483	10.621
1976-77	0.065	0.708	1.152	5.418	2.734	0.515	10.592
1977-78	0.060	0.645	1.049	5.519	2.863	0.748	10.884
1978-79	0.065	0.599	1.012	5.481	2.897	0.728	10.782
1979-80	0.062	0.580	1.034	5.694	2.899	0.753	10.022
1980-81	0.061	0.680	1.007	5.859	2.800	0.784	11.191
1981-82	0.060	0.656	1.025	5.604	2.745	0.927	11.017

ratio during 1968-69—1972-73 there was a decline during the next period ending 1976-77. Once again there was an increase in the next phase of 1977-78 to 1980-81, conforming to the overall pattern. In a way, the trends in overall schedule-staff ratio could be attributed to the increase in the drivers and conductors. It would be of interest to see whether the increase in the schedule-drivers and conductors ratio brought about any increase in the kilometres done per driver and conductor. This would be taken up at a later stage. It is also to be noted that the schedule to 'other' staff ratio increased over the period but there was some aberration during the period 1971-72—1976-77. This could be perhaps because of the changes in the classification of the category of "others". Excluding this period, it is clear that there was a considerable increase in this category of staff. On the whole, the increase in the schedule-staff ratio was accounted for by these categories of staff.

If 1965-66 is taken as the base year, and the schedule-staff ratio of that year is taken as the norm, the percentage increase in the staff per schedule was the highest in the year 1971-72 at 13.37 which gradually came down to 3.0 by 1976-77, and thereafter it gradually increased to 8.84 per cent by 1980-81. As indicated earlier, it came down to 7.15 per cent in 1981-82 (Table 1.10).

Table 1.11 gives the percentage increase in actual staff per schedule in different years taking 1976-77 as the base year with the schedule-staff-ratio of that year as the norm. It could be seen that even with 1976-77 as the norm the staff per schedule has gone up by 5.666 per cent by 1980-81.

The foregoing analysis gave a clear idea of the increase in the schedule-staff ratio in Andhra Pradesh State Road Transport Corporation (APSRTC) during the two periods analysed. It is relevant to see whether the (APSRTC) has surplus staff not only in terms of its earlier schedule-staff ratio but also in relation to other organisations. For this purpose, the following organisations/norms are taken into consideration for the reasons stated. Broadly, two organisations and two norms are taken into consideration. One of these—Gujarat State Road Transport Corporation (GSRTC)—is taken up for comparison for the reason that it is comparable in size, in terms of fleet.

TABLE 1.10 : **Excess staff over 1965-66**

Year	Staff per schedule	No. of schedules	Total staff @ 10.282 (base)	Actual staff	Excess/ shortage of staff	Percentage of excess staff over the base year staff
(1)	(2)	(3)	(4)	(5)	(6)	(7)
1965-66	10.282	1,535	15,783	15,783	—	—
1966-67	10.293	1,635	16,811	16,829	18	0.1071
1967-68	9.923	1,825	18,765	18,110	(—)655	(—)3.4905
1968-69	10.383	1,926	19,803	19,998	195	0.9847
1969-70	10.711	1,929	19,834	20,662	828	4.1746
1970-71	11.068	2,011	20,677	22,258	1,581	7.6462
1971-72	11.657	2,106	21,654	24,550	2,896	13.3740
1972-73	12.056	2,113	21,726	25,474	3748	17 2512
1973-74	10.952	2,645	27,196	28,968	1,772	6.5157
1974-75	11.175	2,905	29,869	32,463	2,594	8.6846
1975-76	10.620	3,565	36,655	37,860	1,205	3.2874
1976-77	10.591	4,071	41,858	43,116	1,258	3.0054
1977-78	10.883	4,498	46,248	48,952	2,704	5.8467
1978-79	10.783	4,973	51,132	53,624	24,92	4.8737
1979-80	11.021	5,470	56,243	60,283	4,040	7.1831
1980-81	11.191	5,784	59,471	64,731	5,260	8.8447
1981-82	11.017	5,922	60,890	65,244	4,354	7.1506

Source : 1. 1968-69 to 1978-79 Annual Administration Reports ;
2. 1979-80 to 1981-82 MIS.

TABLE 1.11 : Excess staff over 1976-77

Year	Staff per schedule	No. of schedules	Total staff @ 10.591	No. of actual staff	Excess/shortage of staff over the base year staff	% of actual increased over the standard
(1)	(2)	(3)	(4)	(5)	(6)	(7)
1976-77	10.591	4,071	43,116	43,116	—	—
1977-78	10.883	4,498	47,639	48,952	1313	2.7561
1978-79	10.783	4,973	52,669	53,624	955	1.8132
1979-80	11.021	5,470	57,931	60,283	2352	4.0600
1980-81	11.191	5,784	61,260	64,731	3471	5.6660
1981-82	11.017	5,922	62,721	65,244	2523	4.0226

Another organisation—Kattabomman Transport Corporation—is selected for this purpose because this undertaking (KTC) had the highest schedule-staff ratio among the eight nationalised road transport undertakings in Tamil Nadu, excluding Pallavan (Metro) (which is not comparable because it is entirely a city transport undertaking) in the year 1980-81. Apart from these two undertakings, as mentioned earlier, two norms are also taken into consideration for comparison. In Tamil Nadu, there is a norm of staff given to the nationalised road transport undertakings for adherence which is 7.50 staff per schedule based on the following norms for different categories :

Administration	0.80
Traffic	5.15
Mechanical & Maintenance	1.55
Total :	7.50

This norm of 7.50 excludes the staff required for the Reconditioning Unit (0.40), Body Building Unit (0.20) and Tyre Retreading Unit (0.05), which together account for another 0.65, thereby increasing the total norm to 8.15. There is a proposal to increase the norms for the Traffic from 5.15 to 5.65 because of the additional requirement of conductors and drivers at 0.25 each per schedule, thereby resulting in an increase in the overall norm to 8.65. It is against these schedule-staff ratios/norms obtaining elsewhere that it is proposed to analyse the excess staff position in Andhra Pradesh State Road Transport Corporation, the data in respect of which are presented in Table 1.12.

It is evident from the table that the schedule-staff ratio was the highest in Andhra Pradesh State Road Transport Corporation when compared with those in other organisations/the norms in Tamil Nadu. When compared with a similar unitary organisation for the entire state, with the same fleet strength, that is, Gujarat State Road Transport Corporation, the Andhra Pradesh State Road Transport Corporation had surplus staff to the extent of 1.58 per schedule. Even after taking into consideration the fact that Andhra Pradesh State Road Transport Corporation has got about 10 per cent of its fleet operating on city services, the excess

TABLE 1.12 : **Staff position : Inter-firm comparison**

Category	Existing staff & schedule staff ratio in APSRTC	Staff required as per KTC staff ratio	Excess (+) shortage (—) in APSRTC (2-3)	Staff required as per GSRTC staff ratio	Excess (+) shortage (—) in APSRTC	Staff required as per 8.15 norm	Excess (+) shortage (—) in APSRTC	Staff required as per 8.65 norm	Difference
(1)	(2)	(3)	(4)	(5)	(6)	(7)	(8)	(9)	(10)
Administration	4,917 (0.85)	7,347 (1.27)	(—)2,430 (—)(0.42)	4,628 (0.80)	289 (0.05)	4,626 (0.80)	291 (0.05)	4,626 (0.80)	291 (0.05)
Traffic	39,625 (6.85)	28,403 (4.91)	11,222 (1.94)	36,444 (6.30)	3,181 (0.55)	29,790 (5.15)	9,835 (1.70)	32,682 (5.65)	6,943 (1.20)
Workshop	20,189 (3.49)	15,156 (2.62)	5,033 (0.87)	14,519 (2.51)	5,670 (0.98)	12,724 (2.20)	7,465 (1.29)	12,724 (2.20)	7,465 (1.29)
Total	64,731 (11.19)	50,906 (8.80)	13,825 (2.39)	55,591 (9.61)	9,140 (1.58)	47,140 (8.15)	17,591 (3.04)	50,032 (8.65)	14,699 (2.54)

KTC=Kattabomman Transport Corporation.

of 1.58 staff per schedule is on the high side. Based on the Gujarat State Road Transport Corporation ratio, the Andhra Pradesh State Road Transport Corporation had surplus staff of 9,140 to operate the Andhra Pradesh State Road Transport Corporation schedules of 1980-81. The financial implications of the excess staff will be analysed at a later stage.

In Tamil Nadu, the Kattabomman Transport Corporation had the highest schedule-staff ratio among all the corporations, excluding the Pallavan (Metro) Corporation which is not comparable. Even against the norm of such an organisation in Tamil Nadu, the Andhra Pradesh State Road Transport Corporation had excess staff to the extent of 2.39 per schedule, implying a total excess staff of 13,825. Two conclusions emerge from the above comparisons. Firstly, the Andhra Pradesh State Road Transport Corporation had a higher schedule-staff ratio or excess staff when compared with a similar organisation. Secondly, the small organisations have lower schedule-staff ratio than large sized organisations, as both Andhra Pradesh State Road Transport Corporation and Gujarat State Road Transport Corporation, which are broadly of the same size, had higher schedule-staff ratios than the Kattabomman Transport Corporation, which is a smaller undertaking with 678 vehicles (as on 31st March 1981), and which has the highest schedule-staff ratio among all the small sized, nationalised road transport undertakings in Tamil Nadu, operating district services. This is a pointer in so far as the policy regarding size is concerned. The reason for this—if one reason could be given—is that the number of levels in the organisation is only two in Tamil Nadu, as against four in Andhra Pradesh and three in Gujarat State Road Transport Corporartion. This clearly shows that the more the tiers in the organisation the more the staff. At the same time, it is not possible in a big organisation to manage effectively a large number of depots with only two tiers, the Head Office directly controlling and co-ordinating the depots. The inevitable inference is that the large organisations shall have to be split if there is to be economy in staff and expeditious decision-making, which is essential in passenger road transport organisations.

This was the position when we compare the APSRTC schedule-staff ratio with those of GSRTC and KTC Worse still is the position of APSRTC when compared with the schedule-staff ratios/norms obtaining in other corporations in Tamil Nadu, which as mentioned earlier is 8.15 or is likely to be 8.65 in future, if approved. Even against the norm of 8.65, the excess staff in APSRTC would come to 2.54 per schedule or a total excess staff of 14,699 which forms a significant part in terms of the total staff. Table 1.13 shows that APSRTC incurred for one year in 1980-81 alone excess expenditure on staff to the tune of Rs. 7.70 crores, based on GSRTC staff ratio ; Rs. 11.60 crores, based on Kattabomman ratio : Rs. 12.40 crores based on 8.65 norm and Rs. 14.84 crores based on 8.15 norm of Tamil Nadu. It is thus evident that a substantial part of the losses—ranging between 45 per cent and 87 per cent were accounted for by the excess staff (as against the norm/ratio obtaining in Tamil Nadu and GSRTC). The remedy for this is not easy in the short-run, as whatever be the organisational set-up, inclusive of split, it is not possible to get rid of the excess staff immediately. The only solution is an immediate step to split the organisation which will bring about gradual reduction of staff in the long run as and when the employees retire, or adoption of a voluntary retirement scheme or augmentation of fleet without further recruitment. But the basic remedy is split.

It is clear from the above that the organisation did not have norms of staff. Even if it had, they were observed more in breach, reflecting the ineffective control systems the organisation had in the vital personnel area. During the course of the discussions with the officers of the organisation it was clear that there was no norm in respect of drivers and conductors in relation to schedules. The requirement of drivers and conductors is based on the crew schedules drawn which are subject to manoeuvring either by Depot Managers themselves or because of pressures from Trade Unions, whereas the schedule-staff ratio is a more rational and unmanoeuvrable basis. Because of this the schedule-bus-crew ratio has gone up resulting in an increase in the overall schedule-staff ratio, apart from the other reasons. Further, the Divisional Managers are empowered to sanction 95 per cent of the requirement of the bus crew as determined by the Depot Managers. Hence, if there is collusion between the Depot Manager and Divisional Manager or if the Divisional Manager

TABLE 1.13 : **Financial implication of surplus staff based on GSRTC and Tamil Nadu norms 1980-81**

Particulars	GSRTC staff ratio (9.6129)	Tamil Nadu: Kattabomman transport corporation (8.8155)	Tamil Nadu: Staff required as per 8.15 norm	Tamil Nadu: Staff required as per 8.65 norm
Existing staff in APSRTC 64,731.				
Staff requirement for operating 5784 schedules based on	55,601	50,989	47,140	50,032
Additional staff in APSRTC based on	9,130 (64731—55601)	13,742 (64731—50989)	17,591 (64731—47140)	14,699 (64731—50032)
Cost of additional staff based on average personnel cost of APSRTC Rs. 8,438.63 (Rs. in lakhs)	770.45 (8438.63 × 9130)	1,159.64 (8438.63 × 13742)	1,484.44 (8438.63 × 17591)	1,240.39 (8438.63 × 14699)

Source : Report on the performance of Nationalised Road Transport Undertakings 1979-80 and 1980-81, Central Institute of Road Transport, Pune.

deliberately wants to recruit additional staff and impose on the depots additional staff, for whatever be the reasons, or if he is apathetic to whatever is happening in the depots it can result in surplus staff. Hence, there is need for fixing scientifically based norms for staff.

The financial implications of excess staff for 1981-82 alone, based upon the schedule-staff ratio of A.P.S.R.T.C. itself in 1976-77, and taking into consideration the average pay of 1981-82, would come to Rs. 3.08 crores. If the cost of staff for manning the schedules of 1981-82, based on its own schedule-staff ratio of 1976-77 and its average pay of the same year (1976-77) is taken into consideration, the additional cost of staff works out to Rs. 42.02 crores. Thus, it is clear that the inefficiency of the organisation in terms of staff contributed Rs. 3.08 crores additional expenditure/loss and the wage inflation accounted for Rs. 38.94 crores ; these two put together accouting for Rs. 42 crores for 1981-82 alone as could be seen from Table 1.14.

TABLE 1.14 : **Financial implications of excess staff and inflation for 1981-82 based on 1976-77 norm**

No. of schedules during 1981-82		5,922
Schedule staff ratio during 1981-82		11,017
Schedule staff ratio during 1976-77		10.591
Existing staff (1981-82)		65.244
Staff required as per 1976-77 schedule-staff ratio		62,720
Excess staff over 1976-77 norm		2,524
Average pay during 1981-82	Rs.	12,207
Extra cost on excess staff as per average pay of 1981-82	Rs.	3,08,10,468
Existing total staff cost	Rs.	79,64,49,000
Average pay during 1976-77	Rs.	5,999
Staff cost as per 1976-77 norms of staff and average pay	Rs.	37,62,57,280
Excess staff cost	Rs.	42,01,91,720
Less : Extra cost resulting from increased staff	Rs.	3,08,10,468
Extra cost due to wage increase	Rs.	38,93,81,252

Table 1.14 (a) shows the additional cost incurred by the organisation, during the period 1977-78—1981-82, on excess staff, taking the 1976-77 schedule-staff ratio as the norm. It shows that the organisation had incurred an additional expenditure of Rs. 9.32 crores during this period because of excess staff, taking

the average pay of the respective years into consideration.

Table 1.14 (b) shows the effect of inflation/wage increase during 1976-77—1981-82, by taking into cosideration the actual staff employed in the respective years and the average pay of 1976-77. The wage increases during the period have resulted in an increase in the staff cost by Rs. 74.15 crores, Rs. 57.00 crores of which was incarred during the last two years only.

As was seen earlier, the main contributing factor for the increase in schedule-staff ratio and consequent increase in the expenditure on staff, was the increase in crew (drivers and conductors) in relation to schedules. An increase in crew in relation to schedules need not necessarily mean inefficiency of the organisation in terms of its operating staff, as the same vehicle with the increase in staff, may be doing mileage proportionate or more than proprtionate to increase in staff which may in turn mean that either the productivity has not gone down or it has increased. In order to have an idea of this, the productivity of drivers and conductors, in terms of effective kilometres done by this category of staff per year, is computed and presented in Table 1.15. The table shows that the productivity of crew in terms of effective kms. done per year has been on the decline since 1978-79. The same trend continued even in the year 1981-82. It should be perplexing to have a decline in productivity in 1981-82 at a time when the schedule-staff ratio as well as schedule-crew ratio came down. A decline in schedule-crew ratio, the average daily mileage remaining the same, should result in an increase in crew productivity in terms of kilometres done. The reason for the decline in crew productivity in terms of kilometres, at a time when schedule-crew ratio came down, must be because of a deliberate policy on the part of the organisation to reduce the unremunerative trips/services which was being pursued during the year 1981-82 and subsequently.

The policy of reducing the schedule-staff ratio is carried to the extreme in a few cases losing the broader perspective of overall efficiency of the organisation by taking a particular parameter as an end in itself. A case may be cited to substantiate this. One of the Depots, inspite of repeated requests for essential requirement of crew for operating the services, could not get the same, thereby resulting in cancellation of trips, implying

TABLE 1.14(a) : **Cost of excess staff**

Year	No. of schedules	Total staff required as per the norm of 1976-77 Bus staff ratio (10.591) (2 × norm)	Average pay of an employee during the year (Rs.)	Total staff cost as per norm (1976-77 Bus staff ratio) and as per the average pay of respective years (3 × 4) (Rs. in lakhs)	Total actual staff cost (Rs. in lakhs)	Difference between staff cost and total staff cost as per norm (Rs. in lakhs) (6—5)
(1)	(2)	(3)	(4)	(5)	(6)	(7)
1976-77	4,071	43,115	5,998.98	2,586.46	2,586.46	—
1977-78	4,498	47,638	6,778.80	3,229.28	3,318.29	89.01
1978-79	4,973	52,669	7,039.39	3,707.58	3,774.66	67.08
1979-80	5,470	57,933	7,283.23	4,219.39	4,390.55	171.16
1980-81	5,784	61,258	8,548.28	5,236.51	5,533.39	296.88
1981-82	5,922	62,720	12,207.24	7,656.38	7,964.49	308.11
					Total :	932.24

TABLE 1.14(b) : **Inflation effect on staff cost**

Year	Actual staff employed	Total staff cost as per 1976-77 average pay (Rs. 5,998.98) (Rs. in lakhs)	Total actual staff cost (Rs. in lakhs)	Difference between actual staff cost and total staff cost as per norm. (4—3)
(1)	(2)	(3)	(4)	(5)
1976-77	43,115	2,586.46	2,586.46	—
1977-78	48,951	2,936.56	3,318.29	381.73
1978-79	53,622	3,216.77	3,774.66	557.89
1979-80	60,283	3,616.37	4,390.55	774.18
1980-81	64,731	3,883.20	5,533.39	1,650.19
1981-82	65,244	3,913,97	7,964.49	4,050.52
			Total :	7,414.51

TABLE 1.15 : **Crew productivity**

Year	Effective kms. (in lakhs)	Average No. of drivers and conductors during the year	Productivity (in effective kms.)
1973-74	2,611.30	13,172	19,824.63
1974-75	3,090.63	15,109	20,455.56
1975-76	3,695.28	17,901	20,642.87
1976-77	4,277.77	20,856	20,510.98
1977-78	4,861.87	23,440	20,741.77
1978-79	5,106.85	26,041	19,610.81
1979-80	5,802.33	29,203	19,868.95
1980-81	6,175.70	32,518	18,991.64
1981-82	6,207.31	33,538	18,508.23

declining vehicle mileage done and loss of revenues, whereas the Depot Manager was given letter of appreciation for bringing down the schedule-staff ratio. The corporation, therefore, while fixing parameters of performance in respect of individual factors should not lose sight of possible slippages in performance elsewhere.

Cost of spares

The corporation presently incurs an expenditure of about Rs. 17 crores per year on spares. The expenditure on spares, in absolute terms, has more than doubled since 1976-77 (vide Table 1.16), the last year of its profits, and by about 400 per cent over 1973-74 when it got the highest profits. The average expenditure on spares per vehicle increased by more than 100 per cent since 1973-74 and by about 50 per cent since 1976-77. It is, therefore, necessary to analyse how far this increased expenditure on spares, especially per vehicle, was due to increase in the cost of spares and how much it was due to inefficiency of the organisation. The methodology for evaluating the organisational effectiveness in regard to cost of stores is as follows : the cost of spares in the base year 1976-77 is taken into consideration and adjusted by the inflation factor, taking into consideration the percentage increase in the cost of vehicle, assuming that the cost of spares would increase at the same rate as that of increase in the cost of vehicle. It is

TABLE 1.16 : **Cost of spare parts per vehicle**

Year	Cost of spare parts (Rs. in lakhs)	Average No. of vehicles held*	Cost of spare parts per vehicle (Rs)
1973-74	342.92	2,748	12,479
1974-75	509.89	3,225	15,811
1975-76	689.58	3,898	17,691
1976-77	792.57	4,325	18,325
1977-78	794.59	4,815	16,502
1978-79	977.40	5,272	18,539
1979-80	1,381.96	5,657	24,429
1980-81	1,730.55	6,329	27,343
1981-82	1,663.10	6,541	25,426

Source : 1973-74 to 1978-79 Annual Administration Reports ; 1979-80 to 1981-82 Annual Performance Reports

* Excluding stabled.

assumed so because spares constitute a part of the vehicle and the cost of spares influences the cost of vehicle. The resultant adjusted cost of spares is multiplied by the average number of vehicles held to arrive at the possible cost of spares, because of inflation. The actual expenditure incurred on spares is compared with the inflation adjusted cost of spares to know whether the organisation was efficient or inefficient in its consumption of spares. It is considered efficient if the actual cost is less than the adjusted costs and vice versa. From the figures in Table 1.17, it is clear that the organisation, though initially efficient in this respect in the years 1977-78 and 1978-79, proved to be inefficient in 1979-80 ; and because of this it incurred an additional expenditure of Rs. 85.71 lakhs in that year. It is, however, heartening to note that there was a slight improvement in the year 1980-81 but spectacular improvement in the year 1981-82, when the organisation in a way saved Rs. 4.27 crores in that year, as the actual cost of spares was less by this extent over the inflation adjusted cost of spares.

At this stage it must be noted that the inflation has resulted in excess expenditure of Rs. 4.64 crores in 1981-82 alone ; and over the last five years, the corporation incurred an additional expenditure of Rs. 13.04 crores on spares because of inflation (vide Table 1.18). Thus, in spite of inflation, the percentage

TABLE 1.17 : **Cost of spares and the impact of organisational efficiency**

Year	Average cost of vehicles	% increase in average cost of vehicles over 1976-77	Average cost of spares per vehicle based on 1976-77 norm as adjusted for inflation based on increase in the average cost of vehicles	Total cost of spares based on average No. of vehicles held x column No. (4)	Actual cost of spares	Excess of actuals over 1976-77 norm adjusted to price increase of vehicle
	(Rs.)		(Rs)	(Rs)	(Rs)	(Rs)
1976-77	1,53,090	100.00	18,235.00	7,92,57,000	7,92,57,000	—
1977-78	1,56,737	102.38	18,669.00	8,98,91,235	7,94,59,000	(—)1,04,32,235
1978-79	1,77,380	115.87	21,128.90	11,13,91,561	9,77,40,000	(—)1,36,51,561
1979-80	1,92,367	125.66	22,914.10	12,96,25,064	13,81,96,000	85,70,936
1980-81	2,36,681	154.60	28,191.31	17,84,22,801	17,30,55,000	(—) 53,67,801
1981-82	2,68,292	175.25	31,956.84	20,90,29,690	16,63,11,446	(—)4,27,18,244
					Total	(—)6,53,98,905

TABLE 1.18 : **Cost of spares and the impact of inflation**

Year	Average No. of vehicles held	Average cost of spares per vehicle	Total cost of spares based on average cost of spares for the year 1976-77	Actual total cost of spares	Excess of actuals over 1976-77 norm
		Rs	Rs	Rs	Rs
1976-77	4,325	18,325	—	—	—
1977-78	4,815	16,502	8,82,34,875	7,94,59,000	77,75,875
1978-79	5,272	18,539	9,66,09,400	9,77,40,000	11,30,600
1979-80	5,657	24,429	10,36,64,525	13,81,96,000	3,45,31,475
1980-81	6,329	27,343	11,59,78,925	17,30,55,000	5,70,76,075
1981-82	6,541	25,426	11,98,63,825	16,63,10,000	4,64,46,175

share of the cost of spares came down during the period 1976-77—1981-82, because of improvement in efficiency in stores consumption and relative increase in other costs. It is a matter for gratification that the corporation could achieve this at a time when the average age of the vehicle has been on the increase particularly since 1977-78. Table 1.19 clearly shows that the average of the vehicles in operation in Andhra Pradesh State Road

TABLE 1.19 : **Age structure of vehicles**

Year	Average age of vehicle in years and months	Cost of spares per vehicle	Inflation adjusted cost of spares per vehicle
		Rs.	Rs.
1973-74	4-1	12,479	—
1974-75	3-1	15,811	—
1975-76	3-1	17,691	—
1976-77	3-7	18,325	—
1977-78	4-0	16,502	18,669
1978-79	4-3	18,539	21,233
1979-80	4-5	24,429	23,027
1980-81	4-5	27,343	28,330
1981-82	4-7	25,426	32,115

Transport Corporation (APSRTC) was consistently on the increase from 1976-77 onwards. It increased from 3 years and 1 month in 1975-76 to 4 years and 7 months in 1981-82. The cost of spares per vehicle also increased but it was less than the inflation adjusted cost of spares per vehicle in all the years since 1977-78, except for 1979-80. The largest difference between the two was in 1981-82 which shows that substantial efforts were put in by the management in that year in this regard. However, a word of caution is necessary in according credit to the management in this respect as efficiency in this respect could sometimes be manoeuvred in the short run ; and, therefore, it is to be judged at least over a period of two or three years. However, the trend is unmistakable.

Any evaluation of an organisations' efficiency over a time span may mean improvement of efficiency only within the organisation by its own standards, which is by itself good.

However, this does not help the organisation unless a comparison is made of its performance in this regard with other organisations. Such comparison can be made from Table 1.20. The table shows that the average cost of spares per vehicle in the case of

TABLE 1.20 : **Average cost of spares per vehicle : Inter-firm comparison (1980-81)**

Name of the undertaking	Total cost of spares (Rs. in lakhs)	Average No. of vehicles held	Average cost of spares per vehicle (Rs. in '000)
APSRTC	1,730.55	6,329	27.34
GSRTC	583.10	6,489	8.99
Pallavan TCL (Dist.)	N.A.	—	—
Pallavan TCL (Metro)	351.58	1,731	20.31
Cheran TCL	229.95	1,281	17.95
Cholan R/W CL	200.95	657	30.59
Kattabomman TCL	169.16	649	26.07
Thiruvalluvar TCL	147.39	408	36.13
Pandiyan R/W CL	211.43	996	21.23

Source : Report on the Performance of Nationalised Road Transport Undertakings 1979-80 and 1980-81 Central Institute of Road Transport, Pune.

(APSRTC) is not a matter for happiness, as the average cost of spares per vehicle in APSRTC was more than 200 per cent over that in Gujarat State Road Transport Corporation, (GSRTC) a comparable organisation in terms of size of fleet. It is also much more than most of the state transport undertakings in Tamil Nadu. This only shows that, despite the improvement in efficiency of the organisation in this regard, in recent years, it is not a matter for complacency and there is still considerable scope for improvement in this regard.

Table 1.21 gives, in financial terms, the extra cost of spares that the corporation has incurred in 1980-81 based upon the GSRTC average cost of spares per vehicle. It shows that if the corporation had been as efficient as GSRTC it would have saved Rs. 11.62 crores in one year that is 1980-81.

To sum up, even though the corporation had shown

TABLE 1.21 : **Comparison of spares cost of APSRTC with GSRTC for the year 1980-81**

	APSRTC	GSRTC
	Rs.	Rs.
Average cost of spares per vehicle	27,343.00	8,990.00
Average No. of vehicles held during the year	6,329.00	6,489.00
Total cost of spares (Rs. in lakhs)	1,730.55	583.10
Cost of spares in APSRTC taking GSRTC consumption as the norm (Rs. in lakhs).	568.98	
Difference (Rs. in lakhs)	1,161.57	

consistent improvement in reducing the spares consumption after adjusting for inflation, there is still considerable room for improvement when compared with other Corporations.

Tyre performance

An analysis of Table 1.7 showed that the percentage increase in cost during 1973-74 – 1981-82 was very high in the case of Tyres and Tubes, next only to that in the case of fuel and lubricants, among the major items of cost. It is, therefore, necessary to analyse the reasons for the same. Table 1.22 gives an idea of tyre performance. The table clearly shows that this is another area where the organisation has shown improvement in performance besides spares, when compared with its own performance in earlier years. The performance of tyres in terms of kilometres done increased in the case of all categories of tyres namely, new tyres and retreaded tyres except in the case of fourth retreaded tyres, even though improvement in performance was marginal in most of the cases. There was improvement in tyre performance even during the period 1976-77 – 1980-81 in all categories except for the first retreaded tyres where there was a slight decline in 1980-81 over 1976-77. However, this improvement in performance of tyres cannot perhaps be attributed to the organisational efficiency as it could have been due to the improvement in the technology of tyres. For example, the introduction of Nylon tyre with 14 ply must have made its own contribution to the improvement in tyre performance. It is difficult to identify the extent of contribution

TABLE 1.22 : **Tyre performance**

Particulars	1973-74 (kms)	1974-75 (kms)	1975-76 (kms)	1976-77 (kms)	1977-78 (kms)	1978-79 (kms)	1979-80 (kms)	1980-81 (kms)	1981-82 (kms)
(1)	(2)	(3)	(4)	(5)	(6)	(7)	(8)	(9)	(10)
New tyres	31,746	31,554	32,916	32,916	32,622	32,750	36,066	35,677	N.A.
	(100)	(99.40)	(103.69)	(103.83)	(102.76)	(103.16)	(113.61)	(112.38)	—
				100*	98.97*	99.36*	109.42*	108.24*	—
First retreaded	21,682	23,086	21,515	22,869	21,134	21,907	21,757	22,467	N.A.
	(100)	(106.48)	(99.23)	(105.47)	(97·47)	(101.04)	(100.35)	(103.62)	—
				100.00*	92.41*	95.79*	95.14*	98.24*	—
Second retreaded	18,296	16,319	20,853	17,722	18,506	17,591	18,701	19,015	N.A.
	(100)	(89.19)	(113.98)	(96.86)	(101.15)	(96.15)	(102.21)	(103.93)	—
				100.00*	104.42*	99.26*	105.52*	107.30*	—
Third retreaded	16,652	20,461	18,191	15,301	16,656	15,310	15,348	17,148	N.A.
	(100)	(122.87)	(109.24)	(91.89)	(100.02)	(91.94)	(92.17)	(102.98)	—
				100.00*	108.86*	100.06*	100.31*	112.07*	—
Fourth retreaded	17,823	16,740	10,364	13,605	15,504	N.A	N.A.	15,242	N·A.
	(100)	(93.92)	(58.15)	(76.33)	(86.99)			(85.52)	—
				100.00*	113.96*	—	—	112.03*	—

Note : Figures in brackets represent change in the performance with 1973-74 as the base.

*These figures represent change in the performance with 1976-77 as the base.

Source : 1 1973-74 to 1978-79 Annual Administration Reports ;

2 1979-80 and 1980-81 MIS Records.

of improvement in the quality of tyres to the improvement in performance.

The improved performance of new tyres is also reflected in the consumption of new tyres as can be seen from table 1.23.

TABLE 1.23 : **New tyre consumption**

Year	Total No. of new tyres issued	Total kms. done (kms. in lakhs)	New tyres consumed per lakh kms.
1976-77	43,653	4,424.00	9.87
1977-78	52,579	5,027.00	10.46
1978-79	62.520	5,302.00	11.79
1979-80	60,544	6,053.00	10.00
1980-81	57,020	6,394.00	8.92
1981-82	56,404	6,402.00	8.81

Source : Information furnished by (1) MIS ;
(2) CCOS.

There was a gradual decline in the number of new tyres consumed per lakh kms. since 1979-80.

An idea of the impact of inflation on the cost of new tyres can be had from Table 1.24. The inflation effect is computed by taking into consideration the average cost of tyres in 1976-77 and the actual consumption of tyres in the respective years. The table shows that the cost of inflation on the new tyres was Rs. 19.19 crores for the period of which Rs. 8.41 crores was for 1981-82 alone.

At this stage, a comparison of tyre performance of APSRTC with that of others may be attempted. Table 1.25 shows that the new tyre performance in the case of APSRTC was next only to that of GSRTC and it was comparable with that of most of the corporations in Tamil Nadu for which data are available on this aspect.

Table 1.26 gives an idea of the financial implications of low mileage given by new tyres in APSRTC when compared with that in GSRTC. It shows that APSRTC incurred an additional expenditure of Rs. 396.82 lakhs in 1980-81 alone on new tyres because of low mileage when compared with the mileage obtained

TABLE 1.24 : **Impact of inflation on tyre consumption**

Year	No. of new tyers issued	Rate of new tyre (Rs.)	Total actual cost of new tyres (Rs. in lakhs)	Total cost of new tyres based on 1976-77 norm (Rs. in lakhs)	Excess of actuals over the norm
1976-77	43,653	1,309.30	571.55	—	—
1977-78	52,579	1,289.50	678.32	688.42	(—)10.10
1978-79	62,520	1,607.00	1,004.86	818.57	186.29
1979-80	60,544	1,943.00	1,176.68	792.70	383.98
1980-81	57,020	2,217.00	1,263.63	746.56	517.07
1981-82	56,404	2,801.00	1,579.91	738.50	841.41
					1,918.65

Source : Information furnished by (1) MIS ; (2) CCOS.

TABLE 1.25 : **Tyre performance : Inter-firm comparison**

Name of the corporation	New tyre mileage (in kms.)
(1) APSRTC	35,677
(2) GSRTC	52,000
(3) *Tamil Nadu*	
(a) Cholan R/W CL	30,345
(b) Pallavan TCL (Dist.)	34,475
(c) Thiruvalluvar TCL	32,979
(d) Pandiyan R/W CL	25,888
(e) Pallavan TCL (Metro)	35,129

Source : Report on the performance of Nationalised Road Transport undertakings 1979-80 and 1980-81 Central Institute of Road Transport, Pune.

TABLE 1.26 : **Comparison of APSRTC with GSRTC in terms of tyre mileage for the year 1980-81**

	APSRTC	GSRTC
New tyre mileage	35,677 kms. (100)	52,000 kms. (145.75)
No. of new tyres consumed	57,020	
Total kms. obtained by new tyres (kms. in lakhs)	20,343.03	
No. of tyres required to operate 20,343.03 lakh kms. if GSRTC is taken as norm	39,121	
Difference : (No. of tyres now consumed— the tyres that would have been consumed, if GSRTC is taken as norm)	=17,899	
Additional cost incurred (Tyres x average rate)	=17,899 × Rs. 2,217 =396.82 (Rs. in lakhs)	

Source : CIRT Report for the year 1980-81.

by tyres in GSRTC.

Table 1.27 shows the financial implications of improvement/deterioration in tyre performance in different years over the base year 1976-77. It can be seen from the table that the organisation incurred an additional expenditure of Rs. 218.23 lakhs during

TABLE 1.27 : **Impact of tyre performance on cost of tyres**

Year	No. of new tyres issued	Tyre performance in kms. (Total kms ÷ No. of new tyres issued)	Total kms done (kms in lakhs)	Total kms based on 1976-77 norms (kms in lakhs)	Efficiency/inefficiency in tyre usage (kms in lakhs)	Extra tyres consumed/tyres saved	Average cost (Rs.)	Extra consumption or saving (in Rs. lakhs)
1976-77	43,653	10,134.47	4,424.00	—	—	—	1,309.30	—
1977-78	52,579	9,560.85	5,027.00	5,328.60	301.60	2,976	1,289.50	38.38
1978-79	62,520	8,480.49	5,302.00	6,336.07	1,034.07	10,204	1,607.00	163.98
1979-80	60,544	9,997.69	6,053.00	6,135.81	82.81	817	1,943.00	15.87
1980-81	57,020	11,213.61	6,394.00	5,778.67	(—)615.33	(—)6,072	2,217.00	(—)134.62
1981-82	56,404	11,350.26	6,402.00	5,716.25	(—)685.75	(—)6,767	2,801.00	(—)189.54
							Total	(—)105.93

Source : Information furnished by (1) MIS ;
(2) CCOS.

1977-78—1979-80 because of its low performance. But over the next two years it had more than made up by improving the tyre performance considerably. The net savings over the five year period because of improved tyre mileage amount to Rs. 105.93 lakhs. As mentioned earlier, this could have been as much because of the improvement in the quality of tyres as for the better usage of the tyres.

Fuel cost

As mentioned earlier, fuel is the second major item of cost, next only to the staff cost and the maximum increase in cost took place during the period 1973-74—1981-82 in the case of this item, thereby necessitating a concerted action to improve the fuel efficiency or kilometres obtained per litre of fuel (KMPL). It is a matter for concern that the fuel efficiency was on decline after 1976-77 when it had the highest KMPL (vide Table 1.28). It is only in the latest year 1981-82 that there is improvement

TABLE 1.28 : **Kilometres obtained per litre of HSD oil**

Year	KMPL
1973-74	4.07
1974-75	4.00
1975-76	4.02
1976-77	4.30
1977-78	4.26
1978-79	4.19
1979-80	4.18
1980-81	4.09
1981-82	4.17

Source : 1973-74 to 1978-79 Annual Administration Reports ; 1979-80 to 1981-82 Annual Performance Reports.

in KMPL over the previous year. The concern on the part of the organisation in respect of this item of cost in view of its share and increasing price was conspicuous by its absence until 1980-81. It was only in 1981-82 that the organisation seems to have tightened up its belt to improve in this regard.

However, it is a matter for consolation that the fuel performance of APSRTC was satisfactory when compared with the fuel performance of other undertakings, except for GSRTC (vide Table 1.29). However, there cannot be an unqualified comparison with GSRTC in this regard, as the APSRTC has about 10 per cent of its fleet operating city services which gives lower KMPL than the district services. Hence, computation of financial implications of lower KMPL in APSRTC when compared with that in GSRTC would be misleading. For this reason, the financial implications of decline in KMPL in APSRTC over its earlier KMPL only, have been computed and presented in Table 1.30. The table shows that the organisation had to spend an additional amount of Rs. 1.40 crores in 1981-82 alone because of decline in KMPL in that year over 1976-77. In fact the additional expenditure would have been much more in that year had it not improved its KMPL over the previous year. The corporation incurred an additional expenditure of Rs. 4.32 crores on fuel during the last five years because of decline in fuel efficiency. However, it must be noted that the organisation has been taking measures, in the last two years, to improve KMPL which had already produced results in 1981-82, when it saved an amount of Rs. 54 lakhs over the previous year.

At this stage, it is relevant to give a brief note on the limitations of data on HSD Oil.

(1) Based upon the figures of HSD Oil, as extracted from the MIS Section, under the Head "HSD Oil issues" (from the register maintained and entitled "HSD Oil Consumption"), an analysis of fuel consumption was originally made and incorporated in the Second Instalment of the Report. These data were disputed by the corporation contending that these data required adjustments for inter-depot and inter-state issues, apart from stock adjustments. However, as the data so extracted were based upon Return MTD 29, which gives details of receipts, issues, and balances of fuel, one should expect that the issues as extracted would only mean issues after making all adjustments.

(2) In veiw of the contention of the Corporation that these were unadjusted figures of issues, data on issues of HSD Oil after all adjustments were asked for. In spite of the written requisition, the Corporation furnished data on HSD Oil purchased only. This indicates that the Corporation had not reconciled the total issues after all adjustments, because of which no accurate data of exact

TABLE 1.29 : **Kilometres obtained per litre of HSD oil : Inter-firm comparison**

Year	APSRTC	GSRTC	PTC (Metro)	PTC (Dist.)	Pandiyan RC	Cheran TC	Cholan RC	Anna TC	KTC (Dist.)	TPTC	TTC
1973-74	4.07	N.A.	N.A.	N.A.	N.A.	N.A.	N.A.	N.A.	N.A.	N.A.	N.A.
1974-75	4.00	4.22	3.60	N.A.	3.70	3.72	3.67	3.80	3.92	N.A.	N.A.
1975-76	4.02	4.35	3.61	N.A.	N.A.	3.70	N.A.	N.A.	3.96	N.A.	N.A.
1976-77	4.30	4.44	3.66	3.91	N.A.	3.82	3.86	N.A.	4.10	3.79	N.A.
1977-78	4.26	4.47	3.64	3.88	N.A.	3.73	3.82	3.89	4.01	N.A.	N.A.
1978-79	4.19	4.52	3.64	3.89	3.61	3.76	3.72	N.A.	3.82	N.A.	N.A.
1979-80	4.18	4.64	3.65	3.80	3.52	3.75	3.72	N.A.	3.75	N.A.	4.18
1980-81	4.09	4.66	3.56	3.83	3.61	4.01	3.85	N.A.	3.74	N.A.	4.06
1981 82	4.17	N.A.	N.A.	N.A.	N.A.	N.A.	N.A.	N.A.	N.A.	N.A.	N.A.

Source : Report on the Performance of Nationalised Road Transport Undertakings from 1974-75 to 1980-81, Central Institute of Road Transport, Pune.

TABLE 1.30 : **Financial implications of fuel efficiency**

Year	Gross kms. (in crores)	Total HSD oil consumed (litres in crores)	Total HSD oil consumed based on 1976-77 norm (litres in crores)	Excess HSD oil consumed over the norm (litres in crores)	Rate per litre (Rs.)	Excess cost (Rs. in lakhs)
1976-77	44.24	10.35	10.35	—	1.29	—
1977-78	50.27	11.68	11.76	(—)0.08	1.30	(—)10.40
1978-79	53.02	12.68	12.40	0.28	1.30	36.40
1979-80	60.53	14.55	14.16	0.39	1.50	58.50
1980-81	63.94	15.88	14.96	0.92	2.25	207.00
1981-82	64.02	15.49	14.98	0.51	3.00	153.00
						444.50

Source : (1) Weighted average cost of HSD oil for 1976-77 and 1977-78—MIS records ;
(2) Remaining data—Reported by the Corporation.

"issues", after all adjustments are available with the corporation. Consequently, data on HSD Oil in stock are not available. Hence the following analysis is based on HSD Oil purchased and HSD Oil as computed based upon the total expenditure on HSD Oil, the weighted average rate of HSD Oil, and Gross kms done.

(3) Further, different sets of figures are furnished by the Corporation, in respect of HSD Oil consumed on different occasions. The fact that there are differences in data in respect of HSD Oil without reconciling the same, leading to confusion and erroneous conclusions, can be seen from the following admission made by the Management in its Budget note for the consideration of the corporation. "There was an inadvertent but significant mistake in the original estimates in regrad to expenditure on power (HSD Oil). A consumption rate of 4.13 revenue yielding kms. per litre was assumed in the original estimates whereas the actual achievement in this regard during 1980-81 was only 3.93 revenue yielding kms. per litre. Instead of the rate of consumption on the revenue yielding kms, the rate on gross operations was adopted for this calculation. As a result of this error the expenditure on power (HSD Oil) was shown less by about Rs. 2.5 crores."*

Table 1.30 (a) gives an idea of efficiency in HSD Oil consumption by "Buses" and for "Departmental Vehicles and other Consumption". It is clear from the table that there has been consistent decline in efficiency in HSD Oil consumption by buses since 1978-79 until 1980-81. The trend has been reserved in the year 1981-82 but the improved KMPL in 1981-82 was an improvement over 1980-81 only and it was still less than what is obtained in any one of the other years.

It must also be noted that there was improvement in KMPL in Departmental and other vehicles in 1981-82 over 1980-81. Once again, it should also be noted that KMPL for other purposes in 1981-82 was less than that obtained in other years, earlier to 1980-81. However, one disconcerting trend is the increase in the precentage of HSD Oil consumed for other purposes during the period 1978-79—1980-81, when it increased from 1.20 per cent in

* Explanatory Memorandum on the Revised Budget Estimates for 1981-82 and Budget Estimates for 1982-83 in respect of APSRTC, p. 11.

TABLE 1.30 (a) : **Efficiency in HSD oil consumption by buses and for other purposes**

(*Litres in crores*)

Year	For buses	HSD oil issued for departmental vehicles and other consumption	Total	KMPL Buses	KMPL for departmental and other vehicles
1976-77	10.17 (98.26)	0.18 (1.74)	10.35 (100)	4.30	2.78
1977-78	11.54 (98.80)	0.14 (1.20)	11.68 (100)	4.30	4.64
1978-79	12.46 (98.27)	0.22 (1.73)	12.68 (100)	4.19	3.46
1979-80	14.28 (98.14)	0.27 (1.86)	14.55 (100)	4.18	3.30
1980-81	15.44 (97.23)	0.44 (2.77)	15.88 (100)	4.09	1.93
1981-82	15.14 (97.74)	0.35 (2.26)	15.49 (100)	4.17	2.69

Source : Data as reported by the corporation.

Note : Figures in brackets represent percentage to the total.

1978-79 to 2.77 per cent in 1980-81. In the year 1981-82, even though the percentage of HSD Oil consumed for other purposes declined over the previous year, it was the second highest figure for the entire period.

Table 1.30 (b) shows the disparity between the computed quantity of HSD oil consumed and the quantity of HSD oil (purchased) as reported by the corporation. In terms of value, this disparity amounts to a shortage of Rs. 24.82 lakhs. This may be because of the fact that necessary adjustments are not made.

The major concern about the HSD oil has been the increase in its prices and the consequent influence on the cost. Table 1.30 (c) shows the impact of inflation on fuel cost. It shows that the organisation had to spend an additional amount of Rs. 45.03 crores during the last five years because of inflation on this item of cost alone.

To sum up, it could be seen that the organization had to spend an additional amount of about Rs. 50 crores during the last five years because of inflation and inefficiency on fuel—Rs. 45.03 crores because of inflation, and Rs. 4.45 crores because of inefficiency.

Motor vehicle, passenger and other taxes on vehicles levied by the state government

It has earlier been mentioned that even though these taxes have increased during the period 1973-74—1981-82, the percentage share of this item of cost out of the total cost declined in the case of APSRTC, because of relative increase in the cost of other items. The fact that the percentage share of this item of cost has declined during the period does not imply awareness, on the part of the government, of the importance of the passenger road transport industry as there has been increase in the tax rates, resulting in increase in tax per vehicle and cost per kilometre. This being a public utility industry, and in view of the inflation adversely affecting the costs of operations, and the difficulties in enhancing the fares, the state government, not only as the owner of this industry, but also as the one charged with the responsibility of fixing reasonable fares for the public should have contributed in its own small way to reduce the costs by restraining itself from periodical increases in the motor vehicle taxes. Unfortunately,

TABLE 1.30 (b) : **Disparity in fuel consumption and its financial implications**

Year	Cost of HSD oil booked to P and L A/c. Rs.	Weighted average cost per litre (Rs.)	Qty. of HSD oil consumed (Litres in crores) (col 2 ÷ col 3)	Qty. of HSD oil issued as reported by the corpn. (Litres in crores)	Difference i.e., stock (Lts. in crores)	Cost of addl. HSD oil consumed as per the cost booked over HSD oil consumed as reported (col 6 × col 3 × 100) (Rs. in lakhs)
1976-77	13,37,14,677	1.29	10.37	10.35	0.02	2.58
1977-78	15,18,44,024	1.30	11.68	11.68	—	—
1978-79	16,93,09,980	1.30	13.02	12.68	0.34	44.20
1979-80	21,90,75,115	1.50	14.61	14.55	0.06	9.00
1980-81	35,59,74,958	2.25	15.82	15.88	(—)0.06	(—)13.50
1981-82	46,29,59,623	3.00	15.43	15.49	(—)0.06	(—)18.00
			Total (Rs. in lakhs)			24.28

Source : (1) Weighted average cost of HSD oil for 1976-77 and 1977-78—MIS Records ;
(2) Weighted average cost of HSD oil for the years from 1978-79 to 1981-82—Reported by the Corporation.

TABLE 1.30 (c) : **Impact of inflation on fuel cost**

Year	Total HSD oil consumed (Lts. in crores)	Weighted average cost (in Rs.)	Actual cost of fuel (Rs. in lakhs) (col 2 × col 3 × 100)	Computed value of fuel cost at 1976-77 average cost (i.e. Rs. 1.29 × col. 2) (Rs. in lakhs)	Excess cost (Rs. in lakhs) (col 4—col 5)
1976-77	10.35	1.29	1,335.15	1,335.15	—
1977-78	11.68	1.30	1,518.40	1,506.72	11.68
1978-79	12.68	1.30	1,648.40	1,635.72	12.68
1979-80	14.55	1.50	2,182.50	1,876.95	305.55
1080-81	15.88	2.25	3,573.00	2,048.52	1,524.48
1981-82	15.49	3.00	4,647.00	1,998.21	2,648.79
				Total (Rs. in lakhs)	4,503.18

Source : 1. Weighted average cost of HSD oil for the years 1976-77 and 1977-78—MIS records ;
2. Weighted average cost of HSD oil for the years 1978-79 to 1981-82 and figures of HSD oil consumption. Reported by the Corpn.

this does not seem to be the attitude of the state government. The fact that the tax per vehicle or the tax per kilometre has been consistently on the increase during the nine-year period of study, except for one year (vide Table 1.31), clearly shows the apathy of the state government to its own child. It looks as though the State Government considers the corporation as a milch cow to extract as much revenue as possible by way of taxes even in times of losses. This has been amply proved by the increase in the taxes that were effected in the year 1978-79.

The seriousness of the problem of taxes is not so much with taxes on mofussil services but with that on city services when compared with the taxes obtaining in other states. A study of Table 1.31 would show that the tax per vehicle in the case of city services was a little lower than that on mofussil services until 1977-78. But thereafter, the tax per vehicle on city services surpassed that of mofussil services, except for the year 1979-80.

The impact of the increase in the tax per vehicle, in the case of city services, when compared with that on mofussil services, is much more in terms of tax per km. as the city services do less kilometrage than the mofussil services. The fact that the city services in their very nature do less kilometrage does not seem to have entered into the consideration of the State Government in levying taxes on city services vis-a-vis the mofussil services. Because of the lower kilometerage done by city services, the tax differential between city and mofussil services being only marginal, the effect is that the tax per km. in the case of city services works out to 50 to 60 per cent more than what it is in the case of mofussil services (vide Table 1.31 (a)). As of now, taking into consideration the existing rates of motor vehicle taxation, the tax on city services amounts to between 75 per cent and 80 per cent of what it is on mofussil services, taking the possible ranges of operation of city and mofussil services, whereas, the vehicle utilisation in city services is round about 60 per cent. Thus, based upon vehicle utilisation alone, the city services are discriminated against and charged a higher tax rate of 15 to 20 per cent more than that on mofussil services. But this is only a part of the problem concerning the tax rates and the inequity in charging tax rates on city services. As is well known, the city services have the the problem of unidirectional traffic, higher cost of operations,

TABLE 1.31 : **Tax per km. and tax per vehicle**

MOFUSSIL

Year	Average No. of vehicles held	Expenditure on licences and taxes (Rs. in lakhs)	Tax per vehicle (Rs.)	Kms operated (effective kms. in lakhs)	Tax per km. (in paise)
1973-74	2256	545.64	24,186	2293.89	23.79
1974-75	2695	723.59	26,849	2766.45	26.16
1975-76	3334	979.85	29,112	3335.70	29.10
1976-77	3804	1,214.78	31,934	3940.04	30.83
1977-78	4275	1,381.37	32,313	4514.82	30.60
1978-79	4671	1,618.84	34,657	4758.65	34.02
1979-80	5052	1,986.56	39,322	5442.05	36.50
1980-81	5693	2,136.25	37,524	5749.94	37.15
1981-82	5832	2,251.28	38,602	5761.77	39.07

TABLE 1.31 : (*Contd.*)

CITY

Year	Average No. of vehicles held	Expenditure on licences and taxes (Rs. in lakhs)	Tax per vehicle (Rs.)	Km. operated (effective kms. in lakhs)	Tax per km. (in paise)	Ratio of tax per kms. in city services to that on mofussil services
1973-74	492	99.42	20,207	307.08	32.38	1.36
1974-75	530	137.37	25,919	324.18	42.38	1.62
1975-76	564	149.58	26,521	359.58	41.60	1.43
1976-77	521	158.29	30,382	337.73	46.87	1.52
1977-78	540	173.59	32,146	347.05	50.02	1.63
1978-79	601	215.16	35,800	348.20	61.79	1.82
1979-80	605	228.27	37,731	360.28	63.36	1.72
1980-81	636	278.06	43,720	425.84	65.30	1.76
1981-82	709	275.77	38,896	445.54	61.90	1.58

TABLE 1.31 : *(Contd.)*

OVERALL

Year	Average No. of vehicles held	Expenditure on licences and taxes (Rs. in lakhs)	Tax per vehicle (Rs.)	Kms. operated (effective kms. in lakhs)	Tax per km. (in paise)
1973-74	2,748	645.06	23,474	2,600.97	24.80
1974-75	3,225	860.96	26,696	3,090.63	27.86
1975-76	3,898	1,129.43	28,737	3,695.28	30.31
1976-77	4,325	1,373.07	31,747	4,277.77	32.10
1977-78	4,815	1,554.96	32,294	4,861.87	31.98
1978-79	5,272	1,834.00	34,788	5,106.85	35.91
1979-80	5,657	2,214.83	39,152	5,802.33	38.17
1980-81	6,329	2,414.31	38,147	6,175.78	39.09
1981-82	6,541	2,527.05	38,634	6,207.31	40.71

Note : Average No. of vehicles held in city excludes vehicles, workshops and headquarters.

Source : (1) 1973-74 to 1978-79, Annual Adminstration Reports ;
(2) 1979-80, Annual Accounts (Provisional) ;
(3) 1980-81 and 1981-82, Main Accounts and City Division Accounts (Provisional).

TABLE 1.31 (a) : **Vehicle utilisation in kilometres per day in city and Mofussil services**

Year 1	Mofussil 2	City 3	Col. (3) as a percentage of Col. (2) 4
1973-74	279	171	61
1974-76	281	168	60
1975-76	274	175	64
1976-77	284	178	63
1977-78	289	176	61
1978-79	279	157	56
1979-80	295	163	55
1980-81	277	183	66
1981-82	271	172	63

Source : 1973-74 to 1978-79 Annual Administrative Reports ;
1979-80 to 1981-82 Annual Performance Reports and MIS Records.

especially in terms of diesel consumption, and the social obligations imposed on it by the state government from time to time, which the mofussil services are not burdened with, apart from lower fares fixed for city services. Further, the motor vehicle tax on city services takes into consideration the standing passengers permitted, thereby resulting in a higer tax per vehicle in the case of city services.

In the light of the above analysis, which showed that, on the one hand, the tax per vehicle and tax per km. have increased during the period, and, on the other, the share of this item of cost, out of the total cost, has declined, it would be relevant to see, how far the organisational efficiency has contributed to decline in the share of this item of cost out of the total cost, even though this decline is partially because of a relatively higher increase in the case of other items of cost. Table 1.31 (b), shows the impact of efficiency on the cost of tax. An idea of the savings in monetary terms on tax because of improved performance can be had from this table. This is computed by taking into consideration the additional passenger kms. done by the organisation based upon the 1976-77 norm of passenger kms. done per vehicle. As the tax rate per seat is fixed, the more the passenger kms. done, the less would be the cost of tax per km. The table shows that the organisation has, in a way, saved Rs. 5.41 crores on tax by better utilisation of fleet, during the period 1976-77—1981-82.

Even though the increased rate of motor vehicle tax has been absorbed to the extent of Rs. 5.41 crores because of improvement in operational efficiency, the increase in motor vehicle tax was high enough to result in substantial amount of excess tax during the period 1977-78 to 1981-82, taking the average tax per passenger km. of 1976-77 as the basis/norm. This additional tax based on the norm, amounted to Rs. 9.46 crores during the period (vide Table 1.31 (c)). But for the improvement in operational efficiency, the burden of increase in motor vehicle tax, during the period, would have been Rs. 14.87 crores.

In view of the various factors mentioned above, making for high cost of operations of city services and lower revenues either because of low kilometerage or lower fares, and also because of the social obligations, there is a strong case either for drastically reducing the tax rate on city services, on par with city services

TABLE 1.31(b) : **Impact of efficiency on cost of tax**

Year	Average No. of vehicles held	Passenger kms done (in lakhs)	Passenger kms per vehicle (in lakhs)	Passenger kms based on 1976-77 norms (kms in lakhs)	Difference between actual passenger kms and passenger kms based on 1976-77 norm (kms in lakhs) (3—5)	Tax per passenger km (in paise)	Savings in money terms (Rs. in lakhs) (6×7)
1	2	3	4	5	6	7	8
1976-77	4,325	1,50,303.00	34.75	—	—	0.9135	—
1977-78	4,815	1,77,087.00	36.78	1,67,331.55	9,755.45	0.8781	85.66
1978-79	5,272	1,97,201.00	37.41	1,83,213.28	13,987.72	0.9300	130.09
1979-80	5,657	2,24,898.31	39.76	1,96,592.85	28,305.46	0.9848	278.75
1980-81	6,329	2,23,625.00	35.33	2,19,946.29	3,678.71	1.0796	39.72
1981-82	6,541	2,27,933.00	34.85	2,27,313.74	619.26	1.1087	6.87
						Total :	541.09

TABLE 1.31(c) : Impact of inflation on MV tax cost

Year	Passenger kms (in lakhs)	Total MV tax (Rs. in lakhs)	Tax per passenger km (in paise)	Computed MV tax as per 1976-77 norm of 0.9135 tax per passenger km (Rs. in lakhs)	Excess of actual over computed tax based on 1976-77 norm (3—5)
1976-77	1,50,303.00	1,373.07	0.9135	—	—
1977-78	1,77,087.00	1,554.96	0.8781	1,617.75	(—) 62.79
1978-79	1,97,201.00	1,834.00	0.9300	1,801.50	32.50
1979-80	2,24,898.31	2,214.83	0.9848	2,054.52	160.31
1980-81	2,23,625.00	2,414.31	1.0796	2,042.89	371.42
1981-82	2,27,933.00	2,527.05	1.1087	2,082.25	444.80
				Total :	946.24

Note : (—) indicates the actual payment of MV tax is less than the norm.

elsewhere, that is, in Tamil Nadu or in the case of Municipal Undertakings of Bombay and Ahmedabad or give a subsidy to the APSRTC on its city services as has been done in Tamil Nadu.

At this stage, it is relevant to compare the taxes on city services in APSRTC with the taxes obtaining on city services elsewhere. For this purpose, comparison is made with Pallavan (Metro), TCL, BEST, and Ahmedabad MTS. These three are only city service organisations, the first one organised as an independent corporation of the State Government, the other two owned and operated by the respective Municipal Corporations. These are selected for the reason that a study of these organisations has been made in connection with this study and data are available for these undertakings. Table 1.32 shows that the tax per km. in APSRTC works out to 158 per cent to 534 per cent more than what it works out to in the case of other undertakings. The Pallavan (Metro) Transport Corporation Ltd., which is a State Government undertaking, and not a Municipal undertaking is charged only about one-third of what the APSRTC is charged. The position is broadly the same vis-a-vis BEST also. The Ahmedabad MTS is charged less than one-sixth of what the APSRTC is charged. A comparison of the absolute tax rates on city services of the undertakings taken up for comparison shows that the APSRTC is charged Rs. 160 per seat per quarter at the slab at which the vehicles may be ordinarily expected to be utilised, while the Pallavan (Metro) is charged only Rs. 50, the BEST Rs. 60 per seat for the first 4 seats and Rs. 55 for every additional seat. The BEST gives 75 per cent exemption for standees upto 25 per cent of the seating capacity. In the case of the Ahmedabad Municipal Transport Services, the tax per seat per quarter works out to less than Rs. 10. Hence, it is a matter for no surprise that the APSRTC should be incurring losses right from the inception on its city services. It is, therefore, recommended that the rate of motor vehicle taxes on city services of APSRTC should be reduced to a minimum of one-third of the present rate. This would result in reduction in losses on city services by Rs. 1.84 crores per annum (based on 1981-82 figures) and would reduce the losses on city services by 45 per cent.

There seems to be a proposal to charge motor vehicle tax based upon passenger revenues instead of basing upon the seating

TABLE 1.32 : **Taxes on city services of APSRTC and other undertakings for the year 1980-81**

(*Rs. in lakhs*)

Name of the undertaking	M.V. Tax	Passenger tax	Other taxes on vehicles	Miscellaneous taxes	Total tax	Tax per effective km. in paise
APSRTC	278.06	—	—	—	278.06	65.30
Pallavan TCL (Metro)	262.17	—	—	6.88	269.05	23.10
BEST	63.80	177.36	5.35	110.29	356.80	25.32
Ahmedabad MTS	19.59	9.50	5.73	—	34.82	10.29

Source : Report on the Performance of Nationalised Passenger Road Transport Undertakings 1980-81, Central Institute of Road Transport, Pune.

capacity and the kilometres scheduled per day. This is not in the interests of the organisation as any increase in fare would automatically imply an increase in tax. Worse still is the fact that any improvement in performance, in terms of vehicle utilisation, occupation ratio, plugging the leakage in revenues, would imply a share of increase in revenues because of these efforts to the Government by way of taxes. In other words, the organisation would be penalised for its efficiency and an increase in fare is not meant for benefiting the corporation alone, but also the Government for no reason. Further, there will be always temptation to raise the percentage of tax on revenues. There is a vital difference between increase in MV Tax on the basis of seat and increase in tax on passenger revenues. In the case of the former, because of increased tax, if the organisation is forced to improve its performance a share of that would not go to the government. In the case of the latter, an increase in the rate of taxation is bound to result in increase in cost to the organisation in terms of tax per passenger km. done, as increase in every paise earned is shared by the government, whereas in the case of the former, it is possible to offset the increase in motor vehicle tax by improved performance in terms of vehicle utilisation and occupation ratio. Thus, the latter in a way has an in-built element of inflation. Hence, it is inadvisable to tax on passenger revenue basis. A better alternative would be to tax the organisation on the basis of vehicles operated in a quarter, irrespective of the route on which they are operated. This would give the operational manoeuvrability to the organisation.

Depreciation

Depreciation as an item of cost may be subjected to different kinds of treatment, each with its own implication to the concern. As is well known there are different methods of depreciating an asset, such as straight line method, diminishing balance method, usage/mileage method and so on. While organisations may follow a particular method, the taxation law may permit another method. For example, the APSRTC follows "usage" method in charging depreciation on its vehicles while the tax law permits written down value method. Hence, the method adopted by an organisation in charging depreciation may be in variance with that allowed by tax law. While the organisation deviates in this regard, in charging depreciation on vehicles, from the tax law, they do not go far enough in this regard to charge depreciation to take care of the replacement cost of the vehicle.

In APSRTC, as is generally the case with any other industrial or business concern in the country, the replacement cost is not taken into consideration in charging depreciation. If this is taken into consideration the organisation would be in a position to replace or renew the vehicles immediately after scrapping without having to look to external agencies for funds for replacement. On the other hand, such a policy would deflate the profit position or inflate the losses position of the undertaking. Hence, public undertakings which are not in good financial position may hesitate to follow a policy of depreciation on replacement cost/current cost basis. This could be one of the reasons for the APSRTC not following replacement cost basis of depreciation.

Unfortunately, the APSRTC has not only been not following the replacement cost policy of depreciating vehicles but also it has changed its policy of depreciating its vehicles completely from 4.8 lakh kms. to 5.5 lakh kms. This has the consequence of showing a lower cost of operations, resulting in showing inflated profits, when the organisation makes profit or deflated losses, when it incurs losses.

Thus, the policy of depreciating vehicles, firstly on original book value and secondly on increased kilometrage results not only in incapacitating the organisation to renew the vehicle when needed but also in showing inflated profits. At least the latter policy of change over to 5.5 lakh kilometers seems to be a deliberate strategy to conceal the losses or to inflate the profits. This strategy actually is a self defeating one, as even though the costs are really higher it shows lower costs ; and, at a time when the organisation incurs losses, it is not in a position to project real losses to ask for an appropriate increase in fares. Even if the vehicle gives improved performance for a longer period because of technological improvements incorporated in the vehicle, it is still advisable to adhere to the policy of depreciating the vehicle at 4.8 lakh kms. for the simple reason that the organisation is not following current cost basis of depreciating the vehicles. If the organisation pursues the old policy, it would at-least be partially offsetting the increased cost of the vehicle.

In this context, it is relevant to note that while the corporation decided shifting from 4.8 lakh kms. depreciation policy to 5.5 lakh kms. policy as early as 1975-76, the Government of Andhra Pradesh which is required by the Act to give its approval in this regard has not done so far.

In the light of the above analysis of depreciation methods and policies being pursued by APSRTC, an attempt is made next to make an empirical analysis of the implications of depreciation policy being pursued by the APSRTC.

It is of interest to note that the impact of the policy pursued by the corporation is perceptible from the trend of share of the cost of depreciation out of the total cost. While its share increased from 10.44 per cent in 1973-74 to 11.66 in 1974-75 it suddenly declined to 10.70 in 1975-76 which continued to be around that level through out the rest of the period except for the last year, that is 1981-82, the figures in respect of which are provisional.

An attempt may be made first to quantify the extent of under costing depreciation because of change over from 4.8 lakh kms. estimated life to 5.5 lakh kms. adopted in the year 1975-76. Table 1.33 shows that had the corporation pursued the policy of depreciating the vehicles at 4.8 lakh kms., throughout the period, the additional cost of depreciation would have been Rs. 13.07 crores, over the six year period. In other words, the cost of depreciation was shown to be less by this amount during this period. Consequently, the total accumulated losses as at the end of the financial year 1981-82 would have been Rs. 64.62 crores instead of Rs. 51.55 crores. So, to this extent the corporation had lost the case for enhancing the fares. As mentioned earlier, this would amount to an additional burden on the corporation in finding sources of finance for replacing/acquiring vehicles.

An idea of the impact of inflation on the cost of depreciation may be had from Table 1.34. As seen earlier (vide Table 1.17) the average cost of vehicle increased by 75 per cent during the short period of six years. Consequently, this is bound to have

TABLE 1.33 : **Impact of change in depreciation policy**

Year	Actual amount of depreciation on vehicles as provided at 5.5 lakh kms. (Rs. in lakhs)	Depreciation calculated @ 4.8 lakh kms. life (Rs. in lakhs)	Under charging of depreciation due to revision of estimated life from 4.8 lakh kms. to 5.5 lakh kms. (Rs. in lakhs)
1976-77	857.46	982.51	125.05
1977-78	1,038.07	1,189.46	151.39
1978-79	1,191.23	1,364.95	173.72
1979-80	1,508.10	1,728.03	219.93
1980-81	1,753.53	2,009.25	245.72
1981-82	1,940.41	2,223.39	282.98
		Total :	1,306.57

its influence on the cost of depreciation. The cost of depreciation per km, increased by about 57 per cent from 19.61 paise per km to 30.76 paise per km. The percentage increase in the cost of depreciation per km. was less than that of the increase in the average cost of vehicle because of the fact that the composition of vehicles in each of these years is such that the average cost of depreciation in terms of paise per km. would be less than that it would be if all the vehicles were new.

The impact of inflation on the cost of depreciation in terms of paise per km. is computed and presented in Table 1.34, assuming that the cost of depreciation per km. remained at 1976-77 level of 19.61 paise. Based upon this calculation, the inflation had cost the organisation, on its depreciation, Rs. 7.03 crores in 1981-82 alone and about Rs. 18 crores over the last six years. Even if the depreciation not provided, because of change to 5.5 lakhs km. depreciation policy, is set off, the impact of inflation still works out to about Rs. 5 crores.

One of the important dimensions of depreciation policy as mentioned in the earlier analysis of depreciation methods and policy is the policy regarding the method of charging depreciation. It has also been mentioned that the corporation has been following the policy of depreciating assets on historical cost basis and not on replacement cost basis which affects the capability of the organisation to renew its operating capital. An idea of the extent of funds required to be mustered by the organisation, just to replace the scrapped vehicles, based on current costs can be had from Table 1.35. In one year, that is, 1980-81 alone, the additional amount required over and above the amounts recouped by way of depreciation was Rs. 5.81 crores, and the amount has been by and large on the increase since 1976-77. It is no surprise that the organisation has been experiencing difficulty in raising adequate resources for financing the acquisition of vehicles. On the one hand the depreciation provision has not been adequate to meet the replacement cost of the vehicle and on the other the contributing governments were not discharging their obligation to meet the requirements of the organisation, forcing it to go in for long term high cost borrowings from outside, thereby further inflating the costs of organisation. This is amply demonstrated by the fact that the long term loans which

TABLE 1.34 : **Impact of inflation on depreciation**

Year	Gross kms in lakhs	Depreciation on vehicles (Rs. in lakhs)	Depreciation cost per km (in paise)	Depreciation on vehicles at 19.61 paise per km (Rs. in lakhs)	Additional depreciation because of inflation (3—5)
1976-77	4,373.36	857.46	19.61	—	—
1977-78	4,961.55	1,038.07	20.92	972.96	65.11
1978-79	5,226.03	1,191.23	22.79	1,024.82	166.41
1979-80	5,925.47	1,508.10	25.45	1,161.99	346.11
1980-81	6,298.19	1,753.53	27.84	1,235.08	518.45
1981-82	6,308.77	1,940.41	30.76	1,237.15	703.26
				Total :	1,799.34

TABLE 1.35 : Number of vehicles sold with their original (acquisition) cost and cost of replacement

Financial year	No. of vehicles sold	Cost of acquisition Rs.	Cost of replacement (proportionate) Rs.	Increase in the cost of replacement Rs	Percentage increase
1971-72	267	1,30,79,806	2,46,45,012	1,15,65,206	88.41
1972-73	390	2,10,49,873	3,58,50,049	1,48,00,176	70.14
1973-74	263	1,35,86,691	2,50,95,119	1,15,08,428	84.56
1974-75	108	66,74,986	1,49,45,151	82,70,165	124.24
1975-76	317	2,16,56,124	4,58,10,360	2,41,54,236	111.52
1976-77	207	1,53,37,287	3,16,89,594	1,63,52,307	106.53
1977-78	396	2,89,71,585	6,20,67,732	3,30,96,147	114.23
1978-79	310	2,55,34,301	5,49,88,077	2,94,53,776	115.35
1979-80	358	3,37,02,843	6,88,67,525	3,51,64,882	104.34
1980-81	419	4,10,76,630	9,91,69,445	5,80,92,815	141.43

accounted for only 18.13 per cent of capital contributions in 1973-74, increased substantially to 29.10 per cent in 1981-82, thereby resulting in a substantial increase in the ratio of interest on long term external borrowings to interest on capital contributions from 22.65 in 1973-74 to 86.05 in 1981-82.

In the light of the above, there is need for reviewing the capital structure policy and the sources of capital and the institutional arrangements for the same in respect of the nationalised passenger road transport undertakings in general. The passenger road transport industry, being a public utility industry in nature, cannot be burdened with high cost finance. The alternatives are as follows :

(i) The Government may meet the entire requirements of the long term funds by way of capital contributions, continuing to charge the present rate of interest, based on the rate of borrowings of the government plus the cost of servicing the same by the government.

(ii) As provided in the RTC Act, it may provide for equity contribution and permit the corporation to raise the funds through debentures by guaranteeing the same so that the corporation may get funds at lower rates of interest.

(iii) Apart from the participating governments providing either equity capital or capital contributions, the central government may set up a specialist financial institution to finance the capital requirements of the State Transport Undertakings for acquisition of fleet either by way of low interest bearing loans or on low interest bearing hire purchase finance.

The above measures cannot be considered in isolation, absolving the corporations of the responsibility of raising their own funds, not by ploughing back of profits, but by charging depreciation at least to replace the vehicles. This is as much an obligation of the user to pay for the replacement of the vehicle which he has used as it is the responsibility of the organisation to recoup the same. The corporation and the government should not feel shy of pursuing such a policy. An alternative to this is to charge depreciation on historical cost basis and appropriate from out of profits additional provision towards replacement of vehicles but this would appear to be unjustified in the eyes of the public in view of the public utility character of the industry as the public loses sight of the very nature of the public utility undertaking and its obligation to replace its vehicles by charging appropriate depreciation.

To revert back to the point of additional cost of replacement of vehicles it can be seen from the table that during the last six years the corporation had to find additional funds to the extent of Rs. 17.22 crores to replace their vehicles over and above the amounts available from out of the accumulated depreciation provisions.

So far an idea has been given of the additional cost of replacing the sold vehicles over and above the cost of acquisition of these vehicles. An attempt is made next to give the financial implications of charging depreciation on replacement cost basis in respect of the vehicles in operation in the respective years. Table 1.36 shows that if depreciation has been provided as per the replacement cost in respect of vehicles in operation, the additonal cost to the organisation would have been Rs. 25.71 crores, assuming that the vehicles would be replaced at 5.5 lakh kms. If the depreciation is to be provided on 4.8 lakh kms. basis, adopted by the corporation earlier to 1975-76, the additional depreciation cost would have been Rs. 40.78 crores. Thus, the dimensions of the problem of replacement cost of the vehicles in operation could be seen very clearly from these figures which further supports the earlier recommendation that the corporation may follow a policy of charging depreciation on replacement cost basis.

When an organisation is appraised, the appraisal is generally done on the basis of its profits or losses, but rarely does one think of the capacity of the organisation to keep the earning power of its assets in tact. The earning power of its assets can be in tact only when the organisation is in a position to renew its assets from out of its own resources. This would mean either the organisation being able to provide funds from out of its general reserves built out of its profits or from out of its specific reserves, which in this case imply depreciation provision. It is only a

TABLE 1.36 : **Implication of depreciation on replacement cost basis**

Year	Depreciation actually provided on vehiles as per original cost of vehicles	Replacement cost of the vehicle	Cost of depreciation per km as per replacement cost (3/5.5 lakh kms of estimated life)	Gross Kms.	Depreciation as per replacement cost	Difference between depreciation as per replacement cost and actual depreciation (6—2)	Cost of depreciation per km as per replacement cost@ 4.8 lakh kms (3/4.8 lakh kms.)	Depreciation as per replacement cost on the basis of 4.8 lakh kms. (8 x 5)	Difference between cost of depreciation based on replacement cost at 4.8 lakh km and actual depreciation
	(Rs. in lakhs)	(Rs.)	(in paise)	(in lakh kms)	(Rs. in lakhs)	(Rs. in lakhs)	(in paise)	(Rs. in lakhs)	
1976-77	857.46	1,53,090	27.835	4373.36	1,217.32	359.86	31.894	1,394.84	537.38
1977-78	1,038.07	1,56,737	28,498	4961.55	1,413.94	375.87	32.654	1,620.14	582.07
1978-79	1,191.23	1,77,380	32,251	5226.03	1,685.45	494.22	36.954	1,931.23	740.00
1979-80	1,508.10	1,92,367	34.976	5925.47	2,072.49	564.39	40.076	2,374.69	866.59
1980-81	1,753.53	2,36,681	43.033	6298.19	2,710.30	956.77	49.309	3,105.57	1,352.04
Total						2,751.11			4,078.08

matter of accounting policy whether an organisation would like to meet its obligation in this regard by charging depreciation or appropriating out of profits. Finally, even if the government were to give, one fine morning, the entire amount of Rs. 51.55 crores and the corporation were called upon to start with a clean slate, it would not be able to do so, as it would require another Rs. 40.78 crores to keep its earning capacity in tact which means that it should replace its vehicles at current cost when they are required to be replaced.

Interest

Interest, as an item of cost, has two components—interest on capital contributions and interest on long-term borrowings. The analysis of interest on capital, as given earlier, based on Table 1.7, relates only to interest on capital contributions paid to the participating governments. The table showed that the interest on capital contributions increased significantly during the period 1978-79—1981-82, in terms of both paise per km, as well as interest as a percentage of total cost. This could be because of a number of reasons. Firstly, it could be because of increase in the rate of interest during this period. This has not happened, in effective terms, in the sense that even though the rate of interest has been raised by the government, in October 1981 and subsequently, with retrospective effect, it has not been paid/not booked in this account as yet. It may be because even though the capital contributions increased they may not have been invested on vehicles and might have been spent on non-earning assets such as bus-stations or might have been used to meet the revenue expenditure. An analysis of the empirical data clearly shows that the investment in new vehicles was more than the capital contributions in those years. A study of this problem from this angle has got a major limitation that a major part of the purchases of new vehicles could have been made from out of depreciation. Hence an analysis of the investment in new vehicles in relation to both capital contributions and depreciation charged during the year put together is also done (vide Table 1.37). No rational inference can be drawn from this analysis also as in some years the investment in new vehicles is almost 100 per cent of capital contributions plus depreciation. For example in 1979-80 and

TABLE 1.37 : **Utilisation of capital contributions and depreciation provision on vehicles for acquisition of vehicles**

(*Rs. in lakhs*)

Year	Capital contributions received during the year	Depreciation on vehicles charged during the year	Total of capital contribution and depreciation	Value of new vehicles bought	Col. 5 as percentage of Col. 4
1973-74	33.81	384.31	418.12	524.80	125.51
1974-75	933.26	618.47	1,551.73	1,205.30	77.67
1975-76	419.76	739.06	1,158.82	1,148.87	99.14
1976-77	726.13	857.46	1,583.59	1,463.54	92.42
1977-78	879.07	1,033.07	1,917.14	1,137.91	59.35
1978-79	1,562.97	1,191.23	2,754.20	1,791.55	65.05
1979-80	927.50	1,508.10	2,435.60	2,439.22	100.15
1980-81	1,401.00	1,753.53	3,154.53	2,115.93	67.08
1981-82	N.A.	—	—	N.A.	—

1975-76, while in other years, it was as low as 59.35 per cent. The years of high utilisation of these funds were also characterised by both higher cost of interest per km, as well as lower cost of interest per km. Logically, the next step would be to see whether the increased cost of interest per km, and its share in the total cost is because of a decline in vehicular utilisation or vehicle utilisation. This study also shows no relationship (vide Table 1.38) between increase in interest on capital contributions on the one hand and vehicular and vehicle utilisation on the other, as

TABLE 1.38 : **Inter-relationship between interest on capital contributions and vehicular utilisation and vehicle utilisation**

Year	Interest on capital contributions (Paise per km.)	Vehicular utilisation (%)	Vehicle utilisation (in K. Ms.)
1977-78	3.33	90.26	312·78
1978-79	4.14	88.05	308.91
1979-80	5.14	92.00	313.00
1980-81	6.03	88.00	312·00
1981-82	7.30	88.00	299.00

the vehicular utilisation almost remained the same during this four year period 1978-79—1981-82. In fact, the vehicular utilisation increased in the year 1979-80 when there was increase in interest on capital contributions in terms of paise per km. Similarly in the case of vehicle utilisation there was higher vehicle utilisation in 1979-80 and 1980-81 over 1978-79. It was only in 1981-82 that there was decline over 1978-79.

A better method of analysing the reason for increase in the cost of interest per km. would be to take the increase in effective kms. in relation to increase in interest on capital contributions, as the measure of effective kms. automatically takes into consideration the utilisation of capital contributions, vehicular utilisation and vehicle utilisation. A study of this aspect from Table 1.39 shows that while there was 27.67 per cent increase in effective kms. during 1977-78—1981-82 there was 179.59 per cent increase in interest on capital contributions. The percentage increase in interest on capital contributions was more than the increase in the capital contributions, which is, of course, because of the fact

TABLE 1.39 : **Percentage change in effective kilometres, capital contributions and interest on capital contributions**

Year	Effective kms. (in lakhs)	% Change	Capital contributions as on 31st March* (Rs. in lakhs)	% Change	Interest on capital contributions (Rs. in lakhs)	% Change
1977-78	4,861.87	100.00	3,917.23	100.00	162.06	100.00
1978-79	5,106.85	105.04	5,480.20	139.90	211.30	130.38
1979-80	5,802.33	119.34	6,407.70	163.58	300.31	185.31
1980-81	6,175.70	127.02	7,808.70	199.34	372.19	229.66
1981-82	6,207.31	127.67	9,150.70	233.60	453.10	279.59

* Excludes Receipts on Capital Account.

that interest is paid on the cumulative amounts. Hence, a proper comparison should be between percentage increase in effective kms. and percentage change in capital contributions where the latter influences directly the percentage increase in interest because of the fact that the rate of interest remained same during this period. As the utilisation of capital contributions was found to be not correlated to increase in interest per km. and further as vehicular utilisation and vehicle utilisation also did not have any perceptible influence on interest, it follows from the figures in Table 1.38 that the increase in cost of interest per km. must be because of inflation in the prices of vehicles. With an increase in the price of vehicle the capital contributions required would increase resulting in a more than proportionate increase in interest than the effective kms. done. This is so because while the capital contributions and interest volume increase there cannot be a commensurate increase in kilometres done because lesser number of vehicles are put on road in relation to capital contributions because of inflation.

This aspect of interest on capital contributions is only a part of the story. The more alarming position regarding interest is the fact that the interest on long term borrowings has been increasing significantly during the recent years (vide Table 1.40). While the interest on capital contributions increased by 180 per cent, the interest on long term borrowings increased by 377 per cent since 1977-78. The increase in the interest on long term borrowings over that on capital contributions was much more, if the peried since 1973-74 is taken—the interest on long term borrowings increased by more than 20 times when compared with 4.7 times increase in the interest on capital contributions. This resulted in an increase in ratio of interest on capital contributions to long term borrowings from 100 : 22.65 in 1973-74 to 100 : 86.05 in 1981-82. While the ratio of interest on long term borrowings to interest on capital contributions increased significantly during the period, the ratio of long term borrowings to capital contributions had not gone up that much, thereby implying that long term borrowing is becoming more expensive. This, coupled with the relative increase in long term borrowings naturally increases the cost of capital to the organisation. This is harmful to the organisation especially at a time when the organisation is incurring losses.

TABLE 1.40 : **Interest on capital contributions and long-term borrowings**

Year	Total capital contributions* (Rs. in lakhs)	Long-term borrowings (Rs. in lakhs)	Capital contributions to long-term borrowings	Interest on capital contributions (Rs. in lakhs)	Interest on long-term borrowings (Rs. in lakhs)	Interest on capital contributions to interest on long-term borrowings
1973-74	1,290.57	234.04	100 : 18.13	79.37	17.98	100 : 22.65
1974-75	1,892.31	52.69	100 : 2.78	89.45	15.96	100 : 17.84
1975-76	2,312.07	673.40	100 : 29.13	118.76	55.25	100 : 46.52
1976-77	3,038.50	730.95	100 : 24.06	132.03	74.37	100 : 56.33
1977-78	3,917.57	639.64	100 : 16.33	162.06	81.71	100 : 50.42
1978-79	5,480.54	1,042.46	100 : 19.02	211.30	75.60	100 : 35.78
1979-80	6,428.12	1,838.09	100 : 28.59	300.31	152.02	100 : 50.62
1980-81	7,829.12	2,039.93	100 : 26.06	372.19	254.74	100 : 68.44
1981-82	9,193.94	2,675.88	100 : 29.10	453.10	389.89	100 : 86.05

*Includes Receipts on Capital Account.

While discussing the cost of interest on capital contributions and the reasons for the significant increase in the same, it has been concluded that the increase must have been because of inflation in the cost of vehicles. Table 1.41 shows that the cost of vehicle, on an average, has gone up by about 55 per cent during the period thereby resulting in additional expenditure of Rs. 15.17 crores on vehicles during the period, taking the 1976-77 average price of vehicle into consideration. Because of this increase in capital expenditure, interest cost has also naturally gone up. The additional interest cost because of increase in the price of vehicles amounted to Rs. 161.59 lakhs during the period.

As mentioned earlier, apart from increase in the cost of interest on capital contributions, there was increase in the cost of interest on long term borrowings for two reasons—firstly, because of increase in the ratio of long term borrowings to capital contributions ; and, secondly, because of possible increase in the rate of interest in the long term borrowings. Table 1.42 gives data on these aspects. The table shows that during the last five years the corporation had to incur an additional expenditure of Rs. 109.62 lakhs, on long term borrowings because of the reasons mentioned above. If the year 1973-74 is taken as the base the additional expenditure on interest on long term borrowings amounts to Rs. 682.96 lakhs.

Finally, it is proposed to analyse from Table 1.43, the impact of inflation on miscellaneous* items of cost, taking 1976 norm of miscellaneous items of expenditure per kilometre as the norm. The table shows that except for the year 1981-82 the organisation had incurred additional expenditure on miscellaneous items (excluding interest on long term borrowings), because of inflation, ranging between Rs. 45.32 lakhs and Rs. 103.79 lakhs. On the whole, during this period, the corporation had to incur an additional expenditure of Rs. 122.36 lakhs on this item because of inflation.

Before the discussion on the costs and cost structure is closed one important accounting practice followed by the corporation in

* Miscellaneous items here include, miscellaneous item excluding interest on long-term loans and includes rent, rates and taxes and insurance.

TABLE 1.41 : **Impact of inflation on the cost of interest on capital contributions**

Year	No. of additional vehicles bought during the year	Cost of the additional vehicles bought (Rs. in lakhs)	Cost per vehicle bought Col.3/Col. 2 (Rs. in lakhs)	Additional cost per vehicle based on 1976-77 cost (Norm= Rs. 1.5309 lakhs) Norm—Col. 4 (Rs. in lakhs)	Total additional cost on vehicles bought Col. 5 × Col 2 (Rs. in lakhs)	Total additional cost on vehicles bought cumulated (Rs. in lakhs)	Interest @ 6.25% on the total additional cost on vehicles bought cumulated (Rs. in lakhs)
1976-77	956	1.463.54	1.5309	—	—	—	—
1977-78	726	1,137.91	1.5674	0.0365	26.499	26.499	1.6562
1978-79	1,010	1,791.55	1.7738	0.2429	245.329	271.828	16.9893
1979-80	1,268	2,439.22	1.9237	0.3928	498.070	769.898	48.1186
1980-81	894	2,115.93	2.3668	0.8359	747.295	1,517.193	94.8246
1981-82	N.A.	N.A.	—	—	—	—	—
						Total :	161.5887

TABLE 1.42 : **Impact of increase in the ratio of interest on long-term borrowings to interest on capital contributions on the cost of long-term borrowings**

Year	Interest on capital contributions (Rs. in lakhs)	Ratio of interest on capital contributions to interest on long-term borrowings	Interest on long-term borrowings based on 1973-74 norm (Rs. in lakhs)	Actual interest on long-term borrowings paid (Rs. in lakhs)	Additional interest on long-term borrowings paid over 1973-74 norm (Rs. in lakhs) (4—5)	Interest on long-term borrowings based on 1976-77 norm (Rs. in lakhs)	Additional interest on long-term borrowings paid on 1976-77 norm (7—5) (Rs. in lakhs)
1973-74	79.37	100 : 22.65	17.98	17.98	—	—	—
1974-75	89.45	100 : 17.84	20.26	15.96	(—) 4.30	—	—
1975-76	118.76	100 : 46.52	26.90	55.25	28.35	—	—
1976-77	132.03	100 : 56.33	29.90	74.37	44.47	74.37	—
1977-78	162.06	100 : 50.42	36.71	81.71	45.00	91.28	(—) 9.57
1978-79	211.30	100 : 35.78	47.86	75.60	27.74	119.02	(—) 43.42
1979-80	300.31	100 : 50.62	68.02	152.02	84.00	169.16	(—) 17.14
1980-81	372.19	100 : 68.44	84.30	254.74	170.44	209.65	45.09
1981-82	453.10	100 : 86.05	102.63	389.89	287.26	255.23	134.66
				Total :	682.96		109.62

TABLE 1.43 : **Impact of inflation on miscellaneous items of cost**

(*Rs. in lakhs*)

1	2	1976-77 3	1977-78 4	1978-79 5	1979-80 6	1980-81 7	1981-82 8
1.	Rent, rates and taxes	13.13	18.14	22.73	27.24	24.53	4.89
2.	Insurance	8.93	8.08	17.66	31.24	7.58	9.00
3.	Adjusted miscellaneous*	764.78	913.58	968.58	1,112.57	1,155.80	979.51
4.	Total miscellaneous costs (1+2+3)	786.84	939.60	1,008.97	1,171.05	1,187.91	993.40
5.	Effective kms.	4,277.77	4,861.87	5,106.85	5,802.33	6,175.70	6,207.31
6.	Total misc. costs per km.	18.394	19.326	19.757	20.182	19.235	16.004
7.	Total misc. costs with 1976-77 as norm.	—	894.28	939.34	1067.26	1135.94	1141.75
8.	Impact of inflation (4—7)	—	45.32	69.63	103.79	51.97	(—) 148.35
	Miscellaneous items as given	839.15	995.09	1044.18	1264.59	1410.54	1369.40
	Less : Interest on long-term loans	74.37	81.71	75.60	152.02	254.74	389.89
	*Adjusted miscellaneous	764.78	913.38	968.58	1112.57	1155.80	979.51

respect of the tyre retreading shop and printing press needs to be noted. The value of various inputs used in these two production units are booked twice on the debit side of the profit and loss account—once under the relevant headings such as 'stores consumed', 'salaries' etc., and for a second time as total costs incurred on 'tyre retreading shops' and 'printing press'. The estimated value of the production of these two units (on cost basis) appears on the credit side of the profit and loss account. During discussions with the officers of the Corporation it was revealed that this particular practice of showing the estimated value of production as an item of revenue on the profit and loss account is being followed at the express suggestion of the Auditor General.

The booking of costs in respect of these items twice on the debit side of the profit and loss account with the simultaneous booking of the value of production (on cost basis) on the credit side of the profit and loss account may not alter the net margin significantly (but for some minor adjustments in respect of work-in-progress, closing stock etc.), but the booking of the costs twice would inflate the costs, thereby resulting in increased costs, which is as much as Rs. 2.78 crores for the year 1981-82.

OPERATIONAL PERFORMANCE

So far an analysis of costs and the impact of inflation and efficiency/inefficiency on costs has been done. While analysing the impact of efficiency/inefficiency on the cost of operation, the impact of certain aspects of organisational efficiency only could be dealt with. Hence, before a comprehensive and integrated analysis of the impact of the efficiency/inefficiency and inflation on the costs of the organisation is made, an attempt will be made to briefly analyse the operational performance of the corporation and the cost implications of operational efficiency/inefficiency since 1976-77.

At the outset, the operational performance of the corporation, in terms of certain major parameters of performance, is attempted from Table 1.44. The table shows the trends in vehicular utilisation, vehicle utilisation, occupation ratio and passenger kms. done. In a way, as mentioned earlier, the passenger kms. done

TABLE 1.44 : **Operational performance**

Year	Vehicular utilisation (%)	Vehicle utilisation (in kms.)	Occupation ratio	Average passenger kms. done per schedule (kms. in lakhs)	Percentage increase in col. 5 over 1973-74	Percentage increase in col. 5 over 1976-77
1973-74	87.54	296.12	72.20	35.03	100.00	—
1974-75	86.98	306.72	66.81	34.79	99.31	—
1975-76	87.51	302.02	69.28	35.44	101.17	—
1976-77	90.61	305.97	69.49	36.92	105.40	100.00
1977-78	90.26	312.78	72.49	39.37	112.39	106.64
1978-79	88.05	308.91	75.35	39.65	113.19	107.39
1979-80	92.00	313.00	76.00	41.11	117.36	111.35
1980-81	88.00	312.00	71.00	38.66	110.36	104.71
1981-82	88.00	299.00	72.00	38.49	109.88	104.25

Note : Staff Productivity, KMPL, Tyre Mileage, have already been studied.

per schedule reflects the integrated effect of the earlier three parameters of performance. It can be seen from the table that while vehicular utilisation has, by and large, declined during 1976-77—1981-82, the vehicle utilisation and the occupation ratio have improved, even though the vehicle utilisation declined perceptibly in the last year that is 1981-82. In the case of occupancy ratio, even though the performance since 1977-78 has been better than that in 1976-77, there was a considerable decline in 1980-81 and a slight recovery in 1981-82 over the previous year. As a result of improved performance in terms of vehicle utilisation and occupancy ratio, since 1977-78, over 1976-77, there was an improvement in average passenger kms. done per schedule, despite the fact that vehicular utilisation came down over 1976-77. The increase in passenger kms. per schedule over 1976-77 was maintained until 1979-80, and since then there was a decline even though the performance in these last two years was better than that in 1976-77. The impact of this improved operational performance on the revenues of the corporation would be analysed later.

The reasons for decline in vehicular utilisation could be broadly attributed to the poor maintenance of vehicles, inadequate supply of units by the workshops and the increasing average age of the vehicles. The statement that the decline in vehicular utilisation could be because of poor maintenance or inadequate supply of units by workshops and stores is amply proved by the fact that cancellation of kms. due to late supply and for want of bus increased considerably during the period 1976-77—1981-82 from 11.85 per cent to 33.72 per cent (vide Table 1.45). The cancellations, on account of mechanical failures, even though came down between 1976-77 and 1978-79, have been on the consistent increase since then, reflecting the state of attention the vehicles are receiving in regard to their maintenance. In fact, the total cancelled kms. have been on the increase not only in absolute terms but also in relation to scheduled kms. Table 1.46 shows that there was generally an increase in the percentage of kms. cancelled since 1973-74, and particularly since 1976-77. In fact, the percentage of cancelled kms. more than doubled between 1976-77 and 1979-80. There was, however, a slight decline in the percentage in 1980-81 and 1981-82. The table also shows that

TABLE 1.45 : **Cause-wise cancellation of kilometres**

Causes for cancellation	1973-74	1974-75	1975-76	1976-77	1977-78	1978-79	1979-80	1980-81	1981-82
Pre-planned cancellation	51.33	41.23	100.48	85.33	94.42	135.89	99.42	—	—
	(30.15)	(17.69)	(31.57)	(33.06)	(30.00)	(22.03)	(13.09)		
Tyre failures	2.94	5.55	6.31	5.29	6.40	13.00	17.20	19.34	24.66
	(1.73)	(2.38)	(1.98)	(2.05)	(2.03)	(2.11)	(2.26)	(2.43)	(3.94)
Mechanical failures	21.87	49.35	54.31	32.36	37.29	60.61	84.67	90.99	82.84
	(12.84)	(21.18)	(17.06)	(12.54)	(11.85)	(9.82)	(11.15)	(11.42)	(13.24)
Late supply and want of bus	27.99	50.84	55.00	30.59	48.06	168.95	301.88	398.12	210.89
	(16.44)	(21.82)	(17.28)	(11.85)	(15.27)	(27.38)	(39.74)	(49.96)	(33.72)
Want of crew	17.38	32.41	26.51	18.76	25.16	52.86	74.24	75.26	69.29
	(10.21)	(13.91)	(8.33)	(7.27)	(7.99)	(8.57)	(9.77)	(9.45)	(11.08)
Poor traffic	30.25	36.18	38.60	52.86	54.62	44.56	39.69	45.93	55.45
	(17.77)	(15.53)	(12.16)	(20.47)	(17.37)	(7.22)	(5.22)	(5.76)	(8.87)
Others	18.51	17.48	37.00	32.95	48.76	141.08	142.61	167.21	182.35
	(10.86)	(7.50)	(11.62)	(12.76)	(15.49)	(22.87)	(18.77)	(20.98)	(29.15)
Total	170.27	233.04	318.30	258.14	314.71	616.95	759.71	796.85	625.48
	(100.00)	(100.00)	(100.00)	(100.00)	(100.00)	(100.00)	(100.00)	(100.00)	(100.00)

Source : MIS Records.
Note : Figures in brackets represent the percentage to the total.

TABLE 1.46 : **Scheduled and effective kms. operated**

(kms. in lakhs)

Year	Scheduled kms.	Cancelled kms.	Scheduled operated kms.	Additional kms. operated (4+5)	Effective kms.	Effective kms. as a % of scheduled kms.
1973-74	2,694.28	170.27 (6.32)	2,524.01	87.29	2,611.30	96.92
1974-75	3,209.73	233.04 (7.26)	2,976.69	113.94	3,090.63	96.29
1975-76	3,886.40	318.31 (8.19)	3,568.09	127.19	3,695.28	95.08
1976-77	4,366.92	258.15 (5.91)	4,108.77	169.00	4,277.77	97.96
1977-78	4,948.65	314.71 (6.36)	4,633.94	227.93	4,861.87	98.25
1978-79	5,548.26	616.97 (11.12)	4,931.29	175.56	5,106.85	92.04
1979-80	6,376.78	759.71 (11.91)	5,617.07	185.26	5,802.33	90.99
1980-81	6,799.83	796.85 (11.72)	6,002.98	172.80	6,175.78	90.82
1981-82	6,604.09	625.49 (9.47)	5,978.60	228.71	6,207.31	93.99

Source : (1) Annual Administration Reports ;
(2) Annual Performance Reports ;
(3) Management Information Systems Records.

Note : Figures in brackets represent Col. 3 as a percentage of Col. 2.

there was a considerable decline in the percentage of effective kms. to scheduled kms. since 1976-77. This trend has been reversed in the latest year, even though it is much below the figure of 1976-77 or 1977-78.

LOSSES OF APSRTC

Impact of inflation and operational managerial efficiency

Now an attempt will be made, in a comprehensive and integrated manner, to account for the losses of Rs. 66.55 crores that the corporation had accumulated after 1976-77. In accounting for these losses, the analysis, made earlier, of the impact of inflation and operational/managerial efficiency/inefficiency on the costs of the operations and the influence of fare revisions from time to time on the operating revenues are brought together to give a comprehensive view of how these have influenced the losses after 1976-77. Apart from making use of the empirical analysis made earlier, the use of data analysed subsequently in respect of the cost incurred by the corporation on hire charges for SETWIN buses is also made. In this context, it is relevant to note that in the following Section of this Chapter the reasons for the losses incurred by the organisation are analysed. The impact of these reasons on the losses of the organisation have already been accounted for in the analysis of empirical data on the impact of inflation and operational efficiency on the losses.

At the outset the aggregate effect of inflation on the cost of different items may be analysed from Table 1.47. The table shows that the corporation had incurred an additional expenditure of Rs. 182.13 crores on different items of expenditure due to inflation since 1977-78, based upon 1976-77 costs, of which a little more than 50 per cent was incurred in the year 1981-82. Of this the increase in emoluments of staff alone accounted for Rs. 74.15 crores that is about 41 per cent of the total inflation effect. The next major item which had substantially influenced the costs of the organisation is fuel which accounted for Rs. 45.03 crores that is, 24.73 per cent of the total increase. Among the other items, tyres and tubes, depreciation, spare parts and taxes may be mentioned as important, in that order, accounting for 10.53,

TABLE 1.47 : Inflation effect on the costs of individual items based on 1976-77 norm

(Rs. in lakhs)

Particulars	1977-78	1978-79	1979-80	1980-81	1981-82	Total for the period
Staff	381.73	557.89	774.18	1,650.19	4,050.52	7,414.51 (40.71)
Spareparts	(—)87.76	11.31	345.31	570.76	64.46	1,304.08 (7.16)
Tyres and tubes	(—)10.10	186.29	383.98	517.07	841.41	1,918.65 (10.53)
Fuel	11.68	12.68	305.55	1,524.48	2,648.79	4,503.18 (24.73)
Taxes	(—)62.79	32.50	160.31	371.42	444.80	946.24 (5.20)

Depreciation	65.11	166.41	346.11	518.45	703.26	1,799.34 (9.88)
Interest on capital	1.66	15.33	31.13	46.71	N.A.	94.83 (0.52)
Miscellaneous items (excluding interest on long-term loans)	45.32	69.63	103.79	51.97	(—)148.35	122.36 (0.67)
Interest on long-term loans	(—)9.57	(—)43.42	(—)17.14	45.09	134.66	109.62 (0.60)
Total	335.28	1,008.62	2,433.22	5,296.14	9,139.55	18,212.81 (100.00)

Source : Staff—Table 1.14 (b) ; Spares—Table 1.18 ; Tyres and Tubes—Table 1.24 ; Fuel—Table 1.30 (c) ; Taxes—Table 1.31 (c) ; Depreciation—Table 1.34 ; Interest on Capital Contributions—Table 1.41 ; Interest on long term loans—Table 1.42. Miscellaneous (excluding interest on long term borrowings)—Table 1.43.

Note : Figures in brackets are percentages to total.

9.88, 7.16 and 5.20 per cent respectively of the increase in the costs.

The impact of operational inefficiency on the costs/losses is only marginal. In fact the influennce of managerial inefficiency in respect of individual items of costs such as staff, spares, tyres and tubes, taxes, depreciation, fuel and interest constitutes an insignificant aspect of the influence of operational inefficiency on costs/losses, whereas the influence of improvement in operational efficiency in terms of effective passenger kilometres done, which in a way reflects vehicular utilisation, vehicle utilisation and load factor, on operating revenues is so outweighing that is more than offsets the costs of inefficiency in respect of different items of costs.

Table 1.48 shows that the impact of inefficiency of the organisation in respect of different items of costs such as staff, spares, tyres and tubes, taxes and fuel together accounted for an additional expenditure or losses to the extent of Rs. 93.73 lakhs only. While the organisation could save on certain items of expenditure because of its efficiency, that is on spares (Rs. 6.36 crores), taxes (Rs. 5.41 crores), and tyres and tubes (Rs. 1.06 crores), it had incurred considerable additional expenditure on such items as staff (Rs. 9.32 crores) and fuel (Rs. 4.46 crores), the latter items more than offsetting the former items.

On the other hand, the corporation as per reported figures, must have earned additional operating revenues to the extent of Rs. 37.75 crores because of improvement in operational efficiency, in terms of additional passenger kilometres done during the period, based on the norms of passenger kilometres per schedule done in 1976-77 as could be seen from Table 1.49.

In this context, it is relevant to note a methodological aspect of computation of the additional revenues derived because of improvement in operational efficiency during the period. As the impact of inflation (i.e., the fare increase over 1976-77) in respect of these additional passenger kilometres done during the period has been taken care of in computing additional traffic revenue realised due to increase in the average fare realised (vide Table 1.50), the impact of operational efficiency on additional revenue is computed by taking into consideration the average fare of 1976-77 and the additional kilometres done in

TABLE 1.48 : **Impact of inefficiency on different items of costs**

(*Rs. in lakhs*)

Particulars	1977-78	1978-79	1979-80	1980-81	1981-82	Total for the period
Staff	89.01	67.08	171.16	296.88	308.11	932.24
Spares	(—)104.32	(—)136.52	85.71	(—) 53.68	(—)427.18	(—)635.99
Tyres and tubes	38.38	163.98	15.87	(—)134.62	(—)189.54	(—)105.93
Fuel	(—) 10.40	36.40	58.50	207.00	153.00	444.50
Taxes	(—) 85.66	(—)130.09	(—)278.75	(—) 39.72	(—) 6.87	(—)541.09
Total	(—) 72.99	0.85	52.49	275.86	(—)162.48	93.73

Source : Staff —Table 1.14(a)
Spares —Table 1.17
Tyres and tubes —Table 1.27
Taxes —Table 1.31(b)
Fuel —Table 1.30

TABLE 1.49 : **Impact of operational efficiency on revenues**

Year	No. of schedules	Passenger kms. done (in lakhs)	Average passenger kms. per schedule (in lakhs)	Computed total passenger kms. (taking 1976-77 average passenger kms. per schedule) Col. 2 × norm of 1976-77 (36.72) (in lakhs)	Extra passenger kms. done over the base year norm (in lakhs)	Average fare per passenger kms. (year-wise) (in paise)	Additional revenue derived because of efficiency in operations based on 5.64 paise per km. for the additional passenger kms. done Col. 6 × Col. 7 (Rs. in lakhs)
1976-77	4,071	150,303.00	36.92	—	—	5.64	—
1977-78	4,498	177,087.00	39.37	166,068.01	11,019	5.45	621.47
1978-79	4,973	197,201.00	39.65	183,605.20	13,596	5.46	766.81
1979-80	5,470	224,898.31	41.11	201,954.65	22,943	5.78	1,293.99
1980-81	5,784	223,625.00	38.66	213,547.66	10,078	6.78	568.40
1981-82	5,922	227,933.00	38.49	218,642.67	9,290	8.49	523.96
						Total :	3,774.63

TABLE 1.50 : **Additional traffic revenue realised due to increase in the average fare realised**

Year	Traffic revenue (Rs. in lakhs)	Passenger kms. (in lakhs)	Average traffic revenue per passenger km. Col. 2/Col. 3. Rs.	Computed traffic revenue (passenger kms. done in the year × average traffic revenue per passenger km. for 1976.77) (Rs. in lakhs)	Excess of actuals over computed traffic revenue Col. 2—Col. 5 (Rs. in lakhs)
1976-77	8,480.91	1,50,303.00	5.64	—	—
1977-78	9,657.02	1,77,087.00	5.45	9,992.21	(—)335.19
1978-79	10,769,81	1,97,201.00	5.46	11,127.14	(—)357.33
1979-80	13,005.43	2,24,898.31	5.78	12,689.98	315.45
1980-81	15,965.66	2,23,625.00	6.78	12,618.13	3,347.53
1981-82	19,361,86	2,27,933.00	8.49	12,861.22	6,500.64
				Total :	9,471.10

respective years.

While the improvement in operational efficiency resulted in netting additional revenues of Rs. 37.75 crores, the increase in fares boosted the traffic revenues of the organisation to the extent of Rs. 94.71 crores during the period as can be seen from Table 1.50. Thus, while the inflation resulted in additional expenditure of Rs. 182.13 crores, the fare increases had helped the organisation to the extent of only Rs. 94.71 crores.

Consequently, the organisation was left with a shortfall of Rs. 87.42 crores, forcing it to either improve its performance and thereby reduce losses or to incur losses to the extent that it could not improve its efficiency. The Corporation as per reported figures, could realise additional revenues by putting in improved operational efficiency to the extent of Rs. 36.81 crores (Rs. 37.75-Rs. 0.94 crores) as could be seen from Table 1.51. Because of this, the organisation could reduce the losses during the period, based on these computations, to Rs. 50.61 crores. However, the figure of loss so arrived at after taking into consideration the impact of inflation and efficiency, is in divergence with the figure of reported losses of Rs. 66.55 crores during the period as per the annual accounts. Thus, a gap of Rs. 15.94 crores is seen between the reported and computed losses. Assuming that the price of lubricants had increased by the same rate during the period as that of HSD oil and taking into consideration the proportion of expenditure incurred on lubricants to the cost of HSD oil (which works out to 12.63 per cent of Rs. 45.03 crores) the corporation may be presumed to have spent an additional amount of Rs. 5.69 crores on lubricants during the period because of inflation. If this is adjusted against the unexplained gap of Rs. 15.94 crores, a balance of Rs. 10.25 crores would be left unexplained. However, account will have to be taken of possible savings in the consumption of lubricants during the period. Further, it is to be noted that the impact of inflation on stores was computed based on the assumption that the price of spares, on an average, would have increased at the same rate as that of increase in the price of vehicles. When all these adjustments are made, the unexplained figure of gap between the reported and computed losses may be negligible. Thus it may be concluded that the organisation could reduce its losses to the extent of at least Rs. 36.81

TABLE 1.51 : Integrated view of reasons for losses of APSRTC since 1977-88

	Rs. in crores		Rs. in crores
1. Inflation effect on the cost of individual items (vide Table 1.47)	182.13	1. Additional traffic revenue realised because of increase in average fare (vide Table 1.50)	94.71
2. Impact of inefficiency on costs of different items (vide Table 1.48)	0.94	2. Additional revenue realised because of improvement in operational efficiency (vide Table 1.49)	37.75
		3. Difference representing losses for the period	50.61
	183.07		183.07

crores due to improved efficiency, of which Rs. 9.62 crores was achieved during the last year 1981-82 alone, Rs. 5.20 crores on operational efficiency and Rs. 4.38 crores on different items of costs (Rs. 2.76 crores plus Rs. 1.62 crores).

In the light of the above, the increasing losses incurred by the corporation, since 1977-78, cannot be attributed to increased inefficiency on the part of the organisation. It must, however, be noted that the organisational efficiency in some respects has gone down ; for example, staff and fuel when compared with its own past performance ; and there is ample scope for improvement in respect of staff, stores and fuel when compared with other organisations. Further, the MV tax increase also contributed to losses when compared with some of the Tamil Nadu corporations.

It is necessary to make note of some of the methodological limitations of the above study, which do not vitiate the validity of the conclusions drawn above, but may only marginally influence the figures. Firstly, the impact of introduction and withdrawal of Jeep Mini-Bus scheme on the costs/losses could not be quantified for want of detailed data. Secondly, while computing the reasons for losses, only those factors which contributed to losses afresh during the period are taken into consideration. In other words, the losses arising out of such reasons as infringement of monopoly right, leakage of revenues, maintenance of staff cars and so on, which have been there earlier to 1976-77 also, have not been included.

In the analysis of losses made so far, the cost of operational inefficiency and its contribution to losses have been computed by taking into consideration the 1976-77 performance of APSRTC itself. In other words, decline in the efficiency of the APSRTC when compared with its past performance has been taken into consideration. It does not give any idea of its performance in relation to the performance of other state transport undertakings. In fact the aim of the organisation should be not only to reach its earlier heights of performance but also the higher levels of performance achieved by the other sister transport undertakings in the country. Hence, an attempt is made to compute the cost of inefficiency of APSRTC in respect of certain major items of costs when compared with the biggest transport undertaking in the country Maharashtra State Road

Transport Corporation (MSRTC), an organisation of comparable size, (GSRTC), and a few of the small sized nationalised transport undertakings in Tamil Nadu (Pallavan (Metro), Pandiyan, Cheran, Kattabomman and Cholan corporations). In making this comparative study, data are computed for the year 1980-81 only, by taking the performance of these undertakings in respect of these items, for that year, as the norm. If the APSRTC's performance is below the level obtaining in other undertakings the difference is computed in monetary terms and shown in the table. It can be seen from Table 1.52 that one item where the performance of APSRTC is much below that of the other undertakings is staff, as the schedule-staff ratio is much more in APSRTC when compared with other undertakings. This item alone for one year accounted for a difference of a minimum of Rs. 7.70 crores when compared with the Gujarat State Road Transport Corporation (GSRTC) which had the highest schedule-staff ratio amongst these other undertakings. The additional cost on staff in APSRTC is much more when compared with other organisations ranging between Rs. 10.84 crores and Rs. 19.53 crores. The remedy for the losses of APSRTC is very clear, that it lies in reducing the schedule-staff ratio, though not possible in the short-run, should be capable of being achieved in the long run. In the analysis on organisational set up, it is pointed out that the remedy lies in splitting the organisation and having smaller corporations which would help in reducing the levels in the hierarchy of organisation to two from the existing four levels. The next major defficiency of the organisation is in the area of spares, where the additional cost incurred by it, when compared with the actual position obtaining in other organisations ranges between Rs. 0.81 crores and Rs. 11.62 crores. It is only in the area of fuel that the APSRTC seems to be faring better than the other undertakings except for G.S.R.T.C. and Maharashtra State Road Transport Corporation (MSRTC) taking the figures as furnished by APSRTC at their face value.

ANALYSIS OF REASONS FOR LOSSES

In the foregoing analysis of costs, cost structure and losses, an idea of losses incurred by the Corporation because of inflation anp

TABLE 1.52 : Cost of efficiency/inefficiency of APSRTC in relation to other state transport undertakings : 1980-81

(*Rs. in lakhs*)

Particulars	MSRTC	GSRTC	PTC (Mofussil)	Pandiyan Road Ways	Chrean	Kattabomman	Cholan
Staff	1,084,24	770.45	1,850.50	1,831.01	1,870.06	1,159.64	1,953.04
Spares	917.16	1,161.57	N.A	386.90	594.49	80.57	205.49
Tyres and tubes	(—)7.95	85.41	(—)9.17	(—)74.66	N.A.	N.A.	(—)40.67
Fuel	58.30	423.80	(—)235.21	(—)460.69	(–)69.12	(—)324.24	(—)215.99
Taxes	(—)403.37	(—)850.62	1,899.73	804.21	N.A.	(—)336.28	N.A.
Total	1,648.38	1,590.61	3,505.85	2,486.77	2,395.43	579.69	1,901.87

Note : Fuel rate is taken as Rs. 2.25 per litre (1980-81)—A.P.S.R.T.C.

the extent of reduction in possible losses because of increase in fares and improvement in operational efficiency (after adjusting for losses on account of inefficiency) has been made. While this analysis shows inflation as one of the main reasons for additional costs/losses incurred, and also the increase in costs because of operational inefficiencies, it has not dealt with in detail various other reasons for losses. Now an attempt will be made to look into these other reasons for losses. It must, however, be noted that the losses arising out of these reasons are not losses exclusive of the analysis made earlier. In other words, the losses arising out of these reasons are already reflected in the figures computed earlier, by way of either additional staff cost or loss of revenue or additional costs under different other items.

These reasons may be broadly analysed under four heads :

(i) the corporation itself,
(ii) the city services,
(iii) the government, and
(iv) the transport authorities.

For the first one, it is the organisation itself that has to take the blame and for the other three it is either the government or its wings, that is transport authorities. The corporation has been losing for its own failure, either because of leakage of revenue, the estimates in respect of which vary between Rs. 3.65 crores and Rs. 4.50 crores per annum or because of the large number of its staff cars, on which it spends a minimum of Rs. 30.22 lakhs per annum. Even if the officers were to be given interest free loans to purchase vehicles and maintenance allowance there would still be a net saving of Rs. 15.74 lakhs per annum.

The corporation had to take up a number of special schemes and give different kinds of concessions at the instance of the state government, the costs in respect of which vary from scheme to scheme. The various kinds of special schemes the corporation undertook at the instance of the government are (1) Special Employment Scheme, (2) Arrangement with Setwin, (3) Village-Link Transport Scheme (VTLS), (4) Jeep Mini-Bus scheme, and (5) Cargo service. The corporation has been incurring additional cost/loss at Rs. 66.65 lakhs per year on excess staff because of special employment schemes, Rs. 55.74 lakhs (cumulative loss) on Setwin Maxi services, Rs. 45.00 lakhs per year on account of Setwin Mini-services, Rs. 12.25 crores (cumulative) loss on VLTS, Rs. 44.37 lakhs (total loss for two years) on cargo services. Besides these, the corporation incurs loss of Rs. 7.22 crores per annum on various kinds of concessions given to city commuters such as students, NGGOs, handicapped persons, committed trips and so on. The Government in a way is responsible for losses of the corporation because of ineffective check on the private operators, infringing the monopoly rights of the corporation, in the operation of stage carriages in those areas where there is complete nationalisation. The estimates of losses because of this infringement vary between Rs. 7.20 crores and Rs. 14.40 crores per annum. On an average the loss on this account may be estimated at about Rs. 10.00 crores per annum.

The unhelpful attitude of the transport authorities is also responsible for the losses of the corporation. The loss on account of infringement of monopoly right is because of the attitude of the transport authorities to the corporotion vis-a-vis the private operators. The Corporation would avoid incurring losses, if only the infringement of monopoly right is checked, the government either charges concessional motor vehicle tax on VLTS or meets the loss on this account by way of subsidies and similarly the government eiher reduces the motor vehicle tax on city services, as suggested earlier, or gives subsidies to meet the various concessions thrust on the corporation by the government.

In the case of losses on VLTS and because of concessions on city services, there are various alternatives. Firstly, as mentioned already, there may be lower rate of motor vehicle tax on the services under VLTS and on city services. Secondly, the government may give subsidy for the losses incurred on VLTS and also because of concessions extended in the case of city services. The third alternative is the usual argument that the corporation has got a social obligation to discharge apart from rendering adequate, economical and efficient services and hence the losses that it incurs on certain services must be made good by profits that it makes on the other services, that is on the whole it should break even. However, in the context of the losses of the corporation on the non-city and non-VLTS services also, there is a case for recommending the first two remedies. It is, therefore, recommended that firstly the motor vehicle taxes on city services should be reduced to the level as recommended earlier, and secondly the motor vehicle tax on VLTS should be reduced to a nominal rate of Rs. 10 per seat per quarter. Further, any loss the corporation incurs on city services for reasons beyond its operational efficiency factors and despite the reduction in the motor vehicle tax rate as suggested must be made good by the government by way of subsidy.

In the light of the above analysis the reasons for losses may now be discussed in detail.

Leakage of revenue

It is ironical that the conductor, who is considered the bread winner for the APSRTC., is subjected to constant vigilance and onslaught by the management. At any point of time, the maximum number of suspensions ordered is against this category. The bulk of disciplinary cases dealt in the corporation relates to the offences committed by conductors. The turn-over of conductors every year is so high that recruitment for this category has been a regular feature. Most of the industrial relations problems encountered by the Managers are offshoots of the disciplinary proceedings initiated against conductors. These are all manifestations of the problem of pilferage or defalcation of revenue by conductors. In other words, the problem of pilferage by conductors concerns not only the fall in the revenue of the corporation but also the various other administrative problems that it leaves in its trail.

Strangely enough, there is no reliable data on this vital subject. In the absence of scientifically collected and processed information, any estimate made quantifying the leakage of revenue of the corporation is liable to be contradicted. For example, the estimate made by the Anantha Rama Krishnan Committee in this regard was later disputed by the corporation. This was way back in the year 1961. In the year 1980, the then Minister for Transport and Chairman of the APSRTC, in an article estimated the extent of loss suffered by the corporation due to pilferage by conductors at Rs. 4.50 crores per year.[1] He claimed that the same had been reduced to 0.50 crores, during his tenure of office. The report of the Vice-Chairman and General Manager disclosed that an additional revenue of Rs. 10,000 per day had been realised on the Hyderabad City routes alone as a result of the special drive launched in ticket checking.[2]

In other words, the quantum of losses suffered by the corporation on the Hyderabad city routes alone works out to Rs. 36.50 lakhs per year. The Hyderabad city services roughly constitute 10 per cent of the total operations. Further, on mofussil routes the pilferage is reported to be rampant for various reasons like the existence of dead-end routes, operation of buses into interior parts and so on. This being so, the pilferage of Rs. 4.50 crores per year as reported by the then Minister for Transport and Chairman of the Corporation in the year 1980, appears to be reasonable.

The study reveals that there has been no scheme or machinery as such to periodically assess the leakage of revenue of the corporation. Computation of the figures for the entire corporation showing the rate of pilferage based on the results of intensive checking on each route and the Jack-Pot-Survey conducted has been a thing of the distant past. The last Jack-Pot-Survey conducted throughout the corporation dated back to the year 1961-62.

Secondly, the high rate of turnover of conductors on charges of pilferage is another indication of the high incidence of defalcation of revenue by conductors. The report of the Vice-Chairman and General Manager shows that as many as 800 conductors were removed from service on this account out of the total strength of 16,000 conductors[3]. The then Minister for Transport and Chairman of APSRTC in an article stated that, on an average, 200 conductors per month were discharged from service.[4] By any standard, this is not a desirable state of affairs. Instead, the management of the corporation will do well if it designs a system which preempts the conductor from indulging in pilferage to the extent possible. In the year 1965, the corporation introduced the system of ground booking at all important termini with a view to realising a large chunk of the revenue outside the bus (nearly 50%). The underlying idea is to reduce the volume of earnings collected throuh conductors to a minimum. For some inexplicable reasons this system was discontinued in course of time. There is a strong case for the immediate revival of the said system.

Thirdly, it is noted that the ticket checking inspectors and the other Traffic Supervisors are interchangeable. This arrangement has led to the posting of supervisors who are unwanted in depots as Checking Inspectors. As a result, the checking squads have become asylums to ineffective supervisors. The checking Inspectors are not exposed to job-oriented training either. The cases framed by these Inspectors suffer from a number of flaws with the attendant conseqences. Therefore, it is suggested that a separate cadre may be created for the Checking Inspectors and youngmen may be recruited for the purpose considering the ardous duties involved.

Fourthly, more jeeps may be allotted to the checking squads to facilitate extensive coverage and to ensure element of surprise in every check exercised. The misuse of jeeps by the officers under the guise of ticket checking may be put an end to. This practice is reported to be endemic at all levels of officers.

Lastly, the corporation has not taken full advantage of the APMV Rule devolving responsibility for ticketless travelling on the passengers. The need for reintroduction of mobile courts in Hyderabad city is strongly felt.

Staff cars

The Corporation is on the brink of financial bankruptacy. To put the corporation back on rails, remedial steps taken shall include austerity measures also. The extravagance and pomp, which could be tolerated during its heydays, are subjected to severe criticism now. Allotment of cars for the use of officers both for private and official work and the liberal use to which these cars are put to attracts immediate attention of the critics.

As part of the austerity drive, the staff cars may be withdrawn and fixed allowance may be paid to officers for maintaining their own vehicles. It is noted that a proposal of this sort was actually considered by the corporation in the year 1978. A study of the said proposals reveals that a saving of Rs. 8.00 lakhs per year was estimated on withdrawing of cars allotted to Heads of Department and abolition of Headquarters depot. At that time only 20 cars were maintained at Head Office. Secondly, the said estimate was worked out on the basis of the costs prevailing in the year 1978. Since then there has been a steep rise in the costs. Thirdly, the cars and jeeps allotted to Divisional Managers, Depot Managers and other officers in the field were not taken into account.

In the light of the above, a new scheme is suggested. Under the new scheme, all the cars/jeeps now allotted to the officers excluding Chairman and Vice-Chairman and General Manager are proposed to be withdrawn. The vehicles allotted to the ticket checking squads and for the other miscellaneous official purposes are to be retained. Officers will be paid a fixed allowance of Rs. 300 each per month as car maintenance allowance. Officers will be provided with a loan assistance of Rs. 50,000 each for purchasing their own cars. This loan is to be interest free. This sort of incentive is necessary to enable the officers to maintain their own cars. For, considering the nature of duties of the officers, it is found necessary that officers shall maintain their own vehicles. The economies of the new scheme are given hereunder :

Expenditure now incurred on fuel (Petrol or HSD Oil), Wages of L.V. drivers (at the rate of one per vehicle), taxes and maintainance charges will be avoided under the new scheme. As such, expenditure on these items is considered as savings under the new scheme. The car maintenance allowance proposed to be paid to the officers and the loss of interest on the loan assistance given are treated as expenditure under the new scheme. From *Annexures 2 and 3*, it may be seen that the approximate savings likely to be realised under the scheme work out to Rs. 30.22 lakhs. Similarly, the approximate expenditure under the new scheme stands at Rs. 14.48 lakhs. The net savings work out to Rs. 15.74 lakhs.

City services

It is a well known fact that the city transport services are generally a losing proposition throughout the world and APSRTC is no exception in this regard. Unlike many other undertakings in the country, the APSRTC operates services in more than one town in addition to the twin cities. Some of the undertakings which provide city services are confined to a single place as is the case with BEST in Bombay, AMTS in Ahmedabad, Pallavan (Metro) in Madras. The Andhra Pradesh State Road Transport Corporation (APSRTC) runs its city/town services, at Vijayawada, Viskhapatnam, Warangal and Kothagudem and though all of them may look alike in so far as being called city/town services, they present problems of varying nature, in terms of growth potential, peak hour traffic, congestion/provided and distances covered on roads, concessions and so on.

In the case of APSRTC, the problems are further compounded on account of the public pressures that are brought upon it, such as pressurising the Corporation to take over city services in Visakhapatnam on an otherwise unwilling corporation ; the severe competition between the private operators and the corporation with overlapping routes in Vijayawada, and the long-distance unpopulated routes operated in Kothagudem and Warangal. Problems of this type are not faced by Pallavan (Metro), BEST (Bombay) and AMTS (Ahmedabad).

The unplanned and hurried nationalisation of town services is a unique feature persent in APSRTC. The corporation was asked to take over part of the services in Vijayawada and the entire services in Visakhaptnam at short notice. It is no secret that the corporation has to take over aged fleet. Further, excess personnel were handed over by the private operators which further aggravated the costs of city operations.

The hurried nationalisation, particularly in Visakhapatnam, resulted in various problems arising out of lack of infrastructural facilites. Even today, depots like Simhachalam and Gajuwaka do not have the basic facilities needed for operating services. This naturally resulted in higher dead killometres. Further, in order to cope with the traffic, the corporation was forced to introduce more number of small sized buses, which it had withdrawn from TTD Operations and deployed them in Visakhapatnam. As the buses intoduced were of small size, more number of buses had to be operated resulting in higher fuel costs and requiring larger crew than otherwise required, contributing to higher costs. As the buses were quite aged, the maintenance costs also went up contributing to higher costs.

Another problem peculiar to city services is the pressure of specific groups demanding concessions, committed trips and so on. Two such prominent groups are government employees and students. As compared to district fares, the city fares are low. This is further eroded due to the concessions provided to the above two groups, that too, at rates prevailing a decade ago. The demand from these groups for certain committed exclusive trips, results in undue pressures on the city services. On the one hand, these groups are entitled for concessional passes, that too on lower fares; and, on the other, they demand that exclusive trips meant for them should be run by the corporation. This, infact, results in a double concession being extended to the groups. The running of these committed trips creates operational problems resulting in the loss of revenue to the corporation. As the corporation has a limited fleet, it has to deploy the same as effectively as possible with least dead kilometrage and best vehicle utilisation. However, the operation of these committed trips is possible only by withdrawing buses from the main and suburban routes during the peak hour period which results in loss of revenue to the corporation. Some of the Depot Managers are of the view that if these trips are discontinued, the corporation's twin city service revenues may go up by as much as 20 per cent and cited an example of increase in revenues when the corporation cancelled committed trips in December 1980.

Further, the concessions granted to the student groups are based on the old fares, and these concessional fares based on old fares continued even when fare hikes are announced and implemented at various places. Besides enjoying substantial concessions, they further want to have exclusive trips to and from their houses to schools and colleges. Obviously, this results in Uni-directional traffic', which is equally true in the case of government servants too. Added to this, whenever the corporation proposes hike in city fares to neutralise the inflationary effect on costs, the student community becomes violent and the corporation buses become the target of fury by this group. Consequently the maintenance costs go up, the earnings decline due to the destruction and damage to its vehicles—all contributing to higher losses. Further, it is to be emphasised that the committed trips usually result in unidirectional traffic consiting of concessional pass holders depriving the corporation of alternative earning opportunities.

Over and above that, due to the congestion of traffic in twin cities/towns, the city buses travel at a lower speed, which results in lower vehicle utilisation. Many a time, curtailment of trips takes place and results in loss of revenue to the corporation, additional wear and tear to the vehicle, and low KMPL. Further, the corporation had to run short distance routes in city operations, which contributes to lower vehicle utilisation, adding to higher costs.

Another contributing factor to city losses is motor vehicle taxation. Though, it appears that the tax amount per seat per quarter is lower in respect of city services as compared to mofussil services, it actually works out to be higher per bus per annum because of inclusion of large number of standees, resulting in higher tax costs on city services, as mentioned in an earlier section.

Further, some of the services hitherto operated as district services in and around twin cities have been converted into suburban services, but there was no change effected in tax rates and they continue to be mofussil rates. Over and above this, the conversion into suburban service results in extension of the suburban pass services, besides slightly lower fares. Thus, the revenues tend to be lower, while taxes remain as earlier, resulting in higher costs on such services.

Another reason for lower revenues on city services is the inadequate and poor quality of checking, besides the corporation employees travelling with their friends and relatives without buying tickets. This naturally, deprives the coporation of its due share of revenues. Poor checking usually encourages lack of integrity on the part of the conductors, by way of either non-issual of tickets to the passengers or re-issue of used tickets to innocent, illiterate and conniving passengers, thereby resulting in higher leakage of revenues. It further encourages development of vested interests by the crew and they would like to continue at the same place to cultivate the various network relationships they developed so that they can carry on their operations silently and successfully. In order to achieve this, they bring the union pressures on officers at the time of transfers and thus indiscipline has become a problem making transfer as an effective instrument to plug the leakage in revenues.

In order to plug the corruption, which results in leakage of revenue, the corporation devised a collection incentive scheme. The scheme has certain loopholes and the norms laid down were quite low contributing to higher costs. Further, when the corporation wanted to tighten the norms, the unions resisted and tried to pressurise the management to retain the old norms resulting in higher incentive payments without commensurate benefits to the corporation in terms of higher revenues. It is a well known fact that when a defective incentive scheme is in operation, making the worker eligible for incentives, it results in higher absenteeism of the crew. From a discussion with the Depot Managers, it is learnt that the city collection incentive scheme enables the conductor to earn amounts ranging between Rs. 500 and Rs. 1,000 or more as incentive alone. It is relevant to note in this context that the staff under this scheme are eligible for incentive even if they put in 21 days of attendance in a month. It is also learnt, that the moment the crew reach the target, they do not exert any more effort to go up further.

City services are laden with higher staff costs for various reasons, some of which have been discussed earlier. The very nature of city service operations require generally a 16 hour working span with peak hour implications requiring almost double crew. This problem is further aggravated due to the inability of the Depot Managers to allot duties in a staggered manner as permitted by the Motor Transport Workers Act. While the Act permits the eight hour work schedule to be staggered in 12 hours, the Depot Managers are not in a position to do so due to Trade Union pressures. Consequently, the average number of hours worked by the crew comes down, requiring additional staff, leading to higher staff costs. Further, many old aged drivers and conductors succeed in getting transferred to twin cities on humanitarian and compassionate grounds. Being seniors, they get higher emoluments which add further to higher staff costs on city services.

It has been mentioned earlier that the running of city services is always a losing proposition. However, the continued presence of private operators in Vijayawada requires an explanation

The private operators succeed in hoodwinking the Motor Transport Worker's Act pertaining to the maximum hours of work. They usually extract work beyond eight hours, besides paying lower wages. Further, their system of close control and checking by appointing their own relatives as supervisors enables them to plug the leakage of revenues. Thus lower costs of operation on the one hand; and assurance of full collection of revenues result in positive margins for them. Further, they succeed in violating the scheduled times and take away the passengers waiting for the RTC buses, by adjusting their timings. Some times, the corporation is persuaded by the Government to operate certain committed trips (e.g., Wagon Workshop, Ajitsinghnagar etc.) resulting in lower revenues while no such pressure is ever brought upon on the private operators.

Another cause for losses on city services is the transfer of Jeep-Mini-buses. Their seating capacity is only fourteen and even when they are operated without a conductor, the CPK comes to Rs. 2.25 as against an EPK ranging between Re. 0.60 and Re. 0.70. The main reason for the continued operation of these buses is the objection that may be raised by the Accountant General, if these are scrapped before they complete their useful life. Further, most of them are vulnerable to failure; and frequent breakdowns are a common feature which results in high staff costs due to the staff idling away time and deprivation of revenues due to breakdowns.

One particular point of interest that has to be noted in Visakhapatnam city operations is that there was a pressure from Headquarters to reduce the losses arising out of city operations and in order to achieve this, it has imposed a ceiling of 33,000 kms, with the hope that this results in curtailing the number of services operated and improving EPK. The occupancy ratio has increased resulting in lower losses. Consequent upon the curtailment of number of trips, over-crowding has become a common feature and the quality of service came down considerably resulting in public dissatisfaction. The issue involved here is the trade off between public dissatisfaction and cutting down losses by reducing trips.

Remedies

While it may not be possible to turn the city losses into profits, it should at least be possible to arrest the increasing trend of city losses by taking certain steps.

1. One of the areas where the corporation can succeed is by lowering its costs through improved performance.

2. Committed trips can be drastically reduced or completely eliminated resulting in availability of these vehicles during peak hours to earn additional revenues. The corporation can approach the concerned educational institutions or employers with a suggestion that they should take RTC buses on special hire for meeting their specific requirements. This would result in higher revenues. Where such a thing is not possible, the corporation may be compensated by the Government through a subsidy to cover the gap.

3. There is need for improved and intensified checking on city routes, which would ensure plugging of leakages resulting in higher revenue collections. The earlier experience with mobile court was a welcome feature. It had to be discontinued because of public criticism and opposition. The corporation should think in terms of reintroduction of mobile courts besides tightening the checking system.

4. One suggestion is to hand over the city services to the Municipalities or to consider the question of creating a separate corporation for city services. The experience with municipalised transport undertakings elsewhere in the country is, however, not that happy. There were instances when such undertakings could not obtain funds for replacing their worn out vehicles.

The creation of a separate city corporation would immediately result in discontinuance of cross-subsidization of city passengers by mofussil passengers, but makes it possible to receive special assistance from institutions like Central Government and World Bank. Further, the problem of city losses gets projected in proper perspective resulting in more sympathetic co-operation from city passengers in the event of inevitable fare hike.

If municipalisation or creation of a separate corporation is not favoured, there is a strong case for the government to consider the question of reduction of taxes on city services and/

or subsidization.

Special employment schemes

The Government of Andhra Pradesh in the year 1978 have designed a special employment scheme to provide increased employment opportunities, exclusively to the educated unemployed candidates belonging to Scheduled Castes, Scheduled Tribes and Backward Classes. Under the normal recruitment rules, the SC/ST and BC candidates enjoy reservation facility to the extent of 14 per cent, 4 per cent and 25 per cent respectively of the total number of posts offered. Under the special employment scheme, however, all the posts are allotted to the SC, ST and BC candidates only. In other words, the special employment scheme is drawn up only to generate employment for the benefit of Scheduled Castes, Scheduled Tribes and Backward classes. For this purpose alone, the rate of recruitment in the APSRTC is fixed at 8 candidates per bus (2 drivers, 2 conductors, 2 mechanics, and 2 cleaners), under the First and Second Phases of the scheme already implemented. The Third Phase of the scheme, which is yet to be implemented by the APSRTC, envisages employment at the rate of 9 per bus.

The corporation, though plagued by the problem of high bus-staff ratio, has agreed for the implementation of the scheme because of the financial crisis that it has been passing through. The corporation has been lured by the loan assistance forthcoming under the scheme at lower rate of interest—13.5 per cent with a rebate of 3 per cent for prompt payment.

The First and Second Phases of the scheme have been implemented by the corporation during the years 1978-79 and 1979-80 respectively. In all 550 buses have been introduced under the scheme with Rs. 11.25 crores received as loan assistance. The implementation of the First and Second Phases of the scheme has led to the absorption of 4,372 candidates as against the 4,400 programmed for the 550 buses introduced. The scheme, however, envisaged introduction of 608 buses under the First and Second Phase and absorption of 4,864 candidates at the rate of 8 per bus. From this, one gets the impression that 28 candidates have been less recruited. Examination of the figures given in Table 1.53 reveals that, for the 550 buses introduced

TABLE 1.53 : **Details of employment under special employment scheme**

	As per Scheme		As per norms of the Corporation		Excess	
Particulars of the phase	No. of buses to be introduced	No. of candidates to be recruited @ 8 per bus	No. of buses introduced	No. of candidates to be recruited	No. of candidates actually absorbed	Absorption over norms
I Phase	300	2,400	300	1,980	2,241	261
II Phase	308	2,464	250	1,650	2,131	481
III Phase	600	5,400 @ 9 per bus	—Not implemented—		299	299
Total	1,208	10,264	550	3,630	4,671	1,041

only, 3,630 candidates need to be recruited, as per the norms of the corporation (drivers 2.6, conductors 2.6, mechanics 0.5 and helpers/cleaners 0.9 per bus). As against this, 4372 candidates have been absorbed in the service of the corporation, under the First and Second phases of the scheme, that is, 742 candidates have been appointed in excess of the number fixed as per the norms. The seriousness of the problem is further aggravated by the employment of 299 more candidates under the Third Phase of the scheme which is yet to be put on ground. Thus the excess employment stands at 1,041.

The excess staff comprise the following categories—conductors 684, mechanics 319 and cleaners 552. The cost of this excess employment, when calculated at the rate of minimum emoluments received in each category, works out to Rs. 66.56 lakhs (vide Table 1.54). This excess staff cost is a recurring expenditure every year and can therefore be taken as loss sustained by the corporation on account of implementation of the seheme. Besides, these candidates (Scheduled Caste, Scheduled Tribes and Backward classes (SC, ST and BCs)) were recruited, relaxing a number of qualifications prescribed for the posts. For example, age, height, educational qualification, experience in driving and so on. As a result, sub-standard candidates were given employment. This had a telling effect on the performance of the corporation. When suitable candidates were not available for the posts of drivers, from the SC and ST communities, required number of candidates of these communities were recruited in the categories of conductors and cleaners, to make good the deficiency in the category of drivers. This contributed for the excess staff being recruited in the categories of conductors and cleaners.

In addition, the corporation has suffered a loss of Rs. 86 lakhs as the training cost of the candidates including payment of stipend sanctioned by the Government is only Rs. 44 lakhs, as against Rs. 130 lakhs estimated during the First and Second phases of the scheme.

From the above figures, one is led to conclude that the special employment scheme is a losing proposition and that the corporation is right in deciding against the implementation of the third phase of the scheme.

But there is the other dimension of the scheme which is often

TABLE 1.54 : **Expenditure on exeess staff**

Category	No. of employees (excess/short) (+) (−)	Minimum rate of emoluments Rs.	Total staff cost per month Rs.	Total staff cost per year Rs.
Drivers	(−)514	662.70 (470+33.5%+7½%) BP DA HRA	(−)3,40,628	(−)40,87,536
Conductors	(+)684	620.40 (440+33.5%+7½%) BP DA HRA	4,24,354	50,92,248
Mechanics	(+)319	634.50 (450+33.5%+7½%) BP DA HRA	2,02,405	24,28,860
Cleaners	(+)552	486.44 (345+33.5%+7½%) BP DA HRA	2,685,51	32,22,180
Total	1,041		5,54,646	66,55,752

overlooked. The gain realised by the corporation in paying lesser rate of interest that is, at the rate of 10.5 per cent on the loan assistance received under the scheme, outweighs the loss sustained. The total interest paid upto 30-6-1982 on the loan assistance o Rs. 11.25 crores works out to Rs. 262.60 lakhs. Had this amount been borrowed by the Corporation from the consortium banks, the interest payable would have worked out Rs. 375.14 lakhs (at the rate of 15%). The net gain thus stands at Rs. 112.54 lakhs. Even this may be taken as understated. For a portion of the loan—margin money advanced by the State Government—carries still lesser rate of interest. It is only 6.5 per cent. Further, a component of the margin money is treated as soft loan and attracts a liability of paying interest at the rate of 1 per cent only, as this is a scheme benefiting the candidates of SC, ST and BC.

The gain on payment of interest is more pronounced now as the corporation has been resorting to borrowings from the banks at the rate of 19 per cent because of the financial stringency experienced.

But then, it may be argued that the gain on payment of interest is only for a short period that is till the loan is redeemed and that the loss on excess staff is going to be a recurring permanent liability. When viewed from this angle, it appears that the special employment scheme is not a welcome feature.

Society for employment and training in twin cities

The Society for Employment and Training in Twin Cities (SETWIN) promoted by the Government of Andhra Pradesh, is an organisation essentially to provide training programmes and self employment to the minorities and weaker sections of the old Hyderabad city. Its transport wing has come into being in the year 1979 and is regulated by G.O.Ms. No. 68 dated 17-10-1979. The unique feature of this scheme, as per the G.O., is to bring about linkage between the APSRTC and the SETWIN. For, the SETWIN Maxi buses (Garuda Services) are proposed for operation on the city routes of the APSRTC on which the corporation has absolute monopoly right. Secondly, the APSRTC shall make use of the buses as stage carriages with its conductors and realise the revenue. Thirdly, the APSRTC shall in return pay hire charges at the rate of Rs. 2.25 per km to the SETWIN, based on the kilometres so operated, followed by a guarantee for a minimum of 75,000 kms of operation per year. Fourthly, the hire charges are subject to revision quarterly. Fifthly, the M.V. taxes on the vehicles have to be reimbursed by the APSRTC.

A detailed examination of the conditions stipulated, reveals that it was totally one-sided. This is another scheme entrusted to the corporation by the State Government, which was not in the interests of the Corporation.

The then Minister for Transport and Chairman of the Corporation reported on 3-11-1980 that the Garuda Maxi buses of the SETWIN contributed for the losses of the corporation to the tune of Rs. 40.00 lakhs during the year ending October 1980.[5] In addition, the mini buses which were originally intended to be operated in the narrow lanes and bylanes of the old city, for the convenience of people in those areas, were actually plying on regular city and district routes of the corporation and were causing a loss of Rs. 45.00 lakhs per year to the corporation, the then Minister admitted.[6]

Table 1.55 shows the performances of the SETWIN Maxi buses during the period starting from October 1979 (time of commission) to February 1982. Information for the month of March 1982 is not available. The total expenditure in this case comprises the hire charges paid to SETWIN as provided in the G.O. and the expenditure on taxes, supervision charges and conductors' wages. The total earnings realised on operation of the SETWIN Maxi Buses stand at Rs. 115.83 lakhs, while the total expenditure works out to Rs. 169.51 lakhs, resulting in a loss of Rs. 53.68 lakhs. To this, Rs. 1.07 lakhs have to be added towards the extra payment made on account of the guarantee of kilometres given from October 1979 to March 1981, for 45,993 kilometres over the actual kilometres operated by the SETWIN buses. This was due to the less number of buses supplied by SETWIN for operation by the corporation than that was scheduled during the period ending with March 1981. In no month, the average number of buses supplied by SETWIN touched the scheduled number that is 50. Yet, the guarantee clause in the G.O. necessitated the corporation to pay for the guaranteed

TABLE 1.55 : **Performance of setwin maxi buses**

(October 1979—February 1982)

Period	Kms operated (in lakhs)	Hire charges paid (Rs. in lakhs)	Other expenditure* incurred (Rs. in lakhs)	Total expenditure (Rs. in lakhs)	Gross earnings realised (Rs. in lakhs)	Loss (Rs. in lakhs)
1. Oct. 1979 to Feb. 1982	50.71	122.01	47.49	169.51	115.83	53.68
2. Payment made due to guarantee of kms from October 1979 to March 1981 for 45,993 kms over the actual kms operated by Setwin.						1.07
Total						54.75

* Taxes+Supervision charges+Conductors' wages.

number of kilometres, though the actual kilometres operated fell short of that. However, after March 1981, the basis of payment on guaranteed kilometres was discontinued. Thus, the total loss for being entangled with SETWIN works out to Rs. 54.75 lakhs upto February 1982. The State Government is to be blamed for this state of affairs. This is another example to show that the State Government's action had adversely affected the autonomy of the Corporation.

Village link transport services (VLTS)

Autonomy in Public Corporations in India, in practice, is conspicuous by absence, experts in the field lament. To quote a retired civil servant who held top executive positions in public enterprises and who was also Director General, Bureau of Public Enterprises, Government of India,

> While the public enterprises do have a fair measure of autonomy on paper, and directives have rarely, if ever been issued by the Government to abridge the powers which they possess, in actual practice there are in fact almost daily inroads into their autonomy which not many enterprise executives have found it possible, or even, from their personal points of view, desirable to resist[7].

The A.P.S.R.T.C. offers a classic example in this regard.

The scheme to connect all the villages in the State by mechanised transport was thrust upon the corporation by the government of Andhra Pradesh in the year 1978. Following the decision taken by the Chief Minister and the Transport Minister, a draft press note was released by the Government on 15-4-1978 which read as follows. "APSRTC itself will participate in a big way by processing into service 300 extra buses and also utilising reconditioned buses. Andhra Pradesh State Road Transport Corporation (APSRTC) will be connecting nearly 3,000 new villages by buses before 31-3-1979. Of these, 1,000 will be connected by end of May 1978". "It was decided that village link transport service scheme should be operative by 2-10-1978". Extract of minutes of the meeting convened by the Transport

Minister on 15-4-1978 runs as follows. "After discussing all these aspects at great length, it was felt desirable that APSRTC should step in, since it has the wherewithal to implement this programme. It was decided finally that the APSRTC should publish schemes under Chapter IV A of M.V. Act on all these routes as identified by the Taluk Level Committees and District Level Committees. Immediately after publication of the schemes, APSRTC shall obtain Temporary Permits and ply their buses". Besides, D.O. letters witten by Secretary and Deputy Secretary, Transport and Roads and Buildings from time to time to the management of the APSRTC, on the subject in question, are replete with directives requiring the corporation to implement the scheme.

The APSRTC which had been reeling under the losses by that time, remained a dumb follower. As a result, the implementation of the scheme was instrumental in accelerating the rate of losses further. For, the village link transport services suffer from certain inherent draw backs. The villages proposed to be connected, by and large, are inaccessible as there are no roads or the roads connecting are not motorable. Unmotorable roads lead to low mobility of the vehicles, low vehicle utilisation, high rate of consumption of fuel, more damages to the tyres, greater wear and tear of the body and premature scrapping of the vehicles. In addition, the traffic potential is very poor, rendering the services unremunerative.

From Table 1.56, it may be seen that the number of village link tranport services had been increasing year after year, despite the fact that the corporation had been progressively sustaining losses there from. The number of buses increased from 207 in 1978-79 to 578 in the year 1980-81 and remained static thereafter. As the corporation had been incurring losses on this scheme, year after year, and as the number of buses operated under the scheme had been on the increase upto 1980-81, obviously, the corporation was under pressure from the State Government to increase the village link transport services till 1980-81.

The rise in earnings per kilometre from 208 paise to 264 paise during the years 1980-81 and 1981-82 respectively, could not be totally attributed to better performance of the services.

TABLE 1.56 : **Performance of village link transport services**

Year	No. of buses	Earnings (Rs. in lakhs)	Kms operated (in lakhs)	EPK (in paise)	Corporation CPK (in paise)	CPK on* VLTS (in paise)	Loss per km (in paise)	Loss per annum (Rs. in lakhs)
1978-79 (2-10-1978 to 31-3-1979) 6 months	207	113.38	62.30	1.82	234	280	0.98	61.05
1979-80	456	368.27	211.65	1.74	252	302	1.28	270.91
1980-81	578	648.00	310.22	2.08	289	346	1.38	428.10
1981-82	578	865.02	327.41	2.64	339	406	1.42	464.92
Total								1,224.98

* Assumption 20 per cent more CPK on VLTS.

The impact of fare revision during the years could be the first plausible reason. Secondly, the restructuring of the village link transport services taken up by the corporation in a big way from the middle of the year 1980-81, from which time the pressure from the Government ceased, had brought about a salutory effect on the performance of the services.

In view of the factors influencing the cost of operations of the village link transport services, an additional amount of 20 per cent is added to the cost of operations in computing the cost per kilometre of operation of twin services. This was the practice adopted in the corporation for determining the costs of operation of the village link transport services. The average loss per kilometre increased at a decreasing rate. During the first two years of operation, the rate of loss per kilometre was as high as 30 paise. This was, however, brought down to 10 paise and then to 4 paise during the years 1980-81 and 1981-82 respectively. This was again an indication of the efforts put in by the corporation-restructuring of routes and so on to peg the rate of losses per kilometre operated. The losses steadily increased since commission and stood at a cumulative total of Rs. 1224.92 lakhs at the end of the year 1981-82.

This was inspite of the reported tax concessions extended by the State Government. On 16-4-1978, the then Chief Minister "promissed to give substantial tax concession on the village link transport services. He said only nominal tax would be levied on the village link transport services."[8] Yet the tax concession actually sanctioned by the State Government subsequently was far from what was promised. It (concession) worked out to be ranging from 20 per cent to 30 per cent of the normal tax payable, depending upon the road surface of the route[9]. In fact, the corporation made out a case for levying a nominal tax of Rs. 10 per seat per quarter, considering the losses that were in store for the corporation, on operation of the village link transport services. But it was in vain.

The action of the state government, in giving a cold shoulder to the corporation in this regard, is unjustifiable. This is more so when the corporation implemented the scheme at the instance of the state government. The argument that a social obligation was cast upon the corporation, because of its monopoly character, is ill conceived. For, the social objective cannot take precedence at a time when the very survival of the corporation is at stake. On the other hand, levying of a nominal tax on the village link transport services should have been the first incentive that the Government could offer, followed by many other concessions of its kind, namely, granting subsidies to the corporation to the extent of the losses suffered on account of the Village Link Transport Services(VLTS). It is unfortunate that the state government has been insisting on its pound of flesh when the corporation (itself a state undertak ng) is passing through a period of crisis for which the Government cannot totally disown responsibility.

Jeep mini buses

This is only an extension of the scheme for introduction of village link transport services, by the APSRTC. The villages which are situated in the hilly and forest areas and have been not connected by any road were proposed to be served by the jeep mini buses, as part of the programme to connect every village by mechanised transport in the State. As many as 60 jeep mini buses were purchased at the rate of Rs. 93,000 each for the purpose. The scheme was formally launched on 1-11-1979. Before long, the mini buses were found unsuitable to meet the desired objective. Except two vehicles operated on narrow roads by Razol depot, all the vehicles were withdrawn from operation and were used for sundry purposes. It is not possible to increase the basic fare to make good the deficiency. The tax concession offered by the government on these vehicles is the same as that on the other village link transport services. As such, the tax concession works out to be insignificant in this case. Twenty eight of these vehicles were also tried on city routes as non-stop services. They were found uneconomical for operation on the Town and city routes either, because of the low seating capacity, which is only thirteen. Finally, it was decided on 29-5-1982 that 30 vehicles might be scrapped and the remaining might be used in Twin Cities, Tirupathi, Vijyawada and Visakhapatnam as contract carriages at the rate of 225 paise per km on special hire basis.

For reviewing the operational performance of these vehicles, information is not available. It may be noted that even at the stage of conception of the scheme losses were estimated on these vehicles. The economics of operation worked out at that time, at 80 per cent occupation ratio with a vehicle utilisation of 200 kms per vehicle per day, revealed a loss of Rs. 46,000 per vehicle per annum. In other words, losses were anticipated in advance. Yet the scheme took off. This only shows that the corporation was sufficiently influenced by the State Government to implement the scheme.

Cargo services

Introduction of the cargo services is a novel scheme primarily designed for the benefit of small farmers of the villages situated within a radius of 40 to 50 kms from the twin cities or other important towns in the state, in that their agricultural produce grown in smaller quantities—vegetables, fruits and so on—is transported from the villages to the nearby city or town. The APSRTC buses which are intended for transporting passengers and their personal belongings, including goods of commercial nature (on the roof of the bus in limited quantities), have not been of the use to the small farmers to market their commodities. It is precisely this need which is proposed to be met by the cargo services. For this purpose alone, the body of the cargo bus is designed in such a fashion as to carry 20 passengers and 3 tonnes of cargo (inside the bus) simultaneously.

Considering the uni-directional nature of cargo movement from villages to cities/towns and that too in two single trips—one in the early morning and the other in the evening—provision has been made for the utilisation of the cargo buses as passenger services during the interlude. In short, it is a double-purpose-vehicle to carry both the passengers and the cargo in combination of passengers only depending upon the exigencies of demand. Undoubtedly the objective and the features of the scheme are laudable.

But, the performance of the cargo services during the last two years (introduced in October 1979) and the economics of operation worked out indicated that the services had not been viable. Table 1.57 clearly shows that the average earning per kilometre obtained was only 185 paise and 232 paise during

TABLE 1.57 : Performance of cargo services for 1980-81 and 1981-82

Year	Average No. of buses under operation	No. of routes under operation	Effective kms (in lakhs)	Passenger earnings (Rs. in lakhs)	Passenger earnings per km (in paise) (5—4)	Cargo earnings (Rs. in lakhs)	Cargo earnings per km (in paise) (7—4)	Total earnings (Rs. in lakhs)	Total earnings per km (in paise) (9—4)	Vehicle utilisation per vehicle per day (in kms)	Break* even cost (in paise)	MV. Tax reduction per km (in paise) @ 60% of tax	Net break even cost per km (in paise)	Loss per km (in paise)	Total loss (Rs. in lakhs)
1980-81	15	178	13.05	22.58	173	1.51	0.12	24.09	185	238	371	23.45	347.55	—162.55	21.21
1981-82	23	271	19.09	41.95	220	2.26	0.12	44.21	232	227	378	24.43	353.57	—121.57	23.21
Total	19	—	32.14	64.53	201	3.77	0.12	68.30	213	232	375	23.94	351.06	—138.06	44.37

Source : Break even chart (from September 1981) Circulated by APSRTC.

the years 1980-81 and 1981-82 respectively.

The average vehicle utilisation was also not encouraging. It stood at 238 kms and 227 kms during the years 1980-81 and 1981-82 respectively. The corresponding break-even cost as shown in the 'Break Even Chart' of September 1981 circulated by the APSRTC was taken into consideration for analysing the profitability or otherwise of the cargo services. Further, allowance was made for reduction of the break even cost per km so obtained because of the lower tax paid on the cargo service buses (for 20 passengers only). When calculated on the above said lines, the break even cost of the cargo services, worked out to 347.55 paise and 353.57 paise during the years 1980-81 and 1981-82 respectively. At this rate, the corporation sustained a loss of Rs. 21.21 lakhs and Rs. 23.21 lakhs during the years 1980-81 and 1981-82 respectively, on operating the cargo services.

Above all, the earnings realised on transporting cargo for which the services were originally designed, present a gloomy picture. The average EPK obtained on lifting cargo alone worked out to 12 paise. The ratio of cargo EPK to the average total Earnings Per Kilometre (both the passenger and cargo earnings put together) was only 5.63 per cent. That is to say the very purpose of the scheme was not served.

Strangely enough, the corporation officials took a stand, during the discussions held, that the loss on cargo services was not a matter of concern and anxiety as the buses earmarked for cargo services would have been operated in any case as passenger buses on the routes identified for the purpose and that the performance of the said routes was comparatively worse prior to the introduction of the cargo services. Infact, the reduction in M.V. Taxes for the cargo services and the resultant fall in cost per kilometre might be taken as a redeeming feature, they argued. This argument does not hold much water, if the concept of "opportunity cost" is applied and analysis made. For, the rate of return on capital earned elsewhere, had the said resources been put to better alternative use, shall be the criterian in deciding the profitability or otherwise of the services.

Concessions

The APSRTC, being a state transport undertaking, has been

extending a number of concessions to the various sections of the society, keeping in view its public utility character. While some of the concessions were forced (vide Annexure 5) on the corporation by the state government, some were of its own making. Whatever be the reasons, the corporation finds itself being saddled with a huge financial burden on account of these concessions. So long as the corporation made profits, the pangs of the concessions had not been felt. Once the corporation started realising losses and the losses reached alarming proportions, the concessions turned out to be the proverbial last straw on the camel's back.

The losses on concessions run to an incredible sum of Rs. 722.13 lakhs a year. The cost of concessions on the city and mofussil routes stands at Rs. 451.25 lakhs and Rs. 270.88 lakhs respectively (vide Table 1.58).

The corporation is now placed in such an irretrievable position that it cannot afford any longer the luxury of granting concessions nor can it revoke them abruptly. The ideal solution will be for the state government to come to the rescue of the corporation by reimbursing the cost of concessions. For the concessions granted are in the nature of welfare measures as the beneficiaries are no other than the students, NGGOs, physically handicapped persons, journalists, MPs, MLAs, and so on.

Apathy of the state government

Special provisions relating to the state transport undertakings were included in Chapter IV A, which was brought about as an amendment to the M.V. Act. Consequently, the various provisions contained in the other chapters of the Act, at times, do not afford operational convenience to the state transport undertakings, as they were not originally framed keeping in the view the needs of the State Transport Undertakings. So is the case with the APMV Rules.

The APSRTC suggested certain amendments to the APMV Rules, in the light of the difficulties experienced in the past. Amendments to the APMV Rules are required for the other reasons also. The rules are interpreted by the Transport Authorities always in favour of the private operators. The repercussions are discussed in detail elsewhere in the report. As such, the

TABLE 1.58 : **Details of losses on concessions granted**

Nature of concession	Loss sustained on city routes (Rs. in lakhs)	Loss sustained on mofussil routes (Rs. in lakhs)	Total loss sustained (City+Mofussil) (Rs. in lakhs)
Student's passes (specified routes)	215.39	—	215.39
Student's general bus ticket	94.92	—	94.92
Student's concessional passes	—	49.16	49.16
For colleges and higher educational Institutions (Mofussil areas)	—	—	—
Student's concessional passes for students of high schools	—	10.10	10.10
Apprentices undergoing training under the Apprenticeship Act.	43.78	—	43.78
Students belonging to SC & ST (extra concessions)	—	45.12	45.12
NGO's bus passes (twin cities and suburban routes)	27.60	—	27.60
Passes for Journalists	1.50	5.55	7 05
Physically handicapped (in twin cities only)	45.12	16.80	61.92
Legislators	—	2.80	2.80
Spouses of legislators	—	1.44	1.44
MPs hailing from A.P.	—	0.49	0.49
General bus ticket (city/town)	20.06	—	20.06
General bus ticket (Sububran)	2.88	—	2.88
Enhancement of age limit of children	—	139.42	139.42
Total	451.25	270.88	722.13

Government may consider the amendments suggested by the APSRTC, to the extent they are not repugnant to the other provisions of the Act. The suggested amendments are given in Annexure 6. Delay in consideration of the amendments may result in some more losses being suffered by the corporation.

Secondly, the schemes published by the corporation to displace the private operators from whom the corporation faces competition in various districts have been pending with the state government for approval for the last five years. Delay on the part of the state government in not taking up these schemes for consideration for such a long time, as this only gave rise to issue of temporary permits to some more private operators, while the old ones have been continuing, causing a severe drain on the revenues of the corporation. This issue was discussed at length elsewhere in the report. Details of the number of schemes published by the corporation and pending with the state government are given in Annexure.

Infringement of monopoly

The Andhra Pradesh State Road Transport Corporation (APSRTC) operates its passenger road transport services on broadly two kinds of routes—firstly, where there is exclusive monopoly in the operation of services on a particular route or in a particular district to the complete exclusion of the private operators, at least in so far as the operation of stage carriages is concerned. Secondly, it may operate services on certain routes and/or in certain distrtcts alongside the private operators. The question of infringement of monopoly right of operation of stage carriages arises in the former case. The violation by private operators takes place in a number of ways. Firstly, the private operators may operate the contract carriages as stage carriages thereby violating not only the permit conditions but also infringing on monopoly right of APSRTC. This constitutes not only illegeal violation of permit rules but also an unfair practice, as the private operator pays a lower M.V. tax on his contract carriage, when compared with the M.V. tax paid by APSRTC on its stage carriages. As a result of the difference in taxes, the private operator is in a position to provide and actually provides the stage carriages at a lower rate than the APSRTC. This culminates in unjustified deprivation of passenger revenue for the APSRTC or to put in relative terms unjustified revenues for the private operators at the expense of APSRTC.

While the infringement of monopoly right deprives unjustifiably revenues of the APSRTC on those routes where the APSRTC has monopoly rights, in the case of the other routes where there is parallel operation of services by APSRTC and private operators, the corporation loses revenue because of violation of scheduled timings. In this analysis, an attempt is made only to assess the possible loss of revenue by the corporation because of infringement only. No attempt is made to quantify the losses incurred because of violation of scheduled timings of operations as no precise data on this aspect are available. However, there is no denial of fact of loss of revenue for the corporation on this count. Besides operating the contract carriages as stage carriages, the private operators infringe on the monopoly right of APSRTC by operating vans.

The infringement of monopoly right of APSRTC cannot take place unless there is hoodwinking by the transport authorities. The fact that there are frequent physical and violent clashes not only between the RTC crew and the private operators but also between the RTC staff and the officials of the Transport Department in the field amply demonstrates not only hoodwinking but also collusion between the private operators and officials of the Transport Department in the field. Another fact to substantiate hoodwinking of illicit operation of contract carriages as stage carriages by private operators is an instance of increase in revenues of APSRTC by amounts ranging between Rs. 2.00 lakhs and Rs. 4.00 lakhs per day overnight because of sudden tightening of check over the illicit operations of the private operators at the instance of the concerned Minister. This clearly establishes that if the Minister is keen, and if there is no political support to the private operators, the Transport Department tightens up its check on the private operators, which results in increased earnings of APSRTC. The continued infringement of monopoly right of APSRTC by private operators would therefore imply only collusion between the Transport Authorities and the private operators and indifference on the part of the concerned Minister. This is further substantiated by the fact that the schemes of nationalisation submitted by the APSRTC have been pending with the State Government for periods ranging up to five years. In addition, whenever the APSRTC asks for modification of routes, undue advantage is taken of this by the Transport Authorities to give temporary permits to private operators resulting in cut throat competition to the Corporation. In this case the Transport Authorities not only make liberal use but also make liberal interpretation of the court judgements to favour private operators, and to victimise the Corporation.

To counteract this, the corporation has from time to time approached the Government to confer on its officials the right to check private vehicles for violation at least in the case of the monopoly routes of the APSRTC. However, for reasons best known to the Government, this power has not been conferred on the officials of the APSRTC. There is no reason why this should not be done especially when such a power is conferred on the officials of the State Transport Undertakings in some of the other States such as Maharashtra and Madhya Pradesh. It is, therefore, recommended that the Government shall confer this power on the officials of the APSRTC forthwith as it has been amply proved that there is absence of willingness in this regard on the part of the Transport Authorities.

Next an attempt may be made to assess the extent of loss of revenues by the APSRTC because of infringement of its monopoly right by the private operators. It is estimated that about 1450 buses covered by contract carriage permits and 2950 vans/motor cabs have been in operation in the State as stage carriages on the nationalised routes. Reasonable estimates of loss of revenue because of infringement vary roughly between Rs. 9.00 crores and Rs. 16.00 crores per annum. For example, the then Minister for Transport and the Chairman of APSRTC, in November 1980 estimated that the income realised by APSRTC consequent on the arresting of illegal operations was Rs. 4.00 lakhs per day.[10] This would amount to a loss of revenue of Rs. 14.60 crores per annum. The Minister, in another context, stated that the loss sustained by the Corporation because of infringement of monopoly right was Rs. 9.00 crores during the year 1979-80.[11] Thus while the estimates of loss of revenue by the concerned Minister himself vary between Rs. 9.00 crores and Rs. 14.60 crores, the figures of loss of revenue as per the statement of the General Secretary of the National Mazdoor Union of APSRTC and the figures furnished by the officers of the APSRTC at various levels also vary. The statement of the General Secretary, National Mazdoor Union estimates the loss of revenue at Rs. 4.75 crores per annum for the Vijayawada Region alone which accounts for only about 23 per cent of the total fleet. On this estimate the Corporation as a whole should be losing about Rs. 21.00 crores per annum. But there is limitation to this estimate for the entire Corporation based on the loss of the Vijayawada Region, as the other Regions may not be so potential in traffic as the Vijayawada Region is. As per the official estimate given by the Vijayawada Region of APSRTC, the loss of revenue on this account is Rs. 2.37 crores per annum for this Region, which works out to a little more than Rs. 10.00 crores per year for the entire Corporation. The figures of losses as furnished by 10 of the 20 divisions in the State (Nizamabad, Karimnagar, Krishna, West Godavari, Guntur, Hyderabad City, Medak, Chittoor, Anantapur, and Kurnool) indicate loss of Rs. 8.13 crores per annum for those 10 divisions put together, which would work out to about Rs. 16.26 crores per annum for the entire Corporation.

Even if the lowest of the estimates is taken into consideration, the minimum loss of revenue of the Corporation is Rs. 9.00 crores per annum. This is no small amount as the Corporation would not suffer losses to this extent, if only the infringement is effectively curbed. Another consequence of infringement of monopoly, which cannot be computed in terms of monetary loss to the Corporation, is that the Corporation is forced to gradually curtail services on those routes on which there is infringement of monopoly by private operators. Thus the policy of complete nationalisation is vitiated by the infringement of monopoly by private operators. In the alternative, at least the augmentation of services on those routes is adversely affected because of inroads made by the private operators into the monopoly domain of APSRTC.

In the light of this, there is not only need for immediately conferring on the Corporation officials the power to check the violations by the private operators but also there is need for total nationalisation of not only the stage carriages but also the contract carriages in the State. In the States where there is complete nationalisation of stage and contract carriages, that is, Maharashtra, there is practically no instance of harassment of RTC staff by Transport Authorities. In fact the contract carriages of GSRTC in Gujarat fetch considerable revenues for the Corporation.

Antagonistic attitude of transport authorities

During the discussions held with the officials of the APSRTC, there was a bitter complaint against the unhelpful attitude of the Transport Authorities. One of the issues raised was the interpretation of the various provisions of the M.V. Act., and rules. It was mentioned that the provisions of the Act and rules were always interpreted to the disadvantage of the APSRTC. Further, it was reported that the various judgements of the High Court given in the recent past complicated the issue.

A study on this subject revealed the following :

The scheme published by the corporation under Section 68(c) to operate a service on a particular route, to the complete exclusion of the other operators (except the ones protected) and approved by the State Government under Sec. 68(D) confers absolute monopoly right of operation on the corporation, on the route so notified. Private operators are permitted to overlap such a notified route to an extent of 8 kms only.

If there is a need for opening a new route covering the entire or a portion of the routes already notified, the corporation may publish a new scheme. The corporation may also apply for the issue of a temporary permit under Sec. 68F(1-A), for conducting operations, on the proposed new route during the intervening period between the date of publication of the draft new scheme and the date of publication of the approved scheme. The Transport Authority may issue the temporary permit applied for by the corporation if it is satisfied that there is need to increase the number of vehicles operated on such route or portion thereof, in the public interest. A temporary permit issued in terms of Section 68F(1-A) is effective till the published scheme is approved under Sec. 68(D) and the permit is granted to the Corporation under Sec. 68F(1).

Section 68F(1-C) provides for the issue of a temporary permit to any other person on the route or portion thereof specified in the scheme published by the Corporation, if no application has been made by the Corporation for the issue of a temporary permit. The temporary permit so granted to the other operator ceases to be effective on the issue of a temporary permit to the Corporation.

Section 68F(1-D) lays down that, under no circumstances except the ones mentioned in the above paragraph, the Transport Authority shall grant a permit in favour of any person during the period intervening between the date of publication of scheme by the corporation and the date of publication of an approved scheme.

The judgement delivered by Hon'ble High Court in W.P. No. 4475 of 1979 concerning two private operators and not the APSRTC, provided for the issue of a temporary permit to a private operator under Sec. 68F(1-c) on a route covered by a draft scheme or portion thereof, even if the approved scheme prohibited such a grant.

This judgement came in handy for the Transport Authorities to issue a number of temporary permits under Sec. 68F(1-c) to Private Operators. The list of routes on which the Private Operators are favoured with the issue of temporary permits by the Transport Authorities is given in the Annexure 8. The routes or portions thereof covered by the said temporary permits issued to private operators are notified routes on which the APSRTC enjoys monopoly right. In other words, the draft scheme, published by the Corporation with a view to providing additional transport facilities to the travelling public by opening a new route covering the notified route or portion thereof on which the Corporation had already been operating its services, was used by the Transport Authorities to the detriment of the Corporation, by granting temporary permits to the private operators under Sec. 68F(1-c), invoking the said judgement.

The judgement delivered in W.P. Nos. 3959/81 and 3871/81 of A.P. High Court further aggravated the severity of the problem. It was held that the temporary permit granted to a Private Operator under Sec. 68F(1-c), would be valid till a permit was granted to the APSRTC in pursuance of an approved scheme or withdrawal of the draft scheme. These judgements would, in a way, affect the spirit of total nationalisation.

As a result, the Transport Authorities started issuing temporary permits to the private operators under Sec. 68F(1-c) without following the procedure laid down under Section 68F(1-A). The permits so granted to the Private Operators would remain valid till the schemes were approved by the State Government, which would normally take a long time. For example, the schemes published by the APSRTC in the year 1977 are still pending approval by the State Government.

In the earlier paragraphs, the action of the Transport Authorities in issuing temporary permits to the Private Operators under Sec. 68F(1-c), when the Corporation published draft schemes covering the notified routes or portions thereof with a view to opening new routes for providing additional transport facilities to the travelling public, were discussed. In addition, the Transport Authorities have been resorting to similar action without following the provisions of Sec. 68F(1-A) even in the cases where the corporation published draft schemes under Section 68E only to modify the existing schemes relating to any routes in respect of which the road transport services are run and operated by the Corporation, to the complete exclusion of the other persons, on matters connected with (a) increase in the number of vehicles or the number of trips, (b) change in the type of vehicles without reducing the seating capacity, and (c) extension of the route without reducing the frequency of the service.

This action of the Transport Authorities is highly unreasonable. For, the schemes published by the Corporation and approved by the State Government at a particular point of time keeping in view the traffic demand then obtaining may become out dated in course of time or may outlive the purpose due to the changed circumstances over a period. In such cases, the Corporation will be forced to publish draft schemes for modification of the existing schemes to the extent required to suit the changed needs. If Transport Authorities take advantage of this situation and start issuing temporary permits to the Private Operators under Sec. 68F(1-c), the Corporation may reconsider the practical utility of invoking Sec. 68E, for providing adequate services to the travelling public. For, without the publication of the draft scheme under Sec. 68E by the Corporation, there would not have been a case for the Transport Authorities to issue temporary permits to the Private Operators. The list of routes on which the Private Operators were issued with temporary permits under Sec. 68F(1-c) where the draft schemes were published by the Corporation under Sec. 68E is given in Annexure 9.

At the time of nationalization of the intra-district routes in Anantapur and Chittoor districts, the State Government, while approving the schemes published by the Corporation gave protection for the continued operation of the then inter-state route buses. This protection is valid till the inter-state routes are taken over on publication of separate schemes by the corporation. In fact the Corporation did publish schemes for the take-over of the said inter-state routes also. But, they are pending with the State Government for approval for one reason or the other. In the meantime, judgement delivered in W.P. No. 3817/79, of A.P. High Court (which was again between two private operators) created problems for the APSRTC. In this case it was held that the permit holder might be permitted to operate more than one bus on the same permit held by him. Similar judgement was given by the High Court of Karnataka. It was held that the conditions of permit could be changed to include an additional bus or additional single trip, even though Sec. 57(8) of the M.V. Act lays down that such variation should be treated as an application for fresh stage carriage permit.

Following the said judgement, the Transport Authorities granted variations to include operation of additional buses and trips on the inter-state routes in question. As these inter-state routes are in essence intra-district routes with only minor extensions into the other state, such variations permitted to increase the number of buses and trips affected the revenues and complexion of the operations of the Corporation on portions of the routes falling within the state. On the top of it, the applications made by the Corporation for the issue of temporary permits on the said routes in terms of the Sec. 68F(1-A) were not given due consideration by the State Transport Authority and the Private Operators were favoured with the variations in the permit conditions to include increase in the number of buses and trips. The list of inter-state routes on which the State Transport

Authority granted increase of buses and trips is given in Annexure 10.

Section 68F(1-A) read with 68FF(1-C) stipulates that, when a draft scheme is published by the Corporation, a temporary permit may be issued to the Private Operator, during the intervening period between the date of publication of the draft scheme and the date of publication of the approved scheme, if no application has been made by the corporation for the issue of a temporary permit and the transport authorities are satisfied that there is need to increase, in the public interest, the number of vehicles operating on the route covered by the draft scheme. In other words, the need to increase the number of buses has to be established before the private operators can be issued with permits. To establish the need, a traffic survey is to be conducted. But the Act and Rules are silent on the procedure to be followed for conducting the traffic survey. As a result, the Transport Department Officials deputed for the purpose adopt their own subjective methods, in conducting the survey, which culminate in the issue of temporary permits to the Private Operators.

Section 68F under Chapter IVA of M.V. Act lays down that, where the scheme published by the Corporation is approved and the corporation puts in an application for the issue of permit in accordance with the approved scheme, the State or Regional Transport Authority, as the case may be, shall issue such permit to the Corporation, notwithstanding anything to the contrary contained in Chapter IV, that is, the function of the Transport Authorities in issuing permit to the corporation in pursuance of an approved scheme is only ministerial in nature. Section 60 under Chapter IV deals with action to be taken by the Transport Authorities against the permit holders for any violations detected. However, the permit issued in pursuance of an approved scheme under Chapter IVA, does not attract disciplinary action for any violations under Section 60. The action contemplated under Section 60 is limited to the permits issued under Chapter IV only. Yet the Transport Authorities in the past imposed penalties extending up to suspension of permits of the Corporation in spite of the fact that the said permits were issued under Chapter IVA. The action of the Regional Transport Authority, Anantapur, in suspending the permits of Corporation in the recent past is an example in point. It is a different matter that the decision of the Regional Transport Authority, Anantapur, is set aside by the State Transport Appelate Tribunal subsequently, on an appeal preferred by the Corporation.

Prior to 1979, G.O.711 of 1965 regulated the payment of Motor Vehicle Taxes by the Corporation. Irregularities committed by the Corporation under this G.O. were looked upon with undue seriousness by the Transport Department officials and huge penalties were levied on the reported arrears of taxes due from the Corporation, disregarding the objections raised by the Corporation against the very basis of the computation of the arrears of taxes. The Corporation was made to pay Rs. 20.00 lakhs as an ad hoc payment, pending settlement of the dues which stood at Rs. 82.61 lakhs as claimed by the Transport Department. The details of the M.V. Taxes claimed from the Corporation as on 31-7-1980 are given in Annexure 10.

The attitude of the Transport Authorities was reported to be partisan in the regions where dual operations existed—Private Operators running buses in competition with the Corporation buses. To illustrate the point, the case of Vizianagaram depot may be examined. During the year 1980-81, the fitness certificates of as many as 44 vehicles of this depot alone were cancelled (CFX Notices issued). This cannot but be branded as unreasonable. The list showing the details of CFX notices issued is given in Annexure 12.

The above instances clearly establish the fact that the Transport Authorities were too anxious to take undue advantage of the awards of the courts to favour Private Operators against the interests of the Government Corporation, thus vitiating the spirit of nationalisation of passenger transport services and the interests of a Government Enterprise. It is beyond doubt that the Transport Authorities, a wing of the Government, is acting against the interest of the Corporation, a Government Undertaking.

COST-FARE RELATIONSHIP AND COMPUTATION OF COST INDEX FOR PERIODICAL AUTOMATIC FARE INCREASES

An idea of cost-fare relationship has already been had while discussing the losses incurred by the Corporation and interpreting

Tables 1.3 and 1.6. It was seen from these tables that the expenditure per km was increasing at a faster rate than the revenue per km since 1973-74, resulting in consistent decline in margins per km. It was only in 1981-82 that this trend has been reversed, slightly reducing the negative margin (vide Table 1.3). It was also seen from Table 1.6 that broadly the position was the same in terms of passenger kilometres also. In spite of the gradual decline in margings leading to negative margins since 1977-78 the fare increases have been sporadic, allowing the Corporation to incur losses. For example, in so far as the fare for the ordinary services (which form significant bulk of the total operations) is concerned there has been no fare increase in between 19th June 1974 and 26th October 1980—a period of six years—when the margin per passenger km came down from (+) 0.36 paise to (—) 0.76 paise. In four out of these seven years the organisation was incurring losses. In other words, the organisation had to wait for about two and a half years after it had started incurring losses on its mofussil services to get fare increase on ordindary services. However, the organisation was permitted to increase fares in respect of Express Services twice in between—on 2-11-1974, and 1-2-1975. However, the fares on express services were reduced on 1-11-1977, in spite of the fact that organisation has started losing, on the whole, though not on the mofussil services in that year. More important is the fact that the fares on city services have not been increased for a period of six and a half years—between 1974 and 3-12-1980—even though the Corporation had been incurring losses on city services all these years. Thus it is clearly established that the Corporation was allowed to suffer losses without giving fare increase at a time when the costs were going up. This is anamolous in view of the fact that when the corporation made profits, the profits were siphoned off by the government by levying surcharge on Motor Vehicle Tax, even though it may have given back the amount to the corporation in the form of non-interest bearing capital contributions towards meeting capital expenditure on passenger amenities. In the light of this policy of surcharge at a time when the corporation makes profits, it is logical to expect the government to allow fare increases at a time when the corporation incurs losses because of cost increase, consequent upon inflation or in the alternative it could have considered, if not reduction in motor vehicle tax, at least doing away with surcharge which was levied at a time when the Corporation made profits. On the other hand, the government has been merging surcharge with the Motor Vehicle Tax, from time to time, and levying again surcharge afresh. The following analysis from Table 1.59 gives an idea of the surcharges levied on Motor Vehicle Taxes from time to time.

The government levied surcharge for the first time in 1968 at 15 per cent on Motor Vehicle Tax. As a consequence of this, two-thirds of the profits of the Corporation were taken away by the government in the form of surcharge in the year 1968-69. The point of interest is that in the year 1976-77, the government through its G.O. of 7-3-1977 increased the surcharge from 30 to 35 per cent with retrospective effect that is from 1-4-1976.

In that year, 75 per cent of the profits were taken away by the government in the form of surcharge. The surcharge was being increased from time to time. It was increased from 15 per cent in 1968 to 30 per cent in 1974 and the same surcharge was maintained after raising the Motor Vehicle Tax by 20 to 30 per cent with effect from 1-7-1974. The surcharge was further increased to 35 per cent with effect from 1-4-1976. Finally, the government abolished the surcharge by increasing the basic motor vehicle tax to more than offset the surcharge with effect from 1-1-1979. Thus the following conclusions emerge from a study of the history of surcharge.

1. The surcharge seems to have been levied to siphon-off profits from the Corporation.

2. There is a temptation to increase not only the surcharge from time to time but also the basic Motor Vehicle Tax.

3. The losses incurred by the Corporation did not deter the government from doing away with surcharge.

4. Further the Motor Vehicle Tax was increased to more than compensate for the surcharge on 1-1-1979, at a time when the Corporation was incurring losses.

It is clear from the above that the Government had no appreciation of the problems of the Corporation at a time when it was in financial straits, not of its own making entirely, but to a great extent because of inflation. Further, this was done without giving any fare increases when the organisation was incurring

TABLE 1.59 : **Surcharge on motor vehicle tax**

Year	Profits/loss (Rs. in lakhs)	Date	Surcharge Rate	Surcharge Amount (Rs. in lakhs)
1973-74	338.44	G.O. dated 23-3-1968 w.e.f. 1-4-1968	15%	96.75
1974-75	364.16	G.O. dated 18-6-1974 w.e.f. 1-7-1974	30%	258.29
1975-76	223.70	—	30%	338.83
1976-77	157.48	G.O. dated 7-3-1977 w.e.f. 1-4-1976	35%	480.57
1977-78	(—)132.23	—	35%	544.24
1978-79	(—)704.60	G.O. dated 23-3-1979 Merging surcharge in the tax	35% for 3/4th of the year	481.425
1979-80		Surcharge is merged with the M.V. Tax		

losses.

In the context of the losses of the organisation, it is to be mentioned that the corporation paid surcharge amounting to Rs. 10.26 crores during 1977-78 and 1978-79. This accounts for about one-fifth of the total accumulated losses of the corporation. This does not take into consideration the fact that the surcharge was more than made good by substantial increase in Motor Vehicle Tax with effect from 1-1-1979 when the surcharge was discontinued. It may also be noted that the corporation would not have incurred losses in 1977-78 and 1978-79 but for the surcharge. In fact it would have made a profit of about Rs. 2.00 crores. Further, the losses since 1979-80 also would not have been that much as it had incurred but for the considerable increase in Motor Vehicle Tax incorporating surcharge also.

Cost computation for fare fixation

In view of the fact that there is considerable time lag betweenthe increase in costs and fare revision, there is need for reducing the time lag between the cost escalation and fare revision. While it is not possible to take care of increase in costs every time that there is an increase in costs of individual items, it should be possible to make annual computations of costs and cost increases for the purpose of fare revision to take care of increase in costs because of inflationary reasons. This exercise should be completed before the end of April of every year and the revised fare may come into force with effect from first of May.

The computation of costs and the extent of fare revision is suggested to be done by the end of April for the reason that usually the cost escalation takes place in the month of April, consequent upon approval of the budget proposals by the parliament/legislature.

The fare revision is to be done based upon computation of costs and cost escalations that take place between the previous fare fixation and the time of computation. The method of cost computation for fare revision may be broadly based on the following lines. The total cost incurred by the organisation for the previous financial year may be taken as the starting point for fare revision and adjustments are to be made for cost escalations and for possible cost savings by improvement of efficiency in areas, such as improvement in KMPL and so on. The likely adjustments to be made in respect of cost increases are the following :

1. Additional depreciation will have to be provided by taking into consideration the costs of replacement and as of now there is need for further adjustment in the case of this item to provide depreciation on vehicles on 4.8 lakh kilometre usage basis instead of 5.5 lakh kilometre usage basis for the reasons already mentioned.

2. As costs on tyre retreading shop and printing press are booked twice to profit and loss account, necessary adjustment will have to be made to eliminate the effect of double booking of this item of cost.

3. The additional financial implication of any wage revisions that took place after the previous fare fixation is to be added to the total cost.

4. The increase in cost of stores based upon the percentage increase in the cost of vehicle over the previous year's average price that is taken into consideration while fixing the fare in the previous year is to be added to the total cost.

5. Similarly, the additional expenditure likely to be incurred because of increases in fuel prices, of motor vehicle tax and cost of tyres is also to be taken into consideration, apart from the increases in interest on capital contributions. While, on the one hand, the cost escalations are to be taken care of, on the other, adjustments are to be made in costs after taking into consideration the targets of improvement set in some of the important parameters of performance wherever the present levels are below the desired norms. For example, there is scope for improvement in KMPL in APSRTC when compared with either its own past performance or the performance of other comparable undertakings in the country. Finally, provision will have to be made for adding up additional cost on miscellaneous items of expenditure based on percentage increase in all other items of expenditure out of the total cost minus miscellaneous items of expenditure. The costs so arrived at will have to be divided by the total expected passenger kilometres computed on the following basis.

In the computation of expected passenger kilometres certain norms of performance in respect of crucial operational areas will have to be fixed by taking into consideration the possible levels of achievement based on either its own past performance or the performance of comparable state transport undertakings. Broadly three parameters of operational performance may be taken into consideration, namely, vehicular utilisation, vehicle utilisation, and occupancy ratio. In the case of vehicular utilisation the norm fixed is 90 per cent of the vehicles held at the end of the year as the corporation is expected to maintain 10 per cent spares. In other words, the corporation is expected to operate 100 per cent of the schedules. In this context, it is relevant to mention that most of the Tamil Nadu Corporations achieved fleet utilisation of 93 to 94 per cent. Secondly, a norm of 310 kilometres of operation per vehicle per day may be taken into consideration as this happens to be the average performance of APSRTC for the last two years, and as the organisation has achieved 310 kilometres in three out of last five years. In the case of occupancy ratio, a norm of 75 per cent is suggested based upon the fact that the organisation achieved a higher occupancy ratio of more than 75 per cent in two of the latest five years. The total passenger kilometres expected to be done in a year is obtained by multiplying the total number of vehicles available for operating the schedules (after providing for 10 per cent spares over this) by 1,13,850 (assuming 310 kilometres of operation per vehicle per day for 365 days) and occupancy ratio of 75 per cent of 52.3 seats per vehicle on an average.

The total cost as arrived at as per the calculation given earlier divided by the expected passenger kilometres would give the average cost per passenger kilometre. The average cost per passenger kilometre so arrived at will have to be adjusted by deducting 0.5 paise per passenger kilometre, in order to arrive at the average fare for ordinary services that the organisation may be permitted to have. This deduction of 0.5 paise per kilometre in arriving at the fare to be permitted on ordinary services is suggested based upon the differential that has been worked out between the average fare realised per passenger and the minimum fare per kilometre per ordinary services as has been obtaining in APSRTC. Further, this assumes that the organisation would continue to have the same mix of ordinary, express and deluxe and city services and that the same fare differential would continue to be maintained among different services.

In the fixation of fares based upon the above methodology, the following further aspects shall be taken into consideration :

1. As the Corporation is presently having excess staff, there shall not be any additional recruitment of staff in the categories in which there is excess staff. Further, while computing the costs at the beginning of each year, the decline in schedule-staff ratio, not so much because of retirements, deaths, and so on but more because of non-replacement of additional staff in these categories, at a time when there is augmentation of fleet, and the saving in cost thereof will have to be taken into consideration.

2. The fare revisions based on the above method are ordinarily to be done only once in a year in the month of May as mentioned earlier. However, if the costs increase substantially during the course of the year for external/uncontrollable reasons, such cost increases may be taken into consideration for fare revision provided such cost increase would amount to or exceed half of the proceeds that are likely to be realised by increase in fare by one paise per kilometre. For example, as of now, an increase in fare by one paise in the basic fare on ordinary services would net approximately Rs. 27.6 crores. Hence, if the cost increases in the middle of the year amount to Rs. 13.8 crores to 27.6 crores per annum, the fare may be increased by one paise per kilometre.

For the purpose of monitoring the trend in costs, a small cell comprising two persons qualified in Transport Economics and Cost Accounts may be constituted and placed under the proposed Passenger Road Transport Rates Tribunal and located in the office of the Secretary, Transport Department, Government of Andhra Pradesh. In order to monitor the costs and decide on the fare revisions a rates tribunal called Passenger Road Transport Rates Tribunal comprising the Secretary, Transport, Government of Andhra Pradesh, Secretary, Finance, Government of Andhra Pradesh, Accountant General, Andhra Pradesh, and a Transport Economist be constituted.

3. As mentioned earlier, the fare revision each year is expected to be done based upon certain norms of operational performance. If the organisation improves its operational performance beyond the norms and thereby gets surpluses over and above its costs as computed, it is recommended

that half of this surplus be paid to its staff right from the chief executive down to the lowest level of employees in the organisation in the form of incentives linked up with improvement in definite parameters of performance because of which surpluses have been realised. The parameters to be taken into consideration for qualifying the surpluses realised may be the passenger kilometres per schedule done, which reflects vehicular utilisation, vehicle utilisation and occupancy ratio, fuel economy, economy in tyre consumption and so on. The norms of performance may be revised periodically taking into consideration its own performance in the last five years and also the performance of sister undertakings in the country, and the pay revisions may be linked with improvement in performance.

Based upon the methodology outlined above, a typical exercise of cost computation for fare revision is done and presented in Statement I. The exercise takes into consideration the total costs as given for 1981-82 and makes adjustments for costs of tyre retreading shop and printing press, wage revision, based upon the latest agreement, increase in costs of items such as stores, fuel, motor vehicle taxes, tyres, interest on capital contributions and miscellaneous expenses. Adjustment is also made for savings on the cost of fuel due to improved KMPL. The cost so arrived at is divided by the passenger kilometres expected to be done by the fleet at the end of the year 1981-82, providing for 10 per cent spares, 310 kilometres of vehicle utilisation and 75 per cent of occupancy ratio.

The average cost per passenger km is computed on the above basis, in two situations—one, taking the existing depreciation policy into consideration and the other based upon the recommended replacement cost on 4.8 lakh km usage basis. As can be seen from Statement I, the cost per passenger km under the first situation works out to 8.80 paise from which 0.5 paise is to be deducted (for the reason mentioned earlier), to arrive at the fare to be permitted for ordinary mofussil services, which comes to 8.30 paise per passenger km. The Corporation is presently permitted to charge 8 paise per km on ordinary services and hence a fare increase of 0.5 paise per km may be allowed to the Corporation with immediate effect, assuming the continuance of the present depreciation policy.

In the second situation, of charging depreciation on 4.8 lakh km usage basis on replacement cost method, the average cost per passenger km would work out to 9.34 paise, from which 0.5 paise is to be deducted to arrive at the fare to be permitted for ordinary mofussil services, which comes to 8.84 paise per passenger km. Hence, a fare increase of 1 paisa per passenger km may be allowed, if the Corporation pursues the depreciation policy as recommended. In either case, there is a small margin left, which would take care of any further increases in prices of inputs. In the cost calculations it is assumed that the M.V. tax would remain constant at the present level.

However, one relevant question that crops up is the problem of dealing with accumulated losses. There are different alternative solutions to this problem. Some of the solutions to this problem are in the nature of traditional solutions in a private enterprise situation which may not be applicable to a public sector public utility concern. For example, revaluation of assets to reflect their true value, especially in a situation where the original value of acquisition was insignificant in relation to market value, is one of the methods suggested. The limitation of this solution is that it is only a technical accounting solution and it does not resolve the problem of accumulated losses. In the case of APSRTC, the organisation acquired land at different places at nominal values which are much below the market values. Hence, revaluation of this asset may no doubt set off the figures of losses to some extent, but it does not solve the problem of losses unless the lands are disposed off at the market value which is not a practicable proposition in many cases, in view of the location of the operational units on those lands.

The next alternative, which is once again a solution in a private enterprise situation, is reduction of capital in the accounts. This is resorted to by a private enterprise or may be resorted to even by a public enterprise in the event of over capitalisation where the capital is not backed by assets with adequate earning power. In the case of APSRTC, however, the accumulated losses are not so much because of the lack of earning capacity of its capital/assets, it is more because of the external agency, that is the government not permitting increase in fares commensurate with increase in costs. Further, it is not advisable to reduce capital, which is a permanent measure, as the assets are expected to earn adequate returns to cover the costs in future. Reduction in capital in such a situation would deprive the owner of return on his capital especially in the situation stated above. Hence, this solution is also ruled out.

A third solution is to leave the losses as they are and to show the same in Balance Sheet until the organisation earns profits and sets off the same against the accumulated losses. This is also not suggested for the reason that the formula for fare revision, as suggested does not deliberately provide for surpluses ; and any surplus that is made due to improvement in operational efficiency is suggested to be utilised partially for paying productivity linked bonus to the employees and partially to augment its fleet.

In the light of the above, it is suggested that, in view of the fact that the government did not allow fare increases in the past to cover increase in costs, resulting in losses, and in view of the high rate of motor vehicle tax levied on city services and further in the light of the heavy surcharge imposed on the motor vehicle tax upto 1 January, 1979, the government shall pay subsidy to the corporation to wipe out the entire accumulated losses of Rs. 66 crores in the next six to seven years. This would work out to about Rs. 10 crores per annum. The amount is reasonable in the light of the fact that the state government gets about Rs. 30 crores per annum from the corporation by way of motor vehicle tax (Rs. 25 crores) and interest on capital contributions (Rs. 5 crores). In a way the state government would be paying this to offset the cost fare lags, high rates of motor vehicle tax on city services and considerable amount of surcharge on motor vehicle tax, for which the state government alone was responsible.

REFERENCES

1. *Andhra Bhoomi*, Telugu Daily, 18th December, 1980.
2. *Indian Express*, 10th June 1982.
3. *Indian Express*, 10th June 1982.
4. *Andhra Bhoomi*, 18th December 1980.
5. *Indian Express*, 4th November, 1980.
6. *Deccan Chronicle*, 4th November, 1980.
7. R.C. Dutt, "Public enterprises : Cavalier erosion of autonomy", *The Economic Times*, Bombay, June 16 1982, p. 9.
8. *The Hindu*, 17th April 1978.
9. *The Hindu*, 17th August 1978.
10. *Andhra Patrika*, 13th November 1980.
11. *Andhra Bhoomi*, 18th December 1980.

STATEMENT I

METHOD OF COST COMPUTATION FOR FARE REVISION

(A) Estimated passenger kilometers :

(1)	Total vehicles held as on 31st March 1982 (on rolls)	7,443
	Less Vehicles claimed to be stabled	600
(2)	Vehicles held as on 31st March 1982	6,843
	Less 10% spares (6843 × 10/110)	622
(3)	No. of vehicles available for operations (i.e., schedules) assuming 90% vehicular utilisation	6,221
(4)	Total effective kilometres likely to be operated assuming vehicle utilisation at 310 kms per vehicle per day (in lakhs)	7,039.06
(5)	Passenger kms (with average seating capacity of 52.3) (in lakhs)	3,68,142.84
(6)	Expected passenger kms with occupancy ratio of 75% (in lakhs)	2,76,107.13

B(i) Estimated costs (based on the existing depreciation policy)

			(Rs. Lakhs)
(1)	Total cost as given for the year 1981-82		22,815.51
(2)	(a) *Less* impact of revised pay scale		1,414.50
			22,401.01
	(b) *Add* amount of RPS for the year		1,100.00
(3)	*Less* double counting of costs in respect of		22,501.01
	(a) Tyre retreading shop	313.06	
	(b) Printing press	51.71	364.77
(4)	Adjusted total costs		22,136.24
(5)	*Add* increase in Depreciation cost (Schedule A-1)		260.18
(6)	*Add* increase in spares cost (Schedule B)		321.27
(7)	*Add* increase in fuel cost (Schedule C)		837.06
(8)	*Add* increase in tyre cost (Schedule D)		513.58
(9)	*Add* increase in cost of lubricants (Schedule E)		83.80
(10)	*Add* increase in MV Tax		—
(11)	*Add* increase in interest on capital contributions (Schedule F)		222.84

(12) *Add* increase in cost towards miscellaneous item (4.35%) (Schedule G)		87.69
		24,462.66
(13) *Less* expected savings on fuel due to improved KMPL (Schedule H)		165.27
		24,297.39

Expected Cost/Fare per passenger km $= \dfrac{\text{Total expected costs}}{\text{Expected passenger kms}}$

$= \dfrac{24,297.39}{2,76,107.13} = 8.80$

Less 0.50 paise for Express/delux 0.50

Fare for ordinary services $= 8.30$

B(ii) Estimated costs (based on depreciation at replacement cost on 4.8 lakh kms usage basis)

		(Rs. lakhs)
(1) Total costs as given for the year 1981-82		22,815.51
(2) (a) *Less* Impact of revised pay scale		1,414.50
		21,401.01
(b) *Add* amount of RPS for the year		1,100.00
		22,501.01
(3) *Less* double counting of costs in respect of		
(a) Tyre retrading shop	313.06	
(b) Printing press	51.71	364.77
(4) Adjusted total costs		22,136.24
(5) *Add* Difference between depreciation at replacement cost on 4.8 lakh kms and depreciation actually provided (Schedule A-2)		1,761.68
(6) *Add* increase in spares cost (Schedule B)		321.27
(7) *Add* increase in fuel cost (Schedule C)		837.06
(8) *Add* increase in tyre cost (Schedule D)		513.58
(9) *Add* increase in cost of lubricants (Schedule E)		83.80
(10) *Add* increase in MV Tax		—
(11) *Add* increase in interest on capital contributions (Schedule F)		222.84
(12) *Add* 4.35% increase in cost towards miscellaneous items (Schedule G)		87.69
		25,964.16

(13) *Less* Expected savings on fuel due to improved KMPL (Schedule H) 165.27

25,798.89

Expected Cost/Fare per passenger km

$$\text{Expected cost per passenger km} = \frac{\text{Total expected costs}}{\text{Expected passenger kms}}$$

$$= \frac{25{,}798.89}{2{,}76{,}107.13} = 9.34$$

Fare per passenger km	=9.34 paise
Less 0.50 paise for Express/delux	=0.50 paise
Fare for ordinary services	8.84 paise

SCHEDULE A—1

Estimated additional cost of depreciation

(1)	Actual cost of depreciation in 1981-82 based on 6,308.00 gross kms (Rs. in lakhs)	1,940.41
(2)	Expected gross kms in lakhs	7,153.80
(3)	Increase in cost due to increased operations (Rs. in lakhs) $\frac{7,153.80 \times 1,940.41}{6,308.00}$	2,200.59
(4)	Increase in cost due to increased operations (Rs. in lakhs) (2,200.59—1,940.41)	260.18

SCHEDULE A—2

(I) Determination of the rate of depreciation per km at replacement cost

(1)	Latest cost of vehicle (Replacement Cost)	Rs. 2,82,261
(2)	Estimated scrap value @ 12%	Rs. 33,871
(3)	Value consumed	Rs. 2,48,390
(4)	Assuming 4.8 lakh kms as estimated life, rate of depreciation per km	51.75 paise

(II) Difference in depreciation

(5)	Total effective kms likely to be operated assuming vehicle utilisation at 310 kms per vehicle per day in lakhs (As per Statement I)	7,039.06
(6)	*Add* expected dead kms as per the proportion in 1981-82 (1.63%)	114.74
(7)	Total expected gross kms likely to be operated (in lakhs)	7,153.80
(8)	Depreciation at replacement cost (Rs. lakhs) 7,153.80 lakh kms × 51.75 paise per km.	3,702.09
(9)	*Less* depreciation now booked as per historical cost based on 5.5 lakh kms of estimated life (Rs. lakhs)	1,940.41
(10)	Additional expenditure to be booked (Rs. lakhs) in respect of depreciation	1,761.68

SCHEDULE—B

Estimated additional cost of spares

(1)	Average cost of vehicle in 1981-82	Rs. 2,68,292
(2)	Cost of vehicie in September, 1982	Rs. 2,82,261
(3)	Percentage increa se in cost of vehicle	5.21
(4)	Actual cost of spares in 1981-82 based on 6,308.00 gross kms (Rs. in lakhs)	1,663.11
(5)	Expected gross kms. in lakhs	7,153.80
(6)	Cost of spares for 7,153.80 Expected gross kms in lakhs $\frac{7,153.80 \times 1,663.11}{6,308.00}$ (Rs. in lakhs)	1,866.11
(7)	*Add* 5.21% increase in the rate	98.27
		1,984.38
(8)	Increase in cost due to increased operations and inflation (Rs. in lakhs) (1,984.38—1,663.11)	321.27

SCHEDULE—C

Estimated additional cost of HSD Oil

(1)	Price of HSD oil per litre (including S.T.) (1981-82)	Rs. 3.060
(2)	Price of HSD oil per litre (including S.T.) (Sept. 82)	Rs. 3.186
(3)	Percentage increase in the cost of HSD oil	4. 12
(4)	Actual cost of IISD Oil in 1981-82 based on 6,308.00 gross kms (in lakhs) (Rs. in lakhs)	4,629.60
(5)	Expected gross kms in lakhs	7,153.80
(6)	Cost of HSD oil for 7,153.80 gross kms (in lakhs) $\frac{7,153.80 \times 4,629.60}{6,308.00}$	Rs. 5,250.35 lakhs
(7)	*Add* 4.12% increase in rate	Rs. 216.31 lakhs
		Rs. 5,466.65 lakhs
(8)	Increase in cost due to increased operations and inflation (Rs. in lakhs) (5,466.66—4,629.60)	837.06

SCHEDULE—D

Estimated additional cost of tyres and tubes

(1)	Weighted average rate of tyres and tubes in 1981-82		Rs. 2,801.00
(2)	(a) Rate pertaining in first half of 1982-83		
	(i) Tyre	Rs. 2,926.16	
	(ii) Tube	Rs. 202.19	Rs. 3,128.35

	(b) Percentage increase in the price	11.69
(3)	Cost of tyres and tubes in 1981-82 (Rs. in lakhs) for 6,308.00 lakh gross kms	1,925.99
(4)	Expected gross kms (kms in lakhs)	7,153.80
(5)	Cost of tyres and tubes for 7,153.80 lakh gross kms (Rs. in lakhs) $\frac{7,153.80 \times 1,925.99}{6,308.00}$	2,184.23
(6)	*Add* 11.69% increase in the rate	255.34
		2,439.57
(7)	Increase in cost due to increased operations and inflation (Rs. in lakhs) (2,439.57—1,925.99)	513.58

SCHEDULE—E

Estimated additional cost of engine oil

(1)	Weighted average rate during 1981-82 (per K.L.)	Rs. 10,587.00	
(2)	Weighted average rate (Current, Sept. 1982)	Rs. 11,373.00	
(3)	Percentage increase in the rate	7.42	
(4)	Cost of Lubricants (including grease) in 1981-82 for 6,308.00 gross kms (in lakhs)	Rs. 384	lakhs
(5)	Expected gross kms in lakhs	7,153.80	
(6)	Cost of Lubricants (including grease) for expected gross kms (Rs. in lakhs) $\frac{(7,153.80 \times 384)}{6,308.00}$	Rs. 435.49	lakhs
(7)	*Add* 7.42% increase in the rate (See item 3)	Rs. 32.31	lakhs
		Rs. 467.80	
(8)	Increase in cost due to increased operations and inflation (467.80−384) (Rs. in lakhs)	Rs. 83.80	lakhs

SCHEDULE—F

Additional cost on account of increase in interest on capital contributions

		Rs. Lakhs
(1)	Capital contributions as on March 31, 1982	9,150.70
(2)	*Less* non-interest bearing capital contributions	701.63
(3)	Interest bearing capital contributions	8,449.07
(4)	**Interest @ 8%**	675.93

(5) *Less* interest charged during 1981-82	453.09
(6) Increase in interest	222.84

SCHEDULE—G

Estimated additional cost of miscellaneous items

(I) (1) Adjusted Total Costs (Rs. in lakhs) for 1981-82	22,501.01
(2) Total adjusted miscellaneous costs (Rs. lakhs)	979.51
(3) Total adjusted miscellaneous costs for 1981-82 as a % of total actual costs for 1981-82	4.35

(II) *Increase in costs*

	(Rs. in lakhs)
on depreciation	260.18
on spares	321.27
on fuel	837.06
on tyres and tubes	513.58
on lubricants	83.80
	2,015.89

4.35% increase in costs as miscellaneous costs based on increase in the costs of above items (Rs. in lakhs)	87.69

SCHEDULE—H

Estimated savings on account of improvement in KMPL

(1) Fuel costs of 1981-82 @ 4.17 KMPL and based on 6,308.00 lakh gross kms (Rs. in lakhs)	4,629.60
(2) *Add* increase in cost of fuel due to increased operations and inflation (Rs. in lakhs)	837.06
(3) Likely fuel cost with 4.17 KMPL (Rs. lakhs)	5,466.66
(4) Expected fuel cost with 4.30 KMPL	5,301.39
(5) Savings on fuel due to improvement in KMPL (Rs. lakhs)	165.27

2

ORGANISATIONAL SET UP

INTRODUCTION

THE organisational structure is one of the important factors which influences the effectiveness of an organisation, eventhough there are a number of other factors which influence the efficiency of an organisation. The passenger road transport industry, with its unique features of geographically widespread operations, labour-intensive nature, the non-storability of the potential service, if not utilised at the time that it is offered, requires a distinct organisational pattern suited to its nature of activity. There is need for the ultimate decision making level, that is, the top management, being nearer the operational level or base of operations that is the Depot. This implies that there shall be as few a number of levels as possible in the hierarchy of the organisation in order to avoid bureaucratic delays. In other words, the number of levels in the organisation is one of the important factors that influences the effectiveness of a passenger road transport organisation.

Another aspect which influences the effectiveness of an organisation is the need for and the extent of centralisation and decentralisation that may be obtaining within the organisation. In the case of smaller organisations where it is possible for decision making authority to be nearer and in constant touch with the operational base, centralisation may help the organisation to be more effective whereas in the case of a large, unitary, monolithic organisation, which covers the entire state in its operations, a highly decentralised set up may perhaps be inevitable if the organisation were to be effective.

In the latter situation, the top level in the organisation will have to confine itself strictly to policy matters and the next level may have to concern itself with sub-policy and operational decisions.

Any set up that is envisaged for an industry, like passenger road transport, will have to avoid parallel functioning of important functionaries at various levels. In the case of passenger road transport industry, it is to be ensured that there is smooth functioning and effective co-ordination of mechanical and operational wings which are crucial to the organisation.

Another factor which has to be taken care of in this industry, is the organisational set up for the workshops and alongwith that stores and the relationship between the workshop organisation and the operational set up. The workshop organisation will have to be dovetailed into the operational set up so that there is effective support from the workshop to operations.

It can be seen from the foregoing discussion that the organisational effectiveness in a road transport industry is influenced by the organisational set up. If the organisational set up is taken care of, to make the organisation effective, it should result in improved operational efficiency, other things remaining the same. At this stage, it must be noted that there are other factors that influence the performance of the organisation such as leadership, the worker attitude, quality of personnel, the political environment and so on. But at the same time, the influence of organisational set up on organisational effectiveness cannot be underestimated.

THE ORGANISATIONAL SET UP OF APSRTC : A BRIEF REVIEW

One of the reasons for reviewing the organisational set up is already made out in the foregoing analysis that is, to ensure organisational effectiveness. The most important factor that necessitates constant review and reorganisation of the organisational set up is the growth of the organisation. As an organisation grows, there is need for review and reorganisation to make it effective.

The APSRTC came into existence on 11 January 1958 with 532 vehicles and 4490 (31st March 1958) staff which increased to 6629 vehicles and about 65,263 employees by 31st March 1982. The size of the organisation increased by 12 times in terms of fleet strength, and 15 times in terms of staff strength. During the period of 24 years of its functioning, the APSRTC has made changes twice in its organisational set up—once in 1965 and the second time in 1978. The first organisational change was made six years after its incorporation and the second 12 years after the first one. It should be surprising that one should think of review and revision of the organisational set up within about 4 years of the previous change. In fact, attempts have been made to bring about drastic changes in the organisational set up within two years of the previous change that is, to regional set up. The fact of the matter is that the previous change to regional set up had not been tried in its spirit, which is discussed in greater detail at a later stage.

The Depot set up of 1965

The Depot set up,* introduced in September 1965, was a radical change that has brought rich dividends and has "stood the test of time". It was a radical change in so far as the set up at the Depot was concerned. This experiment was the first of its kind in the country. The essential features of the Depot set up are and still continue to be :

(1) identification of the Depot as a crucial unit of operations.
(2) introduction of the concept of integrated management at the Depot level, where the Depot Manager is given personnel/disciplinary powers, including "hiring and firing", purchase/financial powers and operational planning.

He has been given the necessary functional assistance in different areas such as traffic, maintenance, personnel, and accounts. Earlier to this Depot set up, there was only a Supervisor Incharge (SIC) who did not have the necessary powers to discharge the functions expected at the Depot level effectively. The Depot set up has strengthened the base level in expediting the decisions regarding requirement of personnel at lower levels, stores and so on, and

* Vide charts 2.1 and 2.2 for organisation charts prior to and after the Depot set up respectively.

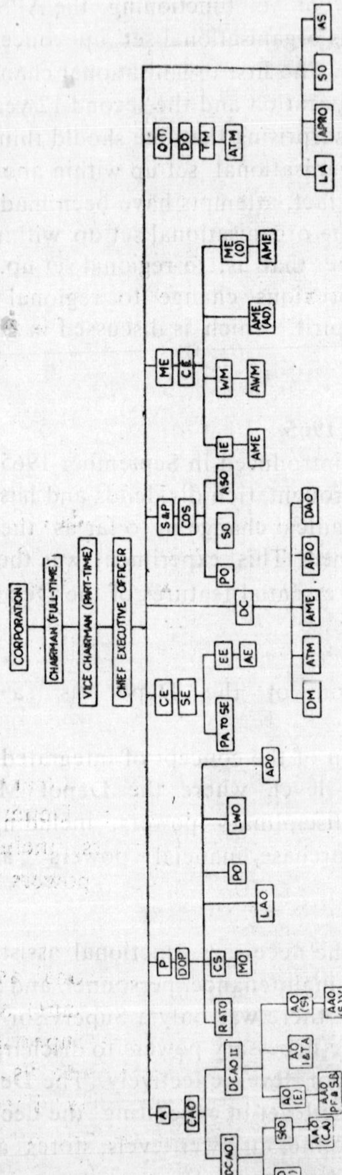

CHART 2.1 : *Organisational structure before Depot set up*

LEGEND TO CHART 2.1

A	=	Accounts
CAO	=	Chief Accounts Officer
DCAO	=	Deputy Chief Accounts Officer
AO	=	Accounts Officer
AO (Estt)	=	Accounts Officer (Establishment)
AO (I & TA)	=	Accounts Officer (Inspection & Test Audit)
AO (S)	=	Accounts Officer (Stores)
AAO (CA)	=	Assistant Accounts Officer (Cost Accounts)
AAO	=	Assistant Acconnts Officer
AAO (S) V	=	Assistant Accounts Officer (Stores) Vijayawada
P	=	Personnel
DOP	=	Director of Personnel
R & TO	=	Recruitment & Training Officer
CS	=	Civil Surgeon
MO	=	Medical Officer
LAO	=	Land Acquisition Officer
PO	=	Personal Officer
LWO	=	Labour Welfare Officer
APO	=	Assistant Personnel Officer
CE	=	Civil Engineer
SE	=	Superintending Engineer
PA to SE	=	Personal Assistant to Superintending Engineer
EE	=	Executive Engineer
AE	=	Assistant Engineer
DVC	=	Divisional Controller
DM	=	Depot Manager
ATM	=	Assistant Traffic Manager
AME	=	Assistant Mechanical Engineer
APO	=	Assistant Personnel Officer
DAO	=	Divisional Accounts Officer
S & P	=	Stores and Purchase
COS	=	Controller of Stores
PO	=	Purchase Officer
SO	=	Stores Officer
ASO	=	Assistant Strores Officer
ME	=	Mechanical Engineering
CE	=	Chief Engineer
IE	=	Industrial Engineer
AME	=	Assistant Mechanical Engineer
WM	=	Works Manager
AWM	=	Assistant Works Manager
AME (Addl)	=	Assistant Mechanical Engineer (Additional)
ME (O)	=	Mechanical Engineer (Operating)
O (T)	=	Operations (Traffic)
DO	=	Director of Operations
TM	=	Traffic Manager
ATM	=	Assistant Traffic Manager
LA	=	Legal Advisor
APRO	=	Assistant Public Relations Officer
SO	=	Security Officer
AS	=	Assistant Secretary

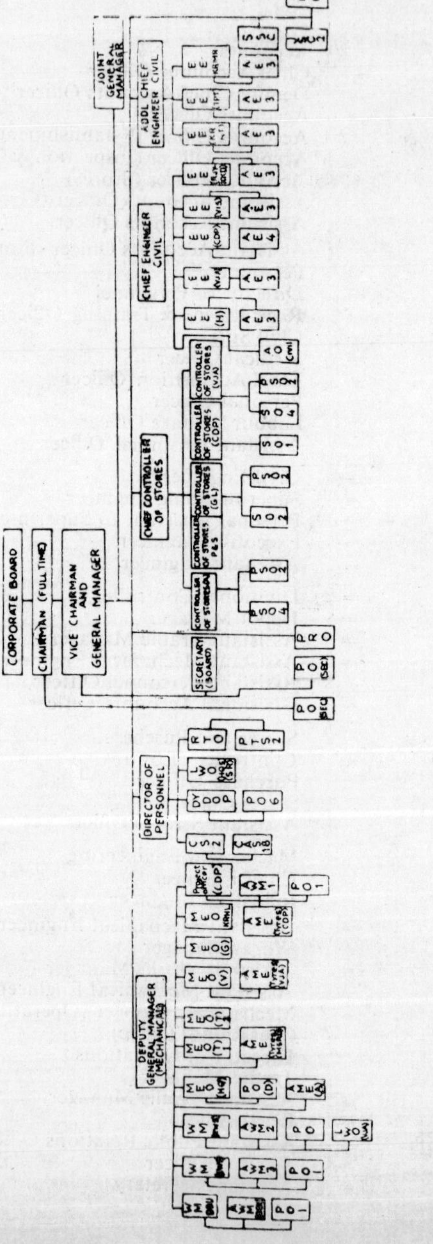
CORPORATE BOARD
CHAIRMAN (FULL TIME)
VICE CHAIRMAN AND GENERAL MANAGER
JOINT GENERAL MANAGER
ADDL CHIEF ENGINEER CIVIL
CHIEF ENGINEER CIVIL
CHIEF CONTROLLER OF STORES
SECRETARY (BOARD)
DIRECTOR OF PERSONNEL
DEPUTY GENERAL MANAGER (MECHANICAL)

CHART 2.2 : (*Contd.*)

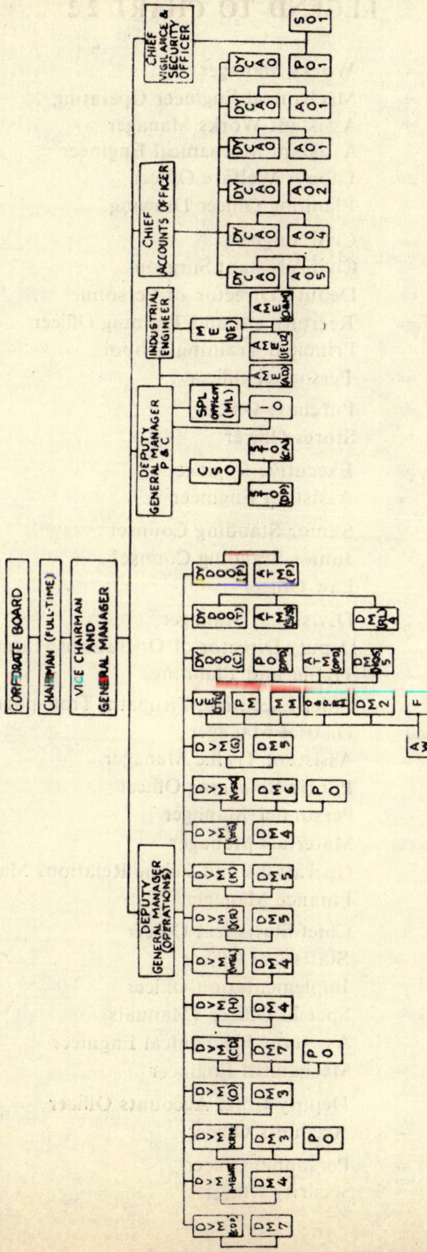

CHART 2.2 : *Organisational structure before regional set up*

LEGEND TO CHART 2.2

W.M.	=	Works Manager
M.E.O.	=	Mechanical Engineer Operating
A.W.M.	=	Assistant Works Manager
A.M.E.	=	Assistant Mechanical Engineer
L.W.O.	=	Labour Welfare Officer
P.O.D.	=	Planning Officer Drawing
C.S.	=	Civil Surgeon
C.A.S.	=	Civil Assistant Surgeon
Dy. D.O.P.	=	Deputy Director of Personnel
R.T.O.	=	Recruitment and Training Officer
P.T.S.	=	Principal Training School
P.O.	=	Personnel Officer
P.S.O.	=	Purchase Officer
S.O.	=	Stores Officer
E.E.	=	Executive Engineer
A.E.	=	Assistant Engineer
S.S.C.	=	Senior Standing Counsel
J.S.C.	=	Junior Standing Counsel
L.O.	=	Law Officer
D.V.M.	=	Divisional Manager
Dy. D.O.O.	=	Deputy Director of Operations (Commercial, Traffic and Planning)
C.E. (T.T.U.)	=	Chief Executive, Tirupathi Transport Unit
D.M.	=	District Manager
A.T.M.	=	Assistant Traffic Manager
P.R.O.	=	Public Relations Officer
P.M.	=	Personnel Manager
M.M.	=	Materials Manager
O. & P.R.M.	=	Operations and Public Relations Manager
F.M.	=	Finance Manager
C.S.O.	=	Chief Statistical Officer
S.T.O.	=	Statistical Officer
I.O.	=	Implementation Officer
SPL Officer (ML)	=	Special Officer (Manuals)
A.M.E.	=	Assistant Mechanical Engineer
M.E.	=	Mechanical Engineer
Dy. C.A.O.	=	Deputy Chief Accounts Officer
A.O.	=	Accounts Officer
P.O.	=	Personnel Officer
S.O.	=	Security Officer

improved the effectiveness of the Depots. As mentioned earlier, this has, in short, paid rich dividends.

Earlier to the introduction of Depot set up, the Divisional Manager (DVM) was taking care of the Depots in respect of personnel, operations, maintenance and accounts which were now decentralised to the Depot at the Depot level. Consequent to the introduction of Depot set up, the DVM became only a co-ordinating agency except for the physical process of recruitment of staff at lower levels, transfers of personnel within the Division upto senior supervisor, and also an appellate authority for all the punishments imposed by the Depot Manager. It could thus be seen that the area of decision making regarding the depot and its operations is shifted from division to depot to make the depot more effective. Incidentally it also became a cost centre.

That the Depot set up has stood the test of time could be seen from the fact that the organisation did not have to think of re-organisation for a period of 10 years even though the fleet strength increased by about 130 per cent and staff strength by about 200 per cent between 1965 and 1977. Infact, even the Regional set up that was introduced in 1978 was only an additional tier where both the Divisional Manager and Regional Manager are actually made ineffective and it is only because of the inherent strengths of the Depot set up that the organisation was able to withstand the stresses and strains of growth, and the problems of industrial relations.

The regional set up

In spite of the fact that the Depot set up has stood the test of time, the APSRTC had to think of changes in the organisational set up some time in the year 1975 in view of the considerable growth in the size of the organisation between 1965 and 1977 in terms of fleet, staff, Depots and Divisions. Next, the span of control of the Chief Executive/Head Office also increased from 5 divisions in 1965 to 14 divisions in 1977, apart from the Heads of Departments in the Head Office. At that time, integrated management existed only at Head Office level and Depot level. Consequently, the top Management became heavy and saddled with too much of work and supervision, as the middle level, that is, the Division was only a co-ordinating unit.

Despite the fact that the Depot set up had given good results, the organisation had to think of changes in its set up in 1975 because of the following reasons :

1. The organisation has grown from 2,120 vehicle in 1965 to 4,900 vehicles as on 31st March 1977 when the regional set up was introduced. This implied an increase in the number of employees from 14,081 to 43,115, number of Depots from 37 to 75 and the number of Divisions from 5 to 14 during this period. Consequently, the span of control of the Head Office—General Manager and Heads of Departments—increased considerably, more so in the case of the former in view of the number of divisions and also the functional heads reporting to him at the Head Office. Naturally, the need was felt to have a tier below the level of the Head Office to co-ordinate the functioning of the Depots and to reduce the number of people reporting to the Head Office.

2. Further, under the earlier set up, there was no integrated managerial unit level between the Head Office and the Depot. There were various functionaries of the level of Class I senior scale officers either in the Division or at the regional workshop—the Divisional Manager to take care of operations in the Division, the Works Manager, Mechanical Engineer, Controller of Stores and the Deputy Chief Accounts Officer to take care of workshop assistance, maintenance, stores and accounts requirements respectively of two or three divisions or a region (which was not a formal one). As all these officers were of the same level and they were all reporting directly to their respective Heads of Departments in the Head Office, there was no integrated management at the level of the Division or anywhere in between the Depot and Head office. Consequently, there was parallel functioning of these different officers reporting vertically to their respective Heads in Head office and the Divisional Manager who was supposed to be responsible for results did not have the necessary authority and functional assistance to render adequate assistance to the Depots. Hence, once again, need was felt in this context too to have an integrated managerial unit between the Head Office and Depot.

3. As mentioned earlier, consequent upon growth and absence of decentralised set up, the organisation became top heavy and everybody was looking straight to Head Office, thereby

choking the functioning of the organisation.

4. Taking into consideration, the future growth of organisation the need for decentralised set up, with the Head office confining itself broadly to policy matters, was felt.

After about three years of deliberations and preparatory work the area/regional* set up was introduced with effect from 16th January 1978. The essential features of the Regional set up as envisaged were as follows :

(1) In terms of the "reorganisation proposals"** as placed before the Corporation Board and approved by the same "the main objective of reorganisation is decentralisation of operations responsibility from Head Office to regional level with commensurate delegation of powers".[1] It is of interest to note that while concluding the discussion on small independent corporations, the reorganisation proposals mentioned that "the advantage resulting from flexibility at organisational level in a small organisation can be secured by measures of providing autonomy and accountability at the Depot and area level".[2] Finally, it was decided "to decentralise the present set up to a further extent with more authority commensurate with responsibility and clear accountability".[3] It was further mentioned that "adequate care has been taken to see that principle of unity of command and unity of direction are maintained in tact and that all powers necessary for maintaing operations at peak level of performance are given to this senior executive"[4] (Area/Regional Manager).

(2) It could also be seen from the Reorganisation Proposals that the Head Office should confine itself only to policy matters. The proposals clearly mention that the "area manager will be coming into contact with Head Office for guidance on policy matters"[5]. The proposals unambiguously state that the "Head Office will be primarily involved in policy decisions and in matters wherever there is an overlap between areas such as long distance routes, cutting across areas, inter-state routes and policies in respect of nationalisation and replacement, staffing

* Originally the set up was called area set up and the chief of the area, the Area Manager, but subsequently changed to Region and Regional Manager, respectively.

** Vide Chart 2.3 for organisation chart after the introduction of the Regional set up.

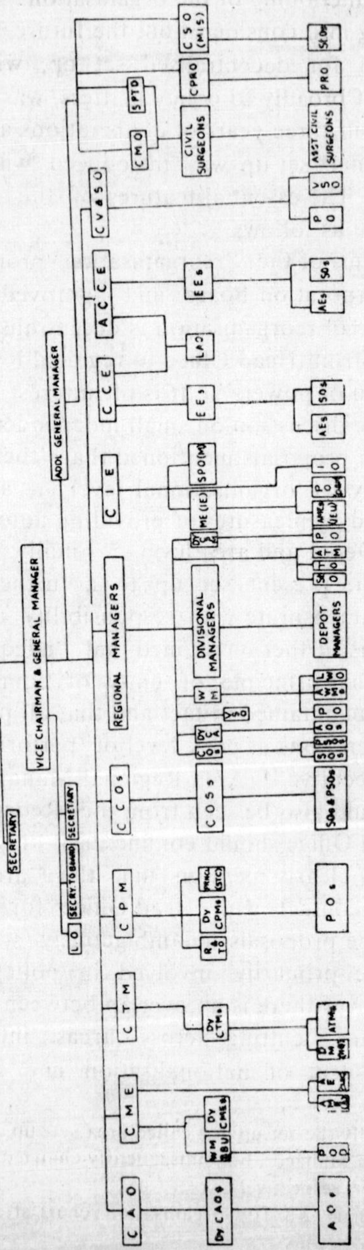

CHART 2.3 : *Organisation structure of APSRTC—April 1981*

norms, corporate objectives, budget, finance, audit and accounts dealing with the Government at corporate level and other corporate policies".[6] The proposals also very clearly mention that the Area Manager "is provided with functional assistance in all the fields ......, with adequate delegation of power to each level so that the Area Manager need not take recourse to Head Office on routine matters except on matters of corporate interest".[7]

(3) The Heads of Departments in the Head Office were assigned only staff role.

> At the Head Office, the Departmental Heads will be available mainly to assist General Manager in formulating corporate policies and appraising the Vice-Chairman and General Manager of the performance of the Areas on various aspects and suggesting appropriate control measures by providing staff assistance to Vice-Chairman and General Manager.[8]

(4) The responsibility of recritument of all categories of staff from the lowest level in Class IV services to one level below the first line supervisors was proposed to be delegated to the area/regional managers. This was thought of evidently to strengthen the Regional Manager so as to enable him to render effective personnel assistance to the Depots and to avoid delays in making the staff available to the Depots, which is likely to happen if there is centralisation of recruitment at Head Office. Further, to make this possible the organisation thought of having regional seniority for all the categories of staff upto one level below the first line supervisors in Class III services. But for some reasons or other, perhaps because of objection from Trade Unions and consequent inaction on the part of management, this could not be given effect to as proposed and Regional Managers are deprived of this authority to make their functioning effective. In order to take care of recruitument at the Area/regional level, the Regional Manager was expected to be provided with functional assistance of Personnel Department headed by Deputy Director of Personnel assisted by three personnel officers.

(5) One of the important changes envisaged, consequent

on the introduction of Regional set up was the conversion of the then Divisional Manager into inspecting and supervising deputy to the Regional Manager, mainly doing field supervision and regular inspection of depots, instead of being another level in the hierarchy of the organisation. The DVM was expected to be stationed in the office of the Regional Manager. It was strongly felt "that a fourth level is not warranted".[9] The proposals further state that "the functions that are presently carried out by the Divisional Manager have been distributed to the functionaries that are available at the Area Manager's office and some to the Depots wherever it is found advantageous to divert them to Depots".[10]

An evaluation of the functioning of the regional set up

An analysis of the functioning of the Regional set up over the last four and a half years shows that the Regional set up has not been implemented as envisaged. In fact there was flagrant violation of everyone of the major features of the set up as envisaged, defeating the very purpose of the set up in spirit and content.

(1) To start with, there was distortion in the role envisaged for the Divisional Manager. Contrary to the Divisional Manager being stationed in the Regional Manager's office, a decision was taken to keep him in the Division itself because of the influence of vested interests within the organisation through political forces. Consequently, both the Divisional Manager, in his role, and the Regional Manager's office have become ineffective especially in so far as rendering support to the Depots in the matter of recruitment of personnel. This is because the Divisional Manager is stripped off his staff which was shifted to the Regional Manager's office. The Divisional Manager is made further ineffective by informally taking away his earlier powers of recruitment and other powers.

The role of Divisional Manager was subverted in practice by placing a Deputy Chief Personnel Manager, a Trojan Horse of the Chief Personnel Manager in the Regional Manager's office, acting above the Head of the Regional Manager and obeying the instructions of the Chief Personnel Manager who is expected to be a staff officer. The Deputy Chief Personnel Manager in many cases happens to be a person without line experience and incapable of appreciating the line manager's problems. Some of the decisions taken and not taken/delayed, because of his lack of appreciation of the needs of the Depots, created problems not only for Depot Managers but also industrial relations problems in general and also in terms of performance of the organisation. One example may be given to substantiate this : The Depot Managers put in their requisitions of requirements of drivers and conductors through their Divisional Managers for operating additional schedules in busy season sufficiently in advance. The Deputy Chief Personnel Manager, because of lack of appreciation of the need, takes his own time for recruiting and giving posting orders. There are instances where the Deputy Chief Personnel Manager has issued orders after the busy season was over and slack season had set in.

As the Divisional Manager is stationed in the Division, he continues to constitute another tier, which was in existence earlier, and Depot Managers continue to envisage for him same role as he was discharging earlier, and the Head Office also was treating him as an administrative head, thereby implying responsibility on the Divisional Managers for the results for the Division. However, as mentioned earlier, he was made ineffective as he was stripped off his staff and further the role envisaged for him as per the Reorganisation proposals was only a co-ordinating and inspecting one.

There were, however, exceptions from this general situation in respect of location and role of Divisional Managers because of the ambiguity of the role of Divisional Manager, the perceptions of his role by Regional Managers and their (Regional Managers) styles of functioning. In all the Regions, the Divisional Managers are stationed in their respective Divisons except in the case of Hyderabad Region, where they are stationed in the Regional Manager's office. In the case of Cuddapah Region, even though the Divisional Managers are stationed in the Divisional Headquarters, the Regional Managers made them function the same way as they were functioning earlier to the introduction of the Regional set up, in the sense that the Divisional Managers in this region were taking all measures regarding recruitment right from requisition to appointment. These distortions took place because of the ambiguity of the role and powers of the Divisional Manager in the reorganisation proposals as approved.

(2) The role assigned for the Head Office and the Regional Managers has been totally violated because of the temptation for centralisation on the part of the Head Office and Heads of Departments. The Regional Managers are supposed to be delegated with all the powers of the Heads of Departments except in respect of stores, purchase and finance.[11] Further, the power of recruitment of staff below the first level of Class III supervisory staff, which was expected to be delegated to the Regional level, has also not been given effect to. It implies, practically, that no tangible authority has been delegated to the Regional level even though a tier has been created with the sole objective of bringing about a decentralised Regional set up. The Region has become only a post office involving itself in too much of paper work, operationally inffective, and therefore, the Depot Managers and the Divisional Managers started looking to the Head Office and also to respective Heads of Departments for any decision, support, assistance and so on. The Depot Managers and Divisional Managers were only marking copies to the Regional Manager. The Chief Executive and the Heads of Departments started dealing with the Depot Managers and the Divisional Managers direct in many instances, ignoring the Regional Manager. Each functional head in Head Office was convening the meetings of functional assistants of Regional Managers, started reviewing their performance and giving direct instructions to them.

Incidentally, too many functionaries from different levels have been inspecting the Depots after the introduction of the Regional set up. This has become a problem for the Depot Managers because of addition of one tier at Regional level and a few more functionaries also at that level, in addition to the chief executive and his functional heads. A considerable time and energy of the Depot Managers had to be devoted for these inspections without at the same time getting adequate support from these functionaries because of the presence of too many levels, resulting in passing the buck and because of absence of definite responsibility for rendering support on the part of various levels.

On the one hand, the Regional Managers have not been delegated necessary powers as envisaged and thus made ineffective, and, on the other, he was also made ineffective because his jusisdiction has become too big in view of the fact that a Region covers 4 to 5 districts with 20 to 25 Depots, apart from the fact that the regional workshop with about 1,000 workers is under him. This (non-delegation) shows lack of trust in the Regional Managers in delivering goods which is borne out by the fact that in spite of lapse of four years, the Regional Managers are not delegated any powers as envisaged. It may be because the top management is not sure of the competence and honesty of some of the persons manning these positions, which may mean a reflection on the selection process itself. It appears from the above that the reasons could be both the temptation to centralise and the incapacity on the part of some of the Regional Managers. Further, there was perhaps a lurking fear that the powers when delegated may be misused by some of the Regional Managers.

It follows from the above that the Chief Executive and Heads of Departments were involving themselves in the day-to-day functioning of the Depots, Divisions and Regions looking into the various aspects of detailed parametres of performance, instead of evaluating the performance of Regions in terms of broad parameters of performance only, such as ultimate costs and profits and variances between the actuals and the budgets. There are many instances where the Regional Manager and the Divisional Manager were ignored and direct explanation was called for from the Depots Managers for the short-fall in performance thereby ignoring and making ineffective the Regional Manager and the Divisional Manager. In other words, the unity of command which was one of the important objectives of the Reorganisation was given a go-by.

(3) The Reorganisation proposals mentioned that "while formulating the Areas set up, utmost care has been taken to see that the increase in staff is marginal except wherever it is inescapable".[12] However, in practice, the Bus-Staff ratio increased in the aggregate from 1:10.59 to 1 :11.19 between 1977 and 1981. It would be of interest to see where and in which categories and for what reasons the staff had increased during the period. It is evident from Table 2.1 that bus-staff ratio increased by 0.60 during a short period of four years after the Regional set up has been introduced. The total staff position at the end of the year 1980-81, which was 64,734, would amount to an excess staff of

TABLE 2.1 : **Bus-staff ratio (based on schedules) for 1976-77 and 1980-81**

	1976-77		1980-81	
	Number	Staff per schedule (No. of schedules : 4071)	Number	Staff per schedule (No. of schedules : 5785
Class I and II Officers	264	0.06	351	0.06
Class III and IV Staff				
(i) Administration	2,882	0.71	4,921	0.85
(ii) Traffic and supervisory	4,688	1.15	5,289	0.91
(iii) Drivers and conductors	22,056	5.42	34,436	5.95
(iv) Workshop and maintenace	11,129	2.73	17,073	2.95
(v) Others	2,096	0.51	2,666	0 46
Total staff	43,115	10.59	64,734	11.19

Source : (1) Annual Administration Reports
(2) Pay Commission Records.

3,471, if the staff required is to be computed for 5785 schedules of 1981, based upon the bus-staff ratio of 1976-77. The two important categories of staff namely, (i) drivers and conductors, and (ii) workshop and maintenance staff, which account for four-fifths of the staff of the entire organisation, accounted for the biggest increase during the period. The drivers and conductors per schedule increased by 0.53 from 5.42 to 5.95. The next biggest increase took place in the workshop and maintenance staff, where it increased by 0.22.

Based upon the pattern expected to be followed by APSRTC in regard to drivers and conductors, which is 5.2 per schedule (calculated at the rate of 2 drivers and 2 conductors plus thirty per cent reserve), there is surplus staff of 4354. Similarly, there is surplus in the case of maintenance and workshop staff. Even giving allowance to the need for additional staff in some of the city and night express services, there is considerable surplus staff in the categories of drivers and conductors.

The essential reasons for this increase are the growth of the organisation and the number of tiers in the organisation because of which there was no effective control over the way the depots were functioning. The Depot Managers who are entrusted with the traffic scheduling had to adopt lenient attitude in the mattter of drawing crew schedules on account of local union pressures.

A number of reasons could be adduced for this but the fact remains that the bus-staff ratio increased during the short period of four years after the Regional set up was introduced.

(4) The regional set up was a failure in one more respect because of lack of planning in bringing about self contained regions. If the regions are to produce results as they are supposed to be decentralised, they need workshop support which implies that the formation of regions should be preceded by the completion of workshop facilities. However, in practice two regions—Vizianagaram and Karimnagar—have been formed without compleling the workshop facillties first. Consequently, there was the problem of lack of adequate workshop facilities for those regions and these regions had to rely on and are still relying on the neighbouring workshops—Vijayawada and Hyderabad respectively. These workshops at Vijayawada and Hyderabad naturally give preference to the requirements of their own regions before they cater to the requirements of other regions. It looks as though these regions were created in haste, rather than on a well planned basis ensuring the requisite facilities, for the reasons best known to APSRTC administration.

(5) Another lacuna that has cropped up in the implementation of Regional set up was the lack of functional expertise at the Regional level/functional assistance to the Regional Manager in respect of the two most crucial functions, namely operations and mechanical, because of the fact that the Divisional Manager was taken away from the Regional office contrary to what was envisaged originally. As per the original proposal, each of the Divisional Managers to be stationed in Regional office was to be provided with Traffic Assistance (ATM) or Mechanical Assistance (AME) depending upon whether the Divisional Manager is a mechanical or traffic officer respectively. As the Divisional Manager himself did not happen to be stationed in the Regional Manager's Office, neither the traffic assistance nor the mechanical assistance was available at the Regional level. Consequently, in between the Depot and the Head Office, there

was no functional assistantant in the area of Mechanical Engineering to ensure monitoring and rendering functional assistance to the Regional Manager at the Regional level. However, on the operations side there were Divisional Managers at the intermediate level, that is, between the Depot and Region located in the Divisions, though not in the Regional office, but made ineffective because of the reasons mentioned earlier. The seriousness of the situation could be seen from the fact that instead of six functional experts—3 Divisional Managers and 3 Assistant Officers for a region—being available for assisting the Regional Manager, nobody was available in his office in crucial functional areas of transport management.

That the Regional set up has not only not delivered goods, but also failed in terms of some key indicators of performance can be seen from Table 2.2. Between 1976-77 and 1981-82 there was decline in operational performance in terms of crucial indicators of performance such as vehicular utilisation and vehicle

TABLE 2.2 : **Operational performance of APSRTC**

Performance indicators	1976-77	1981-82
Vehicular utilisation/fleet utilisation (%)	90.61	88.00
Vehicle utilisation (in kms)	305.97	299.00
Occupancy Ratio/load factor (in %)	69.49	72.00
Bus-staff ratio (staff per schedule) (in nos.)	10.59	11.08
K.M.P.L.	4.30	4.17
Tyre performance (in kms)		
(a) New	32,961	35,677
(b) Average	59,387	68,622
Rate of break downs (per 10,000 kms)	0.81	0.75

Source : Annual Administration Reports and Performance Reports of APSRTC.

utilisation, apart from the bus-staff ratio, to which reference has already been made, not to speak of the steep fall in KMPL (fuel performance). In a road transport organisation, the most important factor is vehicular utilisation because of the fact that a major part of the investment (85%) is made in the vehicles and the utilization of investment means vehicular and vehicle utilisation. This is because of the failure of the organisation to render effective support by way of prompt supply of stores to the workshop and of units and stores to the Depots. This, in turn, is due to too many tiers obtaining in the organisational set up and lack of adequate delegation of powers to the Regional Managers, besides the bureaucratic procedures in the procurement and supply of stores. From the foregoing analysis, it can be seen that there is poor utilisation of both material and human resources resulting indecline in productivity of the vehicle and the crew.

It can thus be concluded that the Regional set up has failed. Nay, it is not implemented. It has resulted in the addition of one more tier to the organisational structure, without serving any purpose, thus adding fifth wheel to the coach.

The introduction of Divisional Accounts Officer's set up (DAO set up)

An instance of confusion that has crept into the organisation, because of growth, monolithic organisation, four tier set up, inadequate delegation and improper controls, is the reintroduction of Divisional Accounts set up on an experimental basis with effect from 1 January 1982 for a period of three months which was further extended by another three months. Earlier to the introduction of the Depot set up in 1965, the DAO set up was in existence, as the Depot was not an integrated unit at that time and managed by a Supervisor Incharge (SIC) who did not have any powers. Consequent on the introduction of Depot set up the Depot was made an integrated unit of management and the Depot Manager had functional assistants in important areas including accounts.

In the light of the repeated mention that the Depot set up has stood the test of time, the latest being as recent as 1977 in the Reorganisation proposals, it is surprising that the organisation should think of taking away this important function from the Depot. The proposed reintroduction of the DAO set up looks all right as the DM is still given the required imprest vested with the necessary purchase powers, there is only post audit of purchases and there is pre-audit of salary bills as per the earlier practice. Thus, it does nct look as though that the DM's power/effectiveness is eroded. In spite of this, the question that arises is as to why this change was thought of and as to the consequences of the same. The ultimate disadvantage is that the DM feels that some thing is taken away from him without any advantage to the organisation and impairing the concept of integrated management at the Depot level.

The apparent reasons for the reintroduction of DAO set up appear to be accumulation of suspense balances and the adverse comments being made repeatedly by the Accountant General. In this context it is of relevance to mention that the phenomenon of suspense balances is not concomitant to the decentralisation of Accounts set up to depot level. This phenomenon was there earlier to the introduction of Depot set up and when the Depot set up was introduced, the suspense balances were handed over to the Depot Managers. This adequately proves that the defect was not with the decentralisation of accounts set up but there is some thing wrong with the accounts system obtaining in the organisation and inaction on the part of the concerned executives in not taking prompt action in settling the balances or taking necessary action against the defaulters. Infact, after the introduction of DAO set up on an experimental basis in Hyderabad region, the accounts set up has not been able to cope up with the problem and consequently, the provident fund and income tax remittances, were not made, thereby, inviting threat of action on the part of the concerned authorities. In many cases, it has been shown that it was Accounts Department that was not taking decisions after necessary clarifications were sent to the Department by the Depot Managers. There is lack of comprehension of the problems on the part of the Accounts Department. There is a need for a further probe into the entire set up and systems obtaining in the Accounts Department. There is perhaps need for decentralised accounts and centralised internal audit.

THE ALTERNATIVES

The prelude

In order to consider the alternatives to the existing organisational set up, an attempt has been made first to find out the strengths and weaknesses of the organisation through constant interaction by way of group discussions with each level of executives namely, the Depot Managers, the Divisional Managers, the Regional Managers, the Heads of Departments and the Vice-Chairman and General Manager and also through individual meetings with the different functionaries, apart from the office bearers of different Associations/Unions of the retired and present employees of the Organisation.

The important factors that should be taken into consideration in designing an effective organisational structure for a nationalised passenger road transport industry have been discussed earlier briefly. Apart from the nature of industry, there are other factors also which should be taken note of in this context. The nationalised passenger road transport industry has been and still continues to be an expanding one because of the scope for further nationalisation or because of need for augmentation, consequent on population growth. Any set up for the industry in a state should take into consideration, apart from organisational effectiveness, the amenability for co-ordination on the part of the government, namely the Minister and the Secretariat in order to ensure effective control in the desired policy areas and monitoring. At the same time, it is necessary to ensure that the decision making level is not far removed from the base of operations.

In the case of the passenger road transport industry, which is in the nature of a public utility service, there is need for ensuring that the entire industry does not come to a standstill because of a localised labour problem being made state-wide problem, which happens when there is only one organisation for the entire state. This may, therefore, require separate undertakings for different parts of the state.

It could be seen from the above that different factors require different organisational patterns. It is, therefore, necessary to see whether a synthesis can be brought about between the needs of effective co-ordination on the part of the Government and the need for having smaller units, for effective functioning and for localising the labour problems. In order to explore the possibility of such a synthesis, avoiding disadvantages and imbibing the merits, a study of the organisational set up of nationalised passenger road transport undertakings in selected states has been made. The selection of the states has been done on the following bases :

(1) Nationalised Passenger Road Transport Undertakings of not only the present size of APSRTC but also the size the APSRTC is likely to acquire in not too distant a future are taken. For example, Gujarat and Tamil Nadu states have got almost similar fleet strength that is., about 7,000 vehicles, while Maharashtra has about 10,000 fleet strength, which the APSRTC may be expected to attain in the next few years. Hence, the Nationalised Road Transport undertakings in these states are selected for detailed study. These undertakings are taken up for study for other reasons too.

(2) The Tamil Nadu and Gujarat undertakings are considered also from the point of view of their operational efficiency.

(3) Tamil Nadu is selected also for the reason of its uniqueness in its organisational set up, in the sense that it is the only state where a number of undertakings were set up, with fleets ranging ordinarily between 500 and 1000 each, which is evaluated to be an effective set up.

(4) The Andhra Pradesh State Road Transport Corporation (APSRTC) organisation has been modelled, by and large, on the pattern of Maharashtra State Road Transport Corporation in a limited sense, there being four levels in both the organisations.

(5) The Gujarat State Road Transport Corporation, which is supposed to be operationally efficient, has the same size and the same unitary monolithic type of organisation for the entire state as APSRTC has got and at the same time the GSRTC is more efficient in its operational performance than the APSRTC. It is of interest to find out as to what makes it more efficient than APSRTC and whether it has already started facing problems of size which may not have surfaced and yet which are felt. It is all these reasons that prompted a study of these undertakings before an effective organisational structure is planned to be evolved for the the APSRTC.

The Maharashtra State Road Transport Corporation (MSRTC) Set Up

The Maharashtra State Road Transport Corporation (MSRTC) is the biggest nationalised road transport undertaking in the conutry with a fleet strength of 10,066 vehicles as on 31 March

1981. Eurlier to the year 1976, it had a three-tier set up, which the APSRTC also had up to the end of 1977 in broad terms of levels, though not in terms of the functions of one of these levels, that is, the Division.

In the year 1976, another tier/level—region—was added because of the large span of supervision of the Head Office over the divisions. Consequently, it has now got four levels, namely, the depot, the division, the region and the Head Office. It may be incidentally mentioned that the APSRTC has followed this pattern with a shift in the emphasis from the division being an integrated unit to the Region being an integrated unit. In the case of MSRTC the Depot is the basic operational unit, the Head Office being the policy making and controlling unit at the apex and the Division being another integrated unit of management with workshop and stores. When the Regional level was created in MSRTC, it was only a co-ordinating, inspecting and monitoring level incharge of a few Divisions in the Region without any workshop attached at that level, with of course a few limited powers in the areas of sanctioning tenders, and staff and creation of certain posts. The Regional officer originally called Deputy General Manager, was to be stationed in the Head Office as per the original proposals, but was ultimately located in the region. The Regional Committee has got the power of sanctioning civil engineering works upto a limit of Rs. 3 lakhs. It has also got powers to sanction staff as per the "Key"/norm laid down by the Head Office in respect of Class III and Class IV staff and power of creation of certain posts, other than officers for a maximum period of two months. There are central workshops directly under the Head Office taking care of body building, engine and unit overhauls, including FIP, the Divisional Workshop taking care of heavy accident repairs and reconditioning and the Depot attending to daily maintenance, docking at 8000 kms and RTO passing. In the case of APSRTC, the roles of Division and Region are the opposite of what they are in the case of MSRTC. Hence, operationally, it is the Depot and the Division that are important in MSRTC while it is the Depot and the Region in the case of APSRTC.

The strong points about the MSRTC set up are the following :

1. The Division/Divisional Manager is in a position to take care of the requirements of the Depots under its/his jurisdiction in terms of workshop support in so far as heavy accident repairs and reconditioning of the vehicle are concerned. Hence, the vehicle condition may be expected to be better than what it is likely to be if there were no Divisional workshops and where the workshop facility is centralised. The level which is charged with the responsibility of producing results had the necessary infrastructure.

2. Another aspect of the MSRTC set up worth mentioning is the constitution of the Regional Committee with appropriate powers delegated to it, to the extent that they were delegated, as mentioned earlier. However, it is to be noted that these are strictly limited powers.

3. The other strengths of MSRTC are not in the area of organisational set up. These pertain to such aspects as 100 per-cent nationalisation of the passenger road transport services in the state of not only stage carriages but also contract carriages operating within the state.

4. Another strength of the MSRTC is checking power conferred on the officers of the MSRTC of and above the rank of Depot Manager over the clandestine operations of the private operators or infringement of monopoly right of MSRTC by the private operators.

However, the MSRTC has some weaknesses and problems which will have to be identified while considering the alternatives to the existing set up of APSRTC.

1. The organisation is already seized of the problem of too many levels/tiers in the organisational structure. As noted earlier, there are Two levels—Division and Region—in between the Depot and the Head Office. The creation of Regional tier has not only not solved the problem of the top heavy management with too much of centralisation at the Head Office level but also added to the paper work and delays in the decision making process. The Head Office is still concerning itself not only with policy matters but also with the regular day-to-day functioning of the operational levels in the organisation, making the regional level redundant and adding to the personnel cost. The organisation seems to have already realised this and appointed a

sub-committee to review the organisational set up and make necessary recommendations.

2. Considering the size of the MSRTC and its existing organitasional set up, what appears to be an optimal alternative may not be practically feasible because of the emotional overtones that it may bring about. It could be perhaps economical and operationally viable if the regional tier is disbanded and size of the Division is increased to about 1000 vehicles, roughly equivalent to two administrative districts, with the workshop facilities taking care of not only the unit overhauls but also engine overhauls and body building where necessary. But, as the present Division is coterminus with the Revenue/Administrative district, disbanding the existing workshop in a district may not be practically feasible in view of the possible local resistance to such an idea. The only alternative left in such a situation would be, assuming that the Regional tier is also done away with, to have a few second level assistants at the Head Office to take care of a few divisions each vested with the necessary powers and directly reporting to the chief executive and with necessary power to give instructions to the Departmental Heads at the Head office directly.

3. Another weakness of the existing set up of MSRTC is that because of the three-tier workshop system and because of the practice of sending the vehicle to the Divisional Workshop for unit replacements and reconditioning the percentage of spares held by the organisation is on the high side, with about 18 per cent, thereby locking up considerable amount of investment in the vehicle. In fact, the inventory of spares was much higher at 25 per cent to 30 per cent prior to the shifting of reconditioning of the vehicle from the central workshop to D visional workshop, which is now reduced to 18 per cent. On a closer evaluation of the workshop structure in MSRTC, one comes to the conclusion that the three-tier workshop structure is an unnecessary luxury. The workshop assistance to the Depots could be taken care of better by having only one more tier of workshop, above the Depot level, by having Regional workshops to take care of about 1000 vehicles, covering about two districts, and undertaking body building, engine and unit overhauls and tyre re-treading. This would be a viable workshop.

The Gujarat State Road Transport Corporation (GSRTC) Set Up

The Gujarat State Road Transport Corporation (GSRTC) is broadly of the same size as that of the APSRTC in terms of the fleet with 6,678 vehicles as on 31 March 1981. It is one among the big organisations, with a three-tier structure—Depot, Division and Head Office. It has already been mentioned that the MSRTC and APSRTC had introduced the fourth tier—the region—in 1976 and 1978 respectively. Except for this, the GSRTC has practically the same organisational structure as the MSRTC has got. In between the depot and the Head Office, there is only the division which is also a level of integrated management with necessary workshop and stores facilities. The workshop organisation in GSRTC is similar to that of MSRTC, the depot workshop taking care of normal maintenance, minor repairs and docking at 36,000 kms, the divisional workshop taking care of major assemblies, R.T.O. passing, body and unit replacements and the central workshop dealing with engine overhaul, F I.P. and tyre re-treading. The strengths of GSRTC are as follows:

(1) To the extent that there are only three tiers in the organisation, it is advantageous for the reason that the depots and divisions are nearer to the Head Office apart from the fact that additional staff is avoided by avoiding another tier. However, this is a limitation in itself, as the span of control of the Head Office is more because of a number of smaller (district-wise) divisions to be controlled by Head Office.

(2) Another strength of this organisation is the divisional workshop because of which the division is able to render effective workshop support to the depots. Here again, another limitation is the size of the division being small and co-terminus with district. It will be of relevance to mention here the recommendation of 40 schedules for depot and 800 vehicles for a division by a study team of Indian Institute of Management, Ahmedabad, which was, however, not implemented in respect of the latter for fear of political repercussions of such a decision, as the implementation of which would imply doing away with the existing divisional workshop which is coterminus with the revenue district.

A distinct feature of this organisation is that it has got the deputationists from civil/police services, both at the chief executive level and at the next level of Deputy General Managers. Consequently, there is lack of continuity in thinking and consistancy in policy and understanding the problems of the organisation.

The real strengths of the organisation are :

(1) The work-culture of its staff ;
(2) Total nationalisation and the Governmental support to the organisation.

The Tamil Nadu set up

As mentioned earlier, Tamil Nadu has got about 7000 vehicles in the nationalised passenger road transport sector, almost the same as the state of Andhra Pradesh has got. While the former has got eight undertakings to manage the fleet, the latter has got only one undertaking. The Tamil Nadu set up is unique in the country not only in the sense of having a number of undertakings within the state to run the nationalised road transport services but also in some of the important respects such as the number of levels within the organisation, the Board set up, the workshop set up, the policy regarding manning the executive positions and so on which are dealt with in greater detail subsequently.

The essential features and strengths

(1) As mentioned above, the foremost feature of the Tamil Nadu set up is that it has a number of undertakings—presently 8—to run the nationalised passenger road transport services. Another distinctive feature is that these are organised in the form of companies, unlike the other states where these are organised in the form of corporations under the Road Transport Corporations (1950) Act, the only exception being Orissa Road Transport Company. The main point of interest is that the Tamil Nadu Government has a deliberate policy of having separate undertakings for a fleet strength of 500-1000 vehicles and to create new undertakings whenever the strength exceeds the stipulated number. Presently the average size of these undertaking is about 800 vehicles.

(2) The strength of this set up lies essentially in the number

of levels within an organisation, apart from the size of the individual undertakings, which is the basic one. Practically, there are only two tiers that is the Head Office and the Depot, the Head Office responsible not only for major policy decisions but also for major operational decisions such as traffic scheduling, workshop support, stores, personnel recruitment and so on, the Depot being responsible for the Depot workshop that is routine maintenance of vehicles and operations.

(3) At the Head Office, the chief executive is the Managing Director (MD) assisted by the General Manager (GM) in the day-to-day functioning of the organisation and the Depots.

The Managing Director is practically free from the day-to-day problems for taking care of the broader policy perspectives and policy matters by way of liaison with the government and co-ordination among MDs of different corporations within the state. He is also the ultimate reviewing authority. Because of the support of the General Manager, the M.D. could devote his time for broader matters and yet, at the same time, the operational base has always somebody to look for, at the Head Office, to take care of their requirements and to attend to their problems promptly. This is further facilitated by the fact that the General Manager is expected to visit the Depots 15 days in a month to appreciate their problems and to render effective support. The very fact that there is no tier in between the Head Office and the Depot makes for quick decisions, prompt assistance and realistic appraisal of the depots and their needs. In short, the decision-making level is nearest to the operational level. Another point of interest is that there is always either the General Manager or the Managing Director available at the Head Office for taking care of any problem that may crop up in the Depots. This is because there is a planned presence at the Head Office or visits to outside places on the part of the Managing Director and General Manager so that whenever the M.D. is away, the G.M. is at Head Office and that the G.M. visits the Depots only when the M.D. is at Head Office. Further, because of the fact that an undertaking in Tamil Nadu encompasses only two districts in its operations, the physical distance to be covered by the G.M. or the Chief Executive in visiting the Depots is short enough to take care of all the Depots effectively.

(4) Even though it looks as though the G.M. has a big span of control over 10 to 12 Depots and Heads of Departments at Head Office, practically it is not a problem because of the informal functioning of the chief executive, routine nature of the business at base level and the capacity to effectively get the work done by the Heads of Departments at Head Office who are his immediate subordinates. This is facilitated also by the absence of conflict of roles, of parallel functioning of the functional heads and so on. In a way he co-ordinates the functional heads at the Head Office and the Branch Managers at the Depots. Further, it is centralised functioning of a decentralised industry that is giving effective results.

(5) Another strength of the organisation is the type of people manning the managerial positions at various levels in the organisation right from the Chief Executive that is the Managing Director down to the Junior Engineer. All the important managerial positions on the operations and maintenance side are manned by qualified mechanical/automobile engineers. The Managing Director invariably and the General Manager generally are deputationist engineers drawn from the Government and they are kept for a reasonably good period so as to ensure continuity. There were instances where the General Managers on deputation were promoted as Managing Directors either in the same organisation or in a sister organisation. There were also instances of promotion within the organisation to the level of General Manager, in either case, the only criterion being efficiency and merit. It is ensured that every officer recruited acquires adequate experience in the depot workshop and ensures knowledge of the vehicle, functioning of the vehicle and maintenance of the vehicles as they are straight away appointed as Junior Engineers in the workshop. One interesting incident which makes clear not only the policy of the Government but also its objectives vis-a-vis the nationalised passenger road transport undertakings, is the clear and emphatic "No" by the Chief Minister to the proposal for having a civil servant as the Managing Director of one of the undertakings.

(6) Despite the fact that there are eight undertakings now in the state in this sector, there is effective co-ordination at the Governmental level and at the industry level :

(a) The former is ensured by the Secretary, Transport, Government of Tamil Nadu, having a small cell in the Secretariat to monitor the functioning of these undertakings. This is a small cell called "chairman's cell" with only four people to assist him namely, a Technical Officer, two Asst. Directors and a Typist. The cell located in the office of the Secretary, Transport in the Secretariat is called the Chairman's cell, as he happens to be the chairman of all the corporations except the Pallavan Transport Corporation (Metro). As the common chairman of the seven undertakings, and through the chairman's cell, a sense of direction is provided to all the corporations by him. He also ensures uniformity in perceptions of Governmental policies vis-a-vis the undertakings.

(b) At the sub-policy level that is at the enterprises' level in terms of norms of personnel, wage policy, nationalisation, route planning, and so on, co-ordination is brought about among different undertakings through the periodical meetings of the Managing Directors without at the same time sacrificing freedom and flexibility of operations and functioning on the part of the individual undertakings so long as an undertaking does not intrude into other's areas.

(c) Co-ordination is also ensured among the contiguous undertakings by having interlocking of directors (i.e., the Chife Executives) of these undertakings in each of the boards.

(7) An important strength of the Tamil Nadu set up lies in its boards and their composition. The boards comprise essentially professional expertise from within the industry, as each of the boards consists of, apart from chairman who happens to be the Secretary, Transport (except for the Pallavan (Metro)), the Managing Director of the concerned enterprise and the Managing Directors of the adjacent undertakings. It is a matter of great relevance and importance that there is no political element at all on these boards in a state which is considered to be one of the enlightened in the country. This avoids unnecessary interference

and external pressures in the functioning of the enterprises. It also ensures that the persons responsible for results have the necessary authority without external influence and that the persons who are not responsible for results do not interfere with the authority responsible for it. Further, it is not desirable to have political element on the boards of public enterprises, not only in view of the central Government policy in respect of its enterprises but also in view of the fact that the legislators, when these legislators represent political element on the boards, have to dispassionately consider, review, criticise and take policy decisions regarding these undertakings when the annual reports of these undertakings are placed on the floor of the legislature. They cannot be expected to play a dual role in respect of these undertakings.

(8) One of the important reasons for the effective functioning of the Nationalised Road Transport Undertakings in Tamil Nadu is the Governmental support to these undertakings. This is partly ensured by the Secretary, Transport, being the chairman of these undertakings. Further, the policy of the Government to keep civil servants in the concerned department in the Secretariat for a reasonable period and to give posting again in the same Department for a reasonable period after promotion would ensure proper appreciation of the policies and functioning of these enterprises under its administrative control.

Further, there is a feeling among the civil servants that the nationalised road transport undertakings are their concerns and consequently there is no harassment of the officials of these undertakings. In fact, there is positive support to these undertakings from the Government not only in Tamil Nadu but also in Gujarat and Maharashtra.

(9) It was a happy sight to see the work environment in the workshops at the central as well as Depot levels in Tamil Nadu. This is a culture by itself, inherited from the earlier private organisations and preserved and nurtured by the nationalised undertakings. In fact, each of these undertakings deliberately attempts at preserving some of the good old traditions. The work ethics/environment is an important factor contributing to the low bus-staff ratio of 1 : 7.5, which the undertakings are planning to raise to 1 : 8.

(10) In so far as the organisational set up for workshop is concerned there are, once again, two levels—the depot workshop and the central workshop. In the case of some of the undertakings, instead of a central workshop, there is a separate Engineering Corporation, though in name, and for reasons of getting financial assistance from central Government under special employment schemes. The depot workshop takes care of the F.C. Work and the unit replacements apart from routine maintenance. The central workshop, takes care of the Engine and unit overhauls, body building and tyre retreading. The policy of ensuring the availability of float units based on well laid down norms makes the central workshop assistance to the Depots very effective. Consequently, the fleet utilisation is as high as 93 per cent. This is a very strong point of the Tamil Nadu set up which is very crucial to a Road transport organisation. This is made possible by the two tier workshop structure and by supplying float units to the Depots effectively.

Some likely problems

(1) The undertakings do not seem to be facing any immediate problems. But there is already a feeling among the chief executives that because of the smallness of the size of the individual undertakings, and consequently the lesser number of levels within the organisation, the managers in the organisation lack career opportunities. In some cases, some of the organisations have created Divisional Managers posts, without creating another tier in the organisational set up, for providing promotional avenues to the lower levels of managerial personnel. The chief executives are already seized of the problem and they seem to be contemplating to have a 'Transport Management Cadre' for the state encompassing all the nationalised passenger road transport undertakings within the state, when there will be possibilities of promotion, though not within the organisation, at least, among the different undertakings within the sector in the state. For this purpose, they also seem to be toying with the idea of creating a 'Trust Fund' to ensure the effective functioning of the cadre to which the individual undertakings would make pension, provident fund, leave salary and other contributions which will be administered by a common agency of all these corporations.

(2) Another problem that may crop up, though not in the immediate future, is the problem of co-ordination, when a number of corporations come up in view of the future growth. Perhaps, the size of the individual corporations may have to be marginally increased to cover about 1000 vehicles operating over two districts instead of about 500-750 vehicles, so as to keep the number of corporations within a reasonable number. This would not be operationally and organisationally uneconomical and unviable.

Conclusion

Thus the Tamil Nadu set up is an example worth emulating in view of the many good aspects of it. It would be ideal, if these features can be incorporated in a unitary set up without allowing the disadvantages of the unitary set up to creep into the organisation, where for some practical reasons split is not possible. This would depend upon a number of factors such as the clarity of the role of the Head office, that being confined strictly to policy matters, the number of levels down this level being only two, practical autonomy to the level below Head office except for major policy areas, the strict instructions to the Chief Executive to confine himself to policy matters, the government being clear of the role of Head office in providing data on only broad parameters of performance and contacting the next level for any further information, rather than the Head office, and the legislature, and the Accountant General being formally informed of the relative roles of the Head office and the next level which may for the immediate convenience be called region. Further, the Board composition should be entirely functional and professional in nature, except for the chairman being the concerned civil servant, and devoid of any political element. How far these conditions could be realised in practice would depend on the will of the Government, the Chief Executive and the Corporation Board.

Organisational set up for APSRTC

In the light of the foregoing analysis of the organisational structures of Nationalised Road Transport Undertakings in three of the States, an attempt is made to suggest a suitable and desirable organisational set up for the nationalised road transport services in Andhra Pradesh. A number of alternatives have been considered in suggesting the organisational set up for APSRTC, which are as follows :

(i) Implementing the Regional set up as envisaged in 1978.

(ii) Splitting the existing corporation and forming smaller companies under the Companies Act, 1956 either as independent ones or under a holding company.

(iii) Splitting the existing corporation and forming smaller corporations under the RTC Act (1950) either as independent corporations or as a holding corporation.

(iv) Continuing the existing unitary corporation form of set up with complete freedom to the regional units in sub-policy and operational matters and leaving only major policy matters to the Head office, with the size of the region being reduced and the regional units having their own management boards.

Splitting the existing organisation and having small units either as independent companies or as subsidiary companies under a Holding Company under the Companies Act, 1956 is not suggested for two reasons. Firstly, a change from the corporate form under the RTC's Act to the Company form under the Companies Act would imply deprivation of capital contributions from the central Government (Railways). The organisation would straightaway be deprived of about one-third of its total capital which it cannot afford under the present financial conditions. Secondly, it is also not suggested for the reason that the overall income-tax liability would be considered enhanced. The Holding Corporate form is also not suggested because it would be no different from a unitary corporation form of organisation in the matter of temptation to centralise at the Head office once an apex organisation exists. Further, the problems of creating subsidiary corporations by an amendment to the RTC Act can perhaps be avoided by making suitable modifications in the existing structure itself namely, by decentralising adequate authority to the Regional units. In addition, the problem of the likely conflicts between the apex corporation and subsidiary corporations can also be avoided.

The alternative of implementing the regional set up as envisaged in 1978 is also not suggested because of its limitations which are discussed hereunder :

Implementation of the regional set up as envisaged in 1978

The defects of the existing Regional set up as implemented and as different from the envisaged set up have already been outlined. If the original proposals were to be implemented, it would imply : (a) delegation of adequate powers to the Regional Managers, (b) location of Divisional Managers in the Regional Manager's office, and (c) the Head office being concerned with policy matters. This may, if implemented, improve the functioning of the organisation to some extent. But it cannot be expected to bring about radical improvement in the functioning of the organisation for the following reasons :

(1) As long as the size of the Head office remains to be the same with all the Heads of Departments with all their paraphernalia remaining at the Head office, there is bound to be temptation to recentralise and to erode the authority of Regional Managers.

(2) The size of the Region is not planned on rational, optimal, operational and organisational considerations. A region should ordinarily not have more than 1000 vehicles and two districts to cover in order to be effective and nearer the operational level and to have a viable workshop.

(3) The idea of two levels for effective functioning of the organisations in Road Transport Industry can be had only in smaller operationally autonomous units which cannot be had unless the Head office (in a three-tier set up) is to concern itself only with policy matters and all other matters to be delegated to the next level that is, the Region. There should be centralisation at Regional level in the matter of operations and operational decisions so as to avoid ambiguity which means direct contact between the Region and Depot.

(4) If the Region is to be really effective and independent from the Head office in operational matters there should be a Regional authority of the type of Regional Management Board vested with sufficient powers and stature, which the originally envisaged set up lacks. Hence, the implementation of the Regional set up as envisaged is not recommended.

Finally, the alternatives left are splitting the organisation into a number of small independent corporations, of the type obtaining in Tamil Nadu, but under a different legal form that is, under the RTC's Act, for the reasons mentioned earlier and the Unitary organisation with practically independent Regions with Regional Management Boards, where the Corporate Board and the Regional Boards are interlinked by its common element of membership to bring about effective liaison between the policy and operational levels that is, the Head office and Regional level.

The splitting of the existing corporation and formation of small independent corporations is suggested for the distinct advantages that this set up confers in the light of the Tamil Nadu experience.

Splitting the existing set up and formation of small independent corporations

In view of the distinct advantages of small, viable and independent corporations, as proved by the results of the Tamil Nadu experience, it is suggested that the same may be adopted with necessary modifications, taking into consideration the shortcomings of Tamil Nadu set up and requirement of the State.

Table 2.3, which gives an idea of comparative operational performance of APSRTC with the Tamil Nadu Corporations, shows very clearly that the small, independent, Tamil Nadu Corporations fared, by and large, better than APSRTC in respect of vehicular utilisation, vehicle utilisation, occupancy ratio, bus-staff ratio, tyre performance and rate of breakdowns. Of particular significance is the performance of the Tamil Nadu Corporations in terms of crucial indicators of performance namely, vehicular utilisation, vehicle utilisation and bus-staff ratio which are distinctly superior to the APSRTC performance.

The Tamil Nadu set up confers the advantages as it satisfies the essential features of organisational set up required in a passenger road transport organisation such as the viability of size of the organisation, the decision making level being nearer the operational level, and the operational level essentially concerning itself with operations, the planning and policy being centralised. Further, the advantages of having an optimal workshop to take care of overhaul of engines and units is also ensured, thereby helping maximum utilisation of fleet.

TABLE 2.3 : **Comparative operational performance of APSRTC and Tamil Nadu corporations as on 31 March, 1981**

Performance indicators	APSRTC City	APSRTC Corpn	Tamil Nadu corporations Pallavan TC (M)	Pallavan TC (D)	Cheran TCL	Cholan R/W CL	Kattabo-mman TC	Anna TC	Pandian RC	Than-thai Peri-yar TC	Thiru-valluvar TC
Vehicular utilisation/ fleet utilisation (%)	93.71	88.00	87.60	92.50	94.00	90.00	92.50	90.80	93.00	92.23	89.00
Vehicle utilisation (kms.)	201.96	312.00	210.00	335.00	219.18	342.00	331.00	N.A.	322.35	N.A.	603.00
Occupancy ratio/ load factor (%)	51.00	71.00	89.80*	78.50*	70.00*	75.00*	70.32*	86.00*	79.06*	74.48*	81.50
Bus staff ratio (staff per schedule in nos.)	10.50	11.19	9.56	7.40	7.36	7.19	8.80	6.95	7.44	6.93	11.30
KMPL	3.36	4.09	3.56	3.83	4.01	3.85	3.74	3.95	3.61	3.81	4.06
Tyre performance (kms.)											
(a) New	—	35,677	35,129	34,475	N.A.	30,345	N.A.	N.A.	25,888	N.A.	32,979
(b) Average	60,204	63,272	99,810*	78,406*	79,426*	84,097*	85,634*	89,996*	84.326*	83,020*	77,231*
Rate of breakdowns (per 10,000 kms.)	0.66	0.79	1.60	3.00	0.32	0.35	0.57	0.23	0.58	0.55	0.25

Source : (1) Report on the performance of Nationalised Road Transport Undertakings 1979-80 and 1980-81 compiled by Central Institute of Road Transport (Training and Research), Pune.

(2) *Figures pertaining to Anna T.C., Thanthai Periyar T.C., and Figures marked* are from Financial and Physical Performance of Transport Corporations of Tamil Nadu issued from the Chairman's cell of Commissioner and Secretary to Govt., Transport Dept., Tamil Nadu, March 1981.

The optimum size of the corporation

Table 2.4 gives an idea of the size of the corporations in Tamil Nadu. It can be seen from the table that the size varies between

TABLE 2.4 : **Fleet strength of Tamil Nadu corporations as on 31 March, 1981**

(*Vehicles in Nos.*)

Particulars	Fleet strength
Anna Transport Corporation Ltd.	512
Cheran Transport Corporation Ltd.	963
Cholan Roadways Corporation Ltd.	764
Kattabomman Transport Corporation Ltd.	678
(a) Pallavan Transport Corporation Ltd. (Metro)	1,794*
(b) Pallavan Transport Corporation Ltd. (District)	502*
Pandiyan Roadways Corporation Ltd.	1,045
Thanthai Periyar Transport Corporation Ltd.	335
Thiruvalluvar Transport Corporation Ltd.	458
Total :	7,051

Source : Report on the performance of Nationalised Road Transport Undertakings, 1979-80 and 1980-81, compiled by Central Institute of Road Transport (Training and Research), Pune.

*Even though they legally constitute one corporation, they are de fact two corporations and taken as such.

300 and 1800 vehicles, with only two of the eight corporations having fleet of more than 1000 vehicles and two less than 500 vehicles and the others in between these two ranges. The average size of the fleet for all the undertakings put together comes to 783 as on 31st March 1981. As a matter of policy, the individual corporations take advance action to split the organisation and create another corporation when the strength is likely to exceed 750 vehicles. There is a feeling that the optional size of a passenger road transport undertaking is 1000 vehicles. The "corporations of smaller sizes with a fleet of not more than 1000 buses catering to a region of 2 or 3 districts could be operationally efficient and viable entities".[13] This feeling expressed by the Special Secretary, Transport Department, Government of Tamil Nadu, who happened to be the Chairman of these undertakings lends realism in the light of the working of these undertakings over a period of time. A fleet

of 1000 vehicles is the essential criterion ; but an incidental consideration is the administrative area that the operation of these 1000 vehicles would imply. Ordinarily, this may be expected to cover two revenue districts after full nationalisation in the light of the figures that are available. It is convenient to identify the fleet of 1000 vehicles in terms of number of revenue districts—ordinarily two, in some cases three and in exceptional cases four depending upon the extent of nationalisation—for the reason that in the case of road transport organisation its officials will have to deal with the concerned district officials such as the Regional Transport Officer (R.T.O.), the Superintendent of Police (S.P.) and the District Collector.

In view of the above, a corporation may cover ordinarily two districts and about 12 to 15 Depots, each with 40 to 80 vehicles. A central workshop of the Corporation would be able to take care of 1000 vehicles in terms of maintenance and also geographically two districts in terms of distance.

Based upon the above considerations, six corporations are suggested for immediate implementation. They are the following :

1. Vizianagaram covering, Srikakulam, Vizianagaram, Visakhapatnam and East Godavari districts with 753 vehicles.
2. Vijayawada covering, West Godavari, Krishna, Guntur and Prakasam districts with 1567 vehicles.
3. Chittoor covering Chittoor and Nellore districts with 702 vehicles.
4. Cuddapah covering Cuddapah, Anantpur and Kurnool districts with 872 vehicles.
5. Hyderabad covering Mahaboobnagar, Nalgonda, Rangareddy, Medak and Hyderabad city with 1616 vehicles.
6. Karimnagar covering Warangal, Khammam, Karimnagar, Nizamabad and Adilabad with 1071 vehicles.

Immediate steps may be taken to organise two corporation workshops within a year and form the corporations for Guntur and Rangareddy, the former covering Guntur and Prakasam districts with 719 vehicles, and the latter covering Mahaboobnagar, Nalgonda, Rangareddy and Medak districts with 880 vehicles.

That would take the total number of corporations to 8 within a year after the implementation of splitting the corporation.

The location of Head office and Central Workshops of the proposed corporations, after the split of the existing corporation, would be as follows :

Jurisdiction of the corporation	Location of the Head office & Central Workshop	Number of vehicles held as on 31-3-1982*
Vizianagaram, Srikakulam, Visakhapatnam, and East Godavari	Vizianagaram	753
West Godavari, Krishna, Guntur and Prakasam	Vijayawada	1,567
Chittoor and Nellore	Tirupathi	702
Cuddapah, Anantapur and Kurnool	Cuddapah	872
Hyderabad, Mahaboobnagar, Nalgonda, Rangareddy and Medak	Hyderabad	1,616
Karimnagar, Warangal, Khammam, Nizamabad and Adilabad	Karimnagar	1,071
First Phase : (immediate implementation)		
Second Phase : (To be implemented within twelve months after the split)		
Guntur and Prakasam	Guntur	719
Mahaboobnagar, Nalgonda, Rangareddy and Medak	Hyderabad	880
Third Phase : (As and when the fleet strength of the Parent Corporation, to which these schedules in these districts belong, exceeds about 1200 and these new areas have at least 500 vehicles to start with)		
Visakhapatnam and East Godavari	Kakinada	
Khammam and Warangal	Warangal	

*For details of fleet held by APSRTC and Private Operators, district-wise, see Annexure 2.1.

Ultimately, when the strength of fleet warrants, there shall be one corporation for two districts. In the next five years after the split, two more corporations may be created—one for Visakhapatnam covering Visakhapatnam and East Godavari and another for Warangal covering Warangal and Khammam districts. This would result in having 10 Corporations for the entire State in the next five years. No corporation shall be created without creating the workshop first.

Immediately the financial implications of the implementation of the split proposal is only marginal to the extent of about Rs. 25 lakh to strengthen the Tirupathi Divisional Workshop for elevating it to the level of a corporation workshop. In the next one year, the additional financial commitment would be Rs. 1.5 crore for the workshops of the two corporations to be created for Guntur and Rangareddy at the rate of Rs. 75 lakh for each workshop approximately. It is to be noted that it is only capital and non-recurring expenditure.

The composition of the boards

The composition of Boards of all the corporations, except the city corporation, is recomended as follows :

1. Secretary, Transport, Government of Andhra Pradesh : Chairman
2. The Finance Secretary of the state Government.
3. The General Manager of the concerned corporation who shall also be Vice-Chairman.

4&5. Representatives of Railways.

6, 7&8. General Managers of adjacent corporations.

9. An expert from industry, business and from academic institutions of repute especially Mechanical/Automobile Engineers/Transport Economist.

In the case of city corporation, the composition of the Board is suggested as follows :

1. Secretary, Transport, Govt. of Andhra Pradesh : Chairman
2. Commissioner of Police, Hyderabad City.
3. Finance Secretary, Govt. of Andhra Pradesh.
4. General Manager of the Corporation.

5&6. Representatives of Railways.

7. Special Officer, Municipal Corporation.

8&9. Two Experts—One an Engineer from an academic institution of repute and second a transport economist/industrialist of repute.

Rationale for the suggested composition : The composition of

Boards of non-city corporations is suggested taking into consideration the need for effective co-ordination among contiguous corporations and representation of the participating governments, apart from an element of professional expertise.

In the case of city corporation, the composition of the Board as suggested takes into consideration the need for representation of all those who contribute to the effective functioning of the organisation.

The success of the proposed set up : The success of the proposed organisational set up, that is, split, is inevitably linked up with the composition of the Boards as recommended. Hence, the recommendations on organisational set up should be taken as a package and *implemented in totality*.

The organisational set up

Features of proposed organisational set up
The essential features of proposed oaganisational set up are :

(1) Viable size in terms of fleet and geographical area covered.
(2) Two levels/tiers in the organisation that is, the Head Office and the Depot and elimination of the other levels in between.
(3) Essentially professional Board.
(4) Possibility of career opportunities within and among different corporation in view of (a) the levels of positions, the tiers of the organisation being two, and (b) suggestion to create a Transport Management Cadre for all the corporations put together from and above the rank of class I senior officers.
(5) Suggestion to create the ADM's level with Engineering qualifications.
(6) Considerably reducing the span of control of the Chief Executive.
(7) Rationalising the grouping of the horizontal functions and bringing about harmony and co-ordination among different functions.

Head office

Chart 2.4 shows the organisational set up of these corporations for Head office.

The Chief Executive of the corporation shall be the General Manager, who is responsible for implementing the policy decisions taken by the Board and for operational and financial results of the corporation. He is assisted by Additional General Manager (AGM) who is responsible for the day-to-day functioning in respect of the two crucial functions of the organisation namely, operations and maintenance. He is expected to free the General Manager from day-to-day operational problems so as to make the General Manager's time available for planning and co-ordination between the Government and the enterprise and amongst different corporations.

The Additional General Manager is expected to render effective assistance to the Depots by visiting the same once in a month, finding out their problems and attending to the same through his functional assistants at the Head office that is the Chief Mechanical Engineer (CME) and Chief Traffic Manager (CTM). This may imply the AGM being away from the Head office for about fifteen days in a month and these visits are to be planned in such a way that either the GM or AGM is always available at Head office. This would also facilitate the GM being away from Head office for liaison with Government and other corporations. The effective functioning of the Depots and assistance to them is ensured by the fact that the Depot Managers (DMs)/ADMs directly report to the AGM and with no intermediary in between. The functional assistants of the AGMs who are of a higher level to the DM's do not interfere in the functioning of the Depots and only render assistance on the instructions of AGMs. In the absence of the AGM from the Head office, who is expected to leave the Head office only when GM is available in Head office, the DMs can directly approach the General Manager regarding any problem confronting the Depots. Hence, either the GM or AGM is always available to the DMs for help.

Under the proposed set up, the stores function is brought under the mechanical function so as to ensure smooth functioning of the workshops by ensuring requisite co-ordination between

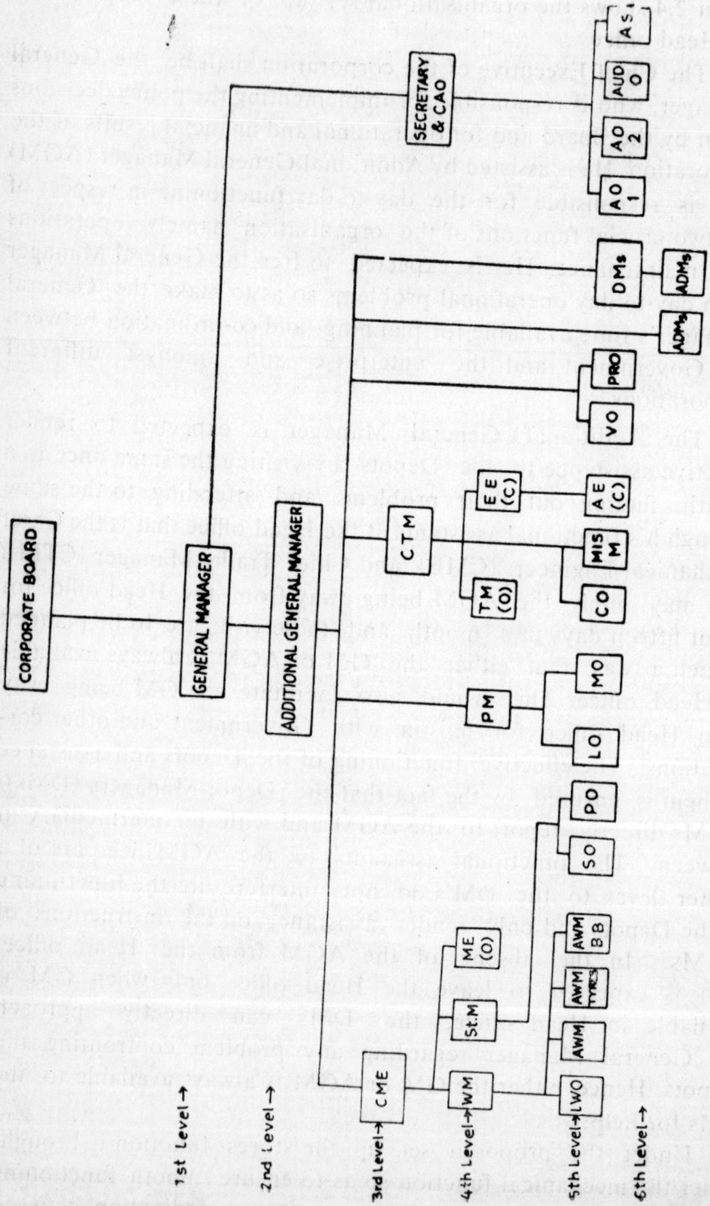

CHART 2.4 : *Organisational structure under split*

LEGEND TO CHART 2.4

CME	=	Chief Mechanical Engineer
CTM	=	Chief Traffic Engineer
Secretary & CAO	=	Secretary and Chief Accounts Officer
WM	=	Works Manager
St. M	=	Stores Manager
ME (O)	=	Mechanical Engineer (Operations)
PM	=	Personnel Manager
TM (O)	=	Traffic Manager (Operations)
EE (C)	=	Executive Engineer (Civil)
LWO	=	Labour Welfare Officer
AWM	=	Assistant Works Manager
AWM BB	=	Assistant Works Manager—Body Building
SO	=	Stores Officer
PO	=	Purchase Officer
LO	=	Legal Officer
MO	=	Medical Officer
CO	=	Checking Officer
MISM	=	Management Information Systems Manager
AE (C)	=	Assistant Engineer (Civil)
VO	=	Vigilance Officer
PRO	=	Public Relations Officer
DM	=	Depot Manager
AO	=	Accounts Officer
AUD. O.	=	Audit Officer
AS	=	Assistant Secretary
ADM	=	Assistant Depot Manager

workshop and stores*.

The depot

It is not proposed to disturb the existing Depot set up in APSRTC in a large way as it has proved its effectiveness. It is only proposed to take care of one or two defects/problems obtaining in the existing set up.

Centralisation of traffic scheduling work

Firstly, it is proposed to take away the traffic scheduling work from the Depot and centralise the work at Head office for the reason of weakness by way of succumbing to the pressures in this regard at the Depot level.

Creation of assistant depot manager's (ADM's) cadre

Secondly, the Depot Manager is presently overburdened, without any senior and capable assistant to assist him. Hence, it is proposed that a new cadre of Assistant Depot Managers (ADMs) in the category of Class II Officers may be created to assist him in the workshop. In future the ADMs will be essentially qualified degree holders in Engineering, but to the extent of 25 per cent of these positions, the diploma holders in Mechanical/Automobile Engineering may be promoted from lower ranks to this position. However, the existing Traffic, Accounts, and Personnel staff would continue to be eligible for promotion to ADM and DM's positions based upon competence. The ADM shall be trained for a period of two years in all the important branches of the Corporation namely, operations, maintenance, personnel, accounts and stores. After the training, the ADMs shall be placed in charge of Depot Workshop for a minimum period of two years.

Afterwards, they may be posted as ADMs to assist the DMs in the case of Depots with 60 or more vehicles and in the case of Depots with less than 60 vehicles they shall be managed by ADMs only.

Cadre of mechanical officers

Further, it is suggested that a separate cadre of Mechanical

* For other details of Head office set up, see Annexure 2.2
For the functions and power of officers, see Annexure 2.3

Officers be developed within each of the organisations with avenues of promotion upto the level of Chief Mechanical Engineer. It is also suggested that, in future, the mechanical and operational positions in the corporation shall be manned by qualified engineers at all levels. The non-technical officers already recruited for traffic/operational positions may be considered for promotions upto the level of Chief Traffic Managers and these officers shall be given first preference for these positions as long as they are available and competent. The positions on personnel side shall be open ordinarily for generalists only.

Workshop set up

Two tier set up: *Central workshop*: A two-tier workshop structure is suggested for these corporations—one at the Central level and the other at the Depot level. The Central workshop is to undertake body building where necessary (not all corporations for the reasons mentioned earlier) and engine and unit overhauls, including F.I.P. Incidentally, the discontinuance of complete overhaul of body is recommended for the reasons discussed in detail under "Losses". The staff rendered surplus, to the extent, may be deployed in body building as the skills required are broadly similar, even though a little more training is required for new body building. They would be required to supply float units to the Depots as per the norms laid down by the organisation. This would ensure avoidance of loss of vehicle time, by eliminating the haulage of vehicle from Depot to Central workshop and back, which would in turn maximise the vehicular utilisation. For example, in the case of Tamil Nadu, the fleet utilisation in different corporations is as high as 92 to 93 per cent because of this reason.

Depot workshop: The Depot workshop would undertake, apart from Fitness Certificate work, routine servicing and maintenance of buses and repairs to and rectify breakdown of vehicles. The Depot is also concerned with unit replacements.

The Head office shall take all decisions regarding procurement and purchase of stores in respect of all standardised items and ensure prompt supply of the same to Central workshop and the Depots.

Some consequential arrangements

Some managerial positions—their equivalent positions in the new set up

Consequent upon the implementation of the suggested split, the present Regional Manager's position would be equated to the Additional General Manager. This does not mean that they can be automatically posted as AGMs in view of the nature and responsibilities envisaged for the position in the proposed set up. The present RMs and other HODs will have to go through a strict screening process to be eligible for posting as AGMs. Wherever they are either found not suitable or where they are unwilling or where they are rendered surplus for being posted as AGMs they may be posted as HODs, that is, CME or CTM, protecting their scale and emoluments. So is the case with staff working in accounts, civil and industrial engineering departments. Similarly, the position of AGM in the present set up may be equated to GM. But, once again, this does not mean automatic eligibility to be posted as GM of small independent corporation, in view of the nature of responsibilities of an independent Chief Executive, unless otherwise selected as GM under the proposed set up. He is eligible for posting as AGM in the new set up with protection of scale and emoluments.

In the proposed split, a new level of intermediary position between the present senior scale officers and the present Heads of the Departments position is proposed to be created. These are the functional heads under the new set up with the designations of CME, CTM and CAO to which the present senior scale officers are eligible for promotion. It is stated earlier that another officer level—Class II (ADM) is suggested for creation between the senior supervisor and Class I junior scale officer. Incidently, for any promotion from one position to another position in the organisation, requirement of 5 years service at the lower level is suggested.

Seniority levels

Maintenance good of industrial relations in the organisation is a sine qua non of better performance. This is more so in a labour-intensive organisation like APSRTC. The APSRTC management has not been oblivious of this fact. For this reason alone, while effecting changes in the organisation structure in the past, the management did not disturb the seniority levels of workers lest it should stir up the hornet's nest. The depot set up introduced in 1965 did not bring about any changes in the seniority levels of workers or supervisors. However, in 1978, creation of regions necessitated the management to re-orient the seniority levels. Considering the sensitivity of the issue involved, decision was taken to retain the divisional seniority of the workers, namely, drivers, conductors, mechanics, cleaners and so on. In the case of supervisors, who were placed one level and more below the first line supervisor, the seniority level was changed from 'State' to 'Region'. But, the seniority levels could not be given effect to as envisaged, on account of stiff opposition from the Trade Unions. The problem eluded solution till 1981, when the management took a final decision to re-fix the seniority of supervisors who were placed three levels and more below the first line supervisor at the 'Region' level. It is implied that the seniority of officers and the other senior supervisors was fixed at the 'State' level.

In the event of splitting up of the corporation and formation of multiple corporations, the seniority levels can be refixed in the following manner :

1. The seniority level of those Class III and IV employees whose seniority is now maintained at the 'Division' level, would now be shifted to the 'District' level.

2. (a) The seniority of all the other Class III employees (Supervisors) has to be fixed at the 'Corporation' level, to which they belong.

(b) The Class II officers now proposed (Asst. Depot Managers) may be given seniority at the 'Corporation' level, as they are proposed to be recruited and appointed at the 'Corporation' level. On promotion as Depot Managers also, they have their seniority fixed at the "Corporation" level.

(c) All the Class I Junior and Senior Scale Officers of Accounts, Personnel and Stores may have the 'Corporation' level seniority.

3. All the Class I Junior Scale Officers of the Traffic and Mechanical Wings may have the 'Corporation' level seniority.

4. The seniority of Class I Senior Scale and Special Scale

Officers of Traffic and Mechanical Departments may be fixed at the 'State' level. For this purpose, it is proposed to have a common "Transport Management Cadre". Promotions, transfers and so on, of officers of this cadre may be regulated by the Chairman's cell proposed to be constituted in the Secretariat.

Recruitment, promotion, postings and transfers of officers belonging to transport management cadre

As mentioned earlier, the ADMs are to be recruited by the concerned corporations and promotions to the levels of DMs may be done by the concerned corporations. In the initial recruitment and appointment of ADMs it shall be clearly stated that they would be shifted to state level Transport Management Cadre once they have to be promoted beyond the level of Depot Manager. Promotions beyond this level are to be done by the Chairman's cell by taking into consideration the requirements of all the corporations. Candidates from all the corporations would be eligible for consideration. On selection of candidates, each corporation will be given required numbers of officers, who will be given appointment orders and postings by the concerned corporation. While allocating the candidates on promotion to different corporations, the preference of the candidates may be taken into consideration to the extent possible. Once allotted to a corporation, they shall continue to be in that corporation until next promotion when the employee can give option, which will be taken into consideration in allocation, to the extent possible. Irrespective of the preference, the GMs may be posted from one corporation to another.

Co-ordination among different corporations and between the corporation and the government—Chairman's cell

In a way co-ordination among different corporations and between the corporations and the concerned department in the Government is built into the composition of the Boards of these corporations, as the Secretary, Transport, Govt. of Andhra Pradesh is the Chairman of all the corporations. Further, there are interlocutory boards which ensure co-ordination among different enterprises. However, there is no central office to co-ordinate, monitor, and review the functioning of the enterprises. Hence, a small cell—Chairman's cell—is suggested in the secretariat located in the office of Secretary, Transport, with skeleton staff of 5 to 6 people. This would also look after the work pertaining to Transport Management Cadre suggested earlier. Further, a common forum for all the organisations, by way of periodical meetings of the GMs of all the Corporations is also suggested to discuss common problems of interest, to exchange experiences and to benefit from each other's experience.

The financial implications of split

The direct financial implications of the proposed split arise broadly on two counts. Firstly, because of the need for creating additional Central workshop facilities ; and secondly, for reasons of changes in the manpower requirements. It is not proposed to analyse the indirect financial benefits, which may accrue because of the better functioning of the organisation. It is also not proposed to attempt at making a detailed exercise of the savings that may be realised because of manpower rendered surplus at lower levels, especially in Class III and Class IV, in view of the fact that there would not be any Head office of the type that is obtaining new in the unitary organisation, which has presently got about 1000 employees in those categories. Further, a detailed exercise is also not done in regard to the personnel that would be rendered surplus at the present regional workshops or in the proposed Central workshops consequent upon doing away with the body overhaul system.

An attempt is made only to highlight the additional expenditure incurred on the creation of Central workshops and the managerial manpower position because of split. The former has already been analysed. The immediate financial implications of split for creating additional Central workshop facilities is Rs. 25 lakh ; and in the next one year Rs. 1.5 crore, as mentioned earlier. It has already been noted that this is a non-recurring expenditure.

The implications of split in terms of manpower is only a saving in recurring expenditure because of the managerial manpower rendered surplus. Table 2.5 shows that consequent upon the split a net of 46 officers of various categories would be rendered surplus in the first phase. The financial saving because

TABLE 2.5 A : **Implications of split in terms of managerial manpower positions (I Phase)**

Category	Existing	Proposed	Difference: Additional staff required	Difference: Staff rendered surplus	Additional expenditure (+) or saving (—) amount per month
	No.	No.	No.	No.	Rs.
VC and GM	1	—	—	—1	— 4,000
GMs	1 (AGM)	6	+5	—	+ 18,725
Addl. GMs	17 (HODs)	6	—	—11	— 37,059
HODs (Intermediary)	—	18	+18	—	+ 57,600
Sr. Scale	88	36	—	−52	—1,66,400
Jr. Scale (others)	199	98	—	—101	—2,54,217
Jr. Scale (DMs)	104	87	—	—17	— 47,889
Class II (ADMs)	—	112	+112	—	+2,12,576
		Total	+135	—181	+2,88,901
					—5,09,565
			Net saving		—2,20,664

TABLE 2.5 B : **Implications of split in terms of managerial manpower positions (II Phase)**

Category	Existing	Proposed	Difference: Additional staff required	Difference: Staff rendered surplus	Additional expenditure (+) or saving (—) amount per month
	No.	No.	No.	No.	Rs.
VC and GM	1	—	—	—1	— 4,000
GMs	1 (AGM)	8	+7		+ 26,215
Addl. GMs	17 (HODs)	8		−9	— 30,321
HODs (Intermediary)	—	24	+24		+ 76,800
Sr. scale	88	48		—40	—1,28,000
Jr. scale (others)	199	130		—69	—1,73,673
Jr. scale (DMs)	104	87		—17	— 47,889
Class II (ADMs)	—	112	+112		+2,12,576
		Total	+143	—136	+3,15,591
					+3,83,883
			Net saving		— 68,292

TABLE 2.5 C : **Implications of split in terms of managerial manpower positions (III Phase)**

Category	Existing	Proposed	Difference: Additional staff required	Difference: Staff rendered surplus	Difference: Additional expenditure (+) or saving (—) Amount per month
	No.	No.	No.	No.	Rs.
VC and GM	1	—	—	—1	— 4,000
GMs	1 (AGM)	10	+9		+ 33,705
Addl. GMs	17 (HODs)	10		−7	− 23,583
HODs (Intermediary)	—	30	+30		+ 96,000
Sr. scale	88	60		—28	— 89,600
Jr. scale (others)	199	162		—37	— 93,129
Jr. scale (DMs)	104	87		—17	— 47,889
Class II (ADMs)	—	112	+112		+2,12,576
					+3,42,281
Total			+151	—90	—2,58,201
			Additional exp.		+ 84,080

of this surplus would be Rs. 2.21 lakh per month. The savings in the second phase of the creation of two more corporations would get reduced to Rs. 0.68 lakh per month. In the third phase, when two more corporations are created, this would result in a marginal increase in expenditure on managerial staff by Rs. 0.84 lakh per month. It is relevant to note, once again, that this does not take into consideration Class III and Class IV personnel, to the extent of about 1000, rendered surplus at the present Head office level.

If for some practical reasons the formation of small independent corporations by splitting the existing corporation is not possible, the following alternative set up is suggested. However, the distinct superiority and advantages of split and formation of small independent corporations are unquestionably clear.

THE SUGGESTED ALTERNATIVE SET UP

The proposed alternative organisational set up also implies a radical change, while keeping the organisation a unitary one in a strictly formal and legal sense, in view of the fact that the Head office shall be concerned only with the following policy matters and the regional unit will be almost an autonomous unit in so far as sub-policy and day-to-day operational matters are concerned :

(1) Nationalisation and inter-state agreements
(2) Investment decisions—choice of chassis
(3) Financing decisions
(4) Pricing decisions
(5) Replacement policy
(6) Depreciation policy
(7) Wage policy excluding bonus and incentives
(8) Recruitment and promotional policies of the rank of Class II officers and above
(9) Policy matters regarding Government and Legislation.

The scope of these policy matters is spelt out and given in Annexure 2.4.

The Board and its composition

The Board of the corporation is the top policy making body of the organisation concerning the policy matters listed above. Broadly, it shall be concerned with planning, monitoring and advising on policy matters. It shall be headed by a Chairman. The Secretary, Transport, Government of Andhra Pradesh shall be the ex-officio chairman of the Board. The Board shall consist of 11 members including the Chairman, the composition of which is as follows :

1. Chairman
2. Vice-Chairman and Chief General Manager
3. Finance Secretary

4 & 5. Representatives from Railways

6—10. General Managers of Regions (50% of the General Managers of the Regions shall be on the Board by rotation once in two years subject to a minimum of 5 General Managers being represented on the Board at any point of time).

11. Professional expert drawn amongst from the following : Transport Economist of repute/Management expert of repute/Industrialist of repute.

It could be seen from the composition of the Board that it is essentially a professional board with expertise drawn mainly from within and to the extent of one from outside.

The Secretary, Transport, Govt. of Andhra Pradesh, is suggested as ex-officio chairman for the reason that he can provide effective co-ordination between the corporation and the Government. This would also facilitate proper understanding and appreciation of the problems of the corporation by the Regulatory wing of the Government concerning Passenger road transport.

The Finance Secretary, and the Representatives of Railways represent the respective financial interests of the participating Governments.

The General Managers are suggested for inclusion in the Board, so that the Board has correct appreciation of the practical implications of the policy decisions taken by it and there is an element of practicability built into the policy decisions taken by the Board.

Similarly, representation of a professional expert is suggested so as to infuse dispassion and freshness of approach to the various policy decisions taken by the Board instead of the policy decisions being taken only by the inside people conditioned by the environment within the organisation.

The representation of political interest is not suggested for the reasons mentioned earlier.

Head office structure

An idea of the organisation structure at the Head office level can be had from Chart 2.5. It can be seen from the chart that the Chairman, Corporation Board, heads the organisation and the chief executive of the organisation is Vice-Chairman and Chief General Manager who is assisted by four advisers— (1) Adviser (Mechanical), (2) Adviser (Operations), (3) Adviser (Industrial Relations & Personnel), and (4) the Financial Adviser.

The regional level

The Regional set up that is proposed would be radically different from the existing one. The region under the existing set up, does not have any stature to assert itself in the matter of its functioning nor is it delegated with adequate powers. Under the proposed set up, the region acquires a stature which is necessary for its effective functioning and would be in a position to confidently deal with the Head office because of composition of the Regional Management Board (RMB). The Regional Management Board consists of the Viec-Chairman and the Chief General Manager, who shall be its Chairman, the General Manager of the region concerned, four General Managers of contiguous regions, two of whom shall be the members of the corporation board, and three advisers from Head office namely, Adviser (Mechanical), Adviser (Operations) and the Financial Adviser. Thus a minimum of three members of the RMB will be members of the corporation board providing an effective link and interaction between policy and practice and also providing the region with adequate stature, thus enhancing the region's status. The fact that three advisers from Head office are represented on the Regional Board would also lend realism to the advice given to the corporation board and the

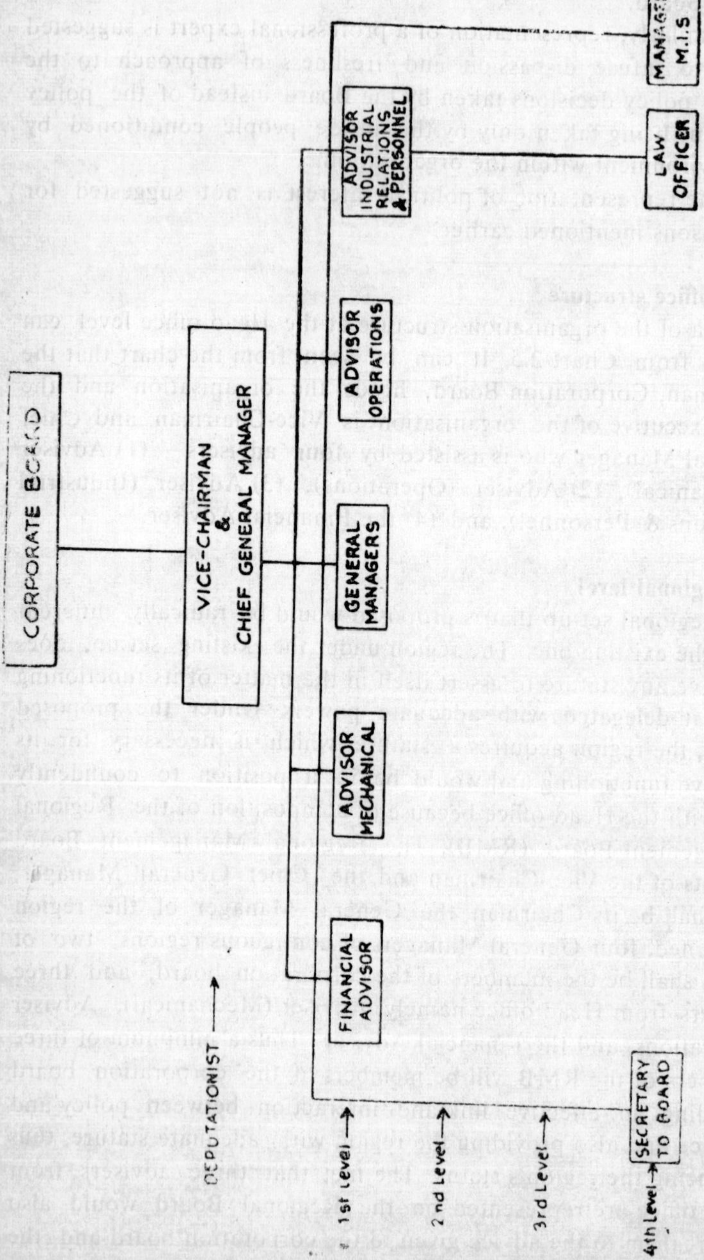

CHART 2.5 : *Head office set up under alternative regional set up*

policy decision taken by the same. Thus there is the process of policy-makers being involved in operational decisions and the operational executives being involved in policy decisions.

Functions of the region-level

A region is broadly responsible for implementation of the policy decisions taken by the Head office/the corporation board. It is the decision making level in all other respects namely, sub-policy decisions, such as bonus policy, incentive policy, preparation of budgets, decisions regarding investments within the budgets, finalisation of draft scheme proposals, fixation of targets of performance and review of performance, creation of posts in Class III and IV categories within the framework of the norms laid down by Head office, laying down norms for stores, workshops, premature scrap, laying down norms for payment of compensation to accident victims and industrial relations. Finally, the region is responsible for costs as well as profits and shall ultimately be judged by the same in relation to the targets set by the RMB and as approved by the Corporation Board. There shall be separate accounts for each of the regions.

A region shall ordinarily have not more than 1000 vehicles on optimal considerations, so that the Central workshop of the region, which is viable in size would be able to take care of the requirements of the fleet of the region. The region will ordinarily be co-terminus with two revenue districts, which may have about 1000 vehicles on full nationalisation. However, in the short-run, where there is partial nationalisation, it may cover more than two districts. A region may also have between 12 and 15 Depots with 40 to 80 vehicles each.

Based on the above criteria, to start with, six regions are suggested for creation, two more within one year after the creation of six regions and two more within five years after the decision to adopt this set up is taken. The criteria for creation of regions here are based on the same criteria as followed for the creation of corporations under split pattern and consequently, the number of regions under this pattern, is the same as under the pattern of split.

The region shall have power to buy all its requirements of stores as per the approved budgets and as per the rate contracts and proprietory items approved by the Head office which shall be conveyed to the region once in a year and in other cases on its own.

The traffic schedules may be taken away from the Depots and centralised at the Regional office so that there is proper planning and co-ordination of the schedules among the different Depots under the Region. The inter-regional co-ordination of the schedules among the contiguous regions is ensured by placing such inter-regional routes for approval by RMB where GMs of contiguous regions are also represented. The long distance routes, traversing beyond the contiguous regions. shall be placed before the meetings of the General Managers of all the Regions, which may be held once in a quarter, where problems of common interest are also discussed and settled. Incidentally, it is not proposed to disturb the existing organisational set up at Depot level except for taking away traffic scheduling and adding Additional Depot Manager.

Each Region may have the following Committees :

Regional selection committee :
To recruit Class III and IV staff, the Committee shall consist of the Chief Traffic Manager, as its Chairman, and Chief Mechanical Engineer and Chief Accounts Officer as its members. The Personnel Manager shall be the member convener. The recruitment and promotion of all other categories of the staff will be done by the Head office. The General Managers of the Regions, who are also the members of the Corporation Board shall also be the members of the Selection Committee for recruitment and promotions to the officers posts.

Regional purchase committee :
The General Manager shall be its Chairman with CME and CAO as its members. The Regional Purchase Committee shall be empowered to make all purchases in accordance with the budgets and as per the rate contracts and proprietory items approved by the headquarters.

Finance & works committee :
It will consist of General Manager as Chairman and CAO, CTM

and Executive Engineer (Civil) as members to approve budget allotments for construction, additions and modifications of workshops, depots, bus-stations, way-side shelters, staff-quarters, and so on.

Workshops

A region may have only two levels of workshops—one at the Depot level and the other at Regional level. The Regional workshop is to be concerned with engine and other unit overhauls, major body repairs and tyre retreading shop. In view of the surplus body building capacity in the industry in Public Sector, the Organisation as a whole may proceed cautiously in the matter of creating additional capacities in body building and the future growth of the body building unit/units within the APSRTC shall be confined only to the extent of the personnel rendered surplus by discontinuance of complete overhaul of bus body and the bus body building units will be located or expanded wherever complete overhaul of body is discontinued. In other words, the new regions will not have body building units and they shall have their requirements from other Regions on a transfer pricing basis. Wherever there is a need for going outside for body building, the external agency/agencies and the rates will be decided by the Head office and the Regions may contact them for their needs.

The Depot workshop is to take care of regular preventive maintenance and general and heavy repairs including F.C. work. The Regional workshops shall have to ensure that the Depots have float units including engines as per the norms laid down by the Head office.

Chart 2.6 gives an idea of the organisational structure of the Region. Under this set up, it is proposed to have an Additional General Manager (AGM) under the General Manager (GM), who would be directly taking the responsibility for the Depots and for assistance to the Depots, thereby eliminating intermediaries between the decision-maker at the Regional level in operational matters and the base of operations which requires support and prompt and timely decisions. His effectiveness is ensured because he is given authority commensurate with responsibility. As the two functional executives, who are expected to render support to

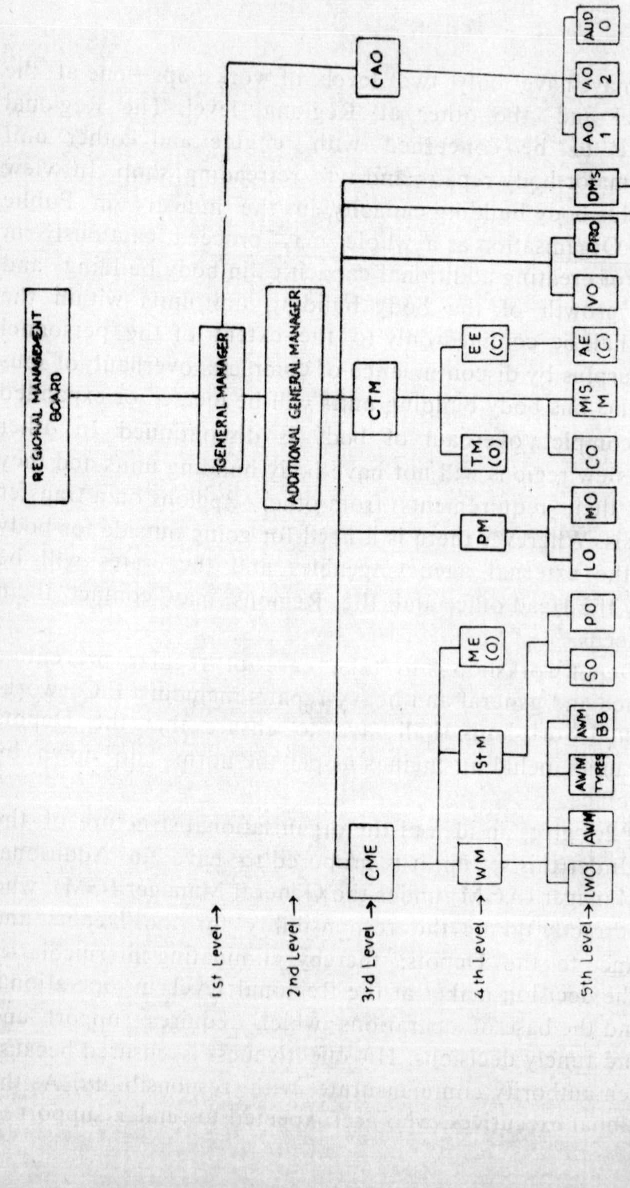

CHART 2.6 : *Regional office set up under the alternative set up*

LEGEND TO CHART 2.6

CME	=	Chief Mechanical Engineer
CTM	=	Chief Traffic Engineer
Secretary & CAO	=	Secretary and Chief Accounts Officer
WM	=	Works Manager
St. M.	=	Stores Manager
ME (O)	=	Mechanical Engineer (Operations)
PM	=	Personnel Manager
TM (O)	=	Traffic Manager (Operations)
EE (C)	=	Executive Engineer (Civil)
LWO	=	Labour Welfare Officer
AWM	=	Assistant Works Manager
AWM BB	=	Assistant Works Manager—Body Building
SO	=	Stores Officer
PO	=	Purchase Officer
LO	=	Legal Officer
MO	=	Medical Officer
CO	=	Checking Officer
MISM	=	Management Information Systems Manager
AE (C)	=	Assistant Engineer (Civil)
VO	=	Vigilance Officer
PRO	=	Public Relations Officer
DM	=	Depot Manager
AO	=	Accounts Officer
AUD. O.	=	Audit Officer
ADM	=	Assistant Depot Manager

the Depot namely CTM & CME, happen to be directly reporting to AGM, proper co-ordination of the concerned functions is automatically ensured and effective assistance is assured to the Depots. Further the AGM is required to visit all the Depots in his jurisdiction, at least, once in a month to acquaint himself with the problems of Depots, and appraise their needs, in order to render support by giving necessary instructions to his functional assistants at the Regional office. Apparently, it looks as though the AGM has got too big a span of control under him. But, looked at from the nature of the work involved, it is not a burdensome span as the nature of transactions is routine at the operational level and he is adequately supported by functional heads under him at the Regional office. Further, he is not concerned with any policy matters and general administration work. The role assigned to the AGM has been tried and proved a success in Tamil Nadu. Incidentally, no other officer, except the General Manager, CME and CTM shall inspect the Depots, the latter two only under advice from the AGM. The availability of AGM to the Depot Managers for looking into all their problems, would free the General Manager from the day-to-day routine work and he will have adequate time available for broader issues, and to deal with Head office and general administration.

The CME at the Regional office will be responsible for the production of the workshop, stores, and mechanical engineering support to the Depots and he is assisted in this regard by Works Manager, Stores Manager and Mechanical Engineer (Operations). The Works Manager, in his turn, is assisted by Labour Welfare Officer and two Assistant Works Managers and the Stores Manager is to be assisted by the Stores Officer and Purchase Officer.

The CTM is to be assisted by Traffic Manager (Operations), who would be in charge of traffic schedules, operational efficiency and so on and an Executive Engineer, who in turn, is assisted by Assistant Engineer, for civil works. The CTM is also to be assisted by a Checking Officer and a Management Information Systems Manager.

Apart from AGM, the CAO also directly reports to the GM. The CAO is to be assisted by two Accounts Officers and one

Audit Officer.

The AGM, in addition to being assisted by CME and CTM, is also assisted by a Personnel Manager to whom the Medical Officer reports. The functions and duties of these different officers and their powers are given in Annexure 2.5.

The suggested organisational structure will provide adequate career opportunities for managerial personnel within the organisation. Under the proposed set up a person recruited as Class II Officer, that is, Assistant Depot Manager (ADM) can look to five promotions within the organisation excluding the Chief General Manager's post, as against practically two levels of promotions possible in the present set up and at the same time reducing the number of tiers in the organisational structure. Creation of Class II Officers, namely, ADMs—an intermediary level between the Class I Junior scale and Class III senior Supervisors (upper subordinates) will increase the avenues of promotion to the Class III employees.

The present Regional Managers may be equated to Additional General Managers. The General Manager and Advisers at the Head office, except for the Financial Adviser, are interchangeable positions. The advisers, shall be men of proven capability drawn from within the organisation, except the Financial Adviser who shall be a nominee of the Government. The General Managers may be drawn either on deputation from civil service, and Engineers from Public Works and Road Transport Department or men of proven ability, honesty and integrity from within the organisation. The AGMs and the General Managers and Advisers selected from within the organisations shall be Engineers by qualification, in course of time. The present Class I Junior Officers and Class I Senior Officers will continue to be in the same position. Incidentally, the designation of Divisional Manager would not be found in the new set up. The persent non-mechanical DVMs will be posted as TM (Operations) and DVMs mechanical would be WMs, SMs and Mechanical Engineering (Operations). In course of time, even the TM (Operations) will be Mechanical Engineer on implementation of the new recruitment policy stated earlier.

Another tier is introduced in the proposed set up in between the present Class I Senior (Divisional Manager) and Class I

Special Grade (e.g., Heads of Departments and Present Regional Managers) posts.

Reorganisation and seniority levels

The existing seniority level of employees coming under Class IV and Class III (other than supervisors), at the level of Division, may be confined to the district. Class III Junior and Senior employees (Supervisors) would have Regional seniority. Consequently, Class III Senior (Traffic Inspector Grade II and above) employees may be given option of Region while allocating them to Region under the new seniority levels. All other officers would be that of state level seniority. However, once posted to Region, based upon option, the officers upto the level of Additional General Manager shall not be transferred to another Region except when he is promoted and posted to a Region based upon his option. They can be transferred within the Region by the Regional Manager to the extent transfers are possible within the Region.

The financial implications of the alternative regional set up

The financial implications of the alternative Regional set up are marginally different from those of split, to the extent of having a corporation Head office, with about 50 personnel, and a few positions less at the Regional level. In the first phase, the saving on managerial manpower would come to Rs. 2.22 lakh per month, which would come down to Rs. 0.80 lakh per month in the second phase, which would ultimately result in additional expenditure of Rs. 0.62 lakh per month (vide Table 2.6), apart from the savings on Class III and Class IV staff to the extent of about 1000 employees as mentioned under split.

1. Implementation of the proposed set up may result in a number of officers now on rolls being rendered surplus in some departments and short in others. This may be avoided by providing inter-departmental transfers to the extent possible. On this premise alone, the financial implications as given in Tables 2.5 and 2.6 have been worked out.

2. Certain departments now existing in the organisation do not find place in the new set up. For example Medical and Industrial Engineering.

TABLE 2.6A : **Implications of alternative regional set up in terms of managerial manpower position (I Phase)**

Category	Existing	Proposed	Difference		Additional expenditure (+) or saving (–) Amount
			Additional staff required	Staff rendered surplus	
	No.	No.	No.	No.	Rs.
VC and GM	1	1	—	—	—
Advisors/GMs	1 (AGM)	6+4=10	+9	—	+33,705
Addle GMs	17 (HODs)	6 (AGMs)	—	–11	–37,059
HODs (Intermediary)	—	18	+18	—	+57,600
Sr. scale	88	39	—	–49	–1,56,800
Jr. scale (Others)	199	86	—	–113	–2,84.421
Jr. scale (DMs)	104	87	—	–17	–47,889
Class II (ADMs)	—	112	+112		+2,12,576
Total			+139	–190	+3,03,881
					–5,26,169
			Net Saving		–2,22,288

TABLE 2.6B : **Implications of alternative regional set up in terms of managerial manpower positions (II Phase)**

Category	Existing	Proposed	Difference: Additional staff required	Difference: Staff rendered surplus	Difference: Additional expenditure (+) or saving (—) Amount
	No.	No.	No.	No.	Rs.
VC and GM	1	1	—	—	—
Advisors/GMs	1 (AGM)	8+4=12	+11	—	+41,195
Addl. GMs	17 (HODs)	8 (AGMs)		–9	–30,321
HODs (Intermediary)	—	24	+24	—	+76,800
Sr. scale	88	51		–37	–1,18,400
Jr. scale (Others)	199	114		–85	–2,13,945
Jr. scale (DMs)	104	87		–17	–47,889
Class II (ADMs)	—	112	+112	—	+2,12,576
Total			+147	–148	+3,30,571 –4,10,555
			Net saving		–79,984

TABLE 2.6C : **Implications of alternative regional set up in terms of managerial manpower positions (III Phase)**

Category	Existing	Proposed	Difference: Additional staff required	Difference: Staff rendered surplus	Difference: Additional expenditure (+) or saving (—) Amount
	No.	No	No.	No.	Rs.
VC and GM	1	1	—	—	—
Advisors/GMs	1 (AGM)	10+4=14	+13	—	+48,685
Addl. GMs	17 (HODs)	10 (AGMs)	—	−7	−23,583
HODs (Intermediary)	—	30	+30	—	+96,000
Sr. scale	88	63	—	−25	−80,000
Jr. scale (Others)	199	142	—	−57	−1,43,469
Jr. scale (DMs)	104	87	—	−17	−47,889
Class II (ADMs)	—	112	+112		+2,12,576
Totai			+155	−106	+3,57,261
					−2,94,941
			Net additional expenditure		+62,320

Medical facilities provided by the organisation for the benefit of its employees form part of the welfare programme drawn up. Therefore, the subject falls outside the ambit of the issue involved—streamlining of the organisation structure.

The functions of Industrial Engineering Unit can be taken care of by the Mechanical Engineer (O) provided for each corporation/Region. For this purpose, the officers concerned may be given intensive training in Industrial Engineering.

REFERENCES

1. Reorganisation proposals, 1977, APSRTC, p. 17.

2&3 Ibid., p. 18.

4. Op. cit, p. 18

5. ,, ,, p. 19

6. ,, ,, p. 22

7. ,, ,, p. 19

8. ,, ,, p. 24

9, Op. cit, p. 22

10. Op. cit, p. 22

11. Circular No. P1/442(13)/77-PD dated 15th January 1978 of APSRTC.

12. Reorganisation proposals, APSRTC, p. 19.

13. PTC Ltd., Madras, Some Salient Features, 1973, p. 63.

3

CAPITAL STRUCTURE AND FINANCIAL POLICIES, PERSONNEL POLICIES AND PRACTICES AND MANAGEMENT INFORMATION SYSTEMS

CAPITAL STRUCTURE

CAPITAL structure refers to the composition of owner's funds and long-term loans. The relation between the two is expected to determine the financial stability in terms of risk. The presence of debt is expected to provide relatively low cost funds, and thus help in lowering the cost of capital and consequently lead to a higher return on the owner's funds, in a situation where the capital structure consists of equity and debt. Thus, the justification for the presence of debt exists because of its ability to help in increasing the returns for the organisation.

APSRTC, being a Public Sector Public Utility with state-wide responsibilities, is expected to be provided with large sums of long-term low cost funds, on a timely basis, without which it would be difficult for the organisation to function efficiently and fulfil the objectives effectively.

The RTC Act provides for two alternative means of raising capital. Under Sec. 23 (1) of the Act, the state and central Governments can provide interest bearing capital contributions. An alternative way of providing capital is provided for in sub Sec. (2) of the Section, according to which the corporation may raise capital by issue of shares. The main point of distinction between the two types of raising capital lies in the method of compensating the providers of the capital. In the first case, where the capital contributions are treated as interest bearing, the organisation will be obliged to make the payment of interest irrespective of the presence of profits and thus it becomes a cost item like any other cost. However, in the second case where capital is raised by way of shares, the question of making payment arises only in the presence of adequate profits, and further it would be the prerogative of the directors to recommend a rate of dividend which they deem fit. Thus, in the former case, the owners will be assured of a fixed rate of return irrespective of the presence of profits, while in the latter case, the return would be subject to the availability of profits and further the amount would be uncertain, as it can vary depending upon the size of profits. Thus, it can be said that the Government chose the former, the more sure and safe way of getting a fixed return, the payment of which is obligatory on the part of the corporation. The impact of this arrangement on the corporation, particularly when it is facing severe losses and cash losses, would be to upset its entire working.

Capital contributions of the APSRTC are made by the AP state Govt. and the central Government (Represented by the Ministry of Railways). These capital contributions require a payment of fixed rate of interest, which will be deemed to be a part of the expenditure of the corporation, [Sec. 28(1) of the RTC Act], the effect of which will be the net profit will be arrived at after providing for interest on capital contributions. Further, the obligation to pay only a fixed interest on capital excludes, by implication, the participating Governments from having any further interest in the surpluses, which is evident from the provisions of Sec. 30 where a specific method regarding the method of disposal of net profits is indicated. Thus, it can be said that the capital contributions have certain special properties that distinguish them from equity funds, in the conventional sense of the term. Generally speaking capital structure of an organisation is supposed to simultaneously help in maintaining/minimising the risk within the acceptable limits and also in maximising the return on owners funds. As stated above, the particular features of capital contributions create a different scenario and conventional theory is inapplicable to the capital structure of this organisation.

The ability of long-term debt to lower the cost of capital is basically dependent on (1) the lower rate of interest compared to the relatively higher cost of equity funds, and (2) the tax deductability nature of even this lower rate of interest. But in view of the unique features of the corporation's capital contributions—a fixed, relatively speaking, low rate of interest, which is also treated as a cost item and hence tax deductable—debt becomes costlier and consequently the presence of debt can only increase the overall cost of funds and not decrease/minimise it. Thus, the coventional logic regarding the financial leverage is not applicable in the context of APSRTC. For this corporation, debt is decidedly disadvantageous. This would remain so, which ever way the income-tax dispute is settled. The contention of the corporation that its profits are not taxable was upheld by the State High Court. The Income-tax Department has gone on appeal and the case is still pending with the Supreme Court. Meanwhile, the corporation is not paying any income-tax and is only regularly submitting the necessary returns. Irrespective of the outcome of the pending case, debt is decidely costly and cannot be considered as conducive to lower the cost of capital and thus maximise the return on investment, if not for the owners, at least for the corporation.

During the period 1973-74 to 1981-82, the total capital contributions (including receipts on capital account) increased by 6.12 times as against 10.43 times increase in respect of long-term borrowings (vide Table 1.40). Consequently, the long-term borrowings as a percentage of total capital contributions increased from 18.13 in 1973-74 to 29.10 in 1981-82. As already stated, this increase in long-term debt has resulted in higher costs of financing. While the interest on capital contributions increased by 4.71 times during the period, the interest on long-term borrowings increased by 20.68 times. It is evident that the long-term borrowings are only 29 per cent of the total capital contributions but the interest thereon amounts to 86.05 per cent of the interest on capital contributions for the year 1981-82.

The more than proportionate increase in long-term borrowings can be stated to have made the capital structure more unfavourable, particularly at a time when the corporation was losing heavily. The question that arises now is why was the corporation forced to accept high cost long-term borrowings ?

If the relatively cheap capital contributions were readily available, then there was actually no need to finance the activities with high cost external borrowings. Part of the long-term loans are due to specific project assistance received under certain schemes. Excepting such scheme assistance, it can be presumed that left to itself the corporation would not have resorted to high cost borrowings, in view of the adverse effect on the cost of capital and consequently on the overall profitability of the corporation.

Cost of capital

The rate of interest on long-term loans ranges between 7½ per cent and 16.3 per cent as on 31 March, 1982. The weighted average cost of long-term loans based on the total interest paid on long-term loans during the year 1981-82 (as per provisional accounts) comes to 14.57 per cent. The capital contributions currently carry 8 per cent rate even though the corporation has not been providing at this rate. The cost of capital on pre-tax basis has been calculated and presented in Table 3.1. The weighted cost of capital has been calculated, based on the weights in the capital structure of the two items namely capital contributions and long-term loans. The cost of capital works out to 9.49 per cent when interest free capital contributions are included and rises slightly to 9.58 per cent when the interest free capital contributions are excluded. Thus, it is evident that the presence of debt has raised the cost of capital instead of reducing it. It is clear that debt is disadvantageous and that the corporation should be provided with adequate funds by the participating Governments so that the cost of funds to the corporation does not go up beyond the 8 per cent which the Governments themselves collect from the corporation.

Capital contributions from participating governments

The enclosed statement furnished by the corporation at the written request of the study team shows that the state Government was almost always forthcoming with whatever capital contributions asked for by the corporation. When enquired, as to why the Corporation did not make a more realistic estimate of its capital requirements and demand the same, particularly in view of the demonstrated attitude of the State Government to give whatever has been asked, the study team was told that the estimation of

TABLE 3.1 : **Cost of capital (pre-tax) as on 31st March, 1982)**

Particulars	Amount (Rs. in lakhs)	Weights in capital structure	Cost of capital: Actual rate	Cost of capital: Weighted rate
I.				
Capital contributions (including interest free contributions)	9,150.70	0.7737	8	6.19
Long-term loans	2,675.88	0.2263	14.57*	3.30
	11,826.58	1.0000		9.49
II.				
Capital contributions (excluding interest free contributions)	8,449,07	0.7595	8	6.08
Long-term loans	2,675.88	0 2405	14.57	3.50
	11,124.95	1.0000		9.58

*Based on long-term loans and total interest paid on long-term loans as per Provisional Accounts for 1981-82.

STATEMENT

(*Rs. in crore*)

Year	Planned capital expenditure	Internal Bnticipated amount	Financing Actual amount realised	Capital contributions asked for as per R.E. from		Capital Contributions committed by*		Capital Contributions Received from	
				State Government	Central Government	State Government	Central Government	State Government	Central Government
1976-77	21.71	8.72	8.84	5.89	2.00			5.26	2.00
1977-78	23.35	9.85	7.28	6.79	2.00			6 79	2.00
1978-79	24.52	12.38	5.51	7.10	2.00			6.90	8.73**
1979-80	29.39	15.11	10.43	8.00	1.28			8.00	1.27
1980-81	55.30	19.84	13.06	10.41	3.60			10.41	3.60
1981-82	50.00	23.51	—	10.35	2.62			10.35	2.62

*"Columns 7 and 8 (of the enclosure) are left blank because the state and central Governments do not give the expected commitment in writing at the time of preparation of the Budget or any time subsequently. As such we are not able to furnish the data in respect of these two columns".

...As per D.O. Letter No. CA/Reogn/DMC/82 dated 14-10-1982, from Sri P. Jeer, Chief Auditor, APSRTC.

**Backlog of previous years is included.

the capital contributions was based more on the past trend in the capital contributions but not so much on the actual requirements. Further, these contributions are not received on some regular basis, like quarterly instalments and there are instances when substantial portions were received just on the last day of the year. Again, there is the problem of the central Government not readily contributing its due share in time. A more important aspect is the directions/suggestion from the state Government to proceed ahead with nationalisation of new areas/routes, extension of city services to new cities, adoption of new schemes like VLTS, by managing with existing resources without readily contributing the additional capital contributions required for such purposes.

If the Governments were so readily forthcoming with whatever the corporation was asking for, there would have been no need to resort to high cost borrowing. It is relevan t to note the statement in the Budget Proposals for 1982-83 which reads as follows :

> Capital contributions by the central Government (Railways) have been constantly falling short of the obligation under the agreed formula in the last few years. This year is likely to be no exception to this trend, as the budget allocations each year have fallen short of the outlays approved by the Planning Commission.[1]

The contradiction is evident and the impact of inadequate and irregular contributions can be clearly seen.

Thus, non-provision of adequate capital on a timely basis must be considered as the cause for the presence of high-cost debt, both long-term and short-term, increasing the cost of interest and adding to losses. It is suggested that the corporation must more realistically estimate its capital requirements, and impress upon the participating Governments the urgent need to contribute the same.

The ratio of capital contributions between the state and central Governments is 2 : 1, implying that the central Government would contribute 50 per cent of the amount contributed by the state Government. It is evident from Table 3.2 that, during the period 1973-74 to 1981-82, in no year the central Govern-

TABLE 3.2 : **Ratio of capital contributions as on 31st March, 1982**

(Rs. lakh)

Year	Capital Contributions from		Ratio
	State Govt.	Central Govt.	
1973-74	959.00	331.53	100 : 34.57
1974-75	1,551.49	340.78	100 : 21.96
1975-76	1,852.50	459.53	100 : 24.81
1976-77	2,378.63	659.53	100 : 27.73
1977-78	3,057.70	859.53	100 : 28.11
1978-79	3,747.70	1,732.50	100 : 46.23
1979-80	4,547.70	1,860.00	100 : 40.90
1980-81	5,588.70	2,220.00	100 : 39.72
1981-82	6,623.70	2,527.00	100 : 38.15

Source : Annual Administration Reports
Provisional Accounts

ment's contributions reached the 50 per cent level. Even if the interest free capital contributions given by the state Government amounting to Rs. 701.63 lakh were to be excluded still the central Government's contributions work out to 42.67 per cent (as on 31st March, 1982), revealing that on this basis the backlog of capital contributions from the central Government can be placed at Rs. 434.08 lakh. It is interesting to note that even the budget estimates do not always show 50 per cent of the expected state contribution as the expected contribution from the central Government. No wonder. the central contributions are less than the expected amount.

An amount of Rs. 600 lakh appears as loan from Andhra Pradesh Government as on 31 March, 1982 (Provisional Accounts). It is stated that this loan carries interest at 7½ per cent compared to the current interest rate of 8 per cent on capital contributions. It is not known as to why the state Government chose to give the sum as a loan and not as a part of the regular capital contributions. The intention of the Government seems to be to collect this amount back as soon as the corporation is able to repay it.

Gap in replacement financing and capital contributions

A sizable portion of the additional capital contributions received each year can be cosidered to have bridged the gap in replacement financing, as the depreciation is provided on historical cost basis. This implies that, to the extent of the funds so used, additional capital contributions did not really provide funds for incurring additional capital expenditure and thus add to the operating capital. Thus, the portion so used only adds a burden on the corporation as the corporation is obliged to pay interest on capital contributions, which implies that the corporation presently incurs a higher finance cost without a net addition to its earning capacity. This point is evident from Table 3.3 which shows that 31.32 per cent of the capital contributions received during the period 1976-77—1981-82 had gone for covering the gap in the replacement finance, which by implication means that the additional 31.32 per cent of the interest paid on capital contributions, so far as it pertains to these capital contributions, was paid just for keeping its earning power intact. Even though the

TABLE 3.3 : **Capital contributions and increase in the cost of replacement of vehicles**

Year	No. of vehicles replaced	Original cost of acquisition of replaced vehicles Rs lakh	Cost of replacement Rs. lakh	Additional cost of replacement Rs. lakh (4—3)	Capital contributions received during the year Rs. lakh
1	2	3	4	5	6
1976-77	207	153.37	316.89	163.52	726.13
1977-78	396	289.72	620.68	330.96	879.07
1978-79	310	255.34	549.88	294.54	1562.97
1979-80	358	337.03	688.68	351.65	927.50
1980-81	419	410.76	991.69	580.93	1401.00
1981-82	NA	NA	NA	NA	—
				1721.60	5496.67
				(31.32%)	100.00

Source : 1. Information furnished by the corporation.
2. Administrative Reports.
3. Provisional Accounts.

main cause for such diversion is non-availability of adequate profits, it is necessary to recognize the impact of a sizeable portion of fresh capital contributions being used to just retain the existing earning capacity.

To sum up, the corporation is an autonomous body according to law and further is expected to be run on business principles in the conduct of its activities as per the provisions of the RTC Act. However, its autonomy in respect of certain vital matters exists only on paper and consequently the ability of the organisation to run on business principles is impaired to a considerable extent. This is more so in the context of a losing situation. The Corporation has no freedom to fix its prices and the Government is usually guided by many non-economic considerations in approving the extent and timing of fare increases. Consequently, costs, pushed up by inflation, overtake revenues and this results in mounting losses. Whatever economies that can be effected, due to improved performance, would yield marginal results and prove inadequate to cover the gap in revenues. Thus, it is necessary for the Government to provide for a timely fare revision to an adequate extent so as not to impair the ability of the corporation to meet its costs of operation and retain its earning capacity.

Inflation has also affected the area of capital expenditure. As mentioned earlier, the depreciation is provided on historical cost basis and the funds so provided are inadequate to finance replacements. The capital contributions are not forthcoming to an adequate extent and in a timely manner, resulting in neglect of its replacement programme besides resorting to high cost long-term and short-term borrowings. This, coupled with mounting revenue losses, makes the position of the corporation unenviable and reduces the autonomy to a mockery and the obligation to act on business principles to a farce.

The corporation has, during the recent past, shown considerable interest in making additions to supporting capital like construction of huge bus stations. This expenditure, besides acting as a drain on already scarce capital, would result in making a permanent addition to the costs. At least during the period of mounting losses one would have expected the corporation to go slow on this, but the unabated enthusiasm of the corporation requires to be checked and looked into.

Losses, during the latest two years*, are higher than the depreciation provisions made, leading to cash losses. This shrinkage in the funds position makes it necessary to raise funds on a costly basis, besides seriously affecting the ability of the corporation to replace its vehicles, resulting in a serious backlog. Neglect of replacement puts the corporation in a vicious circle of increased maintenance costs and reduced earnings, on the one hand, and increased costs due to high cost external borrowings on the other.

The objective of running the corporation on business principles implies the organisation being helped to survive. The corporation must be allowed to at least cover its costs, by suitable and adequate fare revision, without losing sight of the need for continued improvements in the various operational and physical parameters of performance. A qualitative change in the attitude of the Government is necessary to resurrect the corporation from its present pitiable plight.

The releases of capital contributions by the participating Governments, besides being inadequate, are uncertain and irregular, which adds to the cash flow problems. Further, it is gathered that the corporation is finding it difficult to pay in advance the motor vehicle taxes due to over run of costs to such an extent as to result in cash losses in recent years. There were instances when capital contributions were given with one hand and were received back as motor vehicle taxes. The state Government is more insistent on the prompt payment of motor vehicle taxes while it is not regular in giving capital contributions. Just as the Government insists on payment of taxes on a quarterly basis, it is suggested that the participating Governments should also adopt a similar practice of paying the agreed capital contributions in four equated quarterly instalments. This would go a long way in the smooth implementation of capital expenditure programme.

Finally, with accumulated losses appearing at Rs. 66.41** crore as on 31 March, 1982 and estimated losses for 1982-83

* When losses for the year 1980-81 are taken at Rs. 20.72 crore, as per a note prepared by the corporation.

** This would go up to Rs. 69.83 crore, if the revised figure of Rs. 20.72 crores is taken as the loss for the year 1980-81, as per a note prepared by the corporation.

being placed at Rs. 43.22 crore, the total accumulated loss would add upto Rs. 109.63 crores, which would be higher than the total capital contributions made by the participating governmentals by Rs. 4.52 crore (assuming that the participating governments would contribute the budgeted capital contributions amounting to Rs. 13.60 crore during 1982-83). This means that the entire capital contributed by the participating governments can be considered as wiped out. It is high time that the government initiates steps in the right direction to correct such a sorrowful state of affairs. Such steps should be treated as a package deal and must include :

(i) proper estimation and regular provision of capital contributions, keeping in view not only the planned capital expenditure but also the increased working capital requirements, if any.
(ii) immediate grant of additional capital contributions to wipe out high cost debts and overdraft thrust on the corporation.
(iii) willingness to make adequate capital contributions, whenever extension of nationalisation or new schemes involving additional capital expenditure are contemplated.
(iv) realisation of the need for timely fare revision, purely based on economic considerations, and
(v) provision of some special assistance to tide over the current financial problems, or any other alternative measure discussed in pages 188-190 of Chapter I.

Depreciation policy

The corporation provides depreciation on its vehicles on original/historical cost basis. There is nothing wrong with this policy, provided there are adequate profits and sizeable profits are ploughed back to ensure that extra amounts needed for the purpose of replacement will be readily available. The non-availability of profits and further the presence of mounting losses resulted in an unenviable cash loss situation, compelling the corporation to neglect its replacement programme, resulting in (i) diversion of depreciation provided funds on vehicles still in use, to finance replacements, (ii) dependence on additional capital contributions to meet the gap in replacement, and (iii) increased reliance on high cost external debt. The corporation should be allowed to (a) charge depreciation on replacement cost basis, or (b) earn profits, or (c) be provided with grants/subsidies to bridge the gap in replacement. A combination of the second and third method is also possible.

Earlier the corporation was charging depreciation estimating the useful vehicle life at 4.8 lakh kilometres, which it subsequently revised it upwards to 5.5 lakh kilometres. This naturally has the effect of lowering the depreciation charge and consequently result in overstatement of profits or understatement of losses, besides further adding to the problem of widening gap in replacement finance.

The realisation that charging depreciation on historical cost basis does not provide adequate funds for financing replacement made the corporation to constitute a support fund, known as "Fixed Assets and Stock Replacement Fund", to which 10 per cent of the depreciation amount was credited, provided profits were available. This step has helped the corporation, at least partly, only during the periods of adequate profits. Obviously, as losses started appearing from 1977-78, no credits could be made to this Fund, and the problem got aggravated. Thus, any solution, which is dependent on the presence of adequate profits will prove inadequate to meet the challenge of inflation. The alternative seems to be to convince the Government the need to provide depreciation on replacement cost basis. which besides being helpful in ensuring replacement, would give a more realistic estimate of the cost of rendering service and thus ensure proper consideration in respect of this cost item at the time of fare fixation.

It is necessary for the Corporation to devise a method by which it is in a position to show the correct cost on account of depreciation besides being able to find necessary finances for replacement. The alternatives available in this connection have already been discussed in pages 89-92.

Need for costing system

A full-fledged costing system is recommended to support the efficiency drive and its usefulness is all the more great in the context of mounting losses arising mainly due to raising inflationary trends. The introduction of costing would ensure proper and detailed accounting of costs, which step, besides helping the routine accounting function, would usher in greater cost consciousness and result in considerable economies ultimately. Discussions with Depot Managers have revealed that information recorded in various forms/returns is not always correct and complete, for example tyre mileage, spare parts used, maintenance attention, and so on. It is recommended that vehicle-wise costing be introduced as this would ensure proper recording of various costs, facilitating better control over supplies of various spare parts besides ensuring better control on repairs and maintenance.

PERSONNEL POLICIES AND PRACTICES

Introduction

The success of an organisation is largely a product of executive actions in respect of three of the crucial personnel areas viz., (i) selection of right people, (ii) their placement in appropriate job with right amount of training, and (iii) the growth of these people matching with the needs of the organisation. Hence, it is aptly remarked that no organisation is sounder than its men and how they are managed.

Andhra Pradesh State Road Transport Corporation (APSRTC) has an employee strength of nearly 65,000 and can be considered as a 'labour intensive' organisation. In the context of its large numbers, it is necessary that the organisation should pursue sound personnel policies as otherwise, it leads to lot of dissatisfaction among its staff. Further, where the employees perceive that the policies pursued by the organisation are not only unsound but inconsistent, arbitrary and discriminatory, it leads to demoralisation and poor Industrial Relations.

Man-power planning

The foundation for a successful personnel policy is the development of a "man-power planning" in the organisation. There is no man-power planning at all in the organisation and whatever that exists is "of individual oriented than organisational oriented one". The present high bus-staff ratio which the organisation is experiencing is partly on account of lack of man-power planning as the Head Office itself did not have any information flow from the various units regarding its personnel category-wise. In fact, when the Study Team requested the personnel department to supply category-wise staff at the various places, both at Head office and other places, it expressed its helplessness and stated that they have very recently devised a method to monitor this information and they did not have any information pertaining to previous years in this regard. In fact, the Resident Audit Officer has commented on the head-quarter's anxiety to reduce the high bus-staff ratio, "but it did not develop any system to check the excess employment or adjust the excess against further vacancies in that the personnel department of the Head office had no information flow and to the number of men actually employed in various categories vis-a-vis the sanctions recorded."[2] Thus it is clear from the above statement of the Resident Audit Officer, that the Corporation has not developed any information flows with regard to its man-power and as a result of which excess man-power has been recruited and the net result is that the bus-staff ratio of the Corporation has gone up considerably.

The absence of a man-power plan in the organisation was discussed with the Chief Personnel Manager of the organisation. While agreeing on this matter, he commented that it is very difficult to prepare a man-power plan in a public sector transport organisation in view of the various external uncertainties such as Governmental policy on nationalisation, seasonal traffic and so on and sudden spurts in the man-power requirements occur whenever scheme of nationalisation are cleared and taken up by the Corporation or whenever Government wants the Corporation to take over some activities like Special Employment Schemes and Setwin Operations and so on. In view of this, there is bound to be bulges and shortages in various categories of staff which get adjusted in course of time. It was further stated that the Corporation has made a beginning in the preparation of man-power plan and also devised an information flow system so that the man-power strength at various places, category-wise, is obtained and built into the Head Office records for ready reference.

The personnel function

The personnel function is the most neglected function as it is not given its due share of importance in the Corporation in spite of its being a labour intensive one. What goes on in the corporation in the name of personnel function is nothing but 'establishment function' of routine record keeping activities and the person or persons who were/are incharge of the function did/do not have the expertise and professional competence to deal with personnel problems and what is urgently required is that professional expertise must be sought and the function entrusted to a professional man rather than to a non-professional. An outsider should be brought so that he could take a realistic view and implement the policies instead of submitting to pressures, which is what is happening currently. However, one must remember in this context, that earlier, in 1980, an experienced I.A.S. Officer has been posted as Chief Personnel Manager by the state Government but he was not allowed to join duty by the Officers of the Corporation and later the insider continued in the post. However, one must remember that while professionalisation is good, by itself, it will not produce effective results in the area and that ultimately the policies pursued in effect are the outcome from the Chief Executives policy with respect to different functional areas. Where the Chief Executive is drawn from outside, and where his stint with the Corporation is for a period of two or three years, generally he would not like to rock the boat and would like to go back unscathed as far as possible. Further it must also be noted that the policies are often influenced by Government, as its interest in the Corporation is both financial and maintenance of good industrial relations.

The personnel department has multiplied the chances of its members for promotions and created avenues of promotions in the line departments and that the role of the Personnel Officers and Deputy Chief Personnel Managers has been one of more an audit rather than help.

In this context, an examination of the bio-data of the Deputy Chief Personnel Managers, revealed that of the nine Deputy Chie Personnel Managers, four have come from rank and file (i.e. clerks and conductors), and the rest as direct recruitees. Qualification-wise, there are two MBAs and three persons with additional qualifications relevant to the personnel area and the rest do not possess qualifications for holding the posts except attending one or two short-term programmes in the personnel area. Similarly, an examination of the bio-data of Personnel Officers of the corporation reveals that of the 19 Officers, 15 came from the ranks (viz. clerks) with no qualification to man the personnel job except a brief training at CIRT, Pune.

It can be seen from the above that with the type of people coming from the rank and file, one cannot expect more help from the personnel people.

Recruitment

With regard to recruitment policy of the Corporation, it may be, at the outset, pointed out that highly qualified people are being recruited to the conductor's posts and nearly 25 to 30 per cent people recruited into this category are either graduates or post-graduates resulting in a lot of frustration on the part of this group, right on entering the organisation. The problem is further complicated, as these graduate and post-graduate conductors are not willing to go on line duty and work as conductors. Hence, alternative arrangements have to be made to find people to go in their places as conductors.

In view of this, it is suggested that while recruiting conductors, it is better that non-graduate, higher age-group people are recruited so that they stick to their jobs and continue in the organisation as the scope for their securing jobs elsewhere is remote. The present policy of recruiting conductors with graduate and post-graduate qualifications may be discontinued forthwith as it leads to a lot of turnover in this category which is substantiated by the Chief Personnel Manager himself. Nearly eight hundred conductors are annually recruited by the organisation due to the turnover. Further, these relatively high qualified people become a source of indiscipline as they do not have any commitment and consider their stayal in the organisation as purely a temporary one.

Secondly, it may be pointed out that no scrutiny of records of the candidates, who are recruited as conductors, is done at the time of recruitment and there are a number of instances of persons with criminal records being recruited into the Corporation. While a conductor is removed in one division on the grounds of corruption and indiscipline, he gets a job in another division without any difficulty. Even within the same division, the removed conductor is some times coming back as a new recruitee by resorting to stealing of his erstwhile personnel record from the depot and going back to the same depot as conductor. In view of this, it is suggested that extra care should be taken to scrutinise the records of the recruitees ; and inspite of the best efforts, it is but inevitable to have this phenomenon in a large organisation like APSRTC.

Further, it is also suggested that while recruiting conductors and drivers, it is better to specify qualifications for recruitment purposes taking into account the next two higher positions as promotional avenues so that they do not get frustrated and their turnover rate can be reduced. However, at the time of nationalisation of routes and taking over of services from private operators, the specification of these qualifications becomes a bottleneck as there may not be any alternative left except taking over what is given by the private operators.

Thirdly, the APSRTC has in a way become a rehabilitation Centre and people from Srisailam Dam, Nagarjunasagar Canal, Super Bazars, and periodically from Government are being recruited and absorbed by the Corporation. When this issue was raised with the Chief Personnel Manager, he responded that transport industry being a growth industry and that APSRTC because of its growth potential is in a position to absorb the personnel, and the Corporation is, in fact, absorbing them. He further mentioned that the special employment was taken up in a hurry with an eye on seizing an opportunity of securing finances and large number of people were absorbed, particularly in the category of mechanics, and the excess man-power is distributed to all districts without any relation to activity. It was further felt that as the Corporation is itself going through a financial crisis, seizing of an opportunity of this type would mean availability of more funds for further growth. Further, the excess personnel would be absorbed in course of time as nationalisation schemes are implemented in future or because of the growth factor resulting from the acquisition of fleet.

However, it is suggested that whenever the Corporation is asked to absorb personnel from other organisations, the Corporation should first insist that its published nationalisation schemes be approved and cleared along with finances before it absorbs such personnel so that these personnel do not become a drain on the Corporation and the Corporation is not burdened with excess man-power. Since it is the Government, which is insisting on this, it is but fair that Government from its side must clear some published schemes of the Corporation before the Corporation absorbs the personnel as desired by the Government.

Fourthly, it may be mentioned that there are instances where the recruitment was done in more numbers than the posts advertised for and for example, the recruitment of 24, 9 and 30 Depot Managers, Personnel Officers, and Doctors respectively as against 8, 1 and 6 posts respectively advertised in 1977. When the issue was raised with the Chief Personnel Manager, he mentioned that there is no timely recruitment in the Corporation and there is heavy back-log to be cleared on account of which excess number of people are recruited to the posts than the posts advertised for. In the context of this, it was further mentioned that the appreciation of man-power planning upto top level was never done in the organisation.

Further, it was also mentioned that there is no common qualification stipulated to different posts such as AME/ATM/SO/ Purchase Officer, on account of which, it is creating dissatisfaction amongst the employees. It is now proposed by the organisation to have a common recruitment policy stipulating mechanical engineering qualification as a must and the sooner it is implemented the better for the Corporation.

In the re-organised set up, the Deputy Chief Personnel Manager is the real stumbling block and that because of him it is not possible to make timely recruitment and that since recruitment powers were withdrawn from the Depot/Divisional Managers, they have to get the clearance from the Deputy Chief Personnel Manager in so far as the recruitment of drivers and conductors is concerned. The issue was discussed at length in Part II of the Report. However, presently the Corporation had issued Orders restoring the powers of recruitment to Divisional Managers.

Promotions

The issue of promotions is a very sensitive one.

Firstly, it may be pointed out that there is need for promotional avenues in the managerial cadre and today a person who is a direct recruitee to the Depot Manager's level post cannot hope to reach even the next level, that is, the Divisional Manager's level in a reasonable time; and stagnation has set in at the Divisional Manager's level and many people will have to retire as Divisional Managers only.

Further, it may be pointed out that in terms of eligibility of service taken into consideration for promotion to the same level it varies from post to post—for DVMs 5 years of service and Controller of Stores 3 years and so on.

It may be further pointed out that while considering internal candidates for promotions, there is no uniformity in so far as the reservation ratio provided for the internal candidates. For example, for the post of Assistant Mechanical Engineer, the ratio for direct recruitees to internal candidates is 3 : 2, for Assistant Traffic Manager, it is 2 : 2 and for the Personnel Officer it is 1 : 3. This clearly shows that the personnel people have been able to get a major share of their promotions in the ratio for the internal candidates.

Thus different departments have different eligibility ratios for internal candidates besides different periods of qualifying service which was mentioned earlier. Even the qualifying service and the ratios vary from time to time and from batch to batch. The criteria for selection to promotion post is "neither seniority nor merit but one of convenience" and that the selections are based on considerations other than merit and hence they have lost their credibility. In addition to the above, there is a feeling that promotions in the Corporation are not based on the performance of the candidates. It was felt by Line Managers that personnel people protected their interests by closing staff positions to line people and making themselves eligible for line positions. Moreover, traffic related promotional avenues are not created but posts in other areas like Deputy Controller of Stores, Deputy Chief Personnel Manager and so on are created. Further, it was pointed out in this context that Heads of Departments are allowed to sit in the selection committee as members even when they are not members of the selection committee.

In view of the above, it is essential that promotional avenues have to be created, particularly in the managerial cadre, so as to avoid the demoralising tendency that has set in the Officers.

There is a need for common seniority list except for Mechanical Engineers and Accounts people. There should be an 'Accounts test' for those who wish to enter into the Accounts Department and whenever pass the same should be allowed to go into the Accounts Department. Further, the criteria for promotion should be spelt out with at least a minimum qualifying service of 5 years with merit. Sudden promotions should not occur as was happening where promotions from Class III to Class I had occurred.

It is essential that credibility both in selections and promotions must be built as otherwise the managerial cadre will be further domoralised. Time-scale promotions should be instituted and at a time when there is no vacancy and if the candidate is found eligible and suitable for promotion, he should be given the time-scale and as and when vacancy arises, he should be posted into that job without going through the selection process again. Promotion policy should be spelt out in unambiguous terms by the Corporation. When the issue that the personnel people protected their interests in promotions to line jobs by opening up avenues of promotions in the line area was brought to the notice of the Chief Personnel Manager, he pointed out that it was due to the powerful pressures emerging from the personnel department that two more levels of senior clerk and head clerk were created.

There is need for examining the implications of Regulations 30 and 34 of recruitment regulations.

Regulation 30 of 'Recruitment Regulations' refers to temporary promotions. According to this 'whenever the corporation has to meet the emergency requirements of filling up posts, in a higher cadre, in the administrative interest, and when qualified candidates are not available, or if the filling of such vacancy in accordance with these regulations may likely to be delayed unduly', the Corporation can promote temporarily any employee in the lower category from the same department. This rule, gives scope for promoting a junior person who is not qualified in so far as the period of service is concerned. Such a promotee gets an undue advantage at the time of regular selection by the selection committee on account of his service in higher cadre. Further a promotee under Regulation 30 is eligible for increment after the completion of one year of service even without passing the probationary examination where such examination is prescribed.

Such a facility is denied to a regular candidate selected by the selection committee and given promotion with probationary rights until he passes the examination. A case in point to substantiate this is that the directly recruited Personnel Manager who was recruited in to the Corporation on 17 March, 1975, was temporarily promoted as Deputy CPM on 18 September, 1978 under Regulation 30 even though he was not fulfilling the qualification of the five-year qualifying service required for such promotion to the next higher post and later his services were regularised on the completion of his requisite period of qualifying service. Thus, this regulation gives scope for the management to manipulate an undue delay in recruitment, so that they can promote Junior Manager temporarily, till such time, so that later he becomes eligible as a regular candidate for the same. Thus, a backdoor method for promoting people who did not have the required qualified service is available under this regulation.

In view of this, it is suggested that whenever people are being promoted from lower categories to higher categories under Regulation 30, either because there would be undue delay in the recruitment to the higher category or for meeting the needs of administrative interests, the corporation should promote the senior-most in the category temporarily as a matter of policy, subject to unblemished/good record. Since this promotion is purely temporary and cannot be claimed by the promotee as a right which was specifically mentioned in the regulation, it would avoid demoralisation of senior employees. The junior who can be considered under Regulation 30 earlier, for promotion and can enter through back-door cannot do so now if the senior-most employee is considered for promotion.

Where the posts are to be filled by the direct recruitees and when they are not available because of the non-completion of their training period, then, under Regulations 30 and 34 of recruitment regulations, departmental people can be promoted to the posts reserved for direct recruitees on account of which they are placed in an advantage in the reckoning of qualifying service for further promotions and the direct recruitees are put to a disadvantage. In this context, the seniority of the direct recruits is considerably affected in the higher grade, when promoted. As a remedy, it is suggested that the qualifying service of the promotees for consideration to the higher posts may be reckoned from the date on which the post reserved for promotees actually arises. The period of service put in by such promotees against the posts which are reserved for direct recruits may not be reckoned to determine the qualifying service.

Further, promotion channels at the lower levels, particularly at the level of cleaners, drivers and so on have to be planned. Promotional avenues from cleaners to drivers category must be considered and in the context of this, the fixing up of qualifications taking into account the next two levels of promotions should be considered. In fact, in the case of drivers, the scope for promotions is quite meagre while there is no possibility for demotion on account of which indiscipline problems are arising. As there is little that one can do with regard to the job and the attendent dissatisfaction associated with it, they must, at least, be considered for promotion based on their qualification. It was pointed out that the drivers are eligible to be promoted to ADCs and 25 per cent of the vacancies are reserved for them.

Training

The training function is the most neglected function in the Corporation.

It may be pointed out that as of now while there is effective induction programme in respect of Conductors, Traffic Apprentices and 'A' and 'B' grade apprentices, the induction programme in respect of probationary officers and drivers is ineffective. It is ineffective in the case of the former (Probationary Officers) because of disinterestedness on the part of the concerned Departments in imparting training and due to curtailment of training period and in the case of the latter (drivers) it is due to the absence of sophisticated equipment. In the case of Junior Clerks, there is no induction programme at all.

It was stated that the number of trainees sent vary from time to time and usually varies between sixty and hundred. In order to meet the 'urgent needs' of the Corporation, a crash programme of training is necessary. The training schools are equipped with poor infrastructural facilities and sophisticated equipment is not available. There is a feeling that training activity in the Corporation has become an 'orphan activity' and the

Corporation Officers consider training more as a nuisance and many a time the trainee is left on his own. The unfortunate thing is that people who are posted to the training schools, lack themselves the training skills and often they are junior to the persons who are sent for training. The placement of the training officer itself has become a controversial issue and both the training schools and the Officers training college have become rehabilitation centres.

The importance given to the training function in the Corporation can be gauged from Table 3.4.

TABLE 3.4 : **Training function in the corporation**

Year	Staff costs (in lakh of Rs.)	Training costs of Dept. People	Percentage of training costs to total
1977-78	2999.05	23.37	0.78
1978-79	3403.28	20.28	0.60
1979-80	3977.80	21.01	0.53
1980-81	5076.73	17.32	0.34
1981-82	6040.33	21.24	0.35

Source : Administrative Reports, Provisional Accounts of APSRTC.

Except for a marginal increase in the year 1981-82, the training costs as a percentage of total staff costs are coming down over the last five-year period. Even in absolute terms, it was progressively coming down and the 1981-82 figure is less than what it was in 1977-78. Granting that the increase in total staff cost for the year 1981-82 is due to revised pay-scales, it is unfortunate that for a corporation of 65,000 strength, the amount spent on training is not even one per cent of the total staff costs at any given point of time for the above period.

Table 3.5 gives the particulars of training programmes conducted by Staff Training College, Hyderabad.

When it was enquired whether any monitoring is being done about the effectiveness of the training imparted to the trainees, it was stated that not much was done in this regard.

It was further mentioned that when the Staff Training College was located in Nagarjunasagar it was both a problem of getting participants as well as the Faculty to the place and consequently,

TABLE 3.5 : **Particulars of the training programmes conducted by Staff Training College, Hyderabad**

Year	No. of training programmes conducted		
	Officers	Supervisors	Total
1977	91	166	257
1978	99	245	344
1979	98	279	377
1980	67	316	383
1981	85	360	455
1982 (up to Sept. 1982)	59	278	337

Source : Records of Officers Training College, Staff Training College.

it was shifted to Hyderabad in 1981. However, after its shifting to Hyderabad, its budget was slashed nearly by rupees one lakh and fixed at two lakhs of rupee as the College stopped supplying food to the participants. This obviously shows the importance given by the Corporation to the training activity.

During the year 1981-82, the Corporation has spent approximately Rs. 25,000* towards training costs for training Managers at the outside institutes and a total number of 133 officers were sent for training to various institutes. Particulars for other years were not available with the Staff Training College with regard to the expenditure incurred on Officers' training outside the Corporation. However, even if the amount spent in 1981-82 is quadrapled for the purpose of a guess estimate, for each of the other years, which is most unlikely, it is still quite an insignificant amount considering the size of the organisation. Where no effort is made to assess the effectiveness of training, officers who attend these programmes often tend to consider them as a well earned holiday. It was further stated by some Line Managers that those who had been sent earlier for the programmes are being sent again for several training programmes and consequently it is felt that training is meant only for a chosen few in the corporation.

One of the complaints made about training is that training period is not taken into consideration for reckoning the qualifying service for purposes of promotion in the case of direct recruits

**Source* : Annual Administration Report, 1981-82.

for the posts of ATM and AME, while an Accounts Officer, or Personnel Officer who is recruited directly, gets the benefit of his service counted for purposes of eligibility right from the day he joins service. Similarly, in the case of Depot Managers who spend 2 years under training, as probationary ATM/AME, the period of training is not taken into account and the full five-year period has to be completed by them before they become eligible for promotion. In view of this, the relevant recruitment regulations need to be modified making provision for uniform service conditions of treating training period as also active service. When this matter was raised with the Chief Personnel Manager, he stated that the Chartered Accountancy qualification and the training he had undergone, provide him the requisite managerial skills for that function, while the same cannot be said of the Depot Manager—a raw candidate—who starts learning skills step by step from the date of his recruitment. While this is true in the case of Accounts Officers, the same does not hold good in the case of Personnel Officers and Stores Officers recruited directly. Even in the case of Accounts Officers, if they are to be considered for promotion outside their functional area and as Line Managers, they must be given training as the other Line Managers are given and the period of training in such a case is to be treated on par with the other directly recruited Line Officers.

There should be emphasis on the integrated approach to the training activity for Depot Managers but it was unfortunate that the Depot Managers training period was reduced from two years to one year. It is so in view of the importance of the Depot Manager who is entrusted with an investment of nearly 3 crore of rupees and whose abilities and effectiveness influence the working of the Depot which is the base of operation. Even during this short period of training, they were on their own and they were being considered as intruders by the functionaries in the other departments of Corporation.

Over and above this, it was pointed out that the internal promotees straightaway report to duty to the next higher post without being trained and instances are not wanting when a Chief Inspector or Mechanical Foreman is promoted as Depot Manager, they join as Depot Managers without going through any further training. It is very much pertinent to note in this context what the Chief Accounts Officer has said about the DAO set up. It was pointed out, that huge suspense balances were pending and the Depot Managers are not properly trained in the finance function because of which various problems are arising and to set right this it was pointed out that sufficient training in the area should be provided to them.

Exclusive training in the conduct of domestic enquiries is a necessity as the technicalities and intricacies involved in this area are so subtle that if the same is not conducted properly, it would create problems of taking back into service the suspended conductors inviting payment of huge amounts of back wages creating an unnecessary burden on the corporation's already strained finances.

Table 3.6 indicates the enormity of the problem which can be better appreciated in the light of the above remark.

TABLE 3.6 : **Number of conductors reinstated with backwages**

Year	No. of writ peti-tions	No. of conduc-tors reinstated with full back wages and continuity of service	No. of conduc-tors reinstated with part back wages and continuity of service	No. of conduc-tors reappoin-ted without back wages	Amount of money deposi-ted (Rs.)
1979	6	3	—	3	4,000.00
1980	24	15	2	7	75,828.68
1981	37	19	17	—	97,755.09
1982	13	6	4	—	1,03,277.31

Source : Legal Cell—File pertaining to the payment of 1/6 of back wages.

From Table 3.6 it can be seen that the number of writ petitions questioning the suspensions and removals are increasing and the number of people reinstated both with full back wages and part back wages are also increasing. Though the Corporation was asked to deposit 1/6 or 1/4 of the back wages and the amounts in the last column indicate the same, if we take into account the trend towards increased number of reinstatements, in terms of the full or part wages to be paid to the employees, the total amount payable as full or part wages would approximately amount to Rs. 8.43 lakh.

The courts are directing the Corporation to deposit 1/6 of the back wages of the suspended employees. In some instances they were directing the Corporation to deposit 1/4 of the back wages. The amounts shown in Column (6) of Table 3.6 are the deposits made by the Corporation towards 1/6 or 1/4 as directed by courts. Taking 1/6 figure the total of the last column amounts to Rs. 2,80,861.08. If all of them were reinstated with full wages then it would amount to six times the deposit that is made which amounts to Rs. 16.85 lakh. But since some of them are reinstated with full wages, some with part wages and some with no wages, it may not much off the mark to assume that the figure would be around 50 per cent of the deposited money on a very conservative estimate and that amounts to nearly is 8.43 lakh.

Though the Corporation may contest these cases in higher courts and even when the higher courts give them a reinstatement without backwages, it would mean an enormous amount of legal charges besides unnecessary strain on the Corporation. All this arises, many a time, due to the poor conduct of domestic enquiry by people who lack the necessary skills in the conduct of the same.

For example in the case of Sri Shaik Ibrahim—E 42666—ID 17/78, the senior standing council has expressed a genuine doubt about arguing out the case as it is difficult to argue that the domestic enquiry is proper. In the same case the learned judge has observed that the :

> the driver in this case was acquitted of the criminal charges and in the domestic enquiry, the District Manager acted as a witness and the domestic enquiry that was conducted suffered from a serious infirmity in that the District Manager himself acted as a witness as well as a judge which is against principles of natural justice and which cannot be easily got over.[3]

In the light of this, the judge has ordered that Sri Shaik Ibrahim be reinstated with continuity of service and back wages and all other attendant benefits and thus nearly a sum of Rs. 25,000 was paid by the Corporation with a further claim pending to the tune of Rs. 16,000. Similarly, in ID No. 33/1978 of Sri V. Madhuraiah, ex-conductor, E.25705 and in ID No. 132/76 of Sri R. Upender Rao, E. 37245, similar reinstatements with full back wages and all other attendant benefits were given to the claimants. These are cases in point to show that the lacunae in the conduct of domestic enquiries would result in huge expenditures to the Corporation, and hence the need for training. Over and above this, it must also be remembered that a prolonged suspension, till the case is finally disposed off by the court, would also involve the corporation in the payment of huge amounts of continued subsistence allowance, besides paying wages to the people who are appointed in the vacancies that have arisen due to the suspensions.

It may not be inappropriate to cite that the "committee on Public Undertakings (1975-76) at para 137 of its eighth report has recommended that no suspension should be allowed to remain outstanding for over six months. Regulation 19 of employees (CCA) regulations 1967 of the Corporation also envisages that no case of suspension should prolong beynod six months. . . . The Resident Audit Officer in his comments mentioned that there were about 1208 personnel belonging to various cadres of staff under suspension as on 15 August, 1981 and on the basis of minimum eligibility alone assuming that these cases are less than six months old, the financial impact by way of subsistance allowance would amount to Rs. 3.01 lakh per mensun.*

Further, it must also be remembered that where a domestic enquiry case is loosely structured, it loses its original flavour and as time prolongs, it becomes very difficult to establish the facts.

In the light of the above points, it is suggested that effective measures for toning up training have to be taken by the Corporation. Firstly, training instructors or principals should be selected based more on merit and aptitude and posted to the institutes. In other words, training institutes should not be considered as rehabilitation grounds to accommodate organisational misfits.

Source : R.A.O's comments quoted in bus-staff ratio file.

Secondly, infrastructural facilities in the training schools should be improved and equipment of sophisticated nature acquired, so as to provide effective training to the participants. It is further suggested that too much emphasis either on theory or practicals should not be laid and a blend of these two in right proportions should be provided.

Thirdly, when a Depot Manager goes on leave, instead of making the adjacent Depot Manager as additional charge of that Depot, the second in Command of that Depot namely, the Mechanical Foreman or the Chief Inspector, whoever is senior, may hold the additional charge of that Depot, during the leave period. This would provide on the job training to the people so that, when promoted tomorrow, they acquire the necessary skills for the job.

Fourthly, it is better if the trainees are attached to a single officer during the period of training and in the respective functional areas the functional Heads should be held responsible for the training skills of the trainees. Further, at the first line officer level, a generalist with multi level skills should be developed through job rotation and whenever a Chief Inspector or Mechanical Foreman is promoted to the Depot Manager's post, he must work in all the Departments except in the area where he has the skill before joining as Depot Manager. Thus, promotee should also go through prescribed training before he takes over the new job as full-fledged manager. Depot Managers (direct recruits) should have at least a minimum of two years integrated training before they are given independent charge.

Fifthly, in the conduct of domestic enquiries, exclusive training should be provided to the Chief Inspectors, who are now entrusted with the work of conduct of enquiries.

It is further suggested that to make training more effective and monitor the impact, participants should be taken to action points and involve them in the actual situations. This would facilitate the participants to see the changes that have come about in the systems and technology and provide an immediate feed back so that the participants can understand the things better.

Lastly, hostel facilities may be provided, as part of the training institutes and the post-training behaviour of the individual shall be observed by the immediate superior and he should assess the effectiveness of the training that is imparted.

The term training, in its psychological sense, refers to the modification of the behaviour in the individual who has gone through the process of training. In view of this, it is very difficult to point out its effectiveness. The success of training is largely dependent on the trainer and the way training is put to use by the trainee subsequently.

Transfers

There is a policy that any one who has five years of service at a single place can be transferred. However, when it comes to the question of implementing the same, various problems are encountered by the line managers.

The first problem encountered is the peak-slack season problem, and particularly during the peak period if transfers are effected it leads to disturbance of planned schedules particularly at the conductors and drivers level. Over and above this, there is a severe competition for places like Hyderabad and Vijayawada. Earlier, it was also mentioned in the problems of city services that requests for transfers of conductors and drivers on the verge of retirement are sympathetically considered and they are brought to the city.

However, the second and probably the most important problem with regard to transfers is the resistance and interference from the unions in the matter. As a result, many a time, the transfers generally become paper transfers and are never implemented and as and when they are implemented, they are withdrawn and status quo is maintained. Several instances of non-implementation of transfer orders may be cited. It was stated that, though it was established, that thirty typists were considered as excess staff in Head office nothing was done to transfer them. Similarly, whenever the fleet of a Depot is reduced, the question of staff transfers becomes usually a difficult task and many a time they are not effected. Instance of a painter in a particular Depot (Ranigunj) working since last two decades was cited where no transfer could be effected. Similarly, a local president of Mazdoor Union at a particular Depot (Tuni) was transferred by the Depot Manager, as the Manager felt that there was no need for his services at that particular place but the same orders were kept in abeyance and the local president continued at the same place. Similarly, transfers in between two Depots which were located in the same compound (Ranigunj), could not be effected.

When the above matter was brought to the notice of the Chief Personnel Manager, he mentioned that nearly 20 per cent of the Corporation employees that is, approximately 13,000 people are in twin cities and due to historical reasons this has happened. He further pointed out, particularly, with reference to Karimnagar region, that when the Corporation recruited people from the local employment exchange, to avoid the problem of transfers to twin cities, after their joining the Corporation they sought transfer to Hyderabad. In other words, even when local people belonging to the particular place are recruited, later these people seek transfer to the twin cities. In this context, he mentioned that the corporation is changing its transfer policy and that people have to move out whenever they complete their three years of service at a particular place. However, the exception to this rule is ladies and old aged persons.

In the light of the above, it is suggested that wherever the Divisional seniority is finalised, the Divisional Manager should effect transfer when an employee completes the fixed term as per the transfer policies enunciated. Such transfers should be effected always at the end of the peak season, that is, in June, so that the Corporation services are not affected. Such a step, will not dislocate the family and school life of the children of the employee also. The only thing that must be remembered here is that the policy as stipulated is inviolable, and the management should not yield to any pressures from any quarters to modify or cancel the orders.

Incentive schemes

One of the complaints is that the level of wages of productive and non-productive employees were the same. It was pointed out that a golden opportunity of linking wages to incentives is lost.

The Corporation has introduced an "ad hoc depot incentive scheme" from 14 January, 1980. The "scheme envisages about Rs. 50 to each employee per month, if the existing performance level is slightly improved, say by about 10 per cent. In case the performance is improved by about 15 per cent and 20 per cent the incentive amount that could be earned by each of the employee will be about Rs. 75 and Rs. 100 per month respectively. The scheme is purely ad hoc and will be in force only upto 31st March, 1980 initially."[4]

The operation of the scheme was reviewed by the Corporation; and the operation results of the scheme in Hyderabad city division during the month of May 1981 revealed that the "Category of conductors were still being paid very high incentive amount in view of the target being fixed very low and that the targets being not reviewed from time to time. Further, it was found that majority of the conductors got an incentive payment of about Rs. 100 per month. Table 3.7 shows the range of incentive payment to conductors of the city division".[5]

TABLE 3.7* : **Incentive paid to conductors of city division**

Range	No. of conductors	Percentage
Rs.		
Upto 50	255	13.86
50—100	290	15.76
100—150	345	18.74
150—200	302	16.40
200—250	253	13.74
250—300	159	8.64
300—400	165	8.96
400—500	52	2.82
500—600	15	0.81
600 and above	5	0.27
Total	1,841	100.00

*Incentive files of the Corporation.

From the above table it can be seen very clearly that only 29.62 per cent of City conductors are getting an incentive ranging between Rs. 50 and Rs. 100 and nearly 66.5 per cent of the Conductors are getting an incentive ranging between Rs. 100 and Rs. 400. There are five conductors who are getting an incentive of Rs. 600 or more and thus the original expectation that it would range between Rs. 50 and Rs. 100 seems to have overshot by as much as 2.7 times on an average.

It may be pointed out here that the Regional Manager, Hyderabad and Chief Industrial Engineer went round the Depots for getting a first hand information on the performance of the scheme and they found out that there was a "discrepancy in fixing the base which has to be corrected immediately. While analysing the routes which have resulted in incentive payment, a peculiar phenomenon was noticed in that the earnings of EPK of December, 1979 on certain routes was higher than the EPK of January, 1980 even after the fare revision impact was incorporated. Thus it was found out that the conductors and drivers are being rewarded not for their effort but for the growth already achieved."[6]

Further, as per the wage revision instructions, issued vide Circular No. P.D.2/1982-83, dated 24-4-1982, conductors and drivers are also being paid day-out allowance according to the revenue kms performed by them within a spell of 8 hours. Accordingly, where kilometres performed are above 90 kms and up to 100 kms, an amount of Rs. 2 and above 100 kms, an amount of Rs. 3 has to be paid. Hence in the city division, the depot-wise amount payable to conductors and drivers in a month comes to about Rs. 0.52 lakh under this allowance.

In view of the above reasons, it was proposed to modify the existing city incentive scheme which is valid up to 30 June 1982. However, the same old scheme was extended up to 30-9-1982 by the Corporation through its Circular No. XI/1970/IED dated 1-1-1982 and the scheme's validity was further extended by the Corporation up to 30-6-1983, through its Circular No. XII/1980/IED dated 1-7-1982.

In fact, the Chief Industrial Engineer through his letter No. IE/51(1)/80 IED dated 30-1-1981, has pointed out that "in the review of the incentive scheme, it was noted that some of the individual employees are getting incentive in the range of Rs. 250 and above which is substantial. Incentive schemes in Tamil Nadu Corporation prescribe incentive earnings to the extent of only 2 per cent of the earnings and total incentive not exceeding 20 per cent of their wages" and in the APSRTC presently there is no maximum ceiling for the payment of incentive amount. There should be a ceiling fixed taking into consideration the maximum attainable/optimum level of performance.

Over and above this, it was stipulated in the incentive scheme that members to become eligible shall atleast put in 21 days of service during the given month. There were instances where it was not possible for the workers to put in the required number of days of service during a given month due to more number of holidays such as November, October and January and whenever such situation occurred, the Corporation exempted the particular eligibility clause so that the workers become eligible for the same, which is quite understandable.

However, Circular No. XII/1980/IED (Genl.)/1 dated 30-8-1980 stipulated "that the employees who have participated in the strike/work to rule/lightning strike/tool down strike, will disqualify themselves from getting incentive amount payable at the end of the month." The Andhra Pradesh State Road Transport Corporation (APSRTC) employees union, the APSRTC staff and workers' federation have issued strike notice intimating their intention to go on strike on or after 23 September, 1980 and some of the employees have participated in the All India Bundh scheduled on 24 September, 1980. However, the workers were able to get this exempted and thus became eligible for incentive.

Further, the APSRTC employees went on strike on 10th, 11th and 12th of February, 1982 and those who have participated in the strike are not eligible for the incentive under the eligibility clause. However, the unions could get an award from the Deputy Chief Minister, when the management of the Corporation refused to give exemption to the ineligibility arising out of their going on strike. The award given by the Deputy Chief Minister mentions that "Depot incentive bonus may be paid to such of those employees who would have been eligible for such payment but for their going on strike in February, 1982. Absences from duty other than absence due to participation in strike are not condoned by this decision either for purpose of Depot incentive or any other."

The summum bonnum of all this is that the incentive schemes, both for the district and city services, were loosely structured; and whenever the Corporation tried to modify in the light of their experience and implementation the unions resisted it; and, in fact, the Corporation was forced to revert back to the earlier scheme by the employees through their work-to-rule behaviour such as not stopping the vehicles at stages, not picking up passengers, resorting to cancellation of services on flimsy grounds and so on. In fact, the then Vice Chairman and General Manager under the powers conferred in para 4 of Corporation Resolution No. 175/1980 dated 28 November, 1980, has decided to revert back to the scheme that was existing before 1 December, 1980 with effect from 24 December 1980.

Further, the city incentive scheme started as an ad-hoc scheme continued to be ad-hoc and in spite of the various evaluations done and modifications suggested, the old scheme is being extended from time to time and its tenure of life is extended up to 30 June, 1983 for both the district and city schemes. This may imply that the management does not want to have any confrontation with the union in the matter.

It further points out a lacuna in the sense that there is no ceiling to the maximum amount payable as incentive and that the workers are being paid incentive "not for their effort but for the growth that was already achieved." This obviously implies, that the norms were loosely determined and the schemes were implemented in a great hurry without being tried in a limited area for a specified period. Further, the working of the plan indicates that it is most beneficial to the drivers and conductors and is against the interests of the Corporation, in view of the net financial implication to the Corporation.

When the Corporation specifically mentioned that workers were not eligible for incentive if and when they go on strike and when the workers went on strike and when the management refused to accede to their request for condoning the same so that they are become eligible incentive, it is quite unfortunate that Government condoned the action and thus forced the corporation to pay the incentive. This action on the part of the Government clearly shows that it also did not want to have any confrontation with the workers and that the real top management in a public sector corporation is the Government itself, instead of the Managers in the Corporation. In the light of the above Government action, it is not wrong to assume that the Corporation's soft pedalling approach of extending the validity of the otherwise disadvantageous schemes to 30 June, 1983 indicates that if it does not agree, it either has to face an immediate show down in the form of a strike or the Government may give an award as was done earlier in the strike case condoning the eligibility clause. However, it is suggested that the Corporation at the time of its next wage negotiations with unions must make these schemes also negotiable so that it is not put to a disadvantage.

Industrial relations

The Andhra Pradesh State Road Transport Corporation (APSRTC) is a labour intensive organisation which provides transportation service to the public and any problem that arises in the area of industrial relations is immediately reflected in the paralisation of services affecting the public on one side and depriving revenues to the Corporation on the other. Revenues lost are lost for ever and cannot be made good because of the nature of the industry and hence it is important that the Corporation has to evolve an industrial relations policy so that instead of being reactor to situation, it could anticipate and plan for the contingencies. In the process, it enables the corporation to have uninterrupted services and ensure regular earnings which otherwise would be lost if the services are affected. The industrial relations problems are often dealt on a fire fighting basis and there is little time left to think of policy planning in the area and hence there is no clarity of Head office policy in this regard.

Table 3.8 indicates the number of stoppages, kilometres cancelled, man-days lost and loss of earnings to the Corporation, which gives an idea of the magnitude of the problem.

From table it can be seen that nearly Rs. 150 lakh earnings are lost during the above period by the Corporation. In fact particulars of loss of earnings due to general strikes in January, 1982 and in February, 1982 are not included and if these are also taken into account, the total loss of earnings for the Corporation would be definitely more.

It is in this context that the importance of industrial relations policy can be better appreciated. As of now, there is no policy on the industrial relations front and as and when a problem arises it is dealt on an ad-hoc basis creating problems for the line managers. They complain that they were never supported by their

TABLE 3.8 : **Work stoppages and consequences**

Year	No. of stoppages	Man-days lost	Kms cancelled in lakh	Loss of earnings (in lakh of Rs.)
1977	27	1,736	1.59	3.45
1978	65	4,126	6.90	14.39
1979	70	54,902	21.71	48.61
1980	60	23,521	29.27	60.62
1981	69	5,358	6.54	19.24
1982 (Up to Aug.)	12	N.A.	1.03	4.07
				150.38

Source : Industrial Relations Department.

higher ups, consequent upon which, their image before their subordinates is considerably affected and thereby their effectiveness is neutralised in administering discipline.

Over and above this, it was pointed out that the style of the Chief Executive often has its impact and where the Chief Executive is drawn from outside, he may approach the issue as he perceives and, consequently, it is increasingly becoming a difficult task for them at the action points, to adjust to the changing styles of different Chief Executives. In view of this, there is either no policy on the industrial front or if at all anything exists, it is but a weak, vacillating and inconsistent one, depending on the Chief Executive at that point of time.

The existence of several unions and the recognition of the unions give rise to many difficulties and their effectiveness is curtailed because of these realities. It was further mentioned that the discipline of the employees is completely eroded and assaults on officers have become a common feature.

However, their main complaint is that they are not being supported by the higher ups and whenever discipline is administered the higher ups have either set aside the orders issued by the line manager or commented upon to the effect that line manager lacks tact in dealing with the issues. When it was remarked that the line managers are not consistently uniform in administering discipline, it was pointed out that such a thing is well neigh impossible due to the regional variations, and peculiarities of the discipline cases.

It is further stated, that the problems in this area pertain broadly to one of allowing the unrecognised union to collect the subscription fees from its members in the office premises and the recognised union objecting to the same. In the light of this, it is suggested that the facility of subscription collection by any union, whether it is recognised or not, should not be allowed within the premises as matter of privilege and must be made clear to the unions.

Further, it was pointed out that the use of the notice board by the unrecognised unions in the office premises is often a disputed issue by the recognised union and, in order to get over this problem, it is suggested that all the registered unions should have notice boards for displaying notices to its members and it should not be the exclusive privilege of the recognised union alone.

One of the issues leading to confrontation with the unions, as mentioned by the line managers, is the supply of uniforms and tool kits. Many a time, they were never supplied in time leading to problems of indiscipline and hence it is essential that a timely supply of these would go a long way in reducing the same.

Some line managers felt that the Depot Managers are just implementing the union officers' demands in view of the frequent assaults on them and lack of support from above.

It was further felt that the Deputy Chief Personnel Manager has become the breeding ground of all industrial relations problems and compromises on all the nefarious activities are taking place and that Trade Unions are able to short circuit authority and impose their decisions over line managers from the above. With regard to the awarding of punishments by the Depot Managers, though there are guidelines issued at the instance of union, the managers are not in a position to implement them as implementation would lead either to an industrial relation problems or it is set aside by the higher ups.

Conclusion

In retrospect, if we look at the various personnel policies, it is not incorrect to assume that the morale of the officers is on a low side and this is not on account of an overnight phenomenon. The various confusing, inconsistent, ad hoc, and individual oriented personnel policies have contributed to this trend of demoralisation and unless this is arrested, no amount of pressures from above would improve the performance of the organisation.

It has been pointed out that many managers of the DVM and DM's cadre have reconciled to the fact that they would not get any more promotions and promotions are based on considerations other than merit and seniority. Further, the continuous pressures exercised by various functional executives demanding various types of information has multiplied their work load particularly at the Depot level and they feel that only insensitive people can carry on the job in the Corporation and it is difficult for sensitive and loyal people to function in the atmosphere of suspicion and mistrust. Instances are not lacking, where the performance of Depot Managers are monitored through union leaders resulting in total demoralisation.

The line managers further feel that the evaluation system used particularly lacks any logic. As an example, they cited that the "Managerial Productivity Index", which is computed, takes excess staff as one of the variables, and the DM, who is there at a particular point of time, if evaluated on this basis, would be unfortunate as he was not the person who recruited the people. Similarly, when comparing depot performance, incomparable comparisons between depots which have facilities and depots which do not have facilities (e.g., Simhachalam, Gajuwaka) often lead to unfair evaluation and the line manager's major worry is about how he would be finally evaluated by his superiors. When the line managers take decisions their constant worry is as to how the boss views the same and not the merits of the case demanding an effective decision. In the process, the decisions tend to be soft, compromising and often ineffective and poor. Lower level managers feel that there is lack of trust and faith by the higher ups in the lower level managers characterised by a notion of hierarchical set-up and level consciousness. There is a feeling of a social stigma of corruption associated with the R.T.C. people and the line managers feel that the top management has done very little in improving the organisational image in so far as this area is concerned and have let them down with the result they have become quite ineffective. They further feel that the performance evaluation system based on the depot performance is not scientific. It is suggested that as and when the Head Quarters identify the sick depots based on the performance, all the HODs should render assistance to the sick depots as a team along with the Chief and then try to evaluate the various genuine problems of the Depot rather than pulling up the DMs without rendering the necessary assistance. It is further felt that the targets given by the Head-Quarters are often imposed and unrealistic and this top down approach is sapping the energies of the managers and demoralising them completely as they have to continuously battle for accomplishing unrealistic targets entrusted to them.

It is time that the Corporation takes stock of these things before it evolves a more pragmatic, realistic and credible policies so that the morale of the employees may be toned up. Treating these as of inconsequential nature would only alienate further the employees and hence the management may endeavour to remove the various anomalies pointed out, render effective support to the line managers so as to make them effective and thereby help in improving their morale.

MANAGEMENT INFORMATION SYSTEMS

The proposed study is for identifying the deficiencies of the existing set up of the Management Information Systems in the APSRTC and for drawing a new design of the Management Information systems which is in conformity with the new organisational structure recommended.

Existing set-up of M.I.S. in APSRTC

The present organisational structure recognises four levels of management—Head Office, Region, Division, and Depot. Yet, the Management Information System exists at two levels only, that is, Head office and Region. The Depot forms the information source. Basic documents are compiled and furnished by the depot to the Regional Statistical Officer.

The various statements sent by the depot to the Regional

M.I.S. wing are given hereunder.

Sl. No.	Particulars	Form No.	Periodicity	Method of Preparation
1.	Daily Vehicle Position Statement	MTD-151	Daily	In duplicate in the prescribed printed form
2.	Vehicle Log Sheet	MTD-42R	Daily	Vehicle-wise in the prescribed printed form
3.	Vehicle Log Sheet Challan	MTD-42A	Daily	In duplicate in the prescribed printed form
4.	Statement showing the cancellation and delays of services due to traffic, Mechanical and other causes	MTD-110	Daily	In duplicate in the prescribed printed form
5.	Passenger earning Statement	MTD-108R	Daily	—do—
6.	Route wise earnings Statement	MTD-118R and S	Daily	In duplicate in the prescribed printed form
7.	Fleet Strength report	MTD-151A	Fortnightly	In triplicate in the prescribed printed form. First two copies shall be sent to RSTO who will certify the first copy and submit it to CSO every fortnight by the 5th and 20th of every month
8.	Return of receipts, issues and balances of H.S.D Oil	MTD-29(0)	-do-	In duplicate in the prescribed printed form along with relevant vouchers
9.	Return of receipts, issues, and balances of Petrol	MTD-29P	Monthly	In the prescribed printed form along with the relevant vouchers
10.	Return of receipts, issues and balances of Lub. Oil	MTD-29L	-do	—do—

Sl. No.	Particulars	Form No.	Periodicity	Method of Preparation
11.	Statement showing the staff strength and Absenteeism	MDT-29L	Monthly	In theprescribed form
12.	Statement showing the Coaching earnings	—	-do-	-do-
13.	Statement showing the details of Accidents occurred to the Vehicles	—	-do-	-do-
14.	Operational Review	—	-do-	-do-
15.	Statement showing results of Tyre Performance	—	-do-	-do-
16.	ABC Route Effectiveness	—	-do-	-do-
17.	RM Special Squad Statement	—	-do-	-do-
18.	DVM Special Squad Statement	—	-do-	-do-
19.	Tyre Performance Statement	—	-do-	-do-
20.	Inventory of Vehicles	—	Annually	-do-

The information so collected is processed by the Regional MIS Wing and put up to the Regional Manager and the other officers at Regional and Divisional Level for control action. Certain statements, reports, and reviews are also sent to the Chief Statistical Officer, Hyderabad, simultaneously. The statements, reports, and reviews furnished by the Regional MIS Wing to the Chief Statistical Officer and the other officers are given hereunder.

Sl. No.	Particulars	Submitted to	Periodicity
1.	Statement showing daily earnings, kms operated and off road vehicles position at Depots, and Work-Shops	C.S.T.O. & R.M.	Daily

Sl. No.	Particulars	Submitted to	Periodicity
2.	Task Register (Division-Wise)	R.M.	Daily
3.	An abstract of Vehicle Position	C.S.T.O.	Weekly
4.	Statement showing physical performance of region	V.C. & G.M., CSTO, DVMs, Dy. CME, DMs, & Mechanical Officers	Weekly, Fortnightly, and Monthly
5.	Vehicle off-road position	Dy. C.M.E.	Weekly
6.	K.M.P.L. Statement	CSTO, RM, & DVMs	Weekly, Fortnightly and Monthly
7.	An abstract of delays and cancellations of scheduled kms, Scheduled Trips	CSTO	Fortnightly
8.	An abstract of operational results	—do—	—do—
9.	Accidents and breakdown statements	—do—	—do—
10.	Earning statement (Including interest rate)	—do—	—do—
11.	Departmental Vehicles (Non revenue kms)	—do—	Fortnightly and Monthly
12.	Statement showing the fleet strength of the region as on the last day of the month	—do—	Monthly
13.	Account Current of HSD Oil	Dy. CAO (Region) & CSTO	—do—
14.	Account Current of Petrol	—do—	—do—
15.	Region-wise working Results	CAO and CSTO	—do—
16.	Statement showing Revenue kms, Non-Revenue kms, and Gross kms, for the month	Dy. CAO, CSTO & CCOs	—do—
17.	Kilometres operated by Vehicles for the month	—do—	—do—
18.	Coaching earning statement	CSTO	—do—

Sl. No.	Particulars	Submitted to	Periodicity
19.	Statement showing vehicle kms (including Dept. Vehicles)	CSTO	Monthly
20.	Petrol Consumption Statement	CTM	—do—
21.	Depot-wise off-road vehicle statement	CME	—do—
22.	Performance Report (Division-wise)	VC & GM	—do—
23.	Vehicle days statement (Depot-wise)	CSTO	—do—
24.	Average Vehicle Position	—do—	—do—
25.	Statement showing fleet position and performance for the month	CCOS	—do—
26.	Statement showing details of Squad checks	CSTO	—do—
27.	ABC classification	—do—	—do—
28.	Review of Depot-wise buses Dead kms	Dy. CME & RM	—do—
29.	Physical Performance figures	All D.Ms.	Annually

The list of statements prepared and sent to the Divisional Managers and Depot Managers for the purpose of feedback by the Regional MIS Wing is given hereunder.

Sl. No.	Particulars	Prepared by	Feedback to	Periodicity
1.	Statement showing the breakdowns	R.S.T.O.	DMs/DVM	Fortnightly
2.	Statement showing the Analysis of Non-Revenue kms	—do—	—do—	Monthly
3.	Key Indicators of Evaluation of Traffic and Mechanical Departments	—do—	DMs, DM	—do—
4.	Statement showing the vehicle—wise progressive kms and Age in terms of kms and Years.	—do—	DVMs, DMs WM/Dy. CME	—do—

Sl. No.	Particulars	Prepared by	Feed back to	Periodicity
5.	Statement showing the vehicle wise KMPL (Rate of Fuel consumption of each vehicle)	RSTO	DVMs	monthly
6.	Daily Task Register, the average performance (for every 10 days) (Fleet, Earnings, kms) EPK	--do--	DMs/DVM	10 days
7.	Tyre performance	—do—	DMs/DVM/ WM	Monthly

The Chief Statistical Officer, in his turn, compiles various reviews and reports based on the documents received in his office from the Regional Statistical Officers and sends them to the Officers at Head office, Corporation Board, State Government, Central Government and the other outside organisations like the Central Institute of Road Transport, Poona. The list of reports and reviews received in the Central MIS Wing and sent out by the Chief Statistical officer are given hereunder.

List of all periodical returns received from the units (INPUT)

I. Basic documents (Excluded)

1.	Daily Vehicle Position	MTD 151
2.	Vehicle Position Fortnightly	MTD 151 'A'
3.	Daily Operational Statement	MTD 110
4.	Daily Earnings Statement	MTD 108
5.	Daily Vehicle Log-Sheet Challan	MTD 42 'A'
6.	Route-Wise Earnings	MTD 118 (Periodicals)
7.	HSD Oil (FN Statement)	MTD 29 Return
8.	Petrol (Monthly Statement)	MTD 29 Return

II. Traffic

		Periodicity
1.	Daily Earnings (Division-wise)	
2.	Depot-wise Operational Results	Fortnightly
3.	Depot-wise Operational Wastage	Fortnightly
4.	Operational Check Report	Monthly
5.	Route Effectiveness	Monthly

6.	Non Revenue kms Statement	Monthly
7.	Inventory of Routes	Yearly

III. Maintenance

1.	Depot-wise Vehicle Position Statement	Weekly
2.	Depot-wise Vehicle Days Statement	Monthly
3.	Depot-wise Performance of Scrap Tyre Statement	Monthly
4.	Depot-wise Type-wise (Fuel and Lub) KMPL Statement	Monthly
5.	Production Statement of BBU	Monthly
6.	Production Statement of Printing Press	Monthly
7.	Production Statement of Tyres	Monthly
8.	Production Statement of Work-shops	Monthly
9.	Inventory of Vehicles	Yearly

IV. Personnel

		Periodicity
1.	Performance Report of Purchase Depot	Monthly
2.	Performance Report of Stores/Purchase Depots Area-Wise Inventories, Tyres and Tubes/Trade Materials and Key Indicators	Monthly

V. Finance Management

1.	Region-wise Profits and Loss Account	Monthly
2.	Proportionate Budget Allotment Statement	Monthly
3.	Division-wise Profit and Loss Statement	Monthly
4.	Depot-wise Profit and Loss Statement	Monthly
5.	Area-wise working Results Statement	Monthly
6.	Review of Coaching Earnings Statement	Monthly
7.	Cash Flow Statement	Monthly
8.	Review of Audit Objections	Monthly
9.	Review of Suspense Account	Monthly
10.	Financial Statement	Yearly

List of all the statements compiled in central M.I.S. (Output)

I. General

1.	Task Register	Daily
2.	Key Result Area forecast	Monthly
3.	Peak Spotting	Monthly
4.	Managerial Performance Index	Monthly
5.	Inter Corporate Performance	Monthly
6.	Working of APSRTC as on the last day	Monthly

7.	Statistical Data to CIRT	Monthly/Yearly
8.	State Administration Report	Yearly
9.	Administration Report	Yearly
10.	Board Performance	Monthly
11.	Data to other agencies as and when required by them	(No Fixed Programme)
12.	Data to Research Scholars for their Study reports	(No Fixed Programme)

II. Traffic Management

1.	Review and Analysis of Operational Results (Division-wise)	Fortnigthly/Monthly/ Yearly
2.	Review and Analysis of Operational Wastage (Division-wise)	—do—
3.	Review and Analysis of Operational Non-Revenue kms	(Division-Monthly Yearly-wise)
4.	Commuter Satisfaction	Monthly/Yearly
5.	Review and Analysis of Operational Check Report	Monthly/Yearly
6.	Review and Analysis of Route Effectiveness	Monthly/Yearly
7.	Depot Managerial Finance Ranking	Monthly/Yearly
8.	Inter City Performance Report	Monthly/Yearly
9.	Performance Review of Traffic Management (Region-wise)	Yearly

III. Maintenance Management

1.	Review and Analysis of Vehicle Position Statement (Division-wise)	Weekly/Fortnightly
2.	Review and Analysis of Average Vehicle Position Statement (Division-wise)	Monthly/Yearly
3.	Review and Analysis of Scrap Tyre Performance Statement (Division-wise)	Monthly/Yearly
4.	Type-wise HSD and LUB KMPL Statement (Division-wise)	Monthly/Yearly
5.	Tyre Ranking (Depot-wise)	Monthly/Yearly
6.	Fuel Ranking (Depot-wise)	Monthly/Yearly
7.	Performance Review of Production Management (Region-wise)	Monthly/Yearly
8.	Performance Review of Maintenance Management (Region-wise)	Monthly/Yearly
9.	Inventory of Vehicles	Yearly

IV. Personnel Management

1.	Review and Analysis of staff position (Division-wise)	Quarterly

2.	Human Productivity (Division-wise)	Monthly/Yearly
3.	Performance Review of Personnel Management (Region-wise)	Monthly/Yearly
4.	Depot-wise Bus Staff Ratio Ranking	Monthly/Yearly
5.	Employees Productivity Ranking	Quarterly
	V. Material Management	
1.	Performance Review of Material Management (Region-wise)	Monthly/Yearly
	VI. Finance Management	
1.	Review and Analysis Coaching Earnings	Monthly/Yearly
2.	Review and Analysis Region-wise Working Results	Monthly/Yearly
3.	Review and Analysis Financial Results	Monthly/Yearly
4.	Cash Flow	Monthly
5.	Review and Analysis Audit Objections	Monthly
6.	Review and Analysis Suspense Account	Yearly
7.	Review and Analysis Working Results	Monthly/Yearly
8.	Budgetary Review	Monthly
9.	Financial Position of Public Undertakings in A.P.	Yearly
10.	Revised Monthly Regions' Operations and Output of Services	Monthly

The Regional MIS Wing is headed by a Statistical Officer/ Statistical Superintendent. He has ten assistants in Sr. Statistician, Statistician, Statistical Assistant, Jr. Statistician and Computist categories. The Regional Statistical Officer/Statistical Superintendent is under the direct administrative control of the Regional Manager. However, he may receive technical guidance from the Chief Statistical Officer.

The Chief Statistical Officer is incharge of the Central MIS Wing located in Head Office. He reports direct to the Vice-Chairman and General Manager. He is assisted by two Statistical officers and a large contingent of statistical personnel numbering 58 of different capacities.

Deficiencies of the existing management information systems

(1) Depot is the base of operations. It is the place where the end product of the organisation is produced. It is also the place where the raw primary data is available. At such a place as this,

there is no staff trained in MIS Work. The various basic documents that emanate from Depot are compiled by ADCs and Conductors. They are not trained for the job either.

(2) The staff compiling the returns at depot level are under the administrative control of the Depot Manager/Supervisor Incharge. The returns furnished by the Depot Manager/Supervisor Incharge reflect performance of the depot. The performance of the Depot Manager/SIC is evaluated based on the results as shown in the returns. As such there is a tendency for the Depot Manager/SIC to manipulate the figures to his advantage. This is going un-noticed now. Hence, there is need for cross-verification of data and effective control on the correctness of data furnished.

(3) The Regional Statistical Officer/Statistical Superintendent is under the administrative control of the Regional Manager. He is also functionally a subordinate to the Chief Statistical Officer. Thus the Regional Statistical Officer reports to two authorities simultaneously. This is a typical case of the absence of unity of command, with all the attendant evil consequences.

(4) The Corporation is yet to have a management information systems manual which serves as a guide and reference for the statistical personnel in discharging their duties. The manual prepared by an experienced, and retired Statistical Officer under the supervison of another experienced and retired Chief Statistical Officer in the year 1979 is yet to see the light of the day. It has been gathering dust in the office records for reasons best known to the Top Management.

(5) There is duplication of work at various levels. For example, the route-wise earnings registers which are maintained and referred to by the Depot Managers for economic analysis of the individual routes, are also maintained in the offices of the Divisional Managers, Regional Managers and the Chief Traffic Manager in the Head Office.

(6) In the absence of a manual for MIS a number of new statements is required to be submitted by the Regional Statistical Officer and the Depot Managers to the Chief Statistical Officer from time to time while the old ones are continued. There is duplication of work on this account also as no redundant statements have been identified whenever new statements are

introduced. No uniform systems are adopted in all the regions. The work of statistical personnel is not standardised. Nor is there any uniform work list given to them.

(7) There is no MIS wing in the office of the Divisional Manager though the Divisional Manager is considered as a line Manager overseeing the performance of the Depots in his Division. The MIS work in the Divisional Office is carried out with the help of conductors or the clerical staff who are again not trained in the work.

(8) There is no precise demarcation of MIS work at various levels of management resulting in unnecessary repetition of work at all levels. For example, the Depot Managers have to review the daily KMPL figures of his depot for control purpose. It is not necessary that the same shall be done for all the depots at the divisional and regional levels also. It is enough if the weekly KMPL figures are reviewed at the divisional office and the monthly KMPL figures at the regional and Head Office.

(9) Considering the workload of the staff attached to the central MIS wing, the central MIS wing is found to be over-staffed. The industrial engineering unit which conducted a study on this aspect in the recent past found that the central MIS Wing was having surplus staff. The data processing machines hired by the Central MIS Wing on payment of Rs. 10,000 per month towards rent, are underutilised. Only the work relating to the printing of salary bills is done with the help of these machines. Ironically the salary bills are prepared manually before they are fed to the machines for the sake of print-outs.

(10) The functions of MIS do not end with collection of data and presentation of the processed data to Managers for taking decisions. The data collected shall be stored in such a way that retrieval of data becomes possible and easier at a future date. Such a data bank is yet to find place in the existing set up of MIS. For this reason alone, the information relating to category-wise staff position in APSRTC for the years 1973-74, 1977-78 and 1981-82 could not be furnished by the Corporation even though four months had elapsed from the time of requisition.

(11) One of the characteristics of MIS is that the set-up of MIS shall undergo a change with every change in the organisa-

tional structure so that the information needs as identified in the reorganised structure are ably met. The reorganisation done in the year 1978 witnessed only creation of one more tier of MIS in the office of the Regional Manager. The decentralisation of functions of the central MIS wing as envisaged did not take place.

(12) The performance reports put up to the Vice-Chairman and General Manager, Regional Managers and Heads of Departments for the purpose of review in the monthly meetings are so voluminous that one is often lost in the maze of statistics. It can be deduced that the information needs at various levels of management are not assessed based on the types of decisions taken at every level of management. It is a typical example of one of the common misconceptions of MIS the "More Information Better Decisions".

New design of MIS—multiple corporations

The system which provides information to the management for taking decisions is called the 'Management Information System'. Decision-making, the most important function of a manager, is the ultimate objective with which the information is compiled. So much so, the type of information fed to the managers varies depending upon the nature of decisions taken. The nature of decisions taken changes with every change in the level of management in which the managers are placed. For, it is based on the level of management that the tasks assigned to individual managers are determined. The levels of management, the tasks assigned, the inter-relationships of the tasks, etc., form the basic ingredients of the organisational structure. Thus, study of the organisational structure of any organisation without examining the efficacy of the MIS simultaneously is incomplete. While the organisation structure has a bearing on the MIS, the MIS also influences the effectiveness of the organisational structure designed. If the needs of the information and the periodicity with which the information is to be fed to managers are not properly identified, the managers fail to take correct and timely decisions for the accomplishment of the tasks assigned to them. The unfulfilled task is a blot on the management and the organisation.

What has been true of a large scale organisation, is true of a state transport undertaking like the APSRTC as well. For, the APSRTC is also a business organisation in a way. One of the corporate objectives set for the APSRTC is to conduct its activities on business lines.

Corporate objectives

The activities of the APSRTC are governed by the Corporate objectives set by the RTC Act, 1950. The main objective is to provide efficient, adequate, economical and co-ordinated transport services to the travelling public. The other is to organise itself on business lines, while achieving the aforesaid objective.

Determination of tasks and indicators of performance

Corporate Objective	Task	Indicator of Performance
Efficiency	Resource utilisation	Fleet utilisation
		Vehicle utilisation
		Crew utilisation
	Cost Control	Fuel Performance
		Tyre Performance
		Spare parts Consumption
		Lubricants Consumption
	Vehicle condition	Cleanliness of buses
		Seats comfort
	Punctuality	Cancellation and delays
	Reliability of services	Rate of breakdowns
	Safety	Rate of Accidents
Adequacy	Sufficiency of routes	No. of villages connected
		No. of trips operated
	Sufficiency of comfort	Deluxe services
		Express services
		Chartered services
Co-ordination	Internal Co-ordination	Inter-divisional services
		Inter-Corporate services
		Inter-state services
	External co-ordination	Rail connections
		Competition with rail transport
Economical	Reasonable fare	Cost Analysis
		Profitability
		Return on Capital

Corporate Objective	Task	Indicator of Performance
Business lines	Survival Growth	Margin of profit Fleet strength Staff strength Gross Revenue Internal resources generated Capital contributions

Levels of management

For fulfilment of the above said objectives, the new organisational structure provides for two-tier management for each independent corporation suggested—Head office and the Depot. Again, depending upon the functions of the officers, three levels of management can be identified—Top Management, Middle Management and the Lower Management.

The Corporation Board and the General Manager constitute the Top Management. Their functions are to evolve strategies for the realisation of the corporate objectives, to draw long-term and short-term plans, to formulate policies, to determine the tasks, etc. These functions relate to *strategic planning.*

The Additional General Manager and the Heads of Departments—Chief Traffic Manager, Chief Mechanical Engineer, and Chief Accounts Officer—can be grouped under the Middle Management. Officers at this level of management organise execution of policies formulated by the top management, prepare work plans, review the results obtained, and exercise control over the activities at the lower level of Management. These functions relate to *Management Control.*

Management control

The Depot Managers and Assistant Depot Managers are at the lower level of management, as they are responsible for actual implementation of the policies and accomplishment of the tasks assigned. These functions relate to *operational control.*

Types of Decisions

Depending upon the nature of functions as mentioned above, the following decisions are identified at each level of management.

Strategic planning

Decisions relating to capital structure, capital expenditure, long-term and short-term borrowings, Budgetary control, Annual plans, Depreciation, Nationalisation, Operations, Rate fixation, Manpower planning, Personnel policies, Stores purchase, Inventory control, Purchase of vehicles, Scrapping of vehicles, Maintenance systems, Passenger amenities, Labour welfare measures, and so on.

Management centrol

Decisions relating to resources utilisation—Vehicle and crew utilisation, Scheduling, Operations, Recruitment and Training, Industrial relations, Production at Workshops, Stores Management, Facilities at Bus stations, tenders of canteen, Pan shop, etc. Public Relations, Performance of Depots, Review and Control, Ticket checking, and so on.

Operational control

Decisions relating to conduct of operations, maintenance of vehicles, control of staff, Wages of staff, Disciplinary actions, Working hours of staff, Industrial relations, Allotment of duties to staff, Bus station management, Provision of passenger amenities, Public complaints, Motor Vehicle and other taxes, Permits, Implementation of provisions of M.T.W. Act, Factories Act, Route-wise performance, Pilferage, Infringement of monopoly, Retirement and settlement of dues and so on.

Information needs

The following information needs are identified at each level of management.

Level	Type of Information required	Periodicity
Strategic Planning	Operational Performance Reports	Monthly
	Production Reports	,,
	Resources utilisation Reports	,,
	Report on inventory control	,,
	,, Cash flow	,,
	,, Cost analysis	,,
	,, Industrial relations	,,
	,, Incentive scheme	,,

Level		Type of Information required	Periodicity
Strategic Planning	Report on	Manpower planning	Quarterly
	,,	Personnel policies	,,
	,,	Capital and Revenue expenditure	,,
	,,	Capital contributions	,,
	,,	Long-term borrowings	,,
	,,	Interest on capital and borrowings	,,
	,,	Progress of Civil Engg. Works	,,
	,,	Stores purchases	,,
	,,	Nationalisation of passenger services	Annual
	,,	Augmentation of services on the existing routes	,,
	,,	Fare fixation	,,
	,,	Annual plans	,,
	,,	Budget	,,
	,,	Purchase and scrapping of vehicles	,,
	,,	Utilisation of depreciation fund and other internal resources	,,
	,,	Labour welfare activities	,,
Management Control	,,	Report on daily earnings	Weekly
	,,	Vehicle position	,,
	,,	Fuel performance	,,
	,,	Cancellation and delays	,,
	,,	Vehicle failures	,,
	,,	New services introduced	,,
	,,	Cost analysis	Monthly
	,,	Route-wise earnings	,,
	,,	Accidents	,
	,,	Ticket checks	,,
	,,	Public Complaints	,,
	,,	Tyre performance	,,
	,,	Local purchases	,,
	,,	Workshop and Stores supplies	,,
	,,	Absenteeism	,,
	,,	M.V. Act irregularities	,,
Operation Control	,,	Daily earnings	Daily
	,,	Vehicle position	,,
	,,	Fuel performance	,,
	,,	Cancellation and delays	,,
	,,	Breakdowns	,,
	,,	Route-wise earnings	,,
	,,	Vehicle-wise KMPL	,,
	,,	Driver-wise KMPL	,,
	,,	Absenteeism	,,

Level	Type of Information required	Periodicity
	,, Ticket checks	Weekly
	,, Tyre performance	,,
	,, Public complaints	,,
	,, Workshop and stores supplies	,,
	,, Local purchases	,,
	,, Cost Analysis	Monthly
	,, Funds position	,,
	,, Vehicle Maintenance schedule	,,
	,, Miscellaneous revenue	,,
	,, M.V. Act Irregularities	,,
	,, Inventory of Vehicles	Annual
	,, Inventory of stores	,,
	,, Inventory of tyres	,,
	,, Statutory returns	,,

Organisation of MIS

In accordance with the organisational structure recommended for multiple corporations the MIS for each independent corporation is proposed to have two wings – the control MIS Wing located in the office of the General Manager and the Depot" MIS Wing established in all the Depots. Central MIS wing meets the information needs of the Corporation Board, the General Manager, the Additional General Manager and the Heads of the Departments. The Depot MIS Wing primarily generates basic data for processing and use by the Central MIS wing and also feeds the Depot Manager such information as is required by him for control purpose at the Depot level.

There may be an apprehension that the proposal to establish a Depot MIS Wing in all the depots of the Corporation (numbering 112) may come in for criticism on the ground that it results in increase in the number of statistical personnel at a time when the organisation is already overstaffed. There is no need to entertain such an apprehension as the proposal does not entail any extra staff. There are two ADCs allotted to each depot in the existing set up for preparation of the statistical reports. The ADC working in the earning section prepares MTD 108, MTD 110, MTD 118, MTD 230, etc. The ADC attached to maintenance wing compiles MTD 151, MTD 151A, Vehicle Log sheet challan, KMPL returns, tyre reports, etc. These two ADCs who are considered as the depot staff at present may be treated as the statistical personnel and may be brought into the fold of MIS after being given necessary training, wherever found necessary. In the new set up they will continue to be under the administrative control of the Depot Manager/SIC.

The Statistical Personnel now working in the central MIS Wing and the six Regional MIS wings put together will be distributed and attached to the proposed units of the central MIS Wings in all the autonomous multiple corporations recommended.

Information flow

The Depot forms the information source. All the basic data flows from here. At the same time, it is not necessary that whatever data that is generated at the Depot level shall be reported, as collection and compilation of data costs a lot. A judicious filteration is necessary. It is enough if data relating to key-result areas is furnished by the Depot MIS wing to the central MIS wing. Here again there may be two types of information outflows : the on-going information flow and the one-time information flow. The on-going information flow may be in respect of all the key result areas. The one-time information flow may be for specific data required to meet a particular need arising occasionally. For example, review of the performance of an experimental unit fitted to the vehicles.

The frequency of information flow is also a factor to reckon with. It may not be necessary that information relating to every key result area shall be reported daily to the central MIS wing. Periodical reporting may suffice. It depends upon the importance of the item of information communicated in terms of time. For example, information relating to earnings, kilometres operated, cancellation, and vehicle position may be required daily while the fuel performance, tyre performance, route-wise earnings, etc., may be required periodically in the central MIS wing. Similarly, financial information like cost analysis, may be required monthly.

In the new set up of multiple corporations suggested, the structure of depot management was not changed except that an Assistant Depot Manager was provided to assist the Depot Manager in all the cases of depots having a fleet strength of 60 and above. Secondly, only the function of scheduling was proposed to be withdrawn from the Depot Manager for reasons explained and all the other functions were retained as they were at depot level. Thirdly, by and large, the depot management was found to be satisfactory. As such, the pattern now followed for the outflow of information from the depot—the types of reports, the periodicity, and the contents of reports—is to be continued in the new set up also.

Information processing

The processing of information in the central MIS wing, however, undergoes a change in the new set up. For the central MIS wing is required to cater to the needs of two levels of management in the head office—Top Management, and the Middle Management. The reports put up to the Top Management are for the purpose of planning. The reports fed to the Middle Management are for control purposes. It is the purpose that determines the contents of the reports and the periodicity.

Accordingly, the following control reports are recommended for preparation and submission to the Additional General Manager, the Chief Traffic Manager, the Chief Mechanical Engineer and the Cheif Accounts Officer.

Level	Name of the report	Periodicity
To the Additional General Manager	The Report on earnings	Weekly
	,, Kilometres operated	,,
	,, Vehicle position	,,
	,, Fuel performance	,,
	,, Cancellation and Delays	,,
	,, Vehicle failures	,,
	,, Cost analysis	Monthly
	,, Route-wise earnings	,,
	,, Accidents	,,
	,, Public complaints	,,
	,, Tyre performance	,,
	,, Local Purchases	,,
	,, Workshop and stores supplies	,,
	,, Absenteeism	,,
To the Chief Traffic Manager	,, Earnings	Weekly
	,, kms operated	,,

Level	Name of the report	Periodicity
	Report on Vehicle position	Weekly
	,, Cancellation and delays	,,
To the Chief Traffic Manager	,, Cost analysis	Monthly
	,, Route-wise earnings	,,
	,, Public complaints	,,
	,, Absenteeism	,,
	,, Accidents	,,
To the Chief Mechanical Engineer	Report on Workshop and Tyre shop Production	Weekly
	,, Vehicle position	,,
	,. Fuel Performance	,,
	,, Cancellation and delays	,,
	,, Vehicle failures	,,
	,, Cost analysis	Monthly
	,, Tyre performance	,,
	,, Workshop and stores supplies	,,
To the Chief Accounts Officer	,, Cost analysis	,,

The following planning reports may be put up by the Central MIS Wing to the Corporation Board and the General Manager.

To the Corporation Board and General Manager	Report on Operational Performance	Monthly
	,, Production reports	,,
	,, Resourees utilisation	,,
	,, Cost analysis	,,
	,, Industrial Relations	,,
	,, Capital Contributions	Quarterly
	,, Capital expenditure	,,
	,, Progress of Civil Engg. Works	,,
	,, Nationalisation	Annual
	,, Fare Revision	,,

The contents and the formats of the reports as they are adopted now may be continued in the new set up also.

Information for meetings and reviews

One of the functions of the Incharge MIS is to put up performance reports to the Managers for review in the periodical meetings held. At present such meetings are held in the offices of the General Manager, the Regional Manager, and the Divisional Manager. In the meeting convened by the General Manager the Regional Managers and the other Heads of the Departments participate. The meeting convened by the Regional Manager at the Regional level is attended by the Divisional Managers. The Divisional Manager, in his turn, holds meeting of the Depot Managers of his division. All these meetings are at present held once in a month. The performance report put up by the MIS Wing to the General Manager and the Regional Manager are one month old. In the Depot Managers' meeting also one month old information is reviewed. Review of one month old performance reports may be all right as far as the Regional Managers' meeting is concerned. For it may not be feasible and desirable also to convene the meeting of Regional Managers more than once in a month for reviewing the performance of the regions. But in the meetings of the Divisional Managers, and the Depot Managers convened by the Regional Managers and the Divisional Managers respectively, the periodicity needs to be reduced, as the review of performance reports in the periodical meetings held should serve a meaningful purpose. The objective is not merely to review the performance which is already one month old, but to take corrective action so that the damage done during the period under review is immediately checked, and does not recur in the following period.

Therefore, it is suggested that, in the new set up recommended, the periodicity of the meetings of Depot Managers convened by the Additional General Manager to whom they report directly shall be once in ten days so that the corrective action taken for avoiding further damage being done may show results in the next ten days period of the month, rather than postponing the corrective action, for full one month as is happening now. The Central MIS Wing may have to prepare and put up performance reports of the Depots in the new set up suggested to the Additional General Manager once in ten days. For the meetings of the Additional General Manager and the Heads of the Departments convened by the General Manager, however, monthly performance reports may be put up.

Data bank

In the new set up suggested, there is a dire need to organise a data bank in the Central MIS Wing so that the data collected and processed may be stored for its retrieval at a future date. It is not proper to direct the Depot MIS Wing to furnish data of the yester years, whenever need arises, as a large amount of data is generated daily in the depots whether used or not. To preserve all the data that is generated daily is a herculian task, besides the problem of space and the extra expenditure involved. In the case of the Central MIS Wing, however, only selected information is received from the Depots periodically. Hence the suggestion.

Mechanisation

In all the large scale organisations, the order of the day has been computerisation of information, on account of the innumerable advantages derived there from. Yet, mechanisation of information is not suggested for the multiple corporations proposed taking into account the smaller size of the corporation and the huge investment involved. Further, it is noted that the sister organisations like BEST, and MRTC, which have gone in for large computers, are not using the computers for the MIS purposes and have limited the use of computers to inventory control, pay rolls, etc. The experiences of the above said organisations have shown that the manual system of MIS is best suited for a nationalised transport undertaking.

Design of MIS—Modified regional set up

In the earlier chapter, modified regional set up was suggested as an alternative organisational structure to that of the multiple corporations, in case the latter could not be implemented. The chief distinguishing features of the modified regional set up are that the independent regions proposed have Regional Management Boards in the place of the corporation boards and that a small Head Office exists to co-ordinate the activities of all the regions. There is no other major difference in organisational structure suggested for both the proposals. As such, the new design of MIS suggested for multiple corporations can be advantageously adopted in toto for the modified regional set-up also. In addition, there may be an apex MIS wing located in the head office to feed information to the Chairman, Chief General Manager, and the other advisors proposed. This apex MIS wing is designed to play only a limited role in that it receives information relating to performance reports of all the regions (Department wise) and puts up consolidated reports to the Corporation Board, Chief General Manager, and his Advisors for review in the periodical meetings and for feed-forward action. It may be made clear that the apex MIS wing is not to oversee the activities of the Central MIS Wing located in each region and the Depot MIS wings, lest the autonomous character of the regions should be taken away.

The various reports due to be sent to the State Government, the Central Government, and the other outside organisations may have to be sent by the regional MIS wings (Central MIS Wings) direct as in the case of the multiple corporations proposed. Copies of the same may, however, be marked to the apex MIS Wing for information and record.

CORPORATE PLAN

Through our letter dated 12 November 1981, it was made clear that the policy projections in respect of corporate plan and other matters depend upon the policies of the Government, regarding further nationalisation. However, it was also mentioned that those would be covered so far as they are incidental to the recommendations for structural, organisational and financial reforms.

The only recommendation that could be made in this regard at the corporate level is the splitting up of the corporation. No further corporate plan can be given unless the policy regarding the splitting up of the existing corporation is decided. Further, the preparation of the corporate plan would also depend upon the policy of the Government and the corporation regarding further nationalisation of not only stage carriages but also contract carriages. The replies of the Government and the corporation on questions to these issues are vague and not definite. The Government simply stated that its policy is "to progressively nationalise the entire stage carriage services in the state". From this, the pace of nationalisation and time phase of nationalisation are not clear. This is all the more so in view of the fact that the schemes of nationalisation notified by the corporation as early as 1977 are still pending with the Government. The reply to the query on nationalisation of contract carriages is more elusive.

The replies of the corporation are also equally vague as they mention a number of variables which are beyond their control and which influence the pace of nationalisation, such as, availability of funds, chassis, governmental policy, inability of the corporation to take over the private services as contemplated. In so far as contract carriages are concerned, the corporation states that the nationalisation of these services "is also under consideration", and "depending upon the financial position and other factors".

In view of all these constraints, the preparation of a corporate plan would be a futile exercise. It is, therefore, suggested that the Government should come out very clearly and in unequivocal terms, on its policy on completion of nationalisation of stage carriages and extension of nationalisation to contract carriages.

REFERENCES

1. Explanatory Memorandum on the Revised Budget Estimate for 1981-82 and Budget Eetimates for 1982-83, in respect of APSRTC, p. 25.
2. File on Bus-Staff Ratio P. 4/08S/237(1)/81 PD.
3. File pertaining to ID 17/78 Sri Shaik Ibrahim.
4. Vide Corporation Circular No. XI/1979/IED Dated 7-1-1980.
5. Incentive files of the Corporation.
6. Incentive files of the Corporation.

4

SUMMARY OF FINDINGS AND RECOMMENDATIONS

Financial results

1. During the short-period of five years : 1977-78—1981-82, the Corporation had accumulated a loss of Rs. 66.55 crores resulting in capital erosion to the extent of 72.73 per cent.

2. The Organisation has been treating a sizeable portion of the accumulated depreciation fund under the head "Withdrawals from Internal Resources for Capital Expenditure" as a part of investment base for calculating the return on investment. Because of this, the return on investment, as reported, shows a much lower figure than what it is.

3. The losses that the organisation has been incurring in the recent years could be attributed to the cost-fare-lags, to a great extent.

Operating and non-operating results

4. There was a sudden increase in the percentage share of non-operating expenditure from 1979-80 onwards and a steep decline in non-operating revenues during 1980-81 and 1981-82. This was because of the changing capital structure consequent upon increased long-term borrowings which contributed to increased non-operating expenditure. This happened in view of the fact that the government failed in its responsibility in providing adequate capital contributions.

Financial results of mofussil and city operations

5. The corporation has been incurring losses on mofussil services since 1978-79, even though it has been incurring losses

on the whole since 1977-78. Out of the total accumulated loss of Rs. 66.55 crores, the city services alone accounted for 30.93 per cent, while the fleet on the city services constituted about ten per cent of the total.

6. The total losses on city services since 1968-69 amounted to Rs. 29.50 crores, which implies that the organisation had lost more than three times the investment made on fleet in the city services.

Trends in cost structure

7. During the period 1973-74—1981-82, the total cost per km of operations increased by more than 130 per cent. The highest increase in costs took place in the case of fuel—from 24.98 paise in 1973-74 to 80.77 paise in 1981-82—thereby increasing its share in the total cost from 17.04 to 23.83 per cent.

Staff cost

8. The staff cost increased by more than 100 per cent during 1973-74—1981-82. The schedule-staff-ratio increased consistently from 1977-78 till 1980-81. There was relatively more increase in staff in the categories of (1) drivers and conductors and, (2) others. With 1976-77 schedule-staff-ratio as the norm, the staff per schedule has gone up by 5.67 per cent.

9. The schedule-staff-ratio was the highest in APSRTC when compared with that in comparable organisations or the norms in Tamil Nadu. Based on the GSRTC ratio, the APSRTC had surplus staff of 9,140 to operate its schedules of 1980-81. Even against the corporation having the highest schedule-staff-ratio in Tamil Nadu, the APSRTC had excess staff of 13,825 (excess of 2.39 per schedule).

10. The APSRTC incurred for one year in 1980-81 alone excess expenditure on staff to the tune of Rs. 7.70 crores based upon GSRTC staff ratio; Rs. 11.60 crores based on Kattabomman ratio.

11. The solutions for this problem are (1) to split the organisation, (2) adoption of a voluntary retirement scheme and (3) augmentation of fleet without further recruitment.

12. A substantial part of the losses—45 per cent to 87 per cent—was accounted for by excess staff.

13. There is need for fixing scientifically based norms of staff

and adhering to the same.

14. The inefficiency of the organisation in terms of staff contributed Rs. 3.08 crores of additional expenditure/loss and the wage inflation accounted for Rs. 38.94 crores.

15. The productivity of crew in terms of effective kms done per year has been on the decline since 1976-77.

Cost of spares

16. Over the last five years, the corporation incurred an additional expenditure of Rs. 13.04 crores because of inflation. However, the percentage share of cost of spares came down during the period because of improvement in efficiency in stores consumption and relative increase in other costs.

17. The average cost of spares per vehicle in APSRTC was more than 200 per cent over that in GSRTC, a comparable organisation. It is also much more than that of most of the State Transport Undertakings in Tamil Nadu. Hence, there is still considerable scope for improvement in this respect.

Tyre performance

18. Tyre performance is another area where the organisation has shown improvement in performance. However, this cannot perhaps be entirely attributed to the organisational efficiency as it could have been due to the improvement in the technology of tyres.

Fuel cost

19. It is a matter for concern that the fuel efficiency was on decline after 1976-77, when it had the highest KMPL. The corporation incurred an additional expenditure of Rs. 4.45 crores, during the last five years, because of decline in fuel efficiency.

20. The organisation could save an amount of Rs. 54 lakhs due to improvement in KMPL in 1981-82.

21. The organisation had to spend an additional amount of Rs. 45.03 crores on HSD Oil because of inflation, during the last five years.

Motor vehicle and other taxes levied by the state government

22. The fact that the tax per vehicle or tax per km has been consistently on the increase, except for one year, clearly shows

the apathy of the state government to its own child. It looks as though the state government considers the corporation as a milch cow to extract as much revenue as possible by way of taxes, raising the same even in times of losses.

23. The tax per km in the case of city services works out to 50 to 60 per cent more than what it is in the case of mofussil services.

24. The Corporation had, in a way, saved Rs. 5.41 crores on tax by better utilisation of fleet during 1976-77—1981-82.

25. There is a strong case either for drastically reducing the tax rate on city services, on par with the tax on city services elsewhere, that is, in Tamil Nadu or give a subsidy to the APSRTC on its city services.

26. The tax per km, on city services in APSRTC, works out to 158 per cent to 534 per cent more than what it works out to in the case of other undertakings. It is, therefore, recommended that the rate of motor vehicle tax on city services of APSRTC be reduced to a minimum of one-third of the present rate.

27. It is inadvisable to levy motor vehicle tax on passenger revenue basis as it has an inbuilt element of inflation. A better alternative would be to tax the organisation on the basis of vehicles operated in a quarter irrespective of the routes on which they are operated.

Depreciation

28. The policy of depreciating vehicles, firstly on original book value and secondly on increased kilometrage results not only in incapacitating the organisation to renew the vehicles when needed but also handicaps the organisation to project real losses to ask for appropriate increase in fares at a time when it incurs losses.

29. If the corporation had pursued the policy of depreciating vehicles at 4.8 lakhs kms the additional cost of depreciation would have been Rs. 13.07 crores over the six year period.

30. The inflation had cost the organisation, on its depreciation, Rs. 7.03 crores in 1981-82 alone and Rs. 18.00 crores for the last six years.

31. The organisation was forced to go in for long-term high cost borrowings from outside, thereby further inflating the costs

of organisation, because of its depreciation policy and inadequate provisions of capital contributions by the participating governments.

32. If depreciation has been provided on replacement cost basis the additional cost to the organisation would have been Rs. 25.71 crores. If the depreciation is to be provided on 4.8 lakh kilometres on replacement cost basis, the additional depreciation cost would have been Rs. 40.78 crores for the period.

Interest

33. The alarming position regarding interest is the fact that the interest on long-term borrowings has been increasing significantly both in absolute and relative terms during the recent years, resulting in increased cost of capital.

34. The additional interest cost because of increase in the price of vehicles amounted to Rs. 161.59 lakhs during the period.

Miscellaneous costs

35. The Corporation had to incur an additional expenditure of Rs. 122.36 lakhs on miscellaneous items because of inflation.

Operational performance

36. There was an improvement in average passenger kilometres done per schedule since 1976-77 until 1979-80, and since then there was a decline even though the performance in these last two years was better than that in 1976-77.

37. The reasons for decline in vehicular utilisation could be broadly attributed to the poor maintenance of vehicles, inadequate supply of units by the workshops and the increasing average age of the vehicles. The statement that it could be because of poor maintenance or inadequate supply of units by workshops and stores is amply proved by the fact that cancellation of kms due to late supply and for want of bus increased considerably during the period. There was generally an increase in the percentage of kilometres cancelled since 1973-74 and particularly since 1976-77.

Losses of APSRTC : Impact of inflation and operational managerial efficiency

38. The Corporation had incurred an additional expenditure of Rs. 182.13 crores on different items of expenditure due to inflation since 1977-78, based upon 1976-77 costs. Of this, the increase in emoluments of staff alone accounted for Rs. 74.15 crores, that is about 40 per cent of the total inflation effect. The next major item which had substantially influenced the costs of the organisation is fuel which accounted for Rs. 45.03 crores, that is 24.73 per cent of the total increase. Among the other items, tyres and tubes, depreciation, spare parts and taxes may be mentioned as important, in that order, accounting for 10.53 per cent, 9.88 per cent, 7.16 per cent and 5.20 per cent respectively of the increase in the costs.

39. While the inflation resulted in additional expenditure of Rs. 182.13 crores, the fare increases had fetched the corporation additional revenues to the extent of only Rs. 94.71 crores, leaving the organisation with a short-fall of Rs. 87.42 crores. The corporation could realise additional revenues by putting in improved operational efficiency to the extent of Rs. 36.81 crores, thereby reducing the losses during the period, based on these computations, to Rs. 50.61 crores. This figure is in divergence with the figure of reported losses.

40. It cannot be denied that the organisation could reduce the possible losses to the extent of at least Rs. 36.81 crores, by improving its operational efficiency.

41. The increased losses incurred by the corporation since 1977-78 cannot be attributed to increased inefficiency on the part of the organisation. It must, however, be noted that the organisational efficiency, in some respects, has gone down, e.g., staff when compared with its own past performance, and there is ample scope for improvement in respect of staff, stores and fuel when compared with other organisations.

42. The remedy for the losses lies in reducing the schedule-staff-ratio, apart from the improvement in performance in the areas mantioned earlier.

Analysis of reasons for losses

43. Apart from tbe recommendations that the Motor

Vehicle Tax on city services should be reduced to the level as recommended earlier, the M.V. Tax on VLTS vehicles should be reduced to a nominal rate of Rs. 10/- per seat per quarter. Further, any loss the corporation incurs on city service for reasons beyond its operational efficiency must be made good by the Government by way of subsidy.

Leakage of revenue

44. The Corporation is losing approximately Rs. 4.50 crores per year due to leakage of revenue. There is a strong case for the immediate revival of the ground booking system.

45. A separate cadre may be created for the checking inspectors and young men may be recruited for this purpose considering the arduous duties involved.

46. More jeeps may be allotted to the checking squads to facilitate extensive coverage and to ensure element of surprise.

47. The corporation should take full advantage of the APMV Rules devolving responsibility for ticket-less travel on the passengers.

Staff car

48. The staff cars may be withdrawn and fixed allowance may be paid to the officers for maintaining their own vehicles. It is suggested that the officers be provided with a loan assistance of Rs. 50,000 each for purchasing cars and be paid a fixed allowance of Rs. 300 per month as car maintenance allowance. The net savings on this account work out to Rs. 15.74 lakhs per annum.

City Services

49. The hurried nationalisation, particularly in Visakhapatnam, resulted in various problems arising out of lack of infrastructural facilities.

50. Another problem, peculiar to city services, is the pressure of specific groups demanding concessions, committed trips and so on. The committed trips usually result in unidirectional traffic consisting of passholders, depriving the corporation of alternative earning opportunities.

51. The congestion of traffic results in lower vehicle

utilisation in city services.

52. Another contributing factor to city losses is high motor vehicle taxation.

53. The lower revenues on city services are due to inadequate and poor quality of checking.

54. The norms laid down for the collection incentive scheme were quite low, contributing to higher costs.

55. City services are burdened with higher staff costs for various reasons.

56. The following measures are suggested for reducing the losses on city services :

(i) Improved performance ;
(ii) Reduction, if not complete elimination, of committed trips ;
(iii) Improved and intensified checking on city routes, inclusive of reintroduction of mobile courts ;
(iv) Creation of a separate city corporation to make it eligible to receive special assistance from central government and World Bank ;
(v) Reduction of motor vehicle tax on city services ;
(vi) Subsidy for the losses incurred because of the concessions thrust on it by the Government.

Special employment scheme

57. The Special Employment Scheme resulted in excess appointment of 1041 candidates over the norms, resulting in recurring cost on this item to the tune of Rs. 66.56 lakhs per annum.

58. Further, due to various relaxations, ineligible and incompetent persons were selected, adding to the costs.

59. In addition, the corporation had suffered a loss of Rs. 86 lakhs on the training costs over and above what the government has sanctioned.

SETWIN

60. The total loss for being entangled with SETWIN worked out to Rs. 54.75 lakhs upto February, 1982.

61. The link up with SETWIN is an instance of the State Government's deep inroads into the autonomy of the Corporation.

VLTS

62. The losses on VLTS increased since the launching of the scheme and stood at accumulated total of Rs. 12.25 crores, at the end of 1981-82.

Cargo services

63. The corporation sustained a loss of Rs. 44.42 lakhs during the last two years on operating the cargo services.

Concessions

64. The losses due to concessions run to a sum of Rs. 7.22 crores a year. The remedy for this is for the State Government to come to the rescue of the Corporation by reimbursing the cost of concessions.

Apathy of the state government

65. The state government may consider amendments to the A.P. M.V. Rules as suggested by the APSRTC, to the extent that they are not repugnant to the other provisions of the Act.

Infringement of monopoly

66. Even if the lowest of the estimates is taken into consideration, the minimum loss of revenue of the Corporation on account of infringement of monopoly rights is Rs. 9.00 crores per annum.

67. It is recommended that the government shall confer the power to check private vehicles on the officials of the APSRTC.

68. There is need for total nationalisation of not only the stage carriages but also the contract carriages in the state.

Antagonistic attitude of transport authorities

69. One of the issues on which there was hostile attitude of the transport authorities is the interpretation of the various provisions of the M.V. Act and Rules. Some of the instances are listed hereunder :

(a) Granting temporary permits to the Private Operators under Section 68F (1—c), liberally invoking the judgement of the High Court, to the detriment of the corporation.

(b) Transport Authorities resorting to similar action without following the provisions of Sections 68F (1—A), where the Corporation publishes draft schemes under Section 68E.

(c) The schemes published by the Corporation for the take over of inter-state routes in Anantapur and Chittoor districts have been pending with the State Government for approval for a long time, for one reason or the other.

(d) The attitude of the Transport Authorities was reported to be partisan (in favour of private operators), in the regions where dual operations exist.

Cost-fare relationship and computation of cost index for periodical and automatic fare increase

70. The corporation had to wait for about two and a half years after it had started incurring losses on its mofussil services to get fare increase on ordinary services.

71. The fares on city services have not been increased for a period of six and a half years—1974 to 1980—even though the corporation had been incurring losses on city services all these years.

72. The corporation was allowed to suffer losses without giving fare increases at a time when the costs were going up.

73. In the light of the policy of levying surcharge at a time when the corporation made profits, the government should have allowed fare increases at a time when the Corporation incurred losses because of cost increases, consequent upon inflation or in the alternative should have done away with surcharge if not reduce the motor vehicle tax.

Cost computation for fare fixation

74. To take care of increase in costs, because of inflationary reasons, it is suggested that there shall be annual fare revision to be deffective from 1st of May every year, based upon annual computation of cost and cost increases.

75. For the purpose of monitoring the trend in costs, the constitution of a cell comprising a Transport Economist and a Cost Accountant is recommended.

76. The constitution of a Passenger Road Transport Rates Tribunal consisting of the Secretary, Transport, Government of Andhra Pradesh, the Secretary, Finance, Government of Andhra

Pradesh, the Accountant-General, Andhra Pradesh, and a Transport Economist is recommended to consider the cost increases and decide on periodical fare revisions.

77. If the corporation improves its operational performance, beyond the norms of performance set, and gets surpluses, it is recommended that half of this surplus be paid to the staff by way of bonus and the balance be utilised for augmentation of fleet and provision of passenger amenities.

78. Based upon the computation of costs (to the extent data are available), a fare increase of 0.5 paisa per passenger kilometre is suggested, if the present depreciation policy is continued. However, a fare increase of 1.0 paisa per passenger kilometre is recommended if the corporation provides for depreciation on replacement cost basis and on 4.8 lakh kilometre usage basis.

79. In order to wise out the entire accumulated losses of Rs. 66 crores, it is recommended that the State Government shall pay subsidy of around Rs. 10 crores per annum in the next six to seven years.

THE REGIONAL SET UP

1. The Regonal set up, which has been introduced in January 1978, has not been implemented as envisaged in the reorganisation proposals.

2. (a) There was distortion in the role assigned to the DVM.

   (b) The role of DVM was subverted in practice by placing a Deputy Chief Personnel Manager in the Regional Manager's office.

3. The role envisaged for Head office and the Regional Managers has been totally violated because of the temptation for centralisation on the part of the Head Office and Heads of Departments. The Regional Manager has not been delegated powers as envisaged. Consequently, the Regional office has become a post office.

4, The bus-staff ratio increased considerably after the

Regional set up has been introduced. The essential reasons, for this, are the growth of the organisation and the increase in the number of tiers in the organisation, apart from other reasons.

5. There was lack of functional expertise in the office of the Regional Manager, in so far as Mechanical Engineering and Operations Departments are concerned.
6. There was decline in operational performance during 1976-77—1981-82, in crucial areas of performance such as vehicular utilisation, vehicle utilisation, and bus-staff ratio.

ORGANISATIONAL SET UP FOR APSRTC

1. Splitting the existing organisation and having small units, either as independent companies or subsidiary companies under a Holding Company under the Companies Act 1956, is not suggested.
2. The Holding Corporate form is also not suggested as it would be no different from a unitary corporation form of organisation in the matter of temptation to centralise at the Head Office.
3. The alternative of implementing the Regional set up as envisaged in 1978 is also not suggested.
4. Splitting the existing set up and formation of small independent corporations.

   (a) Splitting the existing corporation and formation of small independent corporations is recommended.
   (b) Each Corporation may have a fleet of 1000 vehicles covering two districts and about 12 to 15 Depots with 40 to 80 vehicles each.
   (c) A central workshop of the corporation is to take care of the needs of 1000 vehicles.
   (d) In the first phase, formation of six corporations is recommended.
   (e) In the second phase, that is, within one year after the decision to split is taken, two more corporations are recommended for formation.

(f) In the third phase, that is, within five years after the decision to split is taken, two more corporations are recommended for formation, in addition to the two proposed under the second phase.

(g) No corporation shall come into existence without completion of central workshop facilities first.

(h) The composition of the Boards of the non-city corporations, essentially with professional managers and with no non-expertise non-official element is suggested taking into consideration the need for effective co-ordination among contiguous corporations.

(i) In the case of city corporation, the composition of the Board is suggested taking into consideration the need for representation of all those who contribute to the effective functioning of the organisation.

(j) A two-tier organisational structure is suggested.

(k) Two more cadres of officers namely, Additional General Managers and Assistant Depot Managers are suggested, which do not imply any additional financial commitment.

(l) The stores function is brought under mechanical wing.

(m) It is not proposed to disturb the existing integrated Depot set up.

(n) Traffic scheduling is centralised at Head Office.

(o) A two-tier workshop structure is suggested.

(p) Creation of Transport Management Cadre is suggested.

(q) Policy of recruitment of qualified engineers for mechanical, including stores, and traffic departments, in future is suggested.

(r) Doing away with body overhaul system is suggested.

5. (a) If, for any reasons, splitting the existing organisation and formation of small, independent corporations is not possible, an alternative set up, with Policy Board at the Head office with a small office and a highly decentralised Regional set up, is

recommended.

(b) Under this set up, constitution of Regional Management Boards with stature and with powers in sub-policy areas is recommended.

(c) The size of the Region in terms of vehicles is 1000 covering two districts and about 12 to 15 depots.

(d) A region will have only two levels of workshops—Regional level and Depot level.

(e) Traffic Scheduling function is centralised at the Regional Office.

(f) The Region shall have power to buy all its requirements of Stores.

(g) To start with, formation of six Regions is suggested, two more within one year, and another two within five years after the implementation of the recommendation.

CAPITAL STRUCTURE AND FINANCIAL POLICIES

Capital structure

1. The consequence of having interest-bearing capital contributions at a time when the organisation is facing severe losses, particularly cash losses, is that it would upset the entire working of the organisation.

2. The long-term borrowings as a percentage of total capital contributions increased from 18.13 in 1973-74 to 29.10 in 1981-82. While the long-term borrowings constituted only 29.10 per cent of the total capital contributions, the interest thereon amounted to 86.05 per cent of the interest on capital contributions for the year 1981-82. It follows that debt is disadvantageous and that the corporation should be provided with adequate funds by the participating governments.

Capital contributions from participating governments

3. The non-provision of adequate capital on a timely basis is the cause for recourse to high cost debt.

4. During the period 1973-74—1981-82, the central government's contributions did not reach 50 per cent of State government's contributions in any of the years.

5. The releases of capital contributions by the participating governments, besides being inadequate are uncertain and irregular, which adds to the cash flow problems.

6. As the government insists on the payments of taxes on a quarterly basis, so should the participating governments adopt a similar practice of releasing the agreed capital contributions in four equal instalments.

Depreciation policy

7. Depreciation should be provided on replacement cost basis, which, apart from ensuring replacement, would give a more realistic estimate of the cost of rendering service and thus ensure proper consideration in respect of this item of cost at the time of fare revision.

Costing system

8. A full fledged costing system is recommended to improve efficiency.

PERSONNEL POLICIES

Manpower planning

9. There is no man-power planning at all in the organisation and whatever that exists is individual-oriented than organisation-oriented one.

10. The present high bus staff ratio, is partly on account of lack of man-power planning and of information flows in this respect.

Personnel functions

11. The personnel function is the most neglected function of the corporation, in spite of the organisation being a labour intensive one. What goes on in the organisation in the name of 'Personnel' function is nothing but 'establishment' function.

12. The personnel function should be entrusted to a professional manager.

Recruitment

13. It is suggested that non-graduates of higher age groups be

recruited as conductors.

14. There are instances where the recruitment was done in excess of the number of posts advertised.

Promotions

15. The eligibility of service taken into consideration for promotion to the same level varies from post to post.

16. Different departments have different eligibility ratios for internal candidates for promotion to higher posts.

17. The criteria for selection to promotion posts does not seem to be either seniority or merit but one of convenience ; and, hence, selections have lost their credibility.

18. There is need for common seniority list for all cadres except for mechanical and accounts departments.

19. Time scale promotion should be instituted.

20. There is need for examining the implications of regulations 30 and 34 of recruitment regulations.

21. Promotion channels at lower levels, particularly at the level of cleaners and drivers, have to be planned.

Training

22. The training function is the most neglected function in the corporation.

23. There is need for modifying recruitment regulations making provision for uniform service conditions of treating the training period also as active service.

24. Exclusive training in the conduct of domestic enquiries is a necessity.

25. The officer Trainees should be attached to a single officer during the period of training and the functional heads should be held responsible for training the candidates in their respective functional areas.

Transfers

26. One of the important problems in regard to transfers is the resistance and interference from the unions.

27. It is suggested that wherever the divisional seniority is finalised, the divisional manager should effect transfers when an employee completes a fixed term as per the transfer policy

enunciated.

Incentive schemes

28. The incentive schemes were loosely structured and whenever the corporation tried to modify, in the light of their experience, the unions resisted it.

29. The city incentive scheme, which was originally started as an ad-hoc scheme, continued to be ad-hoc in spite of various evaluations done and modifications suggested.

30. It is suggested that the corporation at the time of next negotiations with unions must make the incentive schemes also negotiable so that it is not put to disadvantage.

Industrial relations

31. There is no industrial relations policy for the organisation and problems are dealt with on ad-hoc basis, creating problems for line managers.

32. The Deputy Chief Personnel Manager has become the breeding ground for all industrial relations problems.

Morale

33. The morale of the officers is poor. Many of the honest and efficient Divisional Managers and Depot Managers have reconciled to the fact that they would not get any more promotions and that the promotions are based on considerations other than merit and seniority.

34. There is a feeling that the system of evaluation of officers is unscientific.

MANAGEMENT INFORMATION SYSTEM

Deficiencies of the existing system

35. There is no staff trained in MIS work at the Depot level.

36. There is absence of unity of command over the Regional Statistical Officer/Statistical Superintendent.

37. There is no management informations systems manual as yet.

38. There is duplication of work at various levels.

39. Considering the work load of the staff attached to the

central MIS Wing, the central MIS Wing, is found to be overstaffed.

40. There is no data bank.

Organisation of MIS

41. In accordance with the organisational structure recommended for multiple corporations the MIS for each independent corporation is proposed to have two wings—the central MIS Wing and the Depot MIS Wing.

ANNEXURES

ANNEXURE 1.1

COST STRUCTURE

(*Rs. in lakhs*)

Sl. No.	Particulars	1973-74	1974-75	1975-76	1976-77	1977-78	1978-79	1979-80	1980-81	1981-82
1.	Staff	1,157.20	1,352.18	1,668.82	2,353.98	2,999.05	3,403.28	3,977.80	5,076.73	6,040.33
2.	Spareparts	342.92	509,89	689.58	792.57	749.59	977.40	1,381.96	1,730.55	1,663.10
3.	Tyres and Tubes	294.45	463.83	751.19	717.85	840.35	1,185.73	1,435.08	1,539.11	1,925.99
4.	Fuel including Lubricants	652.19	1,031.39	1,370.37	1,600.77	1,805.11	1,991.04	2,513.10	3,890.48	5,013.63
5.	Passenger Taxes	—								
6.	M.V. Taxes and Permit Fees	645.07	858.94	1,120.16	1,356.97	1,554.96	1,834.00	2,214.83	2,414.31	2,520.93
7.	Rent, Rates and Taxes	4.48	8.51	10.69	13.13	18.14	22.73	27.24	24.53	4.89
8.	(a) Insurance	1.28	24.49	7.09	8.93	8.08	17.66	31.24	7.58	9.00
	(b) Depreciation	399.60	635.44	759.27	883.72	1,075.91	1,257.53	1,582.33	2,030.54	2,036.34
	Total (a+b)	400.88	659.93	766.36	892.65	1,083.99	1,275.19	1,613.57	2,038.12	2,045.34
9.	Interest on Capital	79.37	89.45	118.76	132.03	162.06	211.30	300.31	372.20	453.09
10.	Development Rebate Reserve	0.68	0.26	—	—	—	—	—	—	—
11.	Miscellaneous	249.98	474.76	601.97	839.15	995.09	1,044.18	1,264.59	1,410.54	1,369.40
	Total	3,827.22	5,449.14	7,097.90	8,699.10	10,253.34	11,944.85	14,728.48	18,496.57	21,036.70

Source : 1973-74 to 1978-79 Annual Administration Reports.
1979-80 to 1981-82 Annual Accounts (Provisional).

ANNEXURE 1.2

APPROXIMATE EXPENDITURE UNDER THE NEW SCHEME (WORKING DETAILS)

		Rs.
1.	Payment of allowance at the rate of Rs. 300/- per month to the Officers— 197 × Rs. 300 =Rs. 59,100. Payment of allowance per year Rs. 59,100 × 12 =Rs. 7,09,250.	7,09,250
2.	Cost of interest on interest free loan Total loan assistance = 197 × Rs. 50,000 =Rs. 98,50,000 @ $7\frac{1}{2}$ per cent interest on the loan amount =Rs. 7,38,750.	7,38,750
		14,48,000

APPROXIMATE SAVING UNDER THE NEW SCHEME (WORKING DETAILS)

		Rs.
1.	Total petrol required for cars/jeeps—17,550 litres per month. Cost of petrol per month 17,550 × Rs. 6/- = Rs. 1,05,300 per month. Cost of petrol per year Rs. 1,05,300 × 12 = Rs. 12,63,600	12,63,600
2.	Total HSD Oil required for jeeps per month—2025 litres Cost of HSD Oil per month— 2025 × Rs. 3/- = Rs. 6,075 Cost of HSD Oil per year— Rs. 6,075 × 12 = Rs 72,900	72,900
3.	Wages of L.V. Drivers— @ one driver per vehicle 197 × Rs. 613/- =Rs. 1,20,761 per month Rs. 1,20,761 × 12 = Rs. 14,49,132 per year	14,49,132
4.	Cost of Taxes and Maintenance at the	

rate of Rs. 100/- per vehicle per month— 197×Rs. 100×12=Rs. 2,36,400 per year	2,36,400
	30,22,032
(—) Approximate Expenditure under the new scheme	14,48,000
Net savings	15,74,032

ANNEXURE 1.3

VEHICLES AND PETROL/DIESEL ALLOTTED TO OFFICERS

Category	Number	Quota allotted per officer	Litres of Petrol/HSD Oil			Total litres petrol	Total litres diesel
			Jeeps		Cars		
			Petrol	Diesel	Petrol		
(1)	(2)	(3)	(4)	(5)	(6)	(7)	(8)
H.O.Ds.	12	200	—	—	2,400	2,400	—
R.Ms.	6	250	—	—	1,500	1,500	—
D.V.Ms.	20	150	—	—	3,000	3,000	—
D.Ms.	104	75	7,800	—	—	7,800	—
Executive Engineers	6	200	—	—	1,200	1,200	—
A.Es.	20	75	—	1,500	—	—	1,500
W.Ms.	6	75	—	—	450	450	—
Dy. C.Ms.	9	75	—	—	675	675	—
C.P.R.O.	1	75	—	75	—	—	75
Law Officer	1	75	—	75	—	—	75
Dy. C.T.M.	5	75	—	375	—	—	375
C.Os.	7	75	—	—	525	525	—
Total	197	—	7,800	2,025	9,750	17,550	2,025

ANNEXURE 1.4

DIRECTIVES OF GOVERNMENT ON CONCESSIONS

I. MLAs/MLCs/Spouses.

1. G.O. Ms. No. 162 dated 28-2-1979.
2. Memo No. 866/Elecs.s/77-11 dated 3-3-1979.
3. G O. Ms. No. 331 dated 8-4-1976.
4. G.O. Ms. No. 94/Elecs.s/79-1 dated 14-5-1979.
5. G.O. Ms. No. 663 dated 20-9-1979.
6. G.O. Ms. No. 207 dated 13-3-1980.

II. General Bus Tickets and NGOs.

1. Letter No. 392/SG. Wed./80-3 dated 16-6-1980.
2. Letter No. 1895/Tr-4/76-1 dated 21-6-1976.
3. G.O. Ms. No. 390 dated 18-7-1981.

III. Passes for Members of Parliament.

1. G.O. Ms. No. 448 dated 11-6-1979.

IV. Encashment of age limit of chargeable children.

1. Govt. Letter No. 1042/WWI/79-3 dated 17-4-1979.

ANNEXURE 1.5

AMENDMENTS TO APMV RULES PROPOSED BY APSRTC

Existing provisions of APMV Rules	Proposed amendment	Necessity for amendment
Rule 212 : **Guiding principles for grant or renewal of stage carriage permits.**	A new sub-rule '3' shall be added as follows : Notwithstanding anything contained in this rule, an application for a stage carriage permit of the S.T.U. shall be given preference over all the other applicants.	M.V. Act contains special provision for the operation of State Transport Undertakings which includes take over of the passenger transport from the private operators (Chapter IV-A). The Corporation is not, however, barred from seeking permits under Chapter-IV of the M.V. Act along with the private operators. The Corporation frequently resorts to this provision especially in the areas already notified as this will avoid huge expenditure involving the publication of schemes. Rule 212 of the A.P. M.V. Rules has been made long before the concept of nationalisation has come into existence and speaks of relative merits and demerits of the competing private operator. An operator who has more than 6 adevrse entries in his history sheet during previous two years relating to overloads, etc., is barred from claiming a permit under this Chapter and the APSRTC automatically gets away in view of a large number of entries in its history sheet proportionate to the fleet at its command. It is therefore proposed to seek exemption from the application of the provisions of Rule 212 of A.P.M.V.

ANNEXURE 1.5 : (*Contd.*)

Existing provision in APMV Rules	Proposed amendment	Necessity for amendment
		Rules. Further, it may be stated that such provision exists under Chapter-IV of M.V. Act vide sub-section 1-H of Section 47 in case of inter-state routes. Hence, there is a need to treat the Corporation on a separate footing. Hence, the need for amendment.
Additional conditions for contract carriage permits :		
Rule 213-IV (v) : The vehicle shall be parked at such taxi stands as may be determined by the Transport Authority, when it is not engaged and it shall be available for hire there at.	A new proviso after the existing sub Rule IV (v) of Rule 213 be added : Provided further that the contract carriages other than a taxi or motor cab shall not be parked within a reasonable distance from the Bus stations authorised for stage carriages namely ; 3 kms. in the Municipal city, 2 kms. in Municipal town and 1 km. in other places.	No specific bus stands have been fixed by the RTAs for parking contract carriages as required under this rule with the result the contract carriages are being regularly parked in front of the bus stations of stage carriages and they are resorting to take the passengers by contacting them personally, resulting in clashes between the persons deployed on stage carriages and those contract carriage vehicles. To avoid this menace, there is a need to incorporate a new proviso prohibiting their parking around the bus stations of Corporation within a reasonable distance. Hence, the new proviso be considered to be added to rule 213-IV (v).

Existing provision in APMV Rules	Proposed amendment	Necessity for amendment
Rule 213-IV (vii) : Every contact carriage, other than a taxi and an autorickshaw, shall maintain list of passengers travelling in the vehicles in the following form in respect of such trip and such list shall be produced before the checking officer on demand by him.	Sub Rule IV (vii) be substituted with the following : Every contract carriage, other than a taxi and an auto-rickshaw, shall furnish a list of passengers included in the contract to the transport Authority which had granted the permit, and an attested copy of which shall be annexed to the trip sheet. Provided that it will be a sufficient compliance if the list of passengers attested by an M.V. Inspector or a Station House Officer of the nearest Police Station is posted to the Transport Authority within 24 hours of the commencement of the contract and a copy of the same is annexed to the trip sheet, if the contract is commencing from a place other than the head quarters of the Transport Authority.	Even though the conditions of the permits attached to contract carriages, stipulate that every contract carriage shall maintain a list of passengers travelling the vehicle there is no provision to ensure that the passengers travelling in the bus do belong to a group who have contracted this bus and are not the persons who have boarded the bus at different points and do not belong to a single group. To ensure a proper implementation of this provision and safeguard the interest of the stage carriage operators, it is proposed that all the contract carriages whether covered by temporary or pucca permits shall furnish a list of passengers to the Transport Authority before the commencement of the trip and maintain a copy of the same so as to make it susceptible for a cross check and prevent the utilisation of these contract carriages as stage carriages.

ANNEXURE 1.5 : (*Contd.*)

Existing provision in APMV Rules	Proposed amendment	Necessity for amendment
***Rule** 212 E* : **Grant of renewal of contract carriage permits—guiding principles.**	A new Rule to rule 212-E be added. I. Nature of permits be classified as : (i) For operation within the home district and one neighbouring district. (ii) For operation within the State. (iii) For operation on inter-state areas. The Transport authorities shall determine the strength of contract carriages required on each of the above, having regard to the following matters : 1. No. of stage carriages held in the district/state. 2. Demand on contract carriages (tourist or otherwise).	Guide-lines have been prescribed under Rule 212-E of A.P.M.V. Rules regarding the procedure to be followed by the Transport authorities in regard to grant/renewal of contract carriages. While formulating the above rule, the following items have not been given due consideration : 1. Nature of permit to be granted i.e., for the entire State or district for which separate tax rates are prescribed. 2. No. of permits required for each of the classes. In the absence of the above, contract carriage permits i.e., pucca or temporary are being granted by the Transport Authorities in the state, with the result, they are being operated illicitly on the notified routes of Corporation which is affecting the operations of STUs. As regards the inter-state needs the existing All India Tourist vehicles which are 50 in number are sufficient to cater to the needs of tourist traffic on Inter-State routes. Hence, there is a need to restrict the number required for each district keeping in view the interest of stage carriages. The contract carriage permit holders are indulging in the

Existing provision in APMV Rules	Proposed amendment	Necessity for amendment
	3. The existing facilities available. Provided further that the total number of contract carriages shall not exceed 5% of the total number of stage carriages held in the district, including those of All India Tourist Permits.	illicit operation deterimental to the interests of the stage carriages. No permit temporary, or pucca, should therefore be issued beyond the authorised strength as in the case of the stage carriages.
Rule : *306* Inspection of public service vehicles.	A new sub-rule to Rule 306 be added after sub rule (v) : (vi) Any officer of APSRTC not below the rank of a Depot Manager.	The officials of the APSRTC are not entitled to check the breach of the permit conditions in respect of the private stage carriages and contract carriages operating illicitly on the notified routes. Statutory definitions of stage carriages and contract carriages are sufficiently flexible to enable the operation of contract carriages as stage carriages. Further, the strength of the officials of the Transport Department and the Police Department are not adequate to keep a check on this infringement, APSRTC is a statutory body constituted under RTC Act, and its officers are available at all important places in the state. Therefore, the Government may authorise the officers of the Corporation to check the vehicles of private operators, as has already been done in Madhya

ANNEXURE 1.5 : (*Contd.*)

Existing provision of APMV Rules	Proposed amendment	Necessity for amendment
		Pradesh and Maharashtra with a view to checking the illicit operation.
Rule 244-A : Payment of compounding fee in case of overload for each excess passenger.	A new rule after the Rule 244-A as 244-B be added: Provisions of section 60 of M.V. Act and Rules 244 and 244 A of APMV Rules shall not be applicable to the permits issued under Chapter IV A of the M.V. Act.	At present, any violation of the permit condition of the stage carriage shall be disposed off under section 60 of the M.V. Act, which stipulates that for any violation the permit can either be suspended or cancelled. However, the RTA, can compound such an offence, if it deems fit, if the permit holder agrees to pay a sum determined by the RTA. However, for historical reasons, the permits issued to STUs under chapter-IV (A) are also being subjected to under Section 60. In a Revision Petition filed by the KSRTC, in the Karnataka S.T.A.T. that the R.T.A. cannot impose penalty for the breach of condition of the permit u/s. 60 of the M.V. Act, as the R.T.A. will merely issue the permit, under Chapter IV-A of the M.V. Act. Therefore, suitable amendment be made exempting the permits issued under Chapter IV-A of M.V. Act from the scope of Section 60 in imposing the compounding fee for breach of permit condition.

Existing provision of APMV Rules	Proposed amendment	Necessity for amendment
Rule 316-A : Publication of scheme modified by State Transport Undertaking with the previous approval of the State Government.	*Rule 316-A after amendment* : Any approved scheme for road transport services relating to any route or area in respect of which the road transport services are run and operated by the STU to the complete exclusion of other persons and extension/deviation of the route without reducing the frequency of services in respect of services relating to any route or area in respect of which road transport services are run and operated by the S.T.U. to the complete exclusion of other person except an overlapping of not more than 8 kms provided no other person is providing transport services in the portion extended/deviated, modified by the S.T.U. with the previous approval and the	The approved schemes of Road Transport services in Andhra Pradesh normally provide for an overlapping of not more than 8 kms in the district where the passenger transport is totally nationalised and provide for operation of existing services and for opening of new routes on the portions of the notified routes in respect of other districts viz., Srikakulam, Visakhapatnam, Vizianagaram, Cuddapah, Nellore and Prakasham. Proviso to sub-section (1) of Section 68-E provides for modifying an approved scheme by the State Transport undertaking with the previous approval of the State Government in respect of the following matters in relation to the routes where the schemes provide for complete exclusion of other persons. (1) Increasing the number of buses/trips. (2) Extension of the route. (3) Variation of the time-table (4) Alteration of the increase in the seating capacity. The Corporation is however not in a position to make use of the above provision even in cases where the operations of the Corporations are more or less on the monopoly basis and the modification especially in respect of extension or deviation of the routes does not affect any other operators as the approved schemes provide for

ANNEXURE 1.5 : (*Contd.*)

Existing provision of APMV Rules	Proposed amendment	Necessity for amendment
	State Government under proviso to sub-section 1 of Sec. 68-E, shall be published in the A.P. Gazette in the manner specified in form STU-MS (Revised form enclosed).	overlapping by private operators to a marginal extent. Extension or deviation of the routes where the operations of the Corporation are on a near monopoly and where no operator is providing any transport service in the portion proposed to be extended or deviated will not affect any private operator. It is, therefore, proposed to amend Rule 316-A providing such variation or extensions. Hence, the amendment.
Payment of taxes on contract carriages : Rs. 300 per passenger plying on inter-state routes (All India Tourist Permits) Rs. 250 per passenger plying on inter-state routes with the T.Ps under section 63 (6) of M.V. Act. Rs. 250 per passenger plying on inter-state routes within the state of Andhra Pradesh. Rs. 150 per passenger plying within Home Dis-	A new proviso to sub-sec. (1) of Sec. 9 of APMVT Act, 1963 be added. The facility of paying M.V. Taxes for a period of less than a quarter may be withdrawn or the rates may be so revised as to make a person opting for payment of M.V. Taxes for less than a quarter at any time pays an amount more than the quarterly tax if he chooses not to use the	M.V. Taxes are normally paid once in every quarter, half yearly or yearly. The taxes payable for a stage carriage are Rs. 200 per seat per quarter for ordinary buses and Rs. 300 per seat per quarter for an express bus. The taxes applicable for a contract carriage until 1980 were Rs. 75 per seat per quarter. To bring the operations of a stage carriage and a contract carriage to an even-keel and to withdraw the unintended concession that was being enjoyed by the contract carriage in competing with the operations of the stage carriages, the taxes in respect of contract carriages were revised. This revision has, more or less made the tax burden on contract carriages as well as stage carriages even.

Existing provision of APMV Rules	Proposed amendment	Necessity for amendment
trict and any one contiguous district.	vehicle for all the 90/91 days in quarter.	
Rs. 8.40 per passenger for minimum of three days for special permits and Rs. 2.80 per passenger per day for the subsequent period. Rs. 5.00 per passenger for a minimum of three days within Home District and any one contiguous district and Rs. 1.70 per passenger per day for the subsequent period.		Payment of taxes for stage carriages or contract carriages done at current level of rates amounts to Rs. 10,000 to 15,000 per quarter to be made at one time. Allowing contract carriage operators, especially those operating on the strength of TPs a facility of payment for a minimum period of 3 days gives them the advantage of lower investment even if they operate through out the quarter regularly in addition to opening up of a possibility of depriving the taxes due to the State Government by mischievous deeds. Further, this facility has defeated the very purpose for which the taxes in respect of contract carriages have been revised upwards. There is, therefore, a need to withdraw the facility of payment of taxes for periods short of a quarter if it is decided to continue this facility, the rates could at least be revised as shown below to make it a little discouraging to adopt the short term payment of taxes when compared to quarterly payment if the operator uses the vehicles for about 50 days in a quarter.

ANNEXURE 1.5 : (*Contd.*)

Sl. No.	Description	Present rate	Proposed rate
1.	Contract carriages plying on intra state routes or on inter-state routes with temporary permits.	Rs. 8.40 for 3 days.	Rs. 15/- for 3 days.
		Rs. 2.80 per day beyond 3 days	Rs. 5/- per day beyond 3 days
2.	Contract carriages operating within the home district and contiguous district.	Rs. 5/- for 3 days	Rs. 9/- for 3 days
		Rs. 1.70 per day beyond 3 days.	Rs. 3.00 per day beyond 3 days.

(52—A)

FORM-STU-MS

(Rule 316-A of the Andhra Pradesh Motor Vehicles Rules, 1964)

Whereas, the State Transport Undertaking is of the opinion that the scheme of Road Transport Service approved by Government in Notification No.... .... dated.........published at pages.........part.........of the Andhra Pradesh Gazette, dated...... requires modification :

"Whereas as no other person is providing transport services in the portion of the route to which the present route is proposed to be extended/deviated".

And whereas, the previous approval of the State Government has been obtained as required under the proviso to section 68-E.

Now, therefore, the scheme as so modified is hereby published as required under Rule 316-A of the Andhra Pradesh Motor Vehicles Rules, 1964.

Approved Scheme	Modified Scheme
1. Route (Starting point and terminus with important intermediate stations and route length).	
2. Area (names of routes with starting point and termini and intermediate stations and route length).	
3. Whether town service or mofussil service or both.	
4. Maximum and minimum number of vehicles proposed to be operated on each route by the State Transport Undertaking to the exclusion, complete or partial, or otherwise, of other persons.	

(a) Maximum number
(b) Minimum number
(c) Type
(d) Capacity

5. Maximum and minimum number of trips proposed to be performed on each route by the State Transport Undertaking to the exclusion, complete or partial, or otherwise, of other persons.
6. No. of stage carriages intended to be kept in reserve to maintain the service and to provide for special occasions.
7. The arrangements proposed for the housing, maintenance and repair of the vehicles.
8. The arrangements proposed for the comfort and convenience of passengers.
9. The arrangements proposed for the stands and halts on the route at which copies of time tables of the services are proposed to be exhibited.
10. Whether it is proposed to permit the carriage of goods in addition to the passengers.

Signature :

Station : Designation :

Date : (State Transport Undertaking)

ANNEXURE 1.6

SCHEMES OF 1977 PENDING APPROVAL BFFORE THE GOVERNMENT

Sl. No.		Schemes	No. of buses involved
1.	Mcfussil Routes in Nationalised Area	82	103
2.	Cuddapah District	69	96
3.	Prakasam District	68	89
4.	Nellore District	99	163
5.	Vijayawada Town Services (Published in 1979)	3	107
	Total :	321	558
6.	V.L.T.S. Schemes (1978)	144	180
7.	Inter-State Schemes (1980 and 1981)	32	66
	Total :	497	804

ANNEXURE 1.7

NUMBER OF PERMITS GRANTED UNDER SECTION 68 F (1—c)

Route	No. of permits
A.S. Pet to Nellore via Atmakur	2
Nellore to Donakonda	2
Nellore—Atmakur	1
Madanapalli—Kadiri	1
Nellore-Turumerla	1
Cuddapah—Badwel	1
Anantapur-Uthakallu	2
Nellore Atakanitippa	1
Srikakulam-Visakhapatnam	1
Nellore-Rapur	2
Nellore-Peddireddipalli	1
Ongole-Chimakurty	1
Ongole-Tangutur	1
Kandukur-Kadiri	1

ANNEXURE 1.8

Visakhapatnam-Palakonda	1
Vizianagaram-Palakonda	1
Vizianagaram-Srikakulam	1

ANNEXURE 1.9

DETAILS OF INTER-STATE ROUTES ON WHICH THE STA HAD GRANTED INCREASE OF BUSES AND TRIPS

Inter-state route	No. of permits granted by variation of permit conditions	Overlapping notified sector/route	Remarks
(1)	(2)	(3)	(4)
Chittoor-Bangalore (via) Palamaner, Mulbagal, Kolar.	1+1	Chittoor-Palamaner Chittoor-Tirupathi	
Tirupathi-Bangalore (via) Chandragiri, and Chittoor.	1	Chittoor-Tirupathi Chittoor-Palamaner Tirupathi-Bangalore	
Rayadurg-Hindupur (via) Gundlapalli and Kalyandurg.	1	Hindupur-Madakasira Kalyandurg-Anantapur (via) Rayadurg	
Hindupur-Kalyanadurg (via) Paidetty and Madakasira	1	Hindupur-Madakasira	
Hindupur-Davangere (via) Pavagada and Chitradurg	1	Hindupur-State Border	
Anantapur-T.B. Dam Site (via) Uravakonda and Bellary	1	Anantapur-Uravakonda	
Chellakere-Guntakal	1		

ANNEXURE 1.9 : (*Conted.*)

Inter-state route	No. of permits granted by variation of permit conditions	Overlapping notified sector/route	Remarks
(1)	(2)	(3)	(4)
Gooty-Bellary	1	Gooty-Guntakal Anantapur-Guntakal (via) Gooty	
Rayadurg-Bellary	1	Kalyandurg-Anantapur (via) Rayadurg	
Chittoor-Voyalpad	1	Chittoor-Voyalpad Border Chittoor-Madanapalli Chittoor-Palamaner	
Gurramkonda-Kodur	1	Rajampet-Chittoor	
Reddam-Doddagatta (extension upto Sira)	1	Dharmavaram-Reddam	
Salvandlapalli-Beimanacheruvu (extension Salevandlapalli to Bathalapalli)	1		
Tirupathi-R.K. Pet variation as Waillijah Road-Tirupathi.	1	Tirupathi-Puttur	
Madanapalle-Vellore (via) Katpadi and Chittoor	2	Madanapalli-Chittoor Madanapelle-Palamaner Chittoor-Palamaner	

Kalahasthi-Kaneheepuram (via) Puttur and Tirupati	3	Kalahasti-Puttur Tirupati-Puttur
Venkatagiri-Madras (via) Sullurpet	2	Nellore-Madras Tirupathi-Satyavedu Tirupathi-Tada
Chittoor-Vellore (via) Bommasamudram	1	
Chittoor-Varadareddypalli(via) Paradarami	1	Chittoor-Kannikapuram
Tirupathi-Kancheepuram (via) Renigunta and Arkonam	2	Tirupathi-Puttur Tirupathi-Nagari
Palamaner-Vellore (via) Chittoor and Katpadi	1	Plamaner-Chittoor
Palamaner-Tiruttani (via) Pallipet	1	Palamaner-Chittoor Chittoor-Pallipet
Tirupathi-Tiruvellore (via) Renigunta, Puttur, Nagalapuram and Uthukotai	1	Tirupathi-Puttur Tirupathi-Nagari
Voyalpad-Vellore	1	Chittoor-Voyalpad Chittoor-Madanapalle Chittoor-Palamaner
Nagaladinne-Bellary (via) Yemmiganur, Adoni, Alur, Chintakunta	1	Yemmiganur-Bagaladinne Yemmiganur-Adoni
Thumbapalyam-Vellore (via) Aragonda, Chittoor, Katpadi	1	Chittoor-Aragonda
Chittoor-Kancheepuram (via) Ponnai, Sholinghur, Tiruttani, Arkonam	1	
Puttur-Vellore (via) Chittoor & Pallipet	1	Puttur-Chittoor
Venkatagiri-Madras (via) Naidupet, Sullurpet and Tada	1	Tirupathi-Satyavedu Nellore-Madras

ANNEXURE 1.9 : (*Contd.*)

Inter-state route	No. of permits granted by variation of permit conditions	Overlapping notified sector/route	Remarks
(1)	(2)	(3)	(4)
Chittoor-Vellore (via) Katpadi	6		
Chittoor-Vellore (via) Katpadi	1		
Aragonda-Vellore (via) Chittoor and Katpadi	1	Chittoor-Bangarupalyam (via) Aragonda	
Vellore-Madanapalle (via) Katpadi, Chittoor Narayanpakala, Kalikiri and Voyalpad	1	Madanapalle-Chittoor Madanapalle-Palamaner Palamaner-Chittoor	
Tirupathi-Arkonam (via) Renigunta, Puttur and Nagari	1	Tirupathi-Nagari Tirupathi-Puttur	
Madanapalle-Vellore (via) Chittoor and Katpadi	1	Madanapalli-Chittoor Chittoor-Palamaner Palamaner-Madanapalle	
Madanapalle-Vellore (via) Punganur, Palamaner, and Chittoor	2	Madanapalli-Chittoor Chittoor-Palamaner Palamaner-Madanapalle	
Kuppam-Pernumbat (via) V. Kota and Nayakaneri	1	Kuppam-Pernambut	

Tirupathi-Tiruttani (via) Renigunta, Puttur, and Nagari	1	Tirupathi-Puttur Tirupathi-Nagari Tirupathl-Kosala-nagaram	
Vellore-Voyalpad (via) Katpadi, Chittoor and Palamaner	2	Chittoor-Palamaner Chittoor-Voyalpad	
Tiruvvellore-Tirupathi (via) Puttur and Uthukotai	1	Tirupathi-Nagari	
Thamballapalli-Chintamani (via) Chowdasamudram, Nolakalacheruvu, P.T.M., B. Kothakota, Gownipalli, Srinivaspur	1	Madanapalli-Chowdasamudram	
Palamaner-Kolar (via) Nangili, Mulbagal	1	Palamaner-Kuppam	
Bellary-Anantapur (via) Uravakonda	1	Anantapur-Uravakonda	
Anantapur-Bellary (via) Kuderu, Jallipalli, Mustur, Uravakonda, Vidupenakal, Hagari	1	Anantapur-Uravakonda	
Kalahasti-Tiruttani (via) Renigunta, Puttur and Nagari	1	Kalahasti-Puttur	
Kalahasthi-Tiruvellore (via) Varadyapalem, Satyavedu, Uthukotai	1	Tirupathi-Satyaveedu	
Madanapalli to K.G.F.	Variation by way of extension	Madanapalli-Kadiri	STA, Bangalore had granted variation of the existing route KGF to Madanapalli as KGF to Kadiri by way of extension from Madanpalli to Kadiri to a Karnataka based operator. The STA/AP has countersigned the variation u/s 68-F(1-C) in pursuance of the draft scheme 26/75 (Kurnool-Vellore).

ANNEXURE 1.9 : (*Contd.*)

Inter-state route	No. of permits granted by variation of permit conditions	Overlapping notified sector/route	Remarks
(1)	(2)	(3)	(4)
B. Kothakota to Kandukur (enclave)	Variation by way of extension	Madanapalli-Chowada-Samudram Madanapalli-Kadiri	STA, Bangalore had granted variation of the existing route B. Kothakota-Kandukur by way of extension from Kandukur to Kadiri to a Karnataka based operator. The Sec., STA, AP has countersigned the said variation u/s 68F(1-C) in pursuance of the draft schemes 26/75 (Kurnool-Vellore)
Madanapalli to Bangalore	Variation by way of extension	Tirupathi-Madanapalli	STA, Bangalore has granted variation by way of extension of the inter-state route Madanapalli-Bangalore, from Madanapalli to Tirupathi. The proceedings of the KSTA are suspended in a writ petition filed by us.

ANNEXURE 1.10

DETAILS OF M.V. TAXES DUE FROM APSRTC AS ON 31-7-1980

Name of the district	No. of vehicles	Amount due from APSRTC vehicles
		Rs.
Srikakulam	2	9,830.50
Visakhapatnam	6	32,171.00
Kakinada	63	2,19,623.30
Eluru	67	3,49,108.70
Vijayawada	81	17,68,206.30
Guntur	100	2,97,910.95
Ongole	19	90,940.85
Nellore	13	96,613.00
Chittoor	144	6,24,953.00
Anantapur	—	14,65,919.65
Kurnool	—	9,52,076.40
Cuddapah	—	7,08,131.20
Warangal	20	1,72,801.05
Khammam	28	2,30,714.75
Adilabad	2	17,023.50
Karimnagar	25	1,30,090.50
Nalgonda	14	1,43,328.80
Medak	22	2,06,748.15
Nizamabad	40	3,57,615.04
Mahabubnagar	42	2,87,618.50
Rangareddy	15	36,814,50
Hyderabad	5	43,433.00
Total	687	82,61,678.64

ANNEXURE 1.11

DETAILS OF CFX NOTICES ISSUED

Sl. No.	Veh. No. APZ/AAZ	Date of F.C. Cancelled/ CFX issued	Actual date of expiry of F.C. before issue of CFX
1.	7932	24.3.81	29.4.81
2.	8757	11.3.81	26.3.81
3.	9705	22.1.81	10.8.81
4.	7931	12.12.80	15.6.81
5.	9756	15.5.81	15.7.81
6.	9756	8.11.81	23.7.82
7.	897	9.5.81	10.6.81
8.	1816	24.5.81	2.3.82
9.	1816	23.7.81	2.3.82
10.	9777	13.5.80	10.8.81
11.	7821	4.5.81	2.3.82
12.	9650	2,10.80	6.5.81
13.	9622	9.11.81	15.5.82
14.	8758	29.11.80	10.3.81
15.	9622	4.10.81	15.5.82
16.	8758	24.7.81	30.3.82
17.	APC 6075	19.8.80	13.2.81
18.	9007	4.5.81	25.6.81
19.	197	28.6.81	26.11.81
20.	7932	14.6.81	29.3.82
21.	9712	22.3.81	21.5.81
22.	9739	2.4.81	25.6.81
23.	9739	13.4.81	25.6.81
24.	9705	6.8.81	10.8.81
25.	9705	9.12.81	5.2.82
26.	7931	3.4.80	16.6.80
27.	897	3.11.81	17.5.82
28.	9783	11.5.81	9.7.81
29.	7230	26.11.81	18.2.81

Sl. No.	Veh. No. APZ/AAZ	Date of F.C. Cancelled CFX issued	Actual date of expiry of F.C. before issue of CFX
30.	7230	18.9.81	4.3.82
31.	7113	6.12.80	15.12.80
32.	7210	4.8.81	20.1.82
33.	9757	5.10.81	30.7.82
34.	9705	15.10.81	5.2.82
35.	7111	29.10.81	1.7.82
36.	9756	2.11.81	23.7.82
37.	7189	7.9.81	1.7.82
38.	7159	15.12.81	15.7.82
39.	9650	14.4.82	15.7.82
40.	9902	20.4.82	16.9.82
41.	197	23.5.82	7.12.82
42.	7160	6.7.82	7.4.83
43.	7180	6.7.82	18.3.83
44.	9705	20.7.82	29.3.83

ANNEXURE 2.1

DISTRICT-WISE FLEET OF MOTOR VEHICLES (STAGE CARRIAGES) HELD BY APSRTC AND BY PRIVATE OPERATORS

Sl. No.	District	No. of vehicles held by A.P.S R.T.C. as on 31.3.1982 (including spares required)	No. of vehicles held by Private operators as on 10.1.1976	Total
1.	Srikakulam	29	263	292
2.	Vijayanagaram	62	)	187
3.	Visakhapatnam	250	) 125	250
4.	East Godavari	412	1	413
5.	West Godavari	361	19	380
6.	Krishna	487	106	593
7.	Guntur	551	112	663
8.	Prakasam	168	136	304
9.	Nellore	125	200	325
10.	Chittoor	577	—	577
11.	Anantapur	354	—	354
12.	Cuddapah	191	108	299
13.	Kurnool	327	19	346
14.	Mahaboobnagar	179	45	224
15.	Nalgonda	246	53	299
16.	Ranga Reddy	109	34	143
17.	Medak	181	18	199
18.	Hyderabad-City	736	—	736
	—District	165	—	165
19.	Khammam	189	7	196
20.	Warangal	287	48	335
21.	Karimnagar	229	46	275
22.	Nizamabad	199	39	238
23.	Adilabad	215	—	215
	Total	6629	1379	8008*

Source of data : APSRTC Records

*Excluding 312 Inter-state route buses operated by private operators in Chittoor, Cuddapah and Anantapur Districts.

ANNEXURE 2.2

OTHER DETAILS OF HEAD OFFICE SET UP

The CME is assisted by, apart from stores manager, works manager, who would be incharge of the workshop and Mechanical Engineering Officer, who would look after the requirements of the Depots on the maintenance side. The Stores Manager will have to ensure uninterrupted and free flow of frequently consumed items to the depots, apart from ensuring the requisite supplies to the central workshop. The works manager is to be assisted by Labour Welfare Officer and two Assistant Works Managers. The Stores Manager is to be assisted by Stores Officer and Purchase Officer. The Chief Traffic Manager is to be assisted by Traffic Manager (Operations) who would take care of traffic scheduling, which is centralised in this set up. He is also assisted by Executive Engineer (Civil), who in turn is assisted by Assistant Engineer (Civil) to take care of civil construction works. The checking officer, and Management Information Systems are also placed under CTM.

Apart from CME and CTM, the Personnel Manager also directly reports to AGM even though he is at the next level in the hierarchy. The legal and medical sections are also placed under him.

In the proposed set up also, the CAO directly reports to the GM apart from the AGM. The CAO is assisted by two Accounts Officers and one Audit Officer.

ANNEXURE 2.3

FUNCTIONS AND POWERS OF GENERAL MANAGER

1. Implement the policy decisions taken by the Board
2. Maintain liaison between the Corporation and the Government
3. Ensure co-ordination among different corporations regarding inter-corporation routes
4. Responsible for achieving targets as per the budgets
5. Ultimately responsible for the financial and operational performance of the undertaking
6. Sanction the expenditure within the budget
7. Give ex-post-facto sanction of expenditure as per the norms fixed by the Board
8. Incur unanticipated expenditure subject to the limits set by the Board
9. Fill in the posts as per budget sanctions
10. Create and fill in Class III and Class IV posts as per the norms prescribed by the Board
11. Create and fill in Class III and IV posts for a period of three months, in emergency situations
12. Review all disciplinary cases
13. Exercise all other powers as delegated to him from time to time by the Board to make him effective.

FUNCTIONS AND POWERS OF ADDITIONAL GENERAL MANAGER

1. Responsible for the day-to-day functioning of Depots, stores and workshops
2. Directly responsible for the performance of Depots
3. Transfer all employees in the rank of DMs and below
4. Exercise all other powers as delegated to him from time

to time by the General Manager, to make him effective.

N.B. : 1. The Heads of Departments, namely, CME and CTM shall be under the administrative control of the Additional General Manager and are responsible for rendering effective assistance to the Depots as instructed by AGM.

2. There shall be Corporation Board Committees/Sub-Committees constituted for major/minor civil works, finance, stores, purchases, recruitment and promotions. The powers delegated to the Depot Managers in respect of the above matters under the present set up may be continued.

ANNEXURE 2.4

The policy matters concerning the Head office :

(a) Nationalisation (including Routes Committee) and inter-state agreements ; while the preparatory work for nationalisation such as conduct of traffic surveys, formulation of proposals and so on will be done by the region, final publication of schemes will be done by the Head office.

(b) *Investment decision* : The Head office shall concern itself only with the choice of chassis and the regions will be empowered to place orders directly with the suppliers in accordance with the budgets approved by the Regional Management Board and the capital allocated by the Head office.

(c) *Financing decision* : The Head office shall take decisions regarding capital structure, procurement of funds for investment and allocation of the same to the regions. The capital structure includes the element of permanent working capital required by the Regions.

(d) As pricing is a policy matter, which is decided in consultation and with the approval of Government, it shall be the concern of the Head office.

(e) The Head office will also decide on the replacement policy of vehicles, taking into consideration the type of vehicle, the nature of service and so on.

(f) *Depreciation policy* : The Head office may also decide on uniform depreciation policy for all the regions.

(g) *Wage policy* : The wage policy for the organisation as a whole may be decided by the Head office. As separate sets of accounts are proposed for the regions, the payment of bonus shall be the concern of the regions so as to motivate the employees to improve their performance. Similarly, incentives also shall be the concern of the regions so as to take into consideration the varying conditions that may be obtaining in different regions.

(h) It shall also be the concern of Head office to recruit personnel of and above the rank of Class II officers (Asst. Depot. Managers). The Head Office may, after recruitment, allot the number required for each region for training and posting by the region, within the region, subject to the preferences of the recruitees, to the extent possible. Once allotted they are transferable within the region and may be posted outside the region only on promotion and subject to preferences to the extent possible. The Head office shall have the power of transfer of General Managers/Advisers, except the Financial Adviser, from one region to another and from Head office to the regions and vice-versa. All the other officers shall be allocated to different regions on a permanent basis subject to transfer from one region to another only on promotion and subject to preference to the extent possible.

(i) The Head office shall also be concerned with policy matters regarding Government and Legislation.

However, it must be made clear that if the suggested alternative set up is to function effectively, the Government, the legislature and the Accountant General shall have to directly deal with regions on matters of detail and day-to-day functioning. The Head office shall be answerable to these agencies only for policies and for broad parameters of functioning of the organisation as a whole.

ANNEXURE 2.5

FUNCTIONS AND POWERS OF VICE-CHAIRMAN AND CHIEF GENERAL MANAGER

1. Implement the policy decisions taken by the Board.
2. Maintain liaison between the Corporation and the Government.
3. Co-ordinate the activities of all the Regions in the State in major policy matters.
4. Settle all inter-regional problems to achieve smooth functioning.
5. Accountable for achieving targets as per budgets.
6. Transfer officers, from one Region to another, of the level of proposed Class II scale officers and above on promotion.
7. All other powers as delegated to him from time to time by the Board to make him effective.

N.B. : All Advisors shall be specialists in their respective departments and perform staff functions only.

FUNCTIONS AND POWERS OF GENERAL MANAGER OF A REGION

1. Implement the policy decisions taken by the Corporate Board and the Regional Management Board.
2. Maintain liaison between corporate Head office and the Region.
3. Espouse and safeguard the interests of the Region concerned while being a member of other Regional Management Boards and also secure inter-regional co-ordination.
4. Responsible for achieving targets as fixed by the Corporate Head Office.
5. Sanction expenditure within the budget approved by the Corporate Head Office.

6. Give ex-post-facto sanction of expenditure as per the norms fixed by the Corporate Head office.
7. Incur unanticipated expenditure subject to the limits set by the Corporate Head office.
8. Fill in the posts within the Region as per directives given by Regional Management Board.
9. Ultimately responsible for the financial and operational performance of the Region.
10. Create and fill in posts, within the Region, of Class III and Class IV employees as per norms prescribed by the Regional Management Board.
11. Review all disciplinary cases of the Region.
12. Exercise any other power as delegated by the Regional Management Board.

FUNCTIONS AND POWERS OF ADDITIONAL GENERAL MANAGER

1. Responsible for the day-to-day functioning of Depots, stores and workshops.
2. Directly responsible for the performance of the Depots.
3. Transfer all the employees in the rank of DMs and below within the Region.
4. Exercise all other powers as delegated to him, from time to time, by the General Manager, to make him effective.

N.B. : The Heads of Departments namely CME and CTM shall be under the administrative control of the AGM and are responsible for rendering effective assistance to the Depots as instructed by AGM.

ANNEXURE 3.1

THE WORKING OF APSRTC—THE VIEWS OF NATIONAL MAZDOOR UNION

The purpose of this brief note is to highlight the views expressed by the National Mazdoor Union leaders—the recognised union of APSRTC.

1. *Organisational set up*

The Union leaders mentioned that the Union had differences with both the Government and the Corporation with regard to the organisational set up. The nature of industry demands decentralisation, as the ultimate operational activity is carried out in the Depots. The Corporation, in the name of re-organisation, has weakened the depots considerably and tried to construct a super-structure over the weak base. The Regional Manager's office is made a replica of the General Manager's Office under re-organisation ; and a big fanfare of autonomy was announced. In the implementation process the whole thing was distorted and there was more of paper autonomy than a real one. There was a feeling that the Reorganisation was hustled through without providing adequate infrastructural facilities, and in spite of lapse of nearly three and half years after reorganisation, two regions, namely Karimnagar, and Vizianagaram, are still operating without full-fledged workshops. It is further pointed out that it is of significance that the losses got identified with the emergence of Regional set up. There are so many levels over the depot resulting in tremendous wastages.

2. *Split*

They further mentioned that splitting the organisation would weaken the organisational unit, as the smaller the unit of organisation the greater is the tendency for the unit to succumb to pressures from the Government. It was further felt that it would be difficult to maintain un-economic routes if split is resorted to and also it would be further difficult to mobilise large number of vehicles to meet the demand requirements of jatras and festivals.

3. *Governmental taxation policies*

The Union Leaders questioned the governmental policies and stated that the Government has no control over the rising prices ; and through their Excise Duty and Sales Tax policies they are contributing to the higher operational costs of the Corporation. The M.V. Tax is quite on the high side and there is a feeling that the surcharge on M.V. Tax was deliberately levied with a view to showing losses but not profits.

4. *Utilisation of Funds*

The Capital contributions given by the Government were spent on Civil Engineering works. There is a feeling that the depreciation fund has been misused and the expenditure on Civil Engineering has resulted in over capitalisation.

5. *Irregularities*

There are instances where the Corporation has placed orders with the same manufacturer at different rates for the same thing—One from Hyderabad and another from Karimnagar. They suspected the bonafides of the Corporation for the delay in the establishment of the workshops and even where facilities were created, buildings were hired from private parties. Further, instances are not lacking where materials like tyres at Karimnagar and crankshaft at Visakhapatnam were given for repairs to outside agencies. Some instances of shady deals were also cited by the Union leaders. There was no co-ordination in the Corporation in the matter of purchases as orders were placed, as pointed out earlier, for the same items in different regions at different rates. Further, purchase orders were also placed despite the fact stocks in respect of the same parts were available in stores and the purchases that were made were of sub-standard quality. Though some of the matters were entrusted for enquiry by a Board Member nothing was heard of it.

6. *Maintenance of vehicles*

They complained that the Corporation buses are not complying with M.V. Tax Acts/Rules and the Corporation is running its buses as in a circus show. According to them, nearly 80 per cent of the Corporation buses do not have hand-breaks and some times the vehicles are run without even being tested.

7. *Personnel*

At the depot level, the Depot Manager is deprived of assistance. New recruitees, without adequate training, are being posted to Depots further complicating the problem. Even where Civil Engineering works are not existing, officers are maintained at various places. With regard to the bus-staff ratio, it was mentioned that the matter has to be examined more at the supervisors and Managerial level than giving more emphasis at the workers level.

They questioned the competence of the Accounts man and felt that competent person from finance should be brought. Similarly, they felt that the Chief Personnel Manager should be an IAS Officer, as the insiders are not very clear about the administrative systems. According to the leaders, the Corporation personnel officers are nothing but "glorified clerks".

The annual turnover of conductors is about 400. The large number of suspensions and dismissals involve financial implication to the Corporation to the tune of nearly Rs. 1½ crores annually as subsistance allowance. By implementing the checking proposals under the concerned G.O., leakage of revenue can be arrested amounting to about Rs. 3 crores. The domestic enquiries are not properly conducted and people who conduct them lack the basic skills in conducting such enquiries. It was felt that it should be done by people belonging to the personnel department or personnel brought on deputation from the Labour Department.

8. *Optimum Size*

A Division must comprise 10-12 depots, and have 1000 vehicles and there should be an embargo on establishing depots having less than 30 vehicles.

9. *Some parameters and norms*

The Mechanical Engineering standards are hopeless and they feel that there is figure magic involved and they are questioning the credibility of the parameters. There should be a standardisation with regard to vehicle-body building and colours used. Frequent change of colours would involve stocking of different kinds of paints. Drivers should be fixed to the vehicles.

10. *Wastage of resources*

Providing vehicles freely to Government and other agencies should be discontinued forthwith.

11. *Effective monitoring of earnings*

The Corporation lacks a commercial outlook and there is no check by the Corporation on the earnings realised by way of advertisements. Similarly travel of police personnel on presentation of police warrants requires utmost control and no control is exercised on the carriage of postal bags in the buses.

12. *Stores*

The stores supply position is very bad and often the stores supply amounts to hardly 40-50 per cent of the requirements of Depots and many a time the stores was not in a position to supply frequently consumed items numbering 25 to 30. They estimated an annual loss of Rs. 6-8 crores on the stores purchase policy of the Corporation. In this context, they further stated that springs consumption for 1979-80 has to be examined in detail. Though rubber bushes and shock absorbers are to be supplied, this was not done, and in fact 80 per cent of the vehicles do not have shock absorbers.

13. *Reconditioning and retrieval*

Regarding the scrap material, no inspection is being done before a thing is scrapped and some check is needed in their reconditioning and retrieval.

14. *Budgeting and accounting*

Depot level budgeting, route-wise profitability, and vehicle-wise accounting should be done.

15. *Conclusion*

In conclusion, a policy of nationalising only the profitable routes, as in the case of Tamil Nadu, might be thought of.

ANNEXURE 3.2

THE WORKING OF APSRTC—VIEWS OF THE EMPLOYEES UNION LEADERS

1. *Costs, fare revision and governmental attitude*

The Union leaders raised the issue by stating that the Corporation must behave in a "business like manner" ; and, in the context of this "business like behaviour", it did not mean passing the buck to the customer by a fare hike. In order to enable the Corporation to behave in a bussiness like manner, sufficient autonomy should be given and decision making power should be located within the undertaking but not in the Secretariat.

They stated that APSRTC does not have operational loss, and that there is a need for re-computation of profits or losses. They opined that whatever losses the Corporation has been showing are mainly due to high M.V. taxes and interest charges. In this context, they raised the question whether the Government is really serious of adhering to a policy of providing an economic public transport. If it is, there is an urgent need for gearing the automobile industry to meet the needs of the public transportation system. In this context, they felt that the multinationals are taking advantage of monopoly position by increasing the chassis and tyre prices, thereby resulting in increased costs ; and the Government is encouraging the same. They further felt that transport sector being a "priority sector" the Government should charge the Corporation only 4 per cent rate of interest instead of charging 6.25 per cent as is being done. While the Corporation is asked to shoulder all the social resposibilities of the Government, the Government probably does not want to take up the responsibility of the Corporation.

2. *Inventories and purchase of stores*

With regard to inventory the leaders doubted whether there is any policy on inventory as such and felt that there is no need for the Corporation to lock up its capital, in readily available stocks in the market. There should be centralised negotiations and decentralised supplies.

3. *Vehicle utilisation and maintenance*
In the name of vehicle utilisation, vehicle condition is neglected. There is no time left for adequate maintenance of the vehicle. The non-availability of spares and shortage of maintenance personnel are also contributing to the neglect of the vehicle condition.

4. *Leakage/loss of revenue*
With regard to the revenue leakage they mentioned that it is more on account of private operators and contract carriages. To tackle the pilferage, they suggested more of ground booking. Suspension of conductors, in fact, is costly for the Corporation. The costs of enquiry and the suspension allowances paid to them are to be taken into account. In view of these, it is suggested that the procedure of enquiry should be simplified. In connection with the pilferage and conductors' suspension, they pointed out that tickets issued to the conductors do not bear consecutive numbers ; and, in between two ticket numbers, some numbers might not have been printed, for which the conductor is being held responsible. In view of this they suggested having only 3 punches and 3 denominations of tickets.

5. *Nationalisation of goods transport*
While the corporation is nationalising only passenger traffic, the goods traffic is left to the private sector, which is quite a profitable sector. In the light of this it is suggested by them that the Corporation should diversify and go into the goods transportation also.

6. *Splitting the corporation*
Regarding the split the leaders are unanimous that it would weaken the nationalised road transport organisation and that they would succumb more easily to the pressures of the Government.

ANNEXURE 3.3

THE WORKING OF THE APSRTC—VIEWS OF THE RETIRED APSRTC OFFICERS' ASSOCIATION

1. Losses

(i) *Reasons for losses*

Shri Gurupershad, ex-General Manager of APSRTC explained the reasons for APSRTC losses the following way :

(a) The policy of the State Government in posting an IAS/IPS Officer as General Manager of APSRTC is wrong. The IAS/IPS officers are like passing birds. They do not possess the technical skills required. The period of their stay in the organisation which usually runs 2-3 years is too short for any one to pick up the required knowledge. By the time they are conversant with the systems and environment of the organisation they are transferred. The post of General Manager requires continuous study of the organisation for a long period. This is not possible in the case of IAS/IPS officers. Instead the insiders may be given the required training and posted as General Managers. Similar system is successfully implemented in Railways.

(b) The other cause of losses is indiscipline among the workers. Trade Unions are patronised by the politicians.

(c) Huge capital expenditure is incurred by APSRTC in constructing Bus Stations while money is not available for augmenting the fleet.

(ii) *Remedies*

He suggested the following remedial measures ;

(a) Insiders should head the organisation. Independent regions may be formed under one Corporation. The regions may function exactly on the same lines as the independent corporations existing in Tamil Nadu. Such a set up would avoid resistance from the Trade Unions as they are opposed to formation of multiple Corporations. The regions may be headed by General Managers. There may be one Chairman for the entire Corporation. The General Managers of the region may be made members of the Corporation board. If it is felt that the Corporation board would be too big in size if all the General Managers were to be included as members, formation of three boards may be thought of.

(b) The body building units of the Corporation should be in a position to compete with the private agencies. Economics may be worked out to provide one body building unit to each autonomous region proposed. Establishment of three Corporations for 8 proposed regions might also be taken as one solution.

2. Mr. Radhakrishna stated that the depot managers should have self-appraisal system.

3. Too many officers are inspecting depots pointing out irregularities without providing assistance to the depots.

4. Out of the 121 officers working in the city, a few might be asked to exercise surprise checks on city operations by rotation. This would improve the rate of earnings in city.

5. Staggering of timings of various Government Offices and other industrial establishments might ease the peak hour congestion and also bunching of buses.

6. Mr. Karunakar reported that too many depots are opened on political considerations. There are depots without any infrastructure facilities. Capital expenditure increased on this account. 60 vehicles might be taken as maximum and 40 as the minimum for determining the size of the depot.

7. Mr. Radhakrishna stated that there is no justification to pay incentive amount to conductors as there is monopoly right enjoyed by the APSRTC on routes.

8. Mr. Rajgopal wondered why employees are paid

incentives for realising the earnings when the earnings are not sufficient to meet the costs of operations.

9. Mr. Karunakar stated that the Depot Managers are functioning as mere administrators. There is no body to take care of operations in the depots as was happening earlier in the case of SIC set up.

10. Incentive amount paid to the conductor is very high. The norms are defective.

11. The problem of absenteeism among drivers might be tackled. Because of the inflow of gulf money, majority of drivers are owning autorickshaws in somebody else name. They are absenting from duties in depots and looking after their business. Severe punishment might be given to such absentees.

INDEX

ECONOMICS OF SOCIAL SECTOR AND ENVIRONMENT

By the Same Author

- Ecology and Quality of Life in Urban Slums: *An Empirical Study*
- Women Empowerment and Family Management in Tribal Region

About the author

Udai Prakash Sinha (*b.* 1956) is Professor of Economics, T.M. Bhagalpur University, Bhagalpur. He has authored many books including Planned Development of Resources in a Developing Region (1985), Socio-Economic Dimensions of Integrated Development in India (1991) and IRDP for Weaker Sections (1996). He is editing 'Journal of Economic Issues' since 2000 published by Planning Forum, and Anga Economic Society, University Department of Economics, T.M. Bhagalpur University, Bhagalpur. He has also completed two UGC Major Research Projects and contributed more than 50 research papers to reputed national and international journals of Economics and other social-sciences. Micro-level planning and the regional economics are the areas of his interest and research.

Based on U.G.C. Syllabus

ECONOMICS OF SOCIAL SECTOR AND ENVIRONMENT

Text Book for M.A. and Honours Students

By

Udai Prakash Sinha

University Professor, Dept. of Economics,
T.M.Bhagalpur University, Bhagalpur

CONCEPT PUBLISHING COMPANY
NEW DELHI-110 059

Cataloging in Publication Data—DK
Courtesy: D.K. Agencies (P) Ltd. <docinfo@dkagencies.com>

Sinha, U. P. (Udai Prakash), 1956-
Economics of social sector and environment / by Udai Prakash Sinha.
p. cm.
In Indian context.
Includes bibliographical references.
ISBN-13: 9788180694691
ISBN-10: 8180694690

1. Environmental economics—India. 2. Environmental policy—India. 3. Sustainable developement—India. 4. Welfare economics. I. Title.

DDC 333.709 54 22

ISBN -10: 81-8069-469-0 (HB)

First Published 2007

Published and Printed at
Ashok Kumar Mittal
Concept Publishing Company
A/15-16, Commercial Block, Mohan Garden
New Delhi-110059 (INDIA)

Phones : 25351460, 25351794
Fax : 091-11-25357103
Email : publishing@conceptpub.com

Preface

Economics is not a comprehensively defined discipline and its frontiers have been changing from time to time. The book seeks to present in a lucid way the modern environmental economic theories, and also the diverse elements of resource analysis for the University students. I claim no originally for this work and the analysis here has been largely based on the contemporary works on economics of social sector and environment, and these books have been referred at the end of the chapter concerned. To quote Edgeworth "we hold that for the mastery of a speculative and controversial science, a certain multiplication of a authorities is desirable' I have very often quoted the authorities on the subject. I have especially relied on C.D. Kolstad's "Environmental Economics", Erach Bharucha's "Environmental Studies", Zimmerman's "Economics of Natural Resources", Todaro's "Economic Development" for the theoretical and empirical treatment in this book. A part from these books, I have taken help from many other works, the names of which cannot be mentioned in this short compass. In the chapter on "Welfare Economics" I have thoroughly dwelt on the famous article of Prof. Mishan and also works of Prof. B.K. Thakur's on Lindahal model and sustainable development have come to my help.

This book especially address the concerns of the students of the Indian Universities and Problems emanting therefrom for the M.A. and Honours Students. In writing this book I have been all through encouraged by my reverred teacher Prof. R.R.L. Das, Head of the University Dept. of Economics, T.M.B.U., Bhagalpur. Sincere thanks are also due to Prof. N. Jha, Prof. A.K. Sinha, Prof. A.K. Tiwari and all the Colleagues of the Department who have gone through the proofs of the most complicated chapter of the work.

At the end, I am very much thankful to my wife Prof. Rekha Sinha who has foregone her holidays and comforts, so that I may complete my work.

Udai Prakash Sinha

Bhagalpur

Contents

1

Welfare Economics

Welfare Economics is that branch of economic theory which investigates the nature of the policy recommendations that the economist is entitled to make. In the present chapter we shall be mainly concerned with the construction of a theoretical framework which can be applied to some actual policy problems.

Resource Allocation and General Equilibrium

The problem of resource allocation, i.e., the problem of finding out an optimum position, the inputs of the factors and the technology being given, plays an important part in modern welfare economics. It is essentially a problem of general equilibrium since, if resources are transferred from one industry into another, the interrelationships of the two industries constitute the heart of the matter. The problem of determining optimum outputs of the various commodities produced in the economy arises because of the relative inelasticity of supply of all resources. Determination of the ideal output or the optimal allocation of resources between the two items is a matter of the relative urgency of the demand functions and their relative cost functions. The optimal output of no product can, therefore, be determined without taking into account the position of other commodities with which it competes for society's limited resources. That is why, Baumol contends that "resource allocation is necessarily a matter for general equilibrium analysis".

Paretian Optimum

The social optimum represents an ideal allocation of resources so that any re-allocation of the resources would make at least one person worse off. Following allocative rule we can say that the social optimum requires that the value, at the point of margin, of any class of factor be the same in all cases in which the factor is used. This allocative rule is decomposed in a number of static marginal or first-order conditions for Paretian maximum welfare. These conditions have elaborately been discussed and then proved by writers like Dr. Little and Reder.

The assumptions on which the marginal conditions of maximum welfare are based are:

(1) that each individual has his own preference function and has definite amounts of each; product and each factor;
(2) that the production function of each firm is given by the state of technology;
(3) that the commodities are divisible;
(4) that each individual purchases certain amount of all commodities; and
(5) that the factors enter each of the goods.

1. Optimum Conditions of Exchange

The first marginal condition for ensuring optimum exchange or optimum allocation of goods among the consumers is that for each individual in the society the marginal rate of substitution between any two goods must be the same. If the marginal rate of substitution between any two goods is not the same for any two individuals, they can enter into an exchange, which would increase the satisfaction of both or of one without leading to diminution of the satisfaction of the other.

We can give the mathematical proof of this condition in the following way:

Let the utility function of the first consumer is $U_1 = f_1 (q_1, r_1)$

Let the utility function of the second consumer
is $U_2 = f_2 (q_2, r_2)$
Total amounts of q and r are fixed so that
$q_1+q_2= Q$ and $r_1–r_2 = R$.

The utility of the first consumer is to be maximized subject to the condition that the utility function of the second consumer remains unaffected.

To find out the maximum, we use the following Lagrangian expression:

$\hat{U} = f_1 (q_1, r_2) = \lambda [f_2 (Q - q_1, R-r_1) - U^1{}_2]$

Where, λ is a Lagrangian multiplier and $U^1{}_2$ = Constant. Now let us differentiate this expression partially in turn in respect of Q_1, R_1

$$\frac{\delta\overline{U}}{\delta q_1} = \frac{\delta f_1}{\delta q_1} - \lambda \frac{\delta f_2}{\delta q_2} = 0 \qquad ......(1)$$

$$\frac{\delta\overline{U}}{\delta q_2} = \frac{\delta f_1}{\delta q_2} - \lambda \frac{\delta f_2}{\delta q_2} = 0 \qquad ......(2)$$

From (1) and (2) we get,

$$\frac{\delta f_1}{\delta q_1}\bigg| \frac{\delta f_1}{\delta q_1}\bigg| = \frac{\delta f_2}{\delta q_2}\bigg| \frac{\delta f_2}{\delta q_2} \qquad ......(3)$$

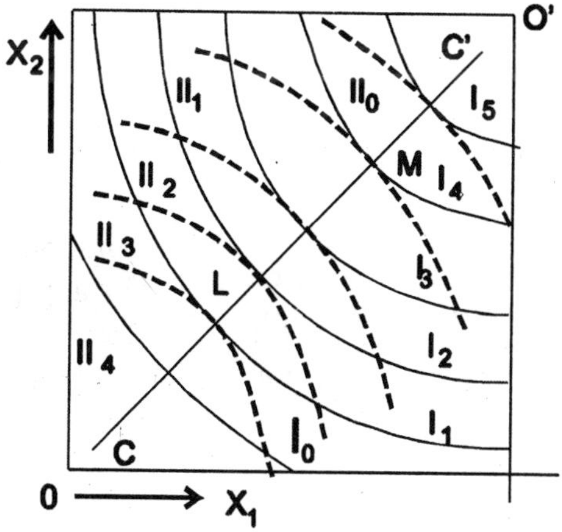

Fig. 1.1

The left hand side of the equation no. (3) is the marginal rate of substitution of the first consumer while the right hand side represents the marginal rate of substitution of the second consumer. The equality of those two sides indicates the fulfilment of the first marginal condition of maximum welfare in the matter of exchange.

In the following figure, we can show the fulfilment of this condition.

We choose an Edgeworth box diagram the vertical and horizontal axes of the rectangle indicating the total available quantities of goods x_1, and x_2. The curves I_0 I_1, I_2, I_3, etc. are the indifference curves of the individual A with O as the point of origin while the curves I_0 I_1, I_2, I_3, etc. are the indifference curves of the individual B with O' as the point of origin. The locus of the points of tangency of these two sets of indifference curves is the contract curve CC'. At the points of tangency the indifference curves of the two individual, having the same slope, the marginal rate of substitution between the two goods is the same for the two individuals who consume them both. Any point off the contract curve indicates the non-fulfilment of this optimum condition of exchange. Welfare is maximized for the community when the community moves from a point off the contract curve to a point on the contract curve. In the words of Boulding, "the assumption that the optimum point must lie on the contract curve itself involves an important value judgment that people ought to get what they want".

2. *Optimum Production Conditions*

Paretian optimality condition in relation to production are the following:

(i) The marginal technical rate of substitution between any pair of factors will be the same for any pair of firms using both to produce a given product.

(ii) The marginal rate of transformation between any two goods is the same for any pair of firms who produce them both.

(iii) The marginal rate of transformation between any factor and any product must be the same for any pair of firms using the factor and producing the product.

For the fulfilment of the first condition, let us refer to Edgeworth diagram which has already been drawn above assuming that I_0 I_1, I_2, I_3, etc. are iso-product curves of the firm A and II_0 II_1, II_2, II_3, etc. are the iso-product curves of the firm B. The locus of the mutual tangencies of these two sets of production indifference curves is known as the production contract curve. (CC′ in the above diagram). Any point on this curve shows that the marginal technical rate of substitution between the two factors for each producer is the same and any point off this curve shows the non-fulfilment of the condition of optimum production.

Mathematically, we can show the proof as follows:

The production function of A is $q_1 = f_1 (y_1, y_2)$
The production function of B is $q_2 = f_2 (y'_1, y'_2)$

Y_1 $(= q_1 + y'_1)$ and Y_2 $(= y_2 + y'_2)$ are the total amounts of inputs and $q_1 + q_2 = q$ the total quantity of output produced.

To find out the maximum output of one producer, the output produced by the other remaining constant, we use the following Lagrangian expression:

$$L = f_1 (y_1 + y_2) + \lambda [f_2 (Y_1 - y_1, Y_2 - y_2) - q'_2]$$

By differentiating,

$$\frac{\delta L}{\delta y_1} = \frac{\delta f_1}{\delta y_1} - \lambda \frac{\delta f_2}{\delta y_1} = 0 \qquad \text{......(1)}$$

$$\frac{\delta L}{\delta y_2} = \frac{\delta f_1}{\delta y_2} - \lambda \frac{\delta f_2}{\delta y_2} = 0 \qquad \text{......(2)}$$

From (1) and (2) we get,

$$\frac{\delta_1}{\delta y_1} \frac{\delta f_2}{\delta y_2} = \frac{\delta f_2}{\delta y_1} \frac{\delta f_2}{\delta y_2}$$

The left hand side shows the marginal technical rate of substitution ($MTSy_1Y_2$) of one firm while the right hand side shows the marginal technical rate of substitution ($MTSy_1Y_2$) of another firm. The second marginal condition of optimum production as stated above is a condition of optimum degree of specialization which determines the optimum output of each product produced by each firm. It states that the marginal technical rate of substitution (MTS) between two products is the rate at which one product must be sacrificed to obtain more of the other product without varying the input used. If this condition is not fulfilled, it is possible to increase the combined output of both the products, or to increase the output of one product without decreasing the output of another. Outputs must be produced in such combinations that the slopes of the product transformation curve, (which are assumed to he concave to the origin) of the two firms are equal.

The third marginal condition of optimum production as stated above shows the optimum factor-product relationship. In terms of this condition, the marginal rate of transformation between any factor and any product must be the same of the two firms using the factor and producing the product. It implies that if the marginal physical productivity of any factor for a given product is not identical for two firms, the total product can be increased by transferring the factor from the low-productivity firm to the high-productivity firm. As has been stated Baumol, "switching around of inputs can give us something for nothing — it can increase one or both outputs without any increase in input use" if this marginal condition of optimum production is not satisfied.

When the find MTS (Marginal technical rate of substitution) MRT (Marginal rate of transformation) and MPP (Marginal physical productivity of a factor) are the same for all the firms, Paretian optimality conditions are fulfilled for the producing sector. If there is any reallocation of resources among the firms, the output level of one firm can be increased only at the expense of a decrease in output level of some other firms.

3. General Paretian Optimality

Paretian condition for general social optimum is fulfilled when the optimum situations in both the consuming sector and the producing sector are reached. But this situation further calls for an equality of the subjective rate of substitution common to all individuals and the objective rate of transformation for all pairs of products. The following figure indicates this.

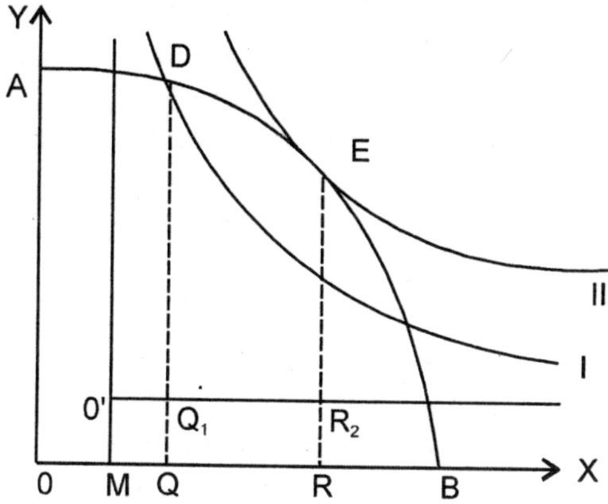

Fig. 1.2

AB is a community transformation curve between two goods x and y, which has been tangent to the indifference curve II of a consumer who consumes both these goods. At the point E, where AB curve has been tangent to the indifference curve, II, the subjective rate of substitution becomes equal to the objectives rate of transformation, D is the point where the indifference curve no.I cuts the AB curves; so D is not an optimum position. For achieving the optimum position, the consumer must be on a higher indifference curve or on a higher welfare level as indicated by the point E.

4. Second-order Conditions

The marginal conditions which have been discussed above are the first order conditions which do not necessarily establish welfare optimality. The fulfilment of these conditions may even lead to a minimum position of welfare as indicated by the point, a, in the following figure. There must be, in addition to these marginal conditions, some stability conditions for equilibrium position which we may call second-order conditions. In the opinion of Prof. Reder, the fulfilment of the second-order conditions in addition to the marginal and the total conditions are essential for achieving welfare optimum. The fulfilment of the second-order condition means that in the neighbourhood of maximum welfare, all indifference curves must be convex to the point of origin and all transformation curves must be concave to it. The convexity of indifference curves implies diminishing marginal rate of substitution between two products for a consumer and the concavity of transformation curves means increasing cost conditions (or diminishing returns) in production. The following figure illustrates this:

In this diagram at the point C, the concave transformation curve is tangent to the convex indifference curve I_3. At the point b, the marginal conditions are fulfilled and it may be treated as a local maximum. In spite of the fulfilment of the second order conditions this position is not the largest maximum. At the point, a, we find minimum position of welfare where only the first order conditions are fulfilled. At the point C, welfare is largest maximum. To attain largest maximum welfare, another set of conditions called "total conditions" by Hicks should be satisfied. Prof. Mishan calls these conditions trite sufficient conditions. When these conditions are fulfilled, "it must be impossible to increase welfare by producing a product not otherwise produced; or by using a factor not otherwise used."

The analysis of Paretian optimum accepts the prevailing income distribution i.e., the prevailing factor endowments. The problem of finding an optimal income distribution is not considered. "The analysis of welfare in terms of Paretian optimum leaves a considerable amount of indeterminacy in the solution. There are an infinite number of points on the contract curve in Edgeworth-box diagram which can pareto optimum. "The indeterminacy is the consequence of considering an increase in welfare to be unambiguously defined only if an improvement in one individual's position is not accompanied by a deterioration of the position of another. This indeterminacy can only be removed by further value judgments."

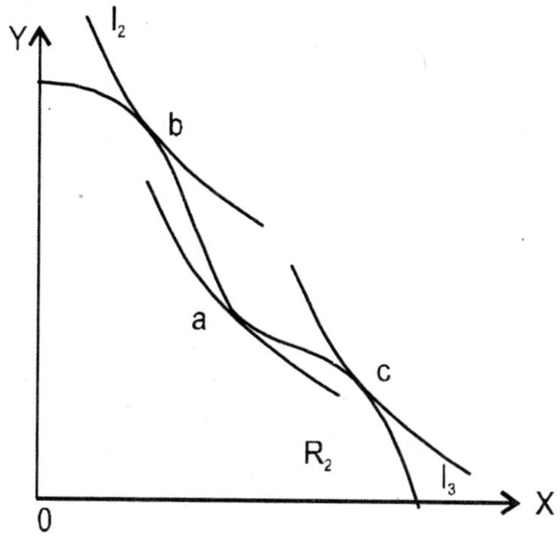

Fig. 1.3

The Efficiency of Perfect Competition

Economic efficiency, often called Paretian optimum, is defined in terms of the outcome of one or more economic activities. The distribution of consumer goods among consumers is efficient if it is satisfied that every possible realization of goods among consumers leads to a reduction of the satisfaction of at least one. Production is efficient if every feasible reallocation of available resources among firms diminishes the output level of at least one firm. We shall now see, that—in the absence of external economies and diseconomies—a perfect competitive equilibrium satisfies the conditions of Paretian optimum.

External economies and diseconomies show that allocation of resources has not been optimum. External economies of production cause marginal social benefits to differ from private benefits, and external economies of consumption arise when a person's consumption favourably affects others.

In both the cases, allocation of resources cannot be ideal. In case of diseconomies also, the same thing happens. Assuming there are no external effects, we can show that Paretian optimum is fully compatible with perfect competition. Welfare is said to increase (diminish) if at least one person's portion improves (deteriorates) with no change in the positions of others. It is clear that no situation can be optimal unless all possible improvements of this variety have been made. Perfect competition is an optimum and a welfare ideal in this sense.

We can deduce the Pareto optimality of perfect competition. In a competitive market the marginal rate of substitution

$$\text{(MRS) between x and y} = \frac{\text{P of x}}{\text{P of y}} \qquad \text{......(1)}$$

If there is perfect competition among entrepreneurs in commodity and factor markets.

$$Px = \frac{r}{MPx} \text{ and } Py = \frac{r}{Mpy} \qquad \text{......(2)}$$

Where, r is the price of the factor capital and MPx and MPy are its marginal products in producing x and y.

$$\text{Therefore, MRS} = \frac{Px}{Py} = \frac{r/MPx}{r/MPy} = \frac{1/MPx}{1/Mpy}$$

$$= \frac{\text{Marginal cost of x in terms of capital}}{\text{Marginal cost of y in terms of capital}}$$

$$= MTSxy. \qquad \text{......(3)}$$

This proves Paretian optimum.

Equation (3) would appear to hold even if the equation (2) does not, provided that

$$\frac{Px}{Py} = \frac{r/MPx}{r/Mpy} \qquad \text{......(4)}$$

$$Px = K\frac{r}{MPx} \; (x = 1, \text{......}, m) \qquad \text{......(5)}$$

Where, k is a factor of proportionality, i.e. if prices are proportional to marginal cost (= r/MP). Equation 5 then becomes

$$R/Px = 1MPx/k \qquad \text{......(6)}$$

The left-hand side of the equation (G) equals the consumer's rate of substitution between the product x and the factor capital; the right-hand side is (l/k) times the producer's rate of transformation between the product z and the factor capital. Here the consumer's and producer's corresponding rates of substitution are not equal. Consumers do not provide the optimal amount of capital, and allocation cannot be Paretian optimum. Since r/MP is the marginal cost of output (MC), the equation (4) can be stated as

$$\frac{P_x}{P_y} = \frac{MC_y}{MC_x} \qquad \text{......(7)}$$

The above proof also implies that for an optimum, P = MC for every commodity; the proportionality of prices and marginal costs is not sufficient. Thus, we find that conditions of Paretian optimum are fulfilled under perfect competition if there is no external effect. Under perfect competition, the households and the firms try to maximize their utilities and profits respectively and as such the consumer seeking maximum utility makes the marginal rate of substitution between any two products equal to the ratio of their prices. Prices being same for all consumers under perfect competition, the marginal rates of substitution between goods must to the ratio of their prices. Since all factors have fixed prices in a perfectly competitive market, the technical all producers using both factors to produce a given output. Again, the marginal technical rate of substitution between any two products are equal to the ratio of their prices ($MTS_{xy} = P_x/P_y$) under perfect competition.

The optimum factor-product relationship also is fulfilled under perfect competition. It implies that the value of the marginal product of any input is equal to its price under perfect competition. Again, in a perfectly competitive market the subjective rate of substitution in the consuming sector is automatically equal to the technical rate of transformation in the producing sector. That is to say, the MRS between any pair of products for any consumer will be the same as the MRT for all producers of the some products. We have seen the compatibility of Paretian optimum with perfect competition. But this is possible if there are no external effects in production and consumption. With constant marginal utility of money, the private marginal economies and diseconomies in production and consumption, there are discrepancies between these elements. In the presence of external effects, a firm's individual maximization differs from social maximization of the firm.

The equation no. (3) above is not fulfilled if there are external economies and external diseconomies of production and consumption. If there are external effects, for maximizing welfare from the standpoint of the society, consumer's MRSs should be equated not with the firm's private MTSs, but with society's MTSs. Price in that case will have to be equal to social marginal cost, and not the private marginal cost.

Paretian Optimum, Monopoly and Oligopoly

The conditions of Paretian optimum fail to be realized in a world of monopoly and monopolistic competition. The marginal conditions of Paretian optimum are not fulfilled also in the presence of oligopolies and monopolies. This assertion is proved by a four stage argument:

(1) Under conditions of monopoly and monopolistic competition among consumers, the corresponding marginal rates of substitution of different consumers are not necessarily equal.
For efficient allocation of resources, price should be equal to marginal cost and the price paid to any factor should be equal to the value of its marginal product. It is possible under perfect competition and not in a market where we find market imperfection. With marginal revenue curve sloping below the average revenue curve. Price is greater than marginal revenue. For maximizing profit, the monopolist will equate his marginal revenue to marginal cost. Therefore, price will be always greater than marginal cost in monopoly. This implies that the factor also is not paid the value of its marginal products. So, misallocation of resources is bound to take place.

(2) Under conditions of monopoly and monopolistic competition among firms in input markets, the corresponding technical rates of substitution of different firms also are not equal when no factor is paid the value of its marginal products.

(3) Under conditions of market imperfection or monopolistic competition among firms in products markets, the corresponding ratio of factor prices of' different firms are not necessarily equal.

(4) Under monopoly or monopolistic competition or oligopoly, optimum factor-product relationship is not maintained and so, resources can never be allocated in keeping with the conditions of Paretian optimum. The equilibrium outputs and prices of the various firms under duopoly and oligopoly are formally indeterminate unless further specification is made concerning the shapes of the "reaction curves." In oligopoly, the demand curve being kinky, it is impossible to find out any suitable device for optimum allocation of resources by a firm in such a market. The marginal technical rate of substitution of one factor for another can never be the same for the duopolists or two firms in an oligopolistic market who use them both.

We have seen that perfect competition results in Paretian optimum allocation. We may now say that every Pareto-optimal allocation must be perfectly competitive one, since Pareto-optimality it cannot be obtained under conditions of an imperfect market.

Pigou's Analysis : A Short Appraisal

Before we discuss any modern interpretation of the determination of ideal output, it is desirable that we should consider the Pigovian welfare economics. All the important theoretical terms applied by Pigou are obtained from Marshallian analysis, but still we find a departure of Pigou from Marshallian analysis. While Marshall concerned himself with surplus analysis, Pigou introduces a marginal analysis, which deals with balancing the advantages and disadvantages of very small changes in the scale of output in different industries.

Pigou is concerned mainly with economic welfare, which is that point of social (general) welfare that can be brought directly or indirectly into relation with measuring rod of money. Pigou is not ready to admit that interpersonal utility comparisons are impossible. He contends that "utilities though not measurable (strictly in cardinal sense), are comparable both interpersonally." Pigou assumes equal capacity for satisfaction, and argues that if it is assumed that real income consists of a single sort of commodity and is subject to the law of diminishing marginal utility, it can definitely be said that persons having more real income will enjoy more satisfaction than those having less of it; if any transfer of real income from the higher income group to the lower income group will necessarily increase aggregate satisfaction or the well-being of society. Thus economic welfare has not only a subjective aspect according to Pigou, it has also an objective or material counterpart. Following Marshall, he defines national income as the flow of goods and services produced annually·after maintaining capital intact which is measurable in terms of money.

For finding out whether any economic change has improved welfare, Pigou applies a double criterion: an increase in the national dividend without any increase in the supply of factors, and a transfer of wealth from the rich to the poor. Pigou refuses to believe in the spentaneous harmony of private and social interests. Modern analysis of external effects is to be found in a crude form in Pigou's distinction between social and private valuation of economic activities. In Pigou's version the social net product is the aggregate contribution made to the national dividend and the private net product is the contribution that is capable of being sold and the proceeds added to the earning of the person for the unit of investment. With external diseconomies or economies resulting from marginal increase in output there must be a divergence between marginal private net product and marginal social net product. The optimum output or the ideal output in Pigou's version is reached when society has maximised the increase in national dividend by equating marginal social products in all industries. In Pigou's analysis, the ideal output is reached when competition equalizes the marginal private products in all uses; it is an economic system where the marginal private net product is equal to marginal social net product automatically.

Dr. Hla Myint points out, the basic difference between Paretian optimum and Pigovian optimum is that while the Paretian optimum is not designed for practical application, Pigovian theory chiefly deals with the practical application of welfare economics. Pigou's distinction between the economic and general welfare and that between marginal private and the marginal social products are meant for serving practical problems. But the main purpose of optimum is to define the concept of optimum free front interpersonal comparisons and value judgments. So, while Paretian optimum provides us with methodological problems of the study of welfare economics Pigovian optimum has contributed to the growth of a welfare economics which is geared to practical applications.

Pigou's analysis of welfare is subject to certain criticisms. In the opinion of Prof. Lionel Robbins, Pigou's welfare economics being based on the assumption of man's equal capacity for satisfaction, rests upon ethical principle, rather than upon scientific demonstration. It is not a judgment of fact "in scientific sense but rather a judgment of value. Thus Pigou's analysis becomes a normative study which cannot provide a positive guide to welfare policy recommendations. Secondly, in examining the course of divergences between private net product and social net product, Pigou has not considered the factors of immobility, indivisibility and imperfect knowledge. Thirdly, Pigou's distinction between economic welfare and the general welfare merely on the basis of distinctions between the national product and the other material or immaterial end-results is not logically convincing. But still, Pigou's contribution to modern welfare economics can hardly be over-estimated. As Dr. Bhabatosh Dutta argue, "Pigou achieved what Marshall could not do in his written work the integration of the nonnative problems with the positive ones, the building-up of a rigorous theoretical analysis which would serve as a scientific theory of economic policy".

Baumol's Interpretation of Ideal Output

Prof. Baumol in his "Welfare Economics and the Theory of the State" has formulated an interpretation related to the ideal allocation of resource among the alternative uses, the level of employment being given, prior to Baumol, R.F.

Kahn of the Cambridge University developed it concept of ideal output which was quit similar to that as a summit or Paretian optimum position. But Baumol has approached this concept from a new angle of vision on the basis of the following assumptions:

(1) The demand side of the market far finished products is perfect in every sense;
(2) all products are evenly distributed among the members of the society at a given time;
(3) tastes and technology are given;
(4) everyone prefers more rather than less of each product;
(5) the level of employment is given;
(6) there are no external effects in consumption for the time being, and
(7) the community indifference curves are here non-intersecting.

In Baumol's view, in a two-commodity economy model we can show (lie determination of the ideal output in the following figure:

The vertical and horizontal axes show the amounts of commodities y and x respectively. The curves I_1, $I_2$and I_3 are the set of non-intersecting community indifference curves indicating the different combinations of the two commodities in the community and showing constancy of real wealth distribution throughout the community. TT' is the transformation curve which has been tangent to the community indifference curve I_2 at the point E. TT curve has been drawn in the concave form on the basis of the assumption that the resources are imperfect substitutes. The slope of this curve at any point measures the ratio of the two social marginal costs. The ideal output position in the above figure has been attained at the position E, where the transformation curve touches the highest possible community indifference curve, which is again tangent to budget line AB at the disposal of the community. Any movement away from E on the TT curve pushes the community to a lower indifference curve.

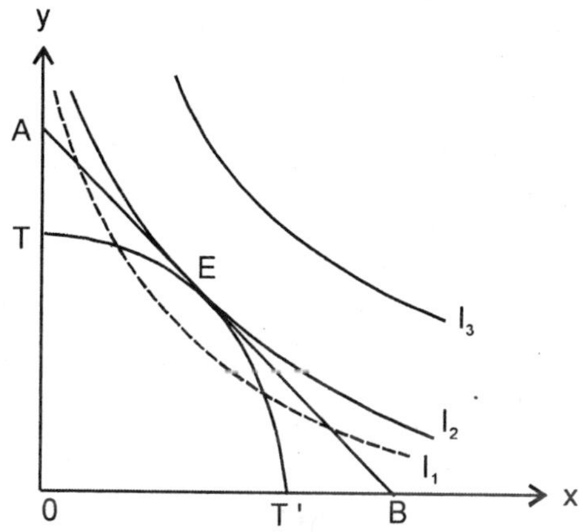

Fig. 1.4

Assuming that external effects are absent under perfect competition, marginal private costs are equal to marginal social costs. In that case, competitive output and ideal output are identical. Once we admit external effects in the industry, the marginal private cost and marginal social cost will differ and in that case the price line will not be tangent to transformation curve and the output will not be an ideal one. As for demand equilibrium, the price line, AB, will be tangent to the highest possible community indifference curve which is I_2 in the above figure. The deviations from ideal output because of the discrepancy between private marginal cost and social marginal cost can be corrected by developing sonic sort of system of taxes and bounties.

Compensation Principle

New Welfare Economics treats the inter-personal comparison of utility as an unscientific method of measuring economic welfare, and introduces the "Compensation Principle" as an objective test of economic efficiency quite detached from art value judgment. This principle has been developed by Kaldor, Hicks Scitovsky, Little and Samuelson and recently new light was thrown upon this subject by Dr. Mishan and Dr. Amartya Sen.

The formulation of the principle of hypothetical compensation arose out of the controversies of 1938-39 in the Economic Journal without challenging Robbins' view of the scientific status of interpersonal comparisons. Kaldor denied their relevance to prescriptive statements. Hicks supported Kaldor's notion of examining the efficiency of alternative economic organizations without reference to the question of distribution, and particularly without reference to the comparisons or satisfactions as between individuals. Scitovsky demonstrated that having shown a position x to be more efficient than a position y on the Kaldor-Hicks criterion, the same criterion might well reveal, following the community's adoption of the x position, that position y was more efficient than position x. With this in mind, Scitovsky criterion was one which required the result of the original Kaldor-Hicks test to be consistent with that of the "reversal" of this test. If was left to Samuelson to push the logic of Scitovsky's initial discovery to its conclusion, that, in general—if we exclude comparisons between situations in one of which there is more of "every" good—it was not possible to rank alternative economic organizations on the basis of compensation tests.

Kaldor-Hicks Criterion

The compensation principle extends Pareto's criterion for increase in welfare to situations where some are better off and some are worse off. This principle seeks to offer all objective stand and of efficiency by isolating the problem of production from that of distribution. Pareto criterion states than "an economic change which harms nobody but makes sonic people better off (in their own estimation) must be considered an improvement" i.e., as a situation which promotes economic welfare. But the compensation principle as originally formulated by Kaldor, can be explained in the following manner: Situation x is socially preferable to situation y, if those who gain from x can compensate the losers and still remain better off than at y. When this is the case, the society call increase its real income (or welfare) by moving from y to x. Hicks further elaborates it as follows: situation x is socially preferable to situation y if the losers in x cannot profitably bribe the gainers into not making the change from y to x.

These two criteria being similar in their contents, they are known by x single name, "Kaldor-Hicks Criterion", which states that "a change is an improvement if the gainers can place a higher value figure on their gains than do the losers on their losses."

Scitovsky Paradox

Scitovsky points out that the Kaldor-Hicks criterion leads to contradictory results. It is possible, Scitovsky argues, that the position x is more efficient than the position y, but once the position x is chosen by the community, the same criterion can reveal that the return move from x back to y is an improvement as well. This contradictory result involved in Kaldor-Hicks criterion as pointed out by Scitovsky is usually known as Scitovsky paradox.

Prof. E.J. Mishan points out that the source of Scitovsky paradox lies in the interconnection between distribution and relative valuations. When we find that distributions of real income are different in two situations, it is quite obvious, Mishan argues, that the possibility of adequate compensation also will differ.

For, the relative valuation of the goods in two situations will not be identical. We may elaborate it further. Let us assume that twc bundle of goods are available respectively in situations x and y: in terms of Kaldor-Hicks list, a comparison of the two bundles depends on the set of relative prices associated with the initial position, and such a comparison may reveal that x is preferable to y: but once x is reached, a comparison of the two bundles, based on the set of relative prices associated with the new situation, may show a different possibility of compensation, so that a return journey from x to y may now be desirable.

Scitovsky, therefore, prescribes a double criterion, which requires the fulfilment of the Kaldor-Hicks criterion plus non-fulfilment of the reversal test.

Little's Criterion

Prof. Little argues that value judgment particular, those about distribution, cannot be avoided in welfare economics. Little criticizes Kaldor and Hicks and argues that compensation is a purely "hypothetical" affair. "Hence, to announce as did Kaldor, Hicks and others, that an objective method of detecting increases in 'wealth' or 'efficiency' had been discovered, is to mislead opinion by the use of persuasive words. Nothing had been discovered. Kaldor had merely coined a definition of efficiency, one whose ethical implications, as it happens, are hardly acceptable." Little explicitly favours "the piece-meal approach to what he calls utopianism, or the all-or-nothing approach of Bergson, Samuelson and others." The criterion Little lays down is that, in so far as welfare is affected only by the economic variables under consideration, the change to a new situation should be made: (a) if the new distribution is no worse than the old, and (b) if it is impossible to make "everyone" as well off in the original position as he would be after the change. Little wants to see whether redistribution of real income as a result of a change in economic policy is good or net. Arrow in the review of the first edition of Little's "A Critique of Welfare Economics" remarks that comparison of relative welfare distributions would require both the possibility of inter-personal comparisons and the measurement of cardinal utility. The second portion of Little's criterion calls for the fulfilment of both the Kaldor-Hicks and the Scitovsky criteria before we are to judge whether the redistribution of real income is good or not.

Dr. A.K. Sen refers to three main features of Little's criterion. In the first place, in line with the Paretian tradition, in Little's criterion, overall economic welfare is related to the welfare of the individual members of the society. Secondly, in the line with Pareto, Little assumes that if at least one person is better off and none worse off than in an alternative situation, then the situation under consideration is better. Thirdly, Little does not throw any light on the exact nature of welfare judgment when some non-Paretian choice is to be made; but such judgments must be in keeping with the principle of transitivity.

Let us now, following Mishan, re-state Little criterion as follows: A social improvement takes place (i) if everyone is made better off, and (ii) if the existing collection of goods is more equally distributed. We may find a desirable economic change in which either the first condition is realized without making the second condition neglected, or the other way round, or both the first and the second conditions are realized. If both the conditions are neglected, the change is not to be desired. In Mishan's explanation, a social improvement occurs "if the existing collection of goods is more equally distributed." Dr. A.K. Sen's contends that the conclusion cannot follow so easily. He argues that Mishan's interpretation of the Little criterion is very restrictive although "the Little criterion is very general."

In Dr. Sen's opinion, the Little criterion is "not based on a dichotomy of the production considerations on one side and distribution considerations on the other." Little's criterion is based on the principle of transitivity.

Construction of the Utility Possibility Curve

In construction, the utility-possibility curve resembles the production- possibility curve except that, along each of the axes, the welfare, or cardinal utility, of one of the individuals is measured on any arbitrary scale. The boundary of all combinations of the individual utilities which are possible with a given bundle of goods forms the utility-possibility curve.

The initial division of the Q, bundle in the Figure is represented as the point C_1' on the utility-possibility curve Q_1Q_1. B's utility can not increase without the corresponding diminution

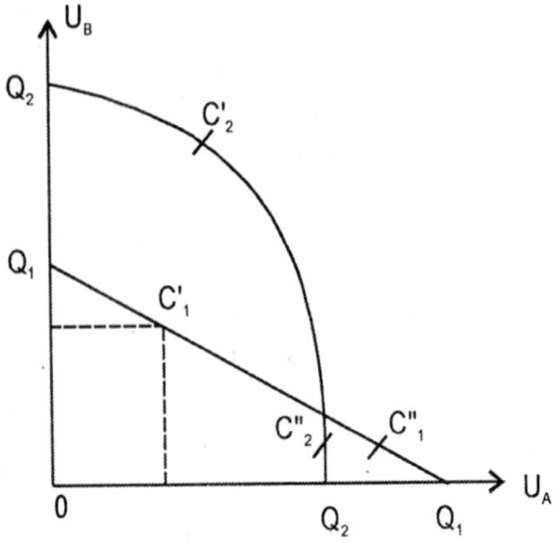

Fig. 1.5

of A's utility, and that is why, the boundary line Q_1Q_1 is downward sloping to the right. Q_2Q_2 is the utility possibility curve corresponding to the Q_2 contract curve, with C_2'' indicating the individual utilities corresponding to the existing division of the bundle. For comparing the alternative bundles Q_1 and Q_2 using, the Kaldor-Hicks criterion, we move along the Q_2Q_2 utility curve from C_2'', the existing distribution increasing B's welfare at the expense of A's to C'_2, t point which is comparable with C'_2 on the Q_1Q_1 curve. The Kaldor Hicks criterion thus being satisfied, we may now try the reversal test, which will be based on C''_2, distribution of the Q_2 bundle. From C'_1 we move along Q_1Q_1 to C''_1 distribution of Q_2 bundle. From C'_1 we more along Q_1Q_1 to C''_1 which is comparable with C_2'' on Q_2Q_2 curve, in this way making both individuals better off with the Q_1 bundle. Since Q_2 is superior to Q_1 by the original test and Q_1 superior to Q_2 by the reveal test, the Scitovsky criterion is not satisfied.

Let us now see the relationship between a production curve and a utility possibility curve. The production possibility curve shows the frontier of the production possibilities open before the economy with its given resources and technological knowledge. A point on the production possibility curve indicates a particular commodity bundles, which can be distributed among the individuals of the community in alternative ways: all these possibilities can be read off from a contract curve. Each point on the production possibility curve gives rise to a contract curve and hence to a different utility possibility curve. Thus a production possibility can be transferred into a set of utility possibility curves which obviously intersect or overlap.

Samuelson Criterion

Samuelson's criterion is a bit stringent criterion for showing a potentially superior position on welfare grounds. A position Q_2 is potentially superior to Q_1 only if for all conceivable distribution of the commodity bundle in Q_2, Q_2 is superior to Q_1. That is to say to requires that the utility possibility curve through Q = is outside the utility possibility curve through Q_1.

Samuelson's criterion states that if Q_2 is potentially superior to Q_1 then this superiority of Q_2 to Q_1 must imply an increase in "potential real income". We are then to assume that for all conceivable welfare distributions, Q_2 should have more of "every" good than Q_1 for the fulfilment of this criterion.

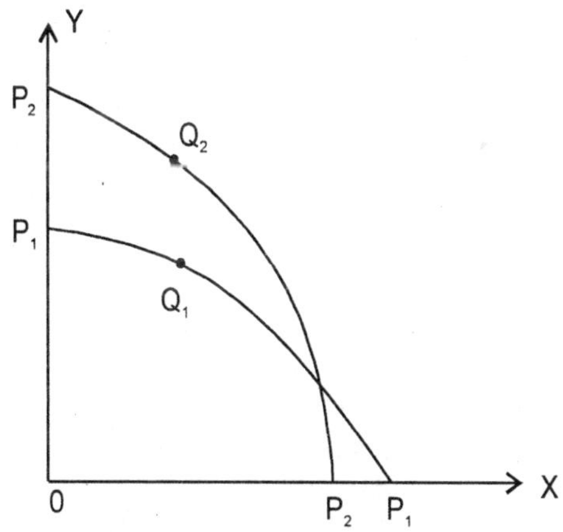

Fig. 1.6

The Samuelson criterion also has certain difficulties. An efficiently produced bundle, if all considerations of distribution are not duly taken into account, cannot be judged to be better than the other efficiently produced bundles. To say that Q_2 is superior to Q_1, we should conceive of a particular case of welfare distribution, and not of all welfare distributions. In the words of Prof. Mishan, "no bundle, then, is superior to any one of the other efficiently produced bundles for all welfare distributions, and therefore no bundle car fulfil the Samuelson criterion."

If Q_1 and Q_2 in the Figure are regarded as bundles of goods on alternative production possibility curves P_1P_1, and P_2P_2 respectively, we run into trouble according to Samuelson. For though the utility-possibility curve generated from bundle Q_2 lies everywhere above that generated from bundle Q, obviously the utility, frontier of the production-possibility curve P_2P_2 will not lie everywhere above that of P_1P_1. If now, the community experiences a shift front Q_1 on P_1P_1 producing more of all goods in the new position, the inference that a potential increase of real income has taken place would be false. This afterthought, however, is not very convincing.

An Appraisal of the Compensation Principle

None of the compensation tests has provided us with an apparatus of mind which may enable its to infer unambiguously if a change in the economic system is better or not. Kaldor and Hicks consider only the production aspect and do not take into the account the distributional aspect of any economic change. But Prof. Little insists that ethical norms being indispensable in welfare economics, we can never overlook the impact of increased production upon the distribution of real income. The implicit promise of value judgment that changes which enable the gainers to overcompensate the losers are good changes is not sufficient to tell its that welfare has really been promoted, unless we are fully aware of who the uncompensated losers are. If a change involves a gain to society, the fact that some members of the society are able to compensate the losers and still remain better off is to accept a peculiar value judgment, which may not have universal favour from the side of the community.

Another criticism against the compensation principle is that the money measure of individual's losses or gains is based on the tacit assumption of the equal marginal utility of money in the hands of both the upper income group and the lower income-group and thus this theory indirectly involves interpersonal comparison of utility which this theory intends to eliminate.

The basic difficulty of the compensation principle is that it simply proves the desirability of an alteration in the social state in which adequate compensation could be paid to the losers. But compensation does not actually have to be paid so as to achieve an improvement. Thus alteration, which would improve welfare, if accompanied by compensation, need not load to improvement if compensation is omitted.

Again the view implicit in Kaldor's argument that the state is responsible for maintaining equitable distribution of income is acceptable only in a socialist state and not in a private enterprise economy. So, Scitovsky concludes, "that while the new welfare economics has, in Kaldor's argument, provided the economist with n guide to policy in some countries, this guide has no universal validity."

Again this principle involves a difficulty of calculating the actual amount of compensation to be paid to the losers and then of examining whether even after the payment of compensation, some people are still better off. This is simply a mathematical puzzle and actually, it is not so easy to find out an accurate calculation of the compensation. In conclusion, me can say, "Any attempt to construct a rigorous and universally applicable criterion for distinguishing what policy change is, an economic improvement most be founded on the problem of interpersonal comparisons. Where a policy charge affects some persons favourably and others adversely, as is usually the case, there is no n priori may of weighing the net result. Of course, we can and must make interpersonal comparisons — we judge, reasonably, that flood victims must occupy the government's, attention and receive emergency assistance at the cost of other taxpayers. However these judgments must be rough ready and can only be handled case by case. No abstract and general formula can be invented which handles all such problems satisfactorily."

Community Indifference—Scitovsky Frontier

Scitovsky Frontier refers to construction of community indifference curves. As an individual has his own tastes, so the society also has social tastes and we can pass from individual tastes to social states. Let us assume that for each me her of the community there is an arbitrary selection of indifference curves and let the selected indifference curves be called prescribed curves. Let us further assume that we have definite amount of all goods but one. The question is, what is the minimum amount of the remaining good, which will be sufficient for placing each man on his prescribed indifference curve? The answer to this question will give us a point on the Scitovsky Community indifference curve corresponding to the prescribed set of individual curves.

Let us illustrate geometric construction of a community indifference map for a community of two individuals. AB whose respective indifference curves are given below.

The community indifference curve to be constructed there from is to have the property that, at all points along it; (i) the individuals A and B maintain their respective levels of welfare, a_1 and b_2 (since community indifference curve call be formed from any pair of the individual curves, let us start by choosing a_1 and b_1, and (ii) the rate of substitution be the same for each individual for any decision of the bundle of goods held in common. Let us now draw the community indifference curve by placing the origin of B's map diagonally opposite to that of A's origin and keeping B's axes parallel to those of A and moving B's map until b_2 just touches a_1 at say c' in the Figure no. 39. Then the point Ob (the origin of B's map) taken with reference to Oa (A's origin) represents a point on the required community indifference map.

Another such point is indicated by the point d^1. B's map having been moved downward to the right and adjusted so that once again, b_2 just touches a_1 at d^1.

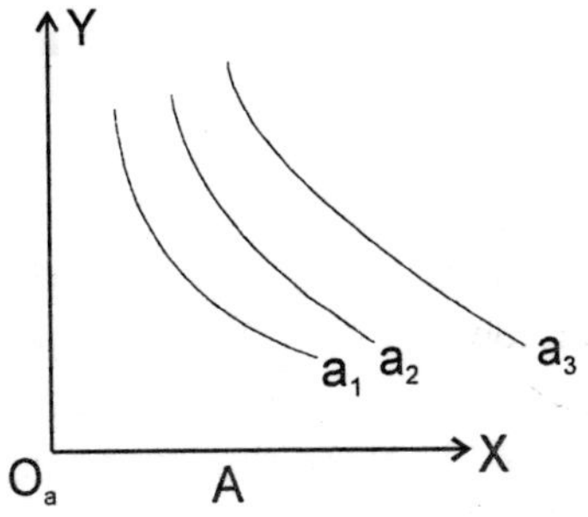

Fig. 1.7

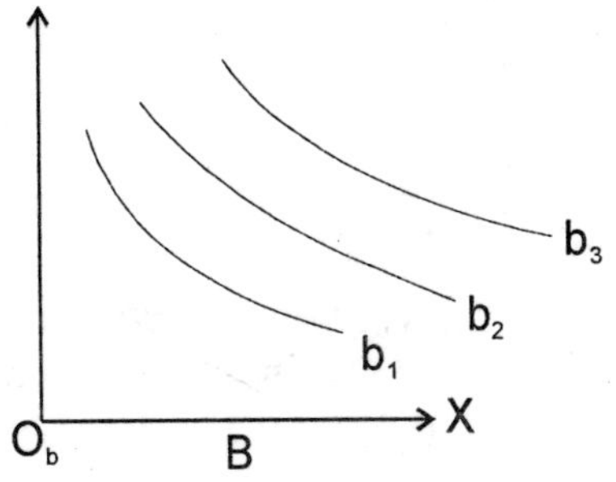

Fig. 1.8

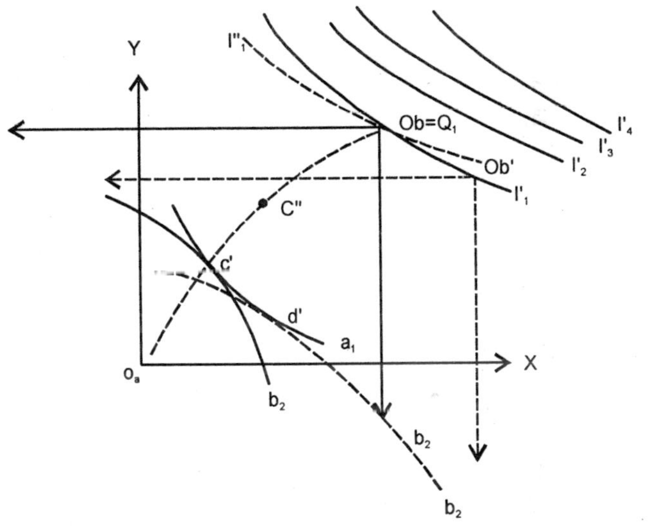

Fig. 1.9

The community indifference curves have two properties:

(i) At any point on the community indifference curve the individuals A and B must be on the same level of welfare; and (ii) at any point on it, the marginal rate of substitution between goods is the same for each individual. Though two individual indifference curves never intersect, community indifference curves do intersect. In the above figure, it is not the only community indifference curve which may pass through Q_1 (=ob) having property (iii) For we could divide this bundle Q_1 between A and B in an indefinite number of ways, taking care that whatever be the distribution, the rate of substitution must be the same for both individuals.

If we use the Paretian criterion to rank the community indifference curves its consistent application present us with a map of non-intersecting community indifference curve. For instance having I'_1 as representing individual welfares a_1 and b_2 we could proceed to construct I'_2 from, say, a_2 and b_2 I'_3 from a_3 and b_3 I_4 from a_3 and b_7 and so on-"everyone" being better off in each successively higher community indifference curve. These curves are comparable and they form part of a consistent community indifference map.

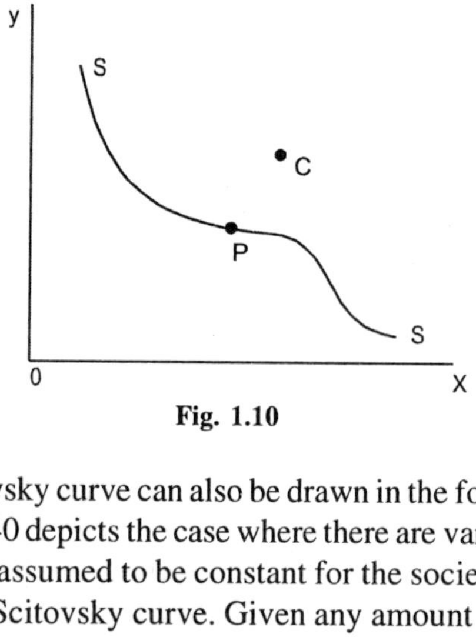

Fig. 1.10

The Scitovsky curve can also be drawn in the following form. The Figure no. 40 depicts the case where there are varying amounts of others being assumed to be constant for the society as a whole. Then SS is the Scitovsky curve. Given any amount of either X or Y, this curve tells us the minimum amount of the other required to keep each member of the community on his prescribed indifference curve. Now let us assume that although each individual is still at his prescribed indifference curve, we have the collection of goods represented by C. Clearly, X and Y cannot have been distributed among the members of the community in an optimal fashion. Foı we can achieve the same result in terms of individual well being by moving to a point like P where the amounts of both X and Y are smaller, So, SS curve here may be referred to as the

Scitovsky Frontier. If the society is on the Scitovsky frontier, the conditions to be fulfilled are quite similar to those necessary for the optimum organization of production. For the society to remain on the Scitovsky frontier the following conditions must be fulfilled:

(i) If society is to be on the Scitovsky frontier, the marginal social rate of substitution between any two goods must be the same in the case of each man who consumes them both.
(ii) If a man consumes one, but not both of the goods, the rate must be less than it is for those me who do consume them both.
(iii) The rates of substitution involved in (i) and (ii) must be maximum ones-not in any absolute sense, but with respect to changes in the distribution of a fixed quantity of goods.

Community Indifference: The Bergson Frontier

The levels of individual welfare prescribed in drawing up the Scitovsky frontier were chosen arbitrarily. But we can arrive at another frontier choosing another set of levels, and there is no reason why it should not intersect the first. Proceeding in this way, we can obtain an infinity of Scitovsky frontiers, intersecting one another indefinitely often. Bergson's social welfare function states.

W (u^1.....u^v). Let us assume that we are given a Pareto W-i.e., the welfare function for which other things remaining constant, increase in one man's welfare increases social welfare and let us assume one of its contours to be constant, i.e., K (u'_1.....u^v) =constant. For any set of U's satisfying this relation we can draw up a community indifference curve. We can draw up such a curve for each of the infinity of sets of the U's satisfying the relation. In the following figure the inner limit of the family of Scitovsky curves we shall call the Bergson Frontier.

In figure (a) the SS curves are convex to the origin; it is the envelope of the family. In figure (b) the SS curves not being so well-behaved. It is no longer the 'true' envelope,—the 'true' envelope would typically be the outer limit of the family, but it is still the inner limit.'

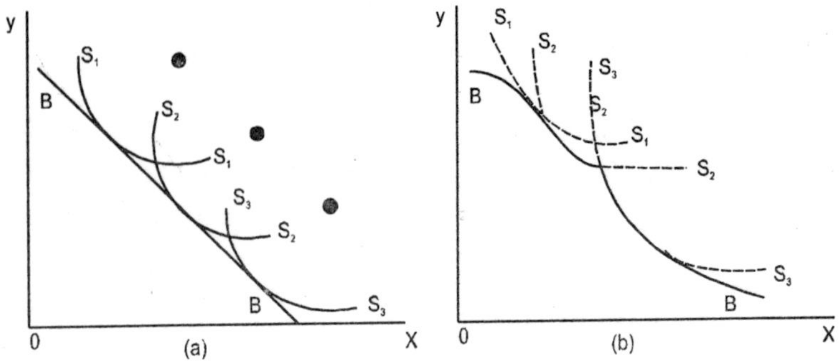

Fig. 1.11

Give any amount of either, X or Y, the Bergson frontier shows the minimum amount of the other good required to attain a given level of social welfare, as defined by W. The Bergson frontier "is thus a community indifference curve depicting social tastes (as defined by W) in the same way its it private one depicts personal tastes."

The properties of Bergson frontier are:

(1) At every point BD is touched by a SS Curve [Fig. 1.11(a)] or coincides with one [Fig. 1.11(b)]. So at every point, the three conditions of the Scitovsky frontier on marginal social rates of substitution should be fulfilled.

(2) In the absence of external effects, individual indifference curves convex to the origin lead to convex Scitovsky frontiers. There is no simple relation between the convexity of individual indifference curves and that of the Bergson frontiers—even in the absence of external effects. Bergson curves can be of any shape.

Social Welfare Function

We have seen that Compensation Principle is not operationally feasible. Pareto criterion also is not determinate. Economists like Kaldor, Hicks and Scitovsky have tried to develop their respective welfare criteria quite independently of the ethical considerations about inter-personal comparisons. But their efforts have not been fully crowned with success. Bergson, Samuelson and their followers have advocated the introduction of value judgments from the sectors outside the domain of the economists; otherwise it is not possible, they argue, to offer meaningful value propositions in the technical sense. Welfare economics, according to a large number of economists, is essentially a normative study.

Since Bentham's preaching of utilitarianism the main objective of any study of economic phenomena from welfare standpoint has been to find out a position of maximum welfare of the society. The Marshal-Pigou formulation of the social welfare function is based on Benthamite social welfare function which consisted in the aggregate of the individual utilities obtained from a change in economic policy. They believe that interpersonal comparisons are possible. But modern writers are keen about avoiding the cardinal measure of utility. Bergson has developed a criterion for social welfare function (which has also been endorsed by Samuelson) with the help of ordinal utility index.

Bergson Criterion or Bergson—Samuelson Formulation of Social Welfare Function

According to Bergson, the only way out of the problem of determining welfare criteria is the formulation of a set of explicit value judgments, which enable the analysis to evaluate the situation. "These judgments as to what constitutes justice and virtue in distribution map's be those of the economist himself, or those set up by the legislature, or by some other governmental authority, or by some other unspecified persons or group."

We can now rank different combination, of the utility which may secure to the various members of society through an indifference map. This indifference map may be treated as social welfare function, and this permits the analyst to examine whether a proposed policy change is important. In this figure, E must be considered better than A so that a change from A to E is an improvement because E lies on a higher indifference curve of the social welfare function. To decide whether E is better than A, we must apply certain value judgments. But "the Bergson criterion, thought it provides us with a highly useful frame of reference, unfortunately does not come equipped with a kit and a set of instructions for collecting the welfare judgments which it requires."

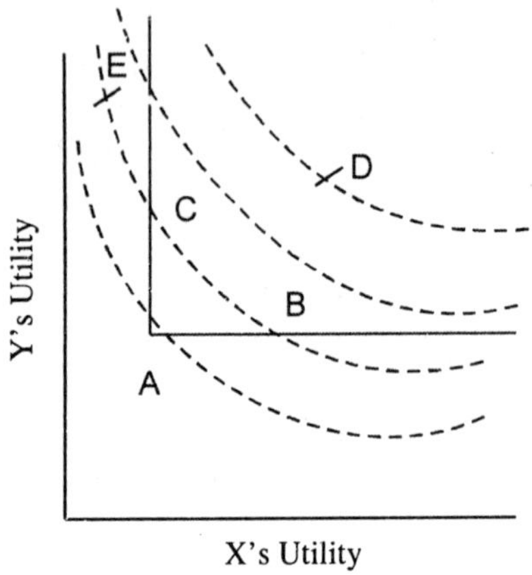

Fig. 1.12

Samuelson also agrees with Bergson on the point that a set of value judgments in the form of a social welfare function should be provided with methods other than those of economics. This social welfare function is a function of utility levels of all persons comprising the society. Since this social welfare function may be the judgments of those who are not economists it may describe "some ethical—that of a benevolent despot, or a complete egotist, or all men of good will."

Bergson's social welfare function can be stated as follows—

$$W = W(u_1, u_2, u_3 \ldots\ldots\ldots u_n)$$

Where, W means welfare, u_1, u_2, u_3, etc. indicate different utility levels of different persons. These different ordinary indices of society's welfare (as represented by u_1, u_2, and u_3) have been shown by the indifference map above. Let us now examine this criterion. In the first place, Bergson criterion involves interpersonal comparisons and value judgments. The function, in essence, is nothing more nor less than a generalization of Marshall-Pigou welfare formulation according to which W is the aggregate of the individual utilities (u_1, u_2, u_3, etc.). Secondly, social welfare function is not something unique and static. A social welfare function can be formulated by applying any set of value judgments. Thirdly, utilities here have been considered not in the cardinal sense but in the ordinal sense. The ethical notions also are obviously ordinal in character. Fourthly, once the social welfare function has been determined by methods other than those of economics, the maximization techniques of Price Theory can be applied to reach the best welfare position of the society. Bergson criterion has been admired by Prof. Little as an outstanding theoretical model which "completes the formal mathematical system of welfare economics" While the Paretian optimum is indeterminate in the sense that any point on the contract curve in Edgeworth box diagram is a Paretian optimum point, the Bergson-Samuelson function has the merit of demonstrating that it is possible to rank all points on the contract curve from the standpoint of social preferability.

But either in a totalitarian or in a democratic system we may face the problem that there are as many vague welfare functions as there are individuals. It has been pointed out by both Paul Streeten and Baumol that Bergson model is not well-equipped with a kit and a set of instructions for collecting required welfare judgments of productions is by no means incompatible with rational allocation of resource since by applying the process of trial and error, a socialist economy, on the basis of the available data or empirical evidences, can impute values to the factors of production valuations. It there is any wrong valuation, it will definitely create an imbalance either in the form of a surplus or in the form of a deficit, and thus it will be detected and duly connected. It is the task of the Central Planning Authority or the Planning Commission to go through the process of valuations in the indicated directions as to determine the accounting prices.

But the view of Mises has been taken by Prof. Robbins and Prof. Hayek. They agree on the point that theoretically, it may be possible to impute rational valuations to the factors of production under socialism. But they find it unworkable for all practical purposes. In their opinion, the Central Planning Board mill then have to draw up "millions of equations on the basis of millions of statistical tables based on many more millions of individual computations. All these calculations can hardly be undertaken in a lifetime."

Prof. Oscar Large challenges the views of Mises, Hayek and Robbins, and says that their views are wholly unjustified. In his view, static welfare analysis provides in argument in favour of a socialist economy. He argues that Mises' standpoint is based on a confusion regarding the nature of prices.

Prof. Arrow has criticized Bergson and, with reference to his own analysis, argues that the majority rule leads to contradictory results and that no social welfare function which takes into consideration all individual preferences can be "social" in the real sense of the term. It will be something which will be imposed upon the society by a dictator. As Mishan points out, the route to the continually changing position of maximum social welfare is too arduous for the most accomplished econometrician to plot, to say nothing of prompting humanity to undertake the journey."

Arrow's Thesis : Social Choice and Individual Values

Arrow contends that it is not easy to develop reasonable procedures for reconciling individual desires into a crucial decision. While in Bergson's analysis, individual's utility depends soley on goods going to himself and not to others, in Arrow's analysis, individual's ordering of social states does not exclusively depend on the bundle of goods which lie obtains from each; for some of the components of the social states are related to collective efforts and these cannot be properly assessed by the individual solely with reference to his personal consumption. To like an illustration such problems as the division of the national income between public and private expenditure cannot be properly assessed by an individual exclusively in terms of his own consumption. In Arrow's opinion the 'external effects' of consumption are no less important than his own consumption in case of an individual when he is to have his own ordering of social states. In Arrow's treatment, the objects of choice are social states. "The most precise definition of a social state would be a complete description of the amount of each type of commodity in the hands of each individual, the amount of labour to be supplied resource invested in each type of productive activity, and the amounts of carious types of collective activity."

Individual orderings of social states represent the desires and aspiration of the individuals. An individual may look upon different social states differently and thus there are different ethical judgments which reflect individual values. Ordering of social states in accordance with individual values is relevant to the achievement of maximum social welfare. In Arrow's analysis of individual ordering is based first on individual tastes and then on individual value. But Rothenberg finds no particular significance in the distinction between tastes and preferences. According to him, individual orderings are always in accordance with desirability of a particular social state to the individual.

Arrow's Five Conditions

In dictatorship, Arrow points out, derivation of a satisfactory social choice from individual decisions is an easy job since it is made by the dictator or the body of dictators. But in a capitalist democracy the problem of achieving a social maximum from a set of individual decisions is a cry scrious job. In a democratic economy each individual has his own conception of a desirable welfare function for society. The question is whether a social ordering call be consistently derived from the set of individual orderings.

Arrow formulates five reasonable conditions, which social choices must meet for giving expression to individual's ordering. These are five value judgments in Arrow's analysis.

Condition 1

"For some sufficiently wide mage of sets of individual orderings the social welfare function gives rise to a tree social ordering." That is to say, a true social ordering can be obtained from a wide range of sets of individual orderings. This social ordering must satisfy the conditions of convexity and transitivity. The property of convexity implies that two alternatives must be related either by presence or indifference; that is to say, of the two alternatives A and B, either A is preferred to B, or B is preferred to A, or the two are indifferent. The property of transitivity shows that if A is better than B and B is better than C, then A is better than C. These properties are considered by Arrow as an index of the rationality of social ordering.

Condition 2

"The social welfare function is such that the social ordering responds positively to alterations in individual values, or at least not negatively." It implies that social choices must move in the same direction, as individual orderings. The alternatives A which society would have preferred to B, must not be rejected in term; of this condition if some individuals of the society would have preferred B more favourably. This condition is thus not related to inter-personal comparison of utility.

Condition 3

The third condition is called by Arrow "the Independences of Irrelevant Alternatives." It implies that the social choice from a given environment depends on individual ordering among the alternatives in that environment and not outside the environment. That is to say, irrelevant opportunities should not be allowed to influence choices among relevant opportunities. To put the condition in other words, if a social state is eliminated as irrelevant, social orderings of the remaining social states must remain unaltered.

Condition 4

The social welfare function is not to be imposed. That is to say, there should be no external interference with a society's choice.

Condition 5

The social welfare function is not to be dictatorial.

The conditions 4 and 5 together imply that the social ordering must not be imposed by any means, even by dictatorship.

Arrow argues that these five value judgments may be called into questions. He demonstrates the impossibility, of deriving a social ordering of all conceivable alternatives social states without violating at least one of these five value judgments. This demonstration is known as General Possibility Theorem.

Arrow first considers a simple case where there are only two alternatives and shows that the method of majority decision provides us with a social welfare function satisfying all the five conditions. But if the number of alternatives is greater than two, no valid social welfare function can be derived accepting the method of majority decision. Every social function satisfying conditions 2 and 3 and yielding a social ordering axioms of rationality may be either imposed satisfying the or dictatorial Arrow uses the following symbols for simplifying his theorem.

(a) xPy means that x is preferred to y.
(b) xIy means that the individual is indifferent to x and y.
(c) xP_1y means that individual 1 prefers x to y.

If in the society there are two persons with exactly opposing interests in the choice between two alternatives x and y, then society will be indifferent between x and y. That is to say, if xP_1y and yP_2x then xIy.

Let us prove the General Possibility Theorem. Let there be to persons in the society with three alternatives A, B, C. In case individual 1 prefers A to B and individual 2 prefers B to A then, by consequence 3, the society is indifferent as between A and B. If this is not the case, then a logical contradiction will emerge. For example, if the society prefers A to B then the individual I will be a dictator and if the society prefers B to A then the individual 2 will be a dictator.

Let us new suppose that the individual I has the ordering A, B, C while individual 2 has the ordering C, A, B. Since individual I prefers B to C and individual 2 prefers C to B, then we can write.

Bp_1C and Cp_2B, then BIC ......(1)

Again for both the individuals A is preferred to B that is to say

AP_1B and AP_2B; then APB ......(2)

From (1) and (2) by the axiom of transivity it follows that

$$A_pB$$
$$B_pC$$
$$\therefore A_pC \qquad ......(3)$$

BA, since individual I prefers A to C and individual 2 prefers C to A, it follows that AIC...........(4) Obviously, (3) and (4) are not compatible. It is not possible that A is both preferred to and indifferent to C. Thus Arrow comes to the conclusion that it is not possible to show a social ordering front more than two alternatives without violating at least one of the live value judgments.

The difficulty of majority rule as a possible social welfare function can also be shown by what is known as "Paradox of voting." Three individuals, Mr. Danish, Mr. Reyaz and Mr. Saquib are to vote among three alternatives A, B, and C, by writing a "3" next to the alternative they like most, a "2" beside the one they rank next highest, etc. Then we get the following record by balloting:

	A	B	C
Mr. Danish	3	2	1
Mr. Reyaz	1	3	2
Mr. Saquib	2	1	3

It is seen that both Mr. Danish and Mr. Saquib prefer A to B, that Mr. Danish and Mr. Reyaz prefer B to C and that Mr. Reyaz and Mr. Saquib prefers A to B and B to C, but it also prefers C to A. Thus the majority voting leads to intransitive social choice pattern. The axiom of rationality in condition 1 is here violated.

In the words of Arrow, the General Possibility Theorem can be stated in the following way: "If the exclude the possibility of interpersonal comparisons of utility, then the only method of passing from individual tastes to social preferences which will be defined for a wide range of sets of individual ordering are either imposed or dictatorial."

Prof. Mishan argues that Arrow's conclusion that the society is indifferent to A and 11 (AIB) when A is not collectively preferred to B nor B is collectively preferred to A, is valid only when these are only alternatives open to the society. But when the interests of the individuals are opposed to each other, one should remain uncommitted to any social ordering. Arrow has discarded the concept of measurable utility and interpersonal comparisons of utility. But his analysis of majority rule certainly involves interpersonal comparisons of utility. If the majority prefer A to B, then the majority decision in favour of A implies A*p*B only if we aim to secure maximum utility and the choice of any individual has the same utility ac that of any other.

Arrow's treatment of A/B as transitivity relation when Ap_1B and Bp_2A is accepted by Mishan only if interpersonal comparison of individual welfares are admitted and if, also, a consistency condition is satisfied with reference to the relationship between B and C. In Mishan's analysis, if the first individual prefers B to C and the second individual prefers C to B, then BIC for society can be accepted provided (a) the aggregate of the individual utilities is sought to be maximized, and (b) the difference in utility having B and haring C, denoted by U_{BC} is the same for the two individuals. Similarly if U_{AB} is the same for the two individuals, one can say AIB when Ap_1B and Bp_2A. These two utility differences being the same (though opposite in sign) for the two persons it follows that for both of them U_{BC} may be either greater than, or equal to, or less than U_{AB} (the signs being ignored). An individual ordering of the alternatives, A, B, and C must follow this consistency condition.

If for one individual U_{BC} is greater than U_{AB} while for the other U_{BC} is either equal to or less than U_{AB}, then the condition is not satisfied and no transitive social indifference can be generally inferred from these elements. Mishan says that no such contradiction can arise when the second individual has the ordering C, B, A (instead of C, A, B as shown above).

Prof. Little in his review of Arrow's book draws in distinction between Bergson's social welfare function and Arrow's social welfare function and says that while in. Bergron's analysis, the individual's tastes are given, in Arrow's analysis, individual tastes do change in the sense of rank ordering. Arrow's social welfare function therefore, examines the relationship between the social judgments under different individual rankings. In Little's opinion Arrow's negative conclusion has no practical significance in welfare economics, and "Arrow's result has no hearing on the possibility or impossibility" of the social welfare function of Bergson. Rothenberg in his book "Measurement of Social Welfare" has argued that on a wider formulation, the Bergson social welfare function can yield the Arrow social welfare function, and "Arrow's conception is not essentially different from the Bergson-Samuelson formulation on this score."

Arrow's theorem gives emphasis on the difficulty, of measuring social welfare on the basis of social choice in I free democratic society.

Graaff's Views on Marginal Cost and the Just Price

A large number of economists believe that public enterprises or nationalized industries should base their price and production policies on the rule that marginal cost should equal price. We should set out all the assumptions which have to be made if the rule is to be given a satisfactory welfare basis. Graaff lay's down the following basic assumptions in this regard:

(i) Individual preference maps are identical with welfare maps;
(ii) the location of the horizon, given so that the group in whose welfare we are interested is properly demarcated;
(iii) We assume that the items of terminal capital equipment if these are not so, they may accept the rule of equality of the marginal cost and price, but may hold different views on what marginal cost actually is:

(iv) risk and uncertainty are absent;

(v) transformation functions arc independent of the distribution of wealth;

(vi) there should be perfect divisibility are one capital goods;

(vii) the necessary conditions for a maximum of welfare are also necessary for minimum welfare;

(viii) the marginal equivalences of the General Optimum are necessary conditions for maximum welfare only if satisfied simultaneously. Thus marginal cost should equal price in a particular industry only if the rule is universally applied;

(ix) The next step is to identify social and private rates of indifference with the assumption that external effects in consumption do let exist'

(x) Social and private rates of transformation are also identical;

(xi) The basic marginal equivalence now is: marginal private rules of transformation and indifference should be equal.

On thc basis of these assumptions Graaff see to show how marginal cost should equal price. In the first place, each consumer will seek, to achieve any given level of welfare in the cheapest possible way. The equality of the ratios of marginal costs (to individual consumers) and marginal private rates of indifference is entailed. Secondly, each producer will produce any given output at the least-cost combination. Thirdly, as the producers and the consumers face the same fixed prices, the equality of marginal private rates of transformation and indifference is second both being equal to the fixed price ratios.

Strictly speaking, the equality of marginal private rates of transformation can be secured by securing the equality of price for marginal units bought and sold by consumers and producers respectively.

With the element of monopoly and monopsony the marginal cost mill diverge from price to the extent of the degree of monopoly power or monopsony power. The equality of price and cost for marginal units can also be achieved under discriminatory pricing initiated by public undertakings. Another assumption which is essential for establishing the principle of marginal cost pricing is that the distribution of wealth to which it leads must be approved.

If the time element is taken into consideration, the basic rule does not change. There is only one kind of marginal cost in the system with which we are concerned: that relating to one of the slices of time used in the classification or commodities. Until quite recently, it was thought that securing the proportionality of prices and marginal costs would do well in securing maximum welfare. But this view is now rejected. Graaff insists that "equating price to marginal cost will lead to the satisfaction of one the necessary conditions for maximum welfare." It is clear that the conditions to be satisfied before it is correct front a welfare viewpoint to set price equal to marginal cost in a particular industry are so restrictive that they are unlikely to be satisfied in practice". "The survival of the marginal cost pricing principle is probably no more than an indication of the extent to which the majority of professional economists are ignorant of the assumptions required for its validity".

Graaff suggests that "the only price a public enterprise or nationalized industry can be expected to set is what we may as well call a just price—a price which is set with some regard as for its effect on the allocation of resources." For the determination of the just price, there should be some definite value judgments and a good deal of positive knowledge. Graaff says that "the task of the economist is to provide the positive knowledge, not to recommend the level at which price should be set".

Allocation of Resources Under Socialism

Economists do not agree on the point as to whether resources call be ideally allocated under socialism. Von Mises has argued that under socialism, rational calculation of resources is impossible, that the, optimum conditions of production and distribution cannot be fulfilled in a socialist economy. Mises and his followers contend that because of the public ownership over the factors of production, a socialist economy cannot have any market for capital goods. It follows for Mises that there is no market for capital goods, there can be no prices for them; and without prices, which indicate the relative importance of the factors of production economic calculation or economic accounting is out of the question. Hence the question of rational allocation of resources cannot arise in such an economy.

Mises argues that in a capitalist system, resources call be properly allocated through the free play of .market mechanism, i.e., through the medium of the price system which is regulated by the market forces of free competition among the independent owners of the factors of production. But in a socialist system, there are no independent owners of the factors to compete with each other in view of the social ownership over the means of production. If the prices of the factors of production are not determined by the market forces, rational economic calculations logically not feasible.

That is why, Mises is the opinion that every step that lakes us away from private ownership of the factors of production, also takes us away from rational economics.

But the Italian economist, Barone, even before Mises, showed that a socialist economy can work as efficiently as a capitalist economy by a method of trial and error; but Barone did not show how such a method could be carried out. But Barone in his essay, "The Ministry of Production in the Collectivist state" proved that by setting up accounting prices for the factors of production, a socialist economy could allocate the resources rationally at least in principle. This view of Barone has been further developed by Taylor. According to Taylor, public ownership of the factors does not stand in the way of determining correct accounting prices by it method of trial and error.

Prof. Lange, criticizes Mises. He, first of all, argues that Mises has not properly interpreted the meaning of 'Prices'. In a narrow sense, Lange argues, prices on a market are simply the exchange ratios regulated by the independent buyer, and sellers; but in a broader sense, prices indicate "the terms on which alternatives are offered". In both the cases, prices serve the purpose of building up an rational costing system. In Lange's view, Mises considered prices in the former sense. But once prices are interpreted in the latter sense. Lange contends socialism finds no difficulty in setting up accounting prices for the purpose of rationally allocating the resources. Hayek and Robbins argue that theoretically rational allocation of resources in a socialist economy is possible: but they doubt the possibility of a satisfactory practical solution of the problem. They further argue that setting up accounting prices may be arbitrary. Even G.D.H. Cole holds this opinion. But Lange replies to them by saying that though arbitrary, these accounting prices are quite significant. To the criticism of Hayek and Robbins that the Central Planning Board will have to draw up millions of equations, simultaneous equations—before economic decisions could be taken, and with any means known at present these calculations could not be solved in a lifetime. Lange replies, "Neither would the Central Planning Board have to sole hundreds of thousands equations. The only 'equations' which would have to be 'solved' would be those of the consumers and managers of production." He further argues that the process of trial and error for determining accounting prices in a socialist economy does not fundamentally differ from the process in terms of which prices are actually determined in a competitive market. Lange contends that socialism can solve the problem of price determination by applying the processor trial and error.

In a competitive market, the conditions of equilibrium are three fold:

(1) All producers and consumers participating in the economic system must achieve maximum profits and maximum satisfaction respectively.
(2) The equilibrium prices are attained by the condition that demand for and supply of each commodity are in equilibrium.
(3) Incomes of consumers are equalized with their receipts from selling productive services plus profits, and the fulfilment of this condition expresses the social organization of the competitive economic system.

In a capitalist economy while the consumers maximize the total utility from their Purchase, the producers maximize their profits by determining the optimum scale of output. The owners of the ultimate factors maximize their income by selling the services of these resources to the highest bidder. Lange shows how economic equilibrium is determined in a socialist system. Just as in a competitive system, the determination of equilibrium consists of two parts: (a) on the basis of given indices of alternatives (which are market prices in the case of consumption goods and the services of labour and accounting price, in all other cases) both the individuals participating in the economic system as consumers and as owners of the services of labour and the managers of production and of the ultimate resources outside labour make decisions according to certain Principles. These managers are assumed to be public officials. (b) The prices (whether market or accounting) ensure that the quantity of each commodity demanded is equal to the quantity supplied.

Lange thinks that these conditions in a competitive economy are met by the parametric function of prices, the market prices being parameters determining the behaviour of the individuals. The method of determining the market in such an economy is also a method of trial and error. In a socialist economy also, Lange argues, there is some place of the freedom of choice of the households. There are markets for consumption goods and for labour in a socialist economy in Lange's analysis. Prices are set in such an economy with the same double purpose as in a competitive economy: (i) just high enough to maintain a balance between the existing supply and demand for consumption goods, and (ii) just high enough to realist, the socially necessary additional costs of production of the commodities so that price may be equal to relative marginal utilities and marginal costs. In the same way wages are to be determined so that people may be given incentives and compensation may be provided for differences between occupations. Thus, resources may be allocated rationally in a socialist economy.

Lange thinks that as welfare ideal Socialism is superior to capitalism. Social wastes are minimized in a socialist economy under the direct regulation or the Central Planning Board. Economic fluctuations, the regular feature of capitalism, are brought under control in a socialist economy by means of economic planning. Secondly while capitalism leads to exploitation and aggravates inequalities of income and wealth, in socialism, exploitation is absent and inequalities of income and wealth are reduced. Economic equality is the main feature of a socialist economy. Thirdly, allocation of resources in a capitalist economy contributes to maximization of individual welfare at the expense of welfare of others. But in a socialist economy allocation of resources in the manner as stated above helps a country to achieve maximum social welfare. Although capitalism has a number of advantages, these are overbalanced by its disadvantages.

Privately Owned Resources

We will review some common economic models of the environment. In each model, the market's failure to account for environmental externalities is the exception rather than the rule, and neoclassical theory is then applied in order to cure or circumvent an inefficiency. Neoclassical theory has been applied to environmental issues to determine what conditions are necessary for the efficient allocation of resources and how market failures lead to inefficiencies and to suggest ways in which these distortions can be corrected.

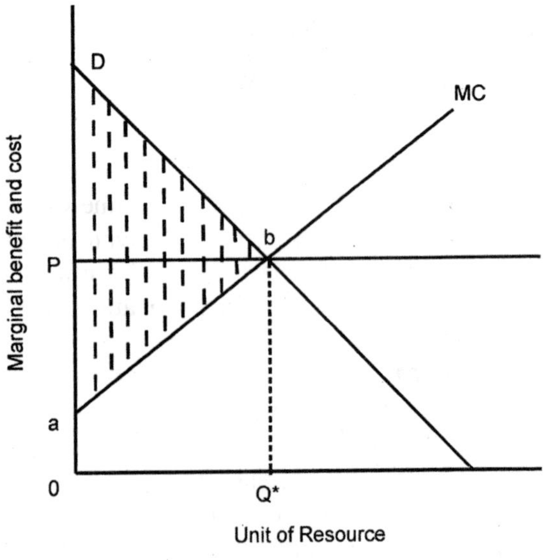

Fig. 1.13

Demonstrates how the market determines the optimal consumption of a natural resource. Finding the optimal market outcome involves maximizing the total net benefits to society from a resource, which is the difference between the total benefits derived from a resource and the total costs to producers of providing it. Total net benefit is maximized when the marginal cost of producing or extracting one more unit of the resource is equal to its marginal benefit to the consumer. This occurs at Static Efficiency in Resource Allocation.

*Q**, where the demand and supply curves intersect. In a perfectly competitive market, the "invisible hand" will ensure that Q* is the quantity produced. The marginal cost curve in Figure 1.13 is upward-sloping because extraction costs increase as a resource becomes more scarce. The resulting producer surplus, or profit, is called a scarcity rent. In the diagram, the producer surplus is area aPb, and the consumer surplus is area DPb. Together they yield a maximum net benefit equal to Dab. In principle, some of these scarcity rents could be taxed and used for environmental protection or other socially useful purposes.

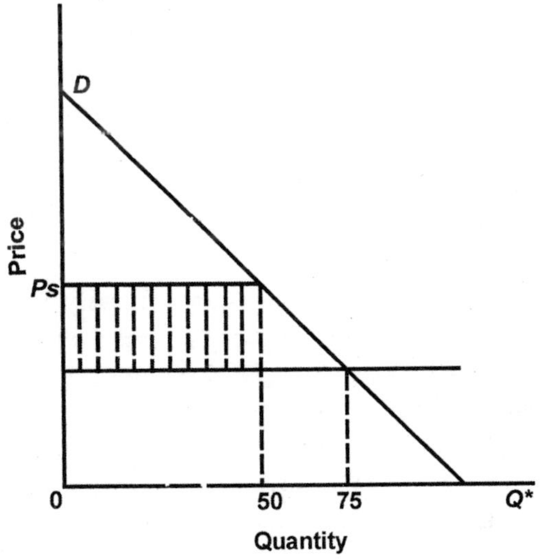

Fig. 1.14: Optimal Resource Allocation Over Time

If resources are scarce and are rationed over time, scarcity rents may arise even when the marginal cost of production is constant, as in Figure 1.14. The owner of a scarce resource has a finite volume of a resource X to sell (75 units) and knows that by saving a portion of it for future sales, she can charge a higher price today. The price of a good that is being rationed inter temporally (over time) must equate the present value of the marginal net benefit of the last unit consumed in each period. That is, the consumer must be indifferent between obtaining the next unit today or tomorrow. In Figure 1.14, assume that a resource owner has 75 units available. If she is willing to offer only 50 units for sale today, the market price for the scarce resource is P_S. The scarcity rent collected by the owner of the resource is equal to $P_S$abP, the shaded region in the diagram between price and marginal cost. It is the owner's ability to collect these rents that creates the rationing effect and is thus necessary to ensure the efficient allocation of resources over time. In the absence of scarcity, all of the resource will be sold at the extraction cost P = MC, 75 units will be consumed at one time, and no rents will be collected.

The proponents of neoclassical free-market theory stress that inefficiencies in the allocation of resources result from impediments to the operation of the free market or imperfections in the property rights system. So long as all resources are privately owned and there are no market distortions, resources will be allocated efficiently. Perfect property rights markets are characterized by four conditions:

(1) *Universality*—All resources are privately owned.
(2) *Exclusivity*—It must be possible to prevent others from benefiting from a privately owned resource.
(3) *Transferability*—The owner of a resource may sell the resource when desired.
(4) *Enforceability*—The intended market distribution of the benefits from resources must be enforceable.

Under these conditions, the owner of a scarce resource has an economic incentive to maximize the net benefit from its sale or use. For example, a farmer who owns his land will choose the levels of investment, technology, and output that maximize the net yield from the land. Because the value of the land may be used as collateral, any viable on-farm investment can be financed by obtaining a loan at the prevailing market rate of interest.

If the foregoing conditions are not met simultaneously, inefficiencies are likely to arise. Thus the way to correct the misallocation of resources is generally to remove any market distortions. A number of models have been designed to explain apparent inefficiencies in resource allocation. We next look at two simple models of inefficiency arising from imperfections in property markets.

Efficient Public Goods Pricing and Lindahal Model

The pricing of public goods is quite a complex issue as they possess qualities quite different from the private goods are those which are excludable and non rivalry in their nature. A good is excludable if it is feasible and practical to selectively allow consumers to consume the good. Reverse applies to the public bad. A bad is excludable if it is feasible and practical to selectively allow consumers to avoid consumption of the bad. Public bads are much relevant in the field of Environmental Economics. Rivalry implies that if one person's consumption of a unit of the bad (good), diminishes the amount of the bad (good) available for others to consume, i.e., there is a negative (positive) social opportunity cost to others associated with consumption. A bad (good) is no rival otherwise.

The problem efficient pricing of public goods needs special discussion, if they are excludable and non-rivalry. Suppose we have a park with a fence around it and thus can restrict entry. Suppose further the park is large so that congestion is never a problem and the cost of operating it is all fixed costs with no cost depending on visitation. What should be the unique efficient admission price for all consumers? To solve this problem, we should first ascertain the efficient amount of use of the park. Since there is no cost associated with letting one more person use the park, efficient use clearly calls for everyone having access to the park. If we exclude anyone to use the park the Pareto optimality condition is violated. Pareto improvement could be attained by allowing whoever has been excluded to use the park-costs would not change, current users would not have their utility reduced, and those newly admitted would have their utility increased. The admission price consistent with Pareto optimality suggests zero price as charging of admission price will restrict some persons to use the park without making, anybody who use the park worse-off. This may be clearly illustrated with the help of following diagram.

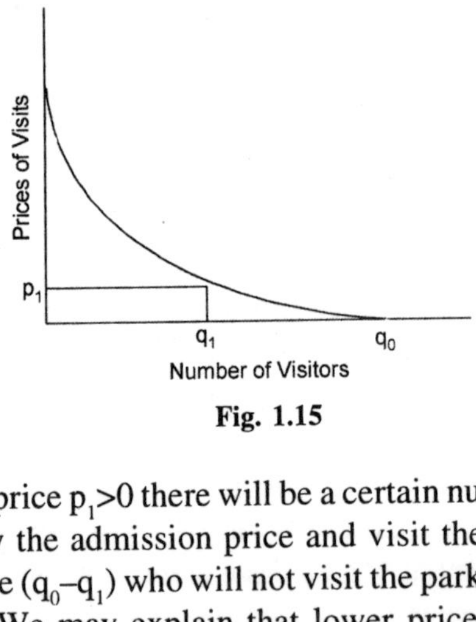

Fig. 1.15

At any price $p_1 > 0$ there will be a certain number of people q_1 who will pay the admission price and visit the park. There will also be people $(q_0 - q_1)$ who will not visit the park because the price is too high. We may explain that lower price would be Pareto preferred. This is because all previous visitors would be just as well off and also some people for whom the price was previously high would be able to enjoy the park site at lower price and the cost of providing the park service is unchanged in the event of lowering down the fee for park visiting. This process will go on continuing till the fee for visiting the park drops to zero. The obvious conclusion is that for a non-rival excludable good, the optimal price from the consumers' angle is zero.

But production of non-rival commodities is similar to production of other commodities. They involve cost and producers must have sufficient revenue to cover it. Even the non-rival and non-excludable goods involve costs and for their optimum amount of production, certain prices for their use are required. Hence, there are two contradictory aspects; on the one hand if the producers raise prices to generate revenue for provision, demand will be depressed and if prices are not charged, budget will not balance and deficit will result on the other.

A theoretical solution, though impractical, to this problem was suggested by Norwegian Economist Erik Lindahal popularly known as Lindahal Model or Lindahal Pricing. Lindahal by means of his voluntary exchange principle based on two persons, single public-good model has shown that it is possible to determine uniquely how much resources should be allocated for provision of public goods and how the share of cost be distributed amongst persons who receive benefit from the public goods.

Explanation of the Model

We suppose there are two persons in a community, A and B. Their total income R is divided optimally as R_A of A's income and R_B of B's income, and R is equal to X+Y+G, where X and Y are two private goods consumed by A and B respectively, and G is public good consumed by equal amount by A and B, Let h represent the percentage share of the cost of G borne by A and if $0 \leq h \leq 100$, then (100–h) represents the cost of G borne by B.

Thus,

$$R = X+Y+G$$

$$R = R_A + R_B$$

$$R_A = X + hG$$

$$G = (RA - X)/h \qquad \text{......(1)}$$

$$R_B = Y + (100 - h)\,G$$

$$G = (R_B - Y)/(100 - h) \qquad \text{......(2)}$$

Since, given X, Y, R_A and R_B, $dG/dh = -(R_A - X)/h^2$ in (1) and

$dG/dh = (R_B - Y)/(100 - h)^2$ in (2), it follows that, for A, G approaches some maximum G as h approaches 0 and, for B, G approaches some minimum G as h approaches 0, given that G is not inferior good in the utility functions of A and B namely, UA = UA(X,G) = Un(RA–hG) and $U_B = U_B(Y,G)$ = UB $[R_B -$ (100–h) G, G].

The same result may be explained through the following diagrams in which the amount of public goods is measured on the horizontal axis, the aa curve shows on the left vertical axis the percentage share of cost which individual A is willing to pay as larger amount of public goods are provided and the bb curve shows on the right inverted vertical axis the percentage share of the cost which individual B is willing to pay as larger amounts of public goods are provided.

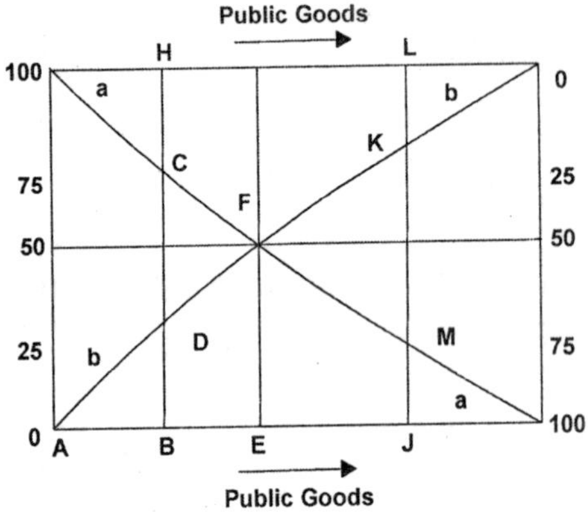

Fig. 1.16

The curves have been drawn on the assumption of diminishing marginal utility which an individual derives from successive increments of consumption of any commodity. Let us suppose that initially AB amount of public goods are provided by the state an individual A is willing to bear 75 per cent of the cost of public goods and individual A is also willing to share more than 75 per cent of cost. The preferences of both individuals warrant larger supply of public goods. Reverse is the case when AJ amount of public goods is provided. Individual A is willing to take the load of only 25 per cent and B is also below the 25 per cent. Total cost of public goods is not borne by the both individuals. The incentive for the provider of public goods would be to reduce the amount of public goods. Thus by process of trial and error it will be found that only at AE amount of public goods the percentage share of the cost or in other words, only at AE output the total cost of provision of the public goods would be just covered by the individual contributions. The AE, in this figure, is the optimum amount of output as the total cost of this output is covered by both the individuals. It is just chance that both the individuals are here covering 50 per cent cost but percentage share may be different depending upon the slopes of their demand curves. The figure-3 shows the demand for A is steeper than the demand for B. Hence, B is sharing higher percentage of cost i.e. GF, more than 50 per cent whereas A is only bearing EF per cent of cost, less than 50 per cent.

It follows from this that the greater the utility or benefit which a person derives from public goods, the greater should be his payment liability for public goods. The principle is consistent with the principle of equity and justice. It is inherently unfair to make some person pay for what others get.

The **Lindahal model** is theoretically well structured but of little practical use for the following limitations:

(1) This model is based on the assumption that individuals are readily revealing their true preference for public goods. This assumption is not likely to correct. As a matter of fact, for public goods persons will not reveal their true preferences, since they can enjoy the benefit of such goods even without revealing their true preferences. The preferences, in the opinion of Prof. Musgrave, can be determined only by a political process of voting.

(2) As Prof Samuelson pointed out, even if individuals true preferences for public/social goods are known somehow or other, it is not possible to determine uniquely how much such goods should be provided by the producer (of course state authority) and for that purpose how much private goods be sacrificed and that again by whom the sacrifice would be made in larger and smaller degree. For example, the provision of some quantity of public goods may be an

ideal solution if individual A is to receive all the benefit from public goods and make the least sacrifice in terms of payment liabilities. This case is much more pertinent in case of social goods while framing the policy of public expenditure and taxation. In general equilibrium setting where social goods are to be provided by the sacrifice of private goods by this individual or that, it is not possible without some extra economic value judgment as to who would benefit by how much by the provision of social goods and how much private goods be sacrificed by whom in order to achieve a given increase in social goods to be provided by the state.

Common Property Resources

If a scarce resource (such as arable land) is publicly owned and thus freely available to all (for, say, farming or grazing animals), as is the case with a common property resource, any potential profits or scarcity rents, inefficiencies will arise. Using a somewhat different framework, we will investigate the misallocation of resources under a common property system. Figure 1.17 describes the relationship between the returns to labour on a given piece of land and the number of labourers cultivating it.

Suppose for the moment that title to this piece of land is privately held. Conventional wisdom tells us that the landowner will hire additional labour to work the land until the marginal product of the last worker is equal to the market wage, W, at point L*. The workload is shared equally among the employees, each of whom produces the average product. However, assuming decreasing returns to labour, each new worker hired reduces the average product of all workers. The marginal product of each additional worker is thus equal to his average product minus the decrease in the average product across all other workers. If an additional employee is hired beyond L*, his cost to the producer, W, will be greater than his marginal product, and the difference will represent a net loss to the landowner. A profit maximizes will thus hire L* workers, with a total output equal to average product.

AP* multiplied by the number of workers, L*. Scarcity rents collected by the landowner will equal AP* CDW.

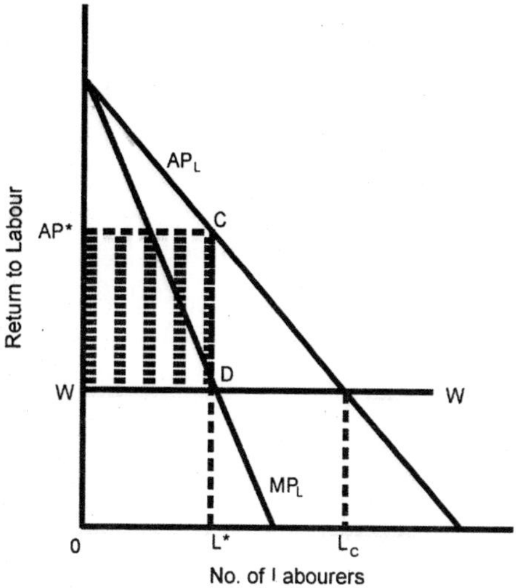

Fig. 1.17

Society's total net benefit from land will be lower under a system of common property, unless workers can coordinate their resource use decisions in a cooperative manner. Generally, if land is commonly owned, each worker is able to appropriate the entire product of his work, which is equal to the average product of all workers. Worker income will continue to exceed the wage until enough workers are attracted so that the average product falls to the level of the wage, at which point the labour force equals L_C. Though total farm output may either rise or fall (depending on whether MP_L is positive or negative—it is negative as drawn in Figure, the marginal product of the additional workers is below the wage. Because we are assuming that all workers could be employed elsewhere with productivity equal to or greater than W it follows that social welfare must fall when marginal product falls below W. No scarcity rent is collected at L_C. The implication of the common property resource model is that, where possible, privatization of resources will lead to an increase in aggregate welfare and an efficient allocation of resources.

Common Property Resources and Misallocation

It should be noted here that these neoclassical models are strictly concerned with efficiency and do not address issues related to equity. Income distribution is not considered, and the theory is unconcerned with the distributional issues arising when all scarcity rents from national resources accrue to a few private owners. Although neoclassical theorists have sometimes suggested that an optimal outcome may be achieved through the taxation and then "lump sum" redistribution of the gains accruing to the owners of scarce natural resources, the historical record for such efforts is not encouraging. This is especially true where the authorities responsible for legislating and coordinating such redistributions are also the owners. Thus the large-scale commercial privatization of resources does not necessarily ensure an improvement in standards of living for the impoverished majority.

Beyond the standard neoclassical arguments, there are a number of alternative reasons why individuals making use of publicly owned resources may make inefficient use of them within the context of farming systems in developing countries. Family farmers, who has saw in generally the most efficient cultivators of land, may be reluctant to make land-augmenting investments if they are afraid of losing tenure on the common property plot. They may also have insufficient funds to hire additional labour or purchase complementary resources due to a lack of collateral, a factor that frequently excludes the poor from competitive credit markets. It is therefore possible that conferring extended tenancy rights or ownership of land to family farmers would raise productivity. The relevant question for the property rights structure is then, who should obtain title to the land if privatization is to occur? A simple auction of publicly owned land to the highest bidder is unlikely to be consistent with development objectives.

Public Goods and Bads

We have detailed how public goods and bads differ from private goods and bads and have intimated that markets will not work for public commodities. We have also examined how much of the public good or bad is desirable. In this section, we take this question further, examining what happens if markets are used. We will see that the basic problem is a mismatch between what is optimal for the producer and what is optimal for the consumer. We will assume excludability is possible; otherwise there is no hope of using prices as a rationing device. The first question is what happens when markets are left to supply the public good?

A. *Market Provision of Public Goods*

What happens if markets are used? We sort of know what the answer is but it is important to understand why: if we let the market operate without intervention, public goods generally will be underprovided. To see this most simply, assume we have a society with *N* identical individuals. Each individual can consume two goods, a rival, excludable private good, x, and a nonrival, nonexcludable public good, *G*. To clarify things, the public good is nonexcludable in consumption (everyone gets to consume it) but it is of course excludable in production—it is produced like any other good at a cost and can be sold at a price to anyone. The price of the private good will be set to one and we will adjust the units with which we measure the public good, so that its price is also one. Assume that each person has income w available to them. The utility of any of the identical people is given by

$$\text{Utility} = u\,(x, G)$$

We might think that G is out of the control of an individual, because it is a public good. However, individuals are free to purchase some of the public good, if that is in their own best interest (they are unlikely to take anyone else's interests into account). Let g be the amount of the good that one individual will purchase and let G be what is provided by everyone else: G = G + g. This of course means that if our individual provides g pp the public good, only w—g of money is available for the private good. Thus we can rewrite the individual's utility as

$$\text{Utility} = u\,(w - g, g + G)$$

Now our individual must decide how much g to choose to consume. The choice depends, of course, on how much of the public good is being provided by everyone else. Figure 1.18 shows indifference curves for our individual with the two goods being g and G. Remember wealth or income (w) is fixed. If we assume that preferences are such that for any utility level it will be desirable for our consumer to spend his money on both private goods and public goods, then indifference curves must be U-shaped. More G is needed to compensate for the extremes of all private good consumption or all public good consumption, in order to keep utility constant. However, at high levels of public goods provision by others, G, it is entirely plausible that no privately provided public goods are necessary. In this case, G needs to increase to keep utility constant as g rises from zero and indifference curves will be upward sloping in g.

Note that if G is fixed, the best choice of g is the point at which one of the indifference curves just touches the horizontal line at the fixed G. As G increases (other people are providing more of the public good), the best choice g falls. If others are providing the public good, then we do not need to provide as much ourselves. The "best response" line in Figure 1.18 indicates the choice of g that will be made in response to the amount of the public good selected by others, G. For a high enough G, no g will be provided.

Now how much will be provided by our little society? Since everyone is the same, everyone will make the same choice about g. Thus G = (n – 1)g, This is a straight line of slope n – 1, also drawn on Figure 1.18. The point at which it intersects the best response line (point N provides the amount of g and G = (n – 1) b that will be generated in this economy: g_N, G_N, So some amount of the public good is provided privately.

Market provision of and efficient provision of a public good. n, Number of identical people in society; g, individual's provision of the public good; G, provision of the public good by everyone else; w, wealth of each individual; N, g_N, G_N, market provision of public good; E, g*, G, efficient provision of public good; U_i, indifference curves.

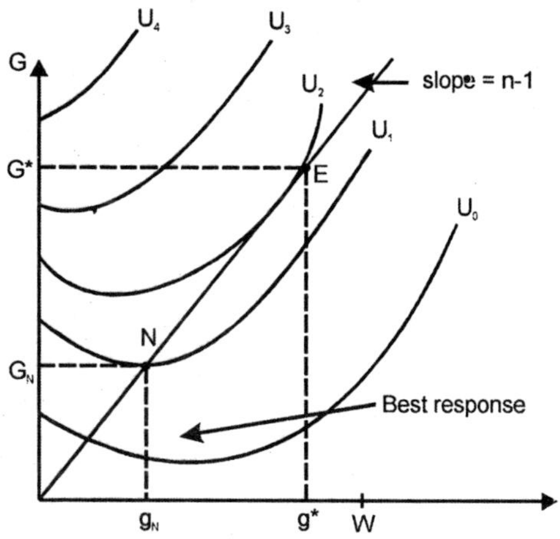

Fig. 1.18

How much should be generated in this society? In other words, what is the efficient level of g and G? The reason we would expect the public good to be underprovided is that if consumers raise their g, they benefit individually but everyone else also benefits and they do not take that into account. Suppose they could be sure that when they raise their g, everyone else matches them by raising their gs? Then consumers see the full benefit of raising g. If we assume that G stays at (n -1) g as consumers raise and lower g, then consumers see all of the advantage of raising and lowering g. In other words, if consumers know that g and G will lie along the upward sloping straight line in Figure, the best choice of g is the point at which an indifference curve is just tangent to the straight line, labeled E in Figure, resulting in public good provision g* and G*.

Note that the non-cooperative provision of the public good is lower than the efficient provision, though still positive. The basic reason for this is that when each person chooses g non-cooperatively, he or she sees some benefits from buying g (thus $g_N > 0$), but most of the benefits occur to others and are ignored in deciding how much to consume (thus $g_N < g^*$).

We know that there is a great deal of private contribution to protect the environment—such contributions support international organizations such as Greenpeace, the Worldwide Fund for Animals/World Wildlife Fund (WWF), and many national organizations such as the Sierra Club. The Nature Conservancy is specifically set up to accept private donations and use these to purchase important natural areas and set them aside for prosperity—a very clear example of private provision of a public good.

The public bad version of this involves a number of polluters. They are injured somewhat by polluting, but most of the damage accrues to someone else. Thus they will control pollution somewhat, reflecting the damage they incur, but they will not control pollution as much as is socially desirable.

The bottom line for both goods and bads is that the market may very well provide some public goods or public bads. However, left to its own devices, the market typically under-provides public goods and over-provides public bads.

B. Efficient Public Good Pricing: Consumers

Now suppose that somehow we could set prices for public goods and bads. Can we do this and obtain efficiency? We approach the case of generating an efficient price for the nonrival bad by first considering the nonrival good. Suppose we have a park with in fence around it and thus can control access. Suppose the park is large so that congestion is never a problem and suppose the cost of operating it is all fixed costs with no costs depending cm visitation. What then should he the efficient admission price (one price for all consumers)? To answer this, we should determine first what is the efficient amount of use of the park. Since there is no cost associated with letting one more person use the park, efficient use clearly calls for everyone having access to the park. If we were to exclude anyone, then a 1'arcto improvement could be attained by allowing whomever has been excluded to use the park-costs would not change, current users would not have their utility reduced, and those newly admitted would have their utility increased.

What admission price would support this Pareto optimum? Clearly only a price of zero. Figure 5.4 shows a typical demand curve for park visits. At any price $p_1 > 0$, there will be a certain number of people (q_1) who will pay the admission price and visit the park. There will also be a number of people (q_0–q1) who will not visit the park because the price is too high. We would argue that a lower price would be Pareto preferred. This is because if the price is lowered, all previous attendees would be just as well off, some people for whom the price was previously too high would be able to enjoy the park at the lower price, and the cost of providing the park services is unchanged. This process continues until the price drops to zero. The consequence is that for a non-rival excludable good, the optimal price from the consumer's point of view is zero.

What is the analog for a non-rival bad? For the sake of simplicity, suppose we have a factory in the middle of nowhere generating smoke that fills a circular area around the factory 2 km in radius. There are no effects outside this circle. Furthermore, there is no good reason for anyone to live inside the circle-assume that workers at the plant are housed at a location 15 km away and are provided free transportation to the plant. The following question is before us: If people decide to live in the polluted area around the plant, what compensation should be paid for the damage they incur?

First it is necessary to determine the Pareto optimal location of consumers. Clearly it is Pareto optimal for nobody to live inside the polluted area. Anyone inside the polluted area can be made better off by moving outside the area, since we assumed there are no advantages to living close to the factory. What level of compensation to people living with the pollution would support this efficient location of consumers? The answer is zero compensation. Any positive level of compensation will attract those consumers for whom damage is less than the compensation offered. It is a Pareto improvement to lower the compensation, inducing those people to move outside the circle (or not move there to begin with). In fact, the optimal compensation is zero since compensation induces people to inefficiently move to the pollution.

This example is a bit stylized since there is no reason for people to live near the pollution. Consider a slightly more realistic example of an airport located within a city. Noise bothers People and the further they are from the airport, the less the noise and the annoyance. People live near the airport because they work near there so commuting is shorter. What compensation should the airport pay to consumers? The same argument applies. Without compensation, consumers optimally trade-off the noise with convenience in finding a place to live. The consumer lives where the marginal convenience cost of moving a little further away just equals the marginal gain to moving in reduced noise. Any positive compensation that is offered will diminish the net damage from the noise and cause the consumer to locate slightly closer to the airport. This is not socially desirable. Key here is the nonrivalry. If the noise were rival (i.e., my consumption of it reduces the amount available to others), then my consumption provides a community service for which I could be paid. Because my consumption of the nonrival bad (noise) imposes no costs, positive or negative, on anyone else, there is no justification for my receiving payment for consumption. In fact, to the extent that such compensation distorts my decisions about where to locate, it is undesirable. However, if compensation does not distort decisions (e.g., lump-sum compensation to land owners is nondistortionary since land cannot be moved), compensation is neutral and perhaps desirable on equity grounds.

Another way of looking at this is that there are actions producers can take to reduce damage (e.g., emit less smoke or noise) and there are actions "victims" can take to reduce damage (e.g., change location or install household noise insulation). The pollution the victim suffers provides sufficient incentive to the victim to take action to reduce damage. Any compensation that distorts those incentives is undesirable. Nondistortionary compensation is fine for equity reasons but of no consequence to efficiency.

This point about the undesirability of compensation for consumption of nonrival bads is difficult to grasp intuitively.

C. Budgets and the Optimal Producer Price

Having discussed consumption we now examine production. We have seen that the optimal provision of nonrival goods involves a price to the consumers of zero. Production of nonrival commodities is similar to production of any other good or bad. There are costs associated with production that are positive for the case of goods and negative for the case of bads. Thus to efficiently supply a nonrival good, the private producer must have revenue sufficient to cover costs. Unfortunately, if the producer must price at zero, which we have just indicated is the efficient consumer price, then the producer cannot afford to provide the right amount of the nonrival good. Budgets will not balance and a deficit will result. If the producer raises prices to generate revenue for provision, demand will be depressed. There will be too little of the public good provided.

For a nonrival bad, a similar thing happens. The cost of production of a bad such as smoke is negative, i.e., the producer saves money by producing the smoke. Since the price is zero (no compensation should be paid), the producer of smoke runs a budget surplus. In other words, the producer saves money by generating smoke and pays no compensation. Smoke is good for the producer; without intervention the smoke producer will ignore damage to the consumer. Now suppose we require a balanced budget, with the producer's savings paid out as compensation to consumers. This would be analogous in the private provision of a public good where the budget must balance. If people are compensated, they desires nore smoke than if they were not compensated. Thus in this case there is an incentive to over provide the public bad. Too much smoke will be generated.

D. Lindahal Prices and Free Riding

A theoretical but impractical solution is available for this problem using prices for public goods and bads. First decide how much of the public good is to be provided by determining where aggregate demand and supply intersect. Then charge each consumer his or her individual willingness to pay for that amount of the good. By construction, the total marginal cost of provision will be the sum of the individual willingness to pay, thus we should have budget balancing. If Anna loves to hike and really values public parks, she should pay her marginal willingness to pay for those parks. If Brewster couldn't care less, perhaps because he has an allergy attack when he goes outdoors, Brewster should pay little toward the public parks. If each pays according to his or her marginal willingness to pay, not only will the right amount of the public good be provided but the budget will balance—the amount collected will equal the amount necessary for provision. This is what is known as a Lindahal equilibrium, and the prices everyone pays are known as Lindahal prices. These are named after the Norwegian economist Erik Lindahal.

One of the main failings of the Lindahal equilibrium is that information is required on individual demand curves. Those demand curves must be provided voluntarily by individuals and they have every incentive to distort their articulated demand. Since the greater your demand, the more you will pay, you have an incentive to understate your demand. This is what is known as *free-riding*. Even if you have a large willingness to pay, you know that if you fib and indicate a low willingness to pay, you will still get the benefits from the good (assuming nonrivalry). You free-ride on everyone else's willingness to provide the public good. Everyone of course has this incentive so that all of the articulated individual demand curves can be assumed to understate demand, although by how much we cannot know.

If we were to seek contributions from consumers to reduce pollution, we would expect some people to claim they were damaged only slightly since their contribution would be based on their announced damage. This is free-riding on the provision by others.

Externalities

An externality occurs when one person's or firm's actions affect another entity without permission. If I like to play my stereo loudly, my neighbours must listen as well. If a laundry is located next to a steel mill, the act of making steel increases costs for the laundry because of all the dirt and smoke generated in making steel. One more additional driver on a congested highway generates externalities for all the other drivers. Of course, there can also be positive externalities. In a classic example of externalities, the owner of an apple orchard provides a positive externality for a neighbouring apiary (in terms of the quantity and sweetness of the honey). And the apiary provides a positive externality to the orchard in terms of the bee pollinating the apple blossoms. The generation of knowledge also provides positive externalities in the sense that its benefits are rarely confined to those who generate the knowledge.

Suppose an individual's utility function is given by U (x, y) where x and y are quantities of two goods (or bads) consumed. The individual chooses how much of x to consume but has no control over consumption of y. How much y will be consumed is chosen by others. This is an externality.

Definition: An externality exists when the consumption or production choices of one person or firm enters the utility or production function of another entity without that entity's permission or compensation.

It is important to exclude from this concept actions between two agents that are mutually agreed and for which payment occurs. When iron ore is sold to a steel mill, the mill's profits are improved, but that is hardly an externality: rather it is a simple transaction. It is unstated, but we also preclude from our definition of externality intentional harm to another (e.g., murder) or intentional good to another (altruism).

Figure illustrates a production externality. Shown are production possibilities for steel and laundry—the maximum amounts of the two that can be produced. Note that with no externality, both can produce some maximum amount and the two firms are essentially independent of one another. With a modest externality involved (e.g., smoke), increased steel production diminishes laundry output. If the externality is strong enough, the possible output combinations can even be noncom ex. leading to potential pricing problems that will not be explored here. What would influence the strength of the externality? Clearly location is important. As we move no firms away from each other, the strength of the externality is bound to decline.

A production externality exists when one firm's profits are involuntarily affected by another's. More specifically, suppose the technology of producing laundry is given by

$$L = f_L (x_1, \text{..........} x_n, e)$$

Where, L is output of laundry and x_1, ...x_n are n different inputs into laundry production. The variable e is smoke emissions from steel manufacturing, which is of course chosen by a steel mill. The steel mill produces steel (S) and smoke emissions (e) using inputs z_1,.........,z_m, according to

$$S = f_s (z_1, \text{.........}, z_m)$$
$$E = f_e(z_1, \text{.........}, z_m)$$

Production possibilities with an externality.

Note that e is chosen by the steel mill [Eq. (5.4b)] but e enters into the production function of the laundry [Eq. 5.3]. The laundry has no say, over what the level of *e is* nor how e enters its production function. Thus the smoke is an externality.

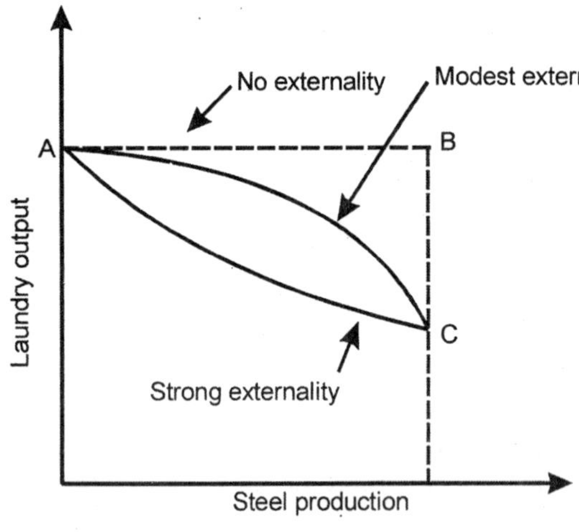

Fig. 1.19

A consumption externality is very analogous. The difference is that we deal with utility functions instead of production functions. Consider the utility function U (w, e), where w is just a basket of goods chosen for consumption and e is levels of pollution, which enters the utility function through no choice of the consumer. This is a consumption externality.

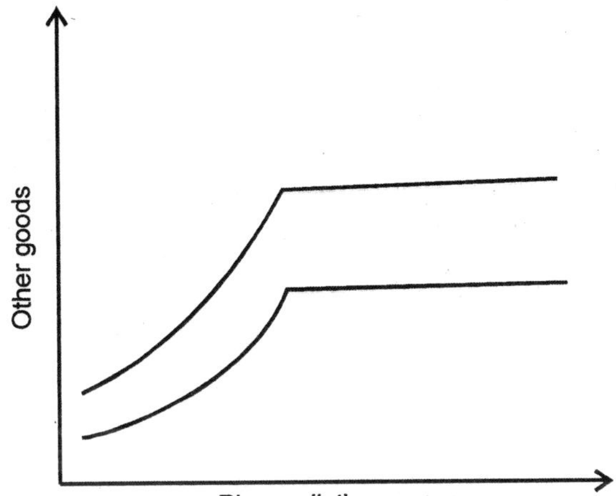

Fig. 1.20

Figure shows an example of a consumption externality. The externality is generated by a paper mill that discharges pollution into a river that is used for swimming. For illustrative purposes, we will assume the water pollution is undesirable only to the extent that it degrades the swimming experience; for instance, the river may totally clean itself (naturally) within a few miles of the paper null. Shown in Figure is a set of indifference curves between pollution and other goods (for some typical consumer).

To the left (low, levels of pollution), swimming and pollution are inversely related. More pollution means the swimming experience is degraded. Thus additional quantities of other goods are needed to keep utility constant. At some point, however, swimming is just not fun anymore: the river has become so polluted that swimming ceases. This is the point of the kink in the indifference curves in Figure. To the right of this point, increased pollution has no effect on utility. One problem with these indifference curves is that they are nonconvex. So why should we be worried about externalities? The basic problem is that the generator of the externality is deciding how much of the externality to produce but is not taking into account the effects of the externality on others. Figure 1.19 illustrates the case of the steel mill and the laundry with a modest externality in the form of smoke from the steel mill. Possible output combinations of laundry and steel given a fixed amount of inputs (production possibilities). The maximum amount of steel that can be produced with these resources is S_0. With no intervention, the steel mill will ignore the effects it might have on the laundry and produce S_0 of steel; the laundry will produce as much as it can, L_0. Assuming prices for steel and laundry (p_s and p_L), the total value of output can be read off the vertical axis as shown in Figure 1.21. Now eliminate the externality by merging the laundry and steel mill into one firm. Steel production will adjust, taking into account the negative effects of the smoke, finding a point at which the total value of output (Y) is greatest, (S_1, L_1). Reading output off the vertical axis, we can see that indeed Y, > Y°. Note that some smoke may still be generated, but the amount is chosen so as to balance the interests of the steel mill with those of the laundry. If there is a transfer from the laundry to the steel mill, this is a Pareto improvement (both the laundry and steel mill are made better off). If no transfer takes place, (S_0, L_0) is a potential Pareto improvement over (S_1, L_1). This is because the pie is bigger when the externality is corrected.

There is a question of semantics about whether we have eliminated the externality at (S_1,*Li*). There is still smoke being produced so there is still an external effect. The convention is to distinguish between Pareto-relevant and Pareto-irrelevant externalities. It is socially desirable to correct a Pareto relevant externality; after the correction, the externality becomes Pareto irrelevant. Thus smoke at (S_0, L_0) is Pareto relevant whereas smoke levels at (S_1, L_1) are Pareto irrelevant.

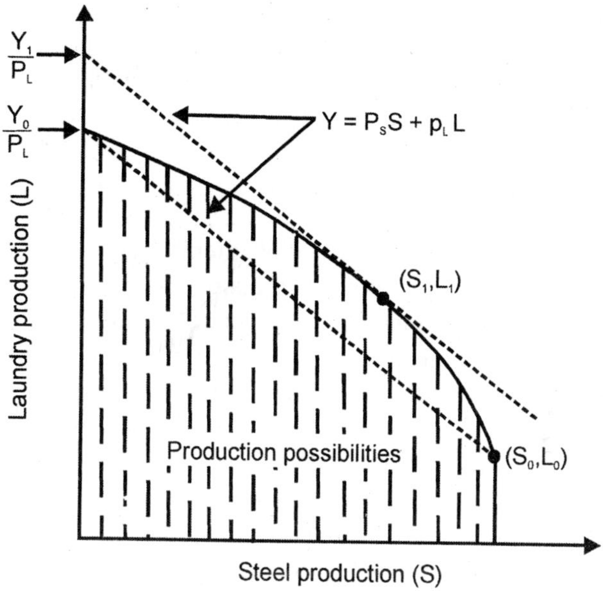

Fig. 1.21

There is another type of externality that can best be illustrated by an example. Suppose you have been a swordfish eater for many years. Recently you have seen the price of swordfish rise dramatically due to the increasing popularity of fish in a healthy diet and depletion of swordfish stocks. The actions of others have driven up the price of fish so that now you have to pay more so you consume less swordfish. This is what is known as a pecuniary externality. Basically, your prices change due to the actions of others. Your utility changes because your income remains fixed. While this is certainly an external effect, it is not something that we will be concerned about. The basic Figure 1.21 Pareto relevance of externality. (S_0, L_0), Steel and laundry production without coordination; (S_1, L_1), steel and laundry production with firms merged; Y_1, value of output without coordination; (p_S, p_L), prices of steel and laundry reason is that there is no inefficiency involved in introducing a pecuniary externality. Prices change, but we have efficiency before and after the price change. We have just moved from one point on the Pareto frontier to another. Although this may have distributional consequences, it does not have the efficiency effects of a conventional externality which involves the inappropriate physical amount of an externality.

Externalities as Public Bads

After having developed the notion of externality, we now wish to argue what as a term it is somewhat redundant with the concept of public bads developed earlier, a concept that is more consistent with conventional consumer and producer theory. An externality involves a good or bad whose level enters the utility functions of several people or firms but is chosen by only one person or firm. This is exactly what happens with a nonrival, nonexcludable good or bad—a public good or bad. When the steel mill generates smoke, it is doing so not intentionally to hurt the laundry but rather because the smoke is nonexcludable. (The fact that smoke is nonrival is not relevant to this example). When I choose to enjoy my blasting stereo, you also listen to it because the sound is nonexcludable. I am a producer of the nonexcludable noise; you are the consumer. Prior to laws prohibiting the dumping of household garbage, my creation of garbage was an externality because simply dumped it into my neighbour's yard or into common areas. With laws making garbage excludable the externality disappears because my garbage no longer enters your utility function without permission.

The notion of externality has arisen because of its intuitive appeal. I do something for my own benefit, ignoring the fact that my action also affects you. However, modern economics starts from the basis of preferences represented by utility functions, with physical quantities of commodities (goods or bads) as arguments, and production functions, also with physical quantities of commodities as arguments. Most externalities can be viewed as a nonexcludable good or bad being produced by one agent and being consumed by one or more agents. The producer chooses how much to produce based on his or her won calculus. The consumer has no choices since the good or bad is nonexcludable. Air pollution fits into this framework, as does noise, and even positive externalities such as knowledge.

The point is that we could just as well dispense with the term externality and fit environmental problems into conventional theory using the concept of public bad or excludability. However, term externality is so common that students should be aware of it. It is sometimes intuitively appealing to discuss an action resulting in an externality than convert the action to a good or bad.

SUGGESTED READINGS

Baumol—Economic Theory and Operations Analysis.

Ganguly, Subrat, Public Finance, A. Nonnative Approach, Navabharat Publishers. Calcutta.

Hasan—An Introduction to Welfare Economics.

Henderson and Quandt—Micro Economic Theory.

Kosstad, Charles, D., Environmental Economics, Oxford University Press.

Little—A Critique of Welfare Economics.

Mishan's Article in the Economic Journal June, 1960 Graaff—Theoretical Welfare Economics.

Musgrave, R.A., The Theory of Public Finance.

Pigou—Economics of Welfare.

Rothenberg—Measurement of Social Welfare.

Samuelson—Foundations of Economic Analysis.

Singh, S.K., Public Finance in Developed and Developing Countries, S. Chand and Company, New Delhi

Todaro Michael, P. and Sterhen C. Smith—Economic Development.

2

Nature, Concept, Scope, Importance and Policy of Environmental Economics

Meaning of Environment

The dictionary meaning of the word environment is a surrounding; external conditions influencing development or growth of people, animals or plants; living or working conditions etc. This involves three questions—

(1) What is Surrounded? The answer to this question is living objects in general and man in particular.

(2) By what Surrounded? If man is taken to be surrounded, physical attributes become the answer to this second question which become environment and where surrounded is the space or habitat. 'Primarily, the concern of all educations is the environment of man. But man cannot exist or be understood in isolation from the other forms of life and from plan life.' So environment of all biological population should be the concern teacher. 'Environment refers to the sum total of conditions which surround man at a given point in space and time.' The environment of early man consisted of only physical aspects of the planet earth; land, air, water and biological communities. With the march of time and advancement of society man extended his environment through his social, economic and political functions.

(3) Where Surrounded? Generally speaking, the environment is equated with 'wherein physical components of the planet

earth, *viz.* land, air, water etc., support and affect life in the biosphere. In his book "The Nature of the Environment" A. Goudie (1984) has, taken environment as the representative of physical components of the earth wherein man is an important factor affecting the environment. Environment has been defined more comprehensively by holistic view of the world as it functions at any point of time, with a multitude of spatial element and socio-economic systems distinguished by quality and attributes of space and mode of behaviour of physical and biological forms. Goudie remarks, "the definition, and in turn the scope, could be governed by our concern and priorities. Our immediate concern is the quality of space we live in, than air we breath, the food we eat, the water we drink and the resources we draw from the environment to support our economy". Goudie has also pleaded for the inclusion of only 'air-land-water-plant' in the concept of environment, thus excluding man and human society from the ambit of environment. In fact, the environment consists of the sum total of the stimulation that the individual receives from conception until death. It covers all those circumstances which exert their influence on the individual since conception of death. Whatever found around the individual, may be covered by the term environment.

Definition of Environment

(1) *Boring*—'A person's environment consists of the sum total of the stimulation which he receives from his conception until his death.'

(2) *Anastasi*—'The term environment is used to describe, in the aggregate, all the external forces, influences and conditions, which affect the life nature, behaviour and the growth, development and maturity of living organisms.'

Environmental includes various types of forces such as physical, intellectual, social, moral, economic, political, cultural and emotional. Environment is the aggregate of all the external forces, influences and conditions, which affect the life, nature, behaviour and the growth, development and maturation of living organisms. A favourable environment helps in the development of native abilities of the child.

Elements of Environment

Though environment has been viewed in different ways with different angles by different groups of people but it may be safely argued that "environment is an inseparable whole and is constituted by the interacting systems of physical, biological and cultural elements inter-related in myriad ways, individually as well as collectively. Physical elements such as space, landforms, water bodies, climate soils, rocks and minerals etc. determine the variable character of the human habitat, its opportunities as well as limitations. Biological elements such as plants, animals, micro-organisms and men constitute the biosphere. Cultural elements such as economic, social and political elements are essentially man-made feature which go into the making of cultural milieu."

Environment as Surroundings

The term 'Environment' refers to the surroundings of an organism which includes both living and non-living components. The literal meaning of environment is to surround and to develop. The words 'surround' and 'develop' raise two basic questions:

(1) What is surrounded and developed? The answer is that man and other organisms.
(2) Man and other living organism are surrounded by what? The simple answer includes all non-living components—land, water, air, atmospheric pressure, etc., and living components such as plants, social, cultural and economic surroundings.

Thus environment includes all the external conditions and influence affecting life and development of an organism.

Man's environment consists of natural as well as socio-cultural environment. Due to present environmental pollution or crisis man has to improve the quality of his environment pollution or crisis man has to improve the quality of his environment. The crisis is due to over consumption of natural resources, over population, urbanization, industrialization and unscientific attitude of human beings. Natural resources have been utilised to meet the demand of better living to such an extent that it has caused serious ecological and environment protection. The best insurance for the environment is a commitment to prevent the deterioration of land, water and air. It requires the introduction of environmental education.

Characteristics of Environment

(1) It is the sum total of the stimulation from man's until his death.

(2) It includes every thing which affects the individual excluding genes.

(3) It includes all the external forces which affect the growth and development of living organism.

(4) It consists of physical, intellectual, social, moral, cultural, emotional, economic and political forces which affect the life and nature of behaviour.

(5) It refers to sum total of conditions which surround man at a given point in space and time.

(6) It includes physical components such as land, air and water and biological components such as plants, animals including man and his several functions, organizations and institutions etc.

(7) It involves physical, chemical, biological, social, economic, political and cultural processes.

Type of Environment

Including biological components under the physical environment Kurt Lewin has enumerated environment into three types which influence the personality of an individual—

(1) Physical Environment,
(2) Social and Cultural Environment, and
(3) Psychological Environment.

(1) Physical Environment—It refers to geographical climate and weather or physical conditions in which an individual lives. The human races are greatly influenced by the climate. The white, black and yellow races live in different climatic conditions. In the cold countries, the people are of white colour and in hot countries people are of black complexion. The human working efficiency also depends on climatic conditions as the individual tries to adjust in his physical environment. The physical environment influences even heredity.

(2) Social Environment—It includes the social, economic and political conditions of an individual in which he lives. The moral, cultural and emotional forces affect the life and nature of individual behaviour. Society may be of two types—closed and open society. Whereas closed society is not very conducive for the development. The contribute for the development of individual potentialities even the classroom climate should be more open.

(3) Psychological Environment—Kurt Lewin has emphasis on the psychological environment of an individual. The physical and social envircnment are common to the individual in a specific situation while every individual has his own psychological environment, in which he lives. Lewin has used the term 'life space', for explaining psychological environment. Psychological environment is very important to understand the personality of an individual. Both the person and his goal from the psychological environment. Unable to overcome the barriers a person can not achieve his goal. It may lead to frustration or has to change his goal for a new psychological environment. This mechanism helps the individual in his adjustment to the environment.

Structure of Environment

Environment is both physical and biological. It includes both living and non-living components. On the basis structure the environment may be divided into two basic types—

(1) Physical or abiotic environment, and
(2) Biological or biotic environment.

1. Physical Environment—On the basis of physical characteristics and state, and physical environment is subdivided into three broad categories viz., (i) solid, (ii) liquid and (iii) gas which represent the lithosphere (solid earth), the hydrosphere (water component) and the atmosphere respectively. Thus, the three basic divisions of physical environment may be termed as (i) lithosphere environment, (ii) atmospheric environment and (iii) hydropheric environment. These may be further broken into smaller units based on different spatial scales e.g., mountain environment, plateau environment, maritime environment, glacier environment, desert environment, coastal environment, etc.

2. Biological Environment—The biological component of the environment consists of plants (flora) and animals (fauna) including man as an important factor. Thus, the biotic environment may be divided into floral environment and faunal environment. All the organisms work to form their social groups and organizations at several levels. Thus, is formed the social environment where in the organisms work to derive matter from the physical environment for their sustenance and development. This process generates economic environment. Of all the organisms is most skilled and civilized and hence his social organisation is most systematic. The three aspects of man, e.g., physical, social and economic, have different characteristics and functions in the biotic environment.

(i) **The Physical Man**—The 'physical man' is one of the organism populations or biological community. He requires basic elements of the physical environment, *viz.*, habitat (space), air, water and food like other biological populations and releases wastes into the ecosystem.

(ii) **The Social Man**—The 'social man' establishes social institutions, forms social organisations, formulate laws, principles and policies to safeguard his existence, interest and social.

(iii) **The Economic Man**—He derives and utilises resources from the physical and biotic environments with his skills and technologies. These may be termed as physical, social and economic and functions of man. The economic function makes the man an environmental/geomorphic process because he transports matter and energy from one component of the ecosystem to the other. So long as the exploitative functions are in harmony with the natural environment this aspect/function does not necessarily involve change in the working of the ecosystem. When these exceed the critical limit, the equilibrium of the environment/ecosystem is disturbed and several environmental and ecological problems crop up. These are detrimental not only to man himself but to whole population of human species in a given ecosystem.

Components of Environment

Environment is a broad concept, which includes all external conditions influencing growth and development of child, animals and plants etc. The environment has been broadly classified into physical and biological components. The physical components include land, animals including man, his functions organisations and institutions. The environmental components can be classified in the following categories—

(1) Physical components—Land, air and water.
(2) Biological components—Plants and animals.
(3) Social components—Population, social system, social changes and social relations, urbanization, etc.
(4) Cultural components—Political, economic moral and values of life, religion, industries, etc.
(5) Psychological components—Facts, self-concepts, level of aspiration, life space, topology, goals of life.

(6) Energy components—Solar energy and geothermal energy.

Today the society is awakened towards environment problems. The public concern about the quality of environment has reached an emotional peak. The environmental improvement measures are costly. Long-term invest of time, money and resources may eclipse the tempo, jeopardise the public interest and taboo the implementation of environment improvement programmes. According to Downs (1972) public interest in environment changes through time and the whole sequence of changes is completed in five stages termed as 'Issue Attention Cycle'.

(i) **First Stage or Pre-problem Stage**—It is characterized by no public attention towards environmental problems except a few experts and interest groups who are seized with such problems.

(ii) **Second Stage**—It is a stage of alarmed discovery and euphoric enthusiasm when the issue of environmental problems catches the public attention. The public are so alarmed and enthusiastic that they readily respond to solve the problem without caring for the cost of investment.

(iii) **Third Stage**—It is marked by realization of the cost of significant progress. The public is aware of the cost of investment. It is realised that the technological development may not always be the best solution to the environment problems.

(iv) **Fourth Stage**—It is characterized by gradual decline in public interest towards environmental improvement programmes due to realizations of higher cost of solution of environmental problems and difficulty in implementing the environmental improvement programme.

(v) **Post Problem Stage**—It is marked by lessening of public interest in the issues of environmental concerns but the public interest in environmental problems erupts in spasmodic manner.

Environmental Factors

What is environment? How does it acts? The environment has various factors which vary with time (temporal variations) and space (spatial variations). These factors are involved both autecological as well as synecological levels of organisation. These factors affect the life and govern the distribution of organisms.

As the term environment etymological means surrounding it is a complex of so many things which surround an organism (light, temperature, soil, water, etc.). Any external force, substance or condition, which surrounds and affects the life of an organism in any way is a factor of its environment. These factors have been variously called as environment factors, ecological factors or simply factors and may be living (biotic) as well as non-living (abiotic). The sum of all these living and nonliving factors makes the environment of an organism.

Various factors of environment have been grouped and discussed in different ways. Sometimes all the factors are classified into two groups—

(1) *Direct Factors*—These are light, temperature, humidity of air, soil air, soil water, soil nutrients etc.
(2) *Indirect Factors*—These include soil structure, soil organisms, altitude, wind, slopes etc.

According to Oosting (1948), the environment is complex of variable factors or causes, which includes (i) Substance (soil, water), (ii) Conditions (temperature, light), (iii) Forces (wind, gravity), (iv) Organisms (plants, animals), and (v) Time. Misra and Puri (1959) preferred to discuss the environment of plants as (i) Environment of roots (geology and soil) and (ii) Environment of shoots (climate, i.e. temperature, light, water, wind etc., and biotic factors).

Daubenmire (1959) classified the factors into seven coordinate headings as (i) Soil, (ii) Water, (iii) Temperature, (iv) Light, (v) Atmosphere, (vi) Fire, and (vii) Biotic factor.

However most of the ecologies prefer to recognize following four categories of factors of environment.

1. *Climatic* or *Aerial Factors*—These include—

(i) Light
(ii) Temperature of air (atmospheric temperature)
(iii) Rainfall (precipitation).
(iv) Humidity of air.
(v) Atmosphere (gases and wind).

2. *Topographic* or *Physiographic Factors*—These are the factors related with physical geography of earth, and include—

(i) Altitude.
(ii) Direction of mountain chains and valleys.
(iii) Steepness and exposure of slopes etc.

3. *Edaphic Factors*—These deal with the formation of soil, its physical and chemical properties and details of related aspects.

4. *Biotic Factors*—These are all kinds of interactions between different forms of life, i.e., plants, animals microorganisms etc.

Importance of Environmental Factors

Under natural conditions at a time, the life or organism is affected by the sum of all environmental factors and not any individual factor. All the factors are so interrelated that variations in one may affect the other. For instance, an increase in temperature would certainly bring out a decrease in humidity values. In addition to affecting the rate of photosynthesis increased light intensity, would affect the atmospheric humidity. Thus, at a given time the effect on the organism's life is all overall effect of interrelated factors, and it is very difficult to say as which of the individual factors is actually responsible for the marked effect on organism's life. Thus in affecting an organism's life under natural conditions environmental factors, operate in conduction and not in isolation following figure shows possible interactions between five principal components of the environment (energy, soil nutrients, organism, water and air). Thus, in considering the environmental factors separately for distinguishing and measuring the effect of each, one must be aware of the fact that in nature these factors even act alone. Organism is subjected to many influences at the same time. The effect of one factor is usually modified by the other factors. The 'real life' of in organism involves the simultaneous and continuing impact of all existing ecological factors.

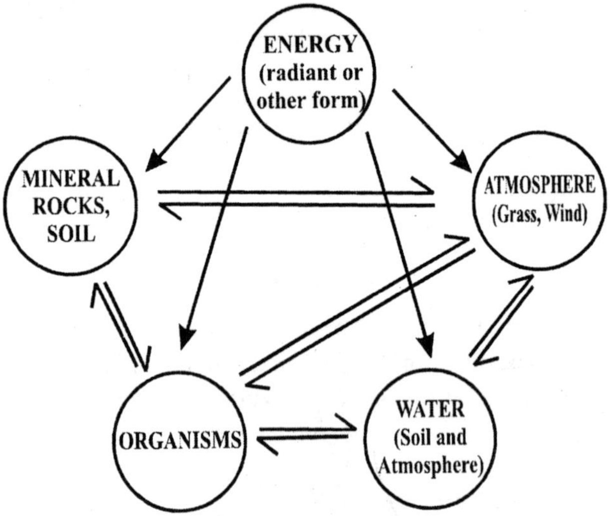

Fig. 2.1

Diagram showing interrelations between principal components of the environment.

Since various environmental factors affect the life of an organism in a holistic manner and all the factors operate in conduction and not in isolation, it is difficult to understand the nature of influence of individual factor. To understand this mechanism of environmental influence, it is essential to study the effect of each factor separately.

Multidisciplinary Nature of Environmental Studies

The components of the environment are broadly classified into two major categories—

(1) Physical components or abiotic components, and
(2) Biological components or biotic components.

The environment is composed of biotic (biological) and abiotic (physical) components. This can be shown with the help of chart.

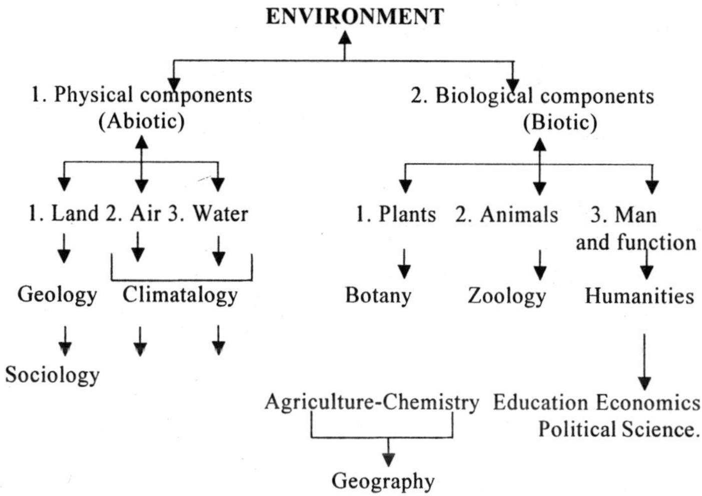

It is evident from the chart that the environment relates to physical science, bio-science; behavioural science and social science. Geography has the widest coverage of environment. The physical components—land, air and water are the areas of geology (land). Agriculture includes plants also. The biological components—plants, man and his functions, organization and institutions are the areas of botany (plants). Zoology (animals), sociology economics, political science, commerce and education study and his function.

Meaning and Concept of Environmental Economics

Environmental economics is concerned with the impact of the economy on the environment, the significance of the environment to the economy, and the appropriate way of regulating economic activity so that balance is achieved among environmental, economic, and other social goals. What distinguishes a morally neutral chemical such as sulfur dioxide from the pollutant sulfur dioxide is the economy. The polluters who emit sulfur dioxide do so because it is a by-product of producing some good the public wants; consumers want the good associated with sulfur dioxide but at the same time obtain disutility (damage) from the sulfur dioxide pollution. The essence of the environment problem is the economy—producer behaviour and consumer desires. Without the economy, most environmental issues are simply research questions of concern to chemists or biologists with no policy significance.

For most goods and services in a modern economy, we rely on markets to match producer costs with consumer demands to yield the "right" amount of pollution (and thus consumption). The problem with pollution is that markets do not work to yield the socially desirable amount of pollution. This illustrates the breadth of problems that need answers: What are the incentives for the generation of pollution? What are the costs of cleaning up pollution? What are the societal gains from pollution control? What is the right balance between costs of control and gains from pollution control? What regulatory mechanisms can be designed to ensure the right balance between costs and gains? Sometimes these issues are straightforward; other times they are exceedingly complex.

Although the field of environmental economics probably dates to the late 1950s and early 1960s with the important contributions emerging from the "think tank". Resources for the future, the field really took off in the 1970s and has been booming ever since. In the 1990s the payoff is beginning to be seen in terms of influence on environmental policy. Marketable permits for pollution control are now embraced, valuation methods are an integral part of environmental prevention, environmental valuation is being used to make decisions concerning major public projects with environmental impacts, and environmental economics is playing a major role in the current climate change debate.

In recent years, economists have become increasingly aware of the important implications of environmental issues for the success of development efforts. We now understand that the interaction between poverty and environmental degradation can lead to a self-perpetuating process in which, as a result of ignorance or economic necessity, communities may inadvertently destroy or exhaust the resources on which they depend for survival. Rising pressures on environmental resources in developing countries can have severe consequences for self-sufficiency, income distribution, and future growth potential in the developing world.

Environmental degradation can also detract from the pace of economic development by imposing high costs on developing countries through health-related expenses and the reduced productivity of resources. The poorest 20 per cent of the world's population will experience the consequences of environmental ills most acutely. Severe environmental degradation, due to population pressures on marginal land, has led to falling farm productivity and per capita food production. Since the cultivation of marginal land is largely the domain of lower-income groups, the losses are suffered by those who can least afford them. Similarly, the inaccessibility of sanitation and clean water mainly affects the poor and is believed to be responsible for 80 per cent of disease worldwide. Because the solutions to these and many other environmental problems involve enhancing the productivity of resources and improving living conditions among the poor, achieving environmentally sustainable growth is synonymous with our definition of economic development.

Though there is considerable dispute concerning the environmental costs associated with various economic activities, consensus is growing among development economists that environmental considerations should form an integral part of policy initiatives. The exclusion of environmental costs from calculations of GNP is largely responsible for the historical absence of environmental considerations from development economics. Damage to soil, water supplies, and forests resulting from unsustainable methods of production can greatly reduce long-term national productivity but will have a positive impact on current GNP figures. It is thus very important that the long-term implications of environmental quality be considered in economic analysis. Rapid population growth and expanding economic activity in the developing world are likely to do extensive environmental damage unless steps are taken to mitigate their negative consequences.

The growing consumption needs of LDC populations may have global implications as well. There is increasing concern in the MDCS that the destruction of the world's remaining forests, which are concentrated in a number of highly indebted developing countries including Brazil, Mexico, Peru, and the Philippines, will greatly contribute to global warming and the greenhouse effect. In this chapter, we examine the economic cause and consequences of environmental devastation and explore potential solutions to the cycle of poverty and resource degradation. We begin, as in previous solutions to the cycle of poverty and resource degradation. We being, as in previous chapters, with a survey of basic issues, including discussions of sustainable development and the linkages among population, poverty, economic growth, rural development, urbanization, and the LDC environment. We next look at the applicability of traditional economic models of the environment, depict some typical environmental situations, and provide some relevant data. We than broaden our scope to examine the global environment and explore policies for seeking worldwide sustainable development. Pakistan's environment problems are this chapter's case study.

Environment and Development : The Basic Issues

Seven basic issues define the environment of development. Many grow out of the discussions in the preceding chapters. The seven issues are (1) the concept of sustainable development, and linkages between the environment and (2) population and resources, (3) poverty, (4) economic growth, (5) rural development, (6) urbanization, and (7) the global economy. We briefly discuss each in turn.

1. Sustainable Development and Environmental Accounting

Environmentalists have used the term sustainability in an attempt to clarify the desired balance between economic growth on the one hand and environmental preservation on the other. Although there are many definitions, basically sustainability refers to "meeting the needs of the present generation without compromising need of future generations." For economists, a development path is sustainable "if and only if the stock of overall capital assets remains constant or rises over time." Implicit in these statements is the fact that future growth and overall quality of life are critically dependent on the quality of the environment. The natural resource base of a country and the quality of its air, water, and land represents a common heritage for all generations. To destroy that endowment indiscriminately in the pursuit of short-term economic goals penalizes both present and, especially, future generations. It is therefore, important that development policymakers incorporate some form of environmental accounting into their decisions. For example, the preservation or loss of valuable environmental resources should be factored into estimates of economic growth and human well-being. Alternatively, policymakers may set a goal of no net loss of environmental assets. In other words, if an environmental resource is damaged or depleted in one area, a resource of equal or greater value should be regenerated elsewhere.

An example of environmental accounting is offered by David Pearce and Jeremy Warford. Overall capital assets are meant to include not only manufactured capital (machines, factories, roads) but also human capital (knowledge, experience, skills) and environmental capital (forests, soil quality, rangeland). By this definition, sustainable development requires that these overall capital assets not be decreasing and that the correct measure of sustainable national income or sustainable net national product (NNP) is the amount that can be consumed without diminishing the capital stock. Symbolically,

$$NNP = GNP - D_m - D_n$$

where, NNP is sustainable national income, D_m is the depreciation of manufactured capital assets, and D_n is depreciation of environmental capital — the monetary value of environmental decay over the course of a year.

An even better measure, though more difficult to calculate with present data collection methods, would be

$$NNP = GNP - D_m - D_n - R - A$$

where, D_m and D_n are as before, R is expenditure required to restore environmental capital (forests, fisheries, etc.), and A is expenditure to avert destruction of environmental capital (air pollution, water and soil quality, etc.).

In light of rising consumption levels worldwide combined with high rates of population growth, the realization of sustainable development will be a major challenge. We must ask ourselves, what are realistic expectations about sustainable standards of living? From present information concerning rapid destruction of many of the world resources, it is clear that meeting the needs of a world population that is projected to grow by an additional 3 billion in the next 50 years will require radical and early changes in consumption and production patterns. We discuss these needed changes later in the chapter.

2. Population, Resources and the Environment

Much of the concern over environmental issues stems from the perception that we may reach a limit to the number of people whose needs can be met by the earth's finite resources. This may or may not be true, given the potential for new technological discoveries, but it is clear that continuing on our present path or accelerating environmental degradation would severely comprise the ability of present and future generations to meet their needs. A showing of population growth rates would help ease the intensification of many environmental problems. However, the rate and timing of fertility declines, and thus the eventual size of world population, will largely depend on the commitment of governments to creating economic and institutional conditions that are conducive to limiting fertility.

Rapidly growing populations have led to land, water, and fuel wood shortages in rural areas and to urban health crises stemming from lack of sanitation and clean water. In many of the poorest regions of the globe, it is clear that increasing population density has contributed to severe and accelerating degradation of the very resources that these growing populations depend on for survival. To meet expanding LDC needs, environmental devastation must be halted and the productivity of existing resources stretched further so as to benefit more people. If increases in GNP and food production are slower than population growth, per capita levels of production and food self-sufficiency will fall. Ironically, the resulting persistence of poverty would be likely to perpetuate high fertility rates, that the poor are often dependent of large families for survival.

3. *Poverty and the Environment*

Too often, however, high fertility is blamed for problems that are attributable in poverty itself. For example, China's population density per hectare of arable land is twice that of India, yet yields are also twice as high. Though it is clear that environmental destruction and high fertility go hand in hand, they are both direct out-growths of a third factor, absolute poverty. For environmental policies to succeed in developing countries, they must first address the issues of landlessness, poverty, and lack of access to institutional resources. Insecure and tenure rights, lack of credit and inputs, and absence of information often prevent the poor from making resource-augmenting investments that would help preserve the environmental assets from which they derive their livelihood. Hence preventing environmental degradation is more often a matter of providing institutional support to the poor than fighting an inevitable process of decay. For this reason, many goals on the international environmental agenda are very much in harmony with the three objectives of development.

4. Growth **Versus** *the Environment*

If, in fact, it is possible to reduce environmental destruction by increasing the incomes of the poor, is it then possible to achieve growth without further damage to the environment? Evidence indicates that the worst perpetrators of environmental destruction are the billion richest and billion poorest people on earth. It has even been suggested that the bottom billion are more destructive than all four billion people in between. It follows that increasing the economic status of the poorest group would provide an environmental windfall. However, as the income consumption levels of everyone else in the economy also rise, there is likely to be a net increase in environmental destruction. Meeting increasing consumption demand while keeping environmental degradation at a minimum will be no small task.

5. Rural Development and the Environment

To meet the expanded food needs of rapidly growing LDC populations, it is estimated that food production in developing countries will have to double by 2010. Because land in many areas of the developing world is being unsustainably over-exploited by existing populations, meeting these output targets will require radical changes in the distribution, use, and quantity of resources available to the agricultural sector. And because women are frequently the caretakers of rural resources such as forests and water supplies and provide much of the agricultural supply of labour, it is of primary importance that they be integrated into environmental programs. In addition, poverty alleviation efforts much target women's economic status in particular to reduce their dependence on unsustainable methods of production.

The increased accessibility of agricultural inputs of small farmers and the introduction (or reintroduction) of sustainable methods of farming will help create attractive alternatives to current environmentally destructive patterns of resource use. Land-augmenting investments can greatly increase the yields from cultivated land and help ensure future food self-sufficiency.

6. Urban Development and the Environment

Demonstrated that rapid population increases accompanied by heavy rural-urban migration is leading to unprecedented rate of urban population growth, sometimes at twice the rate of national growth. Consequently, few governments are prepared to cope with the vastly increased strain on existing urban water supplies and sanitation facilities. The resulting environmental ills pose extreme health hazards for the growing numbers of people exposed to them. Such conditions threaten to precipitate the collapse of the existing urban infrastructure and create circumstances ripe for epidemics and national health crises. These conditions are exacerbated by the fact that under existing legislation, much and renders large portions of urban populations ineligible for government services.

Congestion, vehicular and industrial emissions, and poorly ventilated household stoves also inflate the tremendously high environmental costs of urban crowding. Lost productivity of ill or diseased workers, contamination of existing water sources, and destruction of infrastructure, in addition to increased fuel expenses incurred by people's having to boil unsafe water, are just a few of the costs associated with poor urban conditions. Research reveals that the urban environment appears to worsen at a faster rate than urban population size increases of that the marginal environmental cost of additional residents arises over time.

7. The Global Environment

As total world population grows and incomes rise, net global environmental degradation in likely to worsen. Some trade-offs will be necessary to achieve sustainable world development. By using resources more efficiently, a number of environmental changes will actually provide economic savings, and others will be achieved at relatively minor expense. However, because many essential changes will require substantial investments in pollution abatement technology and resource management, significant trade-offs between output and environmental improvements will occasionally become necessary. The poorer the country, the more difficult it will be to absorb these costs. Yet a number of issues, including biodiversity, rain forest destruction, and population growth, will focus international attention on some of the most economically strapped countries in the world. In the absence of substantial assistance to low-income countries, environmental efforts will necessarily have to be funded at the expense of other social programs, such as education, health services, and employment schemes, that themselves have important implications for the preservation of the global environment.

Exactly what sacrifices need to be made and who should make them will continue to be matters of great controversy. Nowhere was this more evident than at the second United Nations Conference on Environment and Development (UNCED) — the so-called Earth Summit — held in Rio de Janeiro in June 1992 and a follow-up conference in Kyoto, Japan, in 1997. Most cumulative environmental destruction to date has been caused by the developed world. However, with high fertility rates, rising average incomes, and increasing inequality in the developing world, this pattern is likely to reverse sometime in this century. It is thus nuclear how the costs of global reform should be divided. Apportionment of responsibility for reducing environmental damage essentially hinges on the manner in which the question is framed. For example, if a limit is placed globally on levels of per capita pollution emissions, the approach would clearly favour lower-income countries that have much lower per capita consumption levels. Conversely, if international pressures try to limit the growth rate of per capita emissions or even to impose limits on the growth of national emissions, any movement in that direction would tend to freeze incomes in the developing world at a small fraction of those of their developed world counterparts.

8. The Scope of Environmental Degradation

The most pressing environmental challenges in developing countries in the next few decades will be caused by poverty. These will include health hazards created by lack of access to clean water and sanitation, indoor air pollution from biomass stoves, and deforestation and severe soil degradation—all most common where households lack economic alternatives to unsustainable patterns of living. Table 2.1 summarizes the principal health and productivity consequences of environmental damage in the developing world. It divides this damage into seven categories:

Table 2.1: Health and Productivity Consequences of Environmental Damage

Environmental Problem	*Effect on Health*	*Effect on Productivity*
Water pollution and water scarcity	More than 2 million deaths and billions of illnesses a year attributable to pollution; poor household hygiene and added health risks caused by water scarcity	Declining fisheries; rural household time and municipal costs of providing safe water; aquifer depletion leading to irreversible compaction; constraint on economic activity because of water shortages
Air pollution	Many acute and chronic health impacts: excessive urban particulate matter levels are responsible for 300,000 to 700,000 premature deaths annually and for half of childhood chronic coughing; 400 million to 700 million people, mainly women and children in poor rural areas, affected by smoky indoor air	Restrictions on vehicle and industrial activity during critical episodes; effect of acid rain on forests and water bodies
Solid and hazardous wastes	Diseases spread by rotting garbage and blocked drains; risks from hazardous wastes typically local but often acute	Pollution of groundwater resources
Soil degradation	Reduced nutrition for poor farmers on depleted soils; greater susceptibility to drought	Field productivity losses in range of 0.5% to 1.5% of gross national product (GNP) common on tropical soils; offsite siltation of reservoirs, river-transport channels, and other hydrologic investments

Environmental Problem	*Effect on Health*	*Effect on Productivity*
Deforestation	Localized flooding, leading to death and disease	Loss of sustainable logging potential and of erosion prevention, watershed stability, and carbon sequestration provided by forests.
Loss of bio-diversity	Potential loss of new drugs	Reduction of ecosystem adaptability and loss of genetic resources.
Atmospheric changes	Possible shifts in vector-borne diseases; risks from climatic natural disasters; diseases attributable to ozone depletion (300,000) additional cases of skin cancer a year worldwide; 1.7 million cases of cataracts	Sea-rise damage to coastal investments; regional changes in agricultural productivity; disruption marine food chain

Source: From World Development Report, 1992: Development and the Environment, copyright@ 1992 by The International Bank for Reconstruction and Development/The World Bank. (New York: Oxford University Press, 1992) tab.1. Reprinted with permission of Oxford University Press, Inc.

water pollution and water security, air pollution, solid and hazardous wastes, soil degradation, deforestation, loss of biodiversity, and atmospheric changes.

In the 1980s, per capita levels of arable land fell by 1.9 per cent annually, leading to worsening land shortages, which have forced many of the poorest onto marginal land with extremely limited cultivability. It is estimated that over 60 per cent of the poorest peoples residing in developing countries struggle for survival on agriculturally marginal soils. This trend is greatly worsened in some areas of the developing world by strong inequalities in the distribution of land, which force an ever-growing class of landless workers onto increasingly taxed, ecologically sensitive soils. The growing intensification of cultivation of fragile lands leads to rapid soil degradation and loss of productivity.

Roughly 270,000 square kilometres of soil lose virtually all of their productivity each year. An area greater than the size of India and China combined, over 1.2 billion acres, has been significantly degraded. The resulting annual loss in agricultural productivity is estimated to be between 0.5 per cent and 1.5 per cent of annual worldwide GNP. As a result of rapid population increases and the failure of agricultural production to keep pace, per capita food production declined in 69 countries during the 1980s.

An environmental problem shared by both the urban and rural poor is the prevalence of unsanitary conditions created by the lack of clean water and sanitation. This is turn contributes greatly to the spread of infectious diseases. It has been estimated that waterborne pathogens that contribute to typhoid, cholera, amoebic infections, bacillary dysentery, and diarrhea account for 80 per cent of all disease in developing countries and at least in part for up to 90 per cent of the 13 million child deaths each year. Deteriorating environmental conditions were cited as a contributing factor to the spread of cholera epidemics in a number of countries in Latin America and Africa in the 1990s.

Rapid population growth and heavy rural-urban migration make it difficult to extend urban services to many people who need them. For example, to provide clean water to all urban dwellers in Latin American cities by 2030, the numbers served by public facilities will have to be increased by 250 per cent. Though this figure itself is staggering, it excludes the 1.2 billion rural individuals whose needs must also be met. A comparable air for the provision of sanitation would require 400 per cent and 900 per cent increases for urban and rural communities, respectively. On average throughout or slums. In Africa, the proportion is even greater, at 92 per cent, most of which have no access to public services.

Airborne pollutants also take a high toll on the health of citizens in developing countries. Dependence on biomass fuels such as wood, straw, and manure is closely related to poverty. The burning of biomass fuels for cooking and the boiling of water create dangerously high levels of indoor pollution to which 400 million to 700 million people, mostly women and children, are exposed each year. Smoke and fumes from indoor stoves are believed to contribute significantly go up to 4.3 million childhood deaths each year from respiratory diseases and to an ever-larger number of chronic respiratory illness (Table 2.1).

In urban areas, other sources of pollution pose serious threats to physical well-being. According to the World Health Organization, 1.3 billion people live in urban areas with unsafe levels of airborne pollutants. Yet it is projected that by 2030, manufacturing in developing countries will expand to 600 per cent of current levels, vastly increasing potential concentrations of pollutants. Just to maintain current urban air standards until 2030 (which means conceding to conditions much worse than those existing in the urban centers of developed countries), average emissions from LDC industries and electric generators would have to be reduced by 90 per cent to 95 per cent per unit of output.

Environmental Economics and Environmental Policy

Concern with the environment is not a passing fad but a deep-seated concern, brought on in large part by the coincidence of high incomes and high population density. If there were few people in the world, the earth's environment would be very forgiving and capable of absorbing most that human throws at it, cleansing itself automatically. The days of low population on the earth have passed; the total number of people on the planet and particularly the density of people in some parts of the planet magnify the size of environmental insults, overloading the capacity of the earth for self-cleansing. Income is also important, not only because the environment is often viewed as a luxury good. For the poor who struggle to keep food on the table, environmental issues often take a backseat to other more pressing needs related to survival. As people become wealthier, they turn their attention increasingly to the quality of their living environment, which ultimately is the planet. Thus if recent trends toward increasing wealth for the people of the world continue, we can expect concern for the environment to increase over time.

What are the typical issues facing most countries of the world with regard to environmental policy? In developed countries, pollution and the preservation of natural environments (e.g., wilderness areas) are major concerns. Pollution problems usually involve two major issues—what is the right amount of pollution and how can we get polluters to control their emissions?

Determining the right amount of pollution is not easy. Pollution is generated as a by-product of producing goods. To determine the costs of pollution control it is necessary to understand the structure of goods production and how costs will differ for different levels of pollution. Contrary to what most people might think, this is not an engineering question. Although it is easy to find out how much it would cost for a piece of equipment that is placed on a smokestack to reduce pollutants in the smoke (a "scrubber"), to an economist that is only the tip of the cost iceberg. Faced with the prospect of having to reduce pollution levels, the firm has many options. These include end-of-pipe treatment, modifying the production process, modifying the characteristics of the product, relocating the productive activity to reduce damage, and investing in research and development to find new ways of controlling pollution. Consumers can also reduce consumption of the polluting good. Thus characterizing costs at a conceptual level, as well as measuring these costs empirically, is a complex question without easy answers. It is also the domain of environmental economics.

Determining the right amount of pollution also involves determining damages from pollution. The words "damages from pollution" deceptively suggest that this is a natural science question, such as counting the dead fish on a polluted lake or determining the level of pollution at which people begin to get sick. This is an oversimplification of the multitude of ways pollution affects people and the relative seriousness of these effects to people. Air pollution in an urban area can cause physical irritation (itchy eyes, running nose), reduced visibility, degraded visibility (a brown pale), soiled clothes, decreased lung capacity, worry about adverse effects, increased susceptibility to illness, and of course illness itself. Some of these effects are tangible, others are very intangible. Economics is accustomed to condensing this variety of effects into a single measure—the willingness to pay to reduce pollution. If pollution is bad, people are willing to devote some of their resources to eliminating the pollution. Leaving side the fact that most people think the polluter should pay, one way of measuring the overall magnitude or importance of pollution reduction to a person is through his or her willingness to give up something valuable in exchange for improved personal environment quality. Measuring this willingness to pay is not easy and is the subject of much research in environmental economics.

Having characterized the importance of pollution reduction to individuals (their willingness to pay), it is possible to sum up individual preferences to obtain a societal willingness to pay to reduce pollution. It is then easy to combine this with the cost of pollution control to determine the socially optimal amount of pollution reduction. But how to obtain this? The government could tell each polluter how much to emit; but this would be analogous to central planning in the Soviet Union—we know it works up to a point but has severe problems, particularly when there are many firms and polluters involved. It is difficult to determine the best way for the government to intervene in the economy ("regulate") to yield the right amount to pollution control without excessive administrative costs or control costs while at the same time providing the right incentives to undertake research to reduce costs for the future.

So, the "simple" job of fixing the problem of pollution is not so easy at the policy level and can involve hard-to-solve problems, many in the domain of environmental economics. The examples we have used are from developed economies but a very similar analysis could apply to a developing country. Air pollution is a big problem in many cities of the developing world. Water pollution is probably the most severe environmental problem in many developing countries: water contaminated by human waste kills millions of people annually. The same issues of costs, demand for clean-up, and how to regulate apply equally to this question.

Another important type of policy question is the preservation of natural environments, broadly defined. This could involve preserving wild and scenic areas from development or protecting animal and plant species from extinction. Here the primary issue is providing balance between the forces of development that threaten these environmental resources and the social value of preservation. How can both sides of this equation be quantified to help policymakers when they are confronted with very specific decisions (such as whether to allow logging in a virgin forest)?

These examples could go on and on. The point is that environmental protection usually involves the intervention of governments in the economy and it is often difficult to decide on the proper extent and nature of that intervention. Environmental economics as it is applied to real environmental problems can be invaluable in helping make those important decisions.

Environmental Economics and Ecological Economics

This book is concerned with environmental economics. There is another discipline that largely has grown out of systems ecology called "ecological economics." These two fields take quite different perspectives, but are ultimately concerned with helping make social decisions about environmental problems. Unfortunately, in many non-English speaking countries the distinction between the two fields is lost in the translation because of the similarities between the words "environmental" and "ecological."

A simple distinction between the two fields arises from the fact that environmental economics tends to involve economists who have extended their discipline and paradigm to consider the environment, whereas ecological economics tends to involve ecologists who have extended their discipline and paradigm to consider humans and the economy. But this is history; the appropriate question to ask is how do the two fields approach environmental problems and how do they differ?

Ecological economics (as well as conventional economics) is difficult to succinctly define. One of the leading ecological economists defines the subject as a "field of study that addresses the relationships between ecosystems and economic systems in the broadest sense." The emphasis is on the very long-term health of the ecosystem, broadly defined (i.e., with humans as part of it).

One major distinction between the two fields is associated with value and thus the way in which social decisions are made that depend on measures of value of the environment. Conventional economists believe that value to society derives from the individual values held by human members of society. Ecological economists lake a more biophysical view of value. For instance, some ecological economists measure value in terms of embodied energy content. Thus in comparing a typewriter to a computer, the appropriate question is which took more energy to create? Less energy is better. This is a direct extension of ecological theories that ecosystems operate to minimize the throughput of energy. To these researchers, minimizing the energy content of delivered goods and services should drive public policy. The criticism levelled at this "energy theory of value" by environmental economists is that there are many resources in short supply, including land and skilled people. Reducing the value of a good to the embodied content of any factor is an oversimplification. Environmental economists believe the value of a good stems from its embodied content of multiple scarce factors (including energy) as well as how much value individual people place on the final good. In other words, value cannot be reduced to a simple physical metric.

However, the greatest distinction between the fields emerges when considering environmental problems with very long-time horizons, such as global warming or disposal of nuclear wastes. As some environmental economists will readily admit. Economics has a difficult time analyzing problems in which costs and benefits span long time horizons. For instance, storing nuclear wastes can involve potential risks that extend for a quarter of a million years. The benefits of the storage are reaped by the present consumers of nuclear power; the costs, if any, are borne by future generations that must live with the nuclear repositories. The conventional economic approach to this is to add up all of the costs and benefits, whenever they may occur, but to apply a discount factor to reduce the importance of future costs in the sum. Inevitably, this means that what happens a century from now has very little effect on the decisions that are made today. To many people, this is disquieting. Ecological economists have proposed other ways of dealing with the inter temporal decision problem, particularly the notion of sustainability. They argue that we should never undertake any action that is not sustainable in the long run. In the nuclear waste example, they would ask: Can we continue to bury waste forever and ever and be satisfied with the world that results? If the answer is no, then the action is not sustainable. It is not a matter of balancing costs and benefits. There is some intuitive appeal to such a philosophy.

To a large extent, the problem of making decisions over the very long run will not arise in this book. For the most part we are concerned with static issues. Questions of long-run trade-offs and dynamics are the purview of resource economics, to which we now turn.

Environmental Economics and Resource Economics

Nearly all textbooks combine the treatment of environmental and resource economics. In fact, most graduate programs that have a specialization in the area combine environmental and resource economics into one field. Undoubtedly this is because both concern the natural world. Environmental economics involves questions of excessive production of pollution by the market or insufficient protection of the natural world, due to market failure. Resource economics, on the other hand, is concerned with the production and use of natural resources, both renewable and exhaustible. Renewable resources would include fisheries and forests. Nonrenewable would include minerals and energy as well as natural assets such as the Alps and species of plants and animals.

So we see the distinction between the two areas but we also see the overlap. Typically, environmental economies is concerned with static questions of resource allocation. Time is not really an are guided by the efficiency and mental abilities of neighbours. In this sense some areas offer little resources for human use while others do in abundance. As for example, the tribal people of Kerala, Tamilnadu, Manipur, Assam, Jharkhand and Bihar still lead a primitive life because the topography is rugged, the climate is unsuitable for raising and forest gathering. In such an environment people spend much of their time and energy to satisfy a few primitive wants such as food, shelter, fuel, implements and personal adornment. In such an extreme environment inhabitants have little choice in the selection functional activities. On the other hand, the people of Karnataka and Tamilnadu have multitudinous occupations, good accessibility of roads, railways, waterways and airways. The industrial development, location of educational and social institutions, administrative establishment, medical facilities, etc. have given rise to dense population per hectare of land in comparison with Andhra Pradesh and Orissa of South India.

The strength of any nation, whether it be social, economic or political, depends mostly on the resources available at command and their proper utilisation. The evolution of civilisation centres command their spectacular growth in the field of social, economic, cultural and political advancements. History bears testimony to the fact that ancient civilisations flourished because they utilised available water resources; and wherever the growth of civilisations has been slow it has been in areas with less potentialities using the resource and these areas come under the category of under developed countries. It is clear that the capacity of tapping the resources must be developed for the advancement of a country.

Today there is a race among the underdeveloped countries as to how to make the best use of resources at their command to keep the pace of growing necessities set by the growing population and unemployment. Unless these two major problems are solved properly, they will sap the vitality of the nation: and scientists and technologists of the world over must find out ways and means to combat the crucial problems being faced by the underdeveloped countries and must try to make them at par with the developed countries.

It is clear a heavy responsibility lies on the scientists and technologists to uplift the underdeveloped countries by teaching them how to exploit the natural resources and make the best utilisation for the development of the country. The scientists by virtue of their various discoveries must direct the world to foster brotherhood and live in harmony.

The point is that we have not attached importance to the economic-geography of resources in the university curricula. We do not realize that the planning of natural resources cannot be determined without a systematic introduction to the subject. We must know about our natural resources and thereby develop the art of their proper utilisation. This is necessary as the economic development of various nations saturation point and some positive work in this field is most necessary for the survival of the human race. The purpose of this chapter is to shed light on some recent advancement in the concept of resources in introducing the whole book.

Scope of Resources

According to Jones and Darkenwald, resource geography deals with "the productive occupations and attempts to explain why certain regions are outstanding in the production and exportation of various articles and why other are significant in the importation and utilisation of these thing."

The demand for any item used by man is known as resources. In this sense anything in itself is not a resource but the need of such thing for a man makes them resources. In this way, an item as resource if in a certain time and space man has developed technological, cultural and physical abilities to use it. This shows the close relationship between the abilities of man and the resourcefulness of an item.

Generally hunting, fishing, forest gathering, industry, trade, minerals, water, land and soils are known as resources. But all these are the items which supply food, clothes, shelter, fuel, tools, materials of industries and luxuries as the physical base of natural environment, hence all these are known as resource. Besides these, the demand for environmental goods as well as empirical methods for doing so.

There is another set of issues surrounding regulation of environmental goods. The basic problem is that economic incentives need significant refining before they can be relied on to solve many real environmental problems. These difficulties have to do with incentives, different amounts of information possessed by polluters and the government, and the role of technological change in determining future levels of pollution control. This work takes place at various levels, including institutional design, determining empirical properties of different regulatory mechanisms, and theoretical issues of regulatory design.

There are a number of international issues of environmental regulation that are not fully resolved. One major problem is in understanding how environmental regulations interact with trade restrictions (or lack thereof). Are differential environmental regulations compatible with free trade? Can environmental regulations be used effectively as barriers to trade? Does free trade tend to exploit the environments of developing countries due to their less well-developed institutions for environmental protection?

These few paragraphs are meant to suggest the menu of research questions that is being examined by environmental economists. As we travel through the book, it is my sincere hope that the reader identifies other interesting problems for further exploration.

SUGGESTED READINGS

Asthana, D.K. and Meera Asthana, Enviornment Problems and Solution, S. Chand.

Bharucha, Erach, Environmental Studies, University Grants Commission, Universities Press.

Kosstad, Charles D., Environmental Economics, Oxford University Press.

Purohit, S.S. and R. Ranjan, Ecology, Environment and Pollution, Agrobios (India).

3

Economics of Natural Resources

Definition

The sum of all physical, chemical, biological and social factors which compose the surroundings of man is referred to as environment and each element of these surroundings constitutes a resources on which man draws in order to develop a better life. Thus, any part of our natural environment—such as land, water, air minerals, forest, rangeland, wildlife, fish or even human population—that man can utilize to promote his welfare may be regarded as natural resource.

Ramdade (1984) defined a resource as a form of energy and/or matter which is essential for the functioning of organisms, populations and ecosystems. In the particular case of humans, a resource in his words is any form of energy or matter essential for the fulfilment of physiological, socio-economic, and cultural needs both at the individual level and that of the community.

The functioning of ecosystem or of technological civilization involves a continuous flow and consumption of energy sun being the source of it as regards ecosystem and fuels as regards technological civilization. In the light of this fact, a resource may be defined as one of the various forms of primary energy present in the nature.

The five basic ecological variables—energy, matter, space, time and diversity are sometimes combined called natural resource. As such, laws which govern changes in these quantities have great applicability in the resource use.

In resource study the factors of natural environment control the number, energy and abilities of inhabitants. Functional activities issue in deciding on the right amount of air pollution in London. Resource economics on the other hand is concerned with dynamics. Time is what makes renewable and exhaustible resource questions interesting. If we log a forest slowly enough, the forest can regenerate itself and we can continue logging indefinitely. Flow fast we extract an exhaustible resource will determine its scarcity in the future, and thus its price in the future. In both of these cases, market failure is not the essence of the problem (though poorly functioning markets can be important).

There are overlaps between environmental and resource economics. Global warming is an example of a pollution problem with a very long little frame. There are other overlaps, primarily in the preservation of natural environments. These issues involve time so they could be relegated to resource economics. On the other hand, damage to natural environments is often the incidental result of economic activity with a different primary purpose. Species loss is usually the result of conversion of habitat to human use.

Perhaps the best division between environmental and resource economics is between static issues related to the natural world and dynamic issues. For the most part this book concern problems in resource and environmental economics that are static. Typically, we are concerned with pollution.

Positive *versus* Normative Perspectives

There are two fundamental uses of economics. One is to try to explain what we see in the economy around us. Another is to try to explain how we would wish the economy to allocate and distribute goods and services. The terms positive and normative are used to distinguish these two perspectives. Positive economics is more value free, aiming to explain why markets and institutions have evolved as they have and how they work. Examples are understanding why the price of gasoline increases when OPEC meets to restrict output and how the spatial distribution of pollution emissions changes when a marketable permit system is established to regulate sulfur emissions.

Normative economics, on the other hand, attempts to use economic tools to design government policies to intervene in the marketplace. Inevitably the question arises as to the "best" way of intervening in the marketplace. Clearly, this requires away of defining what is best—a much more value—laden process than merely explaining why the economy works as it does.

Unfortunately, when working with environmental problems it is not possible to restrict attention solely to positive economics. Fundamental to environmental economics is the notion of market failure. Repairing that market failure typically requires government intervention. What kind of government intervention. That is a normative question. And that is often the question that environmental economists are asked to help answer. In developing the normative theory of regulation to correct market failure or the public provision of non-market goods, we will try to make clear when value judgments enter the process of policy formulation. The practicing environmental economist should always be aware of the problems of venturing into the territory of normative analysis.

Important Issues in Environmental Economics

This is truly an exciting time in the field of environmental economics. There are relatively few economists who call themselves environmental economists while there are many basic problems that need addressing. We will suggest a few here.

One of the most important contributions of environmental economics to economics generally has been in the area of measuring the demand for non-market goods. Measuring this demand has become central to many public debates over environmental quality. However, some methods for measuring demand have been the subject of great controversy. Stated preference methods involve directly asking people how they value the environment. Such methods have come under strenuous attack by some as at best biased and at worst vacuous. Others argue they are valid and of tremendous importance. A very active area of current research is the theory underlying methods for measuring other items which have an indirect influence in obtaining the resources are health, wants, knowledge, social adjustment, political stability, economic prosperity, national organisation and international cooperation, etc. are also known as resources Commonly coal, iron, gold and silver are known as resources but the same serve the purpose of a man with the advancement of technological knowledge only, without which the resourcefulness of gold or silver cannot be estimated. The value attached to them in terms of capital, marketing, technological knowledge, source of transport and favourable social, economic and political environment makes them resources.

To understand the resourcefulness of a thing, one has to understand the knowledge, habit and external and internal technological knowledge of persons including neutral stuff. There are two forces in physical environment: one is the natural element and other is the natural resistant force. The latter is generally harmful for the development of a nation. In this way, the progress of an economic landscape is determined by the above forces. Primitive people were surrounded by the neutral stuff of physical environment which has no direct influence on man. People in those days tried to fill their belly just like animals; and they had no courage to face the struggle actively. Such conditions are known as the passive adaptation of man which is just like the animal character of the present world.

Primarily the landscape was covered with forests but slowly with the occupation of land, exchange of little surplus with the neighbours and the growth of resources developed with the commercial activities of men. As for example, most of the early civilizations, viz., Egyptian and Mesopotamian in the old world and the Aztec, Melan and Incan in the new world have developed with the growth of subsistence agriculture. In early civilization the impetus for advancement came from European countries by occupying the professions of fishing, tending animals, tilling land, manufacturing, trading etc. With the decline of commercial powers of the Mediterranean, Phoenician, Cretan, Gressian, Carthaginian and Roman (from a. D.1096 to 1270) revived the resource development in most of the American, African and Asian countries of the world.

The resources are dynamic in nature, as for example, many years ago coal was regarded as a blackstone. But nowadays, with the technical advancement of man, coal is regarded as an essential element of the present civilizations. Thus man has developed his technical abilities with the adaptation of nature in comparison with animals and the same is known as the "active adaptation of nature" for the growth of nations. In a natural environment according to the activities of men, the forest clearings give rise to permanent agriculture and in place of wild animals, domestic livestock are reared slowly. Later on fields and settlements developed.

According to Zimmerman and Michell, the knowledge of man is the greatest resource because the elements of physical environment have developed different cultural characteristics such as multifarious knowledge, love, social urbanisation and political organisation, etc. which help in determining an item as resource. The limitation and barrier of human abilities cannot generate energy in itself and the same cannot restore resources. This is because the technical and cultural abilities of man are dynamic which have changed the use of resource in different manner. According to Bowman, the geographical elements of environment are static but with the contact of man the characteristics of those elements have changed like cultural elements. In this way so far as the dynamic relationships of resource and cultural functions are concerned, there is no resource in itself but the same have been made by man as resource. Due to this fact the economic landscape to different nations are different in time and space which ultimately determines the potentialities of consumption and cultural advancement of the societies. Even in a country with the technical abilities of men and physical environment, the concept of resources is changing as for example the resources which are sufficient in peace time are not sufficient for a period of war.

The world's dynamic in its internal structure and so the age-old social, economic and political institutions must change with the advancement of age and time. The factors which once guided

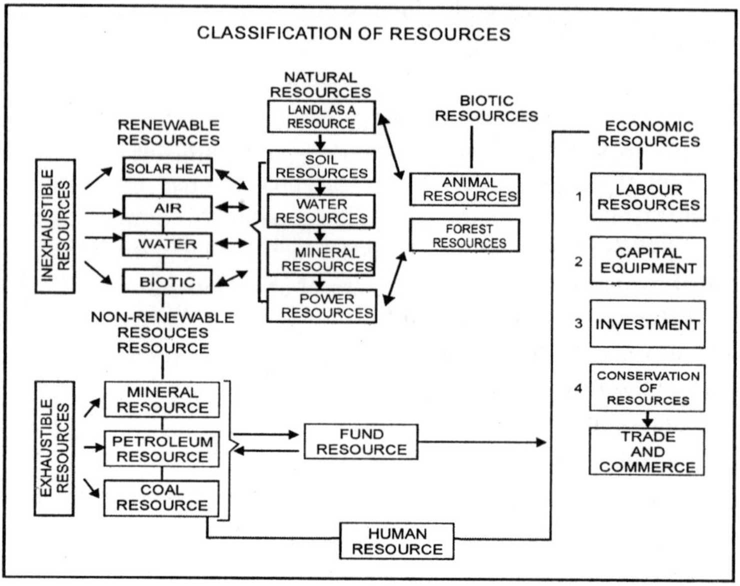

Fig. 3.2: Schematic Representation of Classification of Resources

Human resources can be considered into two ways—first by a study of the actual quantity of the population and then by a study of the qualities of this population. A quantitative assessment would include the total population; the distribution, density, age group, sex-structure, class structure and the actual percentage of working population. A qualitative assessment would include consideration of personality, education, skills, enterprise and ethical values, all of which can affect the economic development of a country to a certain extent.

The classification of natural resources has been attempted by Renner to formulate a conservational programme. Natural resources fall into two major categories: (a) those, which are inexhaustible, and (b) those, which are exhaustible. Fig. shows the distinct components of resources.

(i) *Inexhaustible Resources*: they include the occur water, solar heat, air and biotic.

(ii) *Inexhaustible but maintainable resources*: they include land, soil ground water, mineral and power resources.

(iii) *Inexhaustible but non-reasonable resources*: they include animal life, forest, labour resources etc.

(iv) *Exhaustible resources*: they include, mineral, petroleum and coal resources.

Wantrup uses a system of classification of natural resources (Table 3.1). which is similar to the foregoing in some respects, but differs significantly from it in other ways. While his major breakdown is closely related, his secondary breakdown for the stock resources or fund resources is on the basis of absence or presence of natural deterioration, and for the flow resources is inability or ability of human action to affect the resources. Still other classification are possible; the problem is not simple, and different considerations many loom larger in the minds of some students than in those of others.

Table 3.1: Wantrup's Classification of Natural Resources

1. *Non-Renewable or Stock Resources*
   - (i) Stock not significantly affected by natural deterioration: meal ores in situ, coal, stones, clays,
   - (ii) Stock significantly affected by natural deterioration: refined metals subject to oxidations, oil and gas in case of seepage and blow off, plant nutrients subject to leaching radioactive substance in process of nuclear disintegration, surface water reservoirs subject to evaporation.

2. *Renewals of Flow Resources*
   - (i) Flow not significantly affected by human action: solar and other cosmic radiation, tides, winds.
   - (ii) Flow significantly affected by human action:
     - (a) Reversibility of a decrease in flow not characterized by a critical zone: precipitation, special locations that form the basis of site value, services from a species of durable producer of consumer goods.
     - (b) Reversibility of a decrease in flow characterized by a critical zone, animal and plant species, science resources storage capacity of groundwater basins.

Source: S. V. Ciriacy-Wantrup, Resource Conservation Economics and Policies (rev.ed.: Barkely University of California Press, 1963).

inability to generate the powerful forces of modernisation. The central focus of this complex problem is that unless there is more for mass participations in the cause of advancement, there could be no prospect of rapid progress along a wide front.

Classification

The classic subdivisions of resource include renewal and non-renewable resources. Renewable resources are those, which are reproducible and are obtained from the biomass of living organism, e.g. forests and fish. Resources which are not reproducible and are obtained from the finite non-living reserve are called non-renewable resources e.g. coal and metals. Solar energy although having a finite life, as a special case is considered as renewable resources in an much as solar 'stocks' are inexhaustible on the human scale.

Some authors prefer to classify resources, into biotic (or living) and a biotic (or-non-living) resources, forest, agriculture, fish and wildlife failing in the first category and land, water minerals etc. in the second.

A broader classification of resources, as proposed by Owen (1971), is represented.

Quantity, mutability and reusability are the attributes on which this classification is based. Inexhaustible and exhaustible are main categories of resources based on their stocks in nature. Inexhaustible resources are further divided into two groups. Immutable and mutable resources, depending upon the possibility of their qualitative degradation as a result of man's activity. On the other hand, exhaustible resources, being limited in occurrence, are vulnerable to both quantitative and qualitative degradation. Thus their availability depends upon the method of use, so these are classed into maintainable and non-maintainable resources. Supply of maintainable resources could be made to last for long through wise use, however, some of them have capacity to reproduce called renewable, while other cannot reproduce-called non-renewable resources. Non-maintainable resources have static supply and when destroyed or consumptively used are irreplaceable, yet some of them have potentiality for reuse-called reusable resources, and rest whose permanent exhaustion certain are called non-reusable resources.

Natural Resources

Inexhaustible
Unlimited or un-ending.
Quality may be degraded, not quantity.

Exhaustible
Limited both qualitative and
quantitative degradation possible

Immutable
Quality not degraded by men's activity e.g.,
atomic wind power precipitation,
tidal power of running waters.

Mutable (Mis-usable)
Quality may be degraded man's activity
energy e.g., solar radiation,
water, hydropower

Maintainable
Availability depends upon
method of use by man.

Nonmaintainable
Total quantity static, when
consumptively used, not replaced.

Renewable
Perpetual harvest possible fertility of soil:
bio-products of land fresh
water and sea:haum power.

Nonrenewable
Once gone, no replace-e.g.,
Emnt e.g., species of wildlife

Reusable
Consumptive use small. e.g., gems,
onconsumptively used metals like gold,
platinum, silver, iron copper, zinc.

Nonreusable
Consumptive use high, e.g. fossil fuel:
non-metallic minerals like gypsum, sand,
salt: consumptively used metals like
lead in gasoline and paints, zinc in galvanized iron,
Tin in toothpast containers.

Fig. 3.1: Schematic representation of classification of natural resources.

lassifications of Resources

asically, resources can be divided into two types—(i) Natural esources; and (ii) Human Resources. All the materials, elements d forces of the natural environmental which man adopts to his on ends are called natural resources. Natural resources include nd, soil, water mineral, power forest and animal life.

the development and utilisation of resource now find themselves incapable of ushering in a golden era, and they are now considered to be outdated. For instance, the yield which is produced with old techniques of production to cater the needs of the people now cannot keep pace with the time as there has been a tremendous growth in population and therefore, yields must be treble by using good manure and with the introduction of new crops alongwith modern scientific methods, otherwise we will hardly by able to feed the hungry mouths and to cater the needs of the people. A change in the old order or society is a prerequisite for a more efficient and higher utilisation of resources at a place which will provide proper solution to the fast multiplying problems.

The underdeveloped countries produce a large quantity of the world's raw materials yet they control an insignificant fraction of international trade in finished goods because their resources are being exploited by the market mechanism of the advanced countries. The underdeveloped countries have to face many knotty problems such as illiteracy, limited capital, underdeveloped industry and a primitive agriculture system. Even with limited resource at our disposal there has been a tremendous development after independence in India which managed to steer the ship out of the rough water. India has managed to go ahead with the development strategies with limited resources at its disposal. Poverty stands in the way but it does not hamper progress.

It is most striking to note that the developed countries, over utilised the natural resources and this has had an adverse effect on the underdeveloped countries. On the other hand, the under utilisation of natural resources has kept the Indian economy in abject poverty. This unbalanced exploitation of natural resources may cause immense damage to the quality of human life and the life supporting system of ecology. In case the present trends of industrial and agricultural production, population growth and exploitation of nonrenewable natural resources continue, this would cause immense damage to the earth's carrying capacity of human beings. The oil crisis also continues to be a sore problem in the economic affairs in most of the underdeveloped nations. The crisis of oil may diminish the rate of production of their natural resources.

The value of oil production and prices has added new dimensions to resource development. The prices of raw materials in the international market have been artificially fixed at a lower level, whereas price of finished goods have been inflated to suit the convenience of the developed countries. The prices in most cases do not give the true economic value of the products. After all, self-reliance is the goal of the underdeveloped countries and a rational policy of international trade can help to remove the obstacle in the way of development.

The responsibility for jointly safeguarding the natural resources would rest with the developing countries. This is the only way to eradicate poverty and its consequences.

India represents the paradox of poverty in the land of plenty. The reason is not far to seek. We have not been able to utilise our resources in an orderly manner. There are so many complex problems facing the Indian sub-continent like housing, medical facilities and per capita consumption of food, clothing, energy supply, minerals and other natural resources. The per capita income is very low.

We have not yet gone through the process of raising production in fields and factories to banish poverty from the land of plenty. We have not utilised modern techniques to raise production. We are still using the age-old methods in spite of the fact that if we do not use the modern techniques we cannot feed everyone. The population is a baffling one. It has to be checked by using scientific methods. The illiterate masses must be taught that they have no moral right to increase the number of family members without finding resources for their proper maintenance. Illiteracy is the major cause which stands in the way of the progress of a country. It has to the fought at the war level and if we want to raise the status of the country, illiteracy has to be banished.

Lack of education, inadequate health care and the presence of irrational attitude towards the toiling masses and traditional social institutions are detrimental to the planned development. All these have threatened to thwart the forces of modernisation. Absence of knowledge about development, utilisation and conservation of our natural resources are the root-cause of our

In any event, such classifications while logical and helpful in many ways, generally do not fit any particular beyond the reversible zone, sometime within it. At the same time, these plant associations had the characteristics of flow resources, in the sense that important quantities of plant materials could be removed annually or at other intervals, and yet leave the basic resource fully capable of rejuvenation.

Physical environment is an integrated and composite unit of different materials and biotic resources which have formed different niches in space and time. Thus resources which have formed different niches in space and time are dynamic in availability and use and their presence help directly in the activities of natural environment as a necessary part and parcel of geographical locations, size, accessibility, climate, landscape, features, soil, water, mineral resources, vegetation, livestock and birds including human resources.

Resources and Culture

The culture of a man is the product of his physical environment and mental abilities and the increase of these two have given rise to the cultural advancement of a landscape. According to Karl Sauer, man's deformation of the pristine is assumed as essential. In a real sense cultural landscape is the result of dynamic and deformation of cultural abilities. In this way, culture in itself is the greatest influencing resource of a man. The table of other resources is also changing in time and space according to the cultural attainment which determines the intensity of the usefulness of an item as resource. In order to show the functional importance of this cultural hypothesis, Paul Seers has developed a formula of the physical resource of environment as land/population culture. According to this formula the base of resource is divided by population in a country which is the effect of a cultural landscape. As for example for primitive people coal, petroleum and other minerals are not regarded as resources but for a well-to-do person the same many be a resource.

Industrial Resources

Physical environment is a great source of human living which becomes the base for cultural advancement and the growth of industrial civilisations. On this basis three aspects have highly influenced resource development, such as: (1) technology, (2) social organisation, and (3) the knowledge of inhabitant. In any space and time, and level of industry fully depends on those natural resources which are utilised by the industry. Industries themselves are the product of the cultural landscape and the analysis of specific resources cannot be made keeping out of the cultural make-up of societies. The greater availability of resources, renewability and exploitability, etc. are the result of developed industrialisation. Underdeveloped, uncultured human society receives less resources from the physical environment; for example, petroleum was not known to primitive people as fuel oil but nowadays it is an essential commodity. In this way, the societies which have advanced in industrialisation are great source of the resource base (Figure 3.1)

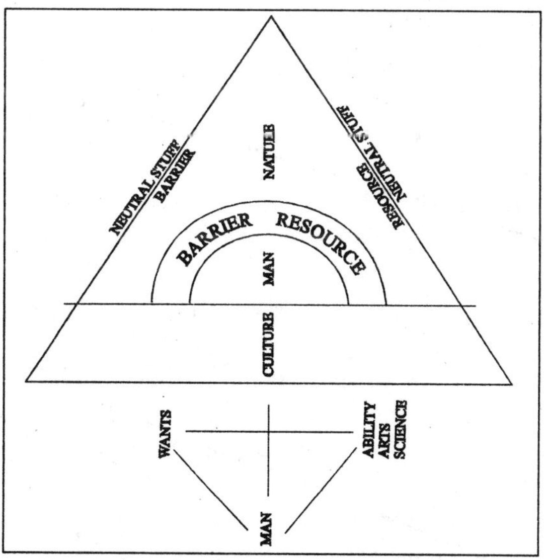

(AFTER-ZIMMERMAN)

Fig. 3.3: Mobilization of Resources

In any region the question of the availability of resources depends on the technological advancement and the amount of resources available in that region. As for example, an area having hundred square kilometers may be an area of under population if the fertility of soil and the productien of crops are better in relation to the inhabiting population. Secondly, if the production of crops in that area is equal to the demand made by the people then it is said that area is under optimum population. Thirdly, if an area has a higher number of people in relation to its productive capacity then it is said that the area is over populated. Fourthly, if the pace of population growth is rapidly increasing in comparison with the growth of production then it is said that the area is under population explosion.

Malthus has studied the relationship between population and resources at the end of nineteenth century and he used the terms "the means of subsistence" in lieu of resources. According to him, in any region population growth is always higher than resources. He suggested that the geometrical progression of population growth takes place in case "the means of subsistence" increase in arithmetical progression. In such a situation malnutrition will automatically bring famine conditions to the region.

In order to show the relationship between population and resources, E. A. Ackerman has classified the whole world into five groups:

(i) The United States Type; developed technology, a case of under population.
(ii) The European Type; developed technology, a case of over population.
(iii) The China or Egypt Type; less developed technology, a case of over population.
(iv) The Brazil Type; less developed technology, a case of under population.
(v) The Arctic Desert Type; less developed technology, a case of intensive over population.

Resources are scarce in nature. Nowhere in this world, the desired level of resource development is possible unless a contentment prevails among the people for the fulfilment of their desires. Wants are unlimited and it is practically impossible to fulfil the desire of all persons at the same time. In areas where the growth of industry, agriculture, urban expansion and accumulation of capital, mineral wealth takes place, it is said that the growth of civilization has reached its peak, e.g., the areas of the Eastern Sea Board of North America. On the other hand, the forested rugged terrain, unfavourable climatic conditions of heavy rains and hot weather in the equatorial belt of the world bears some vulnerable diseases which makes the environment uninhabitable for human beings and as such this belt is the areas of under development from the point of view to resource development.

With the advancement of scientific knowledge, the dimensions of resources are increasing, as now-a-days, the search for tidal power, solar energy, thermal power, atomic energy, are fast changing the scene of resource development. Now the training in agricultural practices is given on the television. The use of the tractor, combine harvester, thresher, and the use of chemical fertilizers in the fields as well as the use of new dwarf varieties of seeds including the growth of agricultural resources beyond imagination. In some areas it is felt that the green revolution has taken place in the cultivation of wheat, rice and maize especially in northern India. Similarly, material culture has also changed because of the change of food habits, clothing, advancement of technical abilities; and the old practices of cultivation through plough and oxen are not altered with the modern method of cultivation through scientific implements and the use of dwarf varieties of seeds, the use of synthetic fibers in place of traditional cotton cloth.

Natural Resources

This is the combination of elements available in nature. Keeping this in mind any element, creature, oxygen, nitrogen, rocks, minerals, landscape, soil, water, vegetation, livestock, etc. are regarded as resources due to their usefulness to man. The combination of a number of natural resources sometimes forms a composite resource as for example agricultural land, forest landscape, mining, etc. The agricultural landscape is the integrated form of land, soil, temperature, rainfall, etc. In this way, different elements and creatures of natural environment form resources both separately and in an integrated manner.

Human Resources

Man as the creator, producer and consumer of natural resources, is a great resource in himself. Natural environment in itself is a dynamic element but without human use it has no importance. In this way, the activeness of man is necessary in order to procure benefit from the unseen resources of nature. The activeness of man is dependent on three things:

(a) Biological hereditary which includes race, physiological behaviour etc.
(b) Social, economic, cultural and political organisations which are acquired and adapted through organisational systems and traditional customs in different time and space as dynamic elements. In this sense living conditions. Level of education, personal and family affairs, occupations and service position, social and economic status, citizenship and the consciousness of nationality, time, region, etc. are dynamic elements which affect population migration; and density, numbers, and behaviour is international relations which in turn, are important factors to affect the use of resources. This can be divided on the basis of several factors in which the following three are important:

    (i) The influence of physical characteristics on natural resources;
    (ii) The influence of cultural factors on resources; and
    (iii) An integrated influence of natural and cultural elements.

The influence of physical characteristics on natural resources includes:

(1) The total resource base and its influence;
(2) The variability of the base of resources;
(3) The characteristics and amount of each resource element;
(4) The inter-relationship amongst different resource elements; and
(5) The locational attributes of resources.

In any space and time the base of human culture is the product of natural resources. The regions which have the greatest endowment of natural resources are the areas of highest technological advancement. Similarly, the availability of resources in greater amount will help in economic development. Recently, in the trade and industrial economic landscape, due to heavy influx of people on food items, raw materials, agricultural land, forest, minerals, water, houses, sources of transport, sources of recreation are developing, keeping in view the demand. In countries like U.S.A., U.S.S.R., China, India and Brazil, the bases of natural resources are vast, and in these countries the economic attainments are also substantial. During the Second World War when international trade was almost stopped, the wheels of the economy of every nation mainly depended on the natural resources base. But in peace time for the countries which have greater potentialities of favourable climatic conditions soil, vegetation, livestock, birds and mineral wealth, the chances of prosperity are enough. In areas of single type of climate, the types of vegetations and crops grown are limited in number while in areas of temperate, sub-tropical and tropical climatic conditions, different types of crop and vegetables are available. Similarly, in a country where only coal is available, the chances of industrial development are less in comparison with the countries where different types of minerals, e.g., coal, petroleum, gas, iron and other minerals are available. With today's competitive economy, the demand for different resources is increasing according to the needs of the society (Figure 3.4). Due to high technological advancement, some items which are in demand these days, may not be so tomorrow or the demand may increase in place of the former.

The priority of resources is generally fixed by man. In any country, the total population, standard of living, wants of living, wants of society, fulfilment of demand of different resources, competitive demand, public opinion, political pressure, national and international political expediency, technological and scientific knowledge, availability of labour and capital resource ownership pattern, projects and legislation of the Government and the factors which are not equally distributed on the earth surface. Their amount, variety, frequency of occurrences are distributed in a haphazard manner. Keeping this in mind, Zimmerman has classified natural resources into four types:

(a) *Ubiquities*—available everywhere such as oxygen in the air;
(b) *Commonalities*—which are generally available in most of the regions as for example soils suitable for agriculture, water, etc.
(c) *Rartities*—those resources which are available rarely such as tin, gold, silver, etc.; and
(d) *Ubiquities*—which are available in a few places very rarely such as the business of cryolite of Greenland.

Zimmerman has classified resources into four groups keeping other ideals in mind such as (i) unused, (ii) unusable, (iii) potential, and (iv) latent.

Those elements, materials, attributes, location and site which have as yet not utilised is known as unused resources. According to present knowledge and a availability of other factors if any element or material is not utilised as resources then the same may be regarded as unusable resources. Those materials which have the chance to be utilised by man in the near future are known as potential resources. Those resources which have attributes of unusability but the same have not been utilised by man in the near future are known as potential resources. Those resources which have attributes of unusablity but the same have not been utilised are known as latent resources, such as solar energy and the availability of carbon dioxide (CO_2).

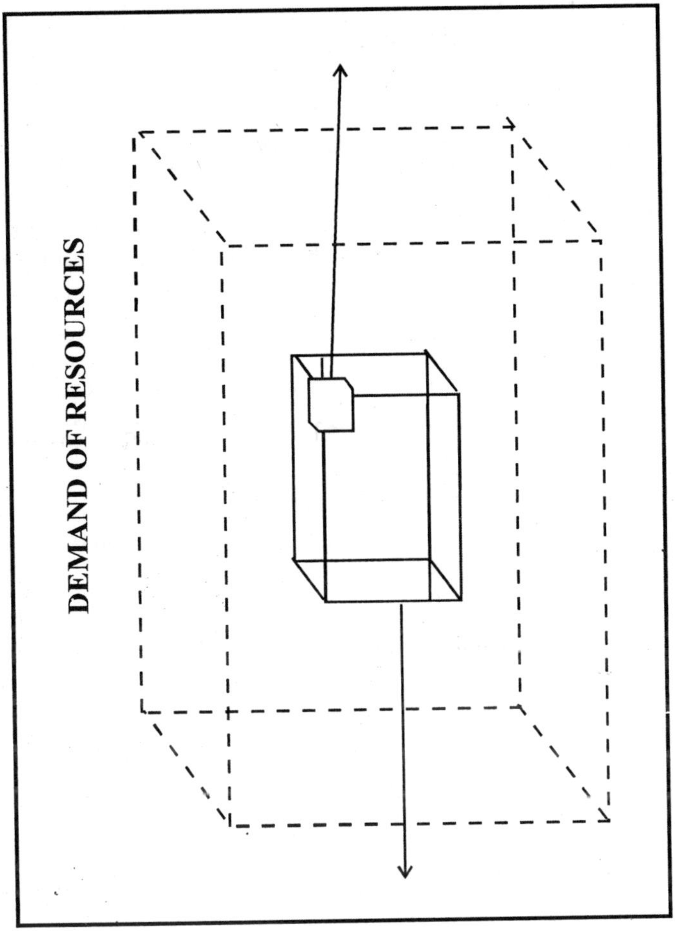

Fig. 3.4: Phantom Resources Theory (After Zimmerman)

Principle of Resource Adequacy

In any country the efficiency of resource is measured by the number of population, the desired level of consumption and the total population, etc. Population and their living standard determine the total demand of resource. Whether the demand on any level can be fulfilled or cannot be determined by human knowledge, technology and the available physical resource. Man is not only the gatherer of resources, he also uses the scarce resources scientifically, increases their production and tries to lessen the pressure of human beings on a particular piece of land with a view to avoiding scarcity of physical resources. During the last two decades the growth of population and the economic development have taken place simultaneously but in order to raise the standard of people, family planning has been introduced in India. In this way, it can be said that the relationship between physical resources and population is a dynamic process.

The coveriance analysis of these two variables has been presented by Ackerman in the form of an equation. Considering the demand and use of resources, the formula is as follows:

$$L = T + S + R \pm S_{ep} - T_r$$

Where, L = Living standard of population;

T = Total base of resource characteristics and attributes of natural and physical resources (physical technology factor, administrative technology factor, resource stability factor);

S = Scale of economies;

R = Resource added in trade;

S_{ep} = Social, economic and political institutions and their characteristics; and

T_r = Techniques of resource use.

Conservation of Natural Resources

The conservation of resources has attracted the mind of scholars mainly after the Second World War due to population explosion, technological industrial revolution and in order to fulfil the increased wants for a good living standard. During A. D. 1600 only a few minerals had been discovered such as clay, whetstone, millstone, iron ore, glass, tin, mica, salt, mercury, etc. But nowadays more than a hundred minerals have been discovered including petroleum, potash, nickel, aluminium, chromium, etc. In 1750 the total population of the world was only 66 crores but in 1978 this rose to about 400 crores. Hence, the resource requirements of these teeming millions also increases with the same rate.

A man can live in flexible manner in any environment which may be designated as an unspecialisation, but the evolutionary characteristics of human beings are of a different nature and the habitat and the scope of his activities are also not restricted. Man as a rational being, utilises the natural environment of the active ecological system. In such a manner that should be the dynamic elements of organic and inorganic world which sometimes used as resources, while at the other created barrier. In order to extract natural resources which have some economic value, a man determines the systems of organisation and space actively. The theory of the conservation of resources considers the base of physical balance of population and living standard of people which not only develop the present social, economic and political activities of man but also controls the future use of resources by less destruction, systematic utilisation and unexpectable exploitation.

The conservation of resources does not mean the use of resources either frugally or preservation. Conservation means the purposeful and planned use of resource and the protection of soil, forest and mineral resources from erosion and restoration. In this way, the conservation of resources always means the optimum use of resources which are intimately related with the population, living standard, technological advancement and cultural characteristics of the region which determines the productive capacity of resources also includes continuous, constant and sustained use of resources. However, the rational use of resources as when and how to use, allocation, depletion, wastage, state of optimum use, planned integrated production come under the conservation of resources.

For planning and conservation of resources the consideration of the following aspects are necessary:

(1) The consideration of a region as a unit is necessary so that the knowledge of total resource base and their types,

amount, characteristics and attributes of resources can be fully estimated for proper utilization.

(2) In any space and time after considering the present resource need, the supply of the resources on lower prices should be immediately stopped in order to prevent destruction and misuse.

(3) For the prosperity and production of resources, all possible methods of conservation must be adopted.

(4) Those resources which are insufficient in quantity or exhaustible should be scientifically used.

(5) Such resources should be invented which are not exhaustible or which may take a long time to exhaust such as solar energy in place of coal and petroleum.

(6) Resources complexes should be utilised in an integrated, balanced and in multiple ways.

(7) Keeping in view the amount and availability of resources the study of a social, economic and political relations are highly needed.

(8) By planning the national resources in a multitude of ways one should try to be self-reliant personally, regionally and socially.

(9) In resource planning full cooperation between the government, public and private institutions is necessary.

(10) The planning and conservation of resources are necessary in order to make the general people good citizens.

Resources Planning and Development

The objective of this study is to make plan for the better use of our resources. These could be rationality, planning for economic development, rise of productivity, rise of level of living, social and economic equalisation, improved institutions and attitudes, national self-reliance, social discipline and participation of people in the task of nation building and so on, although it is difficult to fulfil the desired goals of development planning. Hence it is in this direction that we have to reorient our thinking and plans of action. And as we approach the desired goals, the changed social order will, in turn, accelerate the rate at which resources can be utilised or conserved.

The type of resources which need conservation depend on the availability of other resources, the final demand for them and the level of technology. For example, coal can be utilized for the production of power, fuel and has a potential for conversion into oil and other chemicals. Yet, to meet the demand for power, we have to use our coal reserves for quite sometimes to come. But on account of its exhaustible nature, and its other uses, alternatives have to be found for the production of power. These could be through nuclear energy, or geothermal energy. And till a certain point of time, which we can call the threshold point, we must make the maximum use of our coal and after this point we must conserve our coal resource. The period between the present point of time and the threshold point is the time available to us for the development of alternative methods of power production which are not dependent on non-renewable natural resources. Other modes of conservation and efficient utilisation of resources could be through appropriate technological reforms, recycling of waste, matching of the objectives of organisations engaged in resource exploitation with the national objectives, reform of the social institutions and education of our people in new techniques of resource development and utilisation. In fact, survey, conservation and utilisation are three interlined aspects of resources which cannot be considered in isolation without running the risk of drawing wrong conclusions. Geological and geophysical surveys enable us to identify the available resources, their concentration and their geographical distribution. This combined with the knowledge of distribution of demand for these resources across the country can help us in working out the economics of their extraction, establishing the need for conservation and developing the technology for their optimum utilization. It may be prudent to develop the technology of extraction which simultaneously tackles the problem of utilisation and conservation of resources. This requires an integrated approach to resource planning. For, otherwise there is a risk of unintelligent over exploitation of resources as happened in the advanced countries, or under utilisation of resources as in the developing countries. Economic and social advancement left to "natural forces", is highly unlikely to follow the desired direction. On the contrary, we may end up in a crisis situation as happened during the oil crisis from which it may be difficult and costly to retrieve lost ground and which certainly will impede our advancement. The author has chosen certain specific resources vital to our national development and would like to identify the issues stemming from the broad spectrum of the resources in the order of their importance.

SUGGESTED READINGS

Malthus, T.R., A Summary view of the Principle of Population in Encyclopedia Britannica Supplement, 1824 revised and reprinted in 1990.

Sinha, U.P., Planned Development of Resource in a Developing Region IIP, New Delhi, 1985.

Wantrup, S.V., Resource Conservation and Policies, University of California Press, 1963.

Zimmerman, E.W., World Resources and Industries, Harper and Row, New York, 1961.

4

Environmental Management and Sustainable Development

Environmental management being a too vague, general, or trivial subject has not developed as a full-fledged discipline so far, further, in many developing countries it is viewed as being irrelevant and counter productive, while in advanced industrialized countries it is often interpreted as a means of coping with the 'burden' of environmental legislation and problems put forth by 'overzealous' environmentalists that to talk of underdeveloped world! The global population, however, cannot and should not overlook and deny the last deterioration of environmental world over resulting in dwindling natural resources, pollution of air, water and land, extermination of a number of life forms, down going health status, danger to cultural assets and many socioeconomic backlashes. The root of the problem lies in too many people using too many resources wastefully.

Since the total natural resources available are limited, the way out to the problem seems only through control of population and also the per capita consumption. Because it is difficult to bring down per capita consumption, the recycling and stringent conservation can bring hopes for sustained development without reducing per capita use of resources.

Land

Soil consists of the weathered layer of the earth's crust with living organisms and products of their decay intermingled. Lying on the rocky core of the earth, this complex mixture is one of the four prime requisites for life. Along with sunlight, air and water, soil supports all living beings on land, plants as well as animal. Altogether terrestrial plants have their roots in soil from which they absorb life sustaining water and nutrients. Man and all land animals, in turn, depend on these plants for food directly or indirectly. Foods vegetable oils and fats, forage for livestock, fiber, wood and various other indispensable agricultural products come from soil. Thus, a nations economic well-being is inextricable linked with the fertility and abundance of her soil resource because of mounting demands of swelling population and long mismanagement would put in jeopardy the very survival of man.

Land Use and Abuse

The land although appears to be an unlimited resource but, in fact, its injudicious use would limit the availability of this indispensable life-support system. Thus, a land use may be poor or good, if in a region of low rainfall grasslands are replaced by wheat crops, a temporary desert will eventually result; or if the human habitation and factories and developed on flood plains, the damage is almost inevitable. These are the instances of poor land use. Conversely, if the grasslands are used for moderate grazing by livestock, and it the flood plains are used for forestry or agriculture, these will imply good land use. Ecological principles have great applicability in land use planning. Classification of use should, therefore, be based on natural ecological features of the land in question viz, soil type, slope, biotic communities etc.

Rural Land-use Planning

To a farmer, soil is the essence of survival and his economic well-being is firmly linked with the fertility of his land. In rural land-use planning, concentration is chiefly devoted to creating and developing more farmland be removing forests an natural grasslands, drawing marshes and swamps, channeling streams for irrigation, and so on. Unfortunately, no effort is made to save existing prime farmland from degradation by ill-planned development. Rather than exclusive farm, range or forestry oriented planning, the land use should be made under broad consideration of social, economic, and ecological intricacies.

Urban Land-use Planning

Deterioration quality of urban suburban environment is to a great extent the result of injudicious land use and is a threat to have whole socio-economic system. Thus planned cities are as necessary as planned farms. Although, the implementation of land-use plan is infinitely more difficult in urban areas than in rural ones because of the human problem involved, yet if not heeded it would lead to chronic pollution, epidemic, and social disorder. In any urban land-use planning it should be seen that: (i) at least a third of all land remains as protective open space in the form of parks, green belts, or refuges etc. including adequate space for efficient treatment of domestic and industrial wastes; (ii) residential housing around villages or cities should be developed in cluster with each unit separated by broad green belts; (iii) typical topographic situation like stream valleys steep slopes and marshes etc. should be retained free from houses and other high-density uses; and (iv) waste disposal areas and industrial should be kept apart from human habitations.

Management of Land

From the above account it is clear that major problems emerging out of abuse of land in cities include unsafe and unhygienic dwelling and those in rural areas are of erosion of soil and loss of fertility. While urban problems can be prevented and cured by proper town planning and municipal facilities, the problems relating to rural areas needs long term soil conservation programme.

Prevention and control of soil erosion: The primary purpose of soil conservation is to prevent soil erosion and heal the damage where it has not advanced too far to respond to curative methods. This is possible largely through two means:

(1) The land should wear a vegetational cover throughout the year. Plant roots bind the top soil and prevent it from being drifted so easily with water or air. The vegetative cover also slows up runoff water and causes much of it to percolate into ground the promotes more vegetative growth. The vegetation-whether grasses, trees, or cultivated crops-should fit to the capabilities of the soil and water available.

(2) Engineering and agronomic practices should be applied conjointly to counteract the erosive force of both water and wind on the soil. These include contour cultivation, cover crops and crop rotation, and contour strip cropping, used alone or in combination with terracing where it is required. When terraces are properly constructed and adequately supported by approved cropping and tillage practices, they prove to be one of the most effective erosion-control measures applicable to cultivated sloping lands.

Reclamation of Eroded Lands: Conservationists divided into two camps over the issue of reclamation of land already arrested by ravines. One camp of conservationists and naturalists believes in the policy of "forgive and forget" and advocates that ravines should be allowed to exist, while the other feels that efforts should be made to regain the lost land through bulldozing or some other means. If the ravines are left in there present state, these will spread further and engulf more of productive land. While and violent means to regain the ravines in their near original condition may provoke numerous agencies of nature to take revenge on man. Thus, following consideration are important in negotiating the eroded land:

(i) Ravines should be provided with sufficient and suitable vegetative cover.

(ii) Instead of agriculture, these lands should be reclaimed for forestry, pasture, or horticulture.

(iii) Their deficiency in nutrients and moisture for plant growth should be improved.
(iv) Further misuse of such land should be prevented. Over-trampling by man and cattle should be avoided.
(v) Past damages should be repaired and recompensed understrict ecological consideration. For instance depressions may be filled up, slopes easend out, cattle, trials fenced etc.
(vi) Vegetative cover provided should be protected against reckless destruction by man local population.

Water

The origin of water on the earth is not clear so far. However, the current presumption is that the primordial earth had no oceans, and perhaps very little atmosphere. It is believed that the volatile constituents bound in the earths crust, oozing the surface through volcano's, rock movements, and hot springs, condensed to form the ocean and the atmosphere. This way, perhaps this remarkable combination to hydrogen and oxygen—called water, came into being and eventually became an indispensable component of the earth's environment.

Water moves from the ocean to air to land to ocean in set cyclic pattern called hydrological cycle. In other words, this cycle represents a continuous process of exchange of water from the earth's surface to the atmosphere and *vice versa* under the influence of solar heat.

It is estimated that of the total available water 97.3 per cent is contained in the oceans and out of remaining 2.7 per cent most is in solid form. The amount of water actually available in the atmosphere is a very minute fraction and estimated to be only 1×10^{-5} of the world's total water.

The factors which control the process of evaporation and evapotranspiration include temperature, humidity, and wind. It is a continuous process going on day and night from the ocean surface, ground surface inland waters (like lakes and streams), plant and animal surfaces. Rising in the atmosphere this water forms clouds that float around in gaseous or droplet form. The atmosphere above the earth up to varying heights of 10 to 17 km (depending upon latitude and season) is called the troposphere up to which the clouds float and which all weather changes take place. Water returns to the earth in the form of precipitation, most of which takes place over the ocean and a little on the land surface. Rainfall on the land surface may have following fates: it may percolate through the soil and become a part of ground water regime; accumulate in a pond, lake or reservoir as inland surface water; flow down to the ocean in the form of stream; taken up by plants and animals; or evaporate.

Water Requirements and Uses

Goethe rightly said, "Every thing originated in the water, and everything is sustained by water". Water is needed to fulfil diverse requirements in so many diverse ways. It is vital to life since for all physiological activities of plants and is essential for animals as well. On an average it constitutes 80 per cent of protoplasm ranging from 8 per cent in dry dormant seeds to 95 per cent jelly fish. It serves not only to quench the thirst but also to meet the food requirements because it is an essential raw material in the process of photosynthesis through which green plants make food that is used by all trophic levels directly or indirectly. Ambient humidity which is indeed the invisible form of water that surrounds us in necessary to prevent desiccation of terrestrial life forms. Thus, it can be said that water is a biologically essential and it serves as milieu internal as well as milieu internal.

Flood plain of rivers have been the cradle of civilization and centres of population since ancient times. The reason being their high fertility an easy accessibility to water for various uses like drinking, washing and transport. Egypt was developed on the flood plains of the Nile. Babylon on the flood plain of the Tigris: and North Indian on the flood plains of the Ganges. Even today the Mississippi plain is about the most densely populated area in the USA as flood plains of the Rhine in Europe, and the Yellow river in China.

Beside temperature, water is the other such key factor that influences the global ecology. Covering about 70 per cent of land surface and circulating in hydrologic cycle water influences weather and climate on any region and thus its flora and fauna.

Agriculture is dependent on water, may it be rainfall, or surface or ground water irrigation. It eventually is a more important commodity in a country like India because her largely agrarian economy depends critically or water. Huge amount of protein rich food in the form of fish shell fish, and prawn is obtained from the inland as well as very potent industry.

The kinetic energy of gravitational flow of water is tapped and transformed into electricity, what is called hydro power. This concept of electricity generation is one of the oldest and cheapest tricks largely used world over. Moreover, it leaves no pollution burden on nature as in case of thermal or nuclear power generation.

Hardly any industry can do without water. It has multifarious application in industrial processes *viz.,* a raw material, solvent, chemical reactant, coolant, and cleaning agent.

"Water, water every where not any drop to drink is the situation not only found amidst sea but also at places where industrial and domestic refuse make the benevolent water sources so severely contaminated with pathogens and or toxins that they are lift importable. Being the best dilution medium it is frequently used as the cheapest and convenient way for liquid and solid waste disposal. Further is was practically impossible to maintain sanitary conditions without water for it is needed in all common cleaning and washing practices.

Water at many places serves as a very convenient means of navigation. Besides, it adds to the aeshetic value of the landscape and provides opportunities for recreation and sport.

Water being unevenly distributed over the land, influences interstate and international relations and thus is the cause of what is known as hydro-politics.

It can, therefore, be said that while water is essential for life it is significantly linked with social, economic, political and ecological intricacies.

Problems and Management of Water

Management of water implies making the best use of available water resources for human benefit while not only preventing and controlling its depletion and degradation but also developing it in view of the present and future needs. Water, like forest, is a multipurpose resource and it is important to see that its various uses should not conflict with each other and it can be enjoyed in its totality by man and others. Thus, its right allocation, and quantitative and qualitative conservation are the primary tasks before water managers.

Flood, droughts, improper use, pollution and disease transmission are the important problems related to water. Because usable inland water resources constitute a very minute fraction of the world's total water and because man largely depends upon this minute fraction of water for his various activities, it is important to make efficient use of available water and at the same time prevent abuse of it. This has to be considered not only in giant irrigation projects or industrial and municipal processes but also in every day life. Taps running unpurposeful, leaking water supply pipes, using filtered water for gardens and building construction are a few instances of inefficient and misuse of water in daily life.

Water being the best and convenient dilution medium is the worst affected resource by pollution. To a common man pollution of water means only the drainage of industrial effluents or domestic sewage in natural waters. It may astonish a lay reader that even pure distilled water when released in sea may act as a pollutant since it alters the normal salinity of sea water which adversely affects the marine life. Besides chemical alterations changes in physical condition of water also have grave effects on the biota of system as during thermal pollution caused by the discharge of heated effluents in a body of water. Pathogens, chiefly entering natural water through municipal wastes rich in excreta and other organic filth, also render the water unsuitable for human use.

In fact, it is not only the man who has to use the water resources by these are equally important to land animals and more to those fish and other aquatic animals who live in it. Thus pollution of a body of water does prove detrimental not only to the human society but also to regional ecology and the ecology of very aquatic ecosystem. It is, therefore, essential that the water should not be treated as a simple repository of waste disposal, and if inevitable, the wastes only after proper treatment should be released in it under strict ecological consideration.

The qualitative degradation of water is also in a way quantitative depletion of usable resources. Therefore, recycling of waste water after due treatment would relieve the water scarcity to a great extent, especially in regions marred by water shortage.

Future Needs and Alternate Sources of Water

The demand for usable water like any other resource, is increasing fast with the continuous increase in world population and continuous increase in per capita demand linked with more of sewage disposal and transport prolific use of water-using gadgets (like air cooling and conditioning devices, washing machines etc.) and increased recreational activities. According to an estimate, the daily per capita demand for water of an American was 600 gallons in 1900 which increased to 1,500 gallons in 1960 and is expected to be increased upto 2,700 gallons by 2000. The fact is no different in developing world. Thus, the question is where will be water needed for fulfilling increasing demands come from? The answer is not so simple and can only be found through long term planning. Possible means of meeting out in the pending water deficit problem include: (i) reclamation of sewage and waste water, (ii) development of ground water sources and surface storages, (iii) long range forecasting of rain; (iv) rain making; (v) transfer of sulfur water, and (vi) desalination of sea water.

Agriculture

The practice through which specific plant species are cared and managed so as to obtain maximum yield of consumable parts of the plant is called agriculture. An agricultural field is, in fact, a cropland ecosystem in which ecological principles involving limiting factors and productivity provide great applicability.

The demand for food production, linked with tremendous population growth, has been increasing fast world over. This has been possible to feed increasing number of mouth through increased agricultural production what is called green revolution. It has resulted chiefly from the industrialization of agriculture, which involves highly domestic plant species, sophisticated chemicals, and large fuel energy subsidies. According to an estimate, to double crop yield through industrialized agriculture, a ten fold increase in fertilizers, pesticides and horse power is required.

The green revolution through industrialized agriculture (fuel powered) as compared to conventional agriculture (man-and domesticated-animal powered) has following backlashes;

(i) Such an agriculture involving huge amounts of fuel, and chemicals in the form of fertilizers, pesticides and we dicides, is the chief cause of environmental pollution.
(ii) It may lead to social backlashes when a quick shift from small farms to large industrialized farms takes place. In this process small farmers and agriculture workers are driven off the land to cities where they may not get work, food and housing—a situation of despair and social breakdown.

In retrospect, strong measures should be taken to control the population growth and to improve the conventional agricultural practice with application of current agricultural research under due social and environmental consideration. For a greater and sustained agricultural production following consideration are important:

(i) Available land acreage should be properly and judiciously utilized.
(ii) Soil fertility should be increased through wise use of fertilizers and organic manures.

(iii) High yielding and disease resistant plant varieties should be introduced.
(iv) Mixed cropping should be practicised wherever possible.
(v) Integrated and balanced used of available water sources, surface and ground water should be made.
(vi) Weeds and pests should be efficiently controlled. Integrated pest control practices should be preferred over total reliance on chemical pesticides.
(vii) Soil erosion and loss of nutrients should be prevented through maintaining vegetation cover throughout the year.
(viii) Exotic varieties should be introduced only after due consideration of long term impacts.

Forestry

A forest is a natural ecosystem having multi species and multi aged trees as dominant community. Forests cover about one-third of the earth's land surface of which about 50 per cent is occupied by tropical forest. Of the total geographical area of India 22.74 per cent is forest as against a minimum of 33 per cent forest cover prescribed under National Forest Policy.

Importance of Forest

Functions of a forest may broadly be classified into following three categories:

(i) *Protective functions*: These include the protective role of forest against soil erosion, droughts, floods intense radiation etc.
(ii) *Productive functions*: Forests are the source of wood and many other products like gums, resins, fibers, medicines, katha, honey, bidiwrappers, pulp, paper etc.
(iii) *Accessory functions*: These include the role of forests in recreation, aeshetics, and as habitate of diverge wildlife etc.

Thus, it can be said that forests are important in two ways—ecologically and economically.

Ecological Significance: Environmentally, the forests are very important. They help in balancing oxygen and carbon dioxide level in atmosphere, regulate earth's temperature regime and hydrologic cycle. Forests increase local precipitation and water holding capacity of soil, thus preventing drought situation. Vegetation cover provided by forest impedes the velocity of runoff on soil surface checks soil erosion, silting and landslides, thus reducing the danger of flood. The litter derived from fallen leaves maintains fertility of soil by returning the nutrients. Forests also act as refuge of wild animals and provided protection to them against strong, cold or hot and dry winds, solar radiation, rain and enemies.

Economic Significance: Wood which has various application in domestic and industrial processes, is the chief product of forest. Wood when used as fuel, has certain advantages over coal as its sulphur and ash contents are very low but, at the same times, excessive use of fuel wood mens pressure on forests which have many functions to serve. Wood may also be converted into solid (coke) liquid and gaseous fuels. Timber is an important material in building construction and day-to-day uses. Forest provides raw material for various wood-based industries viz. pulp and paper, composite wood, rayon and other man made fibers, sport goods, furniture, boat building matches etc. Miscellaneous products, like bamboos, resins, gums, some oils, fibers, medicines, katha, lack, shellac etc., are also obtained from forests.

Depletion of Forest

Increase urbanization, industrialization and mining has entailed indiscriminate felling, of trees has denudation of forests. Nobody will, however, ever learn that who set the first assault on which tree in the history, but this practice of logging down trees for human use has been going on or centuries unabated. Colonists used logs for fire wood and making huts. They also made handles for their tools, furniture are fence posts etc. from it. For them forest had only a present and a past-no future; thus they resorted to ruthless and accelerated exploitation of available forest—a story that still continues with more serious backlashes earth has ever witnessed. India alone is losing more than 1.5 million hectare of forest cover in a year and according to Tiwari (1982) 22 million hectare of forests have been destroyed during the last three decades due to over exploitation and misuse and conversion to agricultural field. The depleted forest wealth would simply deprive the man of economic and environmental values offered by forest, as discussed earlier.

Management of Forest

In forestry, the yield chiefly obtained from the accumulated growth of the past, so this industry has to depend upon the annual growth. Forests are management to obtain a sustained yield which is obviously possible through sustained growth. Following considerations are important in this direction:

(i) A forest should have in correct proportion the trees of different ages and classes so that continuous removal of exploitable produce would not affect the future yield.
(ii) Each tree crop should put on normal growth increments.
(iii) No obstacles should exist to the continuous harvest of exploitable stems.
(iv) Unrestrained felling should be prevented.

For all such planning and decision making sound ecological knowledge is desirable that include knowledge about climatic condition, of biotic community, successional trend, life cycle of important tree species methods of arresting growth of undesirable trees and promoting growth of high yield tree species, and biotic inter relationship (such weeds, competition, pets parasites and diseases etc.)

Of various tactics employed in forest management, same deserving special considerations are as follows: (i) restrained felling, (ii) block and selective cutting, (iii) reforestation, (iv) control of disasters, and (v) recycling of forest products.

Rangeland

A range is the grassland that provides natural pasture of grazing animals. Grasslands occur where rainfall is too low to support the forest community but is higher than that which results in desert community. Generally, in grassland precipitation ranges between 25 to 75 cm. However, depending upon edaphic, such as a high water table, grasslands may also occur in regions of forest climates. Soil of a grassland is characterized by having high humus content.

Over, 6,000 species of grasses, adapted for a great variety of climatic regimes, cover about 20 per cent of earth's surface. In size, they vary from as small plants as about 1 cm. to over 35 cm. tall bamboos.

Importance of Rangeland

Man has been cultivating various grass species as his food and as fodder for his domesticated livestock since time immemorial. History of human civilization the witness of dependence of is man on the seeds of various grasses as his own food, for instance, Indo-Chinese, American and Mediterranean cultures were based on ice, maize and wheat respectively while forage was used as fodder for domesticated livestock.

A range, if not serving as a direct source of food for man, still serves the mankind in a number of indirect ways. Solar energy transformed into food energy by the green cover of the range is available to primary consumers (grazers-domesticated or wild) as food, where in a part of is converted into meat. Of considerable importance to; man are these herbivores and their products such as meat, milk, skins, hides, horns and wool etc. It can thus be said that at the root of all biological resources that, man utilized is the forage.

Depletion and Degradation of Rangeland

Man would not destroy an artificial pasture developed by input of his hard labour and money than a natural pasture. Thus, like all natural resources the rangeland, inflicted with human stress is depleted and degraded. Cause of such stress may be ignorance, greed or incompetence of man. Phenomenal growth of cattle industry, on one hand, is responsible for ruthless over grazing. While on the other hand, wide expansion of urbanization, industrialization, and agriculture has resulted in encroachment of rangeland. Often, out of greed too a rancher allows a number of head to graze beyond the carrying capacity of the range being ignorant to the fact that too many sick and weak head would not fetch home as much value as a few head in prime condition of health after grazing on enough good forage.

Community or ecological indicators provide the most practical approach of determining whether or not a range is being utilized properly (Humphery, 1962). Range managers use the term "decreasers" for palatable species vulnerable to grazing their disappearing is an indicate of grazing stress. When such indicators are not heeded unpalatable "weeds". Once established, it may become hard to eradicate the weeds and not only this such vegetation will invite a variety of pest animals like rodents and insects. This makes clear the long-term consequences of overgrazing in a range.

There is increasing need to restore the depleted and degraded rangeland not only out of economic (livestock production) but also ecological consideration since rangeland depletion would also cause problems like soil erosion, spread of pests etc.

Range Management

Stoddard and Smith (1955) defined the range management as "the science and art of planning and direction range use as to obtain the maximum livestock production consistent with conversion of range resources."

Efforts to manage land include: regulation of grazing pressure: manipulation of stock (herd) distribution: burning of range: reseeding of rangeland: selection of cattle breeds: and control of weeds, pests and predators.

Wild Life

Even on global level there appears to be a great deal of ambiguity attached to the term "wildlife". Webster's Dictionary defines wildlife as living things that are neither human nor domesticated, specially mammals, birds and fish hunted by man. In American usage, term 'wildlife' is used to designate the games and exclude fish, thus they have Fish and Wildlife Services at the federal level. In India too, the common understanding of the people regarding wildlife is of wild animals and shikar, more particularly mammals, birds and reptiles. However, a report entitled Wildlife Conservation in India (1970) of the India Board for Wildlife states wildlife as the entire native uncultivated flora and fauna of the country. The Wildlife (Protection) Act, 1972, also defines wildlife as any animal, bees butterflies, crustacea, fish and moth, and aquatic and land vegetation which form part of any habitat.

Thus a comprehensive definition of wildlife may be given as-any or all non-cultivated and non-domesticated life including both, plant and animals.

Importance of Wild Life

The Wildlife resources provide aesthetic, recreational and economic benefits and at the same time are important ecologically. Nature's millions of forms of life on this earth perform some or the other definite biological function which keeps the delicate balance of our exosphere. In nature flora and fauna go hand-in-hand and one cannot exist without the other. Bird and insects are necessary for the cross pollination of flowers and these with other animals also serve for dispersal and propagation of vegetation. Not only this, the health of vegetation also depends on natural browsing and grazing. Needless to mention that animals, directly or indirectly depend on green plants for their food. Besides food plant so provide shelter to a variety of animal species equally important are the relations among animal populations. If too many herbivores are killed, the predators, depriced of their natural food, will leave forest, become vermin, and prey upon domestic livestock or even man. On the other hand if too may carnivores are killed the herbivores because of release of predation pressure will become too numerous and acquire the status of pest for agricultural crops. Thus most important is the balance of nature of which wildlife in an integral and important part.

Abuse and Depletion of Wild Life

One often comes across the headlines in newspapers like 'Last of the blue whales', save the golden langur Tragedy strikes sea turtles, 'major Jownfall' in rhino population. Great India bustard on the road of extinction and so on which narrate the sad story of abuse and depletion of our wildlife heritage. According to an estimate in last 2,000 years the world has lost, by way of extinction about 160 species of animals and 88 species of birds.

India is endowed with rich biological heritage and her various seripuries and epies are full of vivid and beautiful account on wildlife. Over 500 mammalian and 1,200 avian species contribute to the riches of the wealth. Unfortunately today the Indian wildlife as that in many other parts of the world, is threatened because of man's unprecedented intervention with nature. Nearly 134 plant species have been declared threatened as against 71,47 and 15 species of mammal, birds, and reptiles respectively (Khoshboo 1984). Great India bustard Choriotis nigriceps confined to the semi-arid regions of Rajasthan and Gujarat, and the while-winded wood dack cairina scutalata inhabiting the Brahamaputra swamps and the flood plains of Assam are both on the brick of extinction.

Wild Life Management

The conservation, is the practice embracing preservation, maintenance, sustainable utilization, restoration, and enhancement of the natural environment. Wildlife conservation in this sense is the management of nature's living resources if we consider wildlife as consisting both of wild flora and fauna. Since one cannot mange living resources while being indifferent to the non-living environment, the concept of wildlife management becomes the concept of management of natural ecosystems. It also overlaps "forestry" in so far as it is based on multiple land use concept and implies management of wild plants as well as wild animals. However, under the present dispensation wildlife management implies management of wild animals as distinct from forestry, and it implies maintenance of habitats suitable to the different species.

In America and Europe wild animals, particularly mammals, are treated as game crops, as do timber in forestry and food crops in agriculture, and hundint is developed a viable economic activity. In America, wildlife and wildlife related recreation forms multimillion dollar industry. However, in India it is difficult of develop game as in industry because: (i) our forest areas are already overburdened with grazing pressure of domesticated livestock and because of already scarce pasture lands there is little hope of reducing grazing pressure in the forest areas to develop game; and (ii) hunting as a source of recreation is beyond the means of the majority of population.

During past decades the wildlife management implied the understanding, increasing, and controlling of some species. Sanctuaries and national parks were mostly meant of protect a particular species or group of species and to limited extent for tourism and recreation. Today, however, the emphasis is shifting from the management of species to the management of ecosystem. The objective of wildlife management, as outlined in the World Conservation Strategy, are thus as given below:

(i) To maintain essential ecological processes and life support systems in nature ecosystems, on which human survival and development depends. These essential ecological processes and life support systems can be defined to include maintenance of both the biotic and abiotic components of the ecosystems.

(ii) To preserve genetic diversity (i.e., the range and variety of genetic material found in the world's wild plants and animals) on which depend the breeding programmes necessary for the protection and improvement of cultivated plants and domesticated animals, as well as much scientific advance, technical innovation, and the security of the many industries that use living resources.

(iii) To ensure the sustainable utilization the species and ecosystem. This will include the proper utilization of wild animals for game, forest and grazing, and to achieve proper integration for economy both of rural communities as well as trade and industry.

Fortunately, people have been alerted now and the strong measures being taken in favour of restoring, maintaining, and increasing wildlife population given hope that our rich legacy of wildlife will not only be save for future but developed further. Ways and means employed in wildlife conservation include: (i) protection of breeding stock by enacting game laws and developing wildlife refuges; (ii) artificial stocking including introduction of exotics; (iii) control of predators; (iv) habitat improvement, and (v) game farming.

Minerals and their Characteristics

Minerals are the nonliving substances obtained from the earth through the process of mining. Formation of minerals took place predominantly in weak zones like mountains, folded and faulted regions, lakes, troughs, and continental shelves through geological processes going on since billions of year. They hold some peculiar characteristic, as discussed below, which distinguish them from other natural resources.

(i) Exhaustibility

Minerals are non-renewable or depleting assest and once mined out the deposit get depleted and lost for ever without any chance of replenishment. Refuse or waste, however can be consumed after wards through improved benefication technology.

Simply this exhaustible resource cannot be cropped year after year like agricultural products. Therefore, three distinct stages can be identified in the life cycle of a mine: youth-developmental stage;

maturity established stage; and old age-decline ignore reserves. If the rate of mineral consumption is increasing fast, the knowledge about more reserves and potential substitutability of many minerals is also being improved. As such these predictions may prove outlived.

(ii) Localised Occurrence

Minerals are very localised in their occurrence and the total area occupied them is far limited. Most of the mineral deposits are very sproadic in distribution, for instance, Kolar gold fields of India occupy an area of 8 km. by 1.6 km. formations containing coal and petroleum are, in general, bigger as compared to metalliferous deposits. The coal bearing formation of India, for example, occupy about 4 per cent of the country's total area.

(iii) Unpredictable Occurrence

The quantity and quality of a mineral in any region is not easy to predict. Uncertainties prevail with respect to their occurrence, extent of depth, cost of mining (often linked with depth) and the grade.

(iv) Risk Involvement

The process of mining involves large number of problems forminers. Abnormal temperature and pressure variations, rock burst, fire and gas hazard, lack of ventilation and drainage, collapse of roof and side walls are the peculiar problems encountered only in mining industry.

(v) Dependence on Other Factors

Minerals production is largely affected by factors like the changing needs of consumer industries, availability of stock, fluctuation in prices, and reuse of metallic scrap in production process. A technologically poor country possessing richer grades of ores may have to face keen competition in international market with technologically richer countries may, however, possesing poorer grades or ores since in later case the cost of production is considerably low due to improved mining methods.

(vi) International Character

Minerals know no political boundaries. Virtually, no country within its own boundaries has adequate production and reserves of all the minerals needed for its industrial development. The unequal distribution of minerals makes the international trade in its inveitable. Some countries are bestowed with monopolistic rights in respect of certain mineral deposits which result in what is know as geoplotics.

(vii) Development and Conservation of Minerals

Geologists are of general apprehension that the known reserves of minerals may not last for long and most of them will be exhausted within 100 years. New possibilities of mineral reserves in land and beyond the land (as in the seabed are being explored which may reduce, if not totally remove, the futuristic fears of exhaustion of the resource.

Presently, limenite, rutile, tine ore, diamond, sulphur, coal petroleum, and calcareous and ferruginous sea sands are largely being mined from the sea-coast and sea beds. In India, ilmenite, rutile and associated zirocn, monazite, and sillimanite, are obtained from the beach sands of Madras and Kerala coasts. Coral limestone for industrial use like manufacture of calcium carbide, and calcareous sand for cement are being mined from the sea-bed at Tamil Nadu and Dwarka (Gujarat) respectively for quite long time. Indonesia, Thailand, and Burma recover considerable tin ore from the sea-bed, while England recovers coal and Philipplines iron from the sea bed. A number of petroliferous structure occurring off the coast are being mined for petroleum and its products at several places. The ferromanganese nodules or what commonly known as manganese nodules found over the oceanic floors, generally below 4,000 m depth, are perhaps the most spectacular discovery in the field. The most prolific concentrations of such nodules with high metal values have been found in North Pacific between 139 W to 141 W and 4 N. Although precise information about the reserves of manganese nodules is not available but it is estimated that they may run several billion tons and may prove to be potent source of metals like manganese, nickel, copper and cobalt. It is estimated that 1 million tons of manganese nodules from sea-bed provide about 275,000 tons of manganese, 13,000 tons of nickel, 2,5000 tons of cobalt, and 1,000 tons of copper besides other metals like iron, vanadium, molybdenum, silver and lead. Further, it has now been roughly estimated that the metal resources available in molybdenum silver and lead. Further, it has now been roughly estimated that the metal resources available in manganese nodules are several times greater than those available in land, such as cobalt 5,000 times, manganese 4,000 times, nickel 1,500 times copper 150 times.

The conservation of mineral resources does not mean preservation of minerals under ground to be used by future generations but it implies efforts to utilize minerals in best possible way, depending upon the industrial needs and changing technological requirements, so that the life of the deposits is increased without sacrificing out own needs. From the utilization point of view, minerals are placed under two classes: expendable and non-expendable. Expendable minerals have practically no salvage value and ones consumed are lost fore ever, e.g., coal, petroleum, gas and most of the non-metallic minerals. Non-expendable minerals are those which have good salvage value and can be used again and again through recycling, except those quantities that are lost due to corrosion and abrasion, e.g., metallic minerals.

Efforts to Conserve Mineral Resources

(i) Application of efficient methods of mining to take out every possible tonnage lying under ground.

(ii) Utilization of unmarketable ores through the innovative methods or ore dressing and metallurgical practices.
(iii) Use and reuse of scraps.
(iv) Recovering all associated elements as co product or by-product.
(v) Economic use of minerals.
(vi) Substituting the use or rare land costly minerals with those which are abundant and cheaper.

A facility (house, hospital, port), or even in providing a service to society (medical care, public transport). Firewood, fossil duels (coal, petroleum and its products, natural gas), solar energy, biogas, wind and hydro power, and atomic power are chief energy resources. Of these, firewood and fossil fuel are being used for supply of energy since time immemorial and are known as conventional energy sources. Wind and hydro power, solar energy, biogas, and atomic energy are the new and non-conventional sources of energy. Fossil fuels being limited in supply may be termed as exhaustible sources while other, like solar, hydel, wind and atomic energy, that would be available to man for infinite period are regarded as inexhaustible sources. Firewood and other bio fuels (such as, biogas derived from biological wastes, domestic garbages etc.) are indeed renewable energy sources but exploitation of fire woods has great ecological implications since we are already short of forests and whatever forests available should not be squeezed or thinned. However, use of other biofuels is known to be the best option in the light of two important acts: their steady of even increasing supply at low cost; their use in energy production reduces pollution of environment.

Because of rapid depletion and poor regeneration of the exhaustible sources of energy the society should concentrate on tapping the inexhaustible and renewable sources under strict economic and ecological consideration.

Conventional and Exhaustible Energy Sources

Fire wood: No one can trace back in the history that who are made the first assault that is on which tree. However, it is evident that man has been logging down the trees for various purposes, including to get firewood as an important one, since long. Because, in olden days man's knowledge and access for various natural resources were limited, he ruthlessly exploited his own surroundings to meet out his day-to-day requirements. The story still continues in various part of the world at slow ever or faster pace, but often not because of the dearth of knowledge but of vested interests or because of having no other option. Felling of trees for firewood is still a common practice in interior where it is the cheapest and, at times the only available source of energy. This had led to thinning or denudation of woodland that needs serious consideration from both ecological and economic viewpoints. Obviously, the only way out to the problem is making available to the villager the cheaper non conventional energy sources, such as biogas and solar energy in usable form.

Fossil fuel (coal, petroleum, natural gas) are the most extensively used sources of energy today. Like for many other natural resources increase in population and per capita energy demand coupled with the industrialization at a faster pace, are the factors responsible for depletion of fossile fuel world over. According to a report the earth's original stocks of coal and petroleum were about 6,00 billion tons and 1,250 billion barrels respectively, of which by the year 1960,100 billion tons of coal was mined and 100 billion barrels petroleum extracted. The story of natural gas is no different which has acquired the status of irreplaceable commodity of domestic use in modern times. Petroleum and natural gas today fulfil 60 per cent of the world's total energy requirements. It is evident that if the exploitation and consumption of these resources continues at the present incredible rate, there supply may last only for a few one decades.

Non-conventional and Inexhaustible Energy Sources

The rapid depletion conventional energy sources has prompted governments and people to concentrate on finding and tapping some non-conventional energy sources that may last for long. In fact, inexhaustible energy sources, like solar, hydel, tidal, wind and atomic power, can only bring hope for the sustained socio-economic development of humanity for years to come when exhaustible sources will become either in accessible or too costly to afford.

Solar Energy: Research and application in the field of solar energy have opened new vistas in the direction of fulfilling world's future energy requirements. It has especially drawn attention for its practically free steady supply and pollution free use. This energy may be transformed into heat using reflectors and condensers, or into electric energy using solar photovoltaic. The resource can especially be tapped more effectively in the regions where there are long sunshine hours.

Solar-heaters and cookers are becoming popular these days in industry and household. Passive solar architectures provide comfortable housing in extreme cold and hot climates. This engineering has also been successfully applied in warehouse and cold storages. A multipurpose solardryer-cum-warehouse is under construction at Ganaur (Haryana, India) where chillies, potato-chips and other foodstuffs could cried and stored. Solar energy has also been effectively used in desalination of water. College of Engineering Pune has designed a solar furnace that can generate heat up to 20,000 Cu which can be send in various metallurgical and other purposes.

Department of Non-conventional Energy Sources of Govt. of India has prepared a perspective plan that envisages generation of energy through non-conventional sources, chiefly solar to the extent of 250 million tons of coal replacement per annum including 15,000 MW of electricity by the year 2001. Indian's first solar power station, soon to be operated near New Delhi, would be a great breakthrough in this direction. Rural electrification through solar photovoltaics is already in operation at some places in the country. Moreover, photovoltaic irrigation pump sets have also been installed at some places.

Wind Power

The power of wind since olden days is beings used in running mills, irrigation of fields, and carrying out of the farm activities, but its real potential is not so far being realized. According to inventories of Department of Non-conventional Energy Source of Government of India 20,000 MW electricity can be generated from the wind alone in the country. Wind power plants are set up in various parts of the country but they still account for the total capacity of 3.3 MW only. Obviously, this potent resource is still to be tapped optimally.

Hydro Power

Use of gravitational flow of water in generation of electricity, what commonly known as hydro power or hydel power is quite common in various parts of the world. India's, first hydro power station, having a potential of 300 kW, was constructed in 1897 at Darjeeling. Later on, many stations with far high potentiality were set up. The country's economically exploitable hydro power resources have been estimated at 41 million KW (or 41,000 MW) of which only 18 per cent of the potential was utilized by 1979. The Brahmaputra basin has the highest hydro power potential and nearly 30 per cent of the country's total; next to it rank the Indus, Godavari, and Ganga basins respectively.

In world, a total 4,910×109 kW electric power is generated of which hydropower forms of fourth. In highly industrialized countries like USA, USSR, Canada, Japan, Furnace, Sweden, and Norway hydro power is nearly fully developed whereas in the rest of the world it is yet to be developed fully.

Hydel power is considered to be the cheapest source of electricity with the cost of generation ranging from 2 to 3 paise per unit, compared to a minimum of 5 paise per unit of electricity generated coal based thermal power plants. Although the initial cost of hydel project is generally 25 per cent higher but owing to lower recurring cost, the cost of generation of hydro power is the lowest. A part from such economic consideration, development of such projects is beneficial for irrigation and other purposes too.

Tidal power of water in costal areas of India, however not so far being realized. According to an estimate a tidal power potential of 9,000 MW has been identified of which 7,000 to 8,000 MW is in the Gulf of Cambay, 800 to 1,000 MW in the Gulf of Kutch and rest in Sunderbans.

Atomic power (Nuclear power): As already delineated, the fossil fuels beings exhaustible, such sources of energy are not to last for long with the current trend of consumption. Atomic power appears to be the only hope for large scale energy requirements when fossil fuels are exhausted. The reserves of atomic fuels are said to be over 10 times greater than fossil fuels and the advantage of former is that their very small amounts would produce enormous amount of energy. A ton of Uranium^{295} for instance, would provide as much energy as 3 million tons of coal or 12 million barrels of oil. Atomic energy has its application not only in generation of electricity but has successfully been used in marine vessels, spaceships and even in chemical and food processing industry.

Important constraints in atomic energy generation are: (i) cost of construction and maintenance of plants; and (ii) disposal of radioactive wastes cost of construction of an atomic power plant and its maintenance is very high as compared to any other electric power plant. For running one atomic power plant unit 235 MW capacity, heavy water of a worth Rs.10 crore is required per year. Further, as a consequence of frequent failures, the running cost of such plants come to be very high. Moreover after the working capacity of an atomic power plant is over (in about 25 years), these have to be destroyed so as to avoid radiation spillage. Surprisingly the cost and time for destruction of these plants is almost equal to that for construction. Disposal of radioactive wastes is such a problem that still has no satisfactory solution for long term.

Bio Energy (Energy from Biological Matter)

Organic wastes provide an important renewable source of energy. Biogas generated from the decomposition of organic wastes, like manure and domestic wastes is becoming increasingly popular as source of heat and light in many parts. It is considered to be advantageous in view of its relatively cheaper supply, and use of organic wastes in its generation reduces the otherwise impending threat of pollution due to their release in environment. As such, it serves two purposes; fuel production and waste disposal. It has more of practical applicability in villages where organic waste in the form of cattle dung, is available in plenty. Biogas to generated is thus economic and convenient to use as compared to conventional practice of burning of dry dung-cakes. Further, the dung-cakes serve only as a source of heat for cooking and allied and purposes while biogas has multifarious applications. These slurry so produces in a biogas plant can well be used as manure for agricultural fields.

Under the National Biogas Development Programme 8.2 lakh biogas plants were set up by year 1985-86 in different parts of the country. A large-scale urban waste recycling plant at Okhla (New Delhi) generates about 5 lakh cubic feet gas per day. In the VIIIth plan it is proposed that about 12 lakhs cubic feet gas will be generated per day. According to Water Sewage Disposal Undertaking 4,300 gas connections have been given in Delhi.

Conservation of Energy

The need for conservation of energy becomes essential in view of the following simple facts:

(i) Most of the activities of present day large and growing population require massive energy inputs, thus per capita and total demands for energy are fast increasing.

(ii) The fossil fuels we are not endowed with which much are not to last for long at the present rate of consumption. At the same time much talked about possible alternate source of energy are, in fact, still in tentative state of development so far their practical applicability is concerned.

(iii) There are economic constraints for many countries even if they want to develop conventional sources of energy, what to talk about sources like nuclear energy.

(iv) Unplanned exploitation and use of energy result in widespread environmental damage, the cost of which is to be borne by humanity.

Conservation of energy means not simply the curtailment of energy consumption but to curtail unnecessary of wasteful consumption of energy and make thrifty use of energy producting resources to ensure their steady supply for generations.

Energy Resources

In *Rig Veda* it has been mentioned that O'Engery! Thou art the container of the entire Cosmos since Eternity. Thou art bestower of sacrifice, knowledge and technology. O' Respectable One! Thou art the source of light, seasons and all that is beautiful. Thou art the Creator and preserver of all the precious-stones elements. I bow to thee.

In India the concept of energy as Shakti has been almost at the focus of philosophic, scientific and metaphysical though from immemorial. The energy (from the Greek word energy meaning capacity to do work) reported to have been coined by Thomas Young (1973-1829), eighty years, after Newton and applied it to what is now called kinetic energy. The two laws of thermodynamics describe the behaviours of energy first law states list energy may be transformed from one form to the other, but can not be created or destroyed: second law states that because some energy is always dispersed into all unavailable heat energy, no spontaneous transformation of energy from, one, to other form (light to protoplasm far example) is 100 per cent efficient.

The earth's planet cover is equivalent to, over 1,800 billion tones of dry matter, that is energy equivalent of 30.10^{10} Joules, corresponding to the known reserves of fossil energy. Forests make up about 68 per cent of terrestrial biomass, grass ecosystems about 16 per cent, and cultivated lands only 8 per cent. For the earth as a whole, the 173 billion tones of dry matter produced every year by photosynthesis over 20 times the fossil energy consumed in the world, or again 200 times the energy contained in the food of the planet's 4 billion inhabitants.

It is an intrinsic component of any socio-economic development for raising standard of living as also improving the quality of life of the man, in general. Increase in human population and use of energy for new activities to improve life styles has depleted many energy sources. But, today with the challenge to support a large population human society confronts severe limits far many of the energy resources. The conservation of existing energy sources as well as exploration of alternate resources has been engaging the attention of world scientific community.

The conventional energy sources of the world are dwindling last. We have to come to realise that, the world plenty of non-renewable natural sources does indeed have a bottom self. Bio-energy can play an important and vital role to beer energy crisis of the world. It has special relevance to India as its 80 per cent population resides in villages needing energy for cooking, lighting, and operating pumps far irrigation and drinking water, etc. India having largest population of cattle in the world and sizeable forest potentialities, bio-energy can sadly be developed as an alternative source of energy on dependable lines

Energy source scan be divided into two categories:

Conventional Energy Resources

Energy sources, which have been in common, use e.g. wood, coal, lignite, petroleum, natural gas. It is estimated that India has a potential of generating more than 1,00,000 MW from renewable sources. In past 20 years various renewable energy technologies have been developed, including improved chulhas, biogas plants, biomass gasifiers, solar thermal (ST) and solar photovoltaic (SP) systems wind farms wind mills small, small and micro hydel systems, hydrogen energy, ocean energy, fuel cell etc. Some of the products which are being exported include SP systems, wind turbine equipments, selectively coated sheets for thermal applications and solar cookers. The important are as follows:

Table 4.1: Estimated potential and installed power generating capacity from renewable (data are the recent ones or otherwise as specified)

Sources/systems	*Approximate potential/availability*	*Achievements made*
Biogas Plants	12 M	3.31 M"
Biomass power	17,000 MW	222 MW'
Energy from Municipal Wastes	1700 MW	15 MW"
Improved Wood Stoves *(Chulhas)*	120 M	30 M'
Ocean Energy	50,000 MW	
Small Hydro Power	10,000 MW	271 projects with an potential of 217 MW
Solar Cookers		4,87,000 Nos.
Solar Photovoltaic Power		1590 kW (940 kW grid connected) (650 kW non-grid connected)
Solar Photovoltaic	20 MW/km^2	7,50,000 SPV systems aggregate potential of about 58 MW
Solar PV Pumps,		3450 Nos.
Solar Water-Heating Systems (Collector area)	30 Mmz (Collector area)	5,00,000 m^2
Wind Energy	45,000 MW	1175 MW

*As on March 31,1999 **As on March 31, 2000 ***As on April 11, 2000.
Source: India 2000 (A Reference Annual, Ministry of Information's and Broadcasting Govt. of India); H. 21.12.2000; and various websites.

Renewable Energy Resources

Renewable Energy Resources or non-conventional energy sources of energy include solar, wind, "water, geothermal, ocean, hydrogen, biomass, and solid waste. These resources are quickly, renewed and recycled in nature and hence constitute *sustainable energy sources* because the techniques for their exploitation have been developed comparatively recently. In India, the systematic efforts to develop such sources were initiated after setting up of the Commission 1981 for Additional Sources of Energy (CASE) and in 1982 the Department of Non-conventional Energy Sources (DNES). The Ministry of Non-conventional Energy Sources (MNES) created in 1992 is the nodel agency of the Government of India for all matters relating to non-conventional/renewable energy. It undertakes policy making, planning, promotion and coordination of functions relating to all aspects of renewable energy, including fiscal and financial incentives, creation of industrial capacity, promotion of demonstration and commercial programmes, R and D and technology development, intellectual property protection, human resource development and international relations. The production of energy from non-conventional energy sources is based entirely on indigenous know-how.

Bio-energy

Bio-energy includes those processes where biological forms of matter such as plants, vegetables, bacteria, enzyme, etc. provide the basis for energy or its conversion from one form to another. The widest use of bio-energy is the traditional way where wood plants and agricultural matter are directly burnt to provide heat.

Vegetable biomass is a new name for plant organic material wherein solar energy is trapped and stored through the process of photosynthesis in which carbon dioxide and water are transformed and form energy rich compounds. *Biomass* includes both terrestrial as well as aquatic matter and can be conveniently grouped into new plant growth, plant residues and wastes. The new *plant* growth includes wood, short-rotation trees, herbaceous plants. Conventional crops, algae (fresh water and marine), aquatic plants. The *residues* cover not only crop materials, such as straws, husks, bagasse, corn cobs, etc. but also secondary level products such as cow dung, animal droppings, forest based residues like bark, saw dust, wood shaving etc. The term *wastes* has been loosely used. It is matter of vegetable origin in wrong place. It is of disposable nature like garbage, night soil, sewage solids and industrial refuse.

Table 4.2: World energy consumption since 1971 to 1987 (million tonnes of oil equivalent)

Year	*Coal*	*Petroleum*	*Natural Gas*	*Hydroelectric*	*Nuclear*	*Total*
1971	1632	2413	997	318	28	5388
1973	1668	2798	1066	332	49	5913
1975	1709	2725	1709	358	87	5959
1977	1830	2986	1162	376	132	6486
1978	1863	3082	1206	403	150	6704
1979	1976	3124	1273	413	153	6940
1980	2007	3001	1297	421	169	6895
1981	2003	2902	1321	430	198	6854
1982	2047	2825	1316	451	218	6858
1983	2101	2801	1326	475	240	6943
1984	2180	2845	1410	485	282	7202
1985	2273	2809	1494	511	348	7435
1986	2318	2899	1487	517	377	7598
1987	2387	2941	1556	524	404	7811

Source: BP Statistics, World Science News, 29 (5): 19, 1992.

Different Types of Energy Sources

Fossil Fuel

They are nonrenewable fossil resources. They are organic fuel resources found in earth's crust, which have been formed in the past through the effect of heat and compression on forest and other organic matter buried underneath due to landslides, earth quakes and lava. They can be solid (e.g.. coal, lignite), liquid (petroleum) and gaseous (natural gas).

Petroleum or Crude Oil

It is a natural mineral oil, a thick greenish-brown flammable liquid found underground in permeable rocks. Petroleum consists of hydrocarbons mixed with oxygen, sulphur, nitrogen, and other elements in varying proportions. It is though to be derived from ancient organic material that has been converted by, first bacterial action, then heat and pressure (but its origin may be chemical also). From crude petroleum, fuel oil, petrol, kerosene, diesel, lubricating oil, paraffin wax and petroleum jelly.

Table 4.3: Petroleum: Chronology

1859	Edwin Drake drilled the world's first successful oil well in Titusville. Pennsylvania, USA to a depth of 18 m/70 ft.
1865	The first oil pipeline, 9,750 m/32,000 ft long, was constructed at Oil Creek Pennsylvania, USA, to carry oil from well to nearby coalfield.
1896	The first offshore wells were drilled from piers off the California coast.
1899	The first gravity meter was produced.
1914	Reginald Fessenden patented the seismograph.
1939	The aircraft-borne magnetometer was developed to measure magnetism of rocks.
1966	Oil was discovered beneath the North Sea.
1967	The worst oil spill in British waters from the *Torrey Canyon,* which struck rocks at Lands End. Over 108,000 tonnes of oil were spilled.
1974	The world's deepest oil well, 10,941 m/31,441 ft, was drilled in Oklahoma, USA.
1979	In the Gulf of Mexico accidentally released 545,000 tonnes of oil into the sea. The slick spread for 640 km/400 mi. later the same year, the worst tanker spillage occurred. Two tankers, the Atlantic Empress and the Aegean Captain, collided off the island to Tobago, in the Caribbean Sea. More than 230,000 tonnes of oil well spilled.
1984	An exploratory well was drilled off the coast of New England, USA, in water of depth 2,116 m/6,942 ft — a world record.
1988	The Piper Alpha drilling rig in the North Sea caught fire in July, killing 167 people.
1989	The worst spill in American waters occurred when 55,000 tonnes of oil escaped from the Exxon Valdez off the Alaskan coast, near Prince William Sound.
1991	The worst spill to date was a consequence of the Gulf War when Iraqi forces opened the pipeline in the Persian Gulf and coalition forces caused further damage during Operation Desert Storm.

The USA led in production until the 1960s, when the Middle East out produced other areas, their immense reserves leading to a worldwide dependence on cheap oil for transport and industry. In 1961 the Organization of the Petroleum Exporting Countries

(OPEC) was established to avoid exploitation of member countries; after OPEC's price rises in 1973, the International Energy Agency (IEA) was established 1974 to protect the interests of oil-consuming countries. New technologies were introduced to pump oil from offshore and from the Arctic (the Alaska pipeline) in an effort to Global consumption of petroleum in 1993 was 23 billion barrels.

Petroleum products and chemicals are used in large quantities in the manufacture of detergents, artificial fibres, plastics, insecticides, fertilizers, pharmaceuticals, toiletries, and synthetic rubber. Aviation fuel is a volatile form of petrol.

Following indicates deposits, annual production, and potential recovery of fossil fuels at global level.

Table 4.4: World's Conventional Energy Resources

	Petroleum	*Coal*	*Natural gas*
Ultimate deposits	2 Tb	9.9 Tt	204 Tm^3
Confirmed deposits	887.3 Bb	730.8 Bt	104 Tm^3
Annual production	20.4 Bb	3.18 Bt	1.93 Tm^3
Potential recovery	43 years	17-	56 years

They fulfil 70 per cent total energy needs of human society and 87.4 per cent of commercial energy.

Coal and Lignite

In the country, about 60 per cent of the commercial energy consumption is fulfilled by coal and lignite. Coal is used for cooking, heating, in industry and thermal power plants. Over the last 30 years coal production has increased from 55.67 Mt to 211.73 Mt. In the same period lignite production increased from 0.05 Mt to 14.07 Mt. The annual requirement of coal for the year 1987-88, 1992-93, and projected demand for 2011 A.D.

Table 4.5: Annual requirement of coal and oil (1987-2000)

Energy Source	*1987-88*	*1992-93*	*2000-01*	*2000-01*
Coal	214 Mt (20010t)	313 Mt (247 Mt)	530 Mt (426 Mt)	631 Mt (426 Mt)
	44.7 Mt (41 Mt)	57.3 Mt (48 Mt)	92.7 Mt (69.1 Mt)	92.7Mt (69.1 Mt)

The coal resources are limited and may last for over 100 years.

Petroleum

Petroleum is the main fuel for transport, agricultural operations, generators and some industries. Indian economy continues to be highly petroleum intensive. The transport sector consumes about 40 per cent of the petroleum products followed by industry 25 per cent, household 19 per cent, and agriculture 9 per cent. Petroleum fuels are finite. The known reserve of petroleum on the basis of 1989 revised data are sufficient to last up to 2030 A.D.

Natural Gas

It is fast emerging important future energy source India's gas reserves has been increased seven told in the last 10 years. About 2,300 Mm^3 of natural gas was produced during 1980-81, while it rose to 18,000 Mm^3 in 1990-91. Keeping with the trend, the demand by 2000 A.D. is likely to be over 25,000 Mm^3 per year. Even then the resources appear to be adequate because of availability of vast resources of natural gas recently at over 475 Bm^3.

Natural gas is produced in Assam, Tripura, Gujarat, and Western offshore. Reserves of natural gas have also been established in the Krishna-Godavari basin and Cauveri Basin.

Conservation of Fossil Fuels

Recovery of Mines and Wells

Deep mines and wells contain. Lot of fuels, so they should be recovered. Prospecting should be carried out in new areas to find out the existence of more mines. Efforts should be made to develop technology to extract fossil fuels from low yield mines and wells.

Increasing Recovery

Those techniques should be discovered which reduce wastage

during extraction. continuous efforts are required to reduce wastage during refining and washing.

Fires

Fire in mines and wells can destroy fossil fuels so it should be prevented.

Improvement of equipment: Fuel use efficiency of equipment devices and vehicles should be improved with maximization of combustion.

Inter-fuel Substitution

It can be carried out through coal gasification to, producing liquid fuel and Compressed Natural Gas (CNG).

Alternative Sources

Other energy sources such as solar energy, should be use in place of fossil fuels.

Sustainable Development and Environmental Issues

In recent years, economists have become increasingly aware of the important implications of environmental issues for the success of development efforts. We now understand that the interaction between poverty and environmental degradation can lead to a self-perpetuating process in which, as a result of ignorance or economic necessity, communities may inadvertently destroy or exhaust the resources on which they depend for survival. Rising pressures on environmental resources in developing countries can have severe consequences for self-sufficiency, income distribution, and future growth potential in the developing world.

Environmental degradation can also detract from the pace of economic development by imposing high costs on developing countries through health-related expenses and the reduced productivity of resources. The poorest 20 per cent of the world's population will experience the consequences of environmental ills most acutely. Severe environmental degradation, due to population pressures on marginal land, has led to falling farm productivity and per capita food production. Since the cultivation of marginal land is largely the domain of lower-income groups, the losses are suffered by those who can least afford them. Similarly, the inaccessibility of sanitation and clean water mainly affects the poor and is believed to be responsible for 80 per cent of disease worldwide. Because the solutions to these and many other environmental problems involve enhancing the productivity of resources and improving living conditions among the poor, achieving environmentally sustainable growth is synonymous with our definition of economic development.

Though there is considerable dispute concerning the environmental costs associated with various economic activities, consensus is growing among development economists that environmental considerations should form an integral part of policy initiatives. The exclusion of environmental costs from calculations of GNP is largely responsible for the historical absence of environmental considerations from development economics. Damage to soil, water supplies, and forests resulting from unsustainable methods of production can greatly reduce long-term national productivity but will have a positive impact on current GNP figures. It is thus very important that the long-term implications of environmental quality be considered in economic analysis. Rapid population growth and expanding economic activity in the developing world are likely to do extensive environmental damage unless steps are taken to mitigate their negative consequences.

The growing consumption needs of LDC populations may have global implications as well. There is increasing concern in the MDCS that the destruction of the world's remaining forests, which are concentrated in a number of highly indebted developing countries including Brazil, Mexico, Peru, and the Philippines, will greatly contribute to global warming and the greenhouse effect. In this chapter, we examine the economic cause and consequences of environmental devastation and explore potential solutions to the cycle of poverty and resource degradation. We begin, as in previous solutions to the cycle of poverty and resource degradation. We being, as in previous chapters, with a survey of basic issues, including discussions of sustainable development and the linkages among population, poverty, economic growth, rural development, urbanization, and the LDC environment. We next look at the applicability of traditional economic models of the environment, depict some typical environmental situations, and provide some relevant data. We than broaden our scope to examine the global environment and explore policies for seeking worldwide sustainable development. Pakistan's environment problems are this chapter's case study.

Environment and Development: The Basic Issues

Seven basic issues define the environment of development. Many grow out of the discussions in the preceding chapters. The seven issues are: (1) the concept of sustainable development, and linkages between the environment and (2) population and resources, (3) poverty, (4) economic growth, (5) rural development, (6) urbanization, and (7) the global economy. We briefly discuss each in turn.

(1) Sustainable Development and Environmental Accounting

Environmentalists have used the term sustainability in an attempt to clarify the desired balance between economic growth on the one hand and environmental preservation on the other. Although there are many definitions, basically sustainability refers to "meeting the needs of the present generation without compromising need of future generations." For economists, a development path is sustainable "if and only if the stock of overall capital assets remains constant or rises over time." Implicit in these statements is the fact that future growth and overall quality of life are critically dependent on the quality of the environment. The natural resource base of a country and the quality of its air, water, and land represents a common heritage for all generations. To destroy that endowment indiscriminately in the pursuit of short-term economic goals penalizes both present and, especially, future generations. It is therefore important that development policymakers incorporate some form of environmental accounting into their decisions. For example, the preservation or loss of valuable environmental resources should be factored into estimates of economic growth and human well-being. Alternatively, policymakers may set a goal of no net loss of environmental assets. In other words, if an environmental resource is damaged or depleted in one area, a resource of equal or greater value should be regenerated elsewhere.

An example of environmental accounting is offered by David Pearce and Jeremy Warford. Overall capital assets are meant to include not only manufactured capital (machines, factories, roads) but also human capital (knowledge, experience, skills) and environmental capital (forests, soil quality, rangeland). By this definition, sustainable development requires that these overall capital assets not be decreasing and that the correct measure of sustainable national income or sustainable net national product (NNP) is the amount that can be consumed without diminishing the capital stock. Symbolically,

$$NNP = GNP - D_m - D_n$$

where NNP is sustainable national income, D_m is the depreciation of manufactured capital assets, and D_n is depreciation of environmental capital—the monetary value of environmental decay over the course of a year.

An even better measure, though more difficult to calculate with present data collection methods, would be

$$NNP = GNP - D_m - D_n - R - A$$

where D_m and D_n are as before, R is expenditure required to restore environmental capital (forests, fisheries, etc.), and A is expenditure to avert destruction of environmental capital (air pollution, water and soil quality, etc.).

In light of rising consumption levels worldwide combined with high rates of population growth, the realization of sustainable development will be a major challenge. We must ask ourselves,

What are realistic expectations about sustainable standards of living? From present information concerning rapid destruction of many of the world resources, it is clear that meeting the needs of a world population that is projected to grow by an additional 3 billion in the next 50 years will require radical and early changes in consumption and production patterns. We discuss these needed changes later in the chapter.

(2) Population, Resources and the Environment

Much of the concern over environmental issues stems from the perception that we may reach a limit to the number of people whose needs can be met by the earth's finite resources. This may or may not be true, given the potential for new technological discoveries, but it is clear that continuing on our present path or accelerating environmental degradation would severely comprise the ability of present and future generations to meet their needs. A showing of population growth rates would help ease the intensification of many environmental problems. However, the rate and timing of fertility declines, and thus the eventual size of world population, will largely depend on the commitment of governments to creating economic and institutional conditions that are conducive to limiting fertility.

Rapidly growing populations have led to land, water, and fuelwood shortages in rural areas and to urban health crises stemming from lack of sanitation and clean water. In many of the poorest regions of the globe, it is clear that increasing population density has contributed to severe and accelerating degradation of the very resources that these growing populations depend on for survival. To meet expanding LDC needs, environmental devastation must be halted and the productivity of existing resources stretched further so as to benefit more people. If increases in GNP and food production are slower than population growth, per capita levels of production and food self-sufficiency will fall. Ironically, the resulting persistence of poverty would be likely to perpetuate high fertility rates, that the poor are often dependent of large families for survival.

(3) Poverty and the Environment

Too often, h6wever, high fertility is blamed for problems that are attributable in poverty itself. For example, China's population density per acre of arable land is twice that of India, yet yields are also twice as high. Though it is clear that environmental destruction and high fertility go hand in hand, they are both direct out-growths of a third factor, absolute poverty. For environmental policies to succeed in developing countries, they must first address the issues of landlessness, poverty, and lack of access to institutional resources. Insecure and tenure rights, lack of credit and inputs, and absence of information often prevent the poor from making resource-augmenting investments that would help preserve the environmental assets from which they derive their livelihood. Hence preventing environmental degradation is more often a matter of providing institutional support to the poor than fighting an inevitable process of decay. For this reason, many goals on the international environmental agenda are very much in harmony with the three objectives of development articulated.

(4) Growth Versus *the Environment*

If, in fact, it is possible to reduce environmental destruction by increasing the incomes of the poor, is it then possible to achieve growth without further damage to the environment? Evidence indicates that the worst perpetrators of environmental destruction are the billion richest and billion poorest people on earth. It has even been suggested that the bottom billion are more destructive than all four billion people in between. If, in fact, it is possible to reduce environmental destruction by increasing the incomes of the poor, is it then possible to achieve growth without further damage to the environment? Evidence indicates that the worst perpetrators of environmental destruction are the billion richest and billion poorest people on earth. It has even been suggested that the bottom billion are more destructive than all four billion people in between. It follows that increasing the economic status of the poorest group would provide an environmental windfall.

However, as the income consumption levels of everyone else in the economy also rise, there is likely to be a net increase in environmental destruction. Meeting increasing consumption demand while keeping environmental degradation at a minimum will be no small task.

(5) Rural Development and the Environment

To meet the expanded food needs of rapidly growing LDC populations, it is estimated that food production in developing countries will have to double by 2010. Because land in many areas of the developing world is being unsustainably over-exploited by existing populations, meeting these output targets will require radical changes in the distribution, use, and quantity of resources available to the agricultural sector. And because women are frequently the caretakers of rural resources such as forests and water supplies and provide much of the agricultural supply of labour, it is of primary importance that they be integrated into environmental programs. In addition, poverty alleviation efforts much target women's economic status in particular to reduce their dependence on unsustainable methods of production.

The increased accessibility of agricultural inputs of small farmers and the introduction (or reintroduction) of sustainable methods of farming will help create attractive alternatives to current environmentally destructive patterns of resource use. Land-augmenting investments can greatly increase the yields from cultivated land and help ensure future food self-sufficiency.

(6) Urban Development and the Environment

Demonstrated that rapid population increases accompanied by heavy rural-urban migration is leading to unprecedented rate of urban population growth, sometimes at twice the rate of national growth. Consequently, few governments are prepared to cope with the vastly increased strain on existing urban water supplies and sanitation facilities. The resulting environmental ills pose extreme health hazards for the growing numbers of people exposed to them.

Such conditions threaten to precipitate the collapse of the existing urban infrastructure and create circumstances ripe for epidemics and national health crises. These conditions are exacerbated by the fact that under existing legislation, much and renders large portions of urban populations ineligible for government services.

Congestion, vehicular and industrial emissions, and poorly ventilated household stoves also inflate the tremendously high environmental costs of urban crowding. Lost productivity of ill or diseased workers, contamination of existing water sources, and destruction of infrastructure, in addition to increased fuel expenses incurred by people's having to boil unsafe water, are just a few of the costs associated with poor urban conditions. Research reveals that the urban environment appears to worsen at a faster rate than urban population size increases of that the marginal environmental cost of additional residents arises over time.

(7) The Global Environment

As total world population grows and incomes rise, net global environmental degradation in likely to worsen. Some trade-offs will be necessary to achieve sustainable world development. By using resources more efficiently, a number of environmental changes will actually provide economic savings, and others will be achieved at relatively minor expense. However, because many essential changes will require substantial investments in pollution abatement technology and resource management, significant trade-offs between output and environmental improvements will occasionally become necessary. The poorer the country, the more difficult it will be to absorb these costs. Yet a number of issues, including biodiversity, rain forest destruction, and population growth, will focus international attention on some of the most economically strapped countries in the world. In the absence of substantial assistance to low-income countries, environmental efforts will necessarily have to be funded at the expense of other social programs, such as education, health services, and employment schemes, that themselves have important implications for the preservation of the global environment.

Exactly what sacrifices need to be made and who should make them will continue to be matters of great controversy. Nowhere was this more evident than at the second United Nations Conference on Environment and Development (UNCED)—the so-called Earth Summit—held in Rio de Janeiro in June 1992 and a follow-up conference in Kyoto, Japan, in 1997. Most cumulative environmental destruction to date has been caused by the developed world. However, with high fertility rates, rising average incomes, and increasing inequality in the developing world, this pattern is likely to reverse sometime in this century. It is thus nuclear how the costs of global reform should be divided. Apportionment of responsibility for reducing environmental damage essentially hinges on the manner in which the question is framed. For example, if a limit is placed globally on levels of per capita pollution emissions, the approach would clearly favour lower-income countries that have much lower per capita consumption levels. Conversely, if international pressures try to limit the growth rate of per capita emissions or even to impose limits on the growth of national emissions, any movement in that direction would tend to freeze incomes in the developing world at a small fraction of those of their developed world counterparts.

The Scope of Environment Degradation

The most pressing environmental challenges in developing countries in the next few decades will be caused by poverty. These will include health hazards created by lack of access to clean water and sanitation, indoor air pollution from biomass stoves, and deforestation and severe soil degradation—all most common where households lack economic alternatives to unsustainable patterns of living. The principal health and productivity consequences of environmental damage in the developing world. It divides this damage into seven categories: water pollution and water security, air pollution, solid and hazardous wastes, soil degradation, deforestation, loss of biodiversity, and atmospheric changes.

In the 1980s, per capita levels of arable land fell by 1.9 per cent annually, leading to worsening land shortages, which have forced many of the poorest onto marginal land with extremely limited cultivability. It is estimated that over 60 per cent of the poorest peoples residing in developing countries struggle for survival on agriculturally marginal soils. This trend is greatly worsened in some areas of the developing world by strong inequalities in the distribution of land, which force an ever-growing class of landless workers onto increasingly taxed, ecologically sensitive soils. The growing intensification of cultivation of fragile lands leads to rapid soil degradation and loss of productivity. Roughly 270,000 square kilometers of soil lose virtually all of their productivity each year. An area greater than the size of India and China combined, over 1.2 billion acres, has been significantly degraded. The resulting annual loss in agricultural productivity is estimated to be between 0.5 per cent and 1.5 per cent of annual worldwide GNP. As a result of rapid population increases and the failure of agricultural production to keep pace, per capita food production declined in 69 countries during the 1980s.

An environmental problem shared by both the urban and rural poor is the prevalence of unsanitary conditions created by the lack of clean water and sanitation. This is turn contributes greatly to the spread of infectious diseases. It has been estimated that waterborne pathogens that contribute to typhoid, cholera, amoebic infections, bacillary dysentery, and diarrhea account for 80 per cent of all disease in developing countries and at least in part for up to 90 per cent of the 13 million child deaths each year. Deteriorating environmental conditions were cited as a contributing factor to the spread of cholera epidemics in a number of countries in Latin America and Africa in the 1990s.

Rapid population growth and heavy rural-urban migration make it difficult to extend urban services to many people who need them. For example, to provide clean water to all urban dwellers in Latin American cities by 2030, the numbers served by public facilities will have to be increased by 250 per cent. Though this figure it-self is staggering, it excludes the 1.2 billion rural individuals whose needs must also be met. A comparable air for the provision of sanitation would require 400 per cent and 900 per cent increases for urban and rural communities, respectively.

On average throughout or slums. In Africa, the proportion is even greater, at 92 per cent, most of which have no access to public services.

Table 4.6: Principal Health and Productivity Consequences of Environmental Damage

Environmental Problem	*Effect on Health*	*Effect on Productivity*
Water pollution and water scarcity	More than 2 million deaths and billions of illnesses a year attributable to pollution; poor household hygiene and added health risks caused by water scarcity	Declining fisheries; rual household time and municipal costs of providing safe water; aquifer depletion leading to irreversible compaction; constraint on economic activity because of water shortages
Air pollution	Many acute and chronic health impacts: excessive urban particulate matter levels are responsible for 300,000 to 700,000 pre-mature deaths annually and for half of childhood chronic coughing; 400 million to 700 million people, mainly women and children in poor rural areas, affected by smoky indoor air	Restrictions on vehicle and industrial activity during critical episodes; effect of acid rain on forests and water bodies
Solid and hazardous wastes	Diseases spread by rotting garbage and blocked drains; risks from hazardous wastes typically local but often acute	Pollution of groundwater resources
Soil degradation	Reduced nutrition for poor farmers on depleted soils; greater susceptibility to drought	Field productivity losses in range of 0.5% to 1.5% of gross national product (GNP) common on tropical soils; offsite siltation of reservoirs, river-transport channels, and other hydrologic investments
Deforestation	Localized flooding, leading to death and disease	Loss of sustainable logging potential and of erosion prevention, watershed stability and carbon sequestration provided by forests.

Environmental Problem	*Effect on Health*	*Effect on Productivity*
Loss of biodiversity	Potential loss of new drugs	Reduction of ecosystem adaptability and loss of genetic resources.
Atmospheric changes	Possible shifts in vector-borne diseases; risks from climatic natural disasters; diseases attributable to ozone depletion (300,000) additional cases of skin cancer a year worldwide; 1.7 million cases of cataracts	Sea-rise damage to coastal investments; regional changes in agricultural productivity; disruption marine food chain

Source: From World Development Report, 1992: Development and the Environment, copyright@ 1992 by The International Bank for Reconstruction and Development/The World Bank. (New York: Oxford University Press, 1992) tab.1. Reprinted with permission of Oxford University Press, Inc.

Airborne pollutants also take a high toll on the health of citizens in developing countries. Dependence on biomass fuels such as wood, straw, and manure is closely related to poverty. The burning of biomass fuels for cooking and the boiling of water create dangerously high levels of indoor pollution to which 400 million to 700 million people, mostly women and children, are exposed each year. Smoke and fumes from indoor stoves are believed to contribute significantly go up to 4.3 million childhood deaths each year from respiratory diseases and to an ever-larger number of chronic respiratory illness.

In urban areas, other sources of pollution pose serious threats to physical well-being. According to the World Health Organization, 1.3 billion people live in urban areas with unsafe levels of airborne pollutants. Yet it is projected that by 2030, manufacturing in developing countries will expand to 600 per cent of current levels, vastly increasing potential concentrations of pollutants. Just to maintain current urban air standards until 2030 (which means conceding to conditions much worse than those existing in the urban centers of developed countries), average emissions from LDC industries and electric generators would have to be reduced by 90 per cent to 95 per cent per unit of output.

SUGGESTED READINGS

Fisher, A.C., Resource and Environmental Economics.
Sengupta, R.P., Ecology and Economics: An Approach to Sustainable Development.
Tietenberg, T., Environmental Economics and Policy.

5

Environmental Pollution and Policy

Environmental degradation means deteriorating the environmental quality at global, regional and local level by both natural processes and human activities. Population is the adverse changes by human activities on the environmental quality at local level. Sometimes the effects of human activities are so wide that the environmental is degraded at global and regional level as well.

Pollution may be defined as undesirable change in the physical, chemical and biological characteristics of air, water and soil that may harmfully affect the life or create a potential health hazard to any living organism. Pollution is thus direct or indirect change in any component of the biosphere that is harmful of living organisms and man, affecting adversely the industrial progress, cultural and natural resources or general environment.

Meaning of Pollutants

Any substance which causes lowering the quality of environment or pollution is called pollutant.

According to Smith (1977), "Every human society, be it rural, urban, industrial and most technologically advance society dispose of certain kind of by-products and waste. Products which are injected into the biosphere on great quantities and they affect on plants, animals and man are called pollutions."

A pollutant may be defined as 'any solid, liquid or gaseous substance present in such a concentration that may have adverse harmful effects or may be injurious to the environment. Pollutants are the residues of things we make use or throw away. The rivers are polluted by wastes from factories, air by gases, thermal power plants etc., worst pollution occurs in countries where there have been the greatest technological and industrial advances.

Types of Environmental Pollutants

1. Deposited matter such as dust, smoke, tar, grit, etc.
2. Gases such as nitrogen, carbon monoxide, sulphur oxides,
3. Solid waste,
4. Noise,
5. Radioactive waste,
6. Complex organic substances such as ether, acetic acid, benzene, etc.
7. Metals,
8. Florides,
9. Photo chemical oxidants, and
10. Agrochemicals such as fungicides and fertilizers.

Types of Pollution

There are various types of pollutions. These have been classified in different ways and on different-criterion.

1. On the Basis of Environmental Types—On the basis of the type of environment being polluted pollution may be classified in the following categories—

(i) Air Pollution,
(ii) Water Pollution,
(iii) Land Pollution

2. On the Basis of Human Activities—Pollution is generally caused by human activities which can be divided into two broad categories—

(1) *Physical Pollution*— It is caused by human activities due to lowering of the quality of physical components of the environments.

(2) *Social Pollution*— It is causes in different aspects of the society due to cumulative effects of extreme events/hazards and pollution. It may be further subdivided into several categories—

(a) Population explosions,

(b) Sociological Pollution—Educational and social backwardness, etc.

(c) Economic Pollution—Poverty, devolution of currency, lower paratypical income.

3. On the Basis of Nature of Pollutants—Another way to classify the pollution is the nature of pollutants. Pollutants are broadly classified into two categories—

(i) *Non Degradable Pollutants*—These are the materials and poisonous substance which do not degrade or degrade very slowly in nature such as aluminum, mercuric salts, long-chain phjenolics, etc. They are not naturally cycled in ecosystem.

(ii) *Biodegradable Pollutants*—These are the domestic wastes that can are rapidly decomposed under natural conditions and create problems when they accumulate.

4. On the Basis of Cost Pollution —

(i) Damage to crop production.
(ii) Loss of resources by unnecessary wasteful exploitation.
(iii) Medical care of health due to diseases.
(iv) Soiling of buildings and textiles.
(v) Corrosion of metals as iron, steel, copper, brass, zinc, lead, etc.
(vi) Pollution control involving money, funds, manpower, etc., for disposal of pollutants and for control devices developed.

Causes, Effects, Control and Measures of Pollution

Air Pollution

The history of air pollution: The origin of air pollution on the Earth can be traced back to the times when man stated using firewood as a means of cooking and heating. Hippocrates has mentioned air pollution in 400BC. With the discovery and increased use of coal, air pollution became more pronounced specially in urban areas. It was recognized as a problem 700 years ago in London in the form of smoke pollution, which prompted king Edward I to make the first anti-pollution law to restrict people from using coal for domestic heating in the year 1273. In the year 1300 another Act banning the use of coal was passed; the defying the law led to imposition of capital punishment. In spite of this, air pollution became a serious problem in London during the Industrial Revolution due to the widespread use coal of industries. The earliest recorded major disaster was the 'London Smog' that occurred in 1952, which resulted in more than 4000 deaths due to the accumulation of air pollutants over the city for five days.

In Europe, the middle of the 19th century, a black form of the Peppered moth began appearing in industrial areas. Usually, normal-coloured Peppered moth is well camouflaged when on a clean, lichen-covered tree. However, this Peppered pattern was easily spotted and picked up by birds on the smoke-blackened bark of trees in industrial areas. So, while the normal pepper-patterned moths were successful in surviving in clean non-industrial areas, only black-coloured moths were successfully camouflaged in industrial areas. Thus, with the spread of industrialization, an increased incidence of black forms has been observed not only in the Peppered moth, but also in many other moths. This is a classic case of pollution leading to adaptation.

Air pollution began to increase in the beginning of the 20th century with the development of transportation systems and large-scale use of petrol and diesel. The severe air quality problems due to the formation of petrochemical smog from the combustion residues of diesel and petrol engines were felt for the first time in Los Angeles. Pollution due to auto-ehaust remains a serious environmental issue in many developed and developing countries, including India.

The Air Pollution Control Act in India was passed in 1981 and the Motor Vehicle Act for controlling the air pollution was passed in 1981 and the Motor Vehicle Act for controlling the air pollution was passed very recently. These laws are intended to prevent the air from becoming over-polluted.

The greatest industrial disaster leading to serious air pollution took place in Bhopal, were the extremely poisonous methyl isocyanides gas was accidentally released from the Union carbide's pesticide manufacturing plant, on the night of December 2nd, 1984. The effects of this disaster on human health and the soil are felt even today.

Structure of the Atmosphere

The atmosphere is normally composed of 79 per cent nitrogen, 20 per cent oxygen and 1 per cent as a mixture of carbon dioxide, water vapor and trace amounts of several other gases such as neon, helium, methane, krypton, hydrogen and xenon. The general structure of the atmosphere has several important features that have relevance to environmental problems. The atmosphere is divided into several layers.

The innermost layer, the troposphere, extends 17 km above sea level at the equator and about 8 km over the poles. It contains about 75 per cent of the mass of the Earth's air. The fragility of this layer is obvious from the fact that if the Earth were an apple, this particular layer would be no thicker than an apple's skin. Temperature declines with altitude in the troposphere. At the top of the troposphere, temperatures abruptly begin to rise. This boundary where this temperature reversal occurs is called the 'tropopause'.

The tropopause marks the end of the tropopause and the beginning of the stratosphere, the second layer of the atmosphere. The stratosphere extends from 17-48 km above the Earth's surface. While the composition of the stratosphere is similar to that of the troposphere, it has two major differences. The volume of water vapor here is about 1000 times less, while the volume of ozone is about 1000 times greater. The presence of ozone in the stratosphere prevents about 99 per cent of the Sun's harmful ultraviolet (UV) radiation from reaching the Earth's surface, thereby protecting humans from cancer and damage to the immune system. This layer does not have clouds and, hence, airplanes fly in this layer as it creates less turbulence. Temperature rises with altitude stratosphere, until there is another reversal. This point is called the 'stratopause' and it marks the and of the stratosphere.

In the next layer, the mesosphere, the temperature decreases with attitude, falling up to -110°C at the top. Above this a layer where ionization of the gases is a major phenomenon, thus increasing the temperature. This layer is called the thermosphere. Only the lower troposphere is routinely involved in our weather and, hence, air pollution. The other layers are not significant in determining the level of air pollution.

Effect of Air Pollutions on Health

Industrialization and urbanization have resulted in a profound deterioration of India's air quality. The scientific evidence proves that vehicular exhaust is a complex mixture comprising hazardous particles and vapors, some of which are known carcinogens and others probable carcinogens. Diesel and petrol exposure poses a significant and avoidable increase in human health risks. About 3 million premature deaths in the world occur each year due to outdoor and indoor air pollution. The highest numbers are reported to occur in India. According to the World Health Organization, New Delhi is one of the top ten most polluted cities in the world. Various surveys and reports indicate that in New Delhi, the incidence of respiratory diseases due to air pollution is about 12 times higher than the national average. According to another study, India's gross domestic product has increased 2.5 times over the past two decades, while the vehicular pollution has increased eight times and pollution from industries has quadrupled.

Major Sources of Air Pollutants

Transportation

Aeroplanes, cars, ships and trains are leading sources of air pollution. Between 1970 and 1990, the number of vehicles has grown 11.5 times from about a million to more than a million.

At the same time, the figure per 1000 population has increased from 3.4 to 25.31 and is expected to exceed 40 by the year 2007.

The bulk of this vehicular population is found in urban areas. Exhaust from engines contains various kinds of harmful pollutants. Such pollutants include carbon monoxide gas, suspended particulate matter, hydrocarbons (compounds of hydrogen and carbon) and nitrogen oxides (compounds of nitrogen and oxygen). Nitrogen oxides in the air help produce a form of oxygen called ozone. Ozone reacts with hydro-carbons to form a type of air pollution known as smog.

Fuel Combustion

Fuel combustion for heating homes, office buildings and factories sharply increases the level of air pollution in urban areas. Furnaces that burn coal or fuel oil give off nitrogen oxides, particulates and sulphur oxides (compounds of sulphur and oxygen). Electricity generating stations that use fuels also release such pollutants into the atmosphere.

Industrial Process

Industrial processes contribute significantly to air pollution. Industries give off various types of pollutants. For example, factories that produce aluminium expel fluoride dust. Oil refineries discharge ammonia, hydrocarbons, organic acids and sulphur oxides into the atmosphere. Industrial plants that produce plastic foams are a major source of chlorofluorocarbons (CFC's) compounds of chlorine fluorine and carbon.

Solid Wastes

Burning of solid pollution wastes creates a very visible form of air (thick and black smoke). The burning of leaves, scrap cars and other solid other prohibited in some areas.

Other sources of air pollution include chemical sprays, forest and structural fires. Pollution also results from the burning forest, bush and grass to clear land for farming.

Effect of Air Pollution on Health

India's most severe environmental problem arises in several forms, including vehicular emissions and untreated industrial smoke. Due to rapid industrialization, urbanization has led to emergence of industrial centres without a corresponding growth in civic amenities and pollution control mechanisms. India's high concentration of pollution is not due to lack of effort in building a sound environmental legal regime, but rather due to lack of enforcement at the local level. Efforts are currently underway to change this as new specifications are being adopted for auto emissions, which currently accounts for about 70 per cent of air pollution. In the absence of coordinated government efforts, including stricter enforcement, this figure is likely to rise in the coming years due to the sheer increase in number of vehicles.

There are seven primary air pollutants which are considered as health hazard when their concentration exceeds the national ambient air quality standards. These are; SPM (or PM10 and PM2.5), carbon monoxide, nitrogen dioxide, ozone and other photochemical oxidants (smog), lead and sulphur dioxide. Other pollutants include toxic gases and heavy metals. There is little or no information available about these pollutants and they are not independently considered in this article.

Suspended Particulate Matter (SPM)

According to the World Health Organization, health effects of Suspended Particulate Matters (SPM) in humans depend on particle size and concentration, and vary with daily fluctuation in the finer particle level, PM10, and PM2.5 (PM10 is that fraction of total SPM that is less than 10 microns in aerodynamic diameter and PM2.5 refers to the fraction of even particles less than 2.5 Microns in diameter). Health effects of SI'M includes increased daily mortality and increased rates of hospital admissions for respiratory ailments. Long-term effects of SPM refer to mortality and respiratory in morbidity, but only few studies on the long-term effect of SPM is available.

SPM air pollution is an urban phenomenon, but in many areas of developed and developing countries, urban-rural differences in PM10 are small or even absent, including that PM exposure is widespread. This does not imply that exposure to primary, combustion-related PM may not be higher in urban areas. Limited evidence from studies on dust storms indicates that such PM10 particles are less toxic than those associated with combustion sources.

Current epidemiological studies have been unable to define an SPM threshold, below which no health effects occur. Event at low levels of PM (less than 100 microgram/m^3), short-term exposure is associated with health effects.

Recent studies in which PM10 size fractions and/or constituents have been measured, suggest that the observed effects of PM10 are largely associated with finer particles and not with the coarser fraction (PM70 minus PM2.5). In some areas, strong aerosol acidity or sulfate may be the cause of the effects associated with PM2.5. Evidence is also emerging that long-term exposure to low concentration of PM10 in air is associated with mortality and other chronic effects, such as increased rates of bronchitis and reduced lung function. Two cohort studies conducted in the USA suggest that life expectancy may be 2-3 years shorter in communities with high PM exposure compared to those in communities with low PM exposure. This is consistent with earlier cross-sectional studies, which compared age-adjusted mortality rates across a range of long-term average PM concentrations. The results showed that long-term average exposure to low PM levels, starting at about 10 microgram m^3 of fine particulate matter were associated with a reduction in life expectancy.

A recent editorial published the New England Journal of Medicine Comments on a study of PM10 and its correlation to mortality is given below:

The PM10 concentrations were positively associated with daily mortality rates in most of the 20 cities studied and at - concentrations well below the current 24-hour standard of 150 microgram per cubic meter. Moreover, the association was specific to PM10. The concentrations of other regulated air pollutants produced by the combustion of fossil fuels (sulphur dioxide, nitrogen dioxide and carbon monoxide) were weakly and consistently associated with daily mortality rates.

Carbon Monoxide

Carbon monoxide is a colourless, odourless and poisonous gas. A product of incomplete burning of hydrocarbon-based fuels, carbon monoxide consists of a carbon atom and an oxygen atom linked together. It enters the bloodstream through the lungs and forms carboxy-hemoglobin, a compound that inhibits the blood's capacity to carry oxygen to tissues. Persons with heart disease are especially sensitive to carbon monoxide poisoning and may experience chest pain if they breathe the gas while exercising. Infants, elderly persons and individuals with respiratory diseases are also sensitive.

Carbon monoxide (CO) can cause harmful health effects by reducing delivery of oxygen to the body's organs like the heart, brain and tissues. The health threat from lower levels of CO is most serious for those who suffer from heart disease, like angina, clogged arteries or congestive heart failure. For a person with heart disease, a single exposure to CO at low levels may cause chest pain and reduce that person's ability to exercise. Repeated exposures may contribute to other cardiovascular effects.

Even healthy people can be affected by high levels of Carbon monoxide (CO). People who breathe high levels of CO can develop vision problems, reduced ability to work or learn, reduced manual dexterity and difficulty in performing complex tasks. At extremely high levels, CO is poisonous and can cause death. Carbon monoxide can affect healthy individuals, impairing exercise capacity, visual perception, manual dexterity, learning functions and ability to perform complex tasks. The initial symptoms of CO poisoning may include headache, dizziness, drowsiness and nausea. These initial symptoms may lead to vomiting, loss of consciousness. Coma or death may occur if high exposures continue.

Lead

The standard for airborne lead are based on the effects of lead in blood. In adults, critical effects include elevation of free erythrocyte protoporphyrin, whereas for children effects include cognitive defects, hearing impairment and disturbed vitamin D metabolism. All of these effects are considered adverse. A critical level of lead in blood is 100 microgram/1, but much lower levels are dangerous. It should be stressed that all of these values are based on population studies yielding group average, and apply to the individual child only in a probabilistic manner.

For example, in Manila, 33 per cent street vendors in 6-14 years of age who were exposed to high levels of traffic-related lead emission had blood lead level of over 20 microgram/dl. Only 10 per cent of other sampled school children of the same age group exceeded the lead of 20 microgram/dl. Mean IQ decrements due to lead exposure have been estimated at 2.2 per cent in school children, 3.1 per cent in child street vendors, while maximum IQ decrements in these population groups ranged from 4.5 to 6.4 gradients, respectively.

Nitrogen Dioxide

The World Health Organization reports that normal healthy humans, exposed at rest or with light exercise for less than 2 hours to concentrates above 4700 microgram/ml (2.5 ppm), experience pronounced decrease in pulmonary function, but normal subjects do not appear to be affected by concentrations less than 1880 microgram/m^3 (1.0 ppm).

Nitrogen dioxide (NO_2) increases bronchical reactivity, as measured by the response of normal and asthmatic subject following exposure to pharmacological bronchoconstrictor agents, even at level that do not affect pulmonary function directly in the absence of a bronchoconstrictor. Some, but not all, studies show increased responsiveness to bronchoconstrictors at NO_2 levels as low as 376-365 microgram/m^3 (0.2 to 0.3 ppm). In other studies, higher levels had no such effect. Because the actual mechanisms of effect are not fully defined and NO_2 studies with allergen challenges showed no effects at the lowest concentration tested (188 μg/m 3; 0.7 ppm). Full evaluation of the health consequences of the increased responsiveness to bronchoconstrictors is not yet possible. Recent studies have shown an increased reactivity to natural allergens in the same concentration range. The results of repetitive exposures of such individuals or the impact of single exposures on more severe asthmatics are not known.

Long-term exposure to NO_2 at levels up to 1 ppm can cause both reversible and irreversible effects in the lungs resulting in emphysema-like effects. Other effects have been observed in the spleen, liver and in blood.

Ozone and Photochemical Oxidants

The effects of ozone increases with increased concentrations, exposure duration and activity level. Short-term acute effects include pulmonary function changes, increased airway responsiveness and airway inflammation and other symptoms. Adverse effects occur during exercise with one hour exposure to concentrations of 500 $\mu g/m^3$ or higher, particularly in susceptible individuals or sub-groups.

However, the World Health Organization concludes that the health problems of grave concern are from chronic exposure, resulting in increased hospital admission, exacerbation of asthma, inflammatory changes in the lung and structural alternations in the lung. The guidelines value or standard is designed to limit average daily exposure, inhaled dose and dose rate.

Sulphur Dioxide

Acute response to SO_2 occur within the first few minutes after exposure and further exposure does not increase effects. Effects include reductions in the mean forced expiratory volume over one second, increase in specific airway resistance and symptoms such as wheezing or shortness of breath. These effects are enhanced by exercise that increases, the volume of air inspired, as it allows

SO_2 to penetrate further into the respiratory tract. A wide range of sensitivity has been demonstrated, both among normal subjects and among those with asthma, who are predictably most sensitive to the pollutant.

Worsening of symptoms among selected sensitive patients seems to arise in a consistent manner when the concentration of SO_2 exceeds 250 $\mu g/m^3$ in the presence of SPM. Recent studies in Europe have involved mixed industrial and vehicular emissions now common in ambient air.

At low levels of exposure (mean annual levels below 60 $\mu g/m^3$; daily levels usually not exceeding 80 $\mu g/m^3$), effects on mortality and on hospital emergency admissions for total respiratory causes and chronic obstructive pulmonary disease have been consistently demonstrated. Long-term exposure studies examined respiratory symptoms, respiratory illness frequencies, or differences in lung functions values in localities with contrasting concentrations of SO_2 and SPM, using data from the coal-burning era in Europe. The lowest-observed-adverse-effect level of SO_2 was judged to be at an annual average of 100 mg/ m^3, when present with SPM. More recent studies related to industrial sources of SO_2 or to the changed urban mixture of air pollutants have shown adverse effects.

Other Effects

Air pollution causes severe damage to crops and livestock in countries with heavy industries and crowded roads. Plants will not grow alongside many roads in these countries because vehicle exhaust fumes kill them. Air pollution can damage fruit, vegetable and grains.

Some pollutants are not poisonous but can cause damage by altering the earth's atmosphere. For example, the amount of carbon dioxide in the atmosphere has been increasing mainly as a result of the burning of coal, oil, and other carbon-containing fuels. Carbon dioxide allows sunlight to reach the earth and warm its surface, but it prevents some surface heat from escaping out of the atmosphere. This process, called the greenhouse effect, may produce significant climatic changes, which could destroy many kinds of plants and animals. Chlorofluoro-carbons (CFC's) break down the layer of ozone in the earth's upper atmosphere. This layer protects plants and animals from harmful ultraviolet rays.

Most materials deteriorate faster when exposed to the pollutants present in the air. Air pollutants dissolve concrete and stone, metals corrode faster than usual. Air pollutants also damage plastic, rubber and fabrics.

Air pollution is closely related to other forms of pollution. Sulphur dioxide and nitrogen oxides can react with water droplets in the air to produce acid rain. Acid rain pollutes lakes and streams and in high concentrations, can harm soil fertility.

Control of Air Pollution

Adopting latest technologies can reduce air pollution from such stationary sources as factories, furnaces, incinerators and power stations. For examples a plant can install equipment designed to limit the amount of pollutants given off. It can change the method of manufacture. The plant can also switch to a cleaner fuel that causes less air pollution. In some cases, the units must a combination of these steps to reduce air pollution.

Changing the way engines operates, changing the ingredients in fuel and adding pollution control devices to the vehicle control air pollution associated with motor vehicles. Manufacturers and refiners are working in all these areas to find good ways of controlling pollution. In addition, is underway to develop alternative engines that are driven by electricity, methanol, natural gas, steam, or other energy sources that create less air pollution. Increasingly, national and state governments are passing laws and setting requirements designed to control pollution. They also issue information on the effects of air pollutants and the techniques available for controlling them. They set goals called air quality standards for achieving clean air. They then enforce control measures to meet the goals. Governments act directly against polluters if they fail to obey the regulations.

The control measures include emission standards, which restrict the amount of pollution from factories and other sources of pollution. Governments also set emission standards for motor vehicles. In many countries, to meet these emission standards, new cars are equipped with control devices called catalytic converters.

Regulatory Framework

Regulatory reforms aimed at reducing the air pollution problem in cities such as New Delhi have been quite difficult to implement. However, the Supreme Court recently lifted a ruling that it imposed two years ago which required all public transport vehicles in New Delhi to switch to Compressed Natural Gas (CNG) engines by April 1, 2001. This ruling however, led to the disappearance of some 15,000 taxis and 10,000 buses from the city, creating public protests, and widespread "commuter chaos." Last year the Court faced considerable resistance when it attempted to ban all public vehicles that were more than 15 years old and ordered the introduction of unleaded gasoline and CNG.

Now it is necessary to adopt/develop more eco-friendly technology for the vehicles so that the ongoing environmental impact can be minimized to an acceptable level.

Noise Pollution and its Solution

Noise is "unwanted sound"; it is derived from the Latin word "nausea," meaning sea sickness. The American National Standards Institute (ANSI) defines noise as any 'undesired' sound or 'unwanted' sound or sound 'without value'. Its definition can be more appropriately stated as—"Noise is unwanted sound or sounds of a duration, intensity, or other quality that cause some kind of physiological or psychological harm to humans or other living things."

Facts About Noise

- 28 million people in USA, have hearing lass and noise is

one of the leading causes of hearing loss, specially in young people.

- Noise negatively affects learning and behaviour.
- Studies show that children's learning is negatively affected by noise in the classroom.

Animals use sound to stake out territories and to call the attention of all members of the same species to the fact that a territory has been staked out. Sound has other types reproductive significance, mating calls being the most obvious example. Some animals-bats for instance-use high frequency sound to locate prey and to navigate. For every species of animals, including humans, sound is an important means of alerting individuals to danger. But, when this sound crosses the limit, it becomes 'noise and creates problems'. It is a problem for human beings and other species only because they have sense organs that are capable of receiving the information in sound in various survival related ways.

Noise is among the most pervasive Pollutants today. It has a significant impact on the quality of life, and in that sense, it is a health problem in accordance with the World Health Organization's definition of health, which includes, total Physical and mental well-being, as well as the absence of disease. Along these lines, a 1971 WHO group stated, "Noise must be recognized" as a major threat to human well-being. This form of pollution may come from road traffic, jet planes, jet skis, refuse trucks, construction equipment, manufacturing processes, lawnmowers, leaf blowers, radio set, ghetto blasters, etc. From these, unwanted sounds may be routinely broadcast into the air.

The decibel (dB) is a measure of sound intensity; that, the magnitude of the fluctuations in air pressure caused by sound waves. The decibel scale is logarithmic, which means that a doubling of sound intensity is not represented as a doubling of the decibel level. In fact, an increase of just 3 dB means twice as much sound, and an increase of 10 dB means ten times as much sound.

A sound pressure level of 0 dB represents the threshold of hearing in the most sensitive frequency range of a young healthy ear, while the thresholds of tickling or painful sensations in the ear occur at about 130 to 140 dB. The perception of loudness by the human ear is not directly proportional to the decibel level. The intensity of noise diminishes with distance. Outdoors, and in absence of any close reflecting surface, the effective decibel level diminishes at a rate of 6 dB for each factor of two increases in distance. For example, a sound measuring 100 dB at 10 metres would be 64 dB at 20 metres, 88 dB at 40 metres, and so on.

Problems related to noise include hearing loss, stress, high blood pressure, sleep loss, distraction and low productivity and a general reduction in the quality of life.

Noise can interfere with complex task performance. Tasks that demand continuous and sustained attention; and require large working memory capacity are susceptible to adverse effects of noise. It causes brief period of inefficiency when sustained visual attention is required.

On the other hand, since noise increases alertness (arousal), monotonous and boring tasks may be performed better under noise conditions because the organism remains closer to an optimal level or overall arousal.

If a noise is so loud that one needs to shout to be heard, then there is every chance that the inner ear can be injured. Temporary hearing loss can happen after having been exposed to loud noise for only 15 minutes. Permanent hearing loss can happen when someone is exposed to loud noise over and over again. Since hearing loss is most often a very gradual process, many of its symptoms are subtle.

Loud music of any kind can cause temporary and permanent hearing loss. But constant "pounding" music, and noise that goes on for long period of time, are common causes of deafness.

Exposure to noise can induce disturbances of sleep in terms of difficulty to fall asleep, alterations of sleep pattern or depth and awakenings. These effects are referred to as primary sleep disturbance effects. Other primary physiological effects that can be induced by noise during sleep are increased blood pressure, increased heart rate, vasoconstriction, change in respiration and cardiac arrhythmia.

Noise may also contribute to the development and aggravation of stress-related conditions such as high blood pressure, coronary disease, ulcers, colitis and migraine. Growing evidence suggests a link between noise and cardiovascular problems. There is also evidence suggesting that noise may be related to birth defects and low birth-weight babies. The noise exposure can increase susceptibility to viral infection.

Noise can interfere with our ability to communicate. Many noises that are not intense enough to cause hearing impairment can interfere with speech communication. It can mask important sounds and disrupt communication between individuals in a variety of settings. It can also disrupt face to face and telephonic conversation and the enjoyment of radio or television in homes. It can also disrupt effective communication between teachers and pupils in schools and can cause fatigue and vocal strain in those who need to communicate in spite of noise.

Although "Good neighbours keep their noise to themselves" is a popular phrase, but noise from neighbours is a common source of nuisance for a number of reasons:

- the neighbours behaving unreasonably, for instance by playing loud music or allowing their dog to bark all day,
- the neighbours behaving normally, but sound insulation in your home may not be good enough to cut out the sounds of everyday living, and
- the sensitivity of people to noise and different types of noise varies-sounds that are enjoyable to some people may irritate others. "One person's MUSIC may be another person's NOISE".

Modern music and modern music players have brought with them very special noise problems. The CD player or other equipment is designed to boost bass frequencies—in any case the younger listeners seem to prefer the music turned up high and on full bass (low frequencies) settings with virtually no treble (high frequencies)—they like to hear the "beat". What may be identifiable "music" to the person playing it becomes low frequency noise pollution, with no discernible music continue to the person on the other side of the wall.

Noise Pollution in Different Society

The development of society has led to more and more sound sources giving higher and higher noise levels. The major sources of acoustical disturbance now-a-days is due to industrial, çommercial and traffic activities. The impact of such disturbance on human being depends mainly on acoustic energy and duration of exposure. Thus, judicious monitoring of acoustic environment is an important issue before adopting particular control measures against deterioration of environment.

Noise is comparatively a newly recognised problem in the list of occupational hazards. It did not create much public concern, compared to either air or water pollution mainly due to insufficient study of the problem and more because of ignorance of public in general about the insidious effect of noise on both workers in the industry in particular and the public in the community in general.

When considering community reaction to noise, it is therefore necessary to assess the environment in which the noise is being heard and, using suitable bases of judgement, to determine whether or not a definite nuisance exists. Does the noise interfere with sleep or with study, or with the enjoyment of normal amenities of modern community life? It may have to be accepted at the present state of knowledge and under present day economic and social conditions that many industrial workers have to tolerate reasonably, noisy conditions during working hours. And this amount of tolerance gradually affects the person and finally noise deafness (noise induced hearing loss) and other physiological and psychological problems occur due to his/her little knowledge of the subject. Thus, noise acts as a silent killer.

Sources of Noise Pollution

Noise is a major factor of environmental pollution: On the one hand, industrialization, scientific and technological developments have contributed a great deal to the progress of society, on the other, these are main causes of environmental pollution, including noise pollution.

The ill effects of noise pollution are in no way less harmful than those of water, soil and air pollution. It disturbs a person in his normal work. It causes annoyance, tiredness, impaired hearing, high blood pressure and nervous tension. The extent of damage may depend on duration and intensity of noise. Radio, stereo, loudspeakers, generator sets, building construction, honking of horns by vehicles, etc. are supposed to be the main noise sources of human settlements.

In India, the problem caused by noise pollution is more aggravated in view of the fact that there is hardly any celebration, a festival, a marriage or a religious function, where there is no use of loudspeaker at a very high pitch continuously for a long time. Another major factor contributing to the noise pollution in India is that in many of the cities, the industrial and commercial units are either not very far from the residential areas, or they are sometimes set-up in the residential areas.

USA and UK have comprehensive and exclusive Acts, such as Noise Control Act, 1972 of USA and Control of Pollution Act, 1974, Part III of UK. In India recently, Ministry of Environment and Forests has notified "Noise Pollution (Regulation and Control) Rules, 2000", covering various aspects of noise pollution.

Fundamental of Sound

A vibrating sources produce vibration into the medium in which it is placed. These vibrations are propagated as waves in the form of pressure variations and are termed as acoustic waves. If they fall within the range capable of exciting the sense of hearing, they are called as sound waves.

An acoustic wave travels in a given medium at a constant velocity. When the level of the sound becomes objectionable, it is called as noise.

The sound becomes noise, when:

- It annoys and irritates.
- It interferes with normal work.
- It disturbs or prevents sleep.

Thus, in general, the sound can be referred as a physical or mechanical disturbance capable of being detected by the human ear. And the noise can be referred as the random sound phenomena which interferes with communication or human processes of concentration.

Sound Power Level and Sound Pressure Level

Each part of equipment that make noise, radiates certain amount of sound energy, in much the same way as a light bulb which radiates the light energy. The amount of energy that can be radiated by the bulb is measured in Watts. In the similar way, the sound power radiated by a sound source is measured in Acoustic Watts. A relative unit, the decibel (dB) is used as the measure of sound power rather than watts directly. The dB scale is logarithmic.

The sound pressure level is a measure of the amplitude of the sound wave. The sound pressure disturbances that we are capable of hearing are very small (i.e., 2×10^{-5} Pa) relative to the normal atmospheric pressure (1.013×10^{-5} Pa). So the range of pressure from the faintest sound we can hear to the loudest is very large e.g., the lowest audible pressure is 2×10^{-5} Pa whereas the pressure associated with sell, .0ion of pain is approximately 200 Pa. Because of this wide range in the magnitude of these numbers the concept of decibel is introduced here.

Generally the sound intensity is at full strength for a distance that is three times the size of the noise sources itself. For example, if the noise source is of 1 m in diameters than the sound is at full strength at approximately 3 m of distance from the source. Subsequently, the sound strength is reduced by one-half with each doubling of distance. In the above example, the sound will be at

100 per cent strength from 0-3 mt., at 50 per cent strength at 6 mt. and 25 per cent at 12 mt.

The human ear can detect sounds from 20 Hz to 20,000 Hz. The frequencies most important for understanding normal speech lie between 300 Hz—5000 Hz. There are strong individual variations. The 20 Hz sounds are probably felt more than they are heard.

Frequency and A-Weighting

Each vibrating body produces a certain number of complete outward and inward movements or vibrations, in the medium through which it is passing. The number of these completed vibration in a second is known as the frequency of the sound, which is expressed in Hz. The frequency characteristics are important for study because it is generally easier and less expensive to control high frequency noise than the low frequency noise. The audible range of a normal young adult is between 300 to 5000 Hz. The human ears are not equally sensitive to all the frequencies.

Noise measurement can be done by using a Sound Level Meter instrument. Noise measurements are made because it is ultimately desirable to relate the noise to its effects on humans. It is therefore necessary to consider the methods by which noise levels can be evaluated in terms of their subjective effects. Sound level meters have connections to which filters can be added to select particular frequencies of the sound. Most meters have A, B, C scales where the response varies with frequencies. The adjusting of the decibel scale to take into account the different sensitivity to different frequencies is called "weighting". Generally, three weighting networks A, B and C are used. The sound pressure level is expressed normally in dB(A)'s because the reading on A-Scale corresponds most closely to the response of the human ear.

Effects of Noise on Human Beings

The generation of unreasonable noise within the environment is regarded as a form of pollution because it lowers the quality of life. There has been several specific ways in which excessive noise can affect the people adversely. The adverse effect of noise can be described as:

(a) Auditory effect;
(b) Physiological effect;
(c) Effects on task performance; and
(d) Other effects:
  (i) Sleep interference,
  (ii) Speech interference.

Auditory Effect

The excessive noise can cause damage to the human ear. Infact, any continuous noise level above about 85 dBA will cause some damage. This damage is slow, insidious and progressive and is not usually noticed by the recipient until it is far too late. The most prominent effect of noise will be noise induced hearing loss or noise deafness.

The sensitivity to noise varies greatly from person to person. Some of the hearing loss which results from exposure to intense noise is temporary and over a period of time, partial or complete recovery will occur. Such temporary loss is usually referred to as Temporary Threshold Shift (TIS). But, any hearing loss, which persists, is called the permanent threshold shift or Noise Induced Permanent Threshold Shift (NIPTS). The permanent threshold shift is associated with the destruction of the delicate hair cells and their nerve connections in the organ of Corti, which is contained in the Cochlea region (inner ear). Hence, once a permanent threshold shift has occurred, normal hearing cannot be restored. Every exposure to loud noise destroy, some cells, and the prolonged or repeated exposure causes the destruction of large number of cells and ultimately the collapse of the organ of Corti.

Presbycusis—It is the term that describes the loss of auditory sensitivity with increasing age.

Acoustic trauma—If a person is all of a sudden exposed to a high sound situation, then the threshold of audibility shift may become permanent, which is termed as Acoustic tramua.

Physiological Effect

Besides, noise is likely to harm the physiological and psychological well-being of people. Physiological changes include:

(1) changes in heart beat rate and blood pressure,
(2) various glandular changes,
(3) a change in activity of sweat glands.

The frequency of cardiovascular ailments, or atleast of hypertension is higher in workers exposed to loud noise than those who work in less noisy situations. Also the noise interferes with the proper digestive function, particularly when noise is sudden and unexpected. Such type of noise produces a decrease in secretion of digestive juices and also in bowel activity.

Effect on Task Performance

It is likely that any new sound or change in an existing sound may result in at least momentary distraction and that this may impair a person ability to perform some tasks. It has been observed that workers are less accurate when working under noisy environment and may also be liable to make mistakes which produce accidents.

Other Effects

In addition to interference with normal physiological and psychological function of the human system, the excessive noise also causes:

Sleep Interference

Noise has multiple effects on sleep. Aeroplane noise is greater disturbance to sleep than other noises. Noise reduces the depth and quality of sleep and thus may adversely affect the overall mental and physical health. Noise disturbs sleep by leading to more numerous awakenings and/or changes in the stages of sleep.

It has been found that an intermittent noise disturbs sleep more than a continuous noise. Also, elderly persons are more disturbed in their sleep by noise than young adult or children. Children are least disturbed in their sleep.

Speech Interference

Speech reception is the most important and also the most complex use of the auditory system. Noise can either mask the speech to make it inaudible or by masking only some frequencies leaving it audible but of reduced intelligibility.

Noise Standards

For Industrial Noise

The damage risk criteria for hearing as enforced by ISO, DGMS (through its circular no. DG (Tech)/18 of (1975) and CPCB stipulates that noise level upto 90 dBA are acceptable for 8 hours exposure (Leq 8 hr.) per day. That is 90 dBA is the maximum sound level to which an employee can be exposed for 8 hrs. on a given working day.

For Community Noise

The Noise Pollution (Regulations and Control) Rules, 2000 prescribe the ambient air quality standards in respect of noise in industrial, commercial, residential and silence zones area as follows:

Sl.No.	*Area*	*Noise level (Leq. In dBA)*	
1.	Industrial	75	70
2.	Commercial	65	55
3.	Residential	55	45
4.	Silence Zone	50	40

Day time = 0600 hrs to 2200 hrs.
Night time = 2200 hrs. to 0600.

Noise Control Methods

For Industrial Noise

Noise control is the technology for obtaining an acceptable noise environment at one or multiple receivers with economic and operational consideration. Each industrial noise control problem is slightly different and should be treated as an individual basis. The various techniques that could be applied for noise control can be classified as:

(i) control at source;
(ii) control at transmission path; and
(iii) control at receiver by using some protective equipment.

Besides these the following measures could be adopted at sources:

(i) Control of exposure time;
(ii) Job rotation;
(iii) Provision of quite working areas for some time;
(iv) Regular audible monitoring of the hearing levels of personnel; and
(v) Provision of noise barriers close to the receiver.

For Community Noise

(i) Industrial Area

(a) Various machines in the industry should not be allowed to generate more noise by proper designing, maintenance and providing partition.
(b) Residences should not be allowed to grow nearby industrial areas.

(ii) Commercial Areas

(a) The traffic volume should be reduced by diversion of traffic. Parking of vehicles should be restricted to one place only.
(b) The noise generating sources like music system from.
(c) Generators where used should be provided by acoustic hoods.
(d) Unnecessary honking of horns should be banned.

(iii) Residential Areas

(a) Movement of vehicles on the inner colony roads should be banned.
(b) There should be restriction on the use of horns by vehicles passing by the residential areas.
(c) There should be plenty of trees and bushes in open spaces houses and lanes.

(iv) Silence Zones

Area upto 100 meters around certain premises like hospitals, educational institutions and court may be declared as silence zones by the competent authority. The noise control measures are:

(a) Plying of heavy vehicles should be banned near the silence zone area.
(b) Use of horn should be banned.

The world around us is becoming an increasingly noisy place and whether at work in office or factory at home or in a place of entertainment. or even in hospital, unwanted noise is seldom entirely absent. Fortunately, the many sided nature of man's continual search for knowledge leads him to follow every possible like of energy. Appropriate procedure have been developed both for avoiding noise problems and for considerably reducing it by remedial techniques.

Noise pollution is not less hazardous than land, water and air pollution. We must understand that the quality of the environment is every body's responsibility and should contribute by avoiding noisy activities and by supporting anyone who tries to reduce unnecessary noise.

Water Pollution

Water pollution means such contamination of water or such alteration of the physical, chemical or biological properties of water or such discharge of any sewage or trade effluent or of any other liquid gaseous or slid substance into water (whether directly or indirectly) as may, or is likely to create a nuisance or render such water harmful or injurious to public health or safety, or to domestic, commercial, industrial, commercial industrial agricultural or other legitimate uses, or to the life and health of animals or plants or of aquatic organisms.

Fresh water present on the earth's surface is put to multifarious uses. It is used for drinking, domestic and municipal uses, agricultural irrigation, industries, navigation, recreation, etc. The used water becomes contaminated and is called waste water which contains residual of the activities taking place on each of them. Thus passing through these industries, agricultural lands and the urban settlements the water gets soiled up and is rendered harmful to plants, animals and men. These solid wastes are allowed to drain in the natural drain in the natural drainage system of the area and flow down the stream making the life uncomfortable for the people inhabiting areas situated downstream. These water get loaded with organic and inorganic chemicals, pathogenic and non-pathogenic organisms including viruses and cysts. Usually these waters do not remain fit for human consumption and for the life of plants and animals. Finding their ways they bring curse to the habitations downstream.

Non-pointed Source Water Pollution

Non-pointed source water pollution, once known as diffuse source pollution, arises from a broad group of human activities for which the pollutants have no obvious point of entry into receiving water recourses. In contrast, point source pollution represents those activities where wastewater is routed directly into receiving water bodies by, for example, discharge pipes, where they can be easily measured and controlled. Obviously, non-point source pollution is much more difficult to identity, measure and control than point

Table 5.1: Per capita renewable water supplies

Region/Country	*1992*	*2110*	*Change*
	(Cubic metres per person)		%
Africa			
Algeria	730	500	-32
Botswana	710	420	-41
Burndi	620	360	-42
Cape Verde	500	290	-42
Djibouti	750	430	-43
Egypt	30	20	-33
Kenya	560	330	-41
Libya	160	100	-38
Mauritania	190	110	-42
Rwanda	820	440	-46
Tunisia	450	330	-27
Middle East			
Bahrain	0	0	-0
Israel	330	250	-24
Jordan	190	110	-42
Kuwait	0	0	-0
Qater	40	30	-25
Saudi Arabia	140	70	-50
Syria	550	300	-45
United Arab	120	60	-50
Emirates			
Yemen	240	130	-46
Bardados	170	170	0
Belgium	840	870	+4
Hungary	880	570	-2
Malta	80	80	0
Netherlands	660	600	-9
Singapore	210	190	-10

sources. The term "diffuse source should be avoided as it has legal connotation in the United States that can now include certain types of point sources.

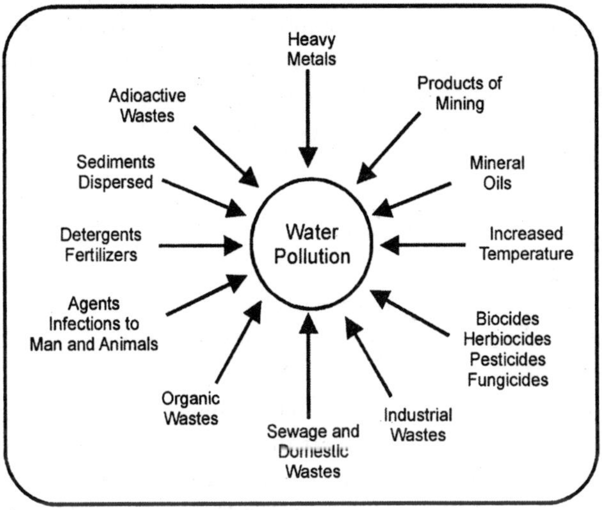

Fig. 5.1: Schematic representation of water pollution

In the United States, the Environmental Protection Agency (US-EPA) has an extensive permitting system for point discharge of pollutants in water courses. Therefore, in that country, non-point sources are defined as any source, which is not covered by the legal definition of point source as defined in the section 502 (14) of the United States Glean Water Act (Water Quality Act) of 1987:

The term *point source* means any discernible, confined and discrete conveyance, including but not limited to any pipe, ditch, channel, tunnel, conduit, well, discrete fissure, container, rolling stock, concentrated animal feeding operation, or vessel or other floating craft, form which pollutants are or may be discharged. This term does not include agricultural storm water discharges and return flows from irrigated agriculture.

The polluted water contains various metallic ions e.g., arsenic, molybdenum, lead, cadmium, mercury, nickel, barium, beryllium, cobalt, tin, vanadium etc. Many of these are highly toxic and when present in river or pond water effect and animal life. Today many of the rivers of the world receive millions of litres of sewage, domestic waste, and industrial and agricultural effluents with different concentrations of pollutants. In America major rivers have become seriously polluted. The Great lakes, which furnish the greatest single source of water to America and Canada have been polluted. Massive pollution turned Rhine into Dead River in the Western Europe.

Scope of the Water Problems

Non-point source pollutants, irrespective of source, are transported overland and through the soil by rainwater and melting snow. These pollutants ultimately find their way into groundwater. Wetlands, rivers and lakes and finally, to oceans in the form of sediment and chemical loads carried by river. As discussed below, the ecological impact of these pollutants range from simple nuisance substances to severe ecological impacts involving fish, birds and mammals, and on human health.

In what is undoubtedly the earlies and still most extensive study of non-pointed source pollution. Canada and the United States undertook a major programme of pointed and non-pointed sources identification and control in 1970s for the entire Great Lakes basin. This was precipitated by public concern (e.g. press reports that "Lake Erie was dead!") over the deterioration in water quality, including the visible evidence of algal blooms and increase in aquatic weeds. Scientifically, the situation was one of Rypertrophic conditions in Lake Ene and eutrophict conditions in Lake Ontario caused by excessive phosphorus entering the Lower Great Lakes from point and non-point sources. The two countries, under the bilateral International Joint Commission, established the Pollution from Land Use Activities Reference Groups (known as "PLUARG") which served as the scientific vehicle for a ten year study of pollution sources from the entire Great Lakes basin, and which culminated in major changes both to point and non-point source control. The study also resulted in an unprecedented increase in scientific understanding of the impacts of land use activities on water quality. This work, mainly done in the 1970s and early 1980s, still has great relevance to non-point source issues now of concern elsewhere in the world.

In most industrialized countries, the focus on water pollution control has traditionally been on point source management. In the United States, which is probably reasonably typical of other industrialized nations, the economics of further increases in point source regulation are being challenged, especially in view of the known impacts of non-point sources of which agriculture has the largest overall and pervasive impact. There is a growing opinion that, despite the billions of dollars spent on point source control measures, further point source control cannot achieve major additional benefits in water quality without significant control over non-point sources. In the, context, it is relevant agriculture is regarded as the main non-point source issue. Table presents the outcome of a study by US-EPA (1194) on the ranking of sources of water quality deterioration in rivers, lakes and estuaries.

Table 5.2: Per cent of assessed river length and lake area impacted (US-EPA, 1994)

Source of pollution	*Rivers %*	*Lakes %*	*Nature of pollutant*	*Rivers %*	*Lakes %*
Agriculture	72	56	Siltation (sediment)	45	22
Municipal point sources	15	21	Nutrients	37	40
Urban runoff/storm sewers	11	24	Pathogens	27	
Resource extraction	11		Pesticides	26	
Industrial point sources	7		Organic enrichment	24	24
Silviculture	7	23	DO		
Hydrologic/habitat	7	16	Metals	19	47
Modification			Priority organic		20
On-site wastewater disposal		13	chemicals		
Flow modification					

In India, all the 14 major rivers including Cooum, Ganga, Gomti, Cauvery, Damoder and Mini-Mahi have been polluted. The river Damodar is perhaps the most heavely polluted river. Many parts of the river do not seems to have any dissolved oxygen and no wonder that they fail to support the growth of desirable aquatic fauna and flora. Only such organisms as bloodworms, sludgeworms, bloodsuckers and certain undesirable animals; pathogenic bacteria and pests are found.

Table 5.3: Some polluted Indian rivers and sources of their pollution.

Name of the river	*Sources of pollution*
Bhadra (Karnataka)	Pulp, paper and steel industries
Cauvery (Tamil Nadu)	Sewage, tanneries, distilleries, paper and rayon mills
Chambal (M.P.)	Rayon mills, caustic soda mills
Cooum (Tamil Nadu)	Automobile workshops
Demodar (Between Bokaro)	Fertilizers, fly ash from steel mills, and Panchet suspended coal particle from washeries and thermal power stations
Ganga (at Kanpur, U.P.)	Jute, chemical, metal and surgical industries; tanneries, textile mills and great bulk of domestic sewage of highly organic nature
Godavari (A.P.)	Paper mill's
Gomti (Near Lucknow, U.P.)	Paper and pulp mills, sewage
Hooghly (near Calcutta)	Power stations; paper, pulp, jute, textile mills; (chemical, paint, varnishes) metal, steel, hydrogenated vegetable oil, rayon, soap, match, shellac and polythene industries; sewage
Jamuna (near Delhi)	DDT factory, Indraprashtha Power Station and Mathura refineries; sewage
Kali (at Meerut, U.P.)	Sugar mills, distilleries, paint, soap, rayon, silk, yarn, tin and glycerine industries
Kulu (H.P.)	Chemical factories, rayon mills and tanneries
Narmada (M.P.)	Paper mills
Siwan (Bihar)	Paper, sulphur and sugar mills; cement industries
Sone (U.P.)	Paper mills

Mahi in Boroda is another heavily polluted river, which contains a variety of industrial and petrochemical wastes. The river Cooum flowing through Madras is polluted by sewage so much that not even the zooplanktons are able to thrive in it. One litre ef Cooum river water contains as much as 900 mg of iron, 275 mg of lead, 1313 mg of nickel and 32 mg of zinc including very high levels of phosphates, silicates and nitrates. Sulphate levels ranging from 80-408 mg/1 were highest recorded among Indian rivers. Gomti river is also polluted by Oudh Sagar Mills of Birlas and a distillary of Mohan Meakins. These units have been accused of polluting a 8 km stretch of the Court. This has caused the death of thousands of fishes. River Cauvery of Tamil Nadu is also polluted (some part) with murcury from the factory located near Mettur Dam on the river.

The river Ganga from Hardwar to Calcutta is treated as one of the unending severs fit only to carry urban liquid wastes, half burned dead bodies, carrion, pesticides and insecticides. All along Ganga's nearly 1500 miles journey to the sea some 27 major towns and cities have been identified among which hardly one-third have anything resembling a sewage treatment plant. Of about 353 industrial units dumping their waste into the river only a dozen have effluent treatment facilities. These 27 towns and cities acd 905 millions litre of waste water into the river every day which affects the health of 251 million people in Northern India.

Water pollution is thc state of deviation from the pure condition, whereby its normal function and properries are affacted. The figure represents the major routes of pollutant interchange among the biotic, terrestrial, atmospheric and aquatic environment. If there occurs any change in dynamic equilibrium existing among the environmental segments (hydrosphere/atmosphere/lithosphere) it gives rise to the state of pollution.

Pollution of Ground Water

If raw sewage is dumped into the soil, the liquid percolates into the ground and this will cause pollution of ground water. Soil acts as filter, but the dissolved toxic substances percolate down, specially the heavy metals. The pollution of groundwater from human sources presents problems that are different from the pollution of surface waters such as lakes and streams.

The oceans are the ultimate sink into which all wastes in rivers and much of that in the air are likely to find their way. For many years people were unconcerned about pollution of the ocean because great mass of sea can dilute a huge volume of foreign matter to the point where it has little effect. Presently the attitude has been changed because of the fact that pollutants are added in such a high concentrations in local areas that environment of the ocean is highly affected. There are six types of major pollutants which can pollute ocean: (i) Sewage and fertilizers, (ii) Chlorinated hydrocarbons and pesticides, incinding DDT, (iii) Heavy metals, (iv) Oil and petroleum products, (v) Radioactive substances, and (vi) Plastics.

Sewage and Fertilizers

The effect of sewage in a sea depends on the extent to which it is treated before being released. The treatment of sewage includes removal of sludge and suspended solid particles, oxidizing polluting organic material sterilizing effluent and removal plant fertilizing compound. If polluted water is continuously being added in ocean it will increase the nutrient budget of the ocean.

Sludge is also dumped in the ocean by the means of tankers or through pipelines. In ocean, sludge decreases light penetration, which results in decreased photosynthetic activity and plant production. There are more chances of pollution of fishes along with the damage of benthic fauna, as the sludge settles. Such events can be observed close to the disposal site. As mentioned earlier that there is a depletion of oxygen in such a waters, therefore, hydrogen sulphide may appear under such situation, which is poisonous. When phosphorous and nitrogen remains of fertilizers are added to ocean they promote an excessive growth of phytoplankton on the surface. This creates several environmental problems like (i) Bacteria that break down the surplus growth themselves use up too much oxygen and the blooms of dinoflagellates release toxic substances, which kill other oceanic organisms mainly larval and adult fish, and shellfish. When these toxic substances are taken up by these organisms, they become poisonous to humans, (ii) This situation causes either departure or death of adult fishes. In case the adult fishes remain there or spawn, there remains insufficient oxygen at the time of egg hatching; and the turbid water influences the growth and development of eggs. (iii) High nutrient levels also cause an excessive death of excess phytoplankton. More phosphorous and nitrogen are released, thus adding much mere of these elements to the water than that in the original sewage, even if it was untreated. An excessive addition of fertilizers in ocean causes the development of red-tide. Some fertilizers are beneficial if the amount is added in correct quantity. Therefore, the use of the sewage fertilizer could be potentially valuable, if bloom (red- tide) is controlled at proper time.

Fate of Pollutants in Aquatic Systems

There are three categories under this: (a) Degradable, (b) Non-degradable (conservative), and (c) Biologically accumulative (persistent).

Degradable pollutants are complex organic substances, which can undergo biological decay by micro-organisms. Radioactive isotopes can also be classified in this category.

Non-degradable substances are referred to as conservative substances. All salts and metals can be categorized in this group. Some organic compounds are also resistant to biological action and are referred to as refractory substances.

The pollutants both degradable and conservative, which can be accumulated by organisms in their bodies, are often called persistent substances. The stable pollutant is distributed in remote places through food chins. For example DDT, a persistent pesticide, has been found even in the of Penguins of Antartica where it has never been used.

The biomagnifications is a process where the concentration of a pollutant increases successively in the higher trophic level along the food chains. This occurs after the pollutant gets accumulated in the lower plant and animal life. Each organism at successively higher trophic level then feeds upon the organisms of the lower trophic level: the food is metabolized and excreted while the persistent pollutants are retained. This leads to the build-up of greater cooperation of pollutants higher in the food chains as the larger organisms consume much more quantity of organisms of the lower trophic levels in their lifetime. Man has greatly suffered in this manner owing to his position often top in the food chains. Several persistent chemicals like organochlorine pesticides and heavy metals have been found to cause longterm pollutional effects.

The degradable pollutants together with some nutrients are degraded or modified and cycle in aquatic systems during some are absorbed by the organisms, some are released to the atmosphere and others may precipitate in the deep sediments of the lakes and oceans.

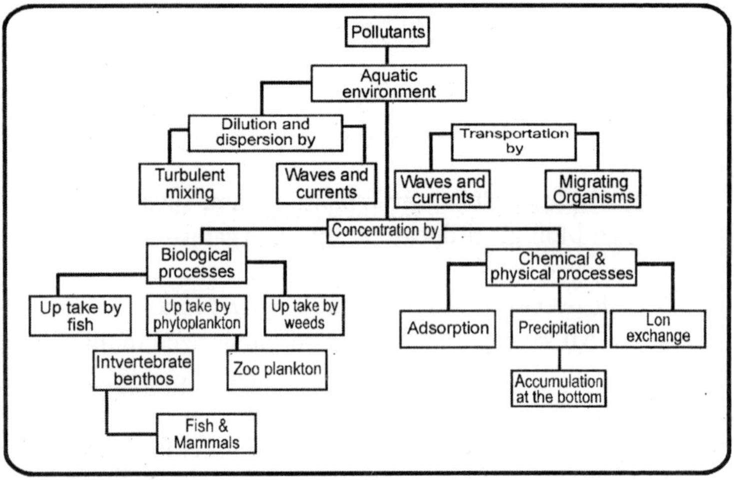

Fig. 5.2: Schematic representation of pollutants.

Signs of Polluted Water

(1) Bad taste of drinking water.
(2) Offensive odour from lakes rivers and ocean beaches.
(3) Unchecked growth of aquatic weeds in water bodies.
(4) Decrease in number of fish in fresh water, and seawater.
(5) Oil and grease floating on surface of the water etc.

(6) Such water cannot be used for public supply, recreation and aesthetic, fish other aquatic life and wildlife agriculture and industry.

The physical characteristics of an unacceptable stream water include temperature, taste and odour, colour, suspended solids and floating matter etc. The changes brought amount in the chemical characteristics through the domestic and industrial effluents cause pollution. It can thus be used as a parameter to indicate the pollution. The important one are pH value, nitrogen, phosphorus, toxic chemicals etc. Naturally flowing water have manually very little or no organic matter in them. The excess organic matter in these wastes indicates the discharge of sewage or industrial effluents into them. Following tests determine the organic matter contents of water. Biochemical Oxygen Demand (B.O.D.), Chemical Oxygen Demand (C.O.D.) and Oxygen absorption.

Octanol: Water Partition Coefficient

Since animals (and also algae) are absorbing organic fat-soluble materials from the surrounding water, a very simplified 'model' for an aquatic animal would be to consider it as a volume of fat, living surrounded by water, with a salute capable of diffusing from one to the ether. Given enough time for equilibration, the solute should reach a steady concentration in the animal which depends on the relative solubility of the solute in fat and water. This relative solubility is usually measured by the octanol; water partition coefficient. Octanol, water and the chemical are shaken up together left for the octanol and water to separate into two layers, and the concentration of the chemical in each layer is then determined. However, the octanol: water partition coefficient does not always correlate so well with concentrations in animals. If animals have better ability to excrete some chemicals than others, clearly that could affect the concentrations in its body. Difference in concentration between species and between different parts of the body can sometimes, though not always, be explained by differences in fat content. Some of the results may be confusing because the experimenters did not wait until equilibrium concentrations had been reached.

Classification of Foreign Substances in Water

The sources of water pollution are as follows:

(1) Sewage and other oxygen demanding wastes, which contain decomposing organic matter and pathogenic agents;
(2) Industrial waste, which contains toxic agents ranging from metal salts to complex synthetic organic chemicals;
(3) Agriculture waste, which comprises fertilizers, pesticides and biocides; and
(4) Physical pollutants, viz., heat (thermal pollutants and, radioactive substances).

Chemically pure water is a collection of H_2O molecules—nothing else. Such a substance is not found in nature—not in wild streams or lakes, not in clouds or rain, not in falling snow, not in the polar ice caps. The foreign substances in water can be classified on the basis of their particles because the size determines the effectiveness of various methods of purification. The particles are divided into three classes on the basis of their fate in aquatic systems. The fate of pollutants in the aquatic systems depends on the nature and stability of the pollutants, and climatological, and ecological.

The pollutants are categorized on the basis of their chemical nature as follows:

(1) Degradable (organic substances and radioactive isotopes).
(2) Non-degradable (all salts and metals and certain organic compounds resistant to biological action; conservative).
(3) Biologically accumulative (persistent).

The pollutants are also classified on the basis of their physical nature:

Suspended Particles

These particles have diameters of more than I micrometer, and are the largest in polluted water. They are large enough to settle out of water quickly and may be retained by filters. They are also large enough to absorb light, thus, making water containing them look cloudy or murky.

Colloidal Particles

These particles are so small that their settling rate is insignificant. They can pass through the holes of most of the filter media, therefore, they cannot be removed from water by settling method or by ordinary filters. Water containing colloidal particles appears cloudy when observed at right angles to a beam of light. The colour of natural waters, such as the blues, greens and reds of lakes or seas are caused largely by colloidal particles.

Dissolved Matter

The dissolved matter of water does not make it cloudy, even when viewed at right angles to a beam of light. Such matter does not settle out, and is not retained on filters. The size of particles is smaller (about one thousandth micrometer). If they are electrically neutral they are known as molecules and if they bear electrical charges, they are known as ions.

Major Water Pollutants

The important water pollutants are organic pollutants, inorganic pollutants, sediments, radioactive materials and thermal pollutants.

Oxygen is required by most of the organisms for metabolic activities especially for mobilization of food and for release of energy, which they need. The process is known as aerobic respiration. (aerobic means with oxygen). Aquatic organisms use the oxygen, which remains dissolved in water. Oxygen is not very soluble in water. Under normal condition at 25°C one litre of water contains 0.0084 g of oxygen, however, one litre of air at 25°C contains 0.27 g of oxygen. When oxygen a removed from water, it takes much time or its replacement, except in places where turbulence mixes water and air, as it does not in the white water of shallow rapids.

The bottom mud of fresh water streams and lakes contains very little oxygen due to the reasons mentioned above, therefore, bottom mud provides the perfect environment for microorganisms that can respire anaerobically (without oxygen). In slow moving water which is rich in nutrients however, the population of various aquatic organism remains high, therefore, under such situation, oxygen consumers may use the oxygen in water faster than it can be replaced by dissolving it from air or by photosynthesis. This situation causes death of the phytoplankton, which require oxygen for respiration. The macroorganisms like trout also die due to high requirement of oxygen.

The greenish scum of bloom of photosynthetic plankton also gives unpleasant smell. When such scum of dead plankton combined with the population of fish and anaerobic bacteria, it gives vary unwanted smell. Similarly, anaerobic sulphur bacteria produces hydrogen sulphide—a gas, which smells like rotten eggs.

The continuous addition of nutrients (as pollutant) in fresh water increases the growth of plankton bloom, oxygen, depletion, and anaerobic decay. Thus, excessive nutrients must be considered as pollutants whether they come from a chemical factory, a farmer's field, municipal sewage works or from any other source.

Pesticide and Biocides

Pesticides cause water pollution. Pesticides means any substance intended for preventing, destroying, attracting, repelling or controlling any pest including unwanted species of plants or animals during production, storage, transport, distribution and processing of food, agricultural commodities, or animal feeds or which may be administered to the animals for the control of ectoparasites. The term includes substances intended for use as a plant growth regulator, defoliant, desiccant, fruit thinning agent or sprouting inhibitor and substances applied to the crops either before or after harvest to protect the commodity from deterioration during storage and transport. The term normally excludes fertilizers, plant and animal nutrients, food additives and animal drugs. Pesticide is a genera: term used in connection with any pest. More specific terms are available for individual pest categories. Pests are any organisms, insects, rodents, nematodes, fungal diseases, weeds, herbs, bacteria etc., which are injurious to the health of man or to man's economic efforts.

Chlorinated Hydrocarbons and Pesticides, Including DDT

Chlorinated hydrocarbons or pesticides are the chemical substances, which are often referred to as biocides, insecticides or simply as pollutants. Most of these substances are non-degradable. These chemicals create problem when they present in high concentration. In fact, all the river pollutants come from agricultural practices enter the same sink — the world ocean. It has been noted that concentration of DDT of various types is high in marine birds. DDE and PCB are other chlorinated hydrocarbons which cause pollution and damage to oceanic organisms. Marine bacteria do not degrade DDE and PCB.

Reasons for use of Pesticides

(1) Pesticides are used to ensure better protection at harvest against unpredictable losses caused by plant diseases and pests.
(2) Pesticides are used to improve both quality and quantity of food.
(3) Pesticides are used to decrease the extent of vector born and other diseases in humans and animals.

Table 5.4: Types of Pesticides

Insecticides:	Substances that prevent, destroy kill mitigate insects (belonging to class insects, Phylum athropoda).
Fungicides:	Substances that prevent, destroy or inhibit the growth of fungi/ diseases in crops.
Herbicides:	Substances, which are use for preventing or inhibiting growth of plants or for killing weeds.
Rodenticides:	Substances that inhibit growth, destroy, or kill rodents (Class Mammalia, order Rodentia).
Nemoticides:	Substances that prevent, destroy, repel or inhibit the nemadode.

Prevention and Control of Water Pollution

It is not always true that biodegradable pollutants alone cause the major pollution load; several kinds of ingredients such as heavy metals, refractory chemical compounds and mineral oil also exist, which cannot be decomposed by mechanical or biological means add to this. Inorganic fertilizers and various biocides are too responsible for contributing to this load. Efforts of control should, therefore, include the reduction in the amounts of waste by reutilizing or recycling of their components. Control of water bodies and of organisms serving the purpose of water protection should be reinforced and carried out by all available means including legal enforcement under the provisions laid down in Water (Prevention and Control of Pollution) Act, 1974 and the Environmental (Protection) Act, 1986. The various ways/ techniques suggested for prevention and control of water pollution are as follows:

Stabilization of Ecosystem

This is the most reliable way to control water pollution. This would involve reduction on in waste input, harvesting and removal of biomass, trapping of nutrients, fish management and aeration. Various physical and biological methods can be adopted to restore species diversification and ecobalance in the water body to prevent pollution.

Some species of algae, such as Chlorella, Scenedesmus and

Spirulina are excellent biological oxidants and are commonly found in polluted waters and stabilization pond effluents in India. These can be used to reduce pollution load in a water body. Water hyacinth, *Eichhornic crassipes*, a luxuriantly growing weed may also be employed for pollution abatement. It can remove phosphorus and nitrogen from a water body. It can also reduce BOD, COD and organic carbon.

Reutilization and Recycling of Wastes

Various kinds of wastes such as paper pulp municipal and industrial effluents, sewage thermal pollutants can be recycled to advantage. For example urban wastes could be generate cheaper fuel gas and electricity. Scientists at the NEERI, Nagpur have evolved inexpensive "know — how" for management of radioactive wastes and the chemical effluents of atomic power plants reclaimed wastes water and have supplied cheaper piped gas and generated electricity by recycling urban wastes. One large size urban wastes recycling plants is already existing at Okhla, New Delhi. The total gas generation from the plant is about 0.6 million cubic feet per day having a heat value of 700-800 BTU per cubic feet. Waste water reclamation through aquaculture, optimum utilization of domestic and industrial waste water in agriculture, detoxification of phenol and cyanide bearing waste by biological methods have been the major areas of investigation at the NEERI. A new technology of waste recycling and disposal has bean introduced by a distillery in Gujarat. This technology would not only help the distillery to the 450,000 litres of waste daily before letting the effluent into streams but also generate energy equivalent to that given by 10 tonnes of coal every day. The regulated use of thermo-nuclear reasons in controlled fusion reactors to produce cheap electricity as suggested can solve the problem of accumulation of waste.

Removal of Pollutants

The various physico-chemical techniques devised for removal of chemical biological or radiobiological pollutants involve adsorption, electrolysis, ion exchange and reverse-osmosis. Of the various techniques, reverse-osmosis deserves special mention. The technique is based on the removal of salts and other substances from water by forcing the later through a semipermeable membrane under a pressure that exceeds the osmotic pressure so that flow is in the reverse direction to the normal osmotic flow. In practice, this involves the use of a porous membrane whose chemical nature is such that, it has a preferential attraction while repulsion for the solute. Reverse-osmosis is commonly used to desalinate brakish water and has also been found suitable effect and economical method for the purification of water polluted by sewage effluents.

Techniques devised by CSIR for the control of water pollution have been successfully employed for the removal and reuse of pollutants from industrial effluents. Some of the achievement are as follows:

(1) *Ammonia removal from the waste water of industry*: Ion-exchange technique employing a weakly acidic cation exchanger based on methacrylic acid is developed to remove ammonia from waste water. The ammonia is removed in the form of ammonium sulphate which can be reduced for the manufacture of fertilizer. The process so developed has good application potential not only for pollution abatement, but also for the recovery of the pollutant in the form of useful salt.

(2) *Removal of mercury from chlor-alkali plants effluents*: Mercury thrown out from chloralkali plants is removed and recovered by mercury-selective ion exchange resin.

(3) *Removal of phenotics*: Phenolics in waste water produced from industries like pulp and paper mills, carbonization plants, petroleum refineries, tanning industries and resin manufacturing units are removed by the use of polymeric adsorbents.

(4) *Decolourisation of water*: An electrolyte decomposition technique developed to decolourise the waste water from saree dyeing and printing industries around Jetpur in Gujarat.

(5) *Removal of sodium salts*: Reverse osmotic technique has been developed to recover sodium sulphate from rayon

mill effluent. The technique is also employed to recover water for reuse. Similarly, 70 per cent of the protein and 80 per cent of the lactose can be recovered from cheese when by reverse osmosis, which otherwise would pose a serious pollution problem.

Water pollution is steadily increasing in quality and noxious contents. The implications of the pollution problems are alarming, and comprehensive legislations are needed to cope with these problems.

Water and Human Diseases

On a worldwide scale, the pollution of water supplies is probably responsible for more human illness than any other environmental influence. The diseases so transmitted are chiefly due to microorganisms and parasites. One example will illustrate the dimensions of the problem. Cholera, an illness caused by ingestion of the bacterium *Vibrio cholerae*, is characterized by intense diarrhea, which results rapidly in massive fluid depiction and death in a very large percentage of untreated patients. Though its distribution in the pas was virtually worldwide, it has been largely restricted during the twentieth century to Asia, particularly the area of the Ganges River in India. During the nine years from 1898 to 1907, about 370,000 people died from this disease, and thousands of Indians continue to die each year even at present.

Water Quality and Health

The main consideration in ensuring the safety of public water supplies is the elimination of the agents of water borne infectious disease. In the last century major epidemics of typhoid and cholera in Britain and elsewhere in Europe were only eliminated when their bacteriological origin was recognized, the contamination of water supplies with sewage was eliminated and disinfection treatment was introduced. There have been no major epidemics in the UK since the Croydon epidemic of 1937 following which all water supplies were chlorinated.

Concern about possible health effects of chemicals in drinking water stemmed from the application of sophisticated analytical techniques, which revealed the presence of traces of many potentially harmful chemicals. The significance to health of these was uncertain although some world undoubtedly cause concern were they present at much higher concentrations. Any fear about the possibility of health effects was reinforced by evidence that environmental factors which could conceivably include drinking water quality are involved in many chronic diseases such as cardiovascular disease and cancer. Public interest in drinking water quality has been stimulated by some specific pollution problems. E.g. detergents, pesticides, lead and asbestos.

Acute health effects of chemical constituents of drinking water are very unlikely but effects due to exposure to low concentrations over a lifetime are just feasible. Such evidence as there is suggests that any such effects are extremely small and difficult to measure, but this is still the subject of much research.

Table 5.5: Compound types identified in drinking water

Compound	*Total number identified*
Carboxylic acids and esters	
Acids	15
Esters	13
Hydrocarbons	
Aliphatic	68
Alicyclic	5
Aromatic	48
Polynuclear aromatic	20
Halogenated compounds	
Aliphatics	53
Aromatics	8
Aromatics	4
Miscellaneous	14
Oxygenated compounds	
Aldehydes	7
Ketones	19
Ethers	11
Miscellaneous	17
Miscellaneous compounds	23

Organic compounds can adversely affect the taste of water at concentrations will below any likely to give rise to toxic effects. This is marked with chlorophenols and certain petroleum products but this natural defense mechanism cannot be depended on. The taste, smell appearance, 'feel' (hardness/softness) is markedly affected by chemical composition as is its corrosiveness to materials including toxic metals.

Table 5.6: Suspected and known carcinogens and promoters identified in drinking water

Compound	*Frequency*	*Compound*	*Frequency*
Acenaphthene	2	n-Docdecane	11
Benzene	13	Eicosane	2
1-Bromobutane	1	Fluoranthe	1
Bromochloromethane	2	Hexachloroethane	3
Bromcdichlorom	14	9-Methyl-fluorene	7
Bromoform	14	Octadecane	7
Carbon tetrachloride	6	Phenanthrene Phenol	5
Chlorodibromomethane	14	Tetrachlorcethylene	11
Chloroform	14	1,1,2,2,-	1
n-Decane	3	Tetrachloroethane	8
Decanoic acid	1	Tetradecane	13
Decanol	1	Trichioroethylene	3
1,2-Dichioroethane	2	1,1,1 Trichloroethane	1
Dibromomethane	7	2,4,6-Trichlorophenol	1
1,4-Dioxane	1	2,4,5-Trichlorophenol	12
		Undecane	

(1) *Gastrointestinal troubles*—the disorders associated with intestinal stress are most common in industrial workers;

(2) *Neuromuscular effects (lead palsy)*—weakness, fatigue, wrist drop, palsy, residual: paralysis and muscular atrophy; and

(3) *Central nervous system effects or CNS syndrome*—involve a panoply of nervous system disorders which may culminate in delirium, convulsions, coma and death.

(4) Constipation, abdominal pain, and pallor have also been described the effects of lead poisoning. The anaemic effect of lead may be due to impairment of the body's

ability to synthesize haemoglobin for more details see under Air Pollution.

Note: Locking to the scope of the book, other diseases caused by mater have not been discussed.

Water Pollution Control through Law

The term water pollution has been used variously in various Indian Acts. Some described it as nuisance, while others as 'negligence'. 3 'Fouling' of water was also the way of describing water pollution. In some enactments water pollution was described as 'poisoning' of water. Some Acts described as rendering water less fit or not fit for consumption by human beings and animals. Interference with or alteration in flow of water to carry away rubbish or causing water to be corrupted in any water way so as to endanger, damage or render it less useful always another mode of explanation of water pollution. Discharge of oil, use of dynamite and casting of blast carries the same meaning.

Almost all the status before the enactment of water (Prevention and Control of Pollution) Act, 1974, stressed upon the mode of causing pollution rather than explaining pollution itself. In a simple sense water pollution is the adding to water of any substance or the changing of waters physical and chemical characteristics in any way which interferes with its use for legitimate purposes. It is also defined as introduction into water of substances of such character and quantity that its natural quality is so altered as to impair its usefulness or render it offensive to the senses of sight, taste or smell. According to Water (Prevention and Control of Pollution) Act, 1974 water pollution means such contamination of water or such alteration of the physical, chemical or biological properties of water or such discharge of any sewage or trade effluent or of any other liquid, gaseous or salic substance into water (whether directly or indirectly) as may or is likely to create a nuisance or render such water harmful or injurious to public health or safety, or to domestic, commercial, industrial, agricultural or other legitimate uses, or to the life and health of animals or plants or of aquatic organisms.

The various inorganic and organic compounds that cause pollution include fertilizers, pesticides, biocides, detergents, phenolic substances, and carboxylic acids. When these compounds negligently or inadvertently are thrown into the sea or a river, water resources get contaminated resulting into threat to aquatic animal and human life. Excess of chemical nutrients also stimulates the luxuriant growth of algae and other plant life to such an extent as to choke waterways and is termed as eutrophication.

All the 14 major rivers of the country, including Cooum, Ganga, Gomti, Cauvery, Damodar and Mini Mahi, have become polluted. The waters of Ganga which were once considered to be pure and sacred are no longer so because of the discharge of sewage and industrial effluents. The industrial effluents are considered more dangerous than the house-hold wastes.

Many of our lakes, notable the Dal lake, have become darkened, smelly and choked with excessive growth of algae. Occasionally certain water bodies become so heavily polluted with oil that they have been seen to catch fire.

WTO and Trade Dispute Settlement Rules and Procedures

The World Trade Organisation is the legal and institutional foundation of the multilateral trading system. It provides the principal contractual obligations determining how Government frame and implement domestic trade legislation and regulations. And it is the platform on which trade relations among countries evolve through collective debate, negotiation and adjudication. The dispute settlement system of WTO is a central element in providing security and predictability to the multilateral trading system.

For variety of reasons enforcing International Law on sovereign National Government is very difficult, no set of International rules can be considered credible without effective mechanism for dispute settlement. GATT (Predecessor of WTO) contained elaborate provisions for resolution of differences between the contracting parties. Several articles of GATT, which embodied individual obligations specified agreements for settling differences as well. In certain matters only bilateral discussion was envisaged and in some other, there was provision for recourse alternatively to bilateral consultation between contracting parties directly concerned or to consultation with the full membership. Certain Articles which governed specific obligations provided for multilateral consultation. Beside these scattered provisions, GATT also had a central dispute settlement machinery in its articles XXII and XXIII and procedures prescribed in them applied to all obligations.

The disputes settlement GATT had been weakened by the general disrespect for GATT rules and insensitivity to moral session that developed in the years, particularly among major economic powers. Therefore, it seems very essential to respect the rules and regulations of the dispute settlement mechanism for better international relations.

The last decade GATT 1985-94, saw greatly increased attention to the dispute settlement procedures, and that attention continued to increase after the Uruguay Round treaty introduced numerous reforms in those procedures. Both WTO and important national leaders have lauded the dispute settlement procedures in WTO, making them almost the centerpiece of the new organization. The WTO Director General R. Ruggiero said in a special report of 30th September 1996 concerning preparations for the first Ministerial Conference in December 1996 in Singapore, "one success that stands out above all the rest is the strengthening of the dispute settlement mechanism". This is the heart of WTO system. Not only has it proved credible and effective in dealing with disputes, it has helped resolve a significant number at the consultation stage. Further more, developing countries have become major users of the system, a sign of their confidence in it which was not so apparent under the old system.

The present chpater focuses a rules and procedurial aspects of World Trade Organization (WTO). The first part of this chapter is introductory and examines the role of dispute settlement process in international law. The second part will explore the vital and dramatic contours of the new dispute settlement procedure and rules, perhaps the most important part of the new organisation. The third part of the chpater deals with the legal implications of actions and penal reports of the Dispute Settlement Bodies (DSB), question of implementation of the results of dispute settlement procedures. The last part will draw some tentative conclusions and suggestions.

The Panel Process

World Trade Organization (WTO) members commit themselves not to take unilateral action against perceived violations of the trade rules but to seek recourse in the multilateral dispute settlement system and to abide by its rules and findings. The aim of the WTO dispute settlement mechanism is to secure a positive solution to a dispute. Thus, finding a mutually acceptable solution to a problem between members consistent with WTO provisions is encouraged. This may be possible through bilateral consultation between the governments concerned.

Thus the first stage of settling disputes requires such consultations. Should they fail and if both parties agree the case at this stage can be brought to the WTO Director-General who acting in an ex-officio, capacity, will offer good offices, conciliation or mediation to settle the dispute. If consultations fail to arrive at a solution after 60 days, the complainant can ask the Dispute Settlement Body (DSB) to establish of a panel to examine the case. The establishment of a panel is almost automatic. Procedure require the DSB to establish a panel request, unless there is consensus against the decision. The determination of the panel's terms of reference as well as its composition is also straight forward. The understanding provides standard terms of reference that mandate the panel to examine the complaint in the light of the agreement cited and to make findings that will assist the DSB in making recommendations or in giving ruling, provided for in that agreement. The panel may operate under different terms of reference, if parties concerned so agree. The panel must be constitute within 30 days of its establishment. The WTO secretariat will suggest the names of three potential panellists to the parties to the dispute, drawing as necessary on a list of qualified persons. If there is real difficulty in the choice, the Director General can appoint the panellists. The panellists serve in their capacities individual and are not subject to government instruction. The panel's final report should normally be given to the parties to the dispute within six months. In cases of urgency, those related to perishable goods, the time frame is shortened to three months. Panels have detailed working procedure set out in the understanding. The main stages are.

Each party to the dispute transmits to the panel its submission on the facts and arguments in the case, in advance of the first substantive meeting.

At that first meeting the complainant presents its case and the responding party its defence. Third parties which notified their interest in the dispute may also present views. Formal rebuttals are made at the second substantive meeting.

- In case where a party raised scientific or other technical matters, the panel may appoint an expert review group to provide an advisory report.
- The panel submits descriptive (factual and argument) sections of its report to the parties, giving them two weeks to comment. The panel then submits an interim report, including its findings and conclusions to the parties, giving them one week to request a review. The period of review is not to exceed two weeks, during which the panel may hold additional meeting with the parties. A final report is submitted to the parties and three weeks later it is circulated to all WTO members.
- Should the panel decide that the measure in question is inconsistent with the terms of the relevant WTO agreement, the panel recommends that the members concerned bring the measure into conformity with that agreement. It may also suggest ways in which the member could implement the recommendation.
- Panel reports are adopted by the DSB within 60 days of issuance, unless one party notifies its decision to appeal or a consensus emerges against the adoption of the report.

The WTO dispute settlement mechanism gives the possibility of appeal to either party in a panel proceeding. However any such appeal must be limited to issues of law covered in the panel report and the legal interpretation developed by the Panel. Appeals are heard by a standing Appellate Body established by the DSB. This Appellate Body is composed of seven persons-broadly representatives of WTO membership who will serve four year terms. They are required to be persons of recognized standing in the field of law and international trade and not affiliated with any government. Three members of the Appellate Body sit at any one time to hear appeals. They can uphold, modify or reverse the legal finding and conclusions of the panel. As a general rule the appeal proceedings are not to exceed 60 days but in no case shall they exceed 90 days. Thirty days after it is issued, Dispute Settlement Body adopts the report of the Appellate Body which is unconditionally accepted by the parties to the disputes—unless there is a consensus against its adoption.

Implementation of Dispute Decisions

Under the GATT consultation. Conciliation and dispute settlement were fundamental to the multilateral trading system, Articles XXII and XXHI of the General Agreement laid heavy emphasis on bilateral consultations as the first step in settling disputes. However, Disputes were not be resolved bilaterally, then the GATT panel system was employed. The panel (consists of three experts) report which was submitted to the council, contains conclusions and recommendations. If the panel report adopted by the GATT council then there was a duty on the part of the contracting parties to act in accordance with the panel's finding. If the violating does not implement the recommendations, the injured party may seek authority from the other members of GATT to make retaliatory action. In fact in only one case had it been found necessary to authorise such retaliation. Pressure stemming from the need of GATT members for negotiating credibility within the multilateral trading system, has proved to be the most effective means of bringing about implementation.

The understanding on Rules and Procedures Governing the Settlement of Disputes, Annex 2 to the final results of the Uruguay Round of Multilateral Trading Negotiations. Done at Marrakesh, April 15, 1994. Entered into the force, January 1, 1995 stresses that "Prompt compliance with recommendations or rulings of the dispute Settlement Body is essential in order to ensure effective resolution of dispute to the benefit of all members."

At a Dispute Settlement Body Meeting held within 30 days of the adoption of the panel or appellate report, the party concerned must state its intentions in respect of the implementation of the recommendations. If it is impractical to comply immediately, the member will be given, a "reasonable period of time"—to be set by the DSB—to do so. If it fails to act within this period, it is obliged to enter into negotiations with the complainant in order to determine a mutually acceptable compensation for instance, tariff reductions in areas of particular interest to the complainant. If after 20 days, no satisfactory compensation is agreed, the complainant may request authorization from DSB to suspend concessions or obligations against the other party. The DSB should grant this authorization within 30 days of the expiry of the "reasonable period of time" unless there is consensus against the request.

In principle, concessions should be suspended in the some sector as that at issue in the panel case. If this is not practicable or effective, the suspension can be made in different sector of the same agreement. In turn, if this is not effective or practicable and if the circumstances are serious enough, the suspension of concessions may be made under another agreement recommendation or ruling, and any outstanding case will remain on its agenda until the issue is resolved.

Procedures

One thing is very clear that the new procedures prescribed in WTO's Dispute Settlement Understanding is tend rather strongly towards a rule oriented approach than negotiations or 'diplomacy' oriented approach. Here rule orientation approach is not contrast with phrases such as rule of law and rule based system but it implies amicable rigidity to rule and possibilities for some bargaining or negotiation. The main idea is that the procedures of rule orientation approach, which often centre on dispute settlement mechanism, should be framed so as to promote as much as possible. the possibility the stability and predictability of the rule system. For this purpose dispute settlement procedures should he creditable, legitimate and reasonably efficient. According to article 3(2) of the Dispute Settlement Understanding of WTO; "The Dispute Settlement System of the WTO is a central element in providing security and predictability to the multilateral trading system. The members recognize that it serve: to preserve the rights and obligations of Members under tile covered agreements and to clarify the existing provisions of those agreements in accordance with customary rules of interpretation of public international law. Recommendations and rulings of the Dispute Settlement Body (DSB) cannot add to or diminish the rights and obligations provided in the covered agreements."

In order to establish that the dispute settlement mechanism relies primarily on reference to rules and their application, the thrust of a mechanism should be the opportunity to obtain an impartial and trusted decision as to the interpretation or application of rule. To avoid tainting the process of that judgement the impartial third party decision of rule interpretations or application should be relatively isolated from other process. Such as process of assisting in negotiation for settlement or the process of rule formulation.

On possible framework for an improved dispute settlement procedure is a "five part approach", which can be out lined as follows:

- Bilateral consultations between the disputing parties, with out outside presence.
- Conciliation process, with the assistance of trained persons probably form file secretarial to assist the parties in resolving their dispute.
- Panel and rulings, similar to the current procedure with more emphasis on the impartiality of the panel members.

Utilization of a broader cadre for panel, and a separation of the conciliation process from the panel process. A goal is to increase the integrity and credibility of the findings, so these can have greater moral force. The panel report should therefore always be published quickly.

- A panel ruling will be submitted to the highest policy body, such as the Dispute Settlements Body (DSB) for approval. This will allow some play in the joints for special circumstances or the recognition of the need for a new rule. Sanction, such as suspending trade concessions as provided. History suggests that there are limited utility far sanctions, and not much willingness by the international community to accept or strengthen sanctions. Thus, at present, the system may well be designed to operate mostly without sanctions.

A very important consideration affecting a nation's willingness to accept the WTO dispute procedures is that nation's view of the role that the treaty and its institutions should play in its international economic diplomacy. India (as well as many other nations) has often expressed the view that the GATT and now WTO treaty texts are vitally important to improving a rule oriented international economic system, which should enhance the predictability and stability of the circumstances of international commerce, which in term should allow private entrepreneurs to plan better for longer term investment and other decisions. In short a basic goal is to reduce the 'risk premium' associated with commerce between nations with vastly differing governmental and cultural structures.

WTO Regime and Environmental Policy

Environment is a non-trade issue. But it has come to dominate the WTO agenda. WTO has come into existence with the twin objective of Free and Fair trade and trade without obstruction. The developed world's pressure on incorporating non-trade issues including environment may lead to a situation where international trade becomes neither free and fair nor without obstructions.

The two agreements in GATT on sanitary and phytosanitary measures and technical barriers to trade have some environmental, health and safety considerations. The basic concerns as reflected in these agreements is that the domestic measures such as policies, rules and regulations should not be a means to restricting trade among nations. This can be best understood by a Canadian example. Ontario—a Canadian province imposes an environmental levy on all beer packaged in cans. They do not distinguish between home and imported products. Canada generally produces beer in bottles. It may take such measures which may protect local manufacturers. If it does so, it mat restrict the trade for those who manufacture beer and pack it in cans as the Americans do. The sanitary and phytosanitary measures under WTO aim at eliminating such causes as to restrict trade among nations.

Sanitary and phytosanitary measures aim at protecting animal, plant life or health within the territory of a member country from risks arising out of diseases carried by plants or products thereof, or from the entry, establishment or spread of pests or additives, contaminants, toxins or disease causing organisms in foods, beverages or foodstuffs.

These measures include all relevant laws, decrees, regulations, requirements and procedures including end product criteria; process and production methods, testing, inspection certification and approval procedures; quarantine treatment and relevant requirements associated with the transport of animals or plants or with the materials necessary for their survival during transport; provisions on relevant statistical methods, sampling procedures and methods of risk assessment directly related to food safety. Member-countries can resort to these measures provided they do not come in conflict with the provisions of agreements in Uruguay Round and are based on scientific principles and not maintained without scientific evidence. Attempts are to be made to harmonize these measures and base them on international standards laid down by relevant international organizations and their subsidiary bodies such as Codex Alimentarius Commission, the International Office of Epizootics and the international and regional organizations operating within the framework of the International Plant Protection Convention. Some concerns have been expressed in some quarters that these international organizations may face undue influence by producer lobbies and may cause harm to consumer interests.

A country may have complaints about sanitary and phytosanitary measures imposed by some other countries. In such cases an explanation of the reasons may be requested and shall be provided by the country retaining the measures. If this is not found satisfactory, Art. 11 of the agreement has provisions for consultations and dispute settlement.

There are separate provisions for developing and least developed countries. Longer time frame for compliance has been accorded on products of export interest to developing and least developed countries to maintain opportunities for their exports. The longer time frame is in the form of specified time-limit exceptions in whole or in part from the obligations taking into account their financial, trade and development needs. Member countries are encouraged to participate proactively in the relevant international organisations.

In the Uruguay Round there is an agreement on technical barriers to trade which lays down the principle followed in the agreement on sanitary and phytosanitary measures. This agreement has got 15 Articles which specifies dos and don'ts for the countries. The most notable among them are:

- One country shall accord to the products of another country a treatment no less than accorded to similar products of national origin except to fulfil a legitimate objective such as national security requirements, prevention of deceptive practices, protection of human health and safety, animal or plant life or health or environment. While evaluating these types of risks, a country has to take into account the various available scientific and technical information-related processing technology or intended end-use of products.
- Countries are supposed to use technical regulations and relevant international standards or relevant parts of them as a basis for their technical regulations unless they are

> ineffective or inappropriate means for the fulfilment of the legitimate objectives pursued because of fundamental climatic or geographical factors or technological problems. Harmonization of technical regulations on as wide a basis as possible, being the basic target of all the member-countries, countries are supposed to discharge full duties within the limited paradigm of their resources. They are supposed to participate proactively in the preparation by appropriate international standardising bodies of international standards for products for which the other have adopted or expect to adopt technical regulations. A country upon the request of another country shall explain the basic reasoning for that technical regulations. Such regulations are rebuttably presumed not to create an unnecessary obstacle to international trade and shall give positive consideration to accepting equivalent technical regulations.

Local government bodies and non-governmental bodies are also supposed to comply with similar principles. A code of good practice forms part of the agreement and they are required to follow the code. There are provisions of special treatment for developing countries. Countries shall if requested, advise other member-countries, especially the other developing countries and shall grant them technical assistance on mutually agreed terms and regarding the establishment of national standardising bodies and participation by the international standardising bodies, shall encourage their national standardising bodies to do likewise. The steps that should be taken by their producers if they wish to have access to systems for conformity, assessment operated by governmental or non-governmental bodies within the territory of the member receiving the request.

Member-countries in the process shall take into account the special development, financial and trade needs of developing countries with a view to preserving their indigenous technology and production methods and process compatible with their development needs. With a view to ensuring that developing countries are able to comply with this agreement, the Committee on Technical barriers to Trade is enabled to grant upon request specified time limited exceptions in whole or in part from obligations under this agreement. The consultation and dispute settlement mechanisms are also set out in the agreement.

The agreements on Sanitary and Phytosanitary measures and Technical Barriers to Trade have generated quite a lot of controversies for different reasons. For example, both the agreements impose disciplines on domestic policies as opposed to measures that are purely border ones. It means political sovereignty of the countries will have to be compromised and it becomes a great political issue in a country. Agreement on Technical Barriers is bound to generate problems in future because of its environmental dimensions. Similarly, there can be regulations that stipulate minimum amount of recycled ingredients. Some guidelines have been introduced to protect the environment but they are interpreted as technical barriers to trade.

As a matter of fact, Uruguay Round originally never had environmental issues on its agenda. But as the negotiations progressed, they came on the scene. For example, United States had banned yellow fish tuna from Mexico on the grounds that it was caught by methods, which destroy dolphins. This decision was challenged in the GATT dispute settlement body, which ruled against USA saying that the decision violated national treatment provisions of GATT. If that is the case, any country trying to protect human plant or animal health or safety within its territory could be held responsible for violating Art XX of GATT.

The net result that everyday one issue or the other of similar nature crops up. It gives rise to many questions. Many international environment agreements impose trade restrictions against countries that are not signatories. If there are cross border environmental issues, countries have tried to impose unilateral restrictions on trade. Environmental damage may be caused by the product or by the production processes or methods. There are many national measures that do not necessarily try to protect the environment within the country. Do they all comply with the provisions of the

WTO? The GATT takes a stand that import restrictions are permissible if the environmental damage is caused by the product but not if it is caused by the production process or methods. GATT had a working group on environmental measures and the International Trade. Though it was mainly nonfunctional since 1991, after Dolphin-Tuna decision it has been revived.

Linkages

Though the environmental issues are non-trade issues, the final Uruguay Round Agreement has highlighted its importance in the international trade. The Ministerial Declaration on Trade and Environment emphasize the linkages between trade policies, environmental policies and the sustainable development. The declaration ensures that this takes a place of priority on WTO Agenda. Following the declaration, a committee on trade and environment was set-up.

The WTO preamble has also recognized the need and objective of protecting and preserving the environment. To quote from the preamble, "Recognising that their relations in the field of trade and economic endeavour should be conducted with a view to raising standards of living, ensuring full employment and a large and steadily growing volume of real income and effective demand and expanding the production and trade in goods and services while allowing for the optimal use of the world's resources in accordance with the objective of sustainable development, seeking both to protect and preserve the environment and enhance the means of doing so in a manner consistent with their respective needs and concerns at different levels of economic development".

The Committee on Trade and Environment shall identify the relationship between trade measures and environmental measures. It shall also work out the response of WTO to environmental agreements and treaties and recommend necessary modifications to multilateral trade agreements. Developed countries are pressing very hard to bring environment on to WTO agenda and have given lots of arguments in its favour. For example:

- Discrimination against products that harm the environment should be and must be allowed,
- Use of low environmental standards to improve a country's competitive advantage constitutes eco-dumping and therefore must be banned,
- Trade restrictions imposed to enforce environmental goals should not be challenged under multilateral rules. The earlier agreements on sanitary and phytosanitary measures and technical barrier to trade had hardly touched upon these issues. But they are definitely going to be hot issues of discussion in future rounds of MTNs. The idea of green WTO may take a while to take shape.

SUGGESTED READINGS

Malaysia (1992).

OECD, Environmentals Indicators, Paris, 1994.

Pearce, D.W. and R.K. Turner, Resource Conservation, 1993

Peet, N.J., Energy and the Environment in the 1990s.

Trivedi, P.R., Ecology and Environment, APH Publication Corporation, New Delhi-110002

World Bank, World Development Report: New Year 1992.

6

Environment and the Decade of Development

Goal, Setting and Policy Challenges in India

The Government of India has proclaimed the new decade as a "Decade of Development", during which India will meet bold targets for economic growth and social development. During his address to the nation from the ramparts of the Red Fort, the Prime Minister announced on August 15, 2000 that the government had set a target of doubling India's per capita income by the year 2001. This is an ambitious target, but one that we believe is certainly achievable. In order to achieve this target, India needs growth in GNP per capita of the order of 7 per cent per year over the next ten years. In light of population growth of around 2 per cent per year, total GNP should increase by around 9 per cent per year and in order to achieve this growth rate on a sustained basis, India needs a well-focussed growth strategy. This paper outlines some of the key policy challenges in meeting these goals.

The starting point for the Decade of Development is the setting of development targets for India. One key target is the rise in national income, but targets should also include improvements in health and education, as well as political participation. We therefore, recommended the following additional targets for the Decade of Development:

- A decline of infant mortality rates from around 80 per 1000 live births to below 30 per 1000 live births by 2010. This should be combined with explicit targets, for halting the AIDS epidemic, and treating, key disease such as malaria, tuberculosis, and other major killers.

- A reduction of a Chill illiteracy from around 45 per cent to less than 20 per cent by 2010. Universal primary education for ages 5-14 for girls and boys by 2010, with a school for within 5 kilometres so home.
- All villages possessing electricity, a trunk road, telephone and internet connectivity, a school, clean water and sanitation, a village health worker, and local self government by 2010.

Pillars of Development

There are two basic pillars of economic development. Broadly speaking, these are human development and economic growth. Human development signifies the ability of every individual to reach their full potential as healthy and educated citizens. This in turn requires major government commitments to health, education, and political participation to fall citizens in the country-with equal opportunity to all, and without discrimination by gender, caste, or region. No individual should be left behind. Economic growth signifies the broad-based and sustained increase in per capita GNP. Sustained economic growth depends on favourable business conditions, high levels of private sector investment technological upgrading and successful integration into, global markets.

There can be no sustained economic development without strong successes in both human development and economic growth. Development strategy therefore requires major public commitments to social sectors (especially health and education) and to improvements in the business environment in order to promote large-scale private investments needed for economic growth.

From a budgetary point of view, government resources need to be shifted towards investments in human development leaving the private sector with the major responsibilities for increased economic growth. The government at both centre all state levels should commit much greater resources. In public health and education. At the same time, the government should turn liver major infrastructure investments (in ports, airports, telecommunications, internet, electricity, large-scale water and sanitation facilities, and major roads) or private investors who call finance these projects using private capital.

The success or failure of the Decade of Development will therefore depend importantly on the quality and direction of public investments.

Only government spending can promote the needed improvements in health and education. Only private spending can promote the needed improvements in infrastructure and productive enterprises. The major budgetary challenge is to shift government spending away from low-priority areas (such as untargeted subsidies, excessive bureaucracy, and investments that can better be left to the private sector) towards high-priority areas such as health and education that can only be met by public spending. India should also mobilize international financial support for the decade of development. This includes larger aid flows for human development as well as much greater flows of private investment to speed economic growth.

Meeting the Human Development Challenge in India

India has not yet met the human development challenge. Adult illiteracy remains almost 50 per cent, and up to 60 per cent far women. Almost half of all children do not finish primary school. Only around 20 per cent are in secondary school. Infant mortality rates are high by international standards, and life expectancy at round 63 years in much lower than is China, other countries in East Asia, and the advanced economics. Fertility rates are still very high, and the population continues in grow rapidly, pressing hard an India's fragile ecosystems and natural environment.

The shortfalls in health, education, and population control are of course mutually interactive. Illiterate mothers are much room likely than literate mothers to suffer the deaths of young children due to disease, since literate mothers are more effective at care giving and all seeking out medical help in emergencies. High infant mortality rates promote high fertility rates, since households have many children to compensate for the risks of childhood deaths. High fertility rates, in turn, promote a social bias against educating young girls, since parents lack the resources to provide a quality education for all of their children, and therefore invest scarce resources in boys, for whom the market returns to investment are higher.

India dramatically under-invests in both public health and education and so do many other developing. In the area of health, the Indian Government (center and states) spends less than 1 per cent of GNP for health, compared to an average of around 3 per cent for all developing countries, and more than 5 per cent for high-income countries. The public health services are broken down, especially at the primary level. Study after study shows that the Primary Health Centres (PHCs) fail to provide an adequate set of services for the population. The poor in India are left with almost no health services, besides the very merger services that they can pay for out of pocket.

The situation in health will get worse, not better, if there is no increase in public investment in health. The AIDS epidemic threatens to rise dramatically in the coming years. Malaria is resurgent, as in tuberculosis linked especially to AIDS.

The governments of India should therefore take the following immediate steps:

- Announce specific and bold targets for health by 2010, which should be adopted nationally and in each state.
- Increase public spending on health at least 3 per cent of GNP within three years. The increase should come mainly at the state level, and mainly to finance prevention and treatment of primary health conditions such as infectious diseases (AIDS, TB, Malaria, respiratory infection, Diarrhoea), nutrition and reproductive health.
- Increase public awareness and public measures to combat the AIDS pandemic, using both domestic budget resources as well as increased international funding.
- Convene a meeting of Chief Minister of all Indian States in 2001 to discuss how the states will meet the health

targets. This meeting will allow stales to present their most successful initiatives, so that all states can adopt "best practices" in public health.

- Support community oversight of village-level health services, including Panchayat responsibilities for oversight of doctors, primary health clinics, and other public health services.
- Aggressively utilize information technology (such as internet connectivity of primary health centres) to improve the performance of the public health facilities.

India needs a similarly bold strategy for universal education, at least through age 14. Special attention is needed to ensure the education of girl on the same basis as boys, and to ensure the continuation of children in school through the ninth year.

Public spending in education should rise from the current level of around 3 per cent of GNP to at least 5 per cent of GNP (and probably more) to meet these goals. This money should be spent mainly by state budgets, but with local responsibility for overseeing the effective operation of schools. In Madhya Pradesh, Panchayats are given responsibility for ensuring school performance at the local level, including the right to withhold teachers' salaries in the event of poor teacher performance.

Studies have shown that more parents would like to send their children to school, but are dissuaded from doing so because of school fees, the poor quality of education in many schools, and great distance from home to school in rural areas. The large distance to schools especially hinder the attendance of' girls. Part of the budgetary increase at the state level should therefore be to ensure the availability of schools within close proximity to every village.

Once of the most effective ways to increase student enrolment is through the provision of fee school meals (e.g. School break fasts or mid-day meals, or both). Tamil Nadu has been very successful in implementing a school meals program, and this example should be generalised throughout the country. International donors especially the United States, maybe prepared to contribute to such a large-scale program, especially if the

Government of India can demonstrate that such a program is an integral step in achieving universal primary education. School meals not only improve school enrolment and attendance, but also childhood nutrition. Regular school meals can be augmented with nutritional supplementation, such as Vitamin A tablets on a six-month basis.

In addition to formal education in schools, the government should promote programs of adult literacy. Students and literate family members can encouraged to help teach the illiterate parents how to read. Small financial incentives can be organized to promote adult literacy. This would also enable the private sector to open private enterprises to promote adult literacy, with income generated by financial incentives provided by the government.

The governments of India should therefore take the following immediate steps:

- Announce specific and hold targets for education by 2010, that should be adopted nationally and ill each state.
- Increase public spending on education.
- In at least 5 per cent of GNP within three years. The increase should come mainly at the state level, and mainly to Finance universal education through age 14.
- Convene a meeting of Chief Ministers of all Indian State in 2001 to discuss how the states will meet the education targets. This meeting will allow states to present their most successful initiatives, so that all states can adopt "best practices" in public education.
- Create fiscal incentives at the Centre and state levels to promote the spread of education into every village in the country.
- Support community oversight of village-level schools, including Panchayat responsibilities for over sight of teachers. Introduce mechanisms such as a school mid-day meals programme to increase school attendance, and to improve the overall health and narration of school children. The government should appeal to international donors to help support such a program thought the country.

- Aggressively utilize information technology (such as internet connectivity of primary schools) to improve the performance of the public school facilities. The social agenda should focus urgently on health and education, bill it should also include other social initiatives, such as increased political participation at the village level (through village councils or Panchayats), and greater social and political equality for girls and women.

Meeting the Economic Growth Agenda

Investments in health and education will have direct and beneficial effects on economic growth, by fostering a healthier, better educated, and therefore more productive labour force. But social investments are not enough. Social investments must be combined with a large improvement in the business environment in India in order to promote a more rapid rate of economic growth.

History has shown that export-led growth is a crucial component of overall economic growth. Without rapid export growth, there cannot be rapid growth of imports. But imports are necessary in order for India to obtain the modem technologies that have been developed abroad. Thus, rapid growth is a sine qua non for rapid economic growth.

Rapid export growth only an achieved in areas of Indian comparative advantage. These include labour-intensive manufacturing sectors such as apparel and textiles, automotive components, footwear and leather goods, jewellery, processed foods, and electronics assembly. They also include high-technology areas in information technology and biotechnology (e.g. pharmaceuticals) that rely on India's tremendous scientific and engineering capacity.

India has achieved some success in export led-growth, but much less than many other Asian countries, notably China. China's exports grew from around $20 billion per year in 1980 to around $200 billion in 2000, or roughly increasing tenfold. India's exports, by contrast, grew Final around $17 billion in 1980 to around $15 billion in 20W or roughly doubling.

There are several barriers to more rapid export growth. Fortunately, most of these barriers call be overcome by regulatory changes and private investments rather than public money. Some of the crucial steps need for a faster growth of exports include:

- Reform of labour laws to ensure the right of enterprise to hire and fire workers for economic cause, subject to the normal rule of law (e.g. prevention of arbitrary dismissals in retribution for union activity).
- Improvements of infrastructure, mainly ports, telecommunications, airports, powers and roads.
- Elimination of remaining administrative barriers to foreign direct investment in export oriented sectors.
- Much more active use of special economic zones and export processing zones as incentive schemes for export-oriented enterprises. State and private enterprises should be free to establish export processing zones according to general legislation.
- Elimination or remaining reservations for small-scale enterprises, especially in export oriented sectors but also generally in the economy.

Improvements in Infrastructure

India's infrastructure in notoriously bad. The road networks are insufficient and in very poor quality. Ports are completely inadequate, so that most exports must be trans-shipped through Singapore or Sri Lanka, rather than shipped directly from Indian ports. Airports are insufficient and the airspace is reserved for just a few carriers. Telecommunications are notoriously poor in quality and coverage. Electricity supplies are irregular, scarce and of low quality. Water supplies are scarce in many areas, and insufficient for key industries (such as chemical processes) as well as household use. And in general, neither the government at the centre or the state levels can afford to upgrade these infrastructure systems out of budgetary funds. Indeed, many of these sectors already impose huge fiscal costs as government provides over and hidden subsidies to these key sectors.

Fortunately, India could enjoy a major—indeed Fundamental—improvement ill infrastructure quality without major budgetary increases. The key is regulatory change, involving two main steps. First, regulatory and oversight responsibilities for almost all infrastructure should be devolved to state level. This includes areas now under central control, such as major ports and airports, and telecommunications. The states have a much better idea of their specific infrastructure needs than do the bureaucracies at the central level. Second, infrastructure should be provided mainly by privately financed projects without state guarantees. The entire cable TV industry in India has grown up without government subsidy, precisely because it was not regulated. Other key areas—telecommunications, internet, water, power—would similarly expand dramatically if private investors were allowed to enter and compete.

Each sector requires its own reforms. Reforms in telecommunications have begun, especially with the end of the VSNL monopoly by 2002 and the intention to disinvest a majority part of the government's holding in the state company. Still, the regulations on local telephony and internet services are blocking a substantiate growth of such services throughout the country. Similarly, barriers to building new airports and to licensing new aviation companies has stymied the development of an efficient and low—priced network of domestic and international flights. Oil can go on and on.

The government of India should therefore take the following steps in infrastructure.

- Devolve major regulatory responsibilities to the state in the following areas of infrastructure: port, airport, power, telecommunications (international long-distance, domestic long-distance, local, data transmission, wireless), internet service, water and sanitation. The individual states should have the powers to liberalize these sectors, permit entry of private firms, and admit foreign investors.
- The enter and the states should set goals for specific areas of infrastructure, including: universal village access by

2010 to telephony, electric power, internet connectivity and roads to major towns and cities.

- Open each infrastructure sector to private-sector competition. Including rights of entry in service provision, by both foreign and domestic providers.

Information Technology and the Decade of Development

The Information Technology sector will have three critical rules in India's development process. First, IT will be a major private - sector industry, providing India with the largest single source of foreign exchange earnings. Second, IT will be critical input into the efficiency of the private sector. India's exporting firms will require low-cost high-quality connectivity to ensure their competitiveness with the international competition. This is true in the whole range of export activities, from the labour-intensive sectors such as horticulture and apparel of the most sophisticated high-teach sectors such as machinery and pharmaceuticals. Third, IT will be a critical input into the social process, since IT will support effective provision of public services (e.g.-governance) health (e.g. telemedicine), and education (e.g. distance).

India is blessed with world leadership in IT, with world-class and world-famous entrepreneurs stretching from Silicon Valley to Chennai, Bangalore and Hyderabad. But within India, the IT sector continues to be hampered by unnecessary government regulation (e.g. the VSNL. monopoly until 2002), low bandwidth, and low take up of IT by government agencies, including the health and education sector.

India needs a specific IT strategy to address the key areas of e-governance, e-commerce, e-health, and e-education. We, therefore, recommended the following steps:

- The centre and state governments should Hold an IT summit in late 2001 in order to spell out further regulatory changes needed to speed the introduction of IT into wide spread use and application in India.
- State governments should be given much more freedom

adopt key technologies (e.g. the wireless local loop developed by IIT Madras).

- The center and states should adopt goals to ensure IT connectivity in all villages in India by 2010. A central fund should be established to provide matching grants to states for programs to support rural IT connectivity.

A Fiscal Strategy for the Decade of Development

The centre and state governments must undertake a fundamental review and reorientation of fiscal policies in order to support the decade development. There are three goals. First, the overall budget deficit must be reduced sharply, from around 10 per cent of GNP (centre plus states) to around 4 per cent of GNP by 2003. Second, the expenditure should be shifted from economic sectors (e.g. infrastructure) where the private sector can carry the investment burden, to social sectors (e.g. health and education) where increased public spending is vital. Third, social program should be redesigned to make a maximal impact per rupee spent. This can best be accomplished by replacing generalized subsidies (such as the public Distribution System or free electricity for farmers) with targeted programmes (such as school meal programs).

The current budget deficit is around 10 per cent of GNP, and this should be reduced to around 4 per cent of GNP to ensure macroeconomic stability, and to prevent an unmanageable buildup of public debt. Thus, the overall deficit should be reduced by around 6 per cent of GNP. At the same time, social spending should rise by around 4 per cent of GNP, for education. This means that the government (centre and state) must find fiscal resources of around 10 per cent of GNP in order to reduce the deficit by 6 per cent of GNP and increase social sending by around 4 per cent GNP at the same time.

Most of this 10 per cent of GNP should come from cuts in existing expanding expenditures rather than from increases in taxation as 10 per cent of GNP. State governments should be given much more freedom adopt key technologies (e.g. the wireless local loop developed by IIT Madras). The center and states should adopt goals to ensure IT connectivity in all villages in India by 2010. A central fund should be established to provide matching grants to states for programs to support rural IT connectivity government spending (centre and state) is already around one-third of GNP, which is quite high by comparison with other developing countries in India's income range. If India were to increase expenditures further as a per cent of GNP, it would have a very difficult time raising the internal tax revenue to cover the spending program.

Of the 10 per cent of GNP needed, perhaps 1 per cent of GNP can be found (negotiated) in the form of increased grant aid from abroad. Given a GNP of around US$ 400 billion, this would mean an additional US$ 4 billion per year in international aid for India, a hefty sum, but not an impossible target for increased support mainly for health and education. The remaining 9 per cent of GNP (or so) will have to be found mainly by cuts or reorganization of current spending programs.

We can identify the following prime areas of potential expenditure reduction over a three-year period:

The net worth of central PSUs is estimated to be Rupees 1324 billion, a little over 6.5 per cent of GDP. The capital employed is placed at around Rupees 2230 billion (See Economic Survey 1999-2000).

Of a total number of 236 central PSUs, there are 104 loss-making PSUs that account for roughly Rupees 60 billion in annual losses to the central exchequer, (see 9th Plan Mid-Term Appraisal, 2000).

A freeze on new employment matched by normal attrition through retirement and death. On an average, about 125,000 central government employees are taken off of government payroll each year due to these reasons. Employment by approximately 12.3 per cent, or a reduction of around half a million employee from the present total of about 4 million. On an average, the government could save about Rupees 20 billion every year on account of reduced wages and salaries, and the associated reduction in the operating expenses. (See Bajpai and Sachs 1997).

	Central expenditures: per cent of GDP		
1.	Disinvestments of PSUs (with revenues used to pay down public debt)	3	1.0
2.	Closure of loss-making PSUs	4	0.3
3.	Reduced bureaucracy	5	0.3
4.	Central power sector undertaking support to SEBs (NTPC, NHPC etc.)	6	0.8
5.	Reduction in subsides, including PDS and transport		0.5
6.	Reduced infrastructure investment, taken over by private-sector projects	7	1.3
7.	Reduced interest payments on account of contractions fiscal measures	8	1.0
	State level expenditures		
1.	SEB commercial losses without subsidy due to differential pricing policy.		1.3
2.	Water sector reform, including rise in water tariffs.		0.3
3.	Transport reform, including rise in transport tariffs.		0.4
4.	Closure of state-level loss-making PSUs		0.6
5.	Reduced bureaucracy		0.6
6.	Reduced in infrastructure investments, taken over by private-sector projects		0.2
	Total Public saving via furthering expenditure		**8.4**

SEBs owe huge sums 10 file central power sector undertakings, such as the National Thermal Power Corporation (NTPC). National Hydro Power Corporation (NHPC), Damodar Valley Corporation (DVC), and Power Finance Corporation (PFC) etc. It is estimated that as of September 1998, the SGDs owed Rupees 16,800 crore (Rupees 168 billion) to these central power sector undertakings. (See Karman and Pillai, 2001).

Annual infrastructure investment for All-India is placed at around Rupees 650 billion (US$ 14 billion) which is roughly 32.2 per cent of GDP. We figure that a little less than half of this amount call be reduced (1.3% of GDP; it the Centre and 0.2% at the states) in investment over a three-year period if the private sector were to take on large-scale in vestments in the infrastructure sector. (For details refer to India Infrastructure Report, 1996).

This additional budgetary saving is a result of a reduction in real interest rates that will come from the file overall package of concretionary fiscal measures suggested above. Interest payments were placed at Rupees 88,000 crores (Rupees 880 billion) in 1999-2000 or 4.5 per cent of GDP.

We estimated expenditure saving that could be achieved by each of these line items to a total of roughly 8.4 per cent GDP over three-years. Of course, we would stress that these are approximate. Perhaps these bold cuts could be augmented by 1 to 2 per cent of GDP in increased tax collections, through credibility in collecting more taxes would depend firmly on making sharp cuts in major areas of waste.

It may seem politically impossible to proceed with such bold cuts, but it should be remembered that these cuts would be combined will substantial increases in public and private politically popular programs such as school locals and increased availability of primary health facility. Private spending in infrastructure would also be politically popular it will mean the much faster diffusion of new technologies (cellular phones, internet connectivity) to rural areas.

The reorientation of spending should also be accompanied by a very different system for delivering public services. The key to collective social service delivery is responsibility of local providers to the local community. For primary schools or primary health clinics to deliver effective and quality services to the community. The teachers and doctors must be monitored effectively by the local communities. We have already mentioned the important experiences of Madhya Pradesh in developing key responsibilities and authority to the Panchayats in the areas of primary health and education. The state providers the funds to him the doctors and teachers, but the Panchayats can withhold payments to these service providers if they are not doing their jobs (such as failing to show up at the clinics and schools).

Environmental Issues in Developed and Developing Economics

The problem of environment have come to the fore only during the recent years. They seem to have gripped the imagination and thinking of enlightened people, organised groups and governments in most of the developed and developing countries. Environment has been defined as the aggregate of all the external condition and influences affecting the life and developed of an organism. It comprises the whole range of external influences acting on an organism, of both the physical and the biological forces of nature surrounding the human individual.

Protection of environment is a problem of the present society. Man's desire for more joy and comfort has led him to exploit natural's free goods to the extent of reducing its natural capacities for self-stabilisation. Environmental problems centre on human activities resulting in pollution of the atmosphere, oceans and land. These range from the global to the regional, national and local. The relevance of such concerns and the priority attached to each varies between the developing and developed countries.

Environmental Issues

The increasing concern about physical limits to global growth in the early 1970s provoked an increasing anxiety about environment degradation on the developed industrialised world. The deterioration in environmental quality is due to the resource.

Such a resource intensive growth-oriented development has resulted in the following pattern of resource allocation.

(1) A decrease in the labour/output ratio.
(2) An increase in capital-intensity of production.
(3) An increase in long-term use of energy and raw-materials per unit of output.
(4) An increase in environmental quality.

Such a growth-oriented development of the industrialised economies has resulted in global problems such as green house effect, acid rain, tropical deforestation and so forth and the world hardly ensuring the criterion of inter-generational equity. Such resource intensive growth is hardly equitable for present generations either. The advanced economics with only twenty-six per cent of the world's population, consume a disproportionately large share of global resources.

The impact of affluent nations on earth's resources is revealed by a look at the United States. An average household in US family affects the environment forty times more than an average Indian or Kenya's household. The average calorie intake per person per day in above 3,500 calories in US. The quantity of waste generated in industrialised countries ranges between 1.5 lbs per day per person to 4 lbs per day per person whereas for lower and middle income countries, it is between 1.1 lbs to 1.9 lbs per day per person. Emissions of carbon from fossil is also very high in the industrialized high income countries.

The advanced economies contributing to population more than developing countries, have simultaneously development pollution control technologies. Advanced economies are hence attempting at a rapid transition to a development path that conserves resources. These industrialized-developed countries should promote less material and less energy-intensive activities and their technological capacity should be used to improve the efficiency of energy and material use. Besides this, committed policies to promote resource-saving development are required.

In developing economies the nature of environmental problems fundamentally differ from that of developed economies. The most important difference is that the Third World is not merely worried about the quality of life. Life in developing world is constantly threatened by poor water, poor sanitation, crowded housing, sickness, diseases and natural disasters. Environmental problems of there poor societies arise not because of excessive technology or development but because of direct dependence on natural resource exploitation to sustain economic livelihoods. In the developing countries poverty, unequal distribution of land and other resources and demographic pressures, have led to over exploitation of natural resources. The developing countries account for 74 per cent of world population which faces environmental treatment facilities etc. provision of these services require faster rate of growth and application of modern technology. Hence developing is considered a cure for environmental problems in developing economies.

The second problem faced by these resource poor developing nations is the inevitable choice between a high rate of growth in conservation of resources, e.g., the choice may be between increased agricultural production through the use of fertilizer, pesticides and herbicides and the preservation of the ecosystem from the adverse effect of such chemical fertilizer, pesticides and future well-being. But there is more crucial choice of a certain pattern and style of development that would cater to basic needs and aspirations of people.

Developing Countries Face Two Choice

(1) The society faces a choice whether to preserve natural resources or destroy environment in the pursuit of economic growth. Knowledge about future damage is essential in this case for a rational choice.

(2) The developing economies are confronted with a choice between satisfying basic needs of the people and between preserving certain natural resources which constitute quality of life.

The poor countries faced with marginal environmental conditions have no choice but to opt for immediate economic benefit at the expense of the long-term sustainability of their livelihood.

The developing countries are also facing difficult choices in international trade because of the various kinds of trade disruptions that can arise from environmental action. A large number of low and lower-middle income economies are directly dependent on natural resources for the majority of their exports.

Damages to environment and natural resources accentuates balance of payments deficit, the depletion of resources increase the cost of natural resources, and weakens exports. At the same time imports increase due to growing need for imported energy, raw materials etc. Trade disruption may also be caused because some less polluting Technology displaces some imports by developed countries. If these displaced imports from major components of export earnings of developing countries, their trade deficit will increase. Developing countries are also affected when developed economies try to impose uniform environmental standards to final products as well as industries manufacturing these final products. Such an environmental standard would mean rise in cost for industries, which developing nations cannot afford, unlike developed nations. Developed nations arguing for uniform environmental standards, it makes their products more expensive and less competitive than imports from developing countries. But it should be realised that enforcement of high environmental standards as a requirements for developed economies is only a price for the social costs ignored by them, their phase of rapid industrialization.

Technology transfer also poses problems similar to that posed by international trade, where environmental objectives are concerned. While it is true that developing national borrow most of their technology from developed nations, it should be remembered that, with respect to pollution control, the same kind of less-polluting technology will not be appropriate for developed and developing nations. The developing countries should be able to alter the available technology according to its needs. It has been suggested by many that if the less polluting technology increases the costs of development in developing countries appreciably, then the additional costs should be shared between developed and developing countries. Whether the developed nations should share the additional costs in the developing countries arising out of their international domestic environmental improvement action is the principal issue of debate today, those who are for it, say so, on grounds than developed nations do not face the cruel choice between sheer survival and better environment. Such a view supported on account of the capability of developed world to tackle both development and environmental problems at a time when developing economies lack the means to do so. The developed world, on account of environmental protection measures should not reduce the flow of assistance to developing nations. In fact it is suggested that the developed nations can set up special fund for environmental protection.

The above analysis makes it clear that the question of environmental protection in developed and developing economies cannot be exclusively treated and watertight compartments in a world open to trade activities. Also it is clear that developing countries should aim for a sustainable society, for sustainable development and for sustainable productive system.

World conservation strategy (1980) has stated that sustainable development requires.

(1) The maintenance of essential ecological process and life support systems.
(2) Preservation of genetic diversity.
(3) Sustainable utilization of species and ecosystems.

Sustainable development is prescribed not only for developing but also for developed economies by the conservational pressure groups. Lester brown and Pamela Shaw of the world watch institute have suggested six steps to be taken by all the countries.

(1) Stabilise world population.
(2) Protect crop land against soil erosion.
(3) Reforest the earth.
(4) Re-cycle more resources.
(5) Conserve energy.
(6) Rely more on renewable energy.

Some Additional Task in the Near Future

There are, of course a large number of additional policy areas that must be addressed to achieve a successful Decade of Development. Without going great length, we want to mention briefly four additional them.

- The Planning Commission and Finance Ministry should work closely with state governments to create new ways for monitoring the fiscal and reform performance of the individuals states. There is not enough information available as to what is really hopping in public policy and development outcomes at the state level.

- The Planning Commission and Finance Ministry should create new incentive mechanisms (e.g. conditionally schemes or matching grants) to ensure that state governments take actions to meet announced targets.
- State governments should be required to come up with plans, within one year (and following working conferences of the centre and state governments) to ensure that all villagers within their states participate in the Decade of Development. They should commit, in particular to policy approach in order it extend basic infrastructure and social services to all villagers within the state.
- The Government should harmonize its international economic policies to support the Decade of Development. India will need several billion dollars of international donor support to achieve the desired goals in the health and education sector. India will also need favourable market access in the rich-country markets in order to achieve the targets for export led growth. India will also need to attract very large-scale foreign investments. And this too will require support of source-country governments, (government policies in U.S., Europe, and Japan can have powerful effects on the direction of foreign investment flows of their multinational firms).

SUGGESTED READINGS

Charles, D. Kolstad, Environmental Economics, Oxford University Press.

Erach, Bharucha, Text book of Environmental Studies.

Michael, Lewis, Inventing Global Ecology, Orient Longman.

Rekha, Sinha and U.P. Sinha, Ecology and Quality of Life in Urban Slums, New Delhi, 2007.

Speth, James Gustave, Global Environmental Challenges, Orient Longman, 2005.

7

Environmental Laws and their Implementation

Background

The post world war period witnessed a phenomenal industrial growth especially in the so called developed nations. The developing nations followed them with equal vigour in fifties and sixties. And that pace is still on. It is estimated that by the end of the century the world output has increased four fold of what was in 1960s. But fifties and sixties also drew the attention of the world, especially of the scientist community to some very uncommon climatic events like recurring draughts and floods, rising average world temperature, thinning of Arctic ice etc. never witnessed before. The investigations and findings of the scientists as to the cause of these events were alarming. Fortunately they did not take long to conclude that these unusual climatic events were due to the environmental degradations which is turn was the result of rapid industrialization. Still all were optimist that science and technology would give us a solution of not only halting but even of reserving this environmental degradation. That hope was dashed when the scientist themselves realised and declared that the pace of degradation was much more rapid than the developments in the field of science and technology. The unprecedented first ever joint statement of the U.S. National Academy of Science and the Royal Society of London.

"*If the current predictions of population growth prove accurate and the pattern of human activity on the planet remains unchanged, science and technology may not be able to prevent either irreversible degradation of the environment or continued poverty of the world*" finally sealed whatever little hope any one had of reviving the degradation and is indicative of the gravity of the situation.

Development is universally accepted and desired. But despite the good progress made over last four-five decades more than one billion people of the world still live in actuate poverty. At the same time in the name of development we have denuded depleted our forests and other natural resources, filled our atmosphere with carbon dioxide and sulphur dioxide, created a giant hole in the protective Ozone layer over Antarctica and North America, and so on so forth. Perturbed over the continued degradation of our environment, the United Nations convened a "Conference of Human Environment" of all member countries at Stockholm in 1972. Important and land mark decision were taken in the conference to take appropriate steps for the preservation of the natural resources. Most of the legislations on environment are direct outcome of the decisions taken in this conference. The objective of these environmental laws is not to stop or retard the industrial growth but (i) to check and restrain its uncontrolled growth, and (ii) to run it in a manner which is least harmful to our environment. Yet some people take these laws as anti-developmental and questions are being asked:

(1) Whether we should give priority to environment or to development; and
(2) Whether development can take place without damaging our environment.

The United Nations took note of these controversies and in order to reach at some consensus created an independent. Commission in 1983, called "The World Commission on Environment and Development". It was headed by Mrs. G.H. Brundtland, the Prime Minister of Norway, and the answer to the above controversy was finally settled by this Commission in its report—"Our Common Future"—Submitted in 1987. It came out with the concept of "sustainable development" and it was defined as "development that meets the needs of the present without compromising the ability of future generations to meet their own needs." Fortunately, this model of development has been accepted in principle globally and has brought the controversy between environment and development to an end at least for the time being.

The first major step to promote sustainable development was the "Earth Summit"—Officially called The United Nations Conference on Environment and Development (UNCED)—held in Rio de Janeiro in June, 1992. Attendance at Rio totalled 35,000 including not less than 106 heads of States and Government—dwarfing the turnout at any other such previous conference. The Earth Summit identified major environmental strategies and challenges with the following concrete objectives:

Rio Declaration: It is non-legally binding statement of 27 general principles. It establishes the fundamental responsibilities and actions of the Governments and other organisations and individuals for the environment and development.

Agenda-20: It is a comprehensive action plan setting out steps that Government, international organisations and others should take to protect the environment and promote long term sustainable development and containing arrangements for financial assistance, technology cooperation and institutional reforms.

Convention: The Rio Summit adopted two important conventions to address two vital global problems. One is on the climate change and the other is on Biological diversity.

Forest Principle: The Summit also adopted a statement of principles for the conservation and use of the World's Forest.

The commitment to action of Government and non-Governmental institutions, including the commercial private sector in each country, will determine the progress made. Since this is an age of privatisation and liberalisation, the private industries have to play a crucial role in the protection of our environment. The desire for industrial growth is universally recognised. But few would agree that our current industrial practices are sustainable. Rather one can safely say that the current pattern of industrial activity is "toxifying" our environment. If the industry has to provide for today's and tomorrow's needs without undue environmental degradation, new processes will be needed that use less virgin materials, produce less waste per unit of product and minimise indirect environmental effects.

The case of clean industry is not only on ecological or humanitarian grounds nor it is because of various regulatory provisions under the prevalent Environmental laws. It is because of *compelling economic reasons* that our industries should go for sustainable practices. There are unnumerable examples where the environmental compulsions have been used as business opportunities by world fame companies.

In the light of these facts, it is not only desirable but essential that all industrial units—whether big or medium or small—must develop an environmental monitoring system and strategy. And to develop it one has to be well acquainted with the controls, regulations and incentives under the prevalent environmental laws.

Acts/Rules

In the last few decades very stringent Acts/Rules have been enacted framed to conserve and protect and our forests and environment. Although two Acts namely Environment (Protection) Act, 1986 and the Forest (Conservation) Act, 1980 needs special mention but it may be relevant to list all these Acts/Rules for better understanding. The other acts/rules are as follows:

(1) Air (Prevention and Control of Pollution) Act, 1981.
(2) Water (Prevention and Control of Pollution) Act, 1974.
(3) Water (Prevention and Control of Pollution) Cess Act, 1977.
(4) Public Liability Insurance Act, 1992.
(5) Hazardous Wastes (Management and Handling) Rules, 1989.
(6) Rules for manufacture, use export and storage of hazardous microorganisms/genetically engineered organism cells, 1989.

(7) Manufacture, storage and important of hazardous chemical Rules, 1989.

These laws are regulatory in nature-not prohibitory and require certain formalities to be completed before an industrial activity is taken up. Ministry of Environment and Forest (MOEF) is the nodal ministry for all these legislations. It is quite common to see inordinate, delays in the setting up of an industry, including cases of expansion or modernisation, either due to:

(1) Delay in obtaining forest clearance under the Forest (Conservation) Act from the Central Government in case involving forest land including mining leases.
(2) Delay in obtaining prior environmental clearances under the Environment (Protection) Act from the Central Government or the State Government, if the project is of a particular type or if is located in certain areas.
(3) Delay in getting no-objection certificates or consents from the Pollution Control Board under Air and Water Acts.

Even if project has got all these clearances and is in a running state, still certain conditions and standards of emission or discharge of environmental pollutants have to be followed rigorously.

The Indian Judiciary as well as large number of NGO's and individuals have become very alert and sensitive as far as forests and environmental issues are concerted. The result is that public interest litigation on environmental/forest issues has increased considerably. Thousands of industrial units have been either closed down or shifted in past few years by the orders of the Hon'ble Courts for causing environmental pollution. Much more units have been directed to installed costly control equipments. These orders have created sheer panic among the industrialists as they were not prepared for it. So much so that most of the planners/industrialists have termed these environmental Acts/Rules and the various decisions/directions of the Court as draconian.

While in some cases the neglect of environment is deliberate, in most of the cases it is because of the lack of knowledge of legal responsibility showered by these environmental laws and rules. Thus, the industries are left with no alternative but to give adequate priority and attention to the alternative but to give adequate priority and attention to the environmental concern and its management. They have to take significant steps for prevention and control of pollution and will have to switch over to environment friendly products sooner or later.

Thus it is better that environment aspect is integrated and incorporated in the project in the planning phase itself so as to avoid future litigation etc.

Important Laws

Under the prevalent forest and environment laws, it is mandatory to obtain certain prior clearances or consents if the project is of certain type and located anywhere in India or for all types if it is located in certain areas. The prior clearances or consents are to be obtained from either Central Government or the State Government or the concerned Pollution Control Board (PCB) depending upon the nature and location of the project. The prior clearness or consent is to be obtained industry or project, if such activity is going to increase the pollution load (air, water and solid).

So it is necessary that in the planning stage itself, it is examined whether the project require—

(i) Forest clearance from the Central or State Government or not.

(ii) Environmental clearance from the Central or State Government or not.

(iii) No objection certificate or consent from the concerned Pollution Control Board or not.

To facilitate, a brief introduction of relevant laws/rules given below:

Forest Conservation Act, (1980)

Check if the Project: Requires any type of forest land whether notified under the Indian Forest Act or is recorded so in the revenue records or is forest in dictionary sense.

If the answer is yes, the project attracts the provisions of the Forest (Conservation) Act, 1980 and prior Forest clearances from the Central Government in mandatory. In order to get the same one has to apply in proforma prescribed under the Forest Conservation Rules alongwith all the documents/informations to the respective state/UT forest department. It may be relevant to mention that every agency has to offer either equivalent non-forest land along with the cost to plant up the land as compensation to the respective state government which is to be ultimately notified as forest under Indian Forest Act. Next, it is necessary to clarify that normally use of forest land in protected areas i.e., national parks and sanctuaries are not permitted unless the activity is beneficial for the wildlife or its habitat. Even outside the protected areas, the permission is given only if there is no alternative available i.e., the project is site specific and can not be located on non-forest land. If unavoidable the use is restricted to the barest minimum. Ministry of Environment and Forests has a well laid down procedure to decide the requests of the state government for use of forest land for non-forestry purposes. The entire guidelines are available in booklet form as well as on the Ministry's website www.envfor.nic.in. Although out the general time frame prescribed in the guideline is 60 days for the state government and 90 days for the central government to decide the same but actual time taken is much more as more often than not incomplete proposals are submitted by the project authorities to the state government resulting by the project authorities to the state government resulting in back referencing. It is also observed that project authorities take a long time in furnishing additional informations sought either by state government or by central government. Therefore, it is advised that before submitting the application one must go through the guidelines carefully and all required documents/informations are furnished with the original application. Identification of non-forest land for compensatory afforestation and its mutation to the state forest department is another very time consuming process and needs timely action. Such agencies who require forest land on regular basis like coal and other mining companies can consider creating advance land bank for compensatory afforestation.

Environment (Protection) Act

(i) In case a project is listed in schedule I of the Notification No. 60 (E) dated 27th January, 1994 issued by Ministry of Environment and Forests, Govt. of India then on and from the date of publication of the above notification in the Official Gazette, prior environmental clearance form the Central Government is necessary for all such projects. It will be necessary even for expansion or modernisation if the Pollution load is to exceed the existing one.

(ii) Is among following site specific projects —

(a) Mining (b) Pit head thermal power stations. (c) Hydro-power, major irrigation projects and/or their combination including flood control. (d) Ports and harbours (excluding minor ports) (e) Prospecting and exploration of major minerals in areas above 500 Ha.

In such cases, the project authorities are to obtain site clearance from the MOEF.

(iii) Is located or proposed to be located in the following designated areas as per notification of the MOEF, Govt. of India —

(a) Ecologically Fragile Area, or (b) Coastal Regulation Zone, or (c) Certain specified area like Doon Valley etc. If yes, then carrying on with certain processes and operation in the areas specified by the notification is prohibited or can be carried out only with the prior permission of the Central Govt. or in certain cases the concerned PCBs. It may be noted that Gurgaon district in Haryana, Alwar district of Rajasthan and Dhanu taluka in Maharashtra have been declared as ecological fragile area under EP Act restricting certain new industrial activity without prior approval from competent authority under EP Act.

Similarly Doon valley in Uttranchal and Murid-Janijra rea in Raigad district of Maharashtra have been declared as specified area where restrictions have been imposed on locating all industries.

(iv) Is likely to cause air pollution and location of the project falls within air pollution control area, as notified under Sec.19 (1) of the Air (Prevention and Control of Pollution) Act, 1981. In majority of cases, entire state has been notified as Pollution Control Area.

If yes, then prior consent of the Pollution Control Board (PCB) is obligatory. The act is applicable to the whole of India and for all types of industries. Complete information for seeking no objection certificate can be obtained from the state PCBs. However, it is necessary to add that all industries are supposed to monitor discharge of pollutants in air continuously even after getting NOC. If the emission level exceeds the specified limits they are liable to punishment including closure.

(v) Is likely to cause sewage discharge anywhere in India unless the State Govt. by notification under section 19 of the Water (Prevention and Control of Pollution) Act, 1974 restricts the application of this Act to certain area/ areas.

If yes, then it is mandatory to obtain prior consent of the PCB. The provisions of the act are similar to the Air act.

Detailed guidelines etc., for all such clearances are also available on MOEF's website for the benefit of industries.

It has already been mentioned above that industries should adopt the best environmental standards not only to conform to the regulations imposed through various legislations but also for, economic reasons. Thus it will be in fitness of things to dwell upon briefly some of the existing instruments through which such benefits can be availed.

Ecomark

The rise in consumer consciousness especially in market aboard has put a tremendous pressure on industries to adopt sustainable practices and produce environment friendly products. With this objective Government of Indian introduced in the year 1991 the scheme of labeling environment friendly products with "Ecomark". The Bureau of Indian Standards (BIS) is implementing the scheme.

Relief for Installing Pollution Control Equipments (PCEs)

The average cost of installing PCEs for all major industries is very high. Therefore it is always advisable to go for modern technologies even if the initial investment is higher. However, there may be existing or even new industry where installation of such equipment may be required. Inspite of the fact that such investment gets recovered over a short period in the form of by products recovered from wastes, reduced medical bills and better labour output, yet there are certain facilities given to the industries in the form of loan facilities by financial institutions to install such facilities, reliefs in income tax and custom duties etc.

National Awards

A large number of awards have been instituted by government, NGOs and Industrial Association for environmental performances to encourage sustainable environmental practices.

SUGGESTED READINGS

Biswas, Dilip, Environmental Legislation: Challenges of Enforcement.
Desai, Justice Ashok A., Environmental Law: An International Perspective.
Prasad, S.N., Environmental Laws at a Glance.
Trividi, R.C., Laws and Institutions for Control of Pollution in India.
Verma, S.B., Environmental Law Pollution and Management.

Index